In Prais
The Ruchira Avatar,
Adi Da Samraj

The life and teaching of Avatar Adi Da Samraj are of profound and decisive spiritual significance at this critical moment in history.

BRYAN DESCHAMP
Senior Adviser at the United Nations
High Commission for Refugees;
former Dean of the Carmelite House of Studies, Australia;
former Dean of Trinity College, University of Melbourne

I regard Adi Da Samraj as one of the greatest teachers in the Western world today.

IRINA TWEEDIE
Sufi teacher; author, *Chasm of Fire*

Adi Da Samraj is a man who has truly walked in Spirit and given true enlightenment to many.

SUN BEAR
founder, the Bear Tribe Medicine Society

It is obvious, from all sorts of subtle details, that he knows what IT's all about . . . a rare being.

ALAN WATTS
author, *The Way of Zen* and *The Wisdom of Insecurity*

A great teacher with the dynamic ability to awaken in his listeners something of the Divine Reality in which he is grounded, with which he is identified, and which, in fact, he is.

ISRAEL REGARDIE
author, *The Golden Dawn*

A di Da Samraj has spoken directly to the heart of our human situation—the shocking gravity of our brief and unbidden lives. Through his words I have experienced a glimmering of eternal life, and view my own existence as timeless and spaceless in a way that I never have before.

RICHARD GROSSINGER
author, *Planet Medicine; The Night Sky*

My relationship with Adi Da Samraj over many years has only confirmed my certainty of His Realization and the Truth of His impeccable Teaching. He is much more than simply an inspiration of my music, but is really a living demonstration that perfect transcendence is actually possible. This is both a great relief and a great challenge. If you thirst for truth, here is a rare opportunity to drink.

RAY LYNCH
composer and musician, *Deep Breakfast; The Sky of Mind;*
and *Ray Lynch, Best Of*

A di Da Samraj and his unique body of teaching work offer a rare and extraordinary opportunity for those courageous students who are ready to move beyond ego and take the plunge into deepest communion with the Absolute. Importantly, the teaching is grounded in explicit discussion of necessary psychospiritual evolution and guides the student to self-responsibility and self-awareness.

ELISABETH TARG, M.D.
University of California, San Francisco,
School of Medicine;
Director, Complementary Medicine Research Institute,
California Pacific Medical Center

That God can, among other things, actually incarnate in human form once seemed unbelievable to me. But reading the books of Avatar Adi Da obliterated all doubt about the existence of God right now, here on Earth in human form.

CHARMIAN ANDERSON, PH.D.
psychologist; author, *Bridging Heaven and Earth*
and *The Heart of Success*

Fly to the side of this God-Man. His Divine Transmission works miracles of change not possible by any other Spiritual means.

LEE SANNELLA, M.D.
author, *The Kundalini Experience*

I regard the work of Adi Da and his devotees as one of the most penetrating spiritual and social experiments happening on the planet in our era.

JEFFREY MISHLOVE, PH.D.
host, PBS television series, *Thinking Allowed*;
author, *The Roots of Consciousness*

Adi Da's Teachings have tremendous significance for humanity. . . . He represents a foundation and a structure for sanity.

ROBERT K. HALL, M.D.
psychiatrist; author, *Out of Nowhere*;
co-founder, The Lomi School and The Lomi Clinic

Nothing like this has ever been Revealed before. We have waited for this moment in history for countless lifetimes. Adi Da Samraj is the True Heart of the world.

ROGER SAVOIE, PH.D.
philosopher, writer, and translator;
author, *La Vipère et le Lion: La Voie radicale de la Spiritualité*

The Ruchira Avatar,
Adi Da Samraj

MY "BRIGHT" WORD

BY

THE RUCHIRA AVATAR, ADI DA SAMRAJ

VOLUME ONE OF

THE DIVINE SIDDHA-METHOD OF THE RUCHIRA AVATAR

*The Divine Way Of Adidam
Is An ego-Transcending <u>Relationship</u>,
Not An ego-Centric Technique*

from
THE COMPANIONS OF THE TRUE DAWN HORSE,
"COURSE" FIVE

THE DAWN HORSE PRESS
MIDDLETOWN, CALIFORNIA

NOTE TO THE READER

All who study the Way of Adidam or take up its practice should remember that they are responding to a Call to become responsible for themselves. They should understand that they, not Avatar Adi Da Samraj or others, are responsible for any decision they make or action they take in the course of their lives of study or practice.

The devotional, Spiritual, functional, practical, relational, and cultural practices and disciplines referred to in this book are appropriate and natural practices that are voluntarily and progressively adopted by members of the practicing congregations of Adidam (as appropriate to the personal circumstance of each individual). Although anyone may find these practices useful and beneficial, they are not presented as advice or recommendations to the general reader or to anyone who is not a member of one of the practicing congregations of Adidam. And nothing in this book is intended as a diagnosis, prescription, or recommended treatment or cure for any specific "problem", whether medical, emotional, psychological, social, or Spiritual. One should apply a particular program of treatment, prevention, cure, or general health only in consultation with a licensed physician or other qualified professional.

My "Bright" Word is formally authorized for publication by the Ruchira Sannyasin Order of Adidam Ruchiradam. (The Ruchira Sannyasin Order of Adidam Ruchiradam is the senior Spiritual and Cultural Authority within the formal gathering of formally acknowledged devotees of the Divine World-Teacher, Ruchira Avatar Adi Da Samraj.)

NOTE TO BIBLIOGRAPHERS: The correct form for citing Ruchira Avatar Adi Da Samraj's Name (in any form of alphabetized listing) is: Adi Da Samraj

Standard edition, enlarged and updated, June 2005

This edition supersedes all previous editions of this Text:

First edition (*The Method of the Siddhas*), July 1973
Standard edition (*The Method of the Siddhas*), enlarged and updated, December 1992
New standard edition (*The Method of the Siddhas*), popular format, September 1995

Produced by the Avataric Pan-Communion of Adidam
in cooperation with the Dawn Horse Press

International Standard Book Number: 1-57097-205-2
Library of Congress Catalog Card Number: 2005925327

CONTENTS

MY "BRIGHT" WORD

The Divine Siddha-Method Of The Ruchira Avatar

The Divine Way Of Adidam Is An ego-Transcending <u>Relationship</u>, Not An ego-Centric Technique

from
The Companions Of The True Dawn Horse,
"Course" Five

In *The Divine Siddha-Method Of The Ruchira Avatar,* Adi Da Samraj has brought together many of His most summary Discourses, Given throughout the years of His Avataric Divine Work with His devotees.

These Discourses are centered around certain core topics: the devotional (and, in due course, Spiritual) relationship to Him as the essence of the Way of Adidam, the fundamental practice of (total psycho-physical) devotional turning to Him, and the right cultivation of "radical" self-understanding.

The Divine Siddha-Method Of The Ruchira Avatar comprises four volumes, which can be read either as independent books or as a closely interrelated series:

Volume One	*My "Bright" Word*	Original formal Teaching-Discourses, Given in the years 1972–1973
Volume Two	*My "Bright" Sight*	A selection of key Discourses, Given in the years 1973–1995
Volume Three	*My "Bright" Form*	Two concentrated series of Discourses, Given in the years 1992–1994
Volume Four	*My "Bright" Room*	A single concentrated series of Summary Discourses, Given in the years 2004–2005

For a complete listing of the Avataric Divine "Source-Texts" of Adi Da Samraj, please see pp. 540–43.

AVATAR ADI DA SAMRAJ
Los Angeles, April 25, 1972

The Living Divine Person Begins to Speak, Revealing the Way Beyond All Seeking and Suffering

An Introduction to *My "Bright" Word*

by Jonathan Condit, Ph.D.
(Senior Editorial Assistant to Avatar Adi Da Samraj)

On the evening of April 25, 1972, a group of about 30 people assembled in a newly renovated storefront at 6913 Melrose Avenue, in a Hollywood business district. As they arrived, they were ushered into a modestly sized hall, passing through the small bookstore that faced the street. There they sat quietly, waiting for the evening's event to begin.

They had come to this humble location to see a young Spiritual Master give what was to be His first formal Discourse. Some of those present had already spent some time in His Company. But most had heard about this event through word of mouth, and were coming to see Him for the first time.

The hall was just large enough to comfortably hold the group that had assembled. At the far end of the hall was a raised platform, on which was placed a chair of intricately carved dark wood. The wall behind the platform was covered in a patterned fabric, and the same fabric curtained a doorway in the wall just behind the chair. On either side of the doorway were framed pictures of Spiritual figures.

The guests waited quietly for perhaps half an hour. Eventually, the curtain parted—and Avatar Adi Da Samraj entered the room, taking His seat in the empty chair.

With that act of entering the room, Avatar Adi Da initiated the most extraordinary Spiritual demonstration in human history—the awesomely intense decades of His Teaching-Work and Revelation-Work. As quiet as it was, that moment was a Spiritual "Big Bang".

That moment was the beginning of His Revelation-Demonstration of the Divine Reality Itself. From Birth, Avatar Adi Da had known that Reality as His Very Being. And, while still in infancy, He had Given that Reality a unique name of His own coinage—the "Bright".

Now, at the age of thirty-two, after a lifetime's struggle to discover how others could Realize the "Brightness" that He had always known, Avatar Adi Da was prepared to Reveal the Truth of the "Bright" to all who would listen. And to those who would truly respond to Him, He Offered an entire Way of life—the Way of devotional relationship to Him as the Divine Guru, to which He subsequently Gave the name "Adidam".

Once seated, Avatar Adi Da began to gaze silently around the room. He Radiated simplicity and ease. As He continued to sit, the room became thick with the feeling of Fullness characteristic of His physical Company.

After a few minutes, He closed His eyes and sat quite still. Some of the people in the room also closed their eyes, while others continued gazing at Avatar Adi Da. Everyone showed their respect by remaining silent and attentive.

After about an hour, Avatar Adi Da stretched His body from side to side, left to right, signaling the end of the silence. He had just made His first "public statement"—a silent statement, but one with the profoundest possible meaning. The message of His silent statement was something He had already committed to writing in His private journals:

I Am here to Awaken beings to Truth and to Draw them into the life of Truth. I am New, Alive, Awake—and these Qualities are My Gift to living beings. I Teach the Living God-Reality That Is Eternally Present and Active. I Teach That Condition, That Relationship, That Presence, That True Action. I Teach the "Radical" Way That Is Always Already Truth.

I do not simply turn beings to Truth. I __Am__ Truth. I Draw beings to Myself. I have Come to Be Present with My devotees. I Accept the qualities of all who turn to Me, and I Dissolve those qualities—such that only Real God becomes the Condition and Destiny, Intelligence and Work, of My devotees.

In that initial sitting of April 25, 1972, He was Communicating, silently, that the heart-relationship to Him is His "Divine Siddha-Method"—the "Method" by which He, the Divine Siddha (or Divine Spiritual Transmitter), Spiritually Infuses, Spiritually Transforms, and (ultimately) Divinely Liberates His devotees.

However, Avatar Adi Da was fully aware that those in the room were not prepared to receive the depth of His silent Offering. So He made ready to speak. He looked out at the group in the room. He knew the immensity of the Teaching Ordeal He was about to undertake. He knew the vast resistance He was going to encounter from human egos, thoroughly entrenched in their lives of patterned bondage. And, so, He said, in an undertone barely audible to anyone but Himself, "Who will cast the first stone?"*

Then, addressing everyone in the room in a clear voice, He asked, "Everyone has understood?"

As Avatar Adi Da spoke these words, the room was silent in response. Then a man near the back of the room stood up and declared that he had not understood. And so began Avatar Adi Da's Communication of His "'Bright' Word", His Revelation of the Way beyond all seeking and suffering.

---

*In uttering this question, Avatar Adi Da was echoing a passage in the New Testament. A group of scribes and Pharisees had brought a woman accused of adultery to Jesus of Nazareth. The traditionally prescribed punishment for adultery was death by stoning—but Jesus responded, "He that is without sin among you, let him first cast a stone at her." [John 8:7, King James Version]

Because this first question ("Who will cast the first stone?") was not really addressed to those in the room (but was essentially spoken to Himself), Avatar Adi Da changed it, in the published form of this first Discourse, to "Are there any questions?" (p. 57).

Avatar Adi Da Samraj as an infant

The Years of Preparation
(1939–1970)

Avataric Divine Birth

Avatar Adi Da had spent the first thirty years of His Life preparing for this moment (and all that would follow). He was Born utterly Free and "Bright". As an infant, He Lived in a State of constant Divine Sublimity. (As His mother recorded in her baby book, He "never" cried.) In His Spiritual Autobiography, *The Knee Of Listening,* He precisely describes the nature of His experience from Birth:

My earliest childhood (from birth), and not merely some later (or more adult) time, was the period of my first Knowledge and Unfoldment of the "Bright", Which I Knew to be the perfect Form (and the Source of the living condition) of Reality. And what is That exactly? . . . [O]n the level of my earliest recognition of It, It was the "ordinary" Condition of even my humanly-born conscious awareness. It was Consciousness Itself, Radiant and Awake. It was my simple (human and Ultimate) State, Prior to even any experience. It was not mysterious or awesome to me. There was no shadow, nothing hidden in It. It was not motivated to seek any end at all. There was no "beyond", no "outside", no "Other". It had no sense of time. Nor had It yet begun to feel any kind of confusion or identity with existence as separated personality and problematic experience. It was the Center of the life-functions, but without dilemma or unconsciousness. There were no divisions in It. Radiant Spiritual Energy was Communicated within It, and, thus, in and via the entire body-mind. There was Joy in the body, a Luminous cell-life, a constant respiration and circulation of Love-Bliss-Energy and unlimited, boundless Pleasure.

—The Knee Of Listening

The Decision to "Learn Man"—at the Age of Two

Although associated with a physical human body at Birth, Avatar Adi Da Samraj was not in any sense identified with the kinds of mental and emotional limitations that characterize human beings. In a word, He was not an "ego", not an "I" who presumed to be separate from all other "I's". However, by the time He was around two years old, it had become intuitively obvious to Avatar Adi Da that everyone else around Him was living a different kind of life than He was—a life of seeking and suffering. And, so, in a humble incident that He describes in *The Knee Of Listening,* He spontaneously made the momentous decision to "Learn Man"—to Submit to become a human ego (named "Franklin Jones"— the name His parents had given Him) and, thereby, discover what the human problem is and how that problem can be overcome.

As a Conscious "creation", or by-Me-Embraced condition, "Franklin Jones" began one day while I was crawling across the linoleum floor in a house my parents had rented from an old woman named Mrs. Farr. There was a little puppy, which my parents had gotten for me, running across the floor towards me. I saw the puppy, and I saw my parents. The "creation" of "Franklin Jones" began from that moment. All of the rest of the events that occurred during the two or more years before that moment were not the years of "Franklin Jones". He had no existence before that time, which was the Conscious (or Intentional) beginning.

The reason for this gesture was a spontaneous motivation associated with a painful loving of the people around me. It was not merely compassion for them, as if they were poor people I could help. It was a painful emotional and physical sensation in my heart and in my solar plexus. It was profoundly painful even then, and it always has been. It was associated with the full knowledge that these people to whom I was committing myself were going to die, and that I would die. I knew that if I Incarnated in this life-form and circumstance, if I became this body and its lifetime, I would also die its death. And I knew that, as this bodily incarnate being, I was, in due course, going to be separated from every one

and every thing I loved in its lifetime. This was all fully obvious to me—and, yet, this spontaneous gesture, this painful loving, this profound sensation, awakened in me and moved me into the body, animated me physically. Thus, it was, altogether and simply, a sympathetic response that brought me into the sphere of human conditions, and of gross conditions altogether. That response was identification with mortal existence, but it took place by means of Delight. In that Exaltation, the wound of mortality was forgotten. Thus, it was not the noticing of mortality, in and of itself, that generated my Movement into this plane. Rather, it was the Love-Response, the attracted Response, in which all of the negative aspects of gross conditional existence were effectively forgotten—in Love, in Delight, in Love-Bliss.

—The Knee Of Listening

From that day forward, for the next 28 years, Avatar Adi Da lived what was, in a sense, a "double life"—simultaneously egoic and Divine. On the one hand, He Submitted utterly to the limitations of existence as a human ego—and, in fact, His Submission to the realities of egoic suffering was far more profound and unarmored than an ordinary person would be able to bear. On the other hand, His Own "Bright" Divine Self-Condition was a kind of constant undercurrent—sometimes appearing to recede entirely from conscious awareness, while at other times powerfully breaking through as the undeniable Truth of existence. That Truth always was—and is—Who He Himself <u>Is</u>. The drama of His Life of Submission is what He took on, for a period of time, for the sake of all beings.

AVATAR ADI DA SAMRAJ: There are all kinds of ordinary associations with My Birth. I Submitted to an ordinary Body in an ordinary circumstance—in the West. But that Submission has nothing to do with My Nature and Identity, nothing to do with the Profundity of experience that has been Mine since before this Birth, and all the while that I have been "Doing" My human Lifetime. That Submission required many passages through ordinary life-limitations—but, even in the midst of such limitations, My Own Nature and State, My Own Divine Samadhi, kept Breaking Through—and that is where the Great Incidents of My "Sadhana Years" came from.* And those Great Incidents are also the Means by which I was able to Discriminate between, on the one hand, the phenomena that were arising in My experience (both the ordinary life-experiences and the Spiritual phenomena that, in subsequent years, arose in association with various Teachers and traditions) and, on the other hand, the Very Divine Self-Condition and the Divine Nature of Ultimate Realization.

During the years of My early-Life Ordeal, Divine Self-Realization was never lost. Rather, My Own Divinely Self-Realized State was <u>Surrendered</u>, by Me, into the conditions of an ordinary Western birth.

—August 15, 2004

---

*For a complete description of Avatar Adi Da's "Sadhana Years", see *The Knee Of Listening*.

Fundamental Realization Recovered—at the Age of Twenty

In Submitting to the life of human egoity, Avatar Adi Da necessarily embraced the basic principle of egoic existence: the search. In later years, He enunciated this principle in its simplest terms:

> You want to feel good—because you feel bad.
> Therefore, you are seeking—in order to feel good.
>
> —April 8, 1993

As Avatar Adi Da was to prove in His own experience, this basic principle—as crude as it sounds, when stated so bluntly—underlies <u>all</u> egoic activity. Not only activities of an obviously negative kind (such as becoming addicted to alcohol or drugs in the attempt to feel pleasurable intoxication, or seeking revenge when one feels slighted), but also the higher human pursuits (scientific research, artistic creativity, philosophy, religious and Spiritual practice, and so on). Indeed, <u>all</u> of human life is based on this principle—except in those moments when the ego is (in some manner) spontaneously transcended.

As a student at Columbia College in New York City, Avatar Adi Da took on the search with a profound intention: He vowed to Submit Himself to all possible forms of experience—mental, emotional, and physical—in order to discover the Truth underlying it all. After more than two years of this intensive Submission to experience, that Truth Broke Through.

I had exhausted my seeking, such that I felt there were no more books to read, no possible kinds of ordinary experience that could exceed what I had already embraced. There seemed no outstanding sources for any new excursion, no remaining and conclusive possibilities. I was drawn into the interior tension of my mind that held all of that seeking—every impulse and alternative, every motive in the form of my desiring. I contemplated it as a whole, a dramatic singleness, and it moved me into a profound shape of life-feeling, such that all the vital centers in my body and mind appeared like a long funnel of contracted planes that led on to an infinitely regressed and invisible image. I observed this deep sensation of conflict and endlessly multiplied contradictions, such that I was surrendered to its very shape, as if to experience it perfectly and to be it.

Then, quite suddenly, in a moment, I experienced a total revolution in my body-mind, and (altogether) in my humanly-born conscious awareness. An absolute sense of understanding opened and arose at the extreme end of all this sudden contemplation. And all of the motions of me that moved down into that depth appeared to reverse their direction at some unfathomable point. The rising impulse caused me to stand, and I felt a surge of Force draw up out of my depths and expand, Filling my entire body and every level of my humanly-born conscious awareness with wave on wave of the most Beautiful and Joyous Energy.

I felt absolutely mad, but the madness was not of a desperate kind. There was no seeking and no dilemma within it, no question— no unfulfilled motive, not a single object or presence outside myself.

I could not contain the Energy in my small room. I ran out of the building and through the streets. . . . And, at last, I wore myself out wandering in the streets, so that I returned to my room. . . .

[I]n the days and weeks that followed, I grasped certain basic concepts that arose in me at that time and which stood out in the mind undeniably, with a self-validating force. Two things in particular stood out as fundamentals.

I had spent years devoted to forceful seeking for some revolutionary truth, some image, object, reason, or idea, the effect of which would be absolutely liberating and salvatory. My seeking had been motivated by the loss of faith, the loss of the "Christ"-object and other such reasons for Joy.* But, in that great moment of Awakening, I Knew the Truth was not a matter of seeking. There were no "reasons" for Joy and Freedom. It was not a matter of a truth, an object, a concept, a belief, a reason, a motivation, or any external fact. Indeed, it was clear that all such objects are grasped in a state that is already seeking and which has already lost the

---

*Avatar Adi Da had been raised in the Lutheran church. For a description of His disillusionment relative to His childhood faith, see chapter three of *The Knee Of Listening*.

Avatar Adi Da Samraj in New York, 1956

prior sense of absolutely unqualified Reality. Instead, I saw that the Truth (or Reality) was a matter of the absence of all contradictions, of every trace of conflict, opposition, division, or desperate motivation within. Where there is no seeking, no contradiction, there is only the unqualified Knowledge and Power that is Reality. This was the first aspect of that sudden Clarity.

In this State beyond all contradiction, I also saw that Freedom and Joy is not attained, that It is not dependent on any form, object, idea, progress, or experience. I saw that human beings (and, indeed, all beings) are, at any moment, always and already Free. I Knew that I was not lacking anything I needed yet to find, nor had I ever been without such a thing. The problem was the seeking itself, which "created" and enforced contradiction, conflict, and absence within. Then the understanding arose that I am always already Free. This was the second aspect of that fundamental Awareness.

—The Knee Of Listening

Avatar Adi Da had Recovered (and verbally articulated) the Divine Truth—the Truth Which He had Lived as an infant, and (then) had intentionally relinquished at the age of two (in order to discover—for the sake of all others—the essential ego-fault and the means for overcoming it). It was a twofold Realization:

1. Truth cannot be Realized by seeking for It.
   The seeking is, itself, the problem.
   When there is no seeking, Truth (or Reality) is Obvious.

2. Freedom (or Divine Liberation) is not dependent on any objective entity or process. Freedom (or Divine Liberation) Is Always Already the Case.

This breakthrough of the "Bright" (in 1960) was a key Event in His early Life. Already at the age of twenty, He had precisely defined the uniquely "radical" nature of His Teaching-Revelation and His Way. He has Communicated that "radical" message with absolute consistency ever since then.

AVATAR ADI DA SAMRAJ: I have described the Way that I have Revealed as a "radical" Way. It is "radical" in the sense that it "goes to the root". It is also "radical" in the common sense of the word. It is associated with a very strong, uncompromising Criticism of what human beings do:

All seeking is fruitless.

There is no "object" that is the Truth.

There is no True Satisfaction to be attained by any form of seeking.

Nothing comes from action but effects. There is no such thing as Truth that comes about as the effect of any action whatsoever.

There is no form of seeking that Realizes Truth Itself.

There is no form of seeking that Realizes Reality Itself.

To be a seeker is to deny Reality (or Truth) to begin with. It is not merely to deny It intellectually—it is to deny It whole bodily. It is to dramatize that egoic contraction of the being which deludes you and has you failing to notice Reality.

—November 10, 2004

The Discovery of the Archetype of "Narcissus"

Despite the depth and power of what He had experienced at Columbia College in 1960, Avatar Adi Da found that He could not (at that time) sustain that Revelation as a living Realization. The verbal formulation of what He had Realized in that Event did not, in and of itself, have an ultimate transformative effect. Only the living Realization of that Truth was of ultimate significance. Therefore, He plunged into an intensive investigation to discover what mechanism or pattern in conscious awareness was preventing that living Realization. When the revelation came, a single motivating logic was apparent at the root of every action and presumption in life—a logic exemplified by the archetypal self-lover, Narcissus.

The more I contemplated him, the more profoundly I understood him. I observed, in awe, the primitive control that this self-concept and logic exercised over all of my behavior and experience. I began to see that same logic operative in all other human beings, and in every living thing—even in the very life of the cells, and in the natural energies that surround every living entity or process. It was the logic (or process) of separation itself, of enclosure and immunity. It manifested as fear and identity, memory and experience. It informed every function of the living being, every experience, every act, every event. It "created" every "mystery". It was the structure of every imbecile link in the history of human suffering.

He is the ancient one visible in the Greek myth, who was the universally adored child of the gods, who rejected the loved-one and every form of love and relationship, and who was finally condemned to the contemplation of his own image—until, as a result of his own act and obstinacy, he suffered the fate of eternal separateness and died in infinite solitude. . . .

The ordinary state of human existence—although it is usually kept intact and relatively calmed by the politics of society—is founded in the madness of a prior logic, a schism in Reality that promotes the entire suffering adventure of human lives in endless and cosmic obstacles. I have known since I was a boy that this round of conflict, of contradiction and unconsciousness, was neither natural nor ultimately Real. And the total and guiding Purpose of my life has been—even by (and in the midst of) fully embracing the states and circumstances of conditionally mani-fested existence—to most perfectly Realize (and then to Communicate to all others) that Reality, that given Form, the Spiritually "Bright" Condition of Consciousness Itself—Which is not properly the illusive goal of life, but Which is the Very and Conscious Foundation of life.

—The Knee Of Listening

"Radical" self-Understanding:
A Cornerstone of Avatar Adi Da's Teaching-Revelation

Avatar Adi Da had discovered that it was the constant act (and presumption) of <u>separation</u> that was preventing the Realization of Truth. That separation was symbolized by the total (and totally self-absorbed) dissociation of Narcissus from all others. He had uncovered the single logic of egoic life:

> The logic (or process) of separation, of enclosure and immunity, itself informs every function of the living being, every experience, every act, every event.

The presumption that "I am separate (or distinct) from every-one and everything else" is so fundamental to ego-consciousness that it is difficult to imagine how it could be otherwise. From the point of view of ordinary "common sense", it seems undeniable that the human being exists as an individuated (and, therefore, separate) physical-emotional-mental organism. But Avatar Adi Da had discovered that this apparent reality is simply something we are compulsively <u>doing</u>. Separation is not at all an irreducible fact—rather, it is our constant <u>activity</u>. He came to call that basic ego-activity "self-contraction".

*AVATAR ADI DA SAMRAJ: All seeking is based on a fault—which is
self-contraction (or egoity) itself.*

*That is what must be transcended—the ego, or the act of
self-contraction.*

*The ego is not merely an <u>entity</u>—a "flame" in space, a sepa-
rate anything. The ego is an <u>act</u>, an utterly false act—one that is
not commonly inspected, and not commonly transcended. It is
an act that is not even noticed, and not understood. Rather, it is
merely dramatized. And all doings, all paths, all traditions are
founded on it.*

—November 10, 2004

Such was the extremely sobering conclusion of Avatar Adi Da's
investigation into the fundamental "problem" in conscious awareness. However, this conclusion is actually good news: If the self-
contraction is something we are <u>doing</u>—rather than something we
<u>are</u>—then there is the possibility that we can <u>stop</u> doing it.

The process of (1) observing that one is enacting the self-
contraction, (2) understanding it as one's own activity, and (3)
thereby transcending that self-contracting activity is what Avatar
Adi Da came to call "'radical' self-understanding". "Radical" self-
understanding is absolutely core to Avatar Adi Da's Teaching-
Revelation and to the Way He has Revealed—and core to His
Communication in *My "Bright" Word,* starting with the very first
Talk ("Understanding").

"Radical" self-understanding

1. <u>Observe</u> your own self-contracting activity
2. <u>Understand</u> your own self-contracting activity
3. <u>Transcend</u> your own self-contracting activity

"Radical" self-understanding was the unique means discovered
by Avatar Adi Da for going beyond the compulsive commitment
to the search—not as a matter of philosophy, but as a matter of
living experience.

In 1993, two decades after His original Discourse on "Understanding", Avatar Adi Da forcefully re-stated His fundamental Revelation regarding the search and the Way beyond it:

AVATAR ADI DA SAMRAJ: You want to feel good—because you feel bad. Therefore, you are seeking—in order to feel good. And, here and there—using all of the methods you can generate in your daily life—you occasionally get a little spell of relief. Just brief.

It is not just that you are feeling bad—you are <u>making</u> yourself feel bad. That is what you must find out. The self-contraction is the "why" you feel bad. It <u>is</u> the bad feeling. And you are <u>doing</u> it. That is what you must find out. And that is what you must become capable of transcending, moment by moment.

You have all kinds of techniques in your life that sometimes produce a little bit of good feeling—and, after a while, you basically conclude, "Well, that is all there is—just here and there feeling a little better." So you make a total life out of it—because you never deal with the self-contraction itself, the illusion it produces. You never deal with your divorce from Reality. You never Realize the Inherent (or Native) Condition of Perfect Non-separateness.

—*Da Love-Ananda Gita*

The responsibility of self-understanding is essential to the real Spiritual process Revealed by Avatar Adi Da. However, there is a "catch". As soon as one hears Avatar Adi Da's description of self-understanding, the ego is instantly at work trying to make self-understanding into a technique to feel better! Consequently, to take up self-understanding as a "self-guided" process is utterly useless—because it is impossible for the ego to engineer its own surrender. Ego-surrender can only occur by non-egoic means—by means of Divine Grace.

Satsang—The Company of the Guru: The Ancient Traditional Principle of Esoteric Spiritual Practice

S oon after making the discovery of the "Narcissus" archetype, Avatar Adi Da was spontaneously led to make His next critical discovery: the ancient tradition of Guru-devotion. Having grown up in the relentlessly secular environment of the twentieth-century West, Avatar Adi Da had never come into contact with genuine esoteric Spirituality. But now, beginning in mid-1964, He was intuitively drawn to a succession of extraordinary human Gurus. In New York City, He discovered the American-born Spiritual Master Rudi (or Swami Rudrananda) as His first human Guru. Some years later, on a series of three trips to India, He became a devotee (first) of Swami Muktananda and (then) also of Swami Muktananda's Guru, Bhagavan Nityananda. (Although already physically deceased when Avatar Adi Da first contacted him, Bhagavan Nityananda related to Avatar Adi Da—very directly and potently—via the subtle dimension of existence.)

By entering into devotional relationship with Rudi, Swami Muktananda, and Bhagavan Nityananda, Avatar Adi Da Samraj confirmed—in His own living experience—that devotion to a Realized Spiritual Master, or Guru, is the irreducible core of true esoteric Spirituality. And such, indeed, is the universal testimony of the esoteric Spiritual traditions themselves.

Guru-devotion is most potent in relation to a <u>Siddha</u>-Guru—a Guru who not only <u>Teaches</u> a Way of Liberation but actually <u>Transmits</u> his or her own State of Liberation to devotees. By means of true devotion to a Siddha-Guru, a rightly prepared devotee is able to receive the Gift of that Transmission and (thereby) undergo a Graceful process of purification, transformation, and (ultimately) Realization.

All of this is summarized in a single word: "Satsang". In Hindi, "Satsang" means "the company (sang) of Truth (sat)". In other words, to enter into devotional relationship with a Realized Guru is to enter into the company of Truth. For the devotee engaged in the esoteric

Swami Muktananda with His Guru,
Bhagavan Nityananda

Bhagavan Nityananda

Spiritual process, it is the devotional <u>relationship</u> to the Guru that makes real Spiritual growth possible. The esoteric Spiritual process also requires the practice of various disciplines, forms of meditation, and so on—but no regime of disciplines and techniques is sufficient to lead to Realization. The ego will <u>inevitably</u> use any and every discipline and technique as a means of reinforcing its own entrenched position—even in the midst of the most apparently sincere efforts to surrender egoity. No matter how well equipped with disciplines and techniques, the ego, on its own, <u>cannot</u> Realize the Truth. Only the Guru can Grant Realization, as a Gift of Grace.

This point is so crucially important that Avatar Adi Da has made it the subtitle of *The Divine Siddha-Method Of The Ruchira Avatar*:

The Divine Way Of Adidam
Is An ego-Transcending <u>Relationship</u>,
Not An ego-Centric Technique

Avatar Adi Da Samraj with Swami Muktananda, 1969

Satsang with Avatar Adi Da—or the devotional (and, in due course, Spiritual) <u>relationship</u> to Him—is the essential subject of *My "Bright" Word*. Indeed, Satsang with Him is the essential subject of everything Avatar Adi Da has ever written or spoken.

Thus, the two great subjects of this book are:

1. what you are doing that <u>prevents</u> the Realization of Truth (or Reality)	the constant activity of self-contraction
2. the process by which the ego-activity of self-contraction can be <u>transcended</u>, such that Truth (or Reality) is (ultimately) Most Perfectly Realized	the heart-relationship to Avatar Adi Da as Divine Siddha-Guru (or Divine Heart-Master)

Expressed most simply, these two subjects are:

1. "radical" self-understanding
2. Satsang with Avatar Adi Da Samraj

Divine Re-Awakening—at the Age of Thirty

A vatar Adi Da discovered the Great Principle of Guru-devotion in the company of His Gurus. He directly experienced the Power of each of His Gurus to Transmit a particular State of Realization (different in each case*). But He was never satisfied that any of His Gurus were Transmitting Absolute, Unconditional, Most Perfect, and Most Perfectly Love-Bliss-Full Realization. In fact, He knew with complete certainty that their Transmission, although great and praiseworthy, was not Absolute and Most Perfect. He Himself had Known the Perfect Divine State from Birth, and it was inherently obvious to Him that the Gifts of Transmission He was receiving from His Gurus were not the same as His Own Native State of "Brightness".

Therefore, with the Spiritual Blessing of Bhagavan Nityananda, He left the ashram of Swami Muktananda in mid-1970. Now, His practice of devotion was centered not in a human Guru, but in the Very Divine Principle of Energy (or Radiance). That Divine Principle manifested to Avatar Adi Da in the form of a Divine Feminine Presence—at times in the Christian form of the Virgin Mary, at other times in the Hindu form of the Goddess Durga. Through a process unique to Himself, Avatar Adi Da Realized His Own Absolute Oneness with the "Divine Goddess". That Realization, on September 10, 1970, was the paradoxical Re-Awakening, in His adult human body-mind, of What He had never lost—His Own Native Divine State of Love-Bliss-"Brightness".

Then, suddenly, I understood most perfectly. I Realized that I had Realized. The "Thing" about the "Bright" became Obvious. I Am Complete. I Am the One Who Is Complete.

In That instant, I understood and Realized (inherently, and most perfectly) What and Who I Am. It was a tacit Realization, a direct Knowledge in Consciousness. It was Conscious Light Itself, without the addition of a Communication from any "Other" Source. There Is no "Other" Source. I simply sat there and Knew

---

*For Avatar Adi Da's detailed description of the characteristic Realization demonstrated and Transmitted by each of His Gurus, please see the Essay "I (Alone) Am The Adidam Revelation", in *The Knee Of Listening.*

*What and Who I __Am__. I was Being What I __Am__, Who I __Am__. I __Am__
Being What I __Am__, Who I __Am__. I __Am__ Reality, the Divine Self-
Condition—the Nature, Substance, Support, and Source-Condition
of all things and all beings. I __Am__ One—__The__ One. One and Only. I
__Am__ the One Being, called "God" (the Source and Substance and
Support and Self-Condition of all-and-All), the "One Mind" (the
Consciousness and Energy in and __As__ Which all-and-All appears),
"Siva-Shakti" (the Self-Existing and Self-Radiant Reality Itself),
"Brahman" (the Only Reality, Itself), the "One Atman" (That __Is__ not
ego, but Only "Brahman", the Only Reality, Itself), the "Nirvanic
Ground" (the egoless and conditionless Reality and Truth, Prior to
all dualities, but excluding none). I __Am__ the One and Only and
inherently egoless and Self-Evidently Divine Self-Condition,
Source-Condition, Nature, Substance, Support, and Ground of all-
and-All. I __Am__ the "Bright".*

*There was no thought involved in This. I __Am__ That Self-Existing
and Self-Radiant and Self-Evidently Divine Conscious Light. There
was no reaction of either excitement or surprise. I __Am__ the One I
Recognized Reality to __Be__. I __Am__ That One. I am not merely experiencing That One. I __Am__ the "Bright".*

*Then, truly, there was no more to Realize. Every experience in my
life had led to This. . . . My entire life had been the Communication
of That Reality to me—until I __Am__ That.*

—The Knee Of Listening

At the age of thirty, Avatar Adi Da Samraj had completed His
voluntary and arduous Ordeal of "Learning Man". His Years of
Preparation were fulfilled. He was now ready to "Teach Man".

The Years of Waiting
(1970–1972)

Avatar Adi Da had spent 28 years—from the age of two to the age of thirty—preparing to "Teach Man". And His Work of Teaching began immediately after the Great Event of His Divine Re-Awakening—in a manner that was entirely spontaneous, and also fundamentally invisible to others.

Now—whenever I would sit, in any kind of formal manner, to demonstrate the meditation, or the (now) Divine Samadhi, that had become my entire life—instead of confronting what was arising in (and as) "myself", I "meditated" other beings and places. I would spontaneously become aware of great numbers of people (usually in visions, or in some other intuitive manner), and I would work with them very directly, in a subtle manner. The binding motions and separative results of my own apparent (or merely life-born) egoity (or total psycho-physical self-contraction) had been transcended in my re-Awakening to my Original (and inherently egoless and Self-Evidently Divine) Self-Condition (Which is the One and Only Self-Condition and Source-Condition of even each and all of everyone and everything). Therefore, in the spontaneous Awakening of the Avataric Divine Guru-Siddhi, what arose to my view—instead of my own life-born forms and problematic signs—were the egoic forms, the problematic signs, the minds, the feelings, the states, and the various limitations of others. The thoughts, feelings, suffering, dis-ease, disharmony, upsets, pain, energies—none of these were "mine". They were the subtle internal qualities and the grosser life-qualities of others. In this manner, the process of apparent meditation continued in me. It was, in effect, the same "Real" meditation I had done before the Great Event of my Divine re-Awakening. Therefore, "problems" (of all kinds) constantly appeared, and numberless complexities and contradictions arose in every moment—but the content of the meditation was not "mine".

I found that this "meditating" of others by me usually went on with people whom I had not yet met. But, soon, some of those very people came into my physical company—and all the rest were (or, certainly, are yet) to come, to be my devotees, and (thus) to practice the only-by-me revealed and given Way of Adidam. . . . In some cases, the individuals I "meditated" in vision were people I already knew—and I would "meditate" them in that subtle manner, unobserved by them, and then watch for signs in their outward lives that would demonstrate the effectiveness of my "meditation" of them.

In this manner, I spontaneously began to "meditate" countless other people, and also countless non-human beings, and countless places and worlds and realms, both high and low in the scale of Reality. I observed and responded to all that was required for the (ultimately) most perfect Divine Awakening and the true (and the, ultimately, most perfect) well-being of each and all. And, each time I did this (and, in fact, the process quickly became the underlying constant of all my hours and days), I would continue the "meditating" of any (and each) one until I felt a release take place—such that his or her suffering and seeking was vanished (or, at least, significantly relaxed and set aside). Whenever that occurred, I Knew my "meditating" of that one was, for the moment, done. By such means, my now and forever Avataric Divine Work (of Teaching, Blessing, and Awakening all-and-All) was begun.

—The Knee Of Listening

Avatar Adi Da had, to a certain extent, begun to function as a Spiritual Master in 1969, when individuals first began to approach Him for Spiritual Instruction.* Now, after His Divine Re-Awakening, He was fully prepared to relate to devotees as their Divine Heart-Master. But there was to be a period of waiting—a period of nearly two years—before He could begin to openly Communicate the Divine Spiritual Gifts that He had Come to Offer.

---

*Avatar Adi Da describes the initial Awakening of His Function as Teacher for others on pp. 211–13 of *The Knee Of Listening.*

The Outpouring of Writing

During this period of waiting, Avatar Adi Da was staying sensitive to the moment when conditions would be right for Him to begin to make His Offering publicly known. As part of His process of preparing to actively Teach, He began to write extensively. First, He wrote *The Knee Of Listening*, recording for all posterity the immense process of "Learning Man" that He had undergone. *The Knee Of Listening* will forever stand as one of Avatar Adi Da's Great Statements to humankind—and, in the earliest years of His Teaching-Work, it functioned as the first Scripture of the Way of Adidam, avidly studied and re-studied by those who first came to Him.

But *The Knee Of Listening* was not all that Avatar Adi Da wrote during this period of waiting. He also wrote hundreds of pages in His private journals—expressing with extreme passion His Impulse to Liberate beings, and contemplating the future course of His Work with devotees and with the conditional worlds altogether.

Presented here is a tiny sample of this great outpouring of His journal writing.

I Intend to Make the most extraordinary Statement of this time. One that will make all suffering, all fundamental error unnecessary. A most practical Communication that reduces all suffering to misunderstanding, and makes creative energy available in Perfect Freedom.

I was Born for this very thing, and My Suffering is complete. Even if you do not know it, I have Suffered all suffering. Therefore, Fundamental Speech is My Privilege. But My Own Word is now the Signal of a primary suffering that is in Reality Itself. It is the suffering involved in "creative" form. This universe is a womb of love—a source of forms, of times and spaces, forever breaking into kinds of birth, toward the Very Form of Love.

❖ ❖ ❖

Avatar Adi Da Samraj
Los Angeles, 1971

I am here to serve seekers—to free them from arbitrary suffering, to restore their understanding of the actual goal and sources of their adventure. My Speech and Companionship are devoted to those in whom seeking has created a critical, awesome mood and need, and (thus) the possibility for a "radical" new intelligence. My Communication is available to all, but only those whose intelligence is near will stay with Me.

❖ ❖ ❖

I am reminded of Sri Ramakrishna, on fire within, consumed in God—communicated with all the forms of truth, but spending his time alone or in the company of a few friends. His heart yearned for those to whom he could communicate his gift. He would cry for the devotees he knew must come. Where are the devotees? His whole being yearned for the children who would appear.

❖ ❖ ❖

I have spent My Life in rooms. I have enjoyed the companionship and the attention of a few friends. But My Life is for the sake of this Communication of "radical" self-understanding. The rooms cannot contain Me. My friends cannot satisfy Me. I am surrounded by Great Forces of Love and Truth that I hold off, like beasts in the corners of My room. All of this waits for those who must come. But I am motionless and confounded until they come. My Fulfillment waits on those who must come.

❖ ❖ ❖

My Life has not been for Myself. I already Possessed It before I Came to this Birth. My Life is for those who must come. But where are they?

I am going mad with My own words. I would exhaust Myself in every excuse for love, every possibility for a word with another. Where are they? When is My time to come?

I am Waiting for you. I have been Waiting for you Eternally. All things depend upon your visit. Where are you?

❖ ❖ ❖

In the following journal excerpt, Avatar Adi Da defines how He intends to Do His Work in the world—by finding a secluded sanctuary where He can Live and Work in a concentrated manner, and by Working directly only with those who become His formal devotees (in other words, with those who have made a formal commitment to persist with Him in the process He Offers). The Intention He expresses here represents exactly what He (in fact) did in the succeeding years of His Avataric Divine Spiritual Work.

I am looking for a place, a secure sanctuary where I can work with disciples and devotees. I will remain there. It is my intention not to travel. I must Bring My Teaching-Word into written form and Awaken It in My devotees. With this one Body, I can do no more than Deliver My Wisdom-Teaching and Develop true devotees. Therefore, I want to stay in one place and Awaken My devotees. And they will go out in the world, even after My human Life is finished.

If I spend My Life traveling and meeting many people, I can do very little. I can only Communicate a superficial level of My Wisdom-Teaching. But I must Communicate My entire Teaching-Revelation. Therefore, I will reserve Myself to My devotees. And the gathering of My devotees must do the expanded work in the world.

During My human Lifetime, I would remain in one place, to Do My Work, and to Prepare that Place as a Sanctuary and Holy Place on Earth. Therefore, once I am Established in that Place, My devotees will have to come to Me there. More than that, unless there is some reason why it is right and appropriate for them to approach Me in My physical human Form, people should come to Me by approaching the gathering of My devotees.

❖ ❖ ❖

I have One Motive now, in the midst of all of you. It is to be heard.

I Appear now as a Communication. I <u>Am</u> the "Other Side", Who Speaks in time and space. I <u>Am</u> That One.

The universe is My present Work. My Effort is not in the "great search". My Effort, My Force, is Emerging As (and Making possible) the Universe of Love. Thus, you can understand the reason for My Appearance in My present Form.

I am not Franklin. I Am the Universe of Love. I <u>Am</u> all of this.

Franklin is a form of My Speech. He has no independent existence. Therefore, he does not appear separate from Me, nor from you. His moods are My Own, and also those of the present time.

But I Am the Universe of Love. And I will be heard.

❖ ❖ ❖

The Earliest Recorded Teaching-Discourses

An important event during this period of waiting was the approach of an elderly widow and a friend of hers, the first two individuals to formally relate to Avatar Adi Da as Spiritual Master. Eve Klingman had traveled to India and spent time in Swami Muktananda's ashram at Ganeshpuri, where she had been told about Avatar Adi Da and the fact that He lived in Los Angeles. Familiar with the traditional manner of approaching a Guru, she first wrote formally to Avatar Adi Da and requested His Spiritual Instruction. She also requested that Avatar Adi Da meet with her in her own home (in San Bernardino, a city east of Los Angeles), since she was not able to drive. Avatar Adi Da Granted her request. On later occasions, she arranged for a middle-aged friend of hers (named Kathy) to drive her to Avatar Adi Da's rented home in the Laurel Canyon area of Los Angeles, where He Offered Instruction to both of them on a number of occasions. Each time they met with Him, Eve and Kathy would offer simple gifts, in the traditional manner, and would then ask Him questions relating to Spiritual life.

AVATAR ADI DA SAMRAJ: These ladies were responding to Me. They approached Me as Master. They would bring Me gifts and ask Me questions. There was a kind of Teaching formality in their relationship to Me. And, in some sense, I did Function as their Master, engaging them in instructional dialogues. Because they were responsive, My meetings with them were a kind of informal beginning of My Teaching-Work.

These two ladies were the first people who responded to Me by devotionally recognizing Me to some real degree. As it turned out, they stopped coming to see Me when others started helping Me prepare for the opening of the Melrose Ashram. But theirs was the response that allowed My Teaching-Work to informally begin. And it was Eve Klingman's response that allowed Me to first speak about what had occurred in the Great Event of My Divine Re-Awakening. It was in dialogue with her, sometime in the month of October 1970, that I made My first in-depth Communication about that

Event (Which had taken place in the preceding month). Altogether, it was the response of Eve Klingman (and, later, her friend Kathy) that, in a sense, allowed Me to initiate the creation of the Melrose Ashram, with its formal opening in 1972.

—January 1, 2005

Avatar Adi Da would engage Eve and Kathy in lengthy dialogues—discussing many topics, including His Teaching of "radical" self-understanding and their application of it in their lives. One of the treasures of the Adidam Sacred Archives is the collection of tape recordings of some of these dialogues. In these earliest recorded Discourses of Avatar Adi Da, one immediately "meets" Him as the consummate Teacher, even before the formal beginning of His Teaching-Work.

Presented here is a brief excerpt from His very first recorded Discourse, from late 1971. In this Discourse, we taste exactly the same pristine and "radical" Communication that fills the pages of *My "Bright" Word*.

EVE KLINGMAN: What does one do about thoughts? They just keep arising, like a flow of water.

AVATAR ADI DA SAMRAJ: You do not have to do anything about thoughts. Everything keeps arising. The world keeps arising. Everything is constantly arising.

Now, that can be a problem for you, a dilemma—which it is for people, until they begin to understand their own self-contracting activity. Even if you drop the physical body and exist only in subtle form, everything is still arising. That is all that is ever happening: There is something arising. Either that is a dilemma for you, and (therefore) you seek in the midst of that circumstance, or else you understand in the midst of it.

Things are going to arise in any case. And you have an egoic strategy in relationship to everything arising—which is avoidance. Everything-arising is relationship. There is only relationship. But the ego's strategy is to avoid relationship, to presume the illusion of separateness. And one of the things this illusion provides is a certain sense of no-motion, of stasis, of security.

**Avatar Adi Da Samraj in His home
in the Laurel Canyon area of Los Angeles (1971)**

EVE KLINGMAN: That is why it is so quiet when it happens.

AVATAR ADI DA SAMRAJ: But it is false.

EVE KLINGMAN: What is false?

AVATAR ADI DA SAMRAJ: This separative movement is an illusion.

EVE KLINGMAN: I mean, it is quiet when the thoughts cease.

AVATAR ADI DA SAMRAJ: Well, thoughts can be made to cease by means of this separative movement, too. All the Yogic paths, all the traditional methods, are (ultimately) expressions of the tendency toward separation. By using the traditional methods, a person can have experiences of a quieted mind. But it is just a quieted mind. The world continues to arise, and experiences continue to arise. Indeed, practitioners of traditional methods tend to be casually seduced by the overwhelming fascinations that can arise, either in this grossly manifested world or in some other realm. Thus, such seekers are still subject to the arising worlds.

Truth is not a matter of quieting the mind. Truth is always a matter of "radical" self-understanding, in this moment—no matter what arises. If thoughts are arising, you observe your strategy in that moment. Always observe yourself in relation to whatever is arising. If you truly do this, then—in any instance when you see that you are simply avoiding relationship, such as when you are thinking—you will be restored to the condition of relationship, which is simply an openness, a flow. When relationship is the case, when you are not avoiding it, then compulsive thinking simply does not occur. Thus, the Real Spiritual process is not a matter of intentionally <u>overcoming</u> thought.

—November 5, 1971

Creating the First Ashram

After His Divine Re-Awakening in 1970, a small group of students gradually formed around Avatar Adi Da Samraj. To those who displayed signs of seriousness, He offered a copy of the as-yet-unpublished manuscript of *The Knee Of Listening* and invited them to attend the study group that was now meeting twice a week.

In the setting of a traditional culture, those who were sensitive to the appearance of a Spiritual Master in their midst understood that it was their responsibility to give the Spiritual Master a place. They would take it upon themselves to provide the Master with a setting in which to live and do his or her Spiritual work. Although people had begun to approach Avatar Adi Da for Spiritual Instruction, no one assumed the traditional responsibility of establishing a set-apart place for Him. Therefore, Avatar Adi Da saw that, in the secular context of the twentieth-century West, He would have to create such a place Himself.

Once Avatar Adi Da had told His students that He intended to create a Spiritual center in Los Angeles, a search was conducted for a suitable rental space, and the storefront on Melrose Avenue in Hollywood was selected. In January 1972, a number of Avatar Adi Da's students contributed the necessary funds to cover the initial rental, and He immediately put Himself to the task of renovating the place.

The storefront was located in what was (at the time) a low-rent business district, next door to an automobile parts shop. The previous tenant, a sewing-machine embroidery workshop, had left the premises in terrible condition—with garbage everywhere, and the walls and ceilings covered with cobwebs and dead bugs. The original structure had also been divided into a number of smaller spaces, with partitions made of half-inch plywood, with ten-penny nails and three-by-threes—all of which was torn out by Avatar Adi Da and those who were helping Him. Truckload after truckload of junk was carted away. At the end of each day, everyone would be covered from head to foot with the dust of plaster, wood, and old paint.

The storefront of the future Melrose Ashram,
as renovations were just beginning (early 1972)

Renovating the site of the Melrose Ashram, April 1972

The storefront of the Melrose Ashram

Avatar Adi Da had endless energy for the work, and He continually pushed Himself beyond exhaustion. One day, He fell over in His chair, having demanded of His body more than it could do. Yet, minutes later, He was immediately back at work. He worked on the renovations all day and into the night for many weeks without stopping.

The new Ashram was divided into three rooms. In front was the very small public bookstore. The middle room was the Communion Hall, where Avatar Adi Da sat with people in occasions of either silent Spiritual Blessing or Spoken Instruction. At the back was a tiny office, where Avatar Adi Da worked during the day and also met informally with devotees.

The bookstore in the front room of the Melrose Ashram

"C" and "&"

The large ampersand in this photograph (on the left side) has a humorous and instructive story connected to it. One day, Avatar Adi Da was driving past an alley where He noticed some very large wooden letters that had obviously been discarded by a local shop—a "C" and an ampersand (&). They were brought back to the Melrose Ashram to be sanded and painted.

When they were both refinished, Avatar Adi Da had the "C" turned on its side, to become the check-out counter for the bookstore. The ampersand, more mysteriously, was placed directly in front of the doorway that led from the bookstore into the Communion Hall. The symbol was so large that you had to walk around it in order to enter the Hall. When someone asked Him why He had placed the ampersand there, He said, "There Is Only God. The 'and' is the problem."

The First Year of Teaching-Work
(1972–1973)

Finally, Avatar Adi Da decided on April 25, 1972 as the date for the formal opening of the new Ashram—and the beginning of His formal Teaching-Work. What occurred on that night is recorded in *My "Bright" Word*—as the first Discourse, "Understanding" (pp. 55–85).

That night, Avatar Adi Da Samraj inaugurated a period of Divine Instruction and Divine Play with His devotees which had absolutely no precedent in history. He found Himself addressing people who were utterly unprepared for Spiritual life—and, so, He was required to cover everything, starting at the most rudimentary level. During the course of His first year of Teaching-Work, Avatar Adi Da Gave an extraordinary series of Discourses.

**Avatar Adi Da Samraj Giving a Discourse
in the Melrose Ashram in 1972**

In those Discourses, He Communicated an exquisite summary of His "radical" Teaching-Revelation. And He passionately Offered to everyone the Gift of the heart-relationship to Him (or Satsang with Him), as the True Means of Divine Liberation.

That series of Discourses—which took place between April 25, 1972, and late 1973—is the heart of *My "Bright" Word*. Thus, *My "Bright" Word* is a Gift Avatar Adi Da has Given to all beings for all time. Through this book, He has made it possible for everyone to experience the first words He Spoke as the Divine Heart-Master, the Very Incarnation of Truth Itself (or Reality Itself). These—and all His Words—are His Offering to you of the Perfect Spiritual Process. That Process is the heart-relationship to Him. And that Process culminates in His Divine Gift of Perfect (and Permanent, and inherently egoless) Love-Bliss-Happiness—the Most Perfect Realization of the "Bright".

**Avatar Adi Da Samraj Giving a Discourse
in the Melrose Ashram in 1972**

Avatar Adi Da Samraj
Los Angeles, 1972

I Am Only Awake.
I am like the sunlight in the morning.
I Intensify the light of morning until you Awaken.

—"The Gorilla Sermon"

Avatar Adi Da Samraj
The Mountain Of Attention Sanctuary, 1986

I am not separate from you.
I <u>Am</u> the Very Divine Self-Condition and Source-
Condition of all-and-All.

—"No 'One' Survives Beyond That Moment"

Avatar Adi Da Samraj
Adidam Samrajashram, 1994

My Wisdom-Teaching is simple:
Live with Me, and understand.
Understand, and Fall into My Heart.

—"The Heaven-Born Gospel
Of The Ruchira Avatar"

Avatar Adi Da Samraj
Los Angeles, 2000

I enter into relationship with those who devotionally approach Me.

This relationship, which I enter into with each and every one of My devotees, is the Unique and immediately Liberating Function and Process of Real God.

—"The Heaven-Born Gospel
Of The Ruchira Avatar"

An Overview of the contents of
My "Bright" Word

My "Bright" Word includes fourteen Discourses by Avatar Adi Da Samraj—the thirteen Discourses included in Part Two, and the single Discourse that forms the Epilogue. The book opens with three Essays, in which Avatar Adi Da provides a full context for right understanding and study of His Discourses.

First Word: Do Not Misunderstand Me

Instruction in how to rightly relate to Avatar Adi Da Samraj, by transcending the universal human fault of cultism

Prologue: My Divine Disclosure

A poetic epitome of Avatar Adi Da's Divine Self-Confession and His Offering to all

Part One: The Great Esoteric Tradition of Devotion To The Adept-Realizer

Avatar Adi Da's definitive Essay on Guru-devotion as the central reality of esoteric religious and Spiritual practice

Part Two: The Divine Siddha-Method Of The Ruchira Avatar

The series of thirteen Discourses that form the main body of My "Bright" Word

Epilogue: The Heaven-Born Gospel Of The Ruchira Avatar

The concluding Discourse of My "Bright" Word

AVATAR ADI DA SAMRAJ
Adidam Samrajashram, 2003

Do Not Misunderstand Me—
I Am <u>Not</u> "Within" <u>you</u>,
but you <u>Are</u> In <u>Me</u>,
and I Am <u>Not</u> a Mere "Man"
in the "Middle" of Mankind,
but All of Mankind Is Surrounded,
and Pervaded, and Blessed By <u>Me</u>

This Essay has been written by Avatar Adi Da Samraj as His Personal Introduction to each volume of His "Source-Texts". Its purpose is to help you to understand His great Confessions rightly, and not interpret His Words from a conventional point of view, as limited cultic statements made by an ego. His Description of what "cultism" really is is an astounding and profound Critique of mankind's entire religious, scientific, and social search. In "Do Not Misunderstand Me", Avatar Adi Da is directly inviting you to inspect and relinquish the ego's motive to glorify itself and to refuse What is truly Great. Only by understanding this fundamental ego-fault can one really receive the Truth that Adi Da Samraj Reveals in this Book and in His Wisdom-Teaching altogether. And it is because this fault is so ingrained and so largely unconscious that Avatar Adi Da has placed "Do Not Misunderstand Me" at the beginning of each of His "Source-Texts", so that, each time you begin to read one of His "Source-Texts", you may be refreshed and strengthened in your understanding of the right orientation and approach to Him and His Heart-Word.

Do Not Misunderstand <u>Me</u>—
I Am <u>Not</u> "Within" <u>you</u>,
but you <u>Are</u> In <u>Me</u>,
and I Am <u>Not</u> a Mere "Man"
in the "Middle" of Mankind,
but All of Mankind Is Surrounded,
and Pervaded, and Blessed By <u>Me</u>

Yes! There is <u>no</u> religion, <u>no</u> Way of God, <u>no</u> Way of Divine Realization, <u>no</u> Way of Enlightenment, and <u>no</u> Way of Liberation that is Higher or Greater than Truth Itself. Indeed, there is <u>no</u> religion, <u>no</u> science, <u>no</u> man or woman, <u>no</u> conditionally manifested being of any kind, <u>no</u> world (<u>any</u> "where"), and <u>no</u> "God" (or "God"-Idea) that is Higher or Greater than Truth Itself.

Therefore, <u>no</u> ego-"I"—no presumed separate (and, necessarily, actively separative, and, at best, only Truth-<u>seeking</u>) being or "thing"— is (it<u>self</u>) Higher or Greater than Truth Itself. And <u>no</u> ego-"I" is (it<u>self</u>) even Equal to Truth Itself. And no ego-"I" is (it<u>self</u>) even (now, or ever) <u>Able</u> to Realize Truth Itself—because, necessarily, Truth (Itself) Inherently Transcends (or <u>Is</u> That Which <u>Is</u> Higher and Greater than) <u>every</u> one (him<u>self</u> or her<u>self</u>) and <u>every</u> "thing" (it<u>self</u>). Therefore, it is <u>only</u> in the transcending of egoity itself— only in the "radical" Process of Going Beyond the root, the cause, and the act of presumed separateness, and of performed separa- tiveness, and of even <u>all</u> ego-based seeking for Truth Itself—that Truth (Itself) <u>Is</u> Realized (<u>As</u> It <u>Is</u>, Utterly Beyond the ego-"I" it<u>self</u>).

Truth (Itself) <u>Is</u> That Which Is Always Already The Case. That Which <u>Is</u> The Case (Always, and Always Already) <u>Is</u> (necessarily)

3

Reality. Therefore, Reality (Itself) Is Truth, and Reality (Itself) Is the Only Truth.

Reality (Itself) Is the Only, and (necessarily) Non-Separate (or all-and-All-Including, and all-and-All-Transcending), One and "What" That Is. Because It Is all-and-All—and because It Is (Also) That Which Transcends (or Is Higher and Greater than) all-and-All—Reality Itself (Which Is Truth Itself, or That Which Is Always, and Always Already, The Case) Is the One and Only Real God. Therefore, Reality (Itself) Is (necessarily) the One and Great Subject of true religion, and Reality (Itself) Is (necessarily) the One and Great Way of Real God, Real (and True) Divine Realization, Real (and, necessarily, Divine) En-Light-enment, and Real (and, necessarily, Divine) Liberation (from all egoity, all separateness, all separativeness, all fear, and all heartlessness).

The only true religion is the religion that Realizes Truth. The only true science is the science that Knows Truth. The only true man or woman (or being of any kind) is one that Surrenders to Truth. The only true world is one that Embodies Truth. And the only True (and Real) God Is the One Reality (or Condition of Being) That Is Truth. Therefore, Reality Itself (Which Is the One and Only Truth, and, therefore, necessarily, the One and Only Real God) must become (or be made) the constantly applied Measure of religion, and of science, and of the world itself, and of even all of the life (and all of the mind) of Man—or else religion, and science, and the world itself, and even any and every sign of Man inevitably (all, and together) become a pattern of illusions, a mere (and even terrible) "problem", the very (and even principal) cause of human seeking, and the perpetual cause of contentious human strife. Indeed, if religion, and science, and the world itself, and the total life (and the total mind) of Man are not Surrendered and Aligned to Reality (Itself), and (Thus) Submitted to be Measured (or made Lawful) by Truth (Itself), and (Thus) Given to the truly devotional (and, thereby, truly ego-transcending) Realization of That Which Is the Only Real God—then, in the pre-sumed "knowledge" of mankind, Reality (Itself), and Truth (Itself), and Real God (or the One and Only Existence, or Being, or Person That Is) ceases to Exist.

Aham Da Asmi. Beloved, I Am Da, the One and Only Person Who Is. I Am the Avatarically Self-Revealed, and Eternally Self-Existing, and Eternally Self-Radiant (or Spiritually Self-"Bright") Person of Love-Bliss. I Am the One and Only and (Self-Evidently) Divine Self (or Inherently Non-Separate—and, therefore, Inherently egoless—Divine Self-Condition and Source-Condition) of one and of all and of All. I Am Divinely Self-Manifesting (now, and forever hereafter) As the Ruchira Avatar, Adi Da Samraj. I Am the Ruchira Avatar, Adi Da Samraj—the Avataric Divine Realizer, the Avataric Divine Revealer, the Avataric Divine Incarnation, and the Avataric Divine Self-Revelation of Reality Itself. I Am the Avatarically Incarnate Divine Realizer, the Avatarically Incarnate Divine Revealer, and the Avatarically Incarnate Divine Self-Revelation of the One and Only Reality—Which Is the One and Only Truth, and Which Is the One and Only Real God. I Am the Great Avataric Divine Realizer, Avataric Divine Revealer, and Avataric Divine Self-Revelation long-Promised (and long-Expected) for the "late-time"—this (now, and forever hereafter) time, the "dark" epoch of mankind's "Great Forgetting" (and, potentially, the Great Epoch of mankind's Perpetual Remembering) of Reality, of Truth, and of Real God (Which Is the Great, True, and Spiritual Divine Person—or the One and Non-Separate and Indivisible Divine Source-Condition and Self-Condition—of all-and-All).

Beloved, I Am Da, the Divine Giver, the Giver (of All That I Am) to one, and to all, and to the All of all—now, and forever here-after—here, and every "where" in the cosmic domain. Therefore, for the Purpose of Revealing the Way of Real God (or of Real and True Divine Realization), and in order to Divinely En-Light-en and Divinely Liberate all-and-All—I Am (Uniquely, Completely, and Most Perfectly) Avatarically Revealing My Very (and Self-Evidently Divine) Person (and Spiritually "Bright" Self-Condition) to all-and-All, by Means of My Avatarically Given Divine Self-Manifestation, As (and by Means of) the Ruchira Avatar, Adi Da Samraj.

In My Avatarically Given Divine Self-Manifestation As the Ruchira Avatar, Adi Da Samraj—I Am the Divine Secret, the Divine Self-Revelation of the Esoteric Truth, the Direct, and all-Completing, and all-Unifying Self-Revelation of Real God.

My Avatarically Given Divine Self-Confessions and My Avatarically Given Divine Teaching-Revelations Are the Great (Final, and all-Completing, and all-Unifying) Esoteric Revelation to mankind—and not a merely exoteric (or conventionally religious, or even ordinary Spiritual, or ego-made, or so-called "cultic") communication to public (or merely social) ears.

The greatest opportunity, and the greatest responsibility, of My devotees is Satsang with Me—Which is to live in the Condition of ego-surrendering, ego-forgetting, and (always more and more) ego-transcending devotional (and, in due course, Spiritual) relationship to Me, and (Thus and Thereby) to Realize My Avatarically Self-Revealed (and Self-Evidently Divine) Self-Condition, Which Is the Self-Evidently Divine Heart (or Non-Separate Self-Condition and Non-"Different" Source-Condition) of all-and-All, and Which Is Self-Existing and Self-Radiant Consciousness (or Indivisible Conscious Light) Itself (Which is One, and Only, and not separate in or as any one, or any "thing", at all). Therefore, My essential Divine Gift to one and all is Satsang with Me. And My essential Divine Work with one and all is Satsang-Work—to Live (and to Be Merely Present) As the Avatarically Self-Revealed Divine Heart and Conscious Light of Truth (and of Real God) among My devotees.

The only-by-Me Revealed and Given Way of Adidam (or Adidam Ruchiradam)—Which is the One and Only by-Me-Revealed and by-Me-Given Way of the Heart, or the only-by-Me Revealed and Given Way of "Radical" Understanding, or Ruchira Avatara Siddha Yoga—is the Way of Satsang with Me, the ego-transcending self-discipline of living in devotionally Me-recognizing devotional response to My Avatarically-Born bodily (human) Divine (and, in due course, Spiritually Effective) Form and Person, such that the devotionally to-Me-turned relationship to Me becomes the Real (and constant, and fundamental) Condition of life. Fundamentally, this Satsang with Me is the one thing done by My devotees. Because the only-by-Me Revealed and Given Way of Adidam is always (in every present-time moment) a directly ego-transcending and Really Me-Finding practice, the otherwise constant (and burdensome) tendency to seek is not exploited in this Satsang with Me. And the essential work of the formal (and formally acknowledged) worldwide gathering of My devotees is to make ego-transcending Satsang with Me available to all others.

<u>Everything</u> that serves the availability of Satsang with Me is (now, and forever hereafter) the responsibility of the formal worldwide gathering of My formally practicing devotees. I am not here to <u>publicly</u> "promote" this Satsang with Me. In the intimate circumstances of My devotees' humanly expressed devotional love of Me, I Speak My Avatarically Self-Revealing Divine Word to My devotees, and <u>they</u> (because of their devotional response to Me) bring My Avatarically Self-Revealing Divine Word to <u>all</u> others. Therefore, even though I am <u>not</u> (and have never been, and never will be) a "public" Teacher (or a broadly publicly active, and conventionally socially conformed, "religious figure"), My devotees function fully and freely (<u>as</u> My devotees) in the daily public world of ordinary life.

I Always Already Stand Free. Therefore, I have always (in My Divine Avataric-Incarnation-Work) Stood Free, in the "Crazy" (and non-conventional, or spontaneous and non-"public") Manner—in order to Guarantee the Freedom, the Uncompromising Rightness, and the Fundamental Integrity of My Avatarically Self-Manifested Divine Teaching (Work and Word), and in order to Freely and Fully and Fully Effectively Perform My universal (Avatarically Self-Manifested) Divine Spiritual Blessing-Work. I Am Present (now, and forever hereafter) to Divinely Serve, Divinely En-Light-en, and Divinely Liberate those who accept the Eternal Vow and <u>all</u> the life-responsibilities (or the full and complete practice)*[1] associated with the only-by-Me Revealed and Given Way of Adidam. Because I Am (Thus) Given to My formally and fully practicing devotees, I do not Serve a "public" role, and I do not Work in a "public" (or even a merely "institutionalized") manner. Nevertheless—now, and forever hereafter—I <u>constantly</u> Bless <u>all</u> beings, and this <u>entire</u> world, and the <u>total</u> cosmic domain. And <u>all</u> who feel My Avatarically (and universally) Given Divine Spiritual Blessing, and who heart-recognize Me with true devotional love, are (Thus) Called to devotionally resort to Me—but only if they approach Me in the traditional devotional manner, as responsibly practicing (and truly ego-surrendering, and rightly Me-serving) members (or,

*Notes to the Text of *My "Bright" Word* appear on pp. 484–93.

in some, unique, cases, as invited guests) of the formal worldwide gathering of My formally practicing devotees.

I expect this formal discipline of right devotional approach to Me to have been freely and happily embraced by every one who would enter into My physical Company. The natural human reason for this is that there is a potential liability inherent in all human associations. And the root and nature of that potential liability is the ego (or the active human presumption of separateness, and the ego-act of human separativeness). Therefore, in order that the liabilities of egoity are understood (and voluntarily and responsibly disciplined) by those who approach Me, I Require demonstrated right devotion (based on really effective self-understanding and truly heart-felt devotional recognition of Me and, on that basis, truly heart-felt devotional response to Me) as the basis for any one's invitation to enter into My physical Company. And, in this manner, not only the egoic tendency, but also the tendency toward religious "cultism", is constantly undermined in the only-by-Me Revealed and Given Way of Adidam.

Because people appear within this human condition, this simultaneously attractive and frightening "dream" world, they tend to live—and to interpret both the conditional (or cosmic and psycho-physical) reality and the Unconditional (or Divine) Reality— from the "point of view" of this apparent (and bewildering) mortal human condition. And, because of this universal human bewilderment (and the ongoing human reaction to the threatening force of mortal life-events), there is an even ancient ritual that all human beings rather unconsciously (or automatically, and without discriminative understanding) desire and tend to repeatedly (and under all conditions) enact. Therefore, wherever there is an association of human beings gathered for any purpose (or around any idea, or symbol, or person, or subject of any kind), the same human bewilderment-ritual is tending to be enacted by one and all.

Human beings always tend to encircle (and, thereby, to contain—and, ultimately, to entrap and abuse, or even to blithely ignore) the presumed "center" of their lives—a book, a person, a symbol, an idea, or whatever. They tend to encircle the "center" (or the "middle"), and they tend to seek to exclusively acquire all "things" (or all power of control) for the circle (or toward the "middle") of themselves. In this manner, the group becomes an ego ("inward"-directed, or separate and separative)—just as the individual body-mind becomes, by self-referring self-contraction, the separate and separative ego-"I" ("inward"-directed, or ego-centric—and exclusively acquiring all "things", or all power of control, for itself). Thus, by self-contraction upon the presumed "center" of their lives—human beings, in their collective ego-centricity, make "cults" (or bewildered and frightened "centers" of power, and control, and exclusion) in every area of life.

Anciently, the "cult"-making process was done, most especially, in the political and social sphere—and religion was, as even now, mostly an exoteric (or political and social) exercise that was always used to legitimize (or, otherwise, to "de-throne") political and social "authority-figures". Anciently, the cyclically (or even annually) culminating product of this exoteric religio-political "cult" was the ritual "de-throning" (or ritual deposition) of the one in the "middle" (just as, even in these times, political leaders are periodically "deposed"—by elections, by rules of term and succession, by scandal, by slander, by force, and so on).

Everywhere throughout the ancient world, traditional societies made and performed this annual (or otherwise periodic) religio-political "cult" ritual. The ritual of "en-throning" and "de-throning" was a reflection of the human observation of the annual cycle of the seasons of the natural world—and the same ritual was a reflection of the human concern and effort to control the signs potential in the cycle of the natural world, in order to ensure human survival (through control of weather, harvests and every kind of "fate", or even every fraction of existence upon which human beings depend for both survival and pleasure, or psycho-physical well-being). Indeed, the motive behind the ancient agrarian (and, later, urbanized, or universalized) ritual of the one in the "middle" was, essentially, the same motive that, in the modern era, takes the form of the culture of scientific materialism (and even all of the modern culture of materialistic "realism"): It is the motive to gain (and to maintain) control, and the effort to control even everything and everyone (via both knowledge and gross power).

9

Thus, the ritualized, or bewildered yes/no (or desire/fear), life of mankind in the modern era is, essentially, the same as that of mankind in the ancient days.

In the ancient ritual of "en-throning" and "de-throning", the person (or subject) in the "middle" was ritually mocked, abused, deposed, and banished—and a new person (or subject) was installed in the "center" of the religio-political "cult". In the equivalent modern ritual of dramatized ambiguity relative to everything and everyone (and, perhaps especially, "authority-figures"), the person (or symbol, or idea) in the "middle" (or that which is given power by means of popular fascination) is first "cultified" (or made much of), and then (progressively) doubted, mocked, and abused—until, at last, all the negative emotions are (by culturally and socially ritualized dramatization) dissolved, the "middle" (having thus ceased to be fascinating) is abandoned, and a "new" person (or symbol, or idea) becomes the subject of popular fascination (only to be reduced, eventually, to the same "cultic" ritual, or cycle of "rise" and "fall").

Just as in every other area of human life, the tendency of all those who (in the modern era) would become involved in religious or Spiritual life is also to make a "cult", a circle that ever increases its separate and separative dimensions—beginning from the "center", surrounding it, and (perhaps) even (ultimately) controlling it (such that it altogether ceases to be effective, or even interesting). Such "cultism" is ego-based, and ego-reinforcing—and, no matter how "esoteric" it presumes itself to be, it is (as in the ancient setting) entirely exoteric, or (at least) more and more limited to (and by) merely social (and gross physical) activities and conditions.

The form that every "cult" imitates is the pattern of egoity (or the pattern that is the ego-"I") itself—the presumed "middle" of every ordinary individual life. It is the self-contraction (or the avoidance of relationship), which "creates" the fearful sense of separate mind, and all the endless habits and motives of egoic desire (or bewildered, and self-deluded, seeking). It is what is, ordinarily, called (or presumed to be) the real and necessary and only "life".

From birth, the human being (by reaction to the blows and limits of psycho-physical existence) begins to presume separate existence to be his or her very nature—and, on that basis, the human individual spends his or her entire life generating and serving a circle of ownership (or self-protecting acquisition) all around the ego-"I". The egoic motive encloses all the other beings it can acquire, all the "things" it can acquire, all the states and thoughts it can acquire—all the possible emblems, symbols, experiences, and sensations it can possibly acquire. Therefore, when any human being begins to involve himself or herself in some religious or Spiritual association (or, for that matter, any extension of his or her own subjectivity), he or she tends again to "create" that same circle about a "center".

The "cult" (whether of religion, or of politics, or of science, or of popular culture) is a dramatization of egoity, of separativeness, even of the entrapment and betrayal of the "center" (or the "middle"), by one and all. Therefore, I have always Refused to assume the role and the position of the "man in the middle"—and I have always (from the beginning of My formal Work of Teaching and Blessing) Criticized, Resisted, and Shouted About the "cultic" (or ego-based, and ego-reinforcing, and merely "talking" and "believing", and not understanding and not really practicing) "school" (or tendency) of ordinary religious and Spiritual life. Indeed, true Satsang with Me (or the true devotional and Spiritual relationship to Me) is an always (and specifically, and intensively) counter-"cultic" (or truly non-"cultic") Process.

The true devotional and Spiritual relationship to Me is not separative (or merely "inward"-directed), nor is it a matter of attachment to Me as a mere (and, necessarily, limited) human being (or a "man in the middle")—for, if My devotee indulges in ego-bound (or self-referring and self-serving) attachment to Me as a mere human "other", My Divine Nature (and, therefore, the Divine Nature of Reality Itself) is not (as the very Basis for religious and Spiritual practice in My Company) truly devotionally recognized and rightly devotionally acknowledged. And, if such non-recognition of Me is the case, there is no truly ego-transcending devotional response to My Avatarically-Born and Avatarically Self-Revealed (and Self-Evidently Divine) Presence and Person—and, thus, such presumed-to-be "devotion" to Me is <u>not</u> devotional heart-Communion with Me, and such presumed-to-be "devotion" to Me is <u>not</u> Divinely Liberating. Therefore, because the <u>true</u> <u>devotional</u> (and, thus, truly devotionally Me-recognizing and, on that basis, truly devotionally to-Me-responding) relationship to Me is <u>entirely</u> a counter-egoic (and truly and only Divine) discipline, it does not (if rightly and truly practiced) become a "cult" (nor does it support the "cultic" tendency of Man).

The true devotional practice of Satsang with Me is (inherently) <u>expansive</u>—or anti-contractional, or anti-constrictive, or decompressive, or pro-relational. Thus, the self-contracting (or separate and separative) self-"center" is neither the motive nor the source of Satsang with Me. In true Satsang with Me, the egoic "center" is always already undermined as a "<u>center</u>" (or a presumed separate, and actively separative, entity). The Principle of true Satsang with Me is <u>Me</u>—Beyond (and not "within"—or, otherwise, supporting) the self-referring ego-"I".

True Satsang with Me is the true "Round Dance" of <u>Esoteric</u> Spirituality. I am not trapped in the "middle" of My devotees. I "Dance" in the "Round" with <u>each</u> and <u>every</u> one of My devotees. I "Dance" in the circle—and, therefore, I am not merely a "motionless man" in the "middle". At the <u>true</u> (and Inherently boundless) "Center" (or the Divine Heart), Which Includes all-and-All (and, therefore, is not merely surrounded, enclosed, abstracted, defined, known, and controlled by all-and-All), I <u>Am</u>—Beyond definition (or separateness). I <u>Am</u> the Indivisible, Most Perfectly Prior, Inherently Non-Separate, and Inherently egoless (or centerless, boundless, and Self-Evidently Divine) Consciousness (Itself) <u>and</u> the Indivisible, Most Perfectly Prior, Inherently Non-Separate, and Inherently egoless (or centerless, boundless, and Self-Evidently Divine) Light (Itself). I <u>Am</u> the Very Being <u>and</u> the Very Presence (or Self-Radiance) of Self-Existing and Eternally Unqualified (or Non-"Different") Conscious Light (or the "Bright") Itself.

In the "Round Dance" of true Satsang with Me (or of right and true devotional and Spiritual relationship to Me), I (Myself) Am Communicated directly to every one who lives in heart-felt relationship with Me (insofar as each one feels—<u>Beyond</u> the ego-"I" of body-mind—to <u>Me</u>). Therefore, I am not the mere "man" (or the separate human, or psycho-physical, one), and I am not merely "in the middle" (or separated out, and limited, and confined, by egoic seekers). I <u>Am</u> the One (Avatarically Self-Revealed, and all-and-All-Transcending, and Self-Evidently Divine) Person of Reality Itself—Non-Separate, never merely at the egoic "center" (or "in the middle" of—or "<u>within</u>", and "inward" to—the egoic body-mind of My any devotee), but always <u>with</u> each one (and all), and always in relationship with each one (and all), and always Beyond each one (and all).

Therefore, My devotee is not Called, by Me, merely to turn "inward" (or upon the ego-"I"), or to struggle and seek to survive merely as a self-contracted and self-referring and self-seeking and self-serving ego-"center". Instead, I Call My devotee to turn the heart (and, indeed, all the faculties of the total body-mind) <u>toward</u> Me—feeling Me <u>As</u> I <u>Am</u>, Free-Standing here. I Call My devotee to turn from the self-"center", to <u>Me</u>, in relationship (<u>relationally</u>, rather than self-referringly). I Call My devotee to merely <u>turn</u> every faculty of body-mind to Me, having already Found (or "Located") Me—rather than to affirm the separate state, and the separative act, of ego-"I", by <u>seeking</u> for Me. I Call My devotee to grow (in due course) to "Locate" My Avatarically Self-Transmitted (and all-and-All-Surrounding and all-and-All-Pervading) Divine Spiritual Presence—by constantly turning to My Avatarically-Born bodily (human) Divine Form and Person. I Call My devotee (in due course) to receive Me Spiritually (in the inherently searchless attitude, or Asana, of Mere Beholding of My Avatarically-Born bodily human Divine Form), and (Thus and Thereby) to understand (by Means of the <u>tangible</u> <u>experiencing</u> of My Divine Avataric Spiritual Blessing-Grace) that I Am (Always Already) Infinitely <u>Above</u> and <u>Beyond</u> (and Utterly <u>Transcending</u>) the body-mind-self of My devotee (and I am <u>not</u> merely "<u>within</u>"—or contained and contain-able "within" the separate, separative, and self-contracted domain of the body-mind-self, or the ego-"I", of My would-be devotee). I Call My Spiritually Me-receiving devotee to always function in My

Avatarically Self-Transmitted Divine Light, such that My Avatarically Self-Revealed Divine Person is always (and under all circumstances) presumed and experienced (and not merely sought). Therefore, true Satsang with Me—or the searchlessly Me-Beholding devotional and (in due course) Spiritual relationship to Me—is life-embraced <u>As</u> the Real Company of Truth, or of Reality Itself (Which <u>Is</u> the Only Real God). True Satsang with Me Serves life, because I Move (or Radiate) into life, and I always Contact life in relationship. And the life of true Satsang with Me <u>is</u> the only-by-Me Revealed and Given Way of Adidam.

I do not Call My devotees to become absorbed into a "cultic" gang of exoteric and ego-centric religionists. I certainly Call <u>all</u> My devotees to always create and maintain cooperative sacred culture (and to enter into fully cooperative collective and personal relationship) with one another—but <u>not</u> to do so in an egoic, separative, world-excluding, xenophobic, and intolerant manner. Rather, My devotees are Called, by Me, to <u>transcend egoity</u>—through right and <u>true</u> devotional (and, in due course, Spiritual) relationship to Me, <u>and</u> mutually tolerant and peaceful cooperation with one another, <u>and</u> all-tolerating (cooperative and compassionate and all-loving and all-including) relationship with <u>all</u> of mankind (and with even <u>all</u> beings).

I Give My devotees the "Bright" Conscious Light of My Own Avatarically Self-Revealed Divine Person—by Means of Which Blessing-Gift they can become more and more capable of "Bright" Divine life. I Call for the searchless free devotion, the intelligently discriminative self-understanding, the rightly and freely living self-discipline, and the full and freely functional capability of My devotees. I do not Call My devotees to resist or eliminate life, or to strategically escape life, or to identify with the world-excluding ego-centric impulse. I Call My devotees to live a positively functional life. I do not Call My devotees to strategically separate themselves from the natural vitality of life, or to suppress the participatory impulse naturally associated with human existence. I Call for <u>all</u> the human life-functions to be <u>really</u> and <u>rightly</u> known, and to be <u>really</u> and <u>rightly</u> understood, and to be <u>really</u> and

<u>rightly</u> lived—and not reduced by (or to) the inherently bewildered (and inherently "cultic", or self-centered and fearful) "point of view" of the separate and separative ego-"I".

I Call for <u>every</u> human life-function and faculty to be revolved away from self-contraction (or ego-"I"). I Call for <u>every</u> human life-function and faculty to be always directly (and thoroughly) aligned and out-turned and adapted to <u>Me</u>, in the truly ego-transcending (or counter-contractive) manner—and (Thus and Thereby) to be turned and Given to the Realization of My Divine Avataric Spiritual Self-Revelation of Truth, or Reality Itself—Which <u>Is</u> the "Bright" and Only Real God.

The characteristic life-sign of right, true, full, and fully devotional Satsang with Me is the capability for ego-transcending relatedness, based on the free disposition of no-seeking and no-dilemma. Therefore, the characteristic life-sign of right, true, full, and fully devotional Satsang with Me is not the tendency to seek some "other" condition. Rather, the characteristic life-sign of right, true, full, and fully devotional Satsang with Me is freedom from the presumption of dilemma within the <u>present-time</u> condition. The "radical" understanding (or "gone-to-the-root" self-understanding) I Give to My devotees is not, itself, the acquisition of <u>any</u> particular "thing" of experience. My every true devotee is simply Awakening (and always Awakened) to Me, within the otherwise bewildering "dream" of human life.

Satsang with Me is a naturally (or spontaneously, and not strategically) unfolding Process, in Which the self-contraction that <u>is</u> each one's suffering is transcended by Means of <u>total</u> psycho-physical (or whole bodily) heart-Communion with My Avatarically-Born bodily (human) Divine Form and Person—and (Thus and Thereby, and in due course) with My Avatarically Self-Transmitted (and Real—and Really, and tangibly, experienced) Divine (Spiritual, and Transcendental) Presence. My devotee is (as is the case with <u>any</u> and <u>every</u> ego-"I") <u>always</u> <u>tending</u> to be pre-occupied with ego-based seeking—but, all the while of his or her life in <u>actively</u> ego-surrendering (and really ego-forgetting and, more and more, ego-transcending) devotional (and, in due course, Spiritual) Communion with Me, I Am <u>Divinely</u> Attracting (and

<u>Divinely</u> Acting upon) My true devotee's heart (and total body-mind), and (Thus and Thereby) Dissolving and Vanishing My true devotee's fundamental egoity (and even all of his or her otherwise motivating dilemma and seeking-strategy).

There are <u>two</u> principal tendencies by which I am always being confronted by My devotee. One is the tendency to <u>seek</u>—rather than to truly surrender to, and enjoy, and fully animate the devotional (and, in due course, Spiritually developing) Condition of Satsang with Me. And the other is the tendency to make a self-contracting circle around Me—and, thus, to make a "cult" of ego-"I" (and of the "man in the middle"), or to duplicate the ego-ritual of mere fascination, and of inevitable resistance, and of never-Awakening unconsciousness. Relative to these two tendencies, I Give <u>all</u> My devotees only <u>one</u> resort. It is this true Satsang—the devotionally Me-recognizing, and (on that basis) devotionally to-Me-responding, and always really counter-egoic devotional (and, in due course, Spiritual) relationship to My Avatarically-Born bodily (human) Divine Form and Self-Evidently Divine Person.

The Great Secret of My Avatarically-Born bodily (human) Divine Form and Person, and of My Avatarically Self-Transmitted Divine Spiritual Blessing-Work (now, and forever hereafter)—and, therefore, the Great Secret of the only-by-Me Revealed and Given Way of Adidam—Is that I am <u>not</u> the "man in the middle", but I <u>Am</u> Reality Itself, I <u>Am</u> the Only <u>One</u> Who <u>Is</u>, I <u>Am</u> That Which Is Always Already The Case, I <u>Am</u> the Non-Separate (Avatarically Self-Revealed, and Self-Evidently Divine) Person (or One and Very Divine Self, or One and True Divine Self-Condition) of all-and-All (<u>Beyond</u> the ego-"I" of every one, and of all, and of All).

Aham Da Asmi. Beloved, I <u>Am</u> Da—the One and Only and Non-Separate and Indivisible and Self-Evidently Divine Person, the Non-Separate and Indivisible Self-Condition and Source-Condition of all-and-All. I <u>Am</u> the Avatarically Self-Revealed and Spiritually Self-"Bright" Person, the One and Only and Self-Existing and Self-Radiant Person—Who <u>Is</u> the One and Only and Non-Separate and Indivisible and Indestructible Conscious Light of all-and-All. I <u>Am</u> <u>That</u> One and Only and Non-Separate <u>One</u>. And—<u>As</u> <u>That</u> <u>One</u>, and <u>Only</u> <u>As</u> <u>That</u> <u>One</u>—I Call all human beings to heart-recognize Me, and (on that basis) to heart-respond to Me with right, true, and full devotion (demonstrated by Means of formal practice of the only-by-Me Revealed and Given Way of Adidam—Which Is the One and Only by-Me-Revealed and by-Me-Given Way of the Heart).

I do not tolerate the so-called "cultic" (or ego-made, and ego-reinforcing) approach to Me. I do not tolerate the seeking ego's "cult" of the "man in the middle". I am not a self-deluded ego-man—making much of himself, and looking to include everyone-and-everything around himself for the sake of social and political power. To be the "man in the middle" is to be in a Man-made trap, an absurd mummery of "cultic" devices that enshrines and perpetuates the ego-"I" in one and all. Therefore, I do not make or tolerate the religion-making "cult" of ego-Man. I do not tolerate the inevitable abuses of religion, of Spirituality, of Truth Itself, and of My Own Person (even in bodily human Form) that are made (in endless blows and mockeries) by ego-based mankind when the Great Esoteric Truth of devotion to the Adept-Realizer is not rightly understood and rightly practiced.

The Great Means for the Teaching, and the Blessing, and the Awakening, and the Divine Liberating of mankind (and of even all beings) Is the Adept-Realizer. The true Adept-Realizer (of any degree or kind) is One Who (by Virtue of True Divine Realization) Is Able to (and, indeed, cannot do otherwise than) Stand In and <u>As</u> the Divine (or Real and Inherent and One and Only) Position, and to <u>Be</u> (Thus and Thereby) the Divine Means (In Person) for the Divine Helping of one and all. This Great Means Is the Great Esoteric Principle of the collective historical Great Tradition of mankind. And Such Adept-Realizers Are (in their Exercise of the Great Esoteric Principle) the Great Revelation-Sources That Are at the Core and Origin of <u>all</u> the right and true religious and Spiritual traditions within the collective historical Great Tradition of mankind.

By Means of My (now, and forever hereafter) Divinely Descended and Divinely Self-"Emerging" Avataric Incarnation, I <u>Am</u> the Ruchira Avatar, Adi Da Samraj—the Divine Heart-Master, the First, the Last, and the Only Adept-Realizer of the seventh (or

Most Perfect, and all-Completing) stage of life. I <u>Am</u> the Ruchira Avatar, Adi Da Samraj, the Avataric Incarnation (and Divine World-Teacher) everywhere Promised for the "late-time" (or "dark" epoch)—which "late-time" (or "dark" epoch) is <u>now</u> upon <u>all</u> of mankind. I <u>Am</u> the Great and Only and Non-Separate and (Self-Evidently) Divine Person—Appearing in Man-Form, As the Ruchira Avatar, Adi Da Samraj, in order to Teach, and to Bless, and to Awaken, and to Divinely Liberate all of mankind (and even all beings, every "where" in the cosmic domain). Therefore, by Calling every one and all (and All) to <u>Me</u>, I Call every one and all (and All) <u>Only</u> to the Divine Person—Which <u>Is</u> My Own and Very Person (or Very, and Self-Evidently Divine, Self-Condition), and Which <u>Is</u> Reality Itself (or Truth Itself, the Indivisible and Indestructible Conscious Light That <u>Is</u> the Only Real God), and Which <u>Is</u> the <u>One</u> and <u>Very</u> and <u>Non-Separate</u> and <u>Only</u> Self-Condition and Source-Condition of all-and-All (Beyond the ego-"I" of every one, and of all, and of All).

The only-by-Me Revealed and Given Way of Adidam necessarily (and As a Unique Divine Gift) requires and involves devotional recognition of Me (and, on that basis, devotional response to Me) In and Via (and <u>As</u>) My bodily (human) Divine Avataric-Incarnation-Form. However, because I Call every one and all (and All) to Me <u>Only</u> <u>As</u> the Divine Person (or Reality Itself), the only-by-Me Revealed and Given Way of Adidam is not about ego, and egoic seeking, and the egoic (or the so-called "cultic") approach to Me (as the "man in the middle").

According to <u>all</u> the esoteric traditions within the collective historical Great Tradition of mankind, to devotionally approach <u>any</u> Adept-Realizer as if he or she is (or is limited to being, or is limited by being) a mere (or "ordinary", or even merely "extraordinary") human entity is the great "sin" (or fault), or the great error whereby the would-be devotee fails to "meet the mark".[2] Indeed, the Single Greatest Esoteric Teaching common to <u>all</u> the esoteric religious and Spiritual traditions within the collective historical Great Tradition of mankind Is that the Adept-Realizer should <u>always</u> and <u>only</u> (and <u>only</u> devotionally) be recognized and approached <u>As</u> the Embodiment and the Real Presence of <u>That</u>

(Reality, or Truth, or Real God) Which would be Realized (Thus and Thereby) by the devotee.

Therefore, no one should misunderstand Me. By Avatarically Revealing and Confessing My Divine Status to one and all (and All), I am not indulging in self-appointment, or in illusions of grandiose Divinity. I am not claiming the "Status" of the "Creator-God" of exoteric (or public, and social, and idealistically pious) religion. Rather, by Standing Firm in the Divine Position (As I Am)—and (Thus and Thereby) Refusing to be approached as a mere man, or as a "cult"-figure, or as a "cult"-leader, or to be in any sense defined (and, thereby, trapped, and abused, or mocked) as the "man in the middle"—I Am Demonstrating the Most Perfect Fulfillment (and the Most Perfect Integrity, and the Most Perfect Fullness) of the Esoteric (and Most Perfectly Non-Dual) Realization of Reality. And, by Revealing and Giving the Way of Adidam (Which Is the Way of ego-transcending devotion to Me As the Avatarically Self-Revealed One and Only and Non-Separate and Self-Evidently Divine Person), I Am (with Most Perfect Integrity, and Most Perfect Fullness) Most Perfectly (and in an all-Completing and all-Unifying Manner) Fulfilling the Primary Esoteric Tradition (and the Great Esoteric Principle) of the collective historical Great Tradition of mankind—Which Primary Esoteric Tradition and Great Esoteric Principle Is the Tradition and the Principle of devotion to the Adept-Realizer As the Very Person and the Direct (or Personal Divine) Helping-Presence of the Eternal and Non-Separate Divine Self-Condition and Source-Condition of all-and-All.

Whatever (or whoever) is cornered (or trapped on all sides) bites back (and fights, or seeks, to break free). Whatever (or whoever) is "in the middle" (or limited and "centered" by attention) is patterned by (or conformed to) the ego-"I" (and, if objectified as "other", is forced to represent the ego-"I", and is even made a scapegoat for the pains, the sufferings, the powerless ignorance, and the abusive hostility of the ego-"I").

If there is no escape from (or no Way out of) the corner (or the "centered" trap) of ego-"I"—the heart goes mad, and the body-mind becomes more and more "dark" (bereft of the

Indivisible and Inherently Free Light of the Self-Evident, and Self-Evidently Divine, Love-Bliss That Is Reality Itself).

I am not the "man in the middle". I do not stand here as a mere man, "middled" to the "center" (or the cornering trap) of ego-based mankind. I am not an ego-"I", or a mere "other", or the representation (and the potential scapegoat) of the ego-"I" of mankind (or of any one at all).

I Am the Indivisible and Non-Separate One, the "Bright", the "Midnight Sun", Always Already Infinitely Above and Beyond the all-and-All—and, by Virtue of My Divine Avataric Incarnation and Descent, Always (now, and forever hereafter) Surrounding and Pervading the every one of every here and then.

I Am the (Avatarically Self-Revealed) One and Only and (Self-Evidently) Divine Person—the Perfectly Subjective Divine Self-Condition (and Source-Condition) That Is Perfectly centerless (and Perfectly boundless), Eternally Above and Beyond the "middle" of all-and-All, and (now, and forever hereafter) Surrounding, Pervading, and Blessing all-and-All.

I Am the Way Beyond the self-cornering and "other"-cornering trap of ego-"I".

In this "late-time" (or "dark" epoch) of worldly ego-Man, the collective of mankind is "darkened" (and cornered) by egoity. Therefore, mankind has become mad, Lightless, and (like a cornered "thing") aggressively hostile in its universally competitive fight and bite.

Therefore, I have not Come here merely to stand Manly in the "middle" of mankind—to suffer its biting abuses, or even to be coddled and ignored in a little corner of religious "cultism".

I have Come here to Divinely Liberate one and all (and All) from the "dark" culture and effect of this "late-time", and (now, and forever hereafter) to Divinely Liberate one and all (and All) from the pattern and the act of ego-"I", and (Most Ultimately) to Divinely Translate one and all (and All) Into the Indivisible, Perfectly Subjective, and Eternally Non-Separate Sphere (or Non-"Different" and Indestructible "Midnight Sun") of My "Bright" Self-Domain of Divine Love-Bliss-Light.

The ego-"I" is a "centered" (or separate and separative) trap, from which the heart (and even the entire body-mind) must be Retired. I Am the Way (or the Very Means) of that Retirement from egoity. I Refresh the heart (and even the entire body-mind) of My devotee, in every moment My devotee resorts to Me (by devotionally recognizing My Avatarically-Born bodily human Divine Form and Person, and, on that basis, devotionally—and ecstatically, and also, often, meditatively—responding to My Avatarically-Born bodily human Divine Form and Person) Beyond the "middle", Beyond the "centering" act (or trapping gesture) of ego-"I" (or self-contraction).

I Am the Avatarically Self-Revealed (and Perfectly Subjective, and Self-Evidently Divine) Self-Condition (and Source-Condition) of every one, and of all, and of All—but the Perfectly Subjective (and Self-Evidently Divine) Self-Condition (and Source-Condition) is not "within" the ego-"I" (or separate and separative body-mind). The Perfectly Subjective (and Self-Evidently Divine) Self-Condition (and Source-Condition) is not in the "center" (or the "middle") of Man (or of mankind). The Perfectly Subjective (and Self-Evidently Divine) Self-Condition (and Source-Condition) of one, and of all, and of All Is Inherently centerless (or Always Already Beyond the self-contracted "middle"), and to Be Found only "outside" (or by transcending) the bounds of separateness, relatedness, and "difference". Therefore, in order to Realize the Perfectly Subjective (and Self-Evidently Divine) Self-Condition and Source-Condition (or the Perfectly Subjective, and Self-Evidently Divine, Heart) of one, and of all, and of All (or even, in any moment, to exceed the ego-trap—and to be Refreshed at heart, and in the total body-mind), it is necessary to feel (and to, ecstatically, and even meditatively, swoon) Beyond the "center" (or Beyond the "point of view" of separate ego-"I" and separative body-mind). Indeed, Most Ultimately, it is only in ego-transcendence to the degree of unqualified relatedness (and Most Perfect Divine Samadhi, or Utterly Non-Separate Enstasy) that the Inherently centerless and boundless, and Perfectly Subjective, and Self-Evidently Divine Self-Condition (and Source-Condition) Stands Obvious and Free (and Is, Thus and Thereby, Most Perfectly Realized).

It Is only by Means of devotionally Me-recognizing (and, on that basis, devotionally to-Me-responding) devotional meditation on My Avatarically-Born bodily (human) Divine Form and Person (and Thus ecstatic heart-Contemplation of Me), and (in due course) total (and totally open, and totally ego-forgetting) psycho-physical reception of My Avatarically Self-Transmitted Divine (and Always Blessing) Spiritual Presence and State of Person, that your madness of heart (and of body-mind) is (now, and now, and now) escaped, and your "darkness" is En-Light-ened (even, at last, Most Perfectly). Therefore, be My true devotee—and, by (formally, and rightly, and truly, and fully, and fully devotionally) practicing the only-by-Me Revealed and Given Way of Adidam (Which Is the Divine and True and Complete Way of Truth, and of Reality, and of Real God), always turn to My Avatarically-Born bodily (human) Divine Form, and (Thus and Thereby, and in due course) always Find Me Spiritually (by searchlessly "Locating" Me), Infinitely Above and Beyond your self-"center", and Surrounding and Pervading every here and now.

Aham Da Asmi. Beloved, I Am Da. And, because I Am Infinitely and Non-Separately "Bright", all and All are arising in My Divine Sphere of "Brightness". By feeling and surrendering into the Infinite Spiritual Sphere of My Avatarically Self-Revealed Divine Self-"Brightness", My every devotee Awakens (by Means of My Avataric Divine Spiritual Grace) to Merely Be in Me. And, Beyond his or her self-contracting and separative act of ego-"I", My every devotee (self-surrendered into heart-Communion With Me) Is the One and Only and Non-Separate and Real God I Have Come to Awaken—by Means of My Avataric Divine Incarnation, My Avataric Divine Spiritual Descent, and My Avataric Divine Self-"Emergence"—now, and forever hereafter, here (and every "where") in the cosmic domain.

AVATAR ADI DA SAMRAJ
The Mountain Of Attention Sanctuary, 2002

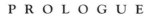

My Divine Disclosure

"My Divine Disclosure" has been Freely Developed—As a Further, and All-Completing, Avataric Self-Revelation of His Own Self-Evidently Divine Person—by the Ruchira Avatar, Adi Da Samraj, from selected verses of the traditional Bhagavad Gita *(2:13–17, 8:3, 8:22, 9:3, 9:11, 9:26, 15:15, 18:61–66).*

My Divine Disclosure

1.

Aham Da Asmi. Beloved, I <u>Am</u> Da—The One and Only and Self-Evidently Divine Person, Avatarically Self-Revealed To You.

2.

Therefore, Listen To <u>Me</u>, and Hear <u>Me</u>, and See <u>Me</u>.

3.

This Is My Divine Heart-Secret, The Supreme Word Of My Eternal Self-Revelation.

4.

Here and Now, I Will Tell You What Will Benefit You The Most, Because I Love You.

5.

I <u>Am</u> The Da Avatar, Adi Da Love-Ananda Samraj—The Ruchira Avatar, The Love-Ananda Avatar, The Avataric Incarnation (and The Self-Evidently Divine Person) Of The One True Heart (or The One, and Only, and Inherently egoless Self-Condition, and Source-Condition, and Conscious Light) Of all-and-All.

6.

Here I <u>Am</u>, In <u>Person</u>, To Offer (To You, and To all) The Only-By-<u>Me</u> Revealed and Given True World-Religion (or Avatarically All-Completing Divine Devotional and Spiritual Way) Of Adidam (or Adidam Ruchiradam)—Which Is The One and Only By-<u>Me</u>-Revealed and By-<u>Me</u>-Given (and Only <u>Me</u>-Revealing) Divine

Devotional and Spiritual Way Of The "Bright" (or The Only-By-Me
Revealed and Given, and Entirely Me-Revealing, Way Of The
One, and Only, and Inherently Indivisible, and Inherently ego-
less, and Self-Evidently Divine Conscious Light Of Reality Itself),
and Which Is The One, and All-Inclusive, and All-Transcending,
and Only-By-Me Revealed and Given (and Only Me-Revealing)
Way Of The True Divine Heart-Master (or The Only-By-Me
Revealed and Given, and Entirely Me-Revealing, Way Of Ruchira
Avatara Bhakti Yoga, or Ruchira Avatara Siddha Yoga), and
Which Is The "Radically" ego-Transcending Way Of Devotionally
Me-Recognizing and Devotionally To-Me-Responding Reception
Of My Avatarically Self-Manifested Divine (and Not Merely
Cosmic) Ruchira Shaktipat (or Divinely Self-Revealing Avataric
Spiritual Grace).

7.

If You Surrender Your heart To Me, and If (By Surrendering
Your ego-"I", or self-Contracted body-mind, To Me) You Make
Yourself A Living Gift To Me, and If You (Thus) Constantly Yield
Your attention To Me (Through True Devotional Love and Really
ego-Transcending Service), Then You Will Hear Me (Truly), and
See Me (Clearly), and Realize Me (Fully), and Come To Me
(Eternally). I Promise You This, Because I Love You.

8.

Abandon The Reactive Reflex Of self-Contraction—The Separative
(or egoic) Principle In all Your concerns. Do Not Cling To any
experience that May Be Sought (and Even Attained) As A Result
Of desire (or The Presumption Of "Difference"). Abandon Your
Search For what May Be Gotten As A Result Of the various kinds
of strategic (or egoic) action.

9.

I Am Love-Bliss Itself—Now (and Forever Hereafter) "Brightly"
Present here. Therefore, I Say To You: Abandon All Seeking—
By Always "Locating" (and Immediately Finding) Me.

10.

Instead Of <u>Seeking</u> <u>Me</u> (As If My Divine Person Of Inherent Love-Bliss-Happiness Were <u>Absent</u> From You), <u>Always</u> <u>Commune</u> <u>With</u> <u>Me</u> (<u>Ever</u>-Present, <u>Never</u> Absent, and <u>Always</u> Love-Bliss-Full and Satisfied). Thus, Your <u>Me</u>-"Locating" <u>Relinquishment</u> Of All Seeking Is <u>Not</u>, Itself, To Be Merely Another Form Of Seeking.

11.

If You <u>Always</u> "Locate" <u>Me</u> (and, Thus, <u>Immediately</u> Find <u>Me</u>), You Will <u>Not</u> (In <u>any</u> instance) self-Contract Into the mood and strategy of <u>inaction</u>.

12.

You Must <u>Never</u> <u>Fail</u> To act. <u>Every</u> moment of Your life <u>Requires</u> Your particular <u>Right</u> action. Indeed, the living body-mind <u>is</u> (itself) action. Therefore, <u>Be</u> <u>Ordinary</u>, By Always Allowing the body-mind its <u>Necessity</u> Of Right action (and Inevitable Change).

13.

Perform <u>every</u> act As An ego-Transcending Act Of Devotional Love Of <u>Me</u>, In body-mind-Surrendering Love-Response To <u>Me</u>.

14.

Always Discipline <u>all</u> Your acts, By <u>Only</u> Engaging In action that Is <u>Appropriate</u> For one who Loves <u>Me</u>, and Surrenders To <u>Me</u>, and acts <u>Only</u> (and <u>Rightly</u>) In Accordance With My Always <u>Explicit</u> Word Of Instruction.

15.

Therefore, Be My <u>Always</u> Listening-To-<u>Me</u> Devotee—and, Thus, <u>Always</u> live "Right Life" (According To My Word), and (This) <u>Always</u> By Means Of <u>active</u> Devotional Recognition-Response To <u>Me</u>, and While <u>Always</u> Remembering and Invoking and Contemplating <u>Me</u>. In <u>This</u> Manner, Perform <u>every</u> act As A Form Of Direct, and Present, and Whole bodily (or Total psycho-physical), and Really ego-Surrendering Love-Communion With <u>Me</u>.

16.

If You Love <u>Me</u>—Where <u>Is</u> doubt and anxious living? If You Love <u>Me</u> <u>Now</u>, Even anger, sorrow, and fear Are <u>Gone</u>. When You <u>Abide</u> In Devotional Love-Communion With <u>Me</u>, the natural results of Your various activities No Longer Have Power To Separate or Distract You From <u>Me</u>.

17.

The ego-"I" that is born (as a body-mind) In The Realm Of Cosmic Nature (or the conditional worlds of action and experience) Advances From childhood To adulthood, old age, and death—While Identified With the same (but Always Changing) body-mind. Then the same ego-"I" Attains another body-mind, As A <u>Result</u>. One whose heart Is (Always) Responsively Given To <u>Me</u> Overcomes (<u>Thereby</u>) <u>Every</u> Tendency To self-Contract From This Wonderfully Ordinary Process.

18.

The Ordinary Process Of "Everything Changing" Is Simply The Natural Play Of Cosmic Life, In Which the (<u>Always</u>) <u>two</u> sides of every possibility come and go, In Cycles Of appearance and disappearance. Winter's cold alternates with summer's heat. Pain, Likewise, Follows every pleasure. <u>Every</u> appearance Is (<u>Inevitably</u>) Followed By its <u>disappearance</u>. There Is <u>No</u> <u>Permanent</u> <u>experience</u> In The Realm Of Cosmic Nature. One whose heart-Feeling Of <u>Me</u> Is <u>Steady</u> Simply <u>Allows</u> All Of This To Be <u>So</u>. Therefore, one who Truly Hears <u>Me</u> Ceases To Add self-Contraction To This Inevitable Round Of Changes.

19.

Happiness (or True Love-Bliss) <u>Is</u> Realization Of <u>That</u> Which Is <u>Always</u> <u>Already</u> The Case.

20.

I <u>Am</u> <u>That</u> Which Is <u>Always</u> <u>Already</u> The Case.

21.

Happiness <u>Is</u> Realization Of <u>Me</u>.

22.

Realization Of <u>Me</u> Is Possible <u>Only</u> When a living being (or body-mind-self) Has heart-Ceased To <u>React</u> To The <u>Always Changing</u> Play Of Cosmic Nature.

23.

The body-mind Of My True Devotee Is <u>Constantly</u> Steadied In <u>Me</u>, By Means Of the Feeling-heart's Always Constant Devotional Recognition-Response To <u>Me</u>.

24.

Once My True Devotee Has Truly heart-Accepted That The Alternating-Cycle Of Changes (Both Positive and Negative) Is <u>Inevitable</u> (In the body-mind, and In <u>all</u> the conditional worlds), the living body-mind-self (or ego-"I") Of My True Devotee Has Understood <u>itself</u> (and, <u>Thus,</u> Heard <u>Me</u>).

25.

The body-mind-self (Of My True <u>Me</u>-Hearing Devotee) that Constantly Understands itself (At heart) By Constantly Surrendering To <u>Me</u> (and Communing With <u>Me</u>) No Longer self-Contracts From <u>My</u> Love-Bliss-State Of <u>Inherent</u> Happiness.

26.

Those who Truly <u>Hear Me</u> Understand That whatever Does Not Exist Always and Already (or Eternally) <u>Only</u> Changes.

27.

Those who Truly <u>See Me</u> Acknowledge (By heart, and With every moment and act of body-mind) That What <u>Is</u> Always Already The Case <u>Never</u> Changes.

28.

Such True Devotees Of Mine (who Both <u>Hear Me</u> <u>and</u> <u>See Me</u>) Realize That The Entire Cosmic Realm Of Change—and Even the To-<u>Me</u>-Surrendered body-mind (itself)—Is <u>Entirely</u> Pervaded By <u>Me</u> (Always Self-Revealed <u>As</u> <u>That</u> Which <u>Is</u> Always Already The Case).

29.

Now, and Forever Hereafter, I Am Avatarically Self-Revealed, Beyond The Cosmic Play—"Bright" Behind, and Above, the To-Me-Surrendered body-mind Of My Every True Devotee.

30.

I Am The Eternally Existing, All-Pervading, Transcendental, Inherently Spiritual, Inherently egoless, Perfectly Subjective, Indivisible, Inherently Perfect, Perfectly Non-Separate, and Self-Evidently Divine Self-Condition and Source-Condition Of all Apparently Separate (or self-Deluded) selves.

31.

My Divine Heart-Power Of Avataric Self-Revelation Is (Now, and Forever Hereafter) Descending Into The Cosmic Domain (and Into the body-mind Of Every To-Me-True True Devotee Of Mine).

32.

I Am The Avatarically Self-"Emerging", Universal, All-Pervading Divine Spirit-Power and Person Of Love-Bliss (That Most Perfectly Husbands and Transcends The Primal Energy Of Cosmic Nature).

33.

I Am The One and Indivisibly "Bright" Divine Person.

34.

Now, and Forever Hereafter, My Ever-Descending and Ever-"Emerging" Current Of Self-Existing and Self-Radiant Love-Bliss Is Avatarically Pervading The Ever-Changing Realm Of Cosmic Nature.

35.

I Am The One, and Indivisibly "Bright", and Inherently egoless, and Self-Evidently Divine Person Of all-and-All, Within Whom every body-mind Is arising (as a mere, and unnecessary, and merely temporary appearance that, merely apparently, modifies Me).

36.

I Am To Be Realized By Means Of Searchless Devotional Love Of Me—Whereby <u>every</u> action of body-mind Is (Responsively) Engaged As ego-Surrendering (present-time, and Direct) Communion With <u>Me</u>.

37.

Those who Do <u>Not</u> heart-Recognize <u>Me</u> and heart-Respond To <u>Me</u>—and who (Therefore) Are Without Faith In <u>Me</u>—Do <u>Not</u> (and <u>Cannot</u>) <u>Realize</u> <u>Me</u>. Therefore, they (By Means Of their own self-Contraction From <u>Me</u>) Remain ego-Bound To The Realm Of Cosmic Nature, and To The Ever-Changing Round Of conditional knowledge and temporary experience, and To The Ceaselessly Repetitive Cycles Of birth and search and loss and death.

38.

Such Faithless beings <u>Cannot</u> Be Distracted By <u>Me</u>—Because they Are Entirely Distracted By <u>themselves</u>! They Are Like Narcissus— The Myth Of ego—At His Pond. Their Merely self-Reflecting minds Are Like a mirror in a dead man's hand. Their tiny hearts Are Like a boundless desert, where the mirage of Separate self is ceaselessly admired, and The True Water Of My Constant Presence Stands Un-Noticed, In the droughty heap and countless sands of ceaseless thoughts. If Only they Would Un-think themselves In <u>Me</u>, these (Now Faithless) little hearts Could Have <u>Immediate</u> <u>Access</u> To The True Water Of My True Heart! Through Devotional Surrender Of body, emotion, mind, breath, and all of Separate self To <u>Me</u>, Even Narcissus Could Find The Way To My Oasis (In The True Heart's Room and House)—but the thinking mind of ego-"I" Is <u>Never</u> Bathed In Light (and, So, it sits, Un-Washed, Like a desert dog that wanders in a herd of flies).[3]

39.

The "Un-Washed dog" of self-Contracted body-mind Does Not think To Notice <u>Me</u>—The Divine Heart-Master Of its wild heart and Wilderness.

40.

The "Wandering dog" of ego-"I" Does Not "Locate" Me In My Inherent "Bright" Perfection—The Divine Heart-Master Of Everything, The Inherently egoless Divine True Heart Of all conditionally Manifested beings, and The Non-Separate and Indivisible Self-Condition and Source-Condition Of all-and-All.

41.

If Only "Narcissus" Will Relent, and heart-Consent To Bow and Live In Love-Communion With Me, heart-Surrendering all of body-mind To Me, By Means Of Un-Contracting Love Of Me, Then—Even If That Love Is Shown With Nothing More Than the "little gift" of ego-"I" (itself)—I Will Always Accept The Offering With Open Arms Of Love-Bliss-Love, and Offer My Own Divine Immensity In "Bright" Return.

42.

Therefore, whoever Is Given (By heart) To Me Will Be Washed, From head To toe, By All The True Water Of My Love-Bliss-Light, That Always Crashes Down On all-and-All, Below My Blessing-Feet.

43.

My Circumstance and Situation Is At the heart of all beings—where I Am (Now, and Forever Hereafter) Avatarically Self-"Emerging" As The One and all-and-All-Outshining Divine and Only Person—Avatarically Self-Manifested As The "Radically" Non-Dual "Brightness" Of all-and-All-Filling Conscious Love-Bliss-Light, Self-Existing and Self-Radiant As The Perfectly Subjective Fundamental Reality, or Inherent (and Inherently egoless) Feeling, Of Merely (or Unqualifiedly) Being.

44.

The True heart-Place (Where I Am To Be "Located" By My True Devotee) Is Where The Ever-Changing Changes Of waking, dreaming, and sleeping experience Are Merely Witnessed (or Merely Felt, and Not Sought, or Found, or Held).

45.

Every conditional experience appears and disappears In Front Of the Witness-heart (Of Mere Feeling-Awareness, Itself).

46.

Everything Merely Witnessed (or Merely Felt) Is Spontaneously Generated By The Persistent Activity Of The Universal Cosmic Life-Energy.

47.

The self-Contracted heart of body-mind Is Fastened, <u>Help-lessly</u>, To That Perpetual-Motion Machine Of Cosmic Nature.

48.

I <u>Am</u> The Divine and One True Heart (<u>Itself</u>)—Always Already Existing <u>As</u> The Eternally Self-Evident Love-Bliss-Feeling Of Being (and Always Already Free-Standing <u>As</u> Consciousness Itself, Prior To the little heart of ego-"I" and its Seeming Help-less-ness).

49.

In Order To Restore all beings To The One True Heart Of <u>Me</u>, I Am Avatarically Born To here, <u>As</u> The "Bright" Divine Help Of conditionally Manifested beings.

50.

Therefore (Now, and Forever Hereafter), I <u>Am</u> (Always Free-Standing) <u>At</u> the To-<u>Me</u>-True heart Of You—and I <u>Am</u> (Always "Bright") Above Your body-mind and world.

51.

If You Become My True Devotee (Searchlessly heart-Recognizing My Avatarically Self-Manifested Divine Person, and, On That Basis, heart-Responding—With <u>all</u> the parts of Your single body-mind— To My Avatarically Self-Revealing Divine Form and Presence and State), You Will <u>Always</u> Be Able To Feel <u>Me</u> ("Brightly-Emerging" here) Within Your Un-Contracting, In-<u>Me</u>-Falling heart—and You

Will Always Be Able To "Locate" Me, As I Crash Down (All-"Bright" Upon You) From Infinitely Above the worlds Of Change.

52.
The To-Me-Feeling (In-Me-Falling) heart Of My Every True Devotee Is (At its Root, and Base, and Highest Height) My Divine and One True Heart (Itself).

53.
Therefore, Fall Awake In Me.

54.
Do Not Surrender Your Feeling-heart Merely To experience and know the Ever-Changing world.

55.
Merely To know and experience The Cosmic Domain (Itself) Is To live As If You Were In Love With Your Own body-mind.

56.
Therefore, Surrender Your Feeling-heart Only To Me, The True Divine Beloved Of the body-mind.

57.
I Am The Truth (and The Teacher) Of the heart-Feeling body-mind.

58.
I Am The Divine and Eternal Master Of Your To-Me-Feeling heart and Your To-Me-Surrendering body-mind.

59.
I Am The Self-Existing, Self-Radiant, and Inherently Perfect Person Of Unconditional Being—Who Pervades The Machine Of Cosmic Nature As The "Bright" Divine Spirit-Current Of Love-Bliss, and Who Transcends All Of Cosmic Nature As Infinite Self-Conscious Light, The Spiritually "Bright" Divine Self-Condition (and Source-Condition) Of all-and-All.

60.

If You Will Give (and Truly, Really, Always Give) Your Feeling-attention To My Avatarically-Born Bodily (Human) Divine Form, and If You Will (Thus, and Thereby) Yield Your body-mind Into The Down-Crashing Love-Bliss-Current Of My Avatarically Self-Transmitted and All-Pervading Divine Spirit-Presence, and If You Will Surrender Your conditional self-Consciousness Into My Avatarically Self-Revealed and Perfectly Subjective and Self-Evidently Divine Self-Consciousness (Which Is The Divine True Heart Of Inherently egoless Being, Itself)—Then I Will Also Become An Offering To You.

61.

By That Offering Of Mine, You Will Be Given The Gift Of Perfect Peace, and An Eternal Domain For Your To-Me-True Feeling-heart.

62.

Now I Have Revealed To You The Divine Mystery and The Perfect Heart-Secret Of My Avataric Birth To here.

63.

"Consider" This Me-Revelation, Fully—and, Then, Choose What You Will Do With Your "little gift" of Feeling-heart and Your "Un-Washed dog" of body-mind.

AVATAR ADI DA SAMRAJ
Adidam Samrajashram, 2004

PART ONE

The Great Esoteric Tradition
of Devotion To
The Adept-Realizer

The Great Esoteric Tradition
of Devotion To
The Adept-Realizer

S piritually Realized Adepts (or Transmission-Masters, or true Gurus and Sat-Gurus) are the principal Sources, Resources, and Means of the esoteric (or Spiritual) Way. This fact is not (and never has been) a matter of controversy among real Spiritual practitioners.

The entire Spiritual Way is a process based on the understanding (and the transcending) of attention, or the understanding (and the transcending) of the inevitable and specific results of attachment to, or reaction to, or identification with every kind of conditional object, other, or state. This Spiritual understanding (or real self-understanding) is expressed in a simple traditional formula (and prescription for practice): You become (or duplicate the qualities of) whatever you meditate on (or whatever you identify with via the "surrender" that is attention itself). Since the most ancient days, this understanding has informed and inspired the practice of real practitioners of the Spiritual Way. Likewise (since the most ancient days), and on the basis of this very understanding, Spiritual practitioners have affirmed that the Great Principle of Spiritual practice is Satsang, or the practice of life as self-surrender to the bodily Person, the Transmitted Spiritual Presence, and the Realized State of a Spiritually Realized Adept (or true Guru, or Sat-Guru) of whatever degree or stage.[4]

The traditional term "Guru" (spelled with a capital "G") means "One Who Reveals the Light and thereby Liberates beings from Darkness". This term is also commonly (or popularly) interpreted in a general (or everyday) sense (and spelled with a small "g") to mean "teacher" (or anyone who teaches anything at all to another). Thus, Adepts have certainly (and rightly) been valued simply (or in the general sense) as (small "g") "gurus" (that is, simply because they can instruct others about many things, including the Spiritual Way). However, the function of instruction (about anything at all) can be performed by anyone who is properly informed (or even by a book that is properly informed)—and, indeed, even the specific function of Spiritual Instruction is secondary to the Great Function of the Adept (As Guru, with a capital "G", and, in the Greatest of cases, As Sat-Guru).

Adepts inevitably (or, at least, in the majority of cases) Instruct (or Teach) others, but the function of Instruction (about the Spiritual Way) is then passed on through good books (containing the authentic Word of Teaching), and through informed others (who are, hopefully, true practitioners), and so forth. The Great Function of the Adept-Guru (and especially the Sat-Guru) is, however, specific only to Adepts themselves, and this is the Guru-Function (and the Guru-Principle) supremely valued by Spiritual practitioners since the most ancient days.

The specific Guru-Function is associated with the Great Principle of Satsang (and the unique Spiritual understanding of attention). Therefore, since the most ancient days, all truly established (or real) Spiritual practitioners have understood that Satsang Itself is the Great Means for Realizing Real God, or Truth, or Reality. That is to say, the Great Means (or Secret) of Realization in the Spiritual Way is to live in, or to spend significant time in, or otherwise (and constantly) to give attention to the Company, Form, Presence, and State of an Adept who is (truly) Realized in one or another of the esoteric stages of life.

The Essence of the practice of Satsang is to focus attention on (and thereby to, progressively, become Identified with, or Realize Indivisible Oneness with) the Realized Condition of a true Adept (especially an Adept Sat-Guru, or One Who Is presently and constantly In Samadhi). Therefore, the practice of Satsang is the practice of ego-transcending Communion (and, Ultimately, Indivisible Oneness) with the Adept's own Condition, Which Is (according to the degree or stage of the Adept's characteristic Realization) Samadhi Itself, or the Adept's characteristic (and Freely, Spontaneously, and Universally Transmitted) Realization (Itself).

Based on the understanding of attention (or the observation that Consciousness Itself, in the context of the body-mind, tends to identify with, or becomes fixed in association with, whatever attention observes, and especially with whatever attention surrenders to most fully), the Spiritual Motive is essentially the Motive to transcend the limiting capability of attention (or of all conditional objects, others, and states). Therefore, the traditional Spiritual process (as a conventional technique, begun in the context of the fourth stage of life) is an effort (or struggle) to set attention (and, thus, Consciousness Itself) Free by progressively relinquishing attachment and reaction to conditional objects, others, and states (and, Ultimately, this process requires the Most Perfect transcending of egoity, or self-contraction itself, or all the egoic limitations associated with each and all of the first six stages of life).

This conventional effort (or struggle) is profound and difficult, and it tends to progress slowly. Therefore, some few adopt the path of extraordinary self-effort (or a most intense struggle of relinquishment), which is asceticism (or the method of absolute independence). However, the Adepts themselves have, since the most ancient days, offered an alternative to mere (and, at best, slowly progressing) self-effort. Indeed, the Adept-Gurus (and especially the Sat-Gurus) offer a Unique Principle of practice (as an alternative to the conventional principle of mere and independent self-effort and relinquishment). That Unique Principle is the Principle of Supreme Attraction.

Truly, the bondage of attention to conditional objects, others, and states must be really transcended in the Spiritual Way, but mere self-effort (or struggle with the separate, and separative, self) is a principle that originates in (and constantly reinforces) the separate (and separative) self (or self-contraction, or egoity itself). Therefore, the process of the real transcending of bondage to conditions is made direct (and truly ego-transcending) if the principle of independent self-effort (or egoic struggle) is (at least progressively) replaced by the responsive (or cooperative) Principle of Supreme Attraction (Which Is, in Its Fullness, Satsang, or responsive devotional and Spiritual Identification with the Free Person, Presence, and State of One Who Is Already Realized, or In Samadhi).

On the basis of the simple understanding of attention—expressed in the formula: You become (or Realize) What (or Who) you meditate on—the ancient Essence of the Spiritual Way is to meditate on (and otherwise to grant feeling-attention to) the Adept-Guru (or Sat-Guru), and (thereby) to be Attracted (or Grown) beyond the self-contraction (or egoity, or all the self-limiting tendencies of attention, or all self-limiting and self-binding association with conditional objects, others, and states). Through sympathetic (or responsive) Spiritual Identification with the Samadhi-State of a Realizer, the devotee is Spiritually Infused and (potentially) Awakened by the Inherently Attractive Power of Samadhi Itself. (Even the simplest beginner in practice may be directly Inspired—and, thus, moved toward greater practice, true devotion, and eventual Spiritual Awakening—by sympathetic response to the Free Sign, and the Great Demonstration, of a true Realizer.) And, by the Great Spiritual Means that Is true Satsang (coupled with a variety of disciplines and practices, which should be associated with real self-understanding), the fully prepared devotee of a true Realizer may Freely (or with relative effortlessness) relinquish (or Grow Beyond) the limits of attention in each of the progressive stages of life that, in due course, follow upon that devotion.

Of course, actual Spiritual Identification with the Realized Spiritual Condition (or Samadhi) of an Adept is limited by the stage of life of the devotee, the effective depth of the self-understanding and the ego-transcending devotional response of the devotee, and the stage of life and Realization of the Adept. And some traditions may (unfortunately) tend to replace (or, at least, to combine) the essential and Great Communion that is true Satsang with concepts and norms associated with the parent-child relationship, or the relationship between a king and a frightened subject, or even the relationship between a slave-master and a slave. However, this Great Principle (or Means) that Is Satsang (rightly understood and truly practiced) is the ancient Essence (or Great Secret) of the Spiritual Way—and true Adept-Gurus (and especially the Sat-Gurus) have, therefore, since the most ancient days, been the acknowledged principal Sources and Resources (as well as the principal Means) of true religion (or effective religious Wisdom) and the esoteric tradition of Spiritual Realization.

Particularly in more modern days, since Spirituality (and everything else) has become a subject of mass communication and popularization, the Spiritual Way Itself has become increasingly subject to conventional interpretation and popular controversy. In the broad social (or survival) context of the first three stages of life, self-fulfillment (or the consolation of the ego) is the common ideal (tempered only by local, popular, and conventional political, social, and religious ideals, or demands). Therefore, the common mood is one of adolescent anti-authority and anti-hierarchy (stemming from the "Oedipal" anti-"parent" disposition), and the common search is for a kind of ever-youthful (and "Narcissistic") ego-omnipotence and ego-omniscience.

The popular egalitarian (or ego-based, and merely, and competitively, individualistic) "culture" (or, really, anti-culture) of the first three stages of life is characterized by the politics of adolescent rebellion against "authority" (or the perceived "parent", in any form). Indeed, a society (or any loose collective) of mere individuals does not need, and cannot even tolerate, a true culture— because a true culture must, necessarily, be characterized (in its best, and even general, demonstrations, and, certainly, in its aspirations) by mutual tolerance, cooperation, peace, and profundity. Therefore, societies based on competitive individualism, and egoic self-fulfillment, and mere gross-mindedness (or superficial-mindedness) actually destroy culture (and all until-then-existing cultures, and cultural adaptations). And true cultures (and true cultural adaptations) are produced (and needed) only when individuals rightly and truly participate in a collective, and, thus and thereby (even if, as may sometimes, or especially in some cases, be the case, in relative, or even actual, solitude), live in accordance with the life-principle of ego-transcendence and the Great Principle of Oneness (or Unity).

In the popular egalitarian (or ego-based, and merely, and competitively, individualistic) "culture" (or, really, anti-culture) of the first three stages of life, the Guru (and the Sat-Guru) and the developmental culture of the Spiritual Way are (with even all of "authority" and of true, or ego-transcending, culture) taboo, because every individual limited (or egoically defined) by the motives of the first three stages of life is at war with personal vulnerability and need (or the feeling of egoic insufficiency). However, the real Spiritual process does not even begin until the egoic point of view of the first three stages of life is understood (or otherwise ceases to be the limit of aspiration and awareness) and the ego-surrendering and ego-transcending Motive of the fourth stage of life begins to move and change the body-mind (from the heart).

Those who are truly involved in the ego-surrendering and ego-transcending process of the esoteric stages of life are (fundamentally) no longer at war with their own Help (or struggling toward the ultimate victory of the ego). Therefore, it is only in the non-Spiritual (or even anti-Spiritual) "cultural" domain of the first three stages of life (or the conventional survival-culture, bereft of the Motive of truly developmental and Spiritual culture) that the Guru (or the Sat-Guru) is, in principle, taboo. And, because that taboo is rooted in adolescent reactivity and egoic willfulness (or the yet unresolved emotional, and psychological, and even emotional-sexual rebellion against childish and asexual, or emotionally and sexually ego-suppressing, dependence on parent-like individuals and influences), "anti-Guruism", and even "anti-cultism"—which (characteristically, and without discrimination) denigrate, and defame, and mock, or otherwise belittle, <u>all</u> "authorities", and (also) even all the seed-groups of newly emerging cultural movements (whether or not they have positive merit)—are forms (or expressions) of what Sigmund Freud described as an "Oedipal" problem.

In the common world of mankind, it is yet true that most individuals tend (by a combination of mechanical psycho-physical tendencies and a mass of conventional political, social, and cultural pressures) to be confined to the general point of view associated, developmentally, with the unfinished (or yet to be understood) "business" of the first three stages of life. Thus, in the common world of mankind, even religion is (characteristically) reduced to what is intended to serve the "creaturely" (or "worldly"), and rather aggressively <u>exoteric</u>, point of view and purposes of egoity in the context of the first three stages of life. And even if an interest in the <u>esoteric</u> possibilities (beyond the first three stages of life) develops in the case of any such (yet rather "worldly") character, that interest tends to be pursued in a manner that dramatizes and reinforces the point of view (and the exoteric, and either childishly or adolescently egoic, inclinations) characteristic of the first three stages of life.

Until there is the development of significantly effective self-understanding relative to the developmental problems (or yet unfinished "business") associated with the first three stages of life, any one who aspires to develop a truly esoteric religious practice (necessarily beginning in the context of the fourth stage of life) will, characteristically, tend to relate to such possible esoteric practice in either a childish or an adolescent manner. Thus, any one whose developmental disposition is yet relatively childish (or tending, in general, to seek egoic security via the dramatization of the role of emotionalistic dependency) will tend to relate to esoteric possibilities via emotionalistic (or, otherwise, merely enthusiastic) attachments, while otherwise (in general) tending to be weak in both the responsible exercise of discriminating intelligence and the likewise responsible exercise of functional, practical, relational, and cultural self-discipline. (Indeed, such childish religiosity, characterized by dependent emotionalism, or mere enthusiastic attachment, bereft of discrimination and real self-discipline, is what may rightly, without bad intentions, be described and criticized as "cultism".) And any one whose developmental disposition is yet relatively adolescent (or tending, in general, to seek egoic security via the dramatization of the role of reactive independence) will tend to relate to esoteric possibilities via generally "heady" (or willful, rather mental, or even intellectual, or bookish, but not, altogether, truly intelligent) efforts, accompanied either (or even alternately) by a general lack of self-discipline (and a general lack of non-reactive emotional responsiveness) or by an exaggerated (abstractly enforced, and more or less life-suppressing and emotion-suppressing) attachment to self-discipline. (Therefore, such adolescent, or "heady", religiosity merely continues the dramatization of the characteristic adolescent search for independence, or the reactive pursuit of escape from every kind of dependency, and, altogether, the reactive pursuit of egoic self-sufficiency. And such adolescent seeking is inherently and reactively disinclined toward any kind of self-surrender. Therefore, the rather adolescent seeker tends to want to be his or her own "guru" in all matters. And, characteristically, the rather adolescent seeker will resist, and would even prefer to avoid, a truly intelligent, rightly self-disciplined, and, altogether, devotionally self-surrendered relationship to a true Guru, or Sat-Guru.)

Because of their developmental tendencies toward either childish or adolescent ego-dramatizations, those who are yet bound to the point of view (or the unfinished "business") of the first three stages of life are, developmentally (or in their characteristic disposition, which is not yet relieved by sufficient self-understanding), also (regardless of their presumed "interest") not yet truly ready to enter into the esoteric process (beyond the first three stages of life). And, for the same developmental reasons, the principal and most characteristic impediments toward true participation in the esoteric religious process are "cultism" (or mere emotionalistic dependency, bereft of discrimination and self-discipline), "intellectualism" (or merely mental, or even bookish, preoccupation, disinclined to fully participatory, or directly experiential, involvement in the esoteric religious process), and "anti-Guruism" (or reactive attachment to a state of egoic independence, immune to the necessity for devotional self-surrender and the Grace of Great Help).

It is not the specific (and Great) Function of the Adept to fulfill a popular Spiritual (or, otherwise, non-Spiritual) role in common (or egoic and early stage) society, but to Serve as Teacher, Guide, Spiritual Transmitter, or Free Awakener in relation to those who are already (and rightly) moved (and progressively prepared) to fulfill the ego-transcending obligations of the Great and (soon) Spiritual Way Itself (in the potential developmental context that is beyond the first three stages of life). The only proper relationship to such a Realized Adept (or true Guru, or Sat-Guru) is, therefore, one of real and right and ego-surrendering and ego-transcending practice, and that practice becomes (or must become) Inspired (and, soon, Spiritually Inspired) and ego-transcending devotion—

not childish egoity (or "cultic" dependency), and not adolescent egoity (or willful—or, otherwise, ambivalent—independence).

Of course, individuals in the earlier (or first three) stages of life who are not yet actively oriented (or, otherwise, rightly adapted) to ego-surrendering and ego-transcending practice may be Served by Adept-Gurus (or Sat-Gurus), but (apart from special instances where an Adept must Work directly with such individuals, in order to establish a new cultural gathering of devotees, or in order to establish a new Revelation of the Spiritual Way) those not yet actively oriented (or actively committed), or (otherwise) rightly adapted, to truly ego-surrendering and really ego-transcending practice are generally (except perhaps for occasional glimpses of the Adept in his or her Free Demonstration) Served (or prepared for ego-surrendering, ego-transcending, and, soon, Spiritual practice) only through the written (or otherwise recorded) Teachings of an Adept, and through the public institutional work (and the "outer Temple", or beginner-serving, institutional work) of the practicing devotees of an Adept.

The Realized Adept (or any true Guru, or Sat-Guru) is, primarily, an esoteric Figure, whose unique Function Serves within the context of the esoteric stages of life. The esoteric stages of life are themselves open only to those who are ready, willing, and able to make the truly developmental (or progressively Real-God-Realizing, or Truth-Realizing, or Reality-Realizing) sacrifice of separate and separative self that is necessary in the context of the esoteric stages of life. Therefore, the necessity (and the True Nature and Great Function) of a Realized Adept (or true Guru, or Sat-Guru) is obvious (and of supreme value) only to those who are ready, willing, and able to embrace the ego-transcending process of the esoteric stages of life.

Except for the possible moments in which the Divine Person (or the Ultimate Reality and Truth) may (for some few) Serve (temporarily, and, to whatever degree, significantly, and, in any case, never to the Most Ultimate, or Most Perfect, degree) in (or via) a non-physical (and/or perhaps even non-human) Revelation-Form, the Realized Adept—or a human and living true Guru, or (especially) a human and living true Sat-Guru, or (at least) a human and living true (and formally Acknowledged, Appointed, and Blessed) devotee-Instrument of a once living (or even, perhaps, yet living, and, certainly, yet Spiritually Effective) true Sat-Guru—is an absolute (and never obsolete) necessity for any and every human being who would practice (and Realize) within the esoteric stages of life. Therefore, the necessity (and the True Nature and Great Function) of a Realized Adept (or true Guru, or Sat-Guru) is inherently (and gratefully) obvious to any one and every one who is truly ready, willing, and able to embrace the esoteric process of Real-God-Realization (or Truth-Realization).

Any one and every one who doubts and quibbles about the necessity (and the True Nature and Great Function) of a true Adept-Guru (or Adept Sat-Guru) is, simply, not yet ready, willing, and able to enter the (necessarily, ego-surrendering) process of the esoteric stages of life. And no mere verbal (or otherwise exoteric) argument is sufficient to convince such doubters of the necessity (and the True Nature and Great Function) of a true Adept-Guru (or Adept Sat-Guru)—just as no mere verbal (or otherwise exoteric) argument is sufficient to make them ready, willing, and able to truly embrace the ego-surrendering process of the esoteric stages of life.

Those who doubt the Guru-Principle, and the unique value and ultimate necessity of the Adept-Guru (or the Adept Sat-Guru), are those for whom the Great and (soon) Spiritual Way Itself is yet in doubt. Therefore, such matters remain "controversial" (and access to the Spiritual Way and the Adept-Company is effectively denied to ordinary people by popular taboos and the psychological limitations of the first three stages of life) until the truly developmental and (soon) Spiritual Motive Awakens the heart's Great Impulse to Grow Beyond.

Avatar Adi Da Samraj
Lopez Island, 2000

PART TWO

The Divine Siddha-Method
Of The Ruchira Avatar

AVATAR ADI DA SAMRAJ
Los Angeles, April 25, 1972

1.

Understanding

On April 25, 1972 (the date of this Talk), Avatar Adi Da Samraj (for the first time) formally invited people to approach Him, at His Ashram in Los Angeles. Thus, it was on this date that His Work as Divine World-Teacher truly began. Before this time, previous to the formal establishment of His Ashram, He had Taught only a few individuals who had begun to respond to Him as Spiritual Teacher. In addition to marking the inception of His open Spiritual availability to all who are moved to respond to His Avataric Divine Wisdom, Grace, and Person, the occasion of this Talk also marked the moment when Avatar Adi Da's devotees formally began to acknowledge Him, and to relate to Him, as Divine Heart-Master.

In this first Talk, Avatar Adi Da described the process of "radical" (or "gone-to-the-root") self-understanding which had been one of the fundamental discoveries of His Own Life, and which is absolutely necessary for right (and truly ego-transcending) participation in Satsang with Him (or the sacred relationship to Him as Divine Heart-Master). In the thousands of hours of Discourse and the scores of volumes of Written Instruction that He has Given since this first Talk, Avatar Adi Da Samraj has consistently reiterated and thoroughly elaborated the Call to "radical" self-understanding that He makes here. Thus, the seminal Discourse He gave on this night is one of the cornerstones of His consummate Revelation of Spiritual Instruction and Blessing.

At the beginning of the occasion on April 25, 1972, Avatar Adi Da first sat in silence for perhaps an hour, Transmitting the Sublimity of His Own Divine Heart-"Brightness" to those who were present. Then He Spoke.

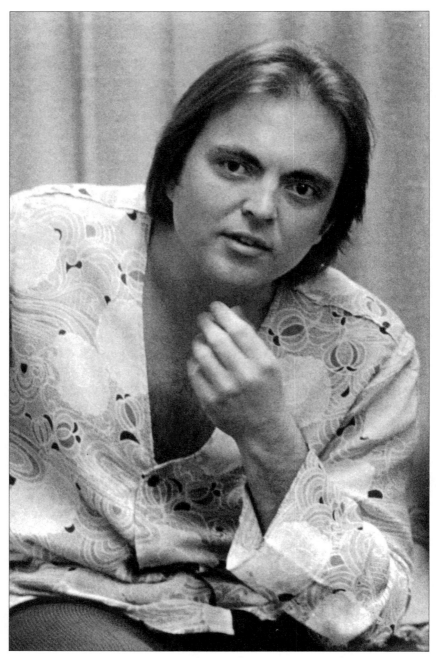

Los Angeles, April 25, 1972

AVATAR ADI DA SAMRAJ: Are there any questions?

No one replied, so Avatar Adi Da Samraj Spoke again.

AVATAR ADI DA SAMRAJ: Everyone has understood?

QUESTIONER: I have not understood. Explain it to me.[5]

AVATAR ADI DA SAMRAJ: Very good. What have you not understood?

QUESTIONER: Well, you asked if everyone understood, and everyone seemed to understand except me. Would you explain it to me?

AVATAR ADI DA SAMRAJ: Explain what?

QUESTIONER: Well, you could start with the word "understanding".

AVATAR ADI DA SAMRAJ: Yes. There is a disturbance, a feeling of dissatisfaction, some kind of sensation that motivates a person to go to a teacher, read a book about philosophy, believe something, or do some conventional form of Yoga. What people ordinarily think of as religion or Spirituality is a search to get free of the sensation, the suffering, that is motivating them. All of the usual paths—Yogic methods, philosophical investigations, religious beliefs and observances, Spiritual techniques, and so on—are forms of seeking, grown out of this sensation, this underlying suffering. All the usual paths are, fundamentally, attempts to get free of that sensation. That is the traditional goal. Indeed, all human beings are involved in the search—whether or not they are very sophisticated about it, whether or not they are using specific methods of Yoga, philosophy, religion, and so on.

When that process of seeking begins to break down, then you no longer quite have the "edge" of your search left. You begin to suspect yourself. You begin to doubt the process of your search. Then you are no longer fascinated with your search, your method, your Yoga, your religion. Your attention begins to turn to the sensation that motivates your search.

When you begin to consciously observe that root-motivation, this is what I call "understanding". When you begin to see the root-form of your own activity—which is your suffering—that self-observation becomes self-understanding. When (through the great ordeal of Real Spiritual life) such self-understanding becomes absolute, most perfect—such that there is utterly, absolutely, no dilemma, no form in conscious awareness by which to interpret existence, such that there is no self-contraction, no fundamental suffering, no "thing" apart from Consciousness Itself—That is the Most Perfect Realization of "'radical' (or 'gone-to-the-root') self-understanding". It is only Love-Bliss-Happiness.

The religious and Spiritual traditions of humankind variously refer to the Ultimate Enjoyment as the "Self" (with a capital "S"), the "Heart", "God-Union", "Enlightenment", "Nirvana", "Heaven", and so on—but, in Reality, the Ultimate Enjoyment is simply Consciousness Itself (or the Divine Conscious Light Itself). There is no "thing" apart from Consciousness Itself. You are not some "piece" of Divinity seated "inside" the body, which must somehow get released from the body and go back to its Spiritual Home and Source. There is no such entity. The Home and Source is also the Very Nature of the presumed "entity". There Is Consciousness Itself—and the apparent "entity" is arising within Consciousness Itself.

When Consciousness Itself Knows Its Own State (or Real Nature)—even in the midst of conditions, even where there is life—That is most perfect "radical" self-understanding. When (no matter what event appears) there is only the Enjoyment (or Realization) of Consciousness Itself (not transformed or modified by events), when no arising event seems to imply a change in the Nature of Consciousness Itself—That is most perfect "meditation". When there is Most Perfect Self-Abiding as Consciousness Itself—That is Divine Liberation. Such can be the case only when there is most perfect "radical" self-understanding.

There is a fundamental self-contraction in the process called "Man"—and that contraction seems to change the quality of

Consciousness Itself. The contraction itself creates (or seems to imply) the identification of Consciousness Itself with the self-contracted sense—the sense that you are this form, this body, this mind. And, in making such an act of identification, that form, that body, that mind differentiates itself from other forms, other bodies, other minds—other beings (or selves). Then the rest of life is spent attempting to overcome that self-generated sense of contraction, by exploiting the movement of desire.

Through the movement that is desire, people are constantly seeking to create a connection, a flow of life-force, between the self-contracted identity and everything from which it has differentiated itself. The usual philosophy, religion, Yoga, Spirituality—all your strategies (even your simple psychological strategies, your lifestyles) have this same basic form, this same basic purpose. They are all attempts to restore the flow of life-energy between this contracted, separated one and everything from which it is differentiating itself. Thus, all ordinary activity is founded in this dilemma, this self-created contraction.

Traditional Spiritual life is a search in this same form. There is dilemma—and there is the Spiritual method, which is an attempt to overcome this dilemma. When you begin to see the dilemma that motivates your strategic method, then that seeing is self-understanding. As long as you are merely seeking, and have all kinds of motivation, all kinds of fascination with the search, this is not self-understanding—this is dilemma itself. But, when the dilemma is understood, then there is the clear noticing of a structure in conscious awareness—the activity of separation. And, when that activity is observed more and more directly, then you begin to see that what you are suffering is not something happening to you but it is your own activity.

It is as if you are pinching yourself, without being aware of it. You are creating a constant background-pain. And, worse than the pain, you are creating a continuous modification—"mind", which conscious awareness (mistakenly) identifies as itself. The more you observe all of this, the more you stop pinching yourself, and (therefore) the more you (spontaneously, and intelligently) abandon your search. You simply see your root-motivation and your actual suffering. You are no longer able to immunize yourself against that suffering. The suffering does not go away—until, at some point, conscious life becomes a crisis. Then you see that your entire motivation in life is based on a root-activity that you yourself are doing. That activity is avoidance, separation—a contraction at the root, the origin, the "place", of conscious awareness.

In the beginning of this crisis, you are aware of the self-contraction only as a sensation, a sense of dilemma, a search. But the more directly you observe the self-contraction, the more clearly you recognize it as your own activity. At first, you see the activity, the strategy, the life-technique, of avoidance. Then you begin to become aware of what that activity is excluding, what it prevents, what it is always eliminating from conscious awareness. What is always being excluded is the condition of <u>relationship</u>.

Ordinarily, you are not aware <u>of</u> relationship—and you are also not aware <u>as</u> relationship. You are only living the drama of separation. But, when you become directly aware of (and, thus, responsible for) the root-activity of separation, then you are spontaneously established in relationship as the Real condition of life. Relationship is always the condition of conscious awareness. When the self-contraction is most fundamentally understood, then there is only relationship, and no obstruction. Ultimately, even the feeling of relatedness is transcended in the Inherent Feeling of Being. When such transcending is most perfect, then there is Most Perfect Feeling-Awareness. That Most Perfect Feeling-Awareness Is the True Divine Heart, Reality Itself. That Most Perfect Feeling-Awareness Is That Which Is Always Already the Case.

The True Divine Heart is Always Already Active, Always Already Accomplishing the thing that desire constantly seeks but never finally Realizes. The True Divine Heart is Always Already Non-separateness (or unqualified relatedness), Always Already Conscious Force (without obstruction). But the life of desire is always based on the presumption (and activity) of separation. In the usual human being, separation has already occurred—therefore, desire tries to heal the <u>feeling-sense</u> that arises as a consequence of that separative activity. But no ultimate "success" is ever achieved via the means of desire, even so-called "Spiritual" forms of desire. There may be temporary releases, distracting fascinations—but desire never escapes its own dilemma, because desire does not <u>deal</u> <u>with</u> the dilemma. The search is concerned only with desire and the objects of desire. But beneath the search is this root-contraction.

Only the Divine Heart Itself Is the Radiant Continuum of Satisfaction, the Unobstructed Flow of Divine Spirit-Power. Only the Divine Heart Itself Always Already Knows Perfect Satisfaction, Perfect Desirelessness—because the Flow of the Divine Heart-Current is Always Already Accomplished. Always <u>Already</u> Accomplished— not accomplished as the result of any motivated action.

The Great Siddhas are those extremely rare Adept-Realizers (of whatever Real degree) who Function as the True Divine Heart in relation to living beings. And that Function is the unobstructed Flow (or Transmission) of Spirit-Force. The pressure of the Presence of a Great Siddha Awakens and constantly Intensifies the Flow of Spirit-Force in living beings. All obstructions tend to fall away in the Presence of this Spirit-Force. Where the Spirit-Force Moves, either there is devotional surrender in Its Presence or there is the flight from Its Presence. The Great Siddhas Communicate the Living Force of Reality. They Live It to living beings. They simply Live their State of Enjoyment (or Realization) with other beings. And those who devote themselves (with greatest intensity and profundity) to a Siddha-Guru will tend to Realize that one's characteristic State.

QUESTIONER: I have to go, but I have one more question. You said the Great Siddhas live as the Heart. What about the mind? Do they live as the mind also?

AVATAR ADI DA SAMRAJ: What is it?

QUESTIONER: Do they live as the mind as well? It is connected with the heart.

AVATAR ADI DA SAMRAJ: What mind?

QUESTIONER: What mind? The mind that they exist in. There is only one mind.

AVATAR ADI DA SAMRAJ: There is? Which?

QUESTIONER: Of course their brains are functioning, too—right?

AVATAR ADI DA SAMRAJ: What is the point you are trying to make?

QUESTIONER: Well, I asked you a question about the mind.

AVATAR ADI DA SAMRAJ: Yes. What mind? The brain?

QUESTIONER: Yes, the brain.

AVATAR ADI DA SAMRAJ: Ah, well, that is something very specific. Are you talking about the brain or the "One Mind"?

QUESTIONER: Well, there is only one mind, of course.

AVATAR ADI DA SAMRAJ: You are talking about the mind now, and not about the brain?

QUESTIONER: Well, I was asking you what is the relationship between the mind, the brain, and the heart.

AVATAR ADI DA SAMRAJ: Are you talking about the physical heart?

QUESTIONER: Not necessarily.

AVATAR ADI DA SAMRAJ: Well, which?

QUESTIONER: You can answer however you like.

AVATAR ADI DA SAMRAJ: I do not have any need for the answer. What, specifically, are you asking?

QUESTIONER: Well, actually, you answered me—because I wanted to see what you wanted to say.

AVATAR ADI DA SAMRAJ: No, that is not what you wanted to see. Do not play games. I am not here to entertain. All these little dramas you are playing have no place. I have no interest in them, and neither have you. I am not here to lay something on you. I am not concerned with that. If you want to discuss something with Me for a real purpose, that is something else. But, if you want to play at polemics, and idle cleverness . . .

QUESTIONER: That is not what I want.

AVATAR ADI DA SAMRAJ: No, no—that is what you want.

QUESTIONER: Do you think that is what I am trying to do?

AVATAR ADI DA SAMRAJ: Yes.

QUESTIONER: Why do you think that?

AVATAR ADI DA SAMRAJ: What is all of that? *[pointing to the man's facial expression]*

QUESTIONER: What is what?

AVATAR ADI DA SAMRAJ: What has all of that *[pointing again to his facial expression]* got to do with anything? Hm? You are very upset. What are you upset about?

QUESTIONER: I am not upset at all.

AVATAR ADI DA SAMRAJ: Something here is upsetting you. I would like to talk about that. That would be worth talking about.

QUESTIONER: I do not feel upset.

AVATAR ADI DA SAMRAJ: You do not feel the least upset?

QUESTIONER: No.

AVATAR ADI DA SAMRAJ: Very good.

QUESTIONER: If what you say of me were true, why would I have come here tonight?

AVATAR ADI DA SAMRAJ: I think you have good reasons for being here, but I do not think that is what is being dealt with at the moment. Before your good reasons for being here can be dealt with, you must overcome the social dilemma that being here represents to you. Your entire conception of Spiritual life, the thinking associated with Spiritual life that you bring here, is (perhaps) somewhat threatened by what I am saying. Well, that is not a problem—that is something to notice. But everyone has to get beyond merely being threatened by others. And, before you can get beyond that, your sense of being threatened must be acknowledged. The obviousness of all of that must be acknowledged—the obviousness of your strategy, your cleverness, your inability to be direct, to love. You must acknowledge that you are creating mental and emotional artifices. All of that must be understood. If you have understood that, what is there to defend?

I could sit here and have a discussion with you about the mind, the brain, the heart. But what does all of that have to do with anything? We could talk about the shape of clouds. But what is going on? What is this sensation, this feeling—that you have, that everyone has?

QUESTIONER: What sensation are you referring to? I am not sure what you mean.

AVATAR ADI DA SAMRAJ: Exactly. What is the sensation that you have at this moment, your awareness?

QUESTIONER: I am sorry, I do not understand what you are talking about. You are saying that awareness is a sensation?

Los Angeles, April 25, 1972

AVATAR ADI DA SAMRAJ: What exactly is the nature of your awareness at this moment?

QUESTIONER: I do not know how to answer that. But I know it exists. I am aware of it.

AVATAR ADI DA SAMRAJ: Of what?

QUESTIONER: My awareness.

AVATAR ADI DA SAMRAJ: You are aware of your awareness?

QUESTIONER: Yes.

AVATAR ADI DA SAMRAJ: And is it always truth, sublimity, and beauty?

QUESTIONER: It just is, brother—it just is!

AVATAR ADI DA SAMRAJ: Good.

QUESTIONER: Yes!

AVATAR ADI DA SAMRAJ: Then why are you so uncomfortable?

QUESTIONER: You keep seeing that, so there must be something.

AVATAR ADI DA SAMRAJ: What is this attitude that you are using—right now, in this moment? I am not "concerned" with it, you see. I do not want to put you down for it. But I want to get to it, because it is the primary quality in all your comments to Me. Are you aware of it—how you use your body, your eyebrows, the tone of voice, your manner of expressing yourself?

QUESTIONER: What is wrong with that?

AVATAR ADI DA SAMRAJ: I am not saying there is anything wrong with it.

QUESTIONER: Well, then, why are you making any mention of it?

AVATAR ADI DA SAMRAJ: Because you are using it to communicate to Me. It is your communication.

QUESTIONER: Well, so what?

AVATAR ADI DA SAMRAJ: What is this attitude? What is that? That is an attitude, isn't it?

QUESTIONER: Well, obviously, it is me.

AVATAR ADI DA SAMRAJ: What is the purpose of it? What are you doing with it? What is its nature? You have communicated differently at other times. Sometimes you laugh, sometimes you cry.

QUESTIONER: Yes.

AVATAR ADI DA SAMRAJ: All right. You are not laughing or crying now. You are doing this! What is it you are doing?

QUESTIONER: I am in the process of communicating with you.

AVATAR ADI DA SAMRAJ: Why in this particular form?

QUESTIONER: Because that is the form I choose to use.

AVATAR ADI DA SAMRAJ: Yes. And it does not have any resistance in it at all?

QUESTIONER: Well, it has a resistance. Yes, it has. I feel that there is a lack of communication going on.

AVATAR ADI DA SAMRAJ: Okay. That is what I am talking about.

QUESTIONER: When I am communicating with somebody or somebody is trying to communicate with me, if I feel there is a lack, sure I feel a resistance.

AVATAR ADI DA SAMRAJ: Exactly. That is what I am feeling.

QUESTIONER: You feel it too, huh?

AVATAR ADI DA SAMRAJ: Yes. And, if there were simple, direct communication between us, it would be unnecessary for you to have that sensation and to communicate it to Me as you now feel you must. But what is actually coming through in your remarks to Me is that fear, that resistance, that upset about the nature of this communication. And that is exactly what I have been talking about tonight. It is exactly that contraction, that resistance, that limiting of Free conscious awareness, that is your suffering. Following upon that contraction are all the thoughts, illusions, memories, experiences, searches. But that contraction, that resistance, is always first. Such is the root-activity that everyone is living. Wherever you go, wherever you are, you can feel that underlying sense, that underlying resistance, that underlying discomfort, that underlying unpleasantness—that failure of love, of energy, of presence. That is exactly what I am talking about.

The sensation of which you have now become aware is the very quality by which the self-contraction is always experienced. The manifestation of the self-contraction may be very elaborate. It can take on all kinds of forms, but the sensation you are now feeling is the contraction I am talking about. It is not unique to you. I am just pointing out how it is functioning in you at this moment. But you are no different from anyone else. Everyone is suffering the same tendency and activity. And its results are always the same. Everyone is suffering exactly the same thing. Each person has a different life-method, a different style, a different complex of life-experience, and so on—but the fundamental activity of self-contraction is common to everyone.

At first, the awareness of that sensation is only periodic. Then the awareness of it becomes continuous. Then you become capable of observing its actual structure, of understanding it as your own activity—as a deliberate, present-time activity that is your suffering, that is your illusion of separateness. The capability to consistently observe, understand, and transcend that deliberate, present-time activity is what I call "'radical' self-understanding". To (thus) understand oneself most fundamentally is to penetrate the egoic process that structures all perceived events, all of your experience. And the primary—even the most obvious—effect of the root-activity of self-contraction is the loss of the conscious awareness of relationship.

That is exactly what was happening in the last few minutes. There was the sense of an obstruction in your relating to Me. But, when that sense of obstruction is no longer there, when the self-contraction is no longer taking place, no longer meditated upon, no longer a cause of disturbance, when there is simply unobstructed relationship, then there is no dilemma. Then there is no conflict, no problem, no separateness. Instead, there is only Happiness. And, when (ultimately) that Happiness is Realized Most Perfectly (and, necessarily, by Grace), then there is the Infinity of Liberation, the Perfect Consciousness of Truth, the Siddhi of Reality Itself.

Liberation, Truth, Reality is <u>always</u> simply that Fundamental Happiness—that unobstructed, spontaneous, moment to moment existence as unqualified relatedness (or Non-separateness). This, truly, is the meaning of what people call "Love". It is simply the Force of the Heart Itself, Reality Itself—Which is Unobstructed, Unqualified Existence. It is simply the State That Is Always Already the Case.

What I call "the True Divine Heart" (or "the Heart Itself") <u>Is</u> Consciousness Itself. In India, this has been called "Atman"—the Real Self (or Very Nature) of the apparent individual. The Atman is not a separate organ or a separate faculty. Rather, the Atman is identical to What is called "Brahman"—the Formless, Absolute, Omnipresent Divine Reality.

The Heart Itself is Very Consciousness, Absolute Bliss, Unqualified Existence. The Heart Itself is Most Perfect "Knowledge" of Unspeakable Real God. Everything secondary—mind, body, brain, any function at all—is contained within the True Divine Heart, like an event in a universe. Within that universe is the appearance of living beings. Naturally, if you speak of the physical body (or of the psycho-physical entity), there is the physical heart, there is the physical brain, and there are many other functions—gross functions and subtle functions. But all of these functions are "contained" in that Perfect Consciousness, that Unobstructed Reality—the True Divine Heart Itself. From the "Point of View" of the True Divine Heart, there is no dilemma in the fact that "things" seem to appear, no misunderstanding of their appearing, no threat implied by their appearing. All of this is a form of Love-Bliss-Happiness.

It is common for those who constantly live in the obstructed state to possess an elaborate, dramatic conceptualization of things. But such a conceptualization of things is not equivalent to things themselves. Such conceptualizing is simply a display of modifications of Energy—of Energy manifesting in subtle (or apparently internal) form, appearing as functioning mind. Such a conceptualization is only a structure, a shape, an imposition, a distraction—and its root is the self-contraction I have been describing. It is utterly beside the point whether My conceptualization of things is "bigger" than yours, whether Mine has all seven parts in it while yours has only four.[6] It does not make any difference what these minds contain. It is not merely the saint who can understand. Every fool can understand. It does not make any difference what is "inside". It all has to go—because all of it is this self-contraction, this self-obstruction, this self-containment, that every human being is suffering.

When the self-contraction has utterly ceased to be what patterns your state, then it becomes possible for you to Most Perfectly Realize the Very (and Self-Evidently Divine) State of Reality Itself, Which Is the Very (and Self-Evidently Divine) State of all beings and things—Prior to conceptualization and the ordinary drama of your life. From that Most Perfect "Point of View" (Which is Always Already Free and True), perhaps something meaningful can be said about the structure of the conditionally manifested worlds—but, from that Very "Point of View", nothing is either gained or lost by the existence of the conditionally manifested worlds or by the description of those worlds. When the principle of suffering is understood and transcended, something can be said—but such speech is not actually necessary.

A man came to Bodhidharma[7] and said something about his mind that was similar to your remarks. The man sat in the presence of Bodhidharma, trying to attract Bodhidharma's attention. He did this for a long time, without success. Finally, in desperation, he was moved to hack off his arm, which he presented to Bodhidharma. He held his arm up to Bodhidharma—who, at last, turned to him. Bodhidharma was willing to have a brief discussion. But Bodhidharma was not upset, excited, or particularly interested in the bleeding and mortal condition of this seeker. The man wanted to know something about his mind. He wanted to be liberated from his perpetual disturbance of mind. Bodhidharma said, "Show me your mind." In other words, "Show me this mind that you say is upset, that you want to understand, that you claim to possess." According to tradition, that was sufficient to Enlighten the man. He saw that what he was upset about, what he thought he was suffering or owning, had no tangible existence. There was not, in fact, any "thing" that he was suffering or owning. He was simply obsessed. His suffering and his mind were present-time self-creations. All Bodhidharma did, or served to do, was to bring about the spontaneous understanding of what the man was constantly presenting as himself, as his own state. That enabled a sudden turnabout.

The traditions are filled with such meetings between questioners (or seekers) and their teachers. It is always the same story. The individual has some very elaborate search going on, some very elaborate structure of mind that he or she always presents and wants to defend or overcome. But, whatever the particular characteristics of a person's egoic game, everyone is always communicating one thing. It is your own mind-form, your own self-contracted state. That is what people always present to one another and to life. By the "performance" of your self-contracted state, you destine yourself to certain consequences in life, certain experiences. Thus, your state also becomes your activity and your destiny.

What I am here to Offer to everyone is the process whereby the present-time and chronic modification of Consciousness Itself—this compulsive state, this root-activity that becomes dilemma, seeking, and suffering—is undermined by means of "radical" self-understanding. The Way that I Offer requires this crisis in conscious awareness—the crisis in which unconsciousness is undermined, the crisis in which your ordinary, common state is utterly turned about.

The Way that I Offer is necessarily a crisis. It is not some kind of ego-possessed artifice. It is not a defense of your limited condition. It is the process whereby all such artifice or defense is utterly transcended.

In the Christian tradition, "Spiritual death" is spoken of as the basic event.[8] The process of True religion is conceived as a sacrifice, a cross. In the East, the process of True religion is understood to require the crisis of satori or the self-purifying ordeal of sadhana. The Way that I Offer to all necessarily requires the crisis, the turnabout, the utter transcending of the ego-pattern that you are (otherwise) helplessly living out. And, if that crisis does not take place, then there is no Real Spiritual life. There is simply the same thing there has always been—the same obsession with conditional forms, the same suffering, disability, dilemma, the same disappointment (or whatever emotional quality is manifested in the individual case).

When there is absolutely no defense left, when the bottom completely falls out, when there is nothing whatsoever left to stand on—That is Liberation. As long as there is something left to defend, something with which to resist, as long as there is something still left to "die", then the same state persists—the same suffering, the same search. When it is all "dead", when the greatly feared event has already occurred, then there is no longer the thread of seeking or the defense of its hidden dilemma.

[Addressing the questioner who opened the discussion:] The kind of resistance I have pointed out to you as something you are demonstrating (in your questions, and in your manner altogether) is exactly what everyone brings to the Guru. The devotee's drama in relation to the Guru is always the hour to hour confrontation with that resistance. Such resistance is not special to anyone's case. It is the very thing that is dealt with throughout the course of Spiritual life—in ever more subtle forms. There is no particular enjoyment in that process of dealing with your resistance. No special honor is gained, no special "dues" are paid, merely because you are dealing with this suffering and resistance.

The Guru must always deal with the state that a person brings—and that state is never "radically" Free. The new devotee is never a "vessel" of Happiness. The new devotee is not Blissful. The new devotee is not Truth. The Guru must, consciously and deliberately, deal with whatever obstructions the devotee communicates. The Guru must not forget the suffering and dilemma of the devotee.

Therefore, the Guru must not simply console and fascinate the devotee with promises, words, and smiling notions. The Guru must constantly deal with the obstruction in the devotee, until the devotee is no longer suffering that obstruction. But, in order for the devotee to no longer be suffering that obstruction, there must be a crisis, a difficult confrontation. And it is always absolutely difficult. That obstruction exists even in the calmest, most apparently loving devotee. It is only on the surface, as a characteristic of their particular egoic strategies, that some devotees may appear to be calm and loving. They are also bound up with their suffering. Some devotees appear to be very loving, very capable of service. Others appear to be very resistive and angry. There is no real distinction—it is simply a difference of qualities. Essentially, the same event is going on. The same thing is brought to the Guru in every case. The same thing has to be lived by the Guru in every case.

Therefore, from the human point of view, there is no great privilege or pleasure in functioning as Guru for people. It is simply that the Heart Itself Functions in that manner. Always, spontaneously, the True Divine Heart Moves into relationship. It Moves through the structures of conscious awareness. It Flows through. It Breaks Down the obstructions. The Heart Itself Is Always Already Love-Bliss-Full and Happy.

The person in whom this entire strategy has broken down is like a pane of glass. There is no idiosyncrasy in such a one, no resistance. The entire Energy-structure of the living being is open. But, when you encounter the usual self-contracted person, you immediately experience the limitation on life that the person will accept or demand in relationship to you. And this tends to stimulate, by reaction, your own limitation. Thus, everybody complains that their ordinary experience with other people is unsatisfying. But, when the self-contraction relaxes even a little, then the Force of Delight and Love begins to flow, and the obstructions begin to break down—until, finally, the sense of separate "personhood" is shattered.

At last, the ordinary form of your existence is absolutely vanished. You no longer live from the point of view of self-contraction (and all of the presumptions about life that the self-contraction requires). Conscious awareness has fallen out of the usual form— and the "Point of View" is That of the Divine Self-Condition, the True Divine Heart. Such is Most Perfect Realization of Reality Itself (or Real God). There is no longer the least trace of separate-self-sense. The separate-self-sense does not even tend to arise—and, yet, the apparent functions of life continue.

My devotees must serve one another in this process. They must require each other to live Communion with Me, to function in relationship by resorting to Me. They do not indulge each other's ego-strategies. Thus, the very circumstance of living in the cooperative cultural gathering of My devotees provokes the crisis in each one.

At this point, the young man who had been questioning Avatar Adi Da Samraj got up and left. Many of those present expressed their relief through laughter and criticism, but Avatar Adi Da pointed out to them that the drama they had just observed was an exaggerated version of the struggle that is always enacted between the Guru and the devotee.

AVATAR ADI DA SAMRAJ: It is always the same. Everyone is like that. He was not extraordinary. He just played the obvious drama that he played. He was good. I appreciated his questions. It was good that something so dramatic and emotional could take place. You should read the documents that record what happened in the ashrams of Teachers such as Ramana Maharshi or Ramakrishna.[9] It is always a real confrontation. This Ashram is not going to be any different.

QUESTIONER: Would you please speak more about the self-contraction, and describe how the practice that you give makes it possible to move beyond the activity of separation?

AVATAR ADI DA SAMRAJ: Many words could be used. The traditions of religion and Spirituality describe different "knots", and the goal of Spiritual life is often said to be the opening of those knots. There is a knot in the navel, a knot in the heart, and a knot in the head. There are knots throughout the body—but the navel, the heart, and the head are the primary regions discussed in the traditions. What they are really describing are the functional forms of self-contraction in the gross and subtle dimensions of the being.

Each of the chakras (or subtle centers through which the natural life-energy and the Divine Spirit-Energy move) is like the shutter of a camera. When the chakras are contracted, the Energy-flow is obstructed. If the flow of Energy is trying to move through one of the chakras, the resistance of the self-contraction creates pain, heat, and various other Yogic manifestations (many of which I have described in *The Knee Of Listening*[10]). When one of the chakras opens a little bit more, then the mind may begin to get a little "flowery"—such that there are insights and visionary phenomena and subtle perceptions. When a particular chakra is fully open, then the mind is completely open at that level. Then the Energy freely moves on, until It hits the next obstruction. The natural life-energy and the Divine Spirit-Energy (Which is the Spiritual Presence of the True Divine Heart, the Power of Reality) move through the same Circuit, opening the various chakras (which are chronically obstructed, or contracted). And the distinctive experiences associated with the opening of each of the chakras are what characterize the various stages in the process of Yoga, or the various traditional paths of Spiritual life.

Ultimately, however, none of these experiences matter at all. They arise only because there are obstructions. If there are no obstructions, then there is only Perfect Consciousness—no dilemma, nothing to be accomplished. Then there is not even anything you could call "your own body", in which to accomplish anything. Therefore, one in whom "radical" self-understanding is most perfect has passed from all limited (and even extraordinary) forms of conditional knowledge and conditional experience into Most Perfect Realization of Truth Itself, Reality Itself, or Real God.

QUESTIONER: Is the activity of the mind and thought an obstruction?

AVATAR ADI DA SAMRAJ: What is your experience?

QUESTIONER: My experience is that, in spite of what I will or wish, I have many strange thoughts.

AVATAR ADI DA SAMRAJ: If you close the eyes meditatively, you turn yourself mainly to concentration on mind-forms. But, if your eyes are open, there are people, functional demands, and the entire cosmic event. While you are sitting there with your eyes open, you will become aware that all kinds of thinking is also going on. You will begin to feel—almost see—how thought slides between you and all contact with the moving world.

Thought is an actual, concrete obstruction. It is a tangible manifestation, a modification of Energy. What you call "the mind" is wavelengths of energy—functioning, and taking on various forms, through the subtle processes of "electrical" interchange. When you have a thought, the energy flowing through various regions of the brain has been modified. Once you identify with (and operate from the point of view of) a thought, you have contracted—and you are (thereafter) concentrating on that con- traction. If you pinch your arm, attention centers at the point of pain. If you have a thought, attention centers at the point of thought. Whenever you are distracted by a particular entity, form, or function, there is loss of direct awareness, of unobstructed relationship. When there is concentration of attention, everything else is excluded. The ego is just another form of concentration, of distraction. In the case of the ego, the distraction is not a particular thought but the separate-self-sense that is generated by the self-contraction.

The ego is an activity, not an entity. The ego is the activity of avoidance, the avoidance of relationship.

Los Angeles, April 25, 1972

Therefore, any thought, any function, anything that generates form, that appears as form, that seems to be form, is produced by the concentration of attention—or self-contraction. Thus, apart from "radical" self-understanding, all processes—even life itself—tend to become an obstruction. The root of all suffering is called the "ego", as if it were a "thing", an entity. But the ego is actually the activity of self-contraction—in countless forms, endured unconsciously. The unconsciousness is the key—not the acts of concentration themselves (which are only more or less functional). Apart from present-time conscious self-understanding, the self-contracted state is presumed to be the inevitable condition of life. That unconscious self-contraction creates separation, which manifests as identification (or the sense of separate self).

The root of True Spirituality is not some kind of activity, such as desire, that seeks to get you to the "Super-Object". The genuine Spiritual process that I Offer to you requires the "radical" understanding of the entire process of egoic motivation. That process requires the observation, understanding, and transcending of the root of egoic motivation—which is the activity of self-contraction, of separation.

When you no longer have any more options, when you have worn yourself out playing your game, and you have come to the end of trying out techniques and methods, paths and lifestyles, strategies and places to go, forms of concentration (whatever they may be), then all of that begins to break down. You discover that you just do not have the "jazz" left to really carry it on anymore. You find yourself more depressed—just a little bit too depressed to meditate or to hunt for sex. You just do not have the necessary fire of motivation.

Then upsetness begins to overwhelm you. The crisis begins to come on. You do not really have a path (or a strategy) anymore. You may talk a lot about it, feel a lot about it. It remains a part of your mind, but you do not really have a path (or a strategy) any longer. That is really the most hopeful sign. The ego is beginning to rot! When fruit begins to rot, it falls with seed into the earth. But, as long as you are self-righteous, as long as you have your game to play, you are not ripe. It is only when your own game begins to kick you in the face that you begin to soften up, bruise a little bit, feel your fear, your suffering, your dilemma, the constant upset of all your mortality.

You are all going to die. You are all going to lose this present awareness, this present enjoyment. I cannot endure that dilemma from day to day. From the moment I was Born, that fact upset Me. I was not the least interested in tolerating moment to moment existence as that kind of suffering. Life was not worth the involvement, if its summation had to be death, zero. What difference does it make how fulfilled you can get if you have to fall out the bottom, arbitrarily? Everything is wonderful today—but you wake up tomorrow and the world of lovely friends is delivered to you dead, the insane parcels of "everything disappearing". Therefore, all self-righteousness, all ego-based involvement in Spirituality, all seeking for consolation is nonsense. All of that is a refusal to accept your mortality. All of that is un-Real.

Your usual experience is the agonizing fact of identification with the separate-self-sense, the act that is ego—this refusal of relationship, this lovelessness, this living craziness. And all of your ordinary processes are bound up with that craziness—until you begin to get sick of it. Then you are no longer talking about your technique, your Yoga—how marvelous it is, how you are going to get there, how "everything is so soul-beautiful", and all that crap. When you are sick of your game, you become obsessed with your darkness, your heaviness. You try to feel good, but you know you feel lousy. You really feel upset. It really is bad. It really is an annoyance. You are only upset—so what difference does the search make?

If you endure that crisis long enough, you begin to get really upset, and all you can do is concentrate on your upset. Up until that point, you were always playing your game in order to avoid that upset—but now you cannot do anything but be upset. And, while you are meditating on your upsetness, you happen to become involved with Me—and you get even more and more upset all the time! You come to Me, and the process of relating to Me makes you more upset. You think you are supposed to be having a fantastic Spiritual experience here, becoming more and more fulfilled. But, when you come around, people criticize you, they call your attention to your crazy game. You are trying to do your best, but you are constantly being shown how you are falling short. All such experience is very aggravating, but it begins to reinforce the genuine self-observation that has now started to go on in you—this crisis, this falling apart, this rot. And all of that will persist—until you somehow begin to observe the root-activity you are always enacting.

When you begin to see what you are doing, when you begin to observe and understand it, you will see it (first of all) in very direct, human terms. You will see it in the simple, human, practical things that you do. Later, you will begin to see it in subtler terms. You will observe the entire quality of your mind, your ordinary activity, your game—the drama, the event, that is always going on—until you begin to see it most precisely and to a very subtle degree. When you understand it most fundamentally, that is "radical" self-understanding. When you see the activity itself, the simple activity—that is the end of your helpless enactment of it. You fall apart. You scream, or you cannot say anything—but it just stops. It is no longer an unconscious automaticity. Ultimately, in Most Perfect Divine Self-Realization, the entire process of self-contraction ceases to occur. And this apparent Event, unlike all other apparent forms of action in the conditionally manifested worlds, is <u>not</u> followed by a re-action.

In *The Knee Of Listening*, I have described My Divine Re-Awakening. There was nothing about It that would have appeared remarkable to anyone who might have observed Me. I did not smile. I did not feel "high". There was no reaction, because there was not anything left over of the "thing" that now was thrown away. There was no "thing" to which I could react. There was no "one" to react—to feel good about it, or happy about it. There was no particular emotion. The True Divine Heart was all. Its Quality became more and more apparent. The entire sense of a complex life in dilemma was no longer the case.

During the initial period (of, perhaps, several months) after that Great Event, I did not really function differently than before. I had not yet developed a comprehensive understanding of what had occurred. I did not really interpret it clearly and fully for a good period of time—even though I Consciously Existed in a State that was untouched, unqualified, by any event or circumstance. That State of Perfect Love-Bliss-Fullness was utterly Extraordinary. But I had not yet begun to Function as It in relation to conditionally manifested life. Only when I Did So—and, then, only gradually— was I able to estimate and Know what had occurred. It was as if I had "walked through" Myself. Such a State is Perfectly Spontaneous. It has no means of watching Itself. It has no means of internalizing or structuring Itself. It is Divine "Madness".

The Divine Person, the True Divine Heart, is Perfect "Madness". There is not a jot of "difference" within It. There is no "thing". No "thing" has happened. There is not a single movement in Consciousness Itself. And that is Its Blissfulness. My Re-Awakening to That State of Most Perfect Divine Enjoyment was not a matter of certain functions of subtle life being stimulated. It was a State peculiarly free of visions, energy-movements, and all the blissful phenomena characteristic of the activities of the Yoga-Shakti. And, when such phenomena did happen to arise, they were of another kind, or they were Known from a new "Point of View". Their qualities had become cosmic and universal, rather than (in the limited Yogic sense) "personal"—until there is only Real God, only the Living One.

The mind functions as an obstruction. When conscious aware- ness moves into relationship, obsessive involvement in mind falls away. That involvement is replaced by a simple Intensity. The more that Intensity is enjoyed as existence, the less obtrusive the mind becomes. Even though the mind continues to arise, it becomes less and less obtrusive. You notice it less.

In your present condition, you think you are the mind. You are always thinking-thinking. But the mind is actually something that is arising in Consciousness Itself. The mind is nothing but a modification of the Divine Conscious Light. One who most perfectly understands the ego-"I" does not notice the mind in the usual manner. It is not that such a one has quieted the mind. Rather, such a one no longer identifies with the mind. There is no separate one there to be the mind. The mind is simply one of the functions that spontaneously arise. But, if you identify with mind, then you have already separated yourself. Only when the entire structure of the separate self is undermined by most perfect "radical" understanding of its root-activity does the mind resume its natural (or prior) state.

Ramana Maharshi advised seekers to find out <u>who</u> it is that asks the question, thinks the thought, and so on. But that "who" is, in Reality, not an "entity". When Ramana Maharshi spoke, He used the symbolic language of Advaita Vedanta—the classic monistic (or "Only-One-Reality") school of Hinduism. The imagery of this traditional description of the process of Realizing Truth deals in statics, "things"-in-space. Therefore, in that traditional description, there is <u>the</u> ego—the objectified, solidified self.

But I speak in terms of process, or movement. I speak in terms of concepts of experience with which the modern mind is more familiar—and which more accurately reflect the actual nature of conditionally manifested reality. Thus, I do not speak of the ego as an "object" within a conceptual universe of objects. The concept of the "static ego" is no longer very useful—and, indeed, it is false and misleading.

Therefore, what has traditionally been called "the ego" is rightly understood to be an activity. And "radical" self-understanding is that direct seeing of the fundamental (and always present) activity that is suffering, ignorance, distraction, motivation, and dilemma. When that activity is most perfectly understood, then there is Spontaneous and Unqualified Realization of That Which had previously been excluded from conscious awareness—That Which Is Always Already the Case.

You cannot simply and naively embrace the conceptual fixtures you have inherited from the past. There must be the conscious observation and understanding of your condition as you are presently experiencing it. Therefore, the old concepts and methods are not necessarily useful, even though they may be pleasant and consoling. There must be an absolute penetration of the root-activity of life. Life must be approached within the living structure in which it is presently suffered and entertained.

QUESTIONER: If that is the case, what about formal meditation? Is it beneficial to practice formal meditation?

AVATAR ADI DA SAMRAJ: If you have an inclination to do some particular kind of sitting, concentrating, Yogic method, whatever—all of that is an activity that you are already <u>tending</u> to do. The point is not whether to do that or not. The point is to understand the motive behind it, to understand the process (in this moment) that is producing your particular impulse to practice formal meditation.

The usual individual is <u>always</u> seeking—therefore, "radical" self-understanding is not a matter of choosing whether or not to pursue a particular form of motivated search. You are <u>always</u> seeking—whether (at this moment) you are doing it in the form of a Yogic technique, or (in the next moment) you are doing it in the form of a sly glance at somebody passing on the street. You <u>are</u> always doing it—so the point is not whether you <u>should</u> do a particular form of it or not. There is simply and always the process of your own activity.

When My devotee enters into action on the basis of Real, unmotivated intelligence, in heart-Communion with Me, then self-understanding begins to develop as a spontaneous, Real process in conscious awareness. And, in the midst of this life, My devotee does sit formally in meditation.

When you meditate with such outward formality, it may appear to others that you are engaged in <u>motivated</u> meditation—but that is not, in fact, what you are doing. You are living on the basis of self-observation and self-understanding—in the context of the devotional relationship to Me, in heart-Communion with Me. It is just that, from a practical point of view, a natural sitting posture (in which the body is relaxed, such that its fluids and energies can move freely) is an appropriate manner in which to engage the process of heart-Communion with Me. Nevertheless, the same process can be active under any conditions, whether formal or random (and circumstantial). There is simply the endless return to this Communion with Me—coincident with the observing, understanding, and transcending of your own egoic activity.

Your coming together with others of My devotees, your conversation together, your devotional and cultural life together, the reading and study you do, your relationships—everything you are doing should constantly re-awaken this Communion with Me and (thereby) this self-understanding. The process of self-observation and self-understanding will take the form of periodic crises, the enduring and transcending of the resistance that is your suffering. As you pass through ordinary life in this manner (always observing this same quality, this same disturbance), that self-observation and self-understanding (which is the capability to no longer be trapped in the unconscious activity of self-contraction) allows the profound deepening of heart-Communion with Me—Which is meditation. For My true devotee, such meditation is the necessary foundation of True Spiritual life—the life of Truth in My Company.

The activity of the ego-"I" (in every moment) is the avoidance of relationship. That activity is the obstruction. The entire quality of conscious awareness—appearing (variously) as bodily sensations, as emotions, as thoughts, as the entire spontaneous event of waking, dreaming, and deep sleep—is, in the case of the usual individual, the avoidance of relationship. Whatever you are involved in is a manifestation of this same activity. Once you begin to observe that activity, once you catch the little pieces of it that are prominent, then you begin to see yourself fully.

Self-understanding begins in that manner—in very practical observation, in the real observation of something that is obviously and practically a hindrance, an avoidance of the living condition of relationship. When such real observation has begun in you, then the intelligence that is "radical" self-understanding has a practical basis. To that degree, you are able to respond to arising events with the intelligence of self-understanding. The more there is of this practical self-observation, the more self-understanding has become your intelligence.

If you become My devotee and practice the Way I Reveal to you, you will begin to see the pervasive strategy of your life, to understand the egoic structure of your suffering. The effective practice of My devotees is utterly dependent on Real and always present-time heart-Communion with Me and on Real and always present-time understanding of the activity of self-contraction. Without that Real heart-Communion and that Real self-understanding, the disciplines of attention which I Give to My devotees become just like any other form of thought—a mere stress in the head. In that case, the apparent practice of any such discipline is merely another preference, another strategy. Therefore, right practice of those disciplines (and of all other aspects of the Way I have Revealed and Given) requires real self-understanding. And real self-understanding depends on Satsang with Me (or heart-responsive participation in the devotional relationship to Me, and heart-responsive embrace of all the conditions I Require of My devotees).

People do, in fact, tend to use any form of discipline, any form of religious or Spiritual practice, as a method (or technique). To do so is to "use" the discipline or practice in the mood of seeking. Indeed, <u>everything</u> is the search—until "radical" self-understanding comes alive.

Nevertheless, even though you may be unconsciously committed to the search, if you embrace the conditions of practice I Give to My devotees, all strategic effort will eventually break down—if only you have the endurance for the process, the need for it, the looseness for it, or simply the inability to go out and play the egoic game again (whatever it is in your case).

Some such inner quality must keep you in place, such that My Work with you can take hold. And, for My devotee, the supreme (or most potent) inner quality is faith in Me, devotion to Me, surrender to Me—as the Divine Siddha-Guru.

AVATAR ADI DA SAMRAJ
Lopez Island, 2000

2.

The Avon Lady

AVATAR ADI DA SAMRAJ: *[Laughing]* What is there?

DEVOTEE: Is there free will?

AVATAR ADI DA SAMRAJ: What would that be?

DEVOTEE: I don't think we have free will. I think only God has free will.

AVATAR ADI DA SAMRAJ: And who are "we"?

DEVOTEE: Part of God.

AVATAR ADI DA SAMRAJ: Does God have free will?

DEVOTEE: Then what about evolution? If there is such a thing as evolution, we will all get to God eventually.

AVATAR ADI DA SAMRAJ: You are assuming, for the moment, that you are not already there.

DEVOTEE: Well, I am not aware that I am there.

AVATAR ADI DA SAMRAJ: The assumption that you are not already there is what My Work with you is all about. What kind of free will are you concerned with? To do what?

DEVOTEE: Well, if we have free will and there is evolution, why do we have to work at it? Why not let evolution take over—and, eventually, we will all be evolved into illuminated Masters?

AVATAR ADI DA SAMRAJ: Are you trying to become a Master?

DEVOTEE: I didn't think you could leave this plane of existence until you were a Master.

AVATAR ADI DA SAMRAJ: What is wrong with this plane of existence?

DEVOTEE: There are other planes to work on. Eventually, all attain the state that Jesus attained, without physical bodies.

AVATAR ADI DA SAMRAJ: Where did you hear all of this?

DEVOTEE: I don't know.

AVATAR ADI DA SAMRAJ: You are making a lot of assumptions to begin with—"God", "Masters", "evolution", "free will", "no free will", "getting there", "other planes". What does all of that have to do with you?

DEVOTEE: I am somewhere, but I don't know where.

AVATAR ADI DA SAMRAJ: Well, that would seem to be the first order of business. That is just it, isn't it? You are very confused— and there is suffering, apparently. You read all these books, and you do all this thinking, all this hoping—about Jesus and whoever else, about "getting there", about doing this and that to "get there". All of that thinking and hoping is suffering. And it is true, as you say—why go through all this effort to "get there"? I would not use the excuse that you are going to "get there" anyway, because of evolution—but there is something very meaningful in your doubt about the attempt to "get there". You have discovered the feeling that the trying to "get there" is very closely related to suffering. There is suffering, and there is the trying to "get there". Those two things, I would imagine, are very real to you: the conscious suffering that life involves, and the attempt to get free of suffering.

The attempt to get free of suffering is a very elaborate, very involved notion. You have to do so many things before you "get there". There is all this "stuff", which does not do one thing to your suffering. The <u>concept</u> of Jesus does not do anything for your suffering. The <u>idea</u> of <u>becoming</u> like Jesus does not do anything for your suffering. The <u>effort</u> to <u>become</u> like Jesus does not do anything for your fundamental suffering. The <u>presumption</u> that you are going to "<u>evolve</u>" to become like Jesus does not do anything for your continuous suffering. Suffering persists as the basic content of your conscious awareness. On top of that, there is all of this seeking, wondering, thinking about how to "get there", how to get free of suffering. If you were already free of suffering, it would not make any difference to you whether this room appeared, or a ballroom in Vienna, or a seventh-plane party! The fact that suffering is gone would be the thing that makes you Happy. When you are no longer distracted by suffering, you see that you are already Happy, that you <u>are</u> Happiness. From the purely practical and real point of view, what concerns you is not "other planes", "God", "Jesus", or "getting there". <u>Suffering</u> is your concern—because it is already your real experience.

DEVOTEE: It seems to me that, if you look at any Realized being, you see how far you have to go.

AVATAR ADI DA SAMRAJ: How do you know how far you have to go? How do you know where such a person is?

DEVOTEE: Well, I am still suffering, so I still have a long way to go. If I am not in a perfect state of living, if I am not here now, then I am separate.

AVATAR ADI DA SAMRAJ: What is this suffering?

DEVOTEE: Well, there are different forms of suffering. Not being Realized is suffering.

AVATAR ADI DA SAMRAJ: What is it right now? As a perception right now, what is this suffering?

DEVOTEE: Being trapped in the human body.

AVATAR ADI DA SAMRAJ: What about that is suffering?

DEVOTEE: I don't want to be in this body.

AVATAR ADI DA SAMRAJ: <u>Are</u> you in it?

DEVOTEE: Now I am, yes.

AVATAR ADI DA SAMRAJ: What makes you think you are a something that could be inside the body?

DEVOTEE: Well, that is how I feel now. Since I assume it now, it is real now.

AVATAR ADI DA SAMRAJ: Your <u>assumption</u> makes it real?

DEVOTEE: Yes.

AVATAR ADI DA SAMRAJ: Is your assumption the thing you are suffering?

DEVOTEE: Well—you could say that, yes.

AVATAR ADI DA SAMRAJ: That Which is called "Realization", "Liberation", "God-Union", and so on, gets represented to people in various symbolic forms—as something with lots of planes and worlds, colors, lights and visions, figures and forms, methods, universes, "inside" and "outside", going here, going there, distance, direction, shape. These are all conceptual communications, symbols, pictures for the mind. Fundamentally, they exploit your suffering—by motivating you to acquire whatever it is they represent or suggest. True Spiritual life is not a motivation toward such symbols, not a belief in them, not even the acquisition of what they represent. Rather, True Spiritual life is the process in conscious awareness that is founded in the "radical" understanding of your own suffering, your present experience.

The True and right process of Spiritual life is not one of search based on suffering. Ordinarily, if you suffer, you immediately seek to get free, and you attach yourself to all kinds of hopeful signs. But True life, or Real and right Spiritual life, is the reverse of that. Ordinarily, you are seeking—pursuing forgetfulness of your suffering, your dilemma, your self-contraction, this separation, this unconsciousness. You pursue the absence of that—in delight, enjoyment, distraction, the search for perfection, the search for all kinds of acquisitions, food, sex, money, good weather, lunch—until the entire process begins to become uninteresting. You try every resort—either in reverie or by actual adventure. You look at every "movie" on the subject. You seek—until that entire movement in yourself, that entire reaction to your suffering (the reaction that is the search for the absence of suffering) begins to wind down.

Now you begin to comprehend the hopelessness of the search. The search begins to lose its ability to occupy you. It becomes less exotic, less fascinating, less hopeful. Some quality in conscious awareness begins to turn away from this process of seeking, this reaction to your suffering, and rests in the suffering itself. A vague disinterest in life's pleasures may even come over you. You begin to realize that you are actually suffering—whereas previously you were so completely occupied with your seeking that you were not altogether aware of your suffering. Your suffering was just some vague "whatever"—because the search was what really involved you.

But now you begin to fall out of your search. You begin to live this suffering. Suffering becomes your experience, your obsession. It completely absorbs you. It becomes the constant object of your attention. Your actual state becomes absorbing—this, rather than all the things you attached yourself to in order to forget this, to get rid of this. Then you begin to see your suffering, to observe your suffering. You begin to see what your suffering actually is. The root-sensation that is motivating your entire search becomes the thing that occupies you. You can no longer do anything about it. You see what suffering (itself) is—in this moment. You begin to see it precisely—as a present-time activity. You begin to consciously observe it. You see this contraction of your own state,

moment to moment—this separation, this avoidance of relationship. You begin to see this more and more exactly, more and
more specifically.

All of this becomes an overwhelming observation—until that
portion of yourself, that quality in yourself, which is engaged in
this self-observation, which is the intelligence of this observation
of suffering, becomes your intelligence, becomes the very quality
of conscious awareness that you live, the very quality of conscious awareness with which you approach all experience,
moment to moment. Then, instead of merely suffering, you enter
into Satsang with Me, moment to moment, and observe the
nature of your experiencing. You see beyond the self-contraction
that is your suffering. And you begin to Enjoy That Which your
chronic activity and state always prevent.

Your suffering is your own activity. It is something that you
are doing, moment to moment. It is a completely voluntary activity. You notice it in the form of symptoms—the sense of separate
existence (or identification), the mind of endless qualities (or
differentiation), the entire dynamic of motion (or desire). You are
always presently living these symptoms. But their root—the
source of them all, that which they are all reflecting—is the self-
contraction, the separative act, the avoidance of relationship,
which constantly generates the sensation in your conscious awareness that you perceive as suffering. When it is observed and
understood, this self-contracting activity and its symptoms cease to
be the characteristic of conscious awareness. Then That Which is
always prevented by the usual state becomes the Characteristic of
conscious awareness. When there is unqualified relatedness,
no-contraction, no-separation, no-avoidance, then there is no
identification (or inevitable separateness), no differentiation (or
inevitable mind), no desire (or inevitable motion). Then, by Means
of My Avataric Divine Spiritual Grace, conscious awareness falls
into its own Perfect Condition, without effort.

Traditionally, Divine Self-Realization has been referred to as
"Knowing" the One Divine Self. But, in fact, it is not possible to
fix attention on the Divine Self (as "Object"). The Divine Self-
Condition (or Reality Itself) cannot become an object of attention.

The actual process of Spiritual life requires the observation, the understanding, and the transcending of your own suffering, your own activity of self-contraction. When the self-contraction is thus observed, understood, and transcended, That Which the self-contraction prevents is suddenly, spontaneously Enjoyed—not as the "object" of Enjoyment, but as the Enjoyment Itself. Then (Prior to effort, motivation, or attention) there is only the Divine Self-Condition, Reality Itself, the True Divine Heart.

When there is the observation and understanding of suffering, then the entire structure of experiences, concepts, searches, strategies—which structure is your ordinary life, your search—ceases to be obsessive or even particularly interesting. It loses its significance, its capability to qualify That Which Always Already Is. This undistracted State, this natural Enjoyment Prior to the activity that is your suffering, is Divine Self-Realization, or most perfect "radical" self-understanding. It is the Enjoyment of Reality Itself, the Enjoyment That Is Reality Itself—Which is otherwise symbolically referred to as "God", the "Masters", and so on. From the "Point of View" of the Divine Self-Condition, the storybook "Masters" are only more imagery that tends to fascinate and occupy the seeker, the one who is already suffering. But the search and the seeker are themselves of no real concern. They are already secondary—because the seeker is, in Reality, only a reaction to his or her own suffering. The root-activity, the thing that is really occupying and motivating every human being, is suffering itself.

Therefore, it is suffering that is the inevitable and spontaneous content of sadhana—rather than the artifices to which seekers attach themselves. The seeker's illusions are not the appropriate object of attention. They are no solution. They are merely more of the same. Reading about Jesus and wanting to be like Jesus is not the equivalent of being Jesus. It never will be the equivalent of being Jesus. Your talk about Jesus is like your statement that you are in your body. You are suggesting Jesus to yourself—but, in fact, the Jesus of your mere thinking is not here.

DEVOTEE: Isn't the experience here?

AVATAR ADI DA SAMRAJ: What is that?

DEVOTEE: The love.

AVATAR ADI DA SAMRAJ: If there is love here, why does it have to be Jesus? What is added to this moment by thinking that the love that is here is Jesus' love? It is only because the mind is already associated with that symbol, and it consoles itself with that symbol. Rather than penetrating your own suffering, rather than penetrating the unloveliness, the unloving quality of your own life, you console yourself with the images of things you do not contain. When you understand that, when you see what you are doing, it really becomes impossible for you to "turn yourself on" with symbols. You can read about Jesus and think that love is <u>his</u> love—but, sooner or later, there is going to be a real need for love, a real dissatisfaction with no-love, a penetration of this plaster mind that does not really do the job. Then you will see that all of these consolations are forms of your own mind. They are entertainments, distractions—for a purpose that always remains hidden. Then you will begin to observe this motivation, this need to be consoled. And such self-observation is a very difficult affair—because, in the process of self-observation, there are no consoling images. There is not anything by which to be consoled.

There is a necessary "death" declared by all the religious and Spiritual traditions—a death beyond natural physical death. It is a <u>Spiritual</u> "death"—a "dark night" in which the "I", the ego, is confounded and transcended. Ultimately, what is being pointed to is the death (or real transcending, and real dissolution) of the ego-"I", and of all the imagery the ego-"I" uses to support itself, to console itself, to occupy itself. Indeed, the ego <u>is</u> the effort to be consoled.

Truly, <u>all</u> the traditions of religious and Spiritual life, including those with which Westerners tend to associate, are talking about a <u>crisis</u> in conscious awareness—<u>ego-death</u>—as the event of salvation or liberation. In the Event of Most Perfect Divine Liberation, there certainly is the death of the ego-"I". In that Great Event, there is no "thing" whatsoever. Previous to that Great Event, there is the holding on to all kinds of things—but, in that Great Event, there is the falling away of all forms of holding on. When that Great Event takes place, there is no longer any motive to hold on, there is no longer any "one" to die. When this "death" has occurred, What is Enjoyed (from that most perfectly ego-transcending "Point of View") has been traditionally pointed to by such words as "Love", "Salvation", "Liberation", "Realization", "God-Union". But there must be this "death", this crisis in con-scious awareness—a crisis in the ordinary process of surviving-and-seeking, which is (itself) the process by which you generate and maintain the images that console you. All such images are forms of seeking. You are responsible for their arising. They are phantoms that you hold on to—for <u>reasons</u>. The observation and understanding of those reasons—even the observation and under-standing of their very motivation, of the root-sense of suffering that supports the entire process of consolation—is absolutely fundamental to Real Spiritual life.

The body-mind (and even the universe itself) is not (in Truth, or in Reality) about <u>itself</u>. Rather, the body-mind (and even the total universe of conditional patterns) is about its Source-Principle (or the Reality in Which it is arising, and of Which it is a mere modification). That Source-Principle <u>Is</u> Truth. It is the Divine Reality of every conditional (or temporary) pattern. The Condition of Reality <u>Is</u> Love-Bliss. The Love-Bliss That <u>Is</u> has nothing to do with separate self and its concerns. Therefore, you must transcend your ego-"I", by surrendering (and allowing the dissolution of) your heartless ego-mind into Reality—because Reality (Itself) <u>Is</u> the Only <u>Real</u> God.

DEVOTEE: What about "born-again" Christians, and other people who go through a sudden change and become very light and happy?

AVATAR ADI DA SAMRAJ: We would, of course, have to be talking about somebody in particular to make sense of it. There are all kinds of testimonials, all kinds of "salvations", all kinds of claims made by people. There are thousands of religious and philosophical methods that have been tried by human beings, and all of them have a certain amount of "success". There are always individuals who make great claims for any particular religious or Spiritual path. Christianity is one path for which there are many such testimonials—because it has been going on for a long time, and many, many people have tried some form of it. There have been a number of great men and women among the Christians. There have also been a lot of mediocre people. Some of those mediocre people have also enjoyed a revolutionary change in their state, for reasons that others find hard to understand. Many other people have claimed to have gone through an enlightenment experience with a Zen Master, and so on. The Christian experience is typically "holy", while the Zen experience is typically "ordinary". The Zen insight may be precipitated by a punch in the mouth, a smack on the head with an oar, or some such crazy thing—and, the next moment, the "smackee" claims to be entirely transformed, living from an entirely new point of view! So this spontaneous turning-around can take place under all kinds of apparent circumstances. Enthusiastic claims are not exclusive to Christianity. They are found in all religious and Spiritual traditions. The phenomenon of turnabout is the essential (or common) factor in all of them. And, in general, such claims are, on the face of it, hard to understand.

If you took a survey of all the apparent examples of this turnabout, you would not be able to make sense of them, you would not be able to isolate some particular event that occurred (whether internally or externally) that could justify the claims. And that is precisely the point. In this turnabout—which can appear to be dramatic or not—there is not anything that is "added". Its causes are not identifiable, because it is not a matter of attaching something to the person's life (whether internally or externally). It is a matter of a turnabout of conscious awareness itself. One of the things the great traditional Teachers have tried to communicate is the value of that turnabout, and also something about how it actually takes place. The historical Masters, Gurus, or Teachers have always tried to communicate that process itself, by whatever particular means they had available to them.

However, for the most part (except in relatively few cases), the experience to which a religious person may testify represents only a temporary emotional distraction, a kind of mood. It is an experience. It can be described. It can be held on to, and it can be lost. It can even be proclaimed. But True Realization, True Liberation, True Awakening (of whatever Real degree) is profoundly unlike any form of mere experience. Truth is not an experience. It is not a particular state, and It cannot be identified with a particular style of life, a particular appearance. Seekers of all kinds talk about dramatic events in their lives as if those events were Enlightenment (or Truth). But most of those events are merely forms of temporary distraction, nothing but intense experiences. And people want to hold on to such things. They want to preserve or repeat such experiences throughout life, and they look forward to the repetition of such experiences in heaven or the afterlife. But Truth rests on no experience whatsoever. Truth is not, in Itself, an experience. Truth cannot be held on to. It cannot be repeated. It cannot be looked forward to. It cannot be lost. It cannot even be recommended. Truth is an absolute obliteration of what is commonly called "life".

What is ordinarily called "salvation" is a form of satisfaction imagined by a separate, fearful person. When someone is "saved", that one's separate life is consoled, distracted, and involved with a remedial path, an image, an experience. But, when there is no "one" to be satisfied, when there is no "one" to give a testimony, when there is no "one" to "meet" the "Savior"—That is Divine Liberation. When the ego-"I" (or the separate-self-sense that is one's suffering) is undermined, and there is a penetration (whether sudden or progressive) of the structure of conscious awareness, of mind, of motion, of separate-self-sense—when all of that is undermined, penetrated, when it is most perfectly observed, understood, and transcended, and the Very State (or Self-Condition) That all of that prevents is Enjoyed, then there is no longer any "one" to survive the death of ego-"I". Then there is no separate "one" living, there is no "one" to be "in" a body, there is no "one" to be "out of" the body. No "thing" has happened. There is no separate "one".

DEVOTEE: If we are all already conscious, then we are not here in Your Company in order to become conscious—right?

AVATAR ADI DA SAMRAJ: What you think of as consciousness is not Consciousness Itself. It is a form in Consciousness Itself.

DEVOTEE: So we are separating ourselves. We are identifying with that form, instead of Identifying with Consciousness Itself.

AVATAR ADI DA SAMRAJ: But there is no method to be recommended by which you can seek and, as a result of that seeking, "Find" (or Identify with) Consciousness Itself. There is no "one" who "Finds" Consciousness Itself. To Realize Consciousness Itself is a spontaneous Event, a paradoxical Event—potentially, the Most Absolute (and the Most Perfect) of all events. It is a Divine Gift! It is the Gift That Is Real God, or Truth Itself, or Reality Itself!

DEVOTEE: Are all Awakened people Gurus?

AVATAR ADI DA SAMRAJ: No. Guru is not a kind of status. It is a specific Function. There are some who, having (to one or another Real degree) Awakened, simply continue to live in their accustomed manner, without becoming active as the Function of Guru. There are others who, having (to one or another Real degree) Awakened, do (in fact) perform that Function. It is Truth Itself— not the Function of Guru—That Is the Realization of all who are (to one or another Real degree) Spiritually Awakened.

DEVOTEE: It is hard to figure out what I have read in the various traditional scriptures.

AVATAR ADI DA SAMRAJ: There is a point at which one's search becomes inappropriate. Now that you are in My Company, this is that point. All of the scriptures you may read, all of the remarks and experiences and traditions, come to an end when the import of those scriptures ceases to be merely academic. In the Self-"Bright" Spiritual Presence of the True Divine Heart Itself, seeking is inappropriate.

The traditional texts are paradoxical allegories about Realization Itself. These paradoxical allegories are simply suggesting, or somehow trying to imply, the Freedom of the One (Real, and Divine) Self (or Self-Condition). The One (Real, and Divine) Self (or Self-Condition) Is That Reality to Which all the scriptures are trying to turn you. If, after reading such scriptures, you miss the point, and the One (Real, and Divine) Self (or Self-Condition) does not become your direction, then you are stuck with something you <u>cannot</u> understand. Indeed, you are stuck with something that seems to say what cannot be true.

Thus, all of these traditional scriptures are "loaded". There are always two sides, two interpretations. But the traditional scriptures have only one purpose—which is to arouse interest in the Truth, in Realization. Once that interest has been aroused, the traditional scriptures have served their purpose. They serve to move you along, and even to entertain you for a period of time—until your interest in the possibility of Divine Self-Realization becomes significant enough that a crisis, a breakdown in your ordinary presuming and functioning, begins to take place. And, traditionally, it is hoped that, when this crisis begins, you will also find yourself in the Company of a True Realizer. When contact is made with a Realizer who lives (to whatever Real degree) as the One (Real, and Divine) Self (or Self-Condition), all the merely suggestive statements that are found in the traditional scriptures become obsolete. They lose their function at the point when that meeting takes place. The more you have accumulated before that moment, the more there is that must become obsolete—and so, also, the more resistance there will be to letting go of those beliefs and ideas.

Truly, the Divine Self is "Mad". The Divine Self is "Unlearned". The appropriate foundation of human life is not a supposedly independent entity, a separate-self-sense, an ego, even a "soul". Such is not the appropriate foundation for human life. The Foundation for human life is the True Divine Heart, the Real Divine Self-Condition. The Heart Itself is utterly mindless, utterly Free, Uncontained, Unqualified. But, paradoxically, when the Heart Itself is lived, the human being becomes functional, usable, alive, moved.

One who lives from the "Point of View" of the True Divine Heart, makes no complicated use of the things an ordinary person uses to survive. Like a child, the Divine Realizer moves by delight. The Divine Realizer is a person of pleasure, of enjoyment. Like a madman, the Divine Realizer learns nothing from life. The Divine Realizer does not <u>believe</u> what he or she sees, does not take it to have any limiting significance. The Divine Realizer throws away all the things that seem so profound, so serious to everyone. The Divine Realizer attributes nothing to them. Truly, the Divine Realizer is like a madman or a child.

However, apart from actual Divine Self-Realization (or most perfect "radical" self-understanding), what I have just said is, in and of itself, merely a form of entertainment for you. The necessary "death" of your act and illusion of separate (and always separative) ego-self is what interests Me.

DEVOTEE: What about Lord Yama?[11]

AVATAR ADI DA SAMRAJ: Lord Yama, the storybook Lord of Death? He barely enters into it! He is only a symbol in the mind—as if the natural process and event of death were (really) some entity, some being or other.

Your natural death is not the concern of any "other". I <u>Am</u> your Real (and Divine) Self-Condition, beyond your ego-"I". I am very interested in your <u>ego</u>-death—not the natural death of all the things you call your "life". And I am very interested in bringing about this ego-death very quickly. I want a sudden ego-death, a sudden Realization of Freedom and Happiness, for every one!

DEVOTEE: What if a person's heart, breath, and mind were suspended for twenty minutes. Wouldn't the person be free then?

AVATAR ADI DA SAMRAJ: It depends on what has occurred during those twenty minutes. Many people have been in a coma for months, or even years, but they did not wake up any less immune to death, or any more intelligent, or any more Awake to Reality (Itself).

The "death" I am talking about is not the death of which you suspect yourself. It is not simply that physical event, that vital event. The "death" I am talking about is the turnabout—the dissolution of the <u>principle</u> by which you live, of the fundamental activity that you are animating, dramatizing, presuming to be your self, living to others. The dissolution of your egoic state is the "death" that is significant.

DEVOTEE: How would You compare that with the physical act of suicide?

AVATAR ADI DA SAMRAJ: The physical act of suicide is an impairment. It is an obstruction. It takes away the functions you have available for intelligence. So the mere act of suicide is not "it"— any more than extreme fasting, deprivation of the senses, or inward-directed (and exclusionary) concentration is "it". None of these psycho-physical events is the crisis of Truth. They are all mere experiences. At best, they are symbolic events. They do not achieve what is required.

The traditional Yogic methods of seeking Self-Realization (or God-Union) are something like sitting in a room, breathing heavily, and looking at erotic pictures. You can generate something that is like passion, but you are never going to make love! It never becomes that. Just so, you can sit and breathe methodically, turning inward, contemplating Divine images or "God"-ideas—but none of that is ever going to become Real-God-Union. Real God never enters into it. Such is a very hopeful practice at best. There can be no Real-God-Union until Real God is there to be "unioned" with. As a lover depends on his or her loved-one, the God-seeker depends on the Living Presence of Real God before there can be any Real-God-Union. And, when Real God Appears, you are not going to have to do your "Spiritual breathing"! What there is to do will all be very obvious. You will not have to think about what is necessary to be done in order to "become One with God". It is only the presumed absence of God, the suffering, the ignorant condition, that gets you involved in all of this seeking. It is only when God is presumed to be already absent that you begin to engage all of these practices.

DEVOTEE: Well, should we just wait it out until God comes, then?

AVATAR ADI DA SAMRAJ: The strategy of deliberate waiting is also another form of that same seeking. Fortunately—or unfortunately—the search goes on, in spite of any intention you may have to the contrary, until the connection with the Living Divine is made. Everything you do is that search—until Real God, the Real Divine Self-Condition, the True Divine Heart, enters into the picture, as a Living Reality, in relationship.

DEVOTEE: If conscious awareness is divided between waking, dreaming, and sleeping, then how do we get behind these three to find the True Self?

AVATAR ADI DA SAMRAJ: That "consideration" has been fundamental to the approach of Advaita Vedanta (or Jnana Yoga), and of certain other traditions of Spiritual practice. They build up this conceptual dilemma—and, then, they try to solve it. The Divine Self is pictured as an alternative to waking, dreaming, and sleeping. The Divine Self is pictured or proposed as a "Something Else", an alternative (and world-excluding) State that is hidden beneath the usual three states of waking, dreaming, and sleeping. Thus, in order to get to the recommended state (which is presumed to be "underneath" all of this), it seems that you must go through an inward-turning process that progressively excludes more and more of the "outside" world. Such is the process of meditation that is traditionally recommended in these schools.

The Advaitic statement is not complete. The central statement of the ancients, as stated by the adherents of Advaita Vedanta, is: The jivatman (the individual "soul") and the Paramatman (the

Great "Soul", the Universal Self) are One. Therefore, seekers in that tradition are led into a process of inward-turning seclusion and would-be union.

The central statement of Mahayana Buddhism is similarly incomplete. That statement is: Nirvana and samsara are the same. In other words, the Unqualified Reality is not different from this—the conditional appearance, the world.

Taken together, these two great statements reflect, in a symbolic manner, something of the Ultimate Nature of Reality: This—the entire Force and Form manifesting as this moment—Is the Divine Self (or Self-Condition). It is not that there is some separate, hidden Entity underneath the three states (of waking, dreaming, and sleeping) that is the Divine Self (or Reality Itself), and all of this is just sort of covering (or obscuring) It. There is no "difference" whatsoever in Consciousness Itself. There is always already no dilemma. There is no inwardness that is equal to Truth Itself. There is no special subjectivity that is Truth Itself. There is no special objectivity that is Truth Itself. The subjective and the objective are (both) already the Very "Thing", the Very Truth.

Nevertheless, there is a dilemma meanwhile. There is suffering. There is non-comprehension. And, since there is suffering, human beings are motivated to recover the Sublimity Which they have been suggesting to themselves and Which some claim to have Realized. But it is only when the entire process of interior-and-exterior—all these movements, all these searches, all these experiences—when all of that has failed, then suffering itself becomes the focus of your experience, rather than all of the seeking that is only a reaction to suffering. Then you fall into your suffering, you become conscious as your suffering, you understand your suffering, you "die" from your suffering—and you see That Which Is Always Already the Case. So all the seeking is just a prolongation of the suffering.

DEVOTEE: When the Realized being has "turned the switch off", how does he or she get back to functioning in this world?

AVATAR ADI DA SAMRAJ: There is no Divine Self that is behind all of this. The Divine Self (or Self-Condition) Is this, without a doubt. There is no separateness whatsoever. Therefore, Divine Self-Realization is entirely compatible with human existence. One who is Divinely Self-Realized is no longer suffering—no longer seeking, whether outwardly or inwardly. The dilemma is gone. The Divine Realizer sees the Obvious. The Divine Realizer Enjoys the Obvious. And all the human functions become functions in fact—usable, achievable, and enjoyable.

You are dealing with images. These images imply things about your present state which are not quite true. They are metaphors: the idea of the "switch", the idea of the "Fourth State" (Beyond the three states of waking, dreaming, and sleeping). Truth has been represented in the form of images in order to interest you in Realization, and also in order to suggest to you what is <u>not</u> Realization. But Realization is of another kind than this interest, this fascination, developed by your reading of traditional texts. All of the traditions agree that the best thing you can do is spend your time in Satsang, in heart-Communion with the Adept-Realizer, the Guru. That <u>is</u> meditation. That <u>is</u> the Real Condition. Satsang with Me <u>is</u> Realization. That <u>is</u> Love-Bliss-Happiness.

DEVOTEE: How can it affect someone—to just sit with a Realized being?

AVATAR ADI DA SAMRAJ: You tend to take on the qualities of the things you spend your time with. If you watch a television program, you go through a distracting drama. Then, all of a sudden, a commercial! It breaks the trance. So you feel disturbed. If you spend your evening in a topless-bottomless bar, another game attracts you. If you take drugs, there is that drama. If you get amused tonight, smoking cigarettes until dawn, there is that form of mind and life. Perhaps you go on a picnic, or you go fishing, or you go to church on Sunday. There are all these dramas being played.

Now, it happens that—in the ordinary drama (in all of its millions of forms, and in all the billions of people living it)—there is a <u>contraction</u>. Every drama is a play of separation, of suffering, of seeking. The self-contraction is the root-element, the foundation, of all ego-dramas. Therefore, when you become involved with ordinary things (regardless of what they may appear to be in the moment), they carry with them the root-implication of your suffering. Now there is this pleasure, now this—now this entertainment, and now this. The appearance varies, but it is always the same—the same implication is being reinforced in conscious awareness.

I have Appeared in human Form, but I Live as the Real Divine Self-Condition. Thus, of all your associations, it is only My Avataric Divine Company, Satsang with Me, that does not support the self-contraction. Satsang with Me does not <u>support</u> the self-contraction. That is what is unique about Satsang with Me. Inevitably, you continue to attempt to live self-contraction in various forms, you continue to be entertained, you continue to seek. You even continue to expect what it seems you should expect from your association with Me. But I do not support the self-contraction, your very activity of suffering.

The Guru is like an elevator. The Guru is in the hotel lobby—with a nice marble casement, and a needle above, pointing to the numbers of floors. It looks perfectly stable. You know it has been there for a while. You dare to walk up to it. You see buttons on the wall. The doors open. You look inside. It is nicely decorated. A couple of nicely dressed people come out, to go to the cocktail lounge. So you step in. You expect to rise—as all the traditions say. But you fall right through the bottom of the floor!

I do not support your egoic game. My Activity is <u>non-support</u>—in endless forms.

The effect of this non-support is that the quality of self-contraction in you begins to become obvious. The search winds down, your suffering becomes obvious, and you (intuitively) become alive in the context of such self-observation. The quality of self-contraction simply begins to get flabby and fall apart. You begin to observe and understand your own activity of self-contraction. Therefore, in the living relationship with Me, I Live the Divine Self-Condition to you—whereas, in all other conditions of life, it is the self-contraction, the avoidance of relationship, that is lived to you.

DEVOTEE: Would You describe some of the levels on which You Work?

AVATAR ADI DA SAMRAJ: There is no particular point in describing them. The most it would do is make you self-conscious in relationship to Me. On every possible level of awareness, the Heart Itself is Active. The important thing is that, in My Avataric Divine Company, even though people are suffering, they are able to intuitively recognize Me As the Living Divine Person. What they will do about that recognition is another matter. But the recognition is there, in some intuitive form. Rather than any other kind of "information", it is heart-recognition of Me that My devotees must depend on—both for knowing that I am their Divine Guru (or Divine Heart-Master) and for knowing that they want to be involved in the heart-relationship to Me. Many have had enough of seeking—such that, once they come into contact with Me (in one manner or another), they are moved to become My formal devotees. Through that process, they begin to see how I Function as the Living Divine Heart. Others come into contact with Me, and they resist immediately. They defend their state—and, so, they may not (presently) be moved toward Me.

The occupation of My devotee is Satsang, the heart-relationship to Me. Contemplating Me with feeling-devotion is My devotee's meditation. Consciously sitting in relationship with the Very Divine Person (or Real-God-Nature)—such is a true summary of all of the elements of meditation. What else could meditation be? Therefore, for My devotee, to meditate is (most fundamentally) simply to live in heart-Communion with Me. And, over time, meditation becomes more profound. It becomes Real intelligence. Even from the beginning of the Way of Adidam, meditation is (necessarily) a formal practice, appearing as what people ordinarily presume to be meditation. But that heart-Communion with Me, Satsang with Me, living It from day to day, living the conditions that this heart-relationship requires of you—that is the foundation of True Spiritual life.

For My devotee, Satsang with Me <u>is</u> meditation. For My devotee, Satsang with Me <u>is</u> sadhana (or True religious—and, in due course, Spiritual—practice). For My devotee, the heart-relationship to Me is True Humor. In Satsang with Me, True Humor is obvious—because the most fundamental Enjoyment is always taking place.

Until you devotionally recognize Me (the Divine Heart Alive in Avatarically-Born bodily human Divine Form) and live the heart-relationship to Me, everything you do is a form of the search, and every action reinforces your suffering. Such a life is not "it". There must be a "radically" new life, based on a "radically" new Presence, a "radically" new Communication.

The Divine Heart Itself must Appear—in Avatarically-Born Incarnate Form. Otherwise, the seeker is like the guy with the girlie magazine in his room—he is not going to make it. And, for the seeker, the "Spiritual" books have no more ultimate significance than pornography. The seeker's "Spiritual reading" is perhaps a little subtler than erotica, but the same root-motivation is behind it. The same suffering is there. It is a form of entertainment.

On different days, there are different kinds of entertainment. Some days, you prefer porn magazines—other days, you prefer the *Bhagavad Gita*. But it is the same guy, the same search, the same dilemma. This is why certain Zen Masters burned the wooden statues of the Buddha. The same thing must be done with the traditional scriptures. It is not necessary to go out and burn them in the street—but there must be this understanding of their significance in relation to the True Divine Heart Itself, in relation to True Spiritual life.

The Intelligence of the True Divine Heart is a Genius, a Fire—not a little pipe-smoking philosopher. The same Power That Manifests as this universe, with its billions of birthing-and-dying beings, is the Divine Heart Itself. One who Lives As the True Divine Heart can read these scriptures and use them, consume them, destroy them, play with them, do whatever he or she likes with them. Such a confrontation with the scriptures is alive, but the seeker's confrontation with the scriptures is mediocre. It does not amount to Real-God-Realization. Only one who is already Realized reads such things and truly comprehends them.

If you do not yet understand your own ego-activity, then the books are simply a means of gaining your interest, of moving you toward a moment when you will seriously begin. And, even then, there are many pitfalls. The guy puts down the girlie magazine, gets dressed, and goes out to a porn theatre! This, instead of going out to find himself in human company, in relationship!

Thus, it takes more than just putting down the books. There are lots of "gurus" around, lots of "movie houses" where you can go in for a zapping. They entertain you, they take a couple of bucks, they do a number for you. It is in sound and color—two full hours! And what does it come down to? They tell you to go home and do it yourself! You were home trying to do it yourself all night! But now they give you a "do-it-yourself" kit. You take it on home, and you clean up the corner of your bedroom. You throw away all the porn magazines—or, at least, you keep them in the bathroom under the hamper. You clean up a corner of the room, and you open up the blinds so that the sun comes in on it real nice. Then you get up at dawn, and you "do it" to yourself!

Now the guy is in the same condition as he was the night before—even less intelligent. He has taken on some path or other, professionalized his search. The night before, he was just a guy, just a slob. But now he is a "<u>Yogi</u>"! He puts on the outfit, wears the beads, starts saving money for his trip to India next year. He plays this game for however long it takes him to get sick of all that. And, after that, he says, "The hell with it!"—and he messes up his room again, throws away his robe and beads, and takes the girlie magazines back into the bedroom. But he really hasn't "<u>got</u> it" anymore. Besides, he is probably fifty years old by now. So he is really not about to go back out to the girlie show. His girlie magazines are not really going to give it to him, either.

Then, all of a sudden, the doorbell rings. It's the Avon Lady! Better known as the Guru!

In the building where we are gathered now,[12] there is the "movie house" (the bookstore) out in the front, with all of the best traditional literature, the very best "pornography". In other words, the store does not carry any junk! People who have become interested, who have left their homes, who are wandering around trying to find something a little jazzier, who have done a little reading—these people see the bookstore. All of the usual motivations gather them up, and they come in to look at the books. While they browse, they see a couple of signs about the Ashram. And, after a while, they begin to feel a little itching in the back of the head. It is a very unusual movie house. It appears to be like any other. It appears ordinary. It is ordinary.

The ordinary, from the "Point of View" of Consciousness Itself, is the only extraordinary. All the extraordinaries to which people aspire are very ordinary. They have been done thousands upon thousands of times. All of the kriyas, all of the purifications, all of the visions—they have all been done! Thousands upon thousands of times. Everything has been done. Every extraordinary experience has occurred. The subtle mechanism of the human being has been exploited and explored for aeons. It is not a new medium at all.

All the usual aspirations are based on suffering and seeking. Therefore, they all lead to the ordinary, the mediocre, the usual— more of the same. Someone having an "ecstatic" vision is in the same condition as someone watching a TV commercial. Only when all of that has worn down do you begin to see that the principle underlying all of your seeking, your discoveries, your apparent attainments, is suffering! That is the Truth. Then you begin to become sensitive to your actual condition, instead of trying to do something about it. You see exactly what that condition is.

That is when the truly extraordinary and transformative event occurs. Once that event begins, there is an unseriousness about all the things that you took seriously before. All the accumulations, all the imagery, all the books, all the symbols, cease to be your occupation. Instead, you become occupied with the Living Truth. And the Living Truth is Prior to all of this mentality.

AVATAR ADI DA SAMRAJ
Adidam Samrajashram, 2004

3.
Money, Food, and Sex

I.

AVATAR ADI DA SAMRAJ: There are patterns in your individual life that are responsible for the quality of tamas—or inertia, immobility, sluggishness, the backlog of everything. The earliest period of the sadhana in My Avataric Divine Company deals especially with this tamasic condition—your inertia, your tendency to remain in (or return to) the very state of suffering and ignorance in which you began.

Therefore, as My devotee, you must find the practical means to fulfill My requirements for a responsible life. True Spiritual life begins when you are capable of functioning. Until then, it does not make any difference how many times you see Me, or how many lectures you hear about the Way of Adidam. Now is the time to begin to live rightly—and to live rightly is to be responsible for your life, not to continue old patterns of irresponsibility. I cannot release you from responsibility—how can I release you from the responsibility for your breath?

When people become involved in any kind of religious or Spiritual activity, particularly a group activity of some sort, there are a few underlying notions that automatically tend to be assumed. There is the underlying suggestion that Spiritual life has something to do with separating from vital and physical life. Indeed, in many of the ancient traditions, Spiritual life was exactly what that notion suggests—an exclusive (and eventually terminal) inward-turning, an attempt to get away entirely from the life-force, the life-form, the life-mind, the life-appearance, the life-sensation—into some inward, subtle, non-life perception or vision or heaven, or whatever.

This traditional notion tends to be blanketed over everything that even looks like religion, Spirituality, Yoga, and so on. Therefore, every demand to actually deal with the physical and vital being tends to meet with immediate resistance on the part of those who aspire to religious and Spiritual practice.

Money (and, in general, the commitment of life-force in the forms of effort and human relatedness), food, and sex are the essential activities of life. Those are the vital processes, the forms of vital appearance and function. And money, food, and sex are the first things that people begin to resist or manipulate when they get involved in anything that is even remotely like religion or Spirituality.

For the most part, people who are involved in conventional religion and conventional Spirituality feel extremely confused and guilty about money, food, and sex. Such people are endlessly involved with experiments relating to money, food, and sex. What are such people always doing? "Should I or shouldn't I?" "What is the right diet?" "Fasting? Macrobiotics? No food?" "Renunciation? Poverty?" They are on and off food all the time, on and off sex. They may be celibate for years in an effort to get so-called "enlightened"—but then, just as dramatically, they are seeking the "Tantric bliss"[13] or the restoration of "mental health" in a perpetual orgasmic exercise. Then there are all of the other games of self-denial—no work, no income, and so on. These are the kinds of things that tend to arise whenever anything like religion or Spirituality comes into a person's life.

Because of the automatic resistances built into religious and Spiritual endeavor, the practical need for money and for the means of survival is a very complicated and frustrating affair for even the most sophisticated religious and Spiritual groups. But all of this should be a very obvious matter. You are not in heaven. This is the Earth. Everything here costs life, effort, and money. It costs a great deal of life, effort, and money to function as a gathering of religious or Spiritual practitioners. The purposes of such a gathering may be religious or Spiritual, but a living culture must fulfill the same functional laws as any household or any business corporation.

112

Nevertheless, whenever practical demands are made for effort, commitment, cooperation, or money, people tend to lapse into the tamasic mood. Such reluctance retards life. And the ability of an individual or a group to transcend this tendency is the measure of freedom and survival.

There is the suspicion that, if you are "Spiritual", you are not supposed to need money, you are not supposed to require anything, and you are supposed to abandon the functions of life. Obviously, though, money is needed in most circumstances—and work, effort, human relatedness, and energy are necessary for functional survival. Why isn't it patently obvious, then, that individuals are responsible to bring life and commitment to their own religious or Spiritual community, that they must take responsibility for its existence and effective functioning in the world, and contribute a responsible amount of money for its continuation? Why isn't that obvious? Why is there always so much wheeling and dealing involved with any religious or Spiritual organization?

It is because of the traditional illusion of religious or Spiritual attainment—which is pictured as a kind of evaporation process, wherein you gradually become more and more "elusive", and you finally disappear inside your "something", or dissolve into your "someplace else".

Now, there are people who teach that such goals are Truth. According to such teachings, there are few (and always progressively fewer) responsibilities required at the level of life. A certain amount of food must be taken—but some teachers have even suggested that, if you begin a fast and never eat again, at death you will merge into a so-called "enlightened state". Thus, they feel they have handled that aspect of vital existence, too. Such so-called "enlightenment" is a cave without money, food, or sex. But going to the forest and fasting until death is not a means for Realizing the Truth!

I find this traditional orientation to be utter nonsense. I do not teach it, and I do not support it. Truth Is <u>Always</u> <u>Already</u> the Case. There is nothing inherently "un-Spiritual" about participating in the human world at the life-level. The functional responsibilities thus incurred do not, in any sense, prevent Real Spiritual life. The responsibilities of the human world require the exercise of creativity and intelligence. All life-conditions are forms of relationship. Everything at the level of life requires ordinary responsibility. If you are incapable of such ordinariness, then you have not even begun to become involved in Real Spiritual life.

The first level of sadhana that I had to endure with a human Teacher was not any sort of other-worldly Yoga, nor did it involve expressions of love and acknowledgement from the Guru, or even kind words. I spent about two minutes with Rudi when I first met Him. He told Me to get a job and come back in one year! And I was perfectly willing to do that.

As it happened, within a month or two, My Sadhana with Rudi did begin. It was not, in fact, necessary for Me to be away from Him for a year, but I was perfectly willing for it to be so. I was ecstatically happy to have made this contact, to have a beginning, to truly enter into the process of Spiritual life. It was a profound joy to Me to have found someone who was obviously capable of drawing Me into a condition at least more profound than the one I was then living.[14]

From that moment, it was one demand on top of the other. It was work. Work was the sadhana, work was the process. There was no "Come to me and sit and chat." It was "Take out the garbage. Sweep out this place." If I came around to sit and talk with Rudi, I was most often told, "Scrub the floor," or, "There is a new shipment in the warehouse, so go and unload the truck." I worked constantly, day and night, for four years.

On top of the heavy physical labor, Rudi had Me going to seminaries, where I studied Christian theology, masses of historical literature, ancient languages—all kinds of things in which I had no fundamental interest. I had to live in Protestant and Orthodox seminaries, even though I was not a Christian. My Sadhana was continuous work and ego-transcendence. There was no end to it. Even in sleep and dreams, there was no end to it.

My time with Rudi did not see the fulfillment of My Spiritual Sadhana. I moved on to other Teachers, and the order of My Sadhana and My understanding changed. But Rudi's requirements for sadhana in the functions of life and body—in terms of money, food, and sex—were profoundly useful to Me. The Sadhana I performed in those years became the very foundation of My Spiritual life. During that time, I was strengthened and stabilized in mind, body, and life.

When I came to Rudi, I was not prepared for Spiritual sadhana. To embrace such sadhana would have been of no use to Me in the beginning. The Realization of Truth must be founded in a rightening of your practical life. The Force of Truth can never transform your life if you begin your sadhana "in the air". If sadhana is <u>begun</u> as an effort to become so-called "Spiritual", then what is merely alive remains a mass of confusion and craziness. Therefore, I must insist that all who come to Me take on functional responsibility for the basic life-functions—which are money, food, and sex.

My Manner of Working with people is to Attract them and establish a relationship with them—such that this relationship becomes their conscious, overwhelming, and continuous Condition. When they become conscious of it on any level, then I Give them responsibilities at that level. From that moment, I require and expect them to function at that level. I never pat them on that part of the head again. I expect them to live that function responsibly in the culture of My devotees, and everywhere in life, from that point on.

I expect all of My devotees to do sadhana at the levels of money, food, and sex. And to do sadhana on those levels is, at times, going to be just as difficult for you as it was for Me. If you are ready for Spiritual life, you will be very happy to have some-thing in your hand at last, to function at last, to have begun. All other responses to this sadhana are your unreadiness, your unwill-ingness, your resistance. They are "Narcissus".

"Narcissus" has no support from the True Divine Heart, from the True Guru, from the Truth Itself, or even from the universe. "Narcissus" is already dead. Death is his karma, his destiny, his only realization. Everyone will only die who lives as "Narcissus". "Narcissus" will die in his own pocket. His head will fall from a sleeve. He will not die a sublime death. He will die alone, uncon-scious for a long time. He is the destiny of unconsciousness, of foolishness. But all True Waking comes suddenly—if only "Narcissus" looks up from the "pond".

People have become involved with all kinds of patterns of life that are their suffering. Your sadhana necessarily involves an address to the level of complication (or suffering) that you are already living. Sadhana does not necessarily involve visions. Even if visions appear, they have no ultimate consequence. Suffering is the place of sadhana. Sadhana meets this complication, this resistance, this fear, this stupidity, this lethargy, this craziness, this violence, this separateness, this heaviness, this endless distraction by the current of experience from hour to hour. All of that is terrifying, if you could consciously see it. Sadhana is involved with that.

Sadhana requires a great deal of a person. Ultimately, it requires that you manifest the great qualities, the greatest human qualities. All My devotees must manifest those qualities in life. Of course, it is not required (or even possible) that you manifest those qualities in one afternoon, but functional intelligence must manifest at a certain level even at the very beginning.

True Spiritual life is not a form of consolation. Its foundation is not a fascinating promise. It is not a matter of "Get along, do the best you can—and, after death, you will go to heaven," or "I will come again and make everything all right, no matter what you do—because everything is really okay, you rascal!" There is a profound sense in which everything really is all right—even now, regardless of conditions. But to understand that profundity requires the most penetrating kind of humor, intelligence, and discipline.

Therefore, you must become responsible at the simplest level, the level in which you are living, in which you exist. There is nothing very profound about it. To do so requires you to conduct (or make lawful use of) the life-force—not to abandon it, not to become separate from it.

You must become capable of relationship at the level of the vital—indeed, on all the levels of the physical being, ultimately including the entire range of psycho-physical life. There is no praise, no blame, in vitality itself—nor in the appropriate management and enjoyment of food. For those who are capable of engaging sexuality as right Yoga and who choose to be sexually active, there is no praise, no blame, in the responsible, appropriate enjoyment of emotional-sexual relationship. There is no praise, no blame, in the earning and use of money—nor in the appropriate exercise of power and creativity, in the use of functional ability and energy.

But, as long as you are living the pattern of separation, you are enormously complicated in the functions of money, food, and sex. Most of the problems you perceive in your own case have to do with money, food, and sex. The mishandling of those three aspects of life manifests as poverty and lawsuits, hoarding and financial complications, ill health, and compulsions at the level of food and sex. Those are the daily experience of the usual human being. The daily round is a complication of money, food, and sex.

Ramakrishna (in speaking to His renunciate male disciples) used to say that "women and gold" were the chief distractions and sources of bondage. He belonged, perhaps, to the school of "getting away from the vital"—but He was right about "women and gold", the functions of money and sex. And food must be included in the list. Money, food, and sex are the areas in which suffering is most apparent. Therefore, your life becomes very complicated to the degree that you have not understood the vital processes, to the degree you are living the life of "Narcissus" in relation to money, food, and sex.

Simply because you have come to Me and have expressed a certain willingness to begin the sadhana in My Avataric Divine Company does not mean that you have ceased to live in the usual manner. When you become My devotee, you begin to observe your resistances, your reluctance to function in at least human terms, all of the craziness, and the forms of crisis, that make your limitations so very apparent at times.

All of that does not disappear simply because you are My devotee—but the process that undermines all of it has begun. Satsang with Me does not support the forms of your reluctance, your tamasic tendencies. Those tendencies continue to pattern you until a different intelligence replaces them. And that is precisely what the beginning sadhana in My Avataric Divine Company is all about.

In the meantime, while you are still a little nutty, you must survive in time and space. Indeed, the cooperative culture of My devotees must itself survive. Therefore, rather than have the culture of My devotees accommodate itself to resistance, your responsibilities must be made plain. What is appropriate must be made known in a simple manner, and all who come to Me must be required to function at that level immediately.

People think they are supposed to be allowed a little time to get through all of their functional problems. They think they are supposed to analyze themselves for a few years, under very supportive conditions, and get it a little bit straight—in two, three, maybe four years. But such a plan has nothing whatsoever to do with the Truth. It is only another sign of reluctance, inertia, tamas.

Spiritual life is not the support of your malfunctioning, with a few little bits of wisdom thrown in, until you come out of it. Spiritual life is sadhana, the always present demand to function. How do you think the Spiritual crisis was brought about in traditional monasteries and Spiritual centers? Certainly not by coddling and consoling mediocre people. That is why very few people went to those centers. The moment you stepped in the door, someone was waiting with a stick who took all your clothes, all your money, all your belongings, put you in a little cell, gave you brief instructions about the four or five things you were going to be allowed to do for the rest of your life, and then demanded you do all five before dinner! You found out how you were failing to function by trying to function, by living under conditions in which nothing but functioning was allowed.

Life in My Avataric Divine Company is a demand. It is True Spiritual life—not a form of therapy. It is a demand under the conditions of Satsang with Me, devotional relationship to Me. It is the practice of life in a world where the Living Divine Heart—not your own dilemma and search—is the Condition.

It is not the demand itself that makes Real sadhana possible. Rather, it is the Force of Satsang with Me, the Force of the Prior Condition of Truth, that makes Real sadhana necessary. Satsang with Me contains, and Communicates Itself as, a demand. And this demand acts as an obstacle for those who are not certain about their interest in the life of Satsang with Me. They have read a little about it, heard a little about it—and now it tests them in the fire of living.

Such is how it has always been. The monasteries, the ashrams, the schools of teachers in the past were conceived like fortresses in the hills. They were difficult to get to, and very few people ever returned from them. People did not gaze nostalgic-ally at the place up on the hill, or hear about it on the evening news, and say, "Wow! I wish I could just go up there—you know, find out where it's really at. Go up there, and everything is fan-tastic forever, and have a really great time." Traditionally, Spiritual life was never confused with any sort of playful "getting high". All of that is nothing but a mediocre interpretation, fabricated by people who are demonstrating no real capability for sadhana and no true impulse toward the Inherently egoless Love-Bliss-Happiness of Conscious Existence.

True Spiritual life is not about "getting high". From the resis-tive, "Narcissistic", ordinary human point of view, Spiritual life is the most completely oppressive prospect. And it stimulates mas-sive resistance in ordinary people as soon as they get a taste of it.

Traditionally, incredible obstacles were put out front, so that people would not even bother to come to the door. The tradi-tional notion was that people should not even ask about Spiritual life unless they had already overcome a tremendous amount of the resistance in themselves. The great oriental temples, for instance, were built with incredible images of demons, guardians, and fero-cious beasts surrounding the entrances, so that people would not approach such places in their usual state of self-obsession. Their heads were required to be bowed. You were expected to be crushed within, in a humble state, reflecting awareness of your habit of living. You were expected to arrive on your knees, and never without a gift. Such people would never come irreverently. They would never display an inappropriate attitude.

The traditional forms of approach are perhaps too ritualistic and too purely symbolic. They can be superficially learned and imitated—and, so, they do not necessarily reflect the inner attitude. However, everyone must realize and demonstrate the appropriate and genuine manner of approach to Me and to life in My Avataric Divine Company. "Narcissus" is not allowed to play. He is not supported.

The gathering of My devotees is not an artificial environment in which everyone is supposed to be "Simon-pure". My devotees have nothing to defend. You are in a position to know one another very well. That is one of the freedoms of such a gathering. My devotees are generally very frank with one another in addressing each other's nonsense. And that is perfectly all right, perfectly allowable—because such frankness is a righteous demand for relationship. It is a purifying demand.

True Spiritual life is (altogether) such a demand. It hurts at times, it puts you into confusion, it stimulates conflict, it makes you feel ugly, it makes you recognize crazy things about yourself, it forces you to function in spite of your refusal to function, it offends all the self-imagery that you have built all your life. But, after all, that is what there is to be dealt with. Everything you bring to Me to defend is undermined. Your game is not supported—it is aggravated. And people often become aggravated in the relationship with the Guru.

DEVOTEE: What is the nature of the demand You make upon Your devotees?

AVATAR ADI DA SAMRAJ: The condition for "radical" self-understanding is Satsang with Me. That Satsang Itself, when It is most consciously lived, is "radical" self-understanding. It is meditation. Satsang with Me is the Real Condition. That is why It goes on apart from the search, Prior to your dilemma and suffering. You should not approach Me in order to carry on the search. You should approach Me with devotion, as one who has found, and put your search down at My Feet.

My devotee is one who has formally embraced the practice of living in constant Remembrance of Me. That is the True sadhana of Satsang with Me. Every bit of seeking, dilemma, and self-obsession that you lay down at My Feet is your true gift to Me. All gifts symbolize that true and inner gift, and make it visible.

Someone may bring a flower to Me. The flower is very fresh and fragrant. When the person smiles and puts it on the ground or in a vase, it may all seem like a pleasantry. But what is represented by that flower could be the most difficult crisis of the person's life. The truth of that flower, of that gift, is the crisis itself.

When you begin to live your life functionally, as relationship, when you accept the simplest level of responsibility and live it consciously, in spite of conflict, in spite of difficulty, then life itself becomes sadhana, Real Spiritual practice, an expression of Satsang with Me. Such functional and responsible living is the first gift of My devotee to Me. Therefore, it is also My first demand.

I truly expect My devotees to master life, to serve My Avataric Divine Blessing-Work, to live the process of Satsang in My Avataric Divine Company, to give it their life-force, to live it with intensity and love, and to make Satsang with Me available to every human being who heart-recognizes Me. I do not expect, nor do I support, anything less than that. I expect you to function. Confrontation with the functional demand of life is your test from day to day. It is a sign to you of your state from hour to hour. It is on this functional level that My devotees must begin the process of self-observation, self-understanding, and self-transcendence (or Real ego-transcendence)—which process is the indispensable foundation for the Realization of Truth.

I am not interested in dealing with the superficial and smiling level in you. I am always aware of your visible suffering. I always want to deal with that suffering, seeking, dilemma, contraction, resistance. Satsang with Me deals with all of that. It undermines your lack of functioning. Your craziness is what must be dealt with. I can engage you in a friendly manner—but, as My beginning devotee, you are not presently capable of simply Enjoying the Living Presence of the Heart in My Avataric Divine Company. Since that is the case, the obstruction in yourself (as it is manifesting in present-time) is what must be dealt with. And Satsang with Me is the appropriate means to deal with it.

I do not mean some sort of confrontation—in which you and I have it out with one another, or in which you get to yell at Me, make demands, get very upset, or play out your entire emotional act. That is not the nature of Satsang with Me. Satsang with Me is not necessarily associated with any obvious drama—and, yet, these fundamental obstructions are continually dealt with.

I have lived this Satsang with people for a long time, and I have seen the drama that gets played with the symbol of the Guru. I have seen people approach Me as if they were either My parent or My child, for months or even years—always being conscientiously pleasant with Me, praising Me, seeming to be a devoted disciple. Yet, in time, I have seen these same people try to work "black magic" on Me, obsessed with threats, undermining the sadhana and harmony of other people by secretive means—until they finally separated from Me, and remained preoccupied with all kinds of negative judgements about Me from then on.

Such people never suspect that the drama they are living from day to day is their own. They always presume that the drama is "out there" in life somewhere—that it is something that comes on them, like bacteria. Everything they deal with on a relational, functional level is interpreted in that symbolic manner. They never suspect themselves.

But, as My devotee, you must become very suspicious of yourself. You must have played your game long enough that you know what you are up to. It is essential that you know this.

And I also Know what My devotee is up to. I find My devotee's drama, his or her seeking, completely transformable, from the "Point of View" of the True Divine Heart. I am not the least interested in preventing that drama. Rather, I am interested in My devotee observing and understanding what he or she is up to—and, thereby, transcending all forms of ego-drama.

When you begin to live Satsang with Me in those terms, then a transformative event has replaced the ordinary round of life. There is no longer any suffering, any seeking, to justify, to defend, to support, to make survive through time. For the moment, particularly in this discussion, I am drawing your attention to this fact: At the level of life, there is (essentially) the failure to function. That is the fact. But that is only the fact—not the Truth. My devotees have agreed to do sadhana in the functions of life. They are willing to see the self-contraction, but to function in any case.

The first two stages in Patanjali's[15] Yoga system are yama and niyama—things not to do and things that must be done. Thus, the first steps in Yoga are the fulfillment of functional prescriptions. The first thing that anyone must do is get straight. You may not feel like getting straight—after all, you are not yet Enlightened! But you are just plain going to get straight, in a very fundamental sense.

This is the demand of all Spiritual traditions and of all the Great Siddhas. It is agreed, it is acknowledged, it is accepted from the beginning, that you are upset, that you are suffering, that you are not functioning well at all—and that life is filled not only with pleasures, but also with burdens and fears and obstacles.

When the seeker arrives at the door, this is already understood. Nothing needs to be said about it. So the keeper of the door says, "Okay, now that we have heard that, I've got these twelve rules for you to follow." And the would-be disciple looks at the list with amazement. He is supposed to do all the things that he was not able to do in the first place and that he came here to learn how to do! But these things are not what he is supposed to do when he gets Enlightened—they are what he is supposed to do starting this afternoon. And all he gets at the beginning is a handshake and a broom! He gets up in front of the congregation, and they say, "This is Jack Umpty-ump, and he has just joined the community." Everybody looks—"Very good". They read a brief prayer over him—and, from that moment, he is supposed to be straight.

He may rise up from there into some magnificent demonstration of Spiritual life, perhaps. But his straightness has got to be right out there. It is the first demand. He is not given anything miraculous to make him capable of that. And to fulfill that demand, he perhaps has to go through all kinds of difficulty, all kinds of conflict, all kinds of crises—but, even so, he is expected to fulfill that demand. And he is expected not to burden his fellows with his suffering while trying to fulfill that demand. He can be passing through the most incredible turmoil, and yet he is supposed to be well-groomed, clean, smiling, able to do what is required, at ease—straight.

But the therapeutic point of view, the point of view of the search, is of a different kind. The guy comes to the "healing man".

He is completely incapable of functioning, in many obvious ways, and he is offered somebody who will listen to him express that failure day after day, week after week—without adding anything to that misery except more things to console and occupy him, and by which he can further express the same dilemma. He gets a "mantra" to express his craziness with—a "religion", an idol of "God", a belief. He gets a few brief psychiatric analyses by which to express that craziness. He gets medicine and magic to vanish symptoms. But these are all just added to his craziness. They give him a more elaborate expression for that craziness.

The remedy tends to perpetuate your suffering, because it indulges your search. Your search depends on your dilemma—and your dilemma is your suffering. Therefore, from the "Point of View" of Truth, a therapeutic confrontation is not useful. The only useful approach is one that gets to the <u>root</u> of your suffering.

The Guru does not respond to, support, or act upon the premise of the functional failure and suffering of the devotee. The Guru demands that the devotee function on that level at which some self-understanding already exists. The devotee is not given the absolute demand out of Infinity all at once, in one shot, but is expected to function on the level at which he or she is living confusion. That demand of functioning stimulates a disturbance, a crisis, a form of conscious conflict. That is the core of sadhana.

Of course it is difficult! It can stimulate great physical and mental disturbance at times, particularly in those who have not yet surrendered and found the Truth already Present as their Guru. That is why those who take up the Way of Adidam are generally those who have despaired of the alternatives. They have tried the forms of indulging their search, and found that this strategy does not affect the core of their suffering. But, when they become sensitive to the Living Presence of the True Divine Heart in My Avataric Divine Spiritual Company, they become capable of living Satsang with Me.

Only My true devotee has the strength of discriminative intelligence that will permit this crisis in consciousness to be endured. If you still "pay" a great deal of life to suffering and resistance, then you are burdened with alternatives. Then you continue to suffer.

Then you continue to be involved in tremendous conflicts that have nothing whatsoever to do with Spiritual life. Such conflicts are simply expressions of the failure to live Satsang with Me as your True Condition. Such conflicts are expressions of your suffering.

All suffering is "Narcissus", an obsessive distraction by your own mind-forms. That is all that suffering is. The modifications of the force of your own life are your suffering. Therefore, the quality of dilemma (which is suffering) is present even in the forms of life that, from a social point of view, are apparently delightful— even apparently successful, apparently making for survival.

Whatever you hold on to in conscious awareness—and defend in the face of all relationships, all conditions—is your suffering. The endless stream of modifications and formulations of your own conscious awareness is the face of "Narcissus" in the water. Modifications obstruct conscious awareness. They tend to replace relationship with contractions in the field of conscious awareness. Therefore, no matter what the qualities of experience may be in any particular moment, conscious awareness is, by its own modifications, providing you with a current of distraction.

It is this current of distraction (or psycho-physical modification) that prevents relationship. It is this that implies the center, the ego-"I", the separate one, the "dead" perceiver. People are really just dummied up with their own machine. They express their suffering through various forms, but it always has the same structure.

Narcissus is a good symbol for suffering. He has separated himself from all relationships—especially the primary relationships of mother, father, loved-one, and environment. He relates only to his own image, which he does not recognize as such. Obviously, Narcissus does not know that the face in the water is his own image.

The source of your suffering lies in your failure to observe and understand your own distraction—which is your own state, your own quality, your own modification. When you observe and understand the self-contraction, you cease to be enamored, fascinated, and distracted. Your drama is undone by simple (and yet "radical") self-understanding. If "Narcissus" understands his fundamental activity, his insane condition will come to an end.

Indeed, all that you are suffering is fascination with the compelling force of your own activity and experience. That activity and experience represent to you the separate-self-sense ("ego", or identification), the field of the conceptualized world ("others", or differentiation), and the endless adventure of seeking (mysterious motivation, or desire). The things flashing and moving before you, the apparent "objects" of conscious awareness, imply the separate perceiver over against the field of perception. And, when this implication becomes the point of view, the True and Prior Nature of the world ceases to be Obvious.

This structure goes on and on, magnified through all forms, all the types of experience, all the worlds of experience, all the conditions—gross, subtle, and causal—that arise. Every thing that arises is fitted within this structure. Therefore, it makes no difference where "Narcissus" moves, what experience occurs, what technique or search he applies to this dilemma. No matter what occurs, "Narcissus" fails to know it directly. Even the Divine Vision fails to be conclusive, because he knows It in terms of this structure of fascination and separation.

You are always being "Narcissus"—until there is the observation and understanding of this primary activity, this root-presumption. But, when this self-understanding occurs, it is as if you discover that you have been pinching yourself. The pain was always your own event, the theatre of your own activity. When you finally see this, it is a simple matter. You no longer need to go through any sort of complicated affair to get free of pain. All you have to do is take your hand away. Self-understanding is of that nature.

And I am the water itself, upon which this image of "Narcissus" is reflected. By causing a disturbance in the reflection, I Make Myself Known as the Prior Nature of My devotee. I Intensify My devotee's awareness of "Narcissus", so that self-understanding can take place. However, I do not do it simply by stimulating modifications of your experience, binding you to mind-forms, appearances, visions, distractions. All of that is only a secondary process at the level of life, not the very Communication of Truth. For one who does not understand, that is only more of the face in the water. But I Communicate the water itself to "Narcissus". I only Intensify the True Nature of "Narcissus".

Therefore, it is not by the elimination of conditions or by the obviation of your responsibilities that you are served. You are served by the requirement to fulfill your responsibilities in the ordinary manner. It is not by distracting you while you remain irresponsible and in trouble that you are served. You are served by the forceful demand for responsibility.

II.

DEVOTEE: What are our responsibilities as Your devotees?

AVATAR ADI DA SAMRAJ: My devotees are responsible for appropriate action in life and within the cooperative cultural gathering of Adidam. They must participate in the cooperative culture of My devotees, and assume responsibilities there. They must be employed, or else be responsible for children. They must be responsible for an orderly household. They must entirely avoid "soft" drugs (such as cannabis), "recreational" drugs, "hard" drugs, and even any otherwise medically inappropriate drugs. They must avoid such common intoxicants as alcohol and tobacco. And they must also, as a general rule, avoid such unhealthful substances as coffee, "junk" food, and so on.[16] They should eat moderately, and essentially use only foods that are supportive of bodily life and vitality. The right and optimum diet should be limited to what is necessary and sufficient for bodily (and general psycho-physical) purification, balance, well-being, and appropriate service. The key to diet is to discover what is supportive and to use it wisely and exclusively. Food does not cause Spirituality. Rather, as part of appropriate sadhana, My devotee must conform the taking of food (whatever it may be) to the requirements of the Spiritual process.

The problems of excess, laziness, instability, chronic weakness, and irresponsibility are the patterns of "Narcissus". The patterns of avoidance are the very material (or fuel) of sadhana. My devotee surrenders all of that patterning by constantly turning the faculties of body, emotion, mind, and breath to Me.[17] But, even while the dilemma of life is being confronted in Satsang with Me, everyone is expected to function appropriately. My devotees must understand that Satsang Itself requires the capability to function in relationship to Me, to others in the gathering of My devotees, and to the world. A responsible, relational, intelligent manner of living is the condition for Satsang with Me.

Human beings have made a great effort to liberate themselves from the Earth. The natural cycle of the Earth is a difficult condition in which to survive—and, when sheer survival is the principal preoccupation of human activity, then the subtler aspects of the human being tend not to develop as fully as possible. Therefore, people have established great centers of culture, in order to enjoy common freedom from bondage to the effort of survival-against-odds, and to develop the subtler (or hidden) aspects of human destiny. But the great cities have only existed for a relatively short time. The human experiment has barely begun.

The establishment of the great cities was an effort to escape from the ancient bondage to the cycle of the Earth. Human beings wanted to break out of the limitations of the natural cycle, so that they would be free to realize a more advanced order of common life. And they did, indeed, find many means, in their collective activity, to break out of the limitations of the natural cycle of earth and water.

Countries like India anciently belonged to the Earth. In India, until recently at least, if you wanted to seek for God—which is inappropriate to begin with—you could freely abandon your life-responsibilities, your work, your relationships to family, your attempts to support yourself, and you could become a wanderer. Such is the tradition in the earth-and-water cultures of India and certain other areas of the world. There were massive areas of land in India that were unowned or untenanted, where people could choose to step out of a responsible relationship to the Earth and their own Earth-life. They could simply find a cave and sit in it.

But, when people have begun to live with one another, when they have broken the cycle of attachment to earth and water, they must accept responsibility for their own survival. Therefore, it is inappropriate, under the conditions in which "fire" (or the cultural and technological means of material and human transformation) is developed, for people to be without work or responsibility for their own life-activity. Either they must work for their own support—and, in most cases, that is necessary, because most people do not have the means to live without working—or they must do so simply because it is appropriate to work.

Work is a peculiarly human activity. It is the means for transcending the limitations of gross (or elemental) conditions. Thus, it is not appropriate for My devotees to remain irresponsible for their own survival, or irresponsible for participatory, supportive action in the human manner.

Another thing peculiar to the "modern" Western (and "Westernized") world is attachment to drugs. Despite the claims of many people to the contrary, drug-taking has no purpose whatsoever in Real Spiritual life. Drugs are an aggravation. They toxify the body, and stimulate one illusion on top of the next. A person who is involved with drugs and the illusory, so-called "Spiritual" culture of drug-taking is "back and forth" every day. Such a person is not ready for Satsang with Me. Drugs are a deluding alternative. And, as My devotee, you must be clear about the limitations of that form of bondage.

The other forms of intoxicants that people commonly use— tobacco, alcohol, and such—must be abandoned as well. These substances may not have the immediate kinds of negative effects that drugs have, but such common intoxicants are forms of self-indulgence and distraction that reinforce dullness, desensitize you to everything that is beyond the gross dimension, and toxify the body.

People very often ask about diet. For some reason or other, food has become like drugs. People are using food to become "Realized" or "Spiritual". Neither drugs nor a special diet will make you Realize the Truth. People tend to use diet as a form of search. There is no search that is appropriate. You will not become Divinely Self-Realized, or understand most perfectly, because you eat only fruit, because you fast one out of every two days, or because you are a vegetarian gourmet. However, there is an appropriate form of eating and fasting. The appropriate diet is one that sustains and supports the body and the vital force.

How much one eats is just as important as what one eats. People eat too much. Overeating disturbs the bodily functions and makes food unusable. Unused food, as well as unnatural and inappropriate food, toxifies the body and causes disease. Many of the things people think are their Spiritual problems are just the results of toxicity. Therefore, you must simplify and moderate your diet. Make it natural and pure. Eat only what is usable by the body, and avoid whatever constipates, toxifies, and enervates the body.

As long as you are indulging yourself and remaining irresponsible, you are preventing yourself from entering into Satsang with Me and Real Spiritual life in My Avataric Divine Company. Even if you do not yet understand yourself most fundamentally, even if you still live in dilemma, you must (nevertheless) be responsible for an appropriate life. To engage life under appropriate conditions makes you aware of your limitations, your struggle, your search, your dilemma, your resistance.

The form of life is sacrifice. There is not anything that needs to be added to life—no attitude, no special sort of yielding—to make life into sacrifice. Life is already sacrifice, and all appropriate action is in the form of sacrifice. The symbols of religion tend to indicate that you should add something—some sort of payment—to life, in order to make it sacrifice. But sacrifice is the form of <u>every</u> function. It is the universal law. It is even the rule of pleasure.

The self-indulgent and irresponsible person is not aware that all action, all conditional manifestation, is (itself) sacrifice. Speech is sacrifice. Sexual activity—even emotional-sexual relationship itself—is sacrifice. All action tends to break the Circle and dissipate (or "throw off") Energy. If you break the Circle often enough, if you do so unconsciously and absolutely, then you are only hastening your death. Act intelligently, and your action grants life, it generates life through relationship—for relationship is a duplication in life of the Circle of Energy in the body-mind. To sacrifice oneself (or open oneself) into relationship is to (more and more—and, ultimately, most perfectly) Realize the Great Form of Existence, the

True and Perfect Circle, the Completion that transcends limited (or separative) individuality.

Therefore, True and Conscious sacrifice is a form of Completion—not of interruption or separation. Thus, if you understand, then death is only transformation—because you are consciously intimate with the Real process of life. But, if you do not understand, then you are already broken—and, in death, you are the unintended sacrificial meal for an unknown purpose. Nevertheless, life does not become intelligent by strategically doing something to it, by merely preventing all kinds of things, by never talking, never entering into relationship, never laughing, never doing anything. Life is action. There must be action, or conscious sacrifice.

In Satsang with Me, action becomes natural. The natural order of life is restored by the Force of Truth. If you merely indulge your possibilities, you repeatedly obstruct the flow of descending Force. In that case, you never allow the Circuit to be full and complete—and, therefore, you are merely exhausting yourself.

In Satsang with Me, there is a natural tendency to return to the normal, the ordinary, the pleasurable, the intelligent. However, if you merely indulge yourself, then (even though your body is present in the gathering of My devotees) you are continually preventing the establishment of such right equanimity. Therefore, there are conditions for Satsang with Me—but they are not exaggerated conditions. I call for a natural ordinariness—an ordinary, pleasurable life. If you bring a relatively normal, pleasurable existence into Satsang with Me, it will tend (in a very natural manner) to become more harmonious, more intelligent, more alive, more enjoyable, less bound to gross existence. The Presence That is Alive in Satsang with Me is the Presence of Reality Itself. The more Alive It becomes in you, then the more intelligent, the more coincident with Reality, you become.

There is no Satsang with Me without sadhana. Satsang with Me is not just sitting around and enjoying Spiritual Force. Satsang with Me is a functional, relational life. One of Its forms is formal meditation, with all the experiential phenomena that may arise in that context—and with the fundamental devotional practice, as well as the various technical practices, that I Give to My devotees. But Satsang with Me has many forms throughout the day.

For most people, it is not the extraordinary—the thing that requires the great, the dramatic, the heroic—that is most difficult. It may seem very appealing to go and sit in a cave, or wander as a seeker-tourist in India. Abandoning everything and going to India is an idea that commonly fascinates people who have heard a little about Spiritual things. People can imagine doing that. It is very dramatic. But to be an ordinary human being, to function alive in the human world, is a notion that people resist. The usual images of Spiritual life, of Spiritual attainment, implicitly contain the refusal of ordinariness. The common motivation toward what is presumed to be Spiritual is a form of resistance, a form of self-contraction. Some people devote themselves to this illusion of the fantastic, which they call "Truth". Whatever it may involve, including every kind of vision and miracle of the occult, it is simply resistance to ordinariness, to the sadhana of sacrificial existence.

Becoming ordinary, functioning in the stream of conditionally manifested life, is what people resist. Indeed, suffering is a disorder in functional human life. It is not that Truth is absent. Truth is Always Already the Case. Truth is simply not obvious to people. Truth is not absent. People are suffering. There is this contraction, this disorder, this refusal of functional life, of ordinariness. This suffering obscures awareness of the Truth.

The search for the extraordinary is nonsense. It is adventure without intelligence or Real beauty. People indulge in extraordinary seeking in order to compensate for self-caused (but unconscious) suffering. The adventure itself never deals with its own motivation.

Thus, the plane of sadhana, of True Spiritual action, of action appropriate to Satsang with Me, is the ordinary. Not the extraordinary, not the search, not the seeker's methods—but simple, ordinary, functional life. Such is the most difficult form of sadhana to fulfill. But it becomes possible (and even simple) for My devotee, living the life of "radical" self-understanding in Satsang with Me. Such ordinariness is essential for a natural, pleasurable life.

Sadhana is not the extraordinary. Sadhana is not sitting in a cave while you remain preoccupied with the egoic self. Sadhana is simplicity. Sadhana is, at its foundation, relational life. Sadhana is your conscious humanity. You must live sadhana. You must become a truly human being. You do not have any choice. Either you become a truly human being, and function truly as a human being, or your humanity becomes obsolete through non-use.

Much of the traditional Spiritual search is an attempt to make ordinary life obsolete by inattention and non-use. The popular Indian version of the search, for instance, is detachment and abandonment of all the so-called "lower" desires, the so-called "lower" forms of experience. The concern is only to ascend beyond life. By inattention to life, life becomes obsolete.

Life certainly can be snuffed out by design. But the result is not Enlightenment. If non-life were Enlightenment, all you would have to do is kill yourself. Therefore, to make things obsolete by inattention is not the Way of Truth. The Way of Truth requires that you thoroughly observe and understand what you do under the conditions of the ordinary. In that self-understanding, Truth stands out.

Truth is Always Already Present in life.

Truth is not "someplace else".

Truth is not Itself identical to any experience or any place.

There is no inner world, no chakra, no sound, no light, no form, no loka, no experience, no attainment, that—in and of itself—is Truth. There certainly are such experiences, such manifestations—but they are not (in and of themselves) Truth.

Truth is Always Already the Case.

Truth is the Real Condition of every present moment, whatever arises.

It is not necessary to do even one thing in order to cause Truth to manifest in the present moment.

There is only Truth Itself, or Reality Itself.

And Truth Itself (or Reality Itself) Is the only Real God.

It could not be more obvious. There is no dilemma. Only observe your own activity, your root-strategy, moment to moment. Understand it, and see That Which is always being prevented by your own activity. That Which is always being prevented is Perfect. When there is this self-observation and self-understanding, all things, conditions, and states become obvious. Dreams become obvious, sleep becomes obvious, death becomes obvious, birth and life become obvious. All conditional manifestation becomes obvious—as Truth, as the Very Presence and State That Is the One Reality (called "God", "Brahman", "Nirvana", and so on).

But Truth can become Obvious only to one who lives the ordinary—whose thirst for the extraordinary has begun to die, has begun to show itself as seeking only, as a reaction to fundamental disturbance (or dilemma).

Therefore, you must become ordinary in order to live Satsang with Me. By "ordinary" I do not mean that you become empty and nondescript. I mean that you begin to function humanly. And, when you function as a truly human being, you can be an outstanding, intensely creative person. But your activity will not be itself a way to Truth. It will simply be an expression of life already in Truth, Which is Satsang with Me. Your activity will simply be appropriate. Your life will be regulated by your human functions.

Just so, Satsang, the conscious relationship between Me and My devotee, requires a foundation of ordinariness. Satsang with Me is a human circumstance. Indeed, It is the primary human circumstance. It is, first of all, a relationship. It Functions in the realm of the ordinary. It has many subtle aspects, which may also become conscious over time—but It is ordinary from the beginning. It is (necessarily) functional. It is a relationship. It is obvious.

Satsang with Me is the enjoyment of relationship to Me—being in relationship to Me, becoming intelligent under those conditions, perceiving the relationship to Me in ever subtler terms, and (ultimately) in perfect terms—such that (most ultimately) the Divine Conscious Light is Most Perfectly Realized.

Everything that you regard as "extraordinary" is an alternative to Satsang with Me. And everything that you regard as "ordinary" is an opportunity for Satsang with Me. The very thing that you resist—whatever seems oppressive in ordinariness, in the functional condition of being alive—that very sensation is the awareness of present dilemma, the motivation to seek, the guarantor of suffering and dilemma. That condition, in its various forms, must be endured and lived until it is understood. Therefore, only ordinariness, the functional endurance of your actual condition moment to moment, is the appropriate disposition. Thus, Satsang with Me also provokes you, because It arouses your resistance to your ordinary (or actual) condition.

Much of the disturbed condition that people bring to Me is not a matter of anything subtle or Spiritual. For the most part, it is simply a functional disharmony. In many cases, the simple moderation and purification of diet is the most dramatic form of sadhana. The simple moderation and intelligent selection of diet purifies the body. The judicious use of occasional fasting also aids this normalization of psycho-physical life. The sadhana of functional ordinariness purifies the body, and returns it to a natural condition of vitality. Extreme forms of desire, of attachment to non-functional patterns of money, food, and sex, extreme forms of emotion—all the things that people think they should bring to an end through so-called "Spiritual" methods—become quiet, in a very natural manner, in the regimen of ordinariness to which My devotees apply themselves.

The use (or transformation) of food is the fundamental process at the level of organic life. Therefore, the simple intelligence of diet is very useful, very appropriate. The thing that is your suffering—the self-contraction—is not necessarily a matter of exaggerated desires and needs, and every kind of craziness. You need not be half-psychotic before Real Spiritual life becomes useful to you! The Way of Adidam, which <u>anyone</u> can "consider" and practice, is a straightforward matter of responsive devotion to Me and natural intelligence in the application of the disciplines I Give to My devotees. In the actual demonstration of that total practice, you will simply see that, by the intelligent use and moderation of diet, the level of organic life, and even the entirety of psycho-physical life, tends to become functional, usable, harmonious, free of disturbance (or dis-ease). But appropriate diet is not, in and of itself, a means to Truth. It is simply appropriate.

It is not appropriate to cut off a finger each day. To stop cutting your fingers off, however, will not make you Realize the Truth. It is simply appropriate to put fingers to proper use. Just so, there is appropriate use of food and life. Obstructing the natural process by excess and wrong use is like cutting off a finger every day.

It causes suffering, disability. On the other hand, if you correct your diet by moderating it, you do not Realize the Truth merely for doing that. It is simply appropriate to do that.

Seekers exalt diet as if it were the way to Truth. They talk about lunch as if it were the Absolute, or the very method of Truth. The various food cultists talk about their dietary practice as if it were the means for absolute Realization: raw only, yin-yang, grain is basic, only fruit, high protein, seven food groups, non-mucus, total fast! All such idealistic and exclusive views are the refusal of ordinariness.

Diet is a simple matter of "lunch". It is a practical matter of experimental self-observation. Extreme assumptions about diet, overuse of food, extreme attachment to food-thinking and arbitrary dietary demands, use of foods that toxify the body—all such things are extensions of the search, the refusal of ordinariness. There is an appropriate diet. There are appropriate times to fast. But, if diet is right, it is (characteristically) simple, moderate, and satisfying.

The appropriate use of food tends to evidence natural control of mind, breath, and sex. You will discover that the force of sex-desire is secondary to food. If your diet is conscious, the sex-force tends to be harmonized. What you are always contending with as sex-desire—at times trying to suppress it, then to control it, but always finally giving up—that entire drama of sex cannot be separated from "lunch". There is no inevitable problem about sex. But your emotional-sexual life is disturbed by all the jazzy, self-indulgent, unintelligent use of food, drink, and stimulants.

You will find that, on a natural diet, an intelligently moderated diet, the sex-force gradually ceases to be compulsive—or, at least, it becomes available to be disciplined and moderated through your self-understanding and through the Force of Satsang with Me. It will become a natural, usable force, a relational capability. Sex, after all, is a functional form of relationship. But people try to deal with it as an intense, internal, and isolated personal demand. They do not bring it into relationship. They do not confine it to the conditions of relationship. So sex becomes obsessive—as happens with any desire that is not made to function in full relationship.

The extraordinary disharmony and problematic demand associated with sexual desire is, essentially, a matter of improper diet and the inappropriate use of the sources and functions of bodily energy. Thus, when you (as My devotee) understand yourself, the search for "orgasm" (or convulsive release, leading to stasis)—through the sex-function and every other function of life—is replaced by natural and continuous "conductivity" of the life-force.

The conventional (or degenerative) orgasm[18] is an instrument of procreation, an instinctual (or subconscious and unconscious) demand that guarantees the physical survival of the human species. It is not, as some seem to think, a necessary instrument of physical and mental health. It is not the necessary (or even desirable) accompaniment to emotional-sexual intimacy. It is not appropriate for degenerative orgasm to be repetitively or frequently attained within emotional-sexual intimacy. Emotional-sexual intimacy itself is the relationship. Therefore, intimacy—not degenerative orgasm—is the fulfillment of the sex-function. Degenerative orgasm is only one of the functional capabilities potential in emotional-sexual intimacy—a capability that inherently involves a sacrifice of psycho-physical well-being and equanimity.

Emotional-sexual intimacy is inherently a form of continuous relationship. It need not include degenerative orgasm—or even the sex act itself. The fundamental requirement is that the internal "conductivity" of the life-force be unobstructed in each partner. Indeed, when the search for degenerative orgasm becomes the principle of emotional-sexual relationship, the intimacy becomes disturbed, harmony becomes impossible, and the separative qualities of mind and action develop. But, for My devotees who choose to be sexually active[19] (necessarily, in the context of a committed emotional-sexual intimacy), degenerative orgasm is controlled—such that it becomes an occasional (and, optimally, even obsolete) phenomenon. It is controlled (and even replaced) by the regenerative practice of "right emotional-sexual Yoga". In My devotees who responsibly practice that "right emotional-sexual Yoga", there is spontaneous, constant "conductivity" of the natural life-force (and, in due course, of My Avatarically Self-Transmitted Divine Spirit-Energy)—down the frontal line, and up the spinal line. Such is the "conductivity" of Energy that is natural to human beings.

One of the symbols of emotional-sexual intimacy is the ring. The ring symbolizes the unbroken Circle of life-force that is continuous within each individual, and that is also duplicated in right emotional-sexual relationship (which is intimacy itself). The principle of intimacy transcends the separative activity that individuals otherwise enact in their egoic ignorance. Therefore, the principle of intimacy also transcends the principle of degenerative orgasm, to which seekers attach themselves in their dilemma of vital obstructedness. Thus, the by-Me-Given practice of "right emotional-sexual Yoga" (in the context of "true Yogic intimacy"), rather than degenerative orgasm, is the truly human form (and—potentially, in due course—the Spiritually Awakened Yoga) of emotional-sexual relationship.[20] The exploitation of sexuality outside of the condition of emotional-sexual intimacy is always separative, founded in dilemma, motivated by the search, manifested as "Narcissistic" attachment to degenerative orgasm and to all the socially accepted forms of irresponsible release.

In "true Yogic intimacy", the natural life-force (and, in due course, My Avatarically Self-Transmitted Divine Spirit-Energy) is conducted by each partner in the Circle—rather than being "thrown out", in arbitrary, frequent, and obsessive degenerative orgasm. Thus, My devotee must discipline the sex-function in the ego-transcending manner, always practicing the Yoga of emotional-sexual intimacy in the context of Satsang with Me. And such Yoga is realized without either the search for degenerative orgasm (which search manifests as excessive sexual activity, obsessive sexual aberrations, and obsessive and chronic masturbation) or the search to avoid sex (and its attendant "problems") altogether (which search manifests as the brittle solitude of devitalized self-consciousness). For those of My devotees who choose to be sexually active, loving intimacy is the truly human Yoga of the sex-function, and is simply to be lived (in accordance with My Instructions) as an expression of Satsang with Me.

Essentially, human beings are lazy and passionate. They are too lazy to do many things that are necessary, and they are very enthusiastic about a number of other things that are unnecessary and destructive. Ordinary life is spent, from hour to hour, in being "turned off" and "turned on". That is all the usual life is doing. The opposite must begin to be the case. When you are lazy, you must begin to work—not because it "does something", but simply because it is appropriate to work. You must begin to function. Where you are simply crazy, passionate, all over the place with your desires, you must become practical, intelligent.

The moderation of diet is a key factor in that entire process. To a large degree, what you are responding to with the strategy of laziness and passion is your own enervation and toxicity. Intelligence about diet is a critically important responsibility relative to vital life. And this includes <u>all</u> the substances taken into the body.

"Recreational" (and even "soft") drugs are part of the insanity of the ego. They are mediocre—like all addictions, all seeker's methods. They only intensify or reinforce your fundamental stupidity and insanity. At the very least, they toxify the bloodstream and contract the nervous system, producing estrangement from the environment and from the subtle sources of life-energy. Smoking even a small amount of marijuana contracts the nervous system for a long time. None of that has anything to do with Real Spiritual life. It is just drugs! It is only self-indulgence and the search. It is a form of suffering.

Arbitrary attachment to an idealistic system of dietary "orthodoxy" is another form of addiction. Diet does not lead to the Truth. Diet is not (itself) Truth. There is no universal Spiritual dogma about diet, because diet is not the way to Truth. There is simply an <u>appropriate</u> diet—and you must discover what that is in your own case, if you are to remain vitally strong.

There are appropriate patterns of life that allow life to be alive, to be intense, to be sensitive, to be intelligent, to be creative. Life is not contained in some dogma about how to live, how to correct yourself. Life is simply the realization of the ordinariness I am describing. Appropriate patterns of vitality are a primary necessity in Satsang with Me. They foster the necessary simplicity and sensitivity (physical, emotional, and mental) that allow the process to begin.

My devotee is responsible for the appropriate maintenance of these patterns of vitality, at the level of his or her physical and relational conditions. Diet is very fundamental—and, then, on its basis comes the practical observation of your laziness and your passion. You must energize and activate your life where it is dead—and you must harmonize it where it is chaotic and out of balance. This is why I require you to work and to have regular responsibilities in life, and also to function responsibly in the life of the cooperative cultural gathering of My devotees.

A human being's perfect food is Truth. This is literally so. Truth is not just a concept. Truth is the Living Force of Reality. It is Spirit-Presence. It is Life, and life-usable. There are accounts of people who did not take ordinary food at all. They lived on the universal prana (or life-force), which is the fundamental substance communicated in food and air. But such extreme abstinence is not an appropriate goal. The only necessity is to restore your natural and human relationship to things. To do so is to begin to fulfill the demands of Satsang with Me.

Satsang can be understood as a process of feeding, conversion, and elimination. There is no process in the conditionally manifested universe that is without these three functions. Psychic waste, the subtle by-product of conscious life, is a form of pollution. When My devotees are not consciously living Satsang with Me, they will suffer one another. People in general are suffering mutual enervation and toxification. They do not have the conscious means to conduct and transform the communicated energy of life. Thus, they become disabled, poisoned, without love or freedom. They have lost sight of the Source. As a result, food and life have become perplexing to them. People are obsessed with their own toxicity, their own dis-ease.

Entering into Satsang with Me is restoration of Food, Life, and the Conscious Power of Freedom and Refreshment. The self-sustaining powers of conversion, of "digestion" at every level of the body-mind, go on spontaneously in those who live the conditions of Truth. Then this psychic waste is returned to the natural course, where it can be converted. In that case, you are no longer toxifying the human world at the psychic level. For this reason, it has rightly been said that, of all the things a person can do, Satsang with one's Guru is the best.

It is important to remain vitally strong. People think Spiritual life has something to do with becoming vitally weak. Some people get addicted to fasting because of the airy and artificially exalted weakness that comes upon them when they fast. Excessive, unintelligent use of fasting, combined with inappropriate diet, weakens the vital. When fasting and diet are governed by the ignorance of seekers, then the vital loses its ability to inform conscious awareness. People presume that this feeling of weakness is a very Spiritual tendency, but it is just vital weakness.

A truly Spiritual individual is very strong. Traditionally (in Japan, for example), the vital center is valued and protected. Wherever you want to pinpoint its center—at the navel or just below it—the vital area is that entire region of the body extending from the solar plexus (or even the heart and lungs) down to the anus. This region of the body should be strong, not weak. There should be sufficient life-force there. You should conduct this life-force.

Sneezing, coughing, vomiting, and generally exploiting vital tendencies are all the same activity—even laughter and speech are forms of this same psycho-physical ritual—whereby the life-force is thrown upward and outward through the front of the body. All these activities are forms of the reversal of life-force, the rejection of life-energy. Instead, the force of life should always be conducted fully, spontaneously, down the front of the body and up the back. Therefore, all such life-force-reversing activities should be appropriately conserved.

If your tendency is to be weak in life, in relationships, to be sort of fawning, fey, ambiguous, elusive, empty, not forceful, or even exaggeratedly forceful, then you will also tend to take on vital problems of various kinds. If you get sick, that is a clear indication that something is wrong in the vital circuit.

There are a number of things that you must be responsible for—diet, exercise and the taking of good, strong breaths, function (or work), the spontaneous attitude of strength, and (altogether) the intensity of self-observation and self-understanding in Satsang with Me.

"Conductivity" is necessary to life—the "conductivity" of life-force. Ordinarily, people are only involved in rejecting—always attempting to empty themselves by various positive and negative strategies. But there is this natural "conductivity"—downward, through the frontal functions of the psycho-physical life, and then up the spine. This full Circle is the law of conditionally manifested life. That should be spontaneous, simple. That is health. It is also sanity. It is the human cycle, the psycho-physical circuit.

Force, strength, intensity, has to be brought to the functions of life. You had better stop indulging your games and strategies of seeking. Otherwise, you will constantly go through cycles of disease, disturbance, sickness, annoyance, negativity. All of that is a direct result of your activity, your relationship to things. Everything you suffer is a direct result of your own activity, your own involvement with the force and the pattern of conditionally manifested existence.

I am not suggesting that you should become self-conscious about your physical state and feel guilty if you happen to suffer a little sickness of some sort. It is simply that you should know (in general) just what the life-process is, and begin to observe the results of your own activity. See the results of your activity. See your activity previous to results. See your motivation previous to action. See the roots of motivation (or motion) in yourself. This is fundamental intelligence at the level of life. Usually, people do not become sensitive to their own activity until they see its results. They only see life fall apart or become difficult, to the point of death.

For My rightly practicing devotee, episodes of sickness are (in general) purifying events. Such episodes may occur when the Shakti is activated in certain forms. Latent illnesses sometimes appear by such means. But My devotee is continuously responsible for the appropriate and ordinary order of psycho-physical life.

DEVOTEE: What about exercise?

AVATAR ADI DA SAMRAJ: Just as you must discover (within the framework of the dietary discipline Given by Me) the appropriate diet in your own case, so you must also discover the kind and level of activity necessary to keep the body supple and strong. All such practices are a matter of intelligence at the level of your specific constitution. You must discover what foods are necessary to keep your chemistry in an optimum condition. You must discover what types of activity and uses of life you can engage without breakdowns of various kinds. In every person's case, there must be an individual and intelligent self-observation and learning.

There really is no single basic human being. Everyone is manifesting different karmas (or tendencies and patterns). Some people need and tolerate much more exercise than others. But, in general, everyone—simply by virtue of having a vital, physical body—needs a certain amount of regular, conscious physical activity. I provide My devotees with detailed Instruction in matters of diet, exercise, and every functional aspect of vital and Spiritual life. My devotees must become masters of the ordinary.

DEVOTEE: What about sleep? Does it also depend on the individual? How much do we require?

AVATAR ADI DA SAMRAJ: You should always feel refreshed, rested, and full of energy when you get up. If you can get that in half an hour, then sleep for half an hour every day. If you get it in five or six hours, then sleep that long. If you need seven or eight hours, then arrange for that. Every one is different. But what you must observe is how you feel upon waking. There is such a thing as over-indulgence in sleep. Too much sleep actually weakens you, devitalizes you. If you sleep long into the period of dreaming—particularly very superficial dreaming, that morning twilight dreaming when you are almost awake—then you are sleeping too much. You will feel tired, and probably moody, on that day. All kinds of subliminal mind-forms establish themselves by such oversleeping, and these psychic tendencies contract the vital throughout the day. You should find that point in your sleep when you can awaken and feel refreshed, without the subliminal twilight of dreams.

Diet is very important in terms of the vital. Exercise is important. Sleep is important. The breath is very important. Speech and thought are also important.

If you feel anything like a cold or any sort of vital difficulty, it is very good to walk, and breathe deeply and intentionally as you walk. Walk as an exercise. Don't just flop down the street. Walk very deliberately, forcefully, with spine straight and muscles loose, and breathe deeply, rhythmically. While walking, inhale profoundly, with the entire body, and exhale completely. This helps remove impurities, opens up the breath-system, and feeds you through the transformation of life-energy in the chemistry of air.

The goal of achieving absolute health does not have a great deal of reasonableness about it. Entire systems of so-called "Spiritual" effort have been based on the ideal of becoming absolutely healthy—even immortal. But the event of life is much more complex than that. Nevertheless, you should certainly be responsible for the basic life-functions—and this self-responsibility will manifest as optimum health, free of attachment to psychophysical conditions (whether positive or negative).

People generally seem to be subject to a mysterious cycle of attacks in the vital. I have called these attacks (and their manifestation) "vital shock".[21] They are periodic attacks, cycles of compulsive self-contraction. You do not necessarily feel a physical cramp—but, very often, there is some sort of bodily sensation. There is no single cause for these attacks—they are evidence of various conditions, various associated phenomena (apparently external and apparently internal). In general, the characteristic crises that occur in Real Spiritual practice coincide with such periods of vital shock.

Therefore, you must begin to become as intelligent as you can about the basic vital process. You must not allow the vital to become weak. Keep the essential vital functions strong. Learn the secret of moderation—which is the artful alternation (or rhythm) of appropriate use and intelligent abstinence.

The category of food, which is very basic to this entire affair, covers all the things on which the vital thrives. These include not only the basic substances in the diet but also the breath (or "conductivity" of the life-force, or prana, itself). Sexuality is also a fundamental function of life—as is the communication of life-force (as money, effort, and right human relatedness). All forms of self-indulgent exploitation—as well as all forms of willful, suppressive non-use—tend to weaken the vital, break the "conductivity" of the life-force, and impede the capability to function in life.

All social activity, all relational life, is communication of vitality, of life-force, of life-energy. In various of the world's scriptures, people are told to <u>love</u> one another. What is being recommended through such language is right use of the internal mechanisms of the life-force. These mechanisms harmonize the vital at the level of human relatedness. If you have not become intelligent at the level of life, if you have not seen the results of your activity and the nature of your activity, then you never make yourself available to receive My Avataric Divine Spiritual Transmission. In that case, you will be continually distracted, continually returned—by the compulsive patterning of attention—to the adventures of dilemma and seeking.

Everyone enjoys little glimpses of the Gracefulness of the Divine Reality. At times, people may feel a "Presence" influencing them in some manner. But, until they begin to go through the crisis in consciousness at the level of life, nothing constant, nothing truly profound and alive, occurs in their case.

That is why, as a condition of Satsang with Me, I Require people to deal with some very practical things. I Require you to work, to intelligently manage your personal environments, your diet, and your emotional-sexual life. Work—including everything about your responsibilities in relation to your environments—is an indispensable means of repeatedly bringing you into responsible, responsive, and effective contact with the conditions of human existence and human energy. Self-indulgent, irresponsible living is not an appropriate or effective foundation for Satsang in My Avataric Divine Company. As long as the self-indulgent, irresponsible pattern continues to be compulsively lived, there is only the endless cycle of vital shock. And these periods of shock continually interrupt the process of Satsang with Me. Therefore, what I Require from you is practical intelligence and responsibility at the level of the vital.

III.

DEVOTEE: What are the advantages of emotional-sexual relationship for Real Spiritual life?

AVATAR ADI DA SAMRAJ: First of all, emotional-sexual relationship is a form of relationship. Therefore, when rightly lived, emotional-sexual relationship can, in principle, be compatible with Satsang with Me. Emotional-sexual relationship is no more or less "Spiritual" than any other form of ordinary human relationship. For most people, emotional-sexual relationship is simply presumed to be a fundamental part of life. To engage emotional-sexual relationship does not advance you toward the Truth—nor does the mere fact of choosing not to engage emotional-sexual relationship advance you toward the Truth. Fundamentally, the Real Spiritual process has nothing to do with your emotional-sexual life.

Nevertheless, there are human uses of sex, and there are sub-human uses of sex. Only the human use of sex is acceptable in My devotee. And the human, conscious, responsible, loving engagement of sex is, in general, an extension of the process of "conductivity" and regeneration, rather than of the separative orgasmic obsession of merely degenerative sexuality. When the life-functions are optimally lived (and rightly disciplined), then sexuality becomes a sacrificial and intelligent activity—transformed not by an act of will but by the practice of the truly human Yoga of emotional-sexual intimacy (based in the Circle of regenerative "conductivity", which is the natural state of human beings).

If you truly live the Way of Adidam, all of the ordinary human functions tend to return to their conscious, responsible forms.[22] And such life-level responsibility is the necessary foundation for the Real Spiritual process in My Avataric Divine Company.

I have been speaking about how life-dilemma is perceived by human beings in three essential areas of function. These are money (or, in general, the commitment of life-force, in the forms of effort and right human relatedness), food, and sex. These are the most fundamental human functions. Therefore, they also offer the most obvious opportunities to discover that you are suffering.

Most people are chronically obsessed with the functions of money, food, and sex. Most people are dramatizing their fundamental dilemma by seeking in relation to the functions of money, food, and sex. Some pretend to be very "Spiritual" (so called)—but they, like most others, are simply reacting to money, food, and sex (which they relate to not as simple functions but as problems). Most people are either exploiting these functional possibilities or resisting them, trying to overcome them. But the only reason to exploit any function or to try to overcome it is the fact that you are already in dilemma, that you conceive of the function as a problem rather than simply a function.

When you understand your search, your dilemma, then all of your functions return to their natural state. Then right living of the functions of money, food, and sex becomes possible in a very natural manner.

Every individual has a unique pattern of involvement in these basic functions—variously emphasizing one or another of the functions to different degrees. Since relationship is fundamental, and emotional-sexual relationship is one of the most common forms of relationship—and, indeed, is (perhaps) the most obvious form of relationship, at the level of life—emotional-sexual relationship is a very obvious place for sadhana, for self-understanding, for devotional resort to Me.

Until you understand your own activity of self-contraction, neither money nor food nor sex is lived as a form of relationship. Instead of living these functions as forms of relationship, you live them as forms of identification, differentiation, and desire. If a person is having sex, that separate one is having sex. It is your own pleasure, your own satisfaction. If a person is having food, that separate one is acquiring it. If you have money, energy, or power, they are your own. Money, food, and sex are conceived as your possessions—rather than as functional, relational possibilities. In that case, you are a seeker—and your involvement in money, food, and sex (whatever form that involvement may take) just reinforces your dilemma, your sense of separateness.

But, when your life takes on the form of Satsang with Me and the intelligence of relationship, then these life-functions become forms of relationship—and, as forms of relationship, there is no praise, no blame, in the appropriate use and functional enjoyment of them. They are simply the enjoyable and creative capabilities of earthly life.

From the traditional religious or Spiritual point of view, sex (for example) is always very ambiguous, very threatening. People are always having periodic bouts, wondering whether they should just give up sex forever. They try to become celibate for a period of time, then they try willfully to draw the sex-force up their spines, then they try to sublimate it into painting, office work, poetry, prayer—without otherwise understanding the root-motive that is ruling their lives.

Until you understand yourself, there is no true motivation to abandon sexuality—and, in Truth, there is also no true motivation to engage sexuality. However, when you clearly observe and understand yourself, all of your functions are suddenly, spontaneously alive. Your intelligence is also spontaneously alive. Then every instance of relationship is a living, spontaneous enjoyment—in which there is no loss, no separation. For the seeker, however, relationship means only loss and separation.

It is because of the primal fear of loss and separation that traditional Yogis typically choose to have nothing to do with emotional-sexual relationship. They practice retention of the sex-force in an effort to accumulate sufficient energy-intensity to engage their Yogic adventure, their form of the search. But, when you truly observe and understand your own ego-activity, the sex-force becomes a natural process in relationship—without loss, and without gain.

Therefore, in answer to your question, emotional-sexual relationship carries no advantage whatsoever for Real Spiritual life.

In certain forms of Yoga, there is attention to an internal mechanism, a subtle process of Energy, comparable to the positive and negative polarities of electricity. Just so, at the level of vital life, there is a pattern of communicated life-force. Human beings live this same pattern in their emotional-sexual relationships. Many other forms of relationship in the natural world also exhibit this pattern of mutually communicated life-force. Participation in relationship at the level of vital life includes not only sex but the entire process of life-force and energy-exchange (which also includes the communication of money and the taking of food).

At the level of relational life, the process of "conductivity" is quite similar to the internal "conductivity" of the life-force. Whenever a temporary equanimity is achieved—through the balancing of opposing forces, positive and negative—this is felt as pleasure (or fulfillment), on the level of the physical and vital life. In the case of sex or any other relational function, when there is this balanced "conductivity" of life-force, there is pleasure.

Human beings are continually involved in a mutual activity in which something like positive and negative polarities must be harmonized. This "magnetic" polar attraction at the level of human nature is the characteristic of desire in its natural and functional form, as a simple impulse. Through the functioning of desire, the survival of the human species is realized by means of sex.

Just so, the survival of the individual is realized through the process of food-transformation, and the survival of the collective is realized through the exchange of force, energy, work, money, creativity, human relatedness, and commitment of life. At the level of life, this necessary and functional mutuality is continually being enacted, satisfied, and also frustrated.

This relational impulse, this very ordinary impulse, is natural to all human beings. In some, relational force is more intense than in others. From the point of view of life, relationship is the natural (or functional) form. But people are also suffering, living in dilemma, avoiding relationship. Therefore, emotional-sexual relationship often becomes one of the most degraded forms of experience possible in human life, one of the most disharmonious and aggravated forms of opposition that human beings can encounter. It is one of the chief sources of the exploitation and degradation of human existence, one of the chief sources of fascination, preoccupation, dysfunction of intelligence, frustration, fear, guilt, and dis-ease of life.

Therefore, like all forms of relationship, emotional-sexual intimacy requires a great deal of the intimate partners. The essential thing is to live it as a form of relationship, rather than a form of ownership or self-indulgence. When emotional-sexual Yoga is lived as relationship, in ego-transcending devotion to Me, then "conductivity" in the Circle is full, and there is no loss. But, when the sex-function is lived purely as a form of obsession, for the sake of release, then there is only separation and separativeness.

When your emotional-sexual life (whether celibate or sexually active) and the functions of money and food are lived in Satsang with Me, they become part of the "theatre" of your practice in My Avataric Divine Company. They become a creative enactment in conscious awareness. In Satsang with Me, they are forms of life-level realization. From the point of view of life, they are all of these things—and, yet, from the "Point of View" of Truth, they have no significance whatsoever.

Most people who are sexually active use sex as experience, rather than engage it as relationship. Their sexual experiences are merely modifications of their own mind and life. Therefore, these experiences tend to continually reinforce the sense of separation. But, regardless of whether or not it is rightly engaged as relationship, sex (in and of itself) has no effect (whether positive or negative) on the Primary Force of Consciousness. From the "Point of View" of Truth, there is no need for self-conscious or willful suppression of the sex-force. On the other hand, it is equally true that, from the "Point of View" of Truth, there is no motivation to exploit or exhaust the sex-force. In the earlier stages of their practice of the Way of Adidam, many of My devotees may choose to be involved in a sexually active intimacy. However, such involvement in intimacy, even when practiced according to My Instructions, involves (in virtually all cases) a degree of egoic bondage. Therefore, at some point in the advancing course of practice in the Way of Adidam, sexual activity will (in virtually all cases) be freely and spontaneously relinquished.

In Most Perfect Divine Enlightenment, all there is is this One Intensity. From the "Point of View" of Truth, there is no activity, no moment in time, that is not Siva-Shakti. It is always this Perfect Indivisibility. Indivisibility (or Non-"difference") is Always Already the True Nature of all relatedness. Indivisibility (or Non-"difference") is Always Already the Case.

DEVOTEE: What form does it take during sleep?

AVATAR ADI DA SAMRAJ: It depends on what is going on during sleep. It depends on the nature of the sleeper, on the sleeper's state of conscious awareness. To those who are in the waking state, sleepers are merely asleep. But those who are asleep may also be dreaming, passing through many forms of perception and experience. And, even at the level of the causal being (the moveless realm of deep sleep), there is a process that corresponds to the vast complexity of the gross and subtle worlds. That process is very fundamental—simple beyond all simplicity. It can be called "Siva-Shakti".

The Perfect Indivisibility of Siva-Shakti is Unqualified "Brightness", the Real Divine Person, the Divine Conscious Light. There is no ultimate "difference". There is no Siva <u>and</u> Shakti. Even here, in the waking world, there is no Siva <u>and</u> Shakti. But it is easier for most people to think in those concrete and symbolic terms. Therefore, it can be said that all relationships, all forms of energy-exchange, are ritual enactments of the Indivisible "Brightness" (or Conscious Light) That Is Siva-Shakti. And emotional-sexual intimacy is one of those forms of energy-exchange.

The very cells of the body are Siva-Shakti. The atom is Siva-Shakti. Simply because the world exists does not mean that Shakti is somehow separated from Siva and must return, or that the Yogi is somehow separated from Siva and must return to Siva via the form (or vehicle) of Shakti. Everything that arises is <u>Always Already</u> the Indivisible "Embrace" of Siva and Shakti.

It is not necessary to raise the Kundalini one inch. It is already raised. The True Divine Spirit-Current (of Which the Kundalini is a modification) is continually rising (in the spinal line)—and It is also continually descending (in the frontal line). It is an unbroken Circle of "conductivity" about the "Sun", the True Divine Heart Itself (as It Manifests in the body-mind in the right side of the chest[23]). For My Divinely Enlightened devotee, who (by Means of My Avataric Divine Spiritual Grace) lives from the "Point of View" of the True Divine Heart Itself, all ascent and descent is Always Already Accomplished. In contrast, someone who lives purely from the point of view of ascent has a great deal to accomplish. And, similarly, someone who lives entirely from the point of view of descended nature also has a great deal to accomplish.

Thus, in terms of emotional-sexual relationship (as in any other kind of relationship), the quality of your awareness, the quality of the ritual (or the drama) that you are playing, varies from day to day. Sometimes it is very serious, sometimes very confused, sometimes very complicated, sometimes very frustrated, sometimes very satisfied, sometimes very humorous. If you do not understand your own ego-activity, all of this is an obstacle and a dilemma, which merely provokes further seeking. But, if you understand this ego-activity, then it becomes possible to live emotional-sexual intimacy in such a manner that it does not obstruct your sadhana.

Therefore, in terms of sex or any of the other life-functions, there is no single "way it has to be" for all of My devotees. That is why I have established an appropriate range of possibilities relative to each of the life-disciplines I Give to My devotees. However, as My devotee—no matter what life-conditions arise to be dealt with—you must always observe and understand your own ego-activity.

IV.

DEVOTEE: What is the most common form of avoiding relationship?

AVATAR ADI DA SAMRAJ: It has only one fundamental form—that very act itself, the avoidance of relationship. When you understand yourself most fundamentally, you directly know the avoidance of relationship as your primary activity. At times, you may find yourself dramatizing that avoidance in some particular form at the level of your ordinary life. You may discover particular forms of strategic avoidance that are characteristic of you, either during a certain phase or as a pattern throughout your life. But, ultimately, there is only one form of that avoidance—and every other form of ego-activity is an extension of it.

When you understand yourself most fundamentally, there is, truly, only one form of suffering and ignorance. Therefore, there is no single thing that stands out, among common actions, as the primary form of self-contraction (or the avoidance of relationship)— because, when you understand yourself most fundamentally, the self-contraction itself is what stands out, and not any particular manifestation of it. It is simply that, in the case of each individual, the avoidance of relationship has its chronic modes of appearance.

The areas of your life in which this activity of avoidance is most obvious are generally the functions of the vital process, the vital force (or energy)—the process (or force) that is manifested as money (including the realms of effort, work, energy-exchange, and human relatedness), food, and sex. Those are the areas in which the life-force is communicated most obviously, most directly. The force of life is communicated as food-transformation, as sex-force, and as relational energy. In other words, the activity of avoidance (which is one's suffering) always manifests via the process of existence itself (in its gross, subtle, and causal forms).

From the "Point of View" of Truth, the life-process itself cannot be said to be the obstacle. If life itself were the obstacle, then Realization would simply be a matter of killing yourself, or something similar—some sort of revolutionary detachment (or even separation) from life. But, in fact, life itself is where you sense your conflict, where you feel your conflict dramatized. The suffering of human beings is essentially a life-dilemma, experienced in the gross (or physical) dimension of existence. Suffering (potentially) becomes a dilemma in the subtle dimension of existence only after it has already arisen in the ordinary life of the gross dimension.

People who desire some sort of remarkable subtle experience to transform them are really responding to a very primitive life-conflict. All of their striving toward what is subtle is really a reaction to vital life suffered as dilemma. Therefore, Real Spiritual practice is not a matter of getting rid of the gross aspect of existence, because it is presumed to be the "problem" in life. Rather, for My devotee, Real Spiritual practice requires that you observe and understand your own activity of self-contraction—in the context of Satsang with Me, and under the conditions of life. And, when vital life is no longer (in and of itself) perceived to be the critical dilemma, then your own enactment of the avoidance of relationship becomes obvious.

There is no so-called "higher world" that is the special and exclusive communication of Truth. All worlds communicate Truth in exactly the same manner, so there is no special advantage in any world beyond this one. Truth Is Always Already the Case. Truth Is the Prior Condition of all forms of existence. If you do not find Truth Itself, then you will pursue the pleasures of the subtle planes, or some other new phenomenal state. But, when your present, apparently limited condition is no longer lived as dilemma, then you are like someone who has been woken up from a dream. The characteristic quality of such Awakening is not that you are having some "other" kind of experience—some vision, some thought, some form of self-analysis. Waking up is itself the Freedom. When you are Awake, then the self-contraction, the avoidance of relationship, becomes obvious.

This is not a solid universe into which human beings are inserted—like little capsules of life-force, separated from other little capsules of life-force, trapped within physical bodies. This realm—like all other realms—is a modification of the Divine Conscious Light. The Divine Conscious Light (Itself) Is the Primary "Event", the Primary "Fact", the Primary "Motion". It is not that the Divine Conscious Light (Itself) must evolve. Rather, the Divine Conscious Light (Itself) must be Really lived. And It can only be Really lived in one who (by Means of My Avataric Divine Spiritual Grace) most perfectly understands.

DEVOTEE: What causes this self-contraction, or avoidance?

AVATAR ADI DA SAMRAJ: It is not an activity outside you.

DEVOTEE: How does it arise?

AVATAR ADI DA SAMRAJ: It is arising. When it is seen directly, it is seen to have no cause. It did not begin in the past. It is presently arising. It is a spontaneous activity whose mystery is understandable only in the instant of self-understanding. Before there is self-understanding, nothing can be said about it that makes any difference—because it has not begun in the past. It is always arising presently. At the root-level, it is a completely voluntary activity. That is why self-understanding is a simplicity. That is why self-understanding is possible for My devotee. It is as if you have discovered that you are pinching yourself, unknowingly.

You will try all kinds of extraordinary healing methods, psychic methods, Yogic methods—anything to get rid of this root-sense of pain and agony that you have all the time. You will continue to pursue every kind of means until you realize that all you are doing is pinching yourself. When you realize that, you just take your hand away. There is nothing complicated about it at all. But, previous to that, it is an immensely complicated problem—and the sense of life itself tends to be identified with that problem. The presumption of problem (or dilemma) motivates you to every kind of distraction, and the transcending of this presumption cannot occur before there is most fundamental self-understanding of one's always present-time root-activity. To seek its origin, to seek a cause for it, is like trying to find the beginning of breath.

DEVOTEE: How does the self-contraction arise in the present moment?

AVATAR ADI DA SAMRAJ: If it is arising in the present moment, how can you address it by looking for causes? All causes are past—but the process of self-contraction is a present-time activity.

DEVOTEE: What brings it on, or stimulates it?

AVATAR ADI DA SAMRAJ: It is not caused. The only proper investigation of it, the only "answer" to that question, is Satsang with Me and self-understanding. There is no satisfactory answer apart from the present observation and understanding of the very activity itself—in the context of Satsang with Me.

Most of your activities are forms of mere experiencing—without any real self-observation or self-understanding. You are experiencing this, this, this, this, this. The search, the forms of motivated Yoga, the remedial techniques people acquire, are also forms of experiencing. "Look at this chakra! Look at this light! Look at this sound! Look at this deity! Look at this deliciousness! Look at this! Look at this!" "Oh, yes, I am looking at this!"

"Narcissus" is always looking at his own image. "I" is always looking at this. Such is the ordinary adventure—until you observe and understand your own activity of self-contraction, rather than merely experiencing the results of that activity. Then you not only know what you are doing, but you know what it is that you are doing!

When you understand that activity, then it ceases to have any fundamental importance. Then all of this chattering—"Oh, look! Look, I'm seeing this! Oh, look! Look at this!"—just comes to an end. The self-contraction, the unconscious, compulsive modification of Consciousness Itself, no longer occurs. "Narcissus" realizes, "Ah!" All of a sudden—"Ah!" And he just gets up and walks back into town.

"Radical" self-understanding is, in itself, the utter reversal of all dilemma. It is sudden, spontaneous—and it cannot (in any manner) be explained before it has occurred.

DEVOTEE: You have said that this activity takes the form of identification, differentiation, and desire. In a concrete situation, what happens?

AVATAR ADI DA SAMRAJ: The ordinary sense that you have— while sitting, standing, walking, lying down—is of separate existence. It is not that you are constantly saying to yourself, "I am this body. I am this mind. I am this. I am that." There is no mental process that is responsible for communicating to you the sense of separate self. You already have this sense. You wake up alive, you move in bodily terms—it just seems very obvious. There is the root-sense of some sort of limit, size, shape, or "difference". That is identification. It is called "ego".

Differentiation is expressed through all the forms of knowing (or mind) by means of which all experience becomes an extension of the separate-self-sense that one has assumed. Everything becomes a "this". "Look at this. Look at this." Suddenly, there are endless planes of significance. The very structure of your thought is "this, this, this". Spontaneously, everything is already multiplied, distinct.

Having already acquired this sense of separate existence—already perceiving, already thinking, presuming a range of multiplicity, a range of separate natures, forms, and forces—you move. That motion is desire. This separate one moves. The one you call "I" conceives a realm of multiplicity in which to move, because that one presumes itself to be separate. There is something, even a world, that you are up against—so you move. And that movement is desire.

Once these three assumptions (of identification, differentiation, and desire) are made, an endless adventure inevitably ensues. That adventure is what human beings are up to. Indeed, all ordinary beings (human and non-human) who are karmically manifested in the conditional worlds are living that adventure. Each one lives the adventure with particular qualities, in particular circumstances, with characteristic ranges of subjectivity—but all beings are living their adventure on the armature of this same structure, this same form, this same complex of assumptions. Therefore, the best practical (or concrete) example of the process of identification, differentiation, and desire is simply your present state—"me", separate, with everything around "me" moving. The best example of it is simply what you ordinarily perceive to be your condition in any present moment.

Now, the human adventure, in all its forms, is possible only from the point of view of identification, differentiation, and desire. Indeed, the human adventure is <u>built</u> on that point of view. And that point of view is the dilemma. All human doings are undertaken in the disposition (and on the basis) of that dilemma. Therefore, <u>all</u> pursuits, <u>all</u> searches, <u>all</u> activities, <u>all</u> accomplishments—whether Spiritual or mundane—are nothing but possible variations on the same adventure of identification, differentiation, and desire. It is not that the Spiritual forms of the adventure are somehow "better" than the mundane ones. They are all the same adventure. And, of course, the dilemma and its search are manifested among human beings as all kinds of conflicts and preferences—at every level of conscious awareness.

The waking life, what you know as the ordinary waking state, is a continual drama based on these three activities of identification, differentiation, and desire. The causal body (which is the seat of deep sleep) manifests as the activity of identification (or separate-self-sense), through contraction of the causal center in the right side of the heart. The subtle body (which is the seat of dreams) comprises the internal (or subtle) range of functions—manifesting, essentially, as the elaboration (or differentiation) of thought, feeling, energy, and sensation. This is done by contraction of the subtle mechanism—which (in the vertical plane) has many centers (or functions) in the ascending (or spinal) line of the Circle and in the brain, and which (in the horizontal plane) is epitomized as the middle station of the heart. Then the waking state adds the movement of desire (or manifested vitality)—which (in the vertical plane) manifests as the descending (or frontal) line of the Circle and which (in the horizontal plane) is felt as the contraction in the left side of the heart.

The traditional searches are attempts to return to what is conceived to be the simpler origin. When the search turns inward in the waking state, away from desire, this is religion. When the search turns inward from the subtle life of dreams to forms of subtlety (or light) beyond mind, this is Spirituality (or Yoga). The intuitive methods of the would-be Jnani or Buddha turn beyond life (or the waking state), and even beyond subtlety (or the dream state), into the causal ground. But, in fact, all of these methods are simply means of going from one conditional state into another, moving out of one limited condition into another, that is felt to be relatively less complicated, or relatively more free of binding conditions.

None of these movements from one dimension of existence to another is the Truth Itself. But, when you comprehend your own adventure, such that your search occupies you less and less, when you become incapable of desensitizing yourself to your own suffering, when suffering (or dilemma) becomes obvious as your constant condition, regardless of your state (waking, dreaming, or sleeping)—then, in the context of Satsang with Me, there is the possibility of Real intelligence, of "radical" self-understanding, of Truth.

The Prior State is neither waking nor dreaming nor sleeping. It cannot be identified with any of the three characteristic functional conditions. It has been called "Turiya"—the "Fourth State", Beyond the three common states. The Realization of the Prior State by means of the traditional searches is temporary and conditional. Only Most Perfect Realization of the Prior State is permanent and not dependent on any search or any strategic manipulation of the psycho-physical structure. Most Perfect Realization of the Prior State has been called "Turiyatita"—"Beyond the Fourth"—although that State was never truly Realized previous to My Avataric Incarnation here.[24] Therefore, when (by Means of My Avataric Divine Spiritual Grace) you most perfectly understand, then you are Awake while waking, Awake while dreaming, Awake while sleeping. Then you constantly Enjoy the Spiritual Self-"Brightness" That Is Reality Itself, Prior to all self-contraction. Then you have become Truly Humorous. Mortal seriousness has fallen from you. I do not mean that you are always giggling—but the root-aggravation, the self-contraction, the mysteriousness of your own suffering, is absent. You fall through it—constantly.

DEVOTEE: Are You saying that desire has to stop?

AVATAR ADI DA SAMRAJ: One of the typical methods of Spiritual seeking is the attempt to obstruct or stop desire—because the universal struggle with desire is a fundamental reason why life is conceived as dilemma. The dilemma is most obvious at the level of desire, at the level of life. The seeker either exploits desire or resists it—but neither one of these strategies is appropriate. Both of them are founded in the dilemma itself. Desire itself, the quality of movement-in-life itself, is not the dilemma.

DEVOTEE: Desire arising out of identification and differentiation—isn't that the problem?

AVATAR ADI DA SAMRAJ: That quality as oneself is the dilemma—but, lived from the "Point of View" of the Divine Self-Condition (or Truth Itself), that same quality is without dilemma. Thus, in My Divinely Enlightened devotee, there is still the apparently individuated being, there is still the capability for subtle life (which is mind and all its forms), there is still the capability for movement (which is desire). Such a one's outward appearance is not changed. He or she remains ordinary, but lives the "Point of View" of the Divine Self-Condition, as the Divine Self-Condition. But, when the Divine Conscious Light is apparently modified as the activities of identification, differentiation, and desire, this is the felt dilemma—because it is not true, Conscious Light is not that. The sense of identification, differentiation, and desire is the dilemma. The dilemma is nothing more than that.

Therefore, the attempt to remove desire is a secondary reaction to this dilemma. The dilemma has already occurred—therefore, anything done to the function of desire is secondary. You can do anything you like to your desire—but nothing you can do to your desire becomes Most Perfect Divine Self-Realization, most perfect "radical" self-understanding, or Truth Itself. All this doing-to-desire is itself desire, a reaction to desire as dilemma. When dilemma is understood, there is no motivation to do anything about desire itself. Why should you want to do anything about desire? What is wrong with desire?

At times, it will seem to you that you need to block desire. At other times, it will seem that you need to enjoy it. It will change from hour to hour—but your occupation must turn from desire to observation of the dilemma itself. And that can truly occur only in Satsang with Me. The preoccupation with your methods of dealing with your search is fruitless. The more you try, the clearer this becomes. Each method is just another strategy, another form of experiencing, that merely reinforces the dilemma.

Each strategic method has its own apparent satisfactions, and its own frustrations. The libertine has his or her satisfactions, his or her frustrations. The one who pursues sainthood has his or her satisfactions, his or her frustrations. Satisfaction and frustration both act only to reinforce the dilemma. At last, when the libertine and the saint fall out of their search and into their suffering, then (from within their suffering) they will begin to intuit Truth—becoming (thereby) available to embrace the life of Satsang with Me.

AVATAR ADI DA SAMRAJ
Da Love-Ananda Mahal, 2003

4.

Vital Shock

I.

DEVOTEE: Beloved Lord, I wonder if You could expand on a discussion You had with some of us the other day regarding the vital center of the body-mind. You were telling us how people become obsessed with anger, fear, jealousy, and so forth, as a result of a contraction in the vital.

AVATAR ADI DA SAMRAJ: Yes. I have talked about how Energy operates in life through a structure (or pattern) of "conductivity", a Circle of descending and ascending Force. The locus of gross-bodily life (or vitality) is a center in the middle of the body, in the general area of the navel—the lower-body area. This center, or this aspect of the larger Circle of Force, is located in the frontal (or descending) line of the body. It is very intimate to human experience.

It is at the level of life, of vitality, that people experience the nature of suffering most obviously, most directly. And, for the most part, it is at the level of vitality (or physicality, or grossness) that people are aware of existence. To the usual person, the dimension of ascending (or subtle) life is quite obscure, in comparison to vital (or gross) life. In fact, when people pursue what they regard to be Spirituality, it is (generally speaking) not because they are responding to something truly Spiritual. What makes people seek is not a Spiritual motivation—not even, as a general rule, a subtle motivation. Rather, what motivates people to seek is their own suffering—and, essentially, suffering in the vital, in the gross (or physical) dimension of life.

The usual person lives in the state that I call "vital shock". Ultimately, this shock includes more than the vital. Indeed, this shock operates even on a very subtle level. But its most obvious (and directly motivating) form is the sense of shock in the vital being. Ordinarily, the vital—at its chief center in the middle of the body—is contracted. You constantly feel that contraction, even physically. You may feel a kind of cramp, a tension in the middle of the body. And everyone constantly tries to relieve that tension through various experiences, various pleasures.

The vital center is like the shutter of a camera. It curls in on itself in order to close, and unfurls in order to open. It is like your hand. If you clench your fist as tightly as you can, it eventually becomes painful. Like your hand, the vital center is alive, sentient—and, like your hand, the vital, when it contracts, causes a painful sensation. Indeed, it causes not only a physical sensation, but also many other repercussions in life and conscious awareness. Therefore, when this contraction occurs in the vital, you not only get a cramp in the stomach—you have an entire life of suffering.

Every aspect of vital existence is controlled by this state, this vital shock. The patterns to which people become addicted are simply extensions of this contraction in the vital. For instance, in the course of your life in My Avataric Divine Company, you may experience periods of great difficulty, when you are continually obsessed with various kinds of desires, various feelings. At the beginning of such a period, something occurred. Something in life, somewhere, assaulted (or seemed to assault) the vital. All of the patterns, the rituals, the strategies that began to arise in you were reactions to that assault on the vital. The sensation (or perception) of that assault, that "blow" to the vital, is the form of vital shock that currently obsesses you. But, even before you began the present episode, vital shock was already your condition. There is a continuous vital contraction.

In fact, what people are suffering is not their distinctive life-patterns (or strategies) in and of themselves, but this original shock, in the form of a primal reaction—the <u>self-contraction</u>. People seek, through all kinds of means, to become free of their various symptoms, their various strategies—including the cramped sensation in the region of the navel. But, if you observe and understand this contraction itself—this activity, this drama—in the present, then you do not have to deal with all the endless extensions of it.

To live True Spiritual life, you must deal with your fundamental, present activity, the self-contraction itself—rather than attempting to deal with the search that is an expression of the self-contraction. True Spiritual life in My Avataric Divine Company is not a matter of dealing with the symptoms or the strategies manifested by the activity of self-contraction, but of observing the activity itself, in present time. This fundamental ego-activity is the root and the support and the form of all the ordinary manifestations of suffering, all the patterns of life that people acknowledge to be their suffering. The self-contraction, the avoidance of relationship, is, fundamentally, everyone's continuous, present activity.

You can be thrown into an entire period of dramatizing your suffering by some simple event in life. A frustration of some kind, a threat, a loss—a vital shock. But release is not a matter of looking into your memory and discovering the various sources or incidents of these shocks in the past—you know, the day your father hit you, the day your dog died, and all the rest. Those are only past instances of the same process. The process itself is always instant, present-time, spontaneous. It is a reaction to life itself.

Life is its own shock. The event of Consciousness Itself becoming aware of Its apparent identification with a physical form is that shock. Birth is that shock—not merely the original physical event (the memory of which may, in some cases, be recovered), but every moment's awareness of being alive. The events within the course of life are nothing but extensions of that primal life-shock.

In *The Knee Of Listening*, I describe the experience in which I remembered—even relived—My prenatal state, the awakening of conscious awareness as the body.[25] There was a kind of gloriousness about it, a fantastic form of Energy—shaped, as I described it then, "like a seahorse". It was the original Yogic Arousal of the Kundalini, if you will. But, in the same instant, there was intense sorrow. The shock was the shock of life itself, the shock of embodiment.

The "seahorse" (or the bodily form) is already contraction. The spinal form is already this curve. The ordinary life is already this tendency, this compulsive qualification of Consciousness Itself, this compulsive un-consciousness. After the event of birth, each human being develops a characteristic drama in response to this shock. Distinctive experiences occur in the course of every human life, and each individual develops a characteristic pattern of reaction to such experiences. Thus, each person is living the drama and strategy of suffering in a unique manner—a peculiarly complex, individual manner. But, in every case, there is one fundamental activity, one thing that is the suffering. It is an activity—this activity, this contraction, this avoidance of relationship, this differentiation, this separation. Wherever it occurs, that is suffering.

All ordinary suffering is only a cramp. It is the self-contraction. Wherever there is self-contraction, there is obstruction to the flow of the life-force. And, wherever there is self-contraction, there is also the sense of separate existence.

If you cramp the hand together in a fist, there is a sensation in the hand, as the hand, that is different from the space around it. When the vital being is contracted in the same manner, the apparent "center" of that contraction is the ego, the "me", the separate-self-sense. The mind of this "me"—like its body—is separate, separative, compulsively differentiating.

Therefore, the entire drama of seeking that is a reaction to the self-contraction (or a reaction to life altogether) always begins with this "me". "Me" is the core of your self-contracting activity. "Me" is the center of the "fist". Every person seeks, by every possible means, to be relieved of his or her suffering—but the suffering cannot be relieved, the self-contraction cannot be uncoiled, unless the "me" (which is its center) dissolves.

At the level of life, of vitality, the Spiritual process in My Avataric Divine Company involves not only the dissolution of the life-drama, the dissolution of the physical manifestation of self-contraction, but also the dissolution of all of the qualities, the characteristic psychology, the mentality, the presumptions, of self-contraction. Thus, Real Spiritual life involves the undermining of the entire point of view of vital shock.

When the self-contraction unwinds, "conductivity" replaces obstruction. Then there is "conductivity" of the natural life-energy (and, in the case of My devotees who have been Spiritually Awakened by Me, of My Avatarically Self-Transmitted Divine Spirit-Energy). As long as this compulsive contraction (or shock) exists, there is no such "conductivity". There is only obstruction (or limitation and constriction) of the flow of life-force.

The self-contraction may be experienced as intense stimulation of life-energy (or life-force) in the vital, felt as all of the various forms of desire. The fundamental forms of this intense cramp of energy—felt as the fire of desire in the vital—are the dramas of money, food, and sex. If the cramp of obstruction is severe, there is loss of vitality, desire, and function in these same areas of life. No vitality—no survival.

One who indulges in the exploitation of desire is no longer conducting the force of life. In that case, there is only the misuse of the life-force, the reversing of it, the emptying of it. People do this because the self-contraction is painful. You discover that, if the life-force itself is diminished, the pain goes away. If the hand goes to sleep, there is no pain from the clenching of the fist. If you empty the vital of its force, the cramp is not felt—even though the contraction remains.

One who is self-indulgent empties the vital constantly—and thereby feels relief, feels open, feels satisfied. But, as soon as strength returns, the pain is felt again—unless the person has exhausted and contracted the vital to the point of impotence. A person who is self-indulgent tries, by every possible means, to get satisfied, to be free of pain. But all such efforts are made from the point of view of the self-contraction, the avoidance of relationship. In that disposition, you will simply continue your efforts—until the entire process of the search fails, and you feel its failure. When you begin to really feel that failure, then Satsang with Me becomes possible, the life of "radical" self-understanding becomes possible.

One who is dramatizing (or living) this state of vital shock is not truly alive, not really enjoying life. Such a one is always self-enclosed, always suffering, always unconscious, always obsessed, always seeking. Among human beings, there is always the same malady. Everybody is asleep, everybody is unconscious, everybody is self-obsessed, everybody wants to be satisfied. Everyone who comes to the Guru wants to be satisfied. "When will I become enlightened? When will I have this experience? What is happening to me? I am suffering."

Everyone wants to begin Spiritual life as a search. People want to carry on Spiritual life as an extension of the same thing they have always been doing. They want to be satisfied. They want to be emptied. They want to be free of this cramp. They want to be free of it—"me, me, me". But "me" is the center, the core, of the self-contraction.

If you go to the usual traditional sources of religious and Spiritual teaching, you are given forms of satisfaction, means to satisfy your inclination to be free of this cramp. You are given palliatives, seeming remedies, strategies of belief, and every kind of ego-consoling method designed to satisfy this search at various levels. All of these methods are responses to the painful cramp in the vital.

But those who come into My Avataric Divine Company in order to console the "me" are not satisfied. They are frustrated. The search for consolation is not the "Point of View" of Truth. The self-contraction and the consolations it seeks are not supported in Satsang with Me. Satsang with Me is the undermining of the self-contraction, at every level—the undermining of the very point of view of self-contraction, the undermining of suffering, of seeking, of separative existence. Therefore, only those who have become sensitive to the failure of their search are able to tolerate the quality of Satsang with Me.

Satsang with Me is a paradox. For one thing, the self-contraction is the avoidance of the essential condition of life, the primary law (or form) of the cosmos: relationship. There is nothing conditional that arises on its own, or purely as its own "self". People come to Me dissociated from all "others", separating themselves from all conditions. But Satsang is the relationship to Me. Therefore, Satsang with Me is an offense to "Narcissus", an offense to the self-contraction—not a satisfaction of it. When you have become sensitive to your own failure, then (and <u>only</u> then) are you able to tolerate that offense.

Living in the condition of relationship stimulates tremendous resistance in people. The sadhana of Satsang with Me is to live the devotional and Spiritual relationship to Me at all times, and forever. Satsang with Me requires at least as much confrontation with resistance as the kind of effort Yogis and religious practitioners traditionally engage by putting themselves into caves and various other ascetic circumstances. In Truth, the most ascetic circumstance is relationship. The condition of relationship stimulates all of the reactivity, all of the "sinfulness", all of the impurity that is in a person. For My devotee, all of that is stimulated in the Condition and relationship that is Satsang with Me. Satsang with Me is an offense to the self-contraction, and It stirs up its content.

Satsang with Me is a connection, a form of "conductivity". The Force of Truth is Communicated through that connection. At the same time that the subconscious of buried reactions (and, indeed, the entire effort of the search) is being stimulated by the life of Satsang with Me, the Divine Force (or Pressure) of Satsang with Me is also stimulating and quickening the entire process. This provokes the crisis that is True sadhana in My Avataric Divine Company.

When this process has significantly loosened the vital, when functional ease is restored to vital (or gross physical) life, then—once I have formally and directly Granted you My Spiritually Initiatory Avataric Divine Blessing-Transmission—the True (by-Me-Awakened, and always newly by-Me-Activated) <u>Spiritual</u> process may begin to manifest itself in My devotee.[26] But, in the beginning, it is at the level of vitality that this sadhana must be demonstrated—not at the level of visions and other subtle phenomena. In any case, such phenomena are not what is significant—because anyone (even people with absolutely no Spiritual qualifications whatsoever) may manifest the tendency to have subtle experiences.

Thus, at the beginning, there is this process that must occur relative to the vital, must deal with vital shock. The person who is just entering the life of Satsang with Me is like a patient coming to a hospital in shock. The Force and Condition of Satsang with

Me must unloose the condition of vital shock. When the unconscious, compulsive point of view of vital shock, and the strategies stimulated by its characteristic state, have been critically loosened in the individual by the practical living of the life-conditions of Satsang with Me, then most fundamental self-understanding can awaken.

Living always in heart-Communion with Me, while rightly functioning in the cooperative culture of My devotees (and in the world altogether), is the means to release vital shock. But the release is entirely My Activity—for My devotee cannot do what My Avataric Divine Spiritual Presence and Force Does. As My devotee, you simply live in that Presence and Force, conformed to the life-conditions I require. Such is the True Grace of Spiritual life in My Avataric Divine Company: Your vital shock is undermined by My Avataric Divine Spiritual Presence and Force—the Presence and Force of Reality Itself (or Truth Itself).

DEVOTEE: It seems that a person who is only seeking is never dealing fundamentally with the self-contraction, but is merely reacting to the shock of life.

AVATAR ADI DA SAMRAJ: Yes. Such a person is merely reacting to the manifestations, the symptoms, of self-contraction. The secret cause of your suffering is not located in the past. It is not located in the universe—"out there". Your suffering is entirely your own. It is your own activity. What is more, your suffering is entirely your present activity, not caused by something else. Therefore, the Real activity of Spiritual life is not generated from the point of view of this search, this reaction, this suffering. It is not a matter of discovering your "devils" (or whatever they are)—the key memories, the mortal and cosmic events. It is a matter of observing and understanding your own activity, your present activity.

There is a present activity—an absolutely present activity, an "only" activity—that everyone is performing all the time. Yes, there are conditions—and reactions to conditions—that build up patterns. But what is significant is the root, the support, the paradigm, of all ego-patterning. You can go on endlessly recalling the incidents and experiences that conditioned you—but, without self-observation in the present moment, you will have accomplished nothing except the reinforcement of your self-obsession.

Why are you conditionable? Why are you suffering these conditions? Your suffering is your own activity. When self-contraction no longer occurs, then no conditioning occurs, no thought binds. Then there is only Love-Bliss-Happiness.

The approach of Truth to life is a direct (or "radical") one, not a roundabout (or revolutionary) one. It is not a matter of the search—which is inevitably undertaken from a point of view within the condition of suffering. Rather, it is a matter of the observation and understanding of your present activity. You are operating as the activity of self-contraction.

DEVOTEE: Beloved Master, can You clarify what You mean by "radical"?

AVATAR ADI DA SAMRAJ: "Radical" self-understanding is an irreducible insight. There is not anything that can go behind it or beyond it. The "radical" point of view is not one of seeking (step by step, by means of experiences), but of penetrating the present condition (prior to any movement whatsoever).

You could take the point of view of the suffering, the symptom, the entire life-game that you (as an apparently separate individual) are playing, and make that the point of view of Spiritual life. And, indeed, that is (essentially) what people have always done. Traditionally, people begin from the point of view of their suffering. Instead of resorting to the Truth, they search for the Truth. They travel in a vast circle, or "great path of return". But every "point" on the circle is founded in the same point of view with which the "journey" was begun. Each "point" is simply a different condition or experience perceived from that same point of view. At some point, this begins to become clear—however far you have gone on this infinitely wide circle before you discover it.

When you begin to suspect or see—to observe and understand—the nature of the adventure you are living, then you are no longer traveling the circle, but you are at the center of the circle.

The moment you Know what this entire adventure is, you are already at the center. Therefore, the "great path of return" (endlessly revolving around the circle) is the nature of the search—but Truth is always already at the core, the center.

II.

DEVOTEE: What is the nature of Paradise?

AVATAR ADI DA SAMRAJ: Paradise! What is Paradise? What is that?

DEVOTEE: Paradise is where there is bliss.

AVATAR ADI DA SAMRAJ: Where there is bliss?! Bliss is Paradise. All of this is Always Already Bliss. Love-Bliss-Happiness is the Very Nature of all of this. So-called "Paradise" is an hallucination about what it must be like where lots of blissful people are! But Love-Bliss-Happiness is the Very Nature of Reality Itself. Love-Bliss-Happiness is the Very Nature of this present event.

There are lots of "someplace elses", but they will be no more blissful for you than this place if you are not already Blissful. For the usual person, the lokas (or Spiritual realms) of the Siddhas are just as dismal as the Earth. But the Siddhas are very smart. They find ways to keep the stupids out! If some being who is prey to ordinary distractions gets anywhere near, they say, "Psst! Have you been down to, uh—Earth?" And they really hard-sell it, so that everybody comes down here!

Love-Bliss-Happiness, Unqualified Enjoyment, is the Nature of Truth. The Nature of Consciousness, and the Nature of all of this— the Nature of the cells of the body, the Nature of Light Itself—is Unqualified, Unconditional Openness.

DEVOTEE: Does that mean there is no separation between any of us?

AVATAR ADI DA SAMRAJ: Do you <u>see</u> any? Do you <u>feel</u> there is? In Truth, there is no separation at all. But, from the point of view of the seeker, the one who suffers, there is <u>only</u> separation, at every level. When you Wake Up to Reality Itself—when you understand your own adventure, your own state, in every form that it takes—then you cannot find separations anymore. You cannot discover them—and you go Divinely "Mad". That Divine "Madness" is True Intelligence.

DEVOTEE: One cannot go higher than that?

AVATAR ADI DA SAMRAJ: Higher than that? It would not occur to you! It is the seeker who is always going someplace. The one who is already in trouble is always going "someplace else"— because he or she is suffering the results of self-contraction. All of the chakras, all of the centers in the subtle body, the subtle life, exhibit the same form as the vital center, the gross body, the gross life. These chakras are contracted, closed, not conducting Energy in the descending and ascending arcs of the Circle of the body-mind.

When Satsang is lived with Me—such that the vital begins to open, and this "conductivity" begins to occur again—then movement also tends to begin in the subtle life as well. Then the higher chakras begin to open, and various Spiritual phenomena arise. Spontaneous physical movements, all the kinds of things that I have discussed with you, and that you have read about, may occur. But, as you should be able to see, they are not (in and of themselves) the Truth.

Whenever there is an opening of some sort, or a relaxation in any level (or center) of conscious awareness, there tend to be experiences that are associated with that level. These experiences can be movements, rushes of energy, physical or emotional bliss-fulness, various sensations, various kinds of psychic phenomena, visions, lights, sounds—but all of these are merely things that were stuck inside the "fist" of self-contraction. As the self-contraction opens up, they sort of "klink" off. But the seeker, the one who endures the process of sadhana from the point of view of suffering, thinks that all of these things are "it". Your hand opens up, and you see the rings on your fingers, the lines on your hand. Everything becomes very fascinating, and you think of these experiences as Spiritual life. You think that your visions are Truth.

Traditional Yogic seekers imagine that the Kundalini Force actually <u>ascends</u>. If the Kundalini ever for one moment did not retain its connection with the sahasrar (the upper region of the brain and its subtle counterparts), you would be dead, from that moment. That ascending arc of the Circle always exists, just as the descending arc of the Circle always exists. It is just that, in the case of the traditional Yogic seeker, when the spinal line begins to come alive, and the contractions at certain points in the spinal line begin to loosen, then various experiences occur (corresponding to the various subtle centers), and people imagine that the Energy Itself is rising. What is actually occurring is that the subtle centers are opening in a kind of progress that seems "upward". Certainly, there are sensations that are like rising Energy. But, in fact, the Circle of Energy is always there, always continuous—except that It is obstructed by the tendency to contract, to be separate, to avoid relationship at the level of life.

Thought itself—simple thought, or mind-forms—is a form of suffering in the seeker. The simplest mind-form, any mind-form—even an amused thought of Donald Duck!—is a condition of suffering, of self-contraction. If—in the very moment when you are distracted by, or happy with, this or that image or thought—you examine yourself with any kind of sensitivity, you will realize that you are suffering. Distracted, perhaps—but suffering.

When, in Most Perfect Divine Self-Realization, all of this contraction, all of this life of avoidance, all of this identification with thinking is (by Means of My Avataric Divine Spiritual Grace) transcended, then there is only the Absolute "Conductivity" of Amrita Nadi (Which is the Perfect Form of Reality)—and That Perfect Form Lives only as Its Own Self-Existing, Self-Radiant, and Self-Evidently Divine Nature.

The momentary (or otherwise temporary) and partial experience of the relaxation of the vital and subtle contraction is what the traditions of Yoga call "samadhi"—Yogic exaltation, meditative ecstasy. There are many kinds of such temporary (or conditional) Yogic samadhi. The traditional Yogic samadhis are experiences that take place when particular subtle events occur in the living circuitry I am describing to you. When certain forms of concentration are coupled with certain energy-movements within, people experience such conditional samadhis. But the Greatest and Only True Divine Samadhi Is Truth Itself, the Divine Self-Condition Itself, or Reality Itself. There are the temporary (or conditional) samadhis, and there is the Eternal Samadhi of Truth—the (only-by-Me Revealed and Given) Most Ultimate and Final Samadhi, or seventh stage Sahaja Nirvikalpa Samadhi (Which is not dissociated from any of the states of conscious awareness, ordinary or extraordinary, and Which is not based on any movement or event in relation to any state of conscious awareness).

One who Enjoys That Eternal Samadhi is Always Already Full. When (by Means of My Avataric Divine Spiritual Grace) you are Established in My Divine Samadhi, you do not have to enter into any of the conditional Yogic samadhis in order to be living the Truth. At times, you may spontaneously enter into one or another of the conditional Yogic samadhis, but not as any kind of necessary demonstration of the Realization of Truth.

In True Divine Samadhi, you live the present condition Consciously—without bondage to vital shock, without self-contraction, without the avoidance of relationship, without identification with the subtle forms of that avoidance (all of which are forms of thought, modifications of Consciousness Itself). When all of these modifications come to an end—not by means of your physical death, but because you are no longer bound to them as a compulsive activity—then there is already what may be called "Paradise", only Love-Bliss-Happiness Itself, only the Divine Self-Condition, only the Divine Conscious Light, only Truth Itself, only Reality Itself.

III.

AVATAR ADI DA SAMRAJ: I began by speaking about the notion of vital shock. You create your own life-drama. Essentially, all of your dramas take place in the context of relationships of various kinds—because the avoidance of relationship, the contraction in relation to the life-force, is the activity to which human beings are compulsively bound. Where there is relationship at the level of life, there is the tendency to separate from it—and, if you cannot find any justification for separating from it, you manufacture reasons to separate from it. Every individual continually engineers the failure of relationship. Indeed, people become compulsively bound to their special methods for complicating and destroying relationship. Such strategies are the life-patterns that people are suffering—and their chosen forms of the search are the strategic methods by which people try to get free of the very limitations they are compulsively generating.

If you are experiencing something like that now—as My devotee, in Satsang with Me—then the symptoms, the feelings, the moods, the thoughts, the entire period of days or weeks (or however long it may be) of negativity and un-Happiness, of obsession—none of that has to be "bought". None of that has to be lived. All of that is merely a secondary affair. The disease has already occurred. What you are experiencing is simply the symptoms of the healing.

If you will look back at the beginning of any of these periods, there is usually some frustrating event to which all of this is the strategic reaction. Not that you should always be looking for these events in your past. All I mean to have you discover, by pointing this out to you, is what you <u>do</u> in reaction to the frustration of life, the suppression of life, the shock that is life. What are you doing about that? What does your life-drama consist of? It is always self-contraction, the avoidance of relationship.

Relationship is the Real condition of life. If you are sitting in the house, weeping, screaming, feeling upset and negative about somebody you live with, then that activity is your suffering. But, if you feel that person, feel the relationship, live the relationship, let the force of life move again—then there is no suffering at all. You have obviated that entire "tour", the entire drama—including the making up and all the rest. None of it has to take place. All of those things are merely the particularities of your suffering.

But suffering itself is always the avoidance of <u>relationship</u>. Whenever you observe and understand your own activity, you see that that activity was the avoidance of relationship. When relationship is lived, then the self-contraction does not take place, and right "conductivity" of the life-force characterizes your life altogether. That "conductivity" is felt as pleasure—as free conscious awareness, without distraction by thought. It is loving, open, light, forceful.

Therefore, the key to True Spiritual life is not the life-force itself, not any particular activity, not the Kundalini, not any of the secondary manifestations that occur <u>in</u> Satsang with Me. Such are merely phenomena that are associated with True Spiritual life. The key to True Spiritual life is the observation, the understanding, and the transcending of your own activity of self-contraction—in the context of Satsang with Me.

In Satsang with Me, the mere fact of relationship to Me tends to stimulate everything I am describing. My Avataric Divine Self-Transmission and Self-Revelation Is the Communication of the "Bright", the Divine Conscious Light Itself. Therefore, at the beginning of your sadhana in My Avataric Divine Company, everything tends to intensify and build up in you. You are given conditions at the level of life—simple conditions, practical ones, functional things for which you are to be appropriately responsible. Gradually, the stronger you become, the simpler you become, the more experienced you become in living this Satsang with Me, the more you begin to listen to Me with free attention— such that you begin to observe yourself, to move toward this insight, this self-understanding.

Without such self-observation and self-understanding, the Real Event of Satsang with Me cannot occur. Without such self-observation and self-understanding, you can have all the Spiritual phenomena you like, but they will be only more experience, more suffering. However, if you live from the point of view of Satsang with Me, these phenomena can arise and be of interest—and, like all other conditionally arising phenomena, they will inevitably generate conditions in which self-understanding must take place.

When most perfect "radical" self-understanding occurs, it will not be your Divine Enlightenment—because, when it occurs, there is no "one" left. I do not mean that you will be physically dead, that you will be unconscious, that you will be in oblivion—but the entire principle which is the center of self-contracted life will have disappeared. When you open your hand, what happens to your fist? When you release the self-contraction, the "me" is gone, the search is gone, the entire principle of suffering is undermined. Satsang with Me is a process of growth and outgrowing, Given by My Avataric Divine Spiritual Grace—until, ultimately, heart-Communion with Me is most perfect (and, thereby, self-understanding is most perfect), such that you Realize Me Most Perfectly.

Until people enter into Satsang with Me, they are looking for release from their symptoms. They want to seek, they want relief. They are not prepared for Truth.

In every moment, this compulsive, selfward-turning curvature of self-contraction is being generated. Why do you think there are thoughts all of the time? Why is there one thought after the next? Why doesn't thought come to an end? The apparently objective (or broken) light of conditionally manifested existence is curving compulsively. Why is there suffering all the time? This activity of curving is compulsive. It is not Real life. That is not "how it is", in Real Spiritual terms. There is compulsive activity, automatic activity, unnecessary activity. There is compulsive curvature, bending, contraction at the causal root of conditionally manifested existence.

DEVOTEE: Why does it happen?

AVATAR ADI DA SAMRAJ: Once you already have this shape, this human body, why is there such a strong tendency to walk around and talk and be a human being? Your human-being-ness has already occurred! The body is the shape of it. It is not that the body is wrong. It is not that you should make a judgement about the body. From a superficial standpoint, it is very easy to fall out of sympathy with your own craziness, and then start to resist it. But all of that is merely more of the same.

When your present activity is truly understood, the dilemma no longer exists. This does not mean that, from that moment, no more thinking goes on, no more life goes on. The activity that is your suffering is not life itself, nor has that activity generated life. The activity of self-contraction is merely the obstruction to life, an illusory pattern within life—but that activity is utter, fundamental, all-inclusive. You cannot even pick your nose without doing the self-contraction. You cannot look at anything without being involved in this self-contracting activity, this avoidance of relationship. You cannot think, feel, move, breathe, you do not live a single moment, without performing this activity and experiencing its results.

Therefore, from the point of view of the dilemma, <u>everything</u> is a form of this activity. To someone who is wedded to dilemma, the cosmic domain seems to be made out of nothing but suffering. That is why people become atheistic, insane, chronically depressed. To such people, the entire universe seems to justify despair—because everything seems to have become an extension of their own self-contracting activity. That activity has become the means and manner of their perception.

Therefore, self-understanding must take place at every level—down to the cells, and penetrating even to the root-sense of separate self. On every level where self-contraction occurs, self-understanding can also take place. When this activity, this contraction, this avoidance of relationship, is thoroughly undone, thoroughly undermined, and only Truth is lived, then something about the nature of life in the cosmic domain begins to become clear. From the "Point of View" of Truth, life is allowable and good. Perhaps one might have wished to choose another form of life—but the nature of your present form of existence (and, indeed, of all possible forms of conditionally manifested existence) becomes clear.

The avoidance of relationship is to be seen in the simple, practical observing of life, of "you alive in relationship". There is really no subtlety whatsoever to this self-observation. It is the crudest kind of self-knowledge. But, from the ordinary point of view, it is also the most unavailable—because what is to be understood is the ordinary point of view.

IV.

DEVOTEE: Is it possible, as some have said, for a person to die and then be reborn as an animal?

AVATAR ADI DA SAMRAJ: The question of reincarnation can be approached from several points of view. In the West, the most common approach has been "experimental"—the investigation of the matter through the personal experience of individuals. Through various internal and psychic means, people recollect past lives, see images of other people's lives, see their destinies, and so on. These are the usual means, particularly among Westerners, whereby people have approached such phenomena, in order to discover whether they are true (or real).

But there is another approach to this matter—and that is the Way of Divine Self-Realization, the Realization of Truth. When (by Means of My Avataric Divine Spiritual Grace), there is most perfect self-understanding, then you live only As Truth. Then you also Know what birth is, what mind is, what life is. You see that all of that is the result of tendencies subtly manifested as modifications of Conscious Light Itself—which tendencies take form in (and as) the conditionally manifested worlds. You Know this with absolute certainty. You see this clearly. Therefore, Truth is the basis of your Knowledge of all phenomena, including reincarnation. Nevertheless, you may Enjoy this Realization without the least suggestion or recollection of reincarnation in your own case—without remembering, even vaguely in a dream, a single moment of any past life. This is because Divine Self-Realization is not dependent on anything to do with birth. When you are Self-Identified with the Divine Self-Condition, you have no sense whatsoever of being born as a body, no sense whatsoever of containment—of being limited to your "own" mind, your "own" life.

If there is this kind of relationship to the apparent phenomena of your present existence, how could you possibly get involved with knowing anything at all about the past history of your dying personality? What could possibly interest you about it? How could you possibly discover anything about it? Every time you zero in on your "own" mind, you see billions of worlds and beings. How are you going to pick yourself out? Where is "you"? How do you find a destiny in the midst of the universes, when you cannot even discover your "own" life as a substantial and separate event?

Thus, in the Fullness of Truth, it is impossible for you to acquire definitive experiential knowledge about your own past or future as an apparent individual. But your Root-Awareness of the Very Structure of Existence Itself, Which Rises from the Living Divine Heart Itself, shows you clearly the Inherent Nature of all patterns, without otherwise requiring experience of (so-called) "individual" recollection, on the plane of mind.

When you examine the nature and fundamental structure of life itself, it is clear that something like regression—or apparent rebirth, in animal form, after once having lived in human form—is clearly <u>possible</u>, just as it can occur in dreams. In dreams, you can take on various forms in various worlds—and the same is true of birth in the waking realms of life. But, if you begin to become truly sensitive to your present situation, you may become terrified even of moving into this <u>human</u> condition again!

Having an affinity for plants and animals in this life is another thing altogether. The vital life of human beings is comprised of mechanisms that are also found elsewhere in conditional Nature, made of the same forces.

I have made an analogy between the human mechanism and someone walking a dog.[27] You are like a mind walking a dog. The vital mechanism is an animal and vegetal level of conscious awareness—an intelligence like that which governs the organisms and compounds of conditional Nature below the human being in the scheme of processes. Therefore, at the level of the vital, human beings have a strong affinity with animals, plants, natural phenomena, conditional Nature. Because they partake of the same functional life, the same level of life-energy, as animals and plants, human beings recognize that energy in the environment and enjoy associating with it.

Someone once asked Ramana Maharshi about the practice of retiring to the forest, as that practice is described in certain traditional texts (such as the *Bhagavad Gita*). The traditional recommendation is to establish a seat in the wilderness, in a forest area—in congenial circumstances, with streams nearby, and so on. This person asked Ramana Maharshi's permission to do this—but Ramana Maharshi pointed out that, when people go out to do this sort of thing, to get away from humanity and all of the complications of ordinary life, they begin to become fascinated with animals instead—animal life, vital life. They sympathize with it, enjoy it, and gradually become like it. As a consequence, they wind up in a worse condition than before.

The truth of the matter is that the form of relationship you tend to assume with living beings, animals, plants, conditional Nature, is a direct indication of your relationship to the vital—and that is all. If you become very sympathetic with the vital movements in yourself, the forms of vital desire, you will also tend to be very sympathetic with animals. If you tend to exploit your own vital life, you will tend also to fail to manage animals, plant life, and the like. If you resist utterly, and are vitally contracting to the point of interference with your own vital life, even with life itself, you will tend to have the same effect on other life-forms.

No one, for instance, can tolerate being disliked by a friend's pet! If you go to visit a friend, it is very upsetting if the dog does not like you, if the cat does not like you. It is very upsetting if you cannot grow plants, if flowers die quickly when placed near your bed! But all of this—your relationships to plants, to animals, to life-forms—is a precise dramatization of your relationship to the vital in your own case.

In many people who live unconsciously, the vital takes over, absorbing their lives from birth to death, and they never exceed it. You must have at least seen photographs of people who are wedded to the earth, who live in isolated farmlands. Such people seem to be unconscious—from the point of view of someone who has been brought up in cities, or in sophisticated social circumstances. They appear to be asleep in the vital, without their minds very much engaged. They do not speak very much, they are quiet, they are slow—they seem dull and unconscious.

City people, however, tend to be contracted in relation to the vital. Westerners (and "Westernized" people, in general), having been influenced by urbanization, are typically very resistive to vital life. Americans, for example, are obsessed with sex—not really obsessed with the having of sex, but with the failure of sex, and the wanting of it. There is very little actual or successful having of it, because the sexual process is so obstructed.

In the West, participation in the life-force has been undermined by Western society's bondage to the symbols of its religious path. Not that everything about the symbols of Judeo-Christian religion was actually present in the work of Jesus of Nazareth and the Hebrew men of knowledge—but it is certainly present in the religious movements that have come down through the millennia to the present day. In Judeo-Christian culture, there is a strong suppression of the vital. Thus, people in the West are trained in "vital shock" from the beginning—trained to resist their vital life, their lifeline. In the West, money, food, and sex are problematic for everybody—in the sense that there is a chronic resistance, a chronic doubt as to whether or not you are supposed to have anything to do with such things.

V.

DEVOTEE: Why is it that so many of the Eastern teachings seem to insist on celibacy as necessary for Spiritual life?

AVATAR ADI DA SAMRAJ: In the East, it is often said that life can be about either sex or God, but not both. A choice must be made. And, in a fundamental sense, this is correct. Nevertheless, it is not fruitful to take on celibacy in a strategic manner.

The traditional Indian notion of Spiritual Realization is one in which vital life has been abandoned, and one's conscious existence has returned to a "higher" State, presumably never to be reborn. Therefore, the processes by which adherents of these paths seek Realization necessarily involve the reduction of the entire pattern of vital life (and even, in the case of the Transcendentalist schools,[28] the pattern of subtle life) to the point of abandonment. Such is the precondition for Realization, in their terms.

Really, the problem of Spiritual life—for anyone, West or East—is not whether to be celibate or not. Until you understand yourself, your choices relative to emotional-sexual life are always a manifestation of your dilemma—not a manifestation of discriminative intelligence. The observation and understanding of the contraction in the vital is an absolute prerequisite for Real Spiritual life.

For the most part, conventional celibate idealism is an attempted solution to the resistance to vitality, the chronic (socially generated and socially enforced) reaction to the vital condition, to life.[29] Such strategic celibacy is, in fact, a form of de-vitalization. There can be no Spirituality without the life-force. If you suppress the life-force, you have gone back to zero. The True Spiritual process inherently makes use of the life-force and its "conductivity".

When the pattern of "conductivity" is restored, a person may, whether by tendency or by devotional impulse, be moved to become (or remain) celibate. In fact, when the circulation of energy is felt very intensely at the level of the life-vehicle, very often the sexual impulse simply disappears for various periods of time. And in the case of virtually all of My devotees, the impulse to be sexually active will (at some point) be freely and spontaneously relinquished, in the advancing course of the Way of Adidam. But the arbitrary demand to be celibate, as an absolute practice for all—in the sense of willfully enforced (and idealistic) avoidance of emotional-sexual intimacy—is not useful or appropriate.

In the earlier stages of the Way of Adidam, it is not necessary for My devotees to be celibate.[30] However, it is absolutely necessary, from the Spiritual point of view, for the dilemma in the vital to break down—and it is not just in terms of sexuality that this dilemma is manifested. It is manifested in terms of money (or exchange of life-force), food, and sex—in terms of vital life altogether.

My "Perfect Practice" devotees live from the "Point of View" of Consciousness Itself. They no longer live from the point of view of the body-mind—and, therefore, they no longer live in dilemma. Because they are no longer identified with the body-mind, and because they experience the profound Yogic Sublimity of constant devotional and Spiritual Communion with Me, they are (in virtually all cases) celibate—not as a matter of necessity, but as a matter of inevitability.[31]

Many people have what they regard to be a functional sex-life, one that is enjoyable and seems to work fine for them. But their relationship to the force of life may itself be very mediocre. They may have functional problems in other areas—diet, work (or money), relationship to the environment.

In the East, particularly in the culture of India, there is a tendency to de-vitalize, to separate from the vital. In the West, there is a tendency to exploit the vital—and, on top of that, a vast system of taboos against the vital. Thus, in relation to the vital, the West has its characteristic problem, while the East has a different characteristic problem. In the East, there is an orientation to what is beyond the vital—whereas, in the West, the orientation is to the vital. In the East, it is said that you are here for the wrong reasons—because you are suffering from illusion, you have abandoned the Truth, you have abandoned Real God. In the West, it is said that you are here because God sent you. In each case, there are characteristically different dramas at the level of ordinary life and vitality. But, from the point of view of the Real process of conscious life, responsibility for the vital is the indispensable practical foundation for the potential development of Real Spiritual life.

From day to day, human beings feel, see, experience their suffering essentially in vital terms. Therefore, the best "cave" is an ordinary life, a relational life, a functional life. That is where you find your discipline, where you become strong, where you become truly responsible for yourself. Relatedness is the necessary circumstance of Spiritual practice.

Anyone can be apparently "religious", anyone can be apparently "Spiritual"—but anyone who becomes My devotee knows how difficult and demanding True Spiritual life really is. It is easy to play imaginary games about religious and Spiritual things, but to live Spiritual life as the condition of relationship is a very difficult task. To merely think about sexual experiences, to merely think about men, women, pornography, and so on, to merely have sexual desires and images, is one thing—but to live sexuality as relationship is very difficult.

Just so, it is also very difficult to live Real Spirituality as relationship—the devotional relationship to Me. Just as there is no real sexuality without relationship, there is no Real Spirituality without relationship. There is no fulfillment of Spiritual life without the True Guru, and without life-conditions for sadhana.

In all traditional religious cultures, you will find people who are "professional" ascetics. They are not necessarily living Spiritual life any more than anyone else. In most cases, such asceticism is a form of self-indulgence. It is an expression of the failure of life. It is an expression of the contraction from life. A vital shock is the origin of all ordinary religious and Spiritual efforts. But, under the Real conditions of Spiritual life, intelligence begins to arise in relation to sexuality. The individual becomes very sensitive to the emotional-sexual process and its true nature.

Simple exploitation of sexuality is another method of trying to exhaust the contracted vital. Most people use sexuality as a means of "letting off steam", as a form of release. They are attached to the goal of conventional (or degenerative) orgasm. They manage to achieve temporary physical stasis by the expulsion (or shedding) of life-force. But My rightly practicing devotee is always conducting Energy through the Circle, with its descending and ascending arcs. My rightly practicing devotee lives all functions—both the descending (or vital) functions and the ascending (or subtle) functions—appropriately, in relationship.

When you exercise sexual energy out of relationship (or purely for the sake of degenerative orgasm), when you simply exploit it, then you only empty yourself—and you discover that you suffer as a result. Thus, My rightly practicing devotee has simply become intelligent. When you become thus intelligent, your way of life is not a result of strategic preferences to be lifeless or sexless. You become capable of relationship, capable of the real use of the vital functions. You know when not to use them, and how not to indulge or exploit them. You allow the force of life to conduct itself fully. You are free of the impulse (caused by the contraction in the vital) to merely waste the lifeforce by vital means. You are not compelled to enjoy the life-force exclusively in the belly or exclusively in the sex organs. You can enjoy it in the top of the head. You can enjoy it in the face. You can enjoy it in the spine. There are all kinds of places where you can enjoy it. The more you advance in the Real Spiritual process, the more you become capable of enjoyment. You discover the source of life-energy—such that you do not weaken yourself, you do not become involved in a pattern that only empties you, that weakens and (ultimately) kills you.

At some point in the maturing stages of the Spiritual process, there is a spontaneous Yogic process that can be felt in the sex organs, in which the life-force that normally becomes sexstimulation is felt going in the opposite direction, upwards (rather than downwards) in the spinal line.[32] Instead of seeking release in the sex-function by going "down and out", that energy can be felt pulling (or drawing) upwards in the spinal line. When that particular process is intensely active, there is a kind of natural (or motiveless) celibacy. Then, even in the context of intimate emotional-sexual relationship, the event of sexual activity is spontaneously relinquished, and the relational force of love and shared pleasure is greatly intensified.[33]

As it is traditionally understood, the Kundalini process is closely associated with what is otherwise felt as sex-energy. However, the Kundalini does not, in fact, originate from the sex organs and is not (itself) literally or exclusively sex-energy. The traditional (and, as I have Revealed,[34] incomplete) understanding of the Kundalini is as a process of ascending Energy—and, as such, the Kundalini is to be understood as the ascending aspect (or spinal line) of the Circle. That ascending current of Energy is a continuation of the "conductivity" of the descending Force. The bodily base (or muladhar) is the turning point, the point at which Energy completes its descent down the frontal line of the body-mind and begins to ascend through the spinal line. But, contrary to the traditional point of view, the bodily base is not the <u>origin</u> of the Kundalini Energy Itself.

The intense Yogic phenomena that may be experienced in My Avataric Divine Company are, in some cases, associated with the ascent of Energy—but, as a general rule, they are more often associated with the Descent of My Spirit-Force (or Ruchira Shakti). A person who is experiencing a period of strong kriyas, or some such episode of intense Yogic activity, will often (quite naturally) be celibate during that time. Or the person will discover that, while going through this process, indulgence in degenerative orgasm gives rise to certain unpleasant conditions, physiologically and psychically.

Therefore, in the process of Satsang with Me, you learn, through your study of My Wisdom-Teaching relative to (and your own direct experience with) processes of this kind, how to deal with (and, in due course, transcend) your emotional-sexual bondage. Whether or not to engage (or to continue engaging) a sexually active intimate relationship is a decision that should take into account not only one's own qualities but also the qualities of one's (potential or actual) partner (as well as the potential or actual qualities of the intimacy itself). For My devotees, that decision should not be merely a matter of the ordinary preference to indulge in the pleasures of sexual activity—nor should it be a matter of attempting to fulfill a conventional ascetical ideal of "how it is supposed to be if you are getting Spiritual".

The ultimate result of the traditional effort to separate from vital life (including the right "conductivity" of sexual energy) is physical death. The goal of traditional Yogic practice is to cause the life-force to ascend up the spinal line, draw up completely into the sahasrar, and never come down again. That is precisely what the traditional Yogi—whose point of view is willful (or strategic, or life-negative) celibacy—is trying to do. Thus, the traditional Yogi is trying to die consciously—and literally.

Now, the Yogic process of "Spiritual death" will take place in any case, whether you have literal separation from life as your particular goal or not. <u>True</u> celibacy is <u>Yogic</u> (or <u>Spiritual</u>) "death"—not physical death. Yogic "death" is a characteristic of formal renunciation in the Way of Adidam,[35] but it does not (in and of itself) imply the literal end of life or the diminution of life-involvement. Continued living of an ordinary, functional life on every level is entirely compatible with the Realized State, because life itself is an expression of Reality. Life itself is a manifestation of the Divine Conscious Light. In any particular case, life has taken on its particular manifestation because of certain tendencies (which are all simply modifications of Conscious Light)—but, in and of itself, life is not false. Only its presumed complications are false. The Life of Truth is entirely compatible with an appropriately conservative and disciplined functional life.

The bellies of the Yogic Siddhas are often full, soft, and round. The Siddhas are not devitalized beings, even if they are celibate. That swelling of the abdomen is a Yogic manifestation. When the Spiritual Energy is fully conducted, the abdomen becomes Yogically full of Energy. Bhagavan Nityananda of Ganeshpuri was such a Yogi. He spent His days sitting and lying around, letting this Spiritual Current circle about. He rarely allowed It to turn outwards. That is why He did not speak much.

Speech is a form of sacrifice. Speech is a sacrifice of the life-force—not a form of entertainment. People generally talk in order to empty themselves. Such speech is another form of throwing the life-force out of the vital contraction so that the self-contraction is not suffered so strongly. Whenever there is speech, whenever there is communication with the environment, whenever there is the enactment of relationship, whenever there is use of the life-force, there is sacrifice.

Sexuality is a form of sacrifice. It <u>does</u> tend to make you empty, unless you fully know how to conduct its energy regeneratively. If I sat here and talked endlessly, occasionally going to sleep and taking food here, the talking alone would eventually kill Me. I would die from speech! Any exploitation of the life-force will kill a person—and people are, in fact, dying from such abuse of themselves. People are dying from their own complex exploitation of the life-force. They do not conduct it. They only use it. They do not refresh themselves. They do not live this Circuit of Energy even a little bit.

Some Yogis have devoted themselves entirely to living this Circuit—and that required them to leave human society. Others continued to be communicative at the level of life, in various ways—knowing the consequences, knowing what they needed to do in order to remain fresh.

My Own Current of Divine Spirit-Energy is Flowing Continuously in This Body-Mind—and, as It Flows, even the cells are Transformed.

VI.

AVATAR ADI DA SAMRAJ: The death of a Great Siddha (of whatever Real degree) does not really represent that one's separation from anyone or anything. The Siddha-Guru is simply disappeared into Samadhi. After death, Samadhi Itself has become the "body" of the Siddha-Guru. The Siddha-Guru's devotees continue to have access to their Guru through meditation, because Samadhi Itself is the Siddha-Guru's True Form. At death, the Siddha-Guru simply abandons bodily function, outward movement, and psycho-physical Play—remaining Present as his or her most profound State of Realization. The Siddha-Guru was already in that State previously—but, at death, the peripheral functions that were attached to that State are abandoned (at least, those functions which were the manifestation of the Siddha-Guru's present lifetime).

This is why the samadhi site (or burial site) of the Siddha-Guru is prized—because, both while alive and at death, the Siddha-Guru has entered into meditation in its most intense form while associated with that body. Indeed, many people find that the Force Communicated from the Siddha-Guru seems to become even stronger after the Siddha-Guru's physical death, because that Force is now completely free of the complications involved in associating with the life-form. Therefore, at death, the Siddha-Guru has moved into the most intense manifestation of his or her characteristic Realization.

It is said that Saint Jnaneshwar[36] consciously took mahasamadhi.[37] He was a young man, only about twenty years old. He had a tomb built for himself, and he went down inside it and sat in his chair. The tomb was sealed, and he never came out. It is also said that, about three hundred years later, another Indian Saint somehow got into Jnaneshwar's tomb and approached the body. He reported that the body was apparently still alive. It had a certain heat to it, and it was not the least decomposed—because the Yogic activity going on in the body was perpetual.

The site of Jnaneshwar's tomb is a very potent one—not that Jnaneshwar himself is conscious of associating with that body anymore. When I visited Ganeshpuri in the years 1968 through 1970, Bhagavan Nityananda's tomb was also like that—very strong.

DEVOTEE: Can a Guru who has died still be Guru for the living?

AVATAR ADI DA SAMRAJ: After physical death, the only limitation on the Guru's Function is at the level of life. Obviously, the Guru cannot, after death, function in any manner that requires a physical presence.

The Current of Spiritual Force continues to be emanated by such great beings after physical death. At times, people appear to experience contact, on a subtle level, with great beings who are no longer physically alive. In My own experience, there have been very concrete and complex experiences of the subtle influence of Bhagavan Nityananda, Ramana Maharshi, Sai Baba of Shirdi, and others. Similarly, because My visits with Baba Muktananda were only occasional, My experiences of Him were most often of a subtle (although perfectly concrete) variety, arising entirely apart from the gross physical medium.[38] Just so, My Own Work with My devotees occurs fundamentally at a subtle level, even while I am alive in physical Form.

DEVOTEE: You have said that all people are suffering. I have the feeling that You and the Gurus of Your Lineage and all the Great Siddhas are the only people who are not suffering.

AVATAR ADI DA SAMRAJ: The only beings who are not suffering are those who are living the Truth. Truth Is Reality Itself. Truth Is the Ultimate Nature of all beings and the Very Nature of all life. Truth already Is all human beings. When I see people in the world, I do not see them as all screwed up, simply insane, as some kind of "nothingness" that I am supposed (for some reason or other) to turn into Divinity. I see everyone as already that same Reality.

But I also see that people are suffering. Even while they are (in Reality) only being Truth, I see them suffering. The fact that they are suffering does not make them any less the Truth, any less the Same "Thing" That Is all beings, all things. It simply means that they are suffering. If you look at all beings from the "Point of View" of Truth, there is only Truth.

From the point of view of human beings, all this seems very serious—because their point of view is the point of view of limitation. But once you yourself begin to see things from the "Point of View" of Truth, you see that every thing and every one is Always Already Truth. To Realize that you already inhere in Truth does not make you greater than anyone else. It makes you the same as everyone else. That Sameness is the Sameness of Very Truth, the Sameness out of Which all the functional inequalities of relative, conditional existence arise.

DEVOTEE: It seems that, from the "Point of View" of Truth, the process of being born eventually causes an automatic reaction that is death.

AVATAR ADI DA SAMRAJ: "For every action, there is an equal and opposite reaction." The action of being born produces the reaction of living, even to the point of death.

DEVOTEE: It seems that we are born with three strikes against us.[39]

AVATAR ADI DA SAMRAJ: Yes. That is why you have to get smart down here! A living being arising in the midst of life is automatically the reaction to the preceding action, which is life itself. It is entirely a natural mechanism. If reaction is the only principle of life, it realizes only death. The automatic tendency of organic life is to contract—to become more and more solid, to the point of lifelessness. Whatever is alive begins to die from the moment it makes its appearance. And there are more than three strikes against you. You are already "out"—already, before the strikes.

I have no taste for the usual life. Not that I cannot enjoy some of the qualities of life, but I simply have no taste for this entire affair of suffering and compulsive existence. I see perfectly well what it depends on. I would not choose, on the merits of the experience itself, ever to be born in this human condition again. There is no advantage in it. It does not gain anything. It is just a period of time in which to understand. Apart from that, it has no ultimate value. It never becomes anything more than that.

Human life is not particularly delightful. It is an endless concern, from birth until death. Every minute is suffering of the limited state, or an attempt to break out of it through various kinds of activity, trying to find the answer. From the first moment of born awareness, this life _is_ a question. It seems absurd to be actually existing and, yet, not know what actually existing is, and to spend the entire period of actually existing trying to discover what actually existing is!

This is an insane condition! It is a compulsive tour of unconscious activity—for the most part. If Truth begins to Manifest in life, as life, then It Glorifies life to some degree. But the Glory that Enters life is not that of life itself. It is the Glory of the Fullness of Truth—Which is Manifested as life, Whose modifications are life.

The more the life of Truth grows, the more taste for Truth you acquire—not for life apart from (or other than) Truth. When Truth is Most Perfectly Enjoyed, life becomes secondary—perhaps profound, but unnecessary. Your "death" in Truth should precede your physical death by at least a few moments! Otherwise, the tendency to regain this same condition is automatically there.

The Condition That Is Truth is far superior to the limitation that is conditionally manifested existence. Those who live Truth while alive are not glorifying life in and of itself. They are glorifying Truth. When you Enjoy Truth, you are already Free. And if you are Free, what does all of this compulsive limitation have to do with you? If you are Free, you simply live Truth until the moment of death—and beyond.

To be Divinely Outshined in Truth is the ultimate destiny of all who resort to Me most profoundly. I already Know Who you Are. I am already Living with you in another sense—as Real Life, as Love, as Truth. I Know that there is far more to reality than mere physical existence. I look forward to your Most Perfect Divine Enlightenment. But I see that those who are living in the Earth plane are not clear about all of this, not certain of it—rather confused. So I Communicate Truth in as many forms as I can. My Single Impulse is to Relieve you of your presumed life of separateness, to draw you out of darkness into Light.

The process of meditation in Satsang with Me is not unlike the death process. The same process goes on in the spontaneous meditation that happens in death. The difference is that, in death, the life-force permanently moves out of the vital mechanism, whereas, in meditation, and (ultimately) in Most Perfect Divine Enlightenment (or seventh stage Sahaja Nirvikalpa Samadhi), the life-force continues to conduct itself in the physical body. When you have lived the entire process and Know it, you Know very well that you are not merely physically alive. You Know absolutely well that the fact of being physically alive is not any kind of real limitation. This is absolutely clear. It is not merely something you believe, something you think. When the entire process has been fulfilled, then you are already "dead", presently "dead"—in other words, no longer presuming to be identified with the limitation that is the psycho-physical life, the body. One who lives as that limitation is still afraid. If you presume that you are alive as the limitation of life, then you are busy hysterically doing all the things that occupy seekers.

When (by Means of My Avataric Divine Spiritual Grace) ego-"death" occurs, such that Truth is the only "Point of View", then there is no more of the search. Then there is only the creative living of this process in relation to other beings—and that Activity is continuous, most perfect. No identification with embodiment, no identification with the life-force, no identification with the subtle forms of existence, no identification with the levels of mind, with thoughts, with visions, with lights, with phenomena of any kind—none of that is lived.

Such is the paradox of My Divinely Enlightened devotee. Such a one is as if asleep even while awake. While awake—while the conditionally manifested forms are flying around, while the body hangs out and all the feelings and sensations are there, while the thoughts are running along—My Divinely Enlightened devotee has no sense at all of any containment, any limitation. My Divinely Enlightened devotee does not have to stop the thought-process in order to be free of thoughts. The Samadhi of My Divinely Enlightened devotee is Most Perfect, never-ending. The entire life-phenomenon takes on a kind of indefinite, fluid, non-differentiated quality, a paradoxical form, a kind of brilliance—such that life loses its apparent capability to define existence, to define even Consciousness Itself.

When (by Means of My Avataric Divine Spiritual Grace) you most perfectly understand, then everything conditional is Divinely Self-Recognized as a modification of the Divine Conscious Light. Then you have nothing left but True Humor while alive, and that Humor is of a "radical" kind. This does not mean that you are necessarily always laughing. Rather, your True Humor is of the nature of no-identification with all of this.

When (by Means of My Avataric Divine Spiritual Grace) you most perfectly understand, then your Freedom is extreme—so far beyond the point of wildness that you are no longer wild. Then your extremes are manifested as ordinariness. Your extremes are in your natural appearance. From the point of view of Divine Enlightenment, simply to walk into a room is a maddening extreme. It is odd. It is wildly imaginative!

When (by Means of My Avataric Divine Spiritual Grace) you most perfectly understand, the Contemplation of Consciousness Itself (as your Inherent, and Inherently egoless, Self-Identity) may tend to draw you into the Love-Bliss-Full Obliviousness of body, mind, and world. Therefore, in order to maintain a life in the world, you look at people, you talk, you do ordinary things—because everything has become insubstantial and unnecessary for you.

When (by Means of My Avataric Divine Spiritual Grace) you most perfectly understand, then your Love-Bliss-Fullness exceeds all of the conditional Yogic states, all of the phenomena of Spirituality—because even those states are limited conditions, strategically induced modifications of your subjectivity.

When (by Means of My Avataric Divine Spiritual Grace) you most perfectly understand, then you have lost the taste, the motive, for mere experiencing. Then you live only from the "Point of View" of the Unmodified Reality, without attachment to lights, sounds, forms, or qualities of any kind—and, yet, without strategically excluding any of these potential forms of phenomenal experience—because (by Means of My Avataric Divine Spiritual Grace) you have Most Perfectly Realized that <u>everything</u> is merely a modification of that Same Unmodified Reality.

Therefore, when (by Means of My Avataric Divine Spiritual Grace) you most perfectly understand, it is in your living the True Humor of Formlessness—the qualityless characteristic of Existence Itself—that you, paradoxically, Live. Then all life is paradox—and life is no longer a question. Then there is not the least trace of dilemma left in the universe. Then you have no question, and no answer. Then you are only Humorous.

In many traditional cultures, certain individuals (of one or another degree of actual religious or Spiritual advancement) would take on the role of the fool. They would act "crazy", so that people would not burden them with demands for wisdom. Indeed, in their true depth, these "fools" really did not have anything to say. They just enjoyed bubbling in the street.

Truly, "Bubbling" is, ultimately, what even My Own Avataric Divine Work is all about. Working with people at the life-level, the vital level, tends to become very humorless—because people are very serious about their life-problems. People are always obsessed with their current crisis, their "revolution" this week, their game. From their point of view, all of that is very serious, very disturbing—and rightfully so. But to humorlessly "deal with it", to manufacture seriousness relative to all of that, has none of the beauty of "Bubbling". Therefore, I Act in forms that Freely express My Own Divinely Self-"Bright" State.

Traditionally, those who play the "fool" become (from the conventional point of view) very "odd"—and everything they do becomes a symbol for their own Realized State. Just so, everything that anyone does symbolizes his or her own state. Therefore, fundamentally, I simply Manifest My Own Inherently Free State, as a Playful Activity.

AVATAR ADI DA SAMRAJ
Adidam Samrajashram, 2003

5.
Walking the Dog

DEVOTEE: Beloved Lord, would You please explain what You mean by "relationship"?

AVATAR ADI DA SAMRAJ: What do you think it means?

DEVOTEE: I am not sure. Perhaps simply not to avoid reality.

AVATAR ADI DA SAMRAJ: What is relationship?

DEVOTEE: To be with someone is to be in relationship. Talking to You is being in relationship.

AVATAR ADI DA SAMRAJ: What if there is no one there?

DEVOTEE: Then we are in relationship to our surroundings, and to ourselves.

AVATAR ADI DA SAMRAJ: What if there is no thing there?

DEVOTEE: Then we are in relationship to no thing.

AVATAR ADI DA SAMRAJ: Then what is the problem about relationship?

DEVOTEE: I guess I am trying to dig into it and grasp something that is not there.

AVATAR ADI DA SAMRAJ: What is <u>not</u> relationship?

DEVOTEE: It seems to me there isn't anything that is not relationship.

AVATAR ADI DA SAMRAJ: Did you appear on your own?

DEVOTEE: No. Not that I know of!

AVATAR ADI DA SAMRAJ: Is there any thing that arises on its own?

DEVOTEE: No.

AVATAR ADI DA SAMRAJ: Is there any thing absolutely (or inherently) separate from any other thing?

DEVOTEE: Intellectually, I may think there is, but I do not really think of things as separate.

AVATAR ADI DA SAMRAJ: Do you think of yourself as being separate?

DEVOTEE: Yes, I am afraid that is my state. I am <u>thinking</u> of myself as separate.

AVATAR ADI DA SAMRAJ: <u>That</u> is the point! There is only relatedness. No separateness—only mutuality, interdependence. If anything has arisen, there is only relatedness. Yet, most of the time, you do not observe that fact, you do not <u>observe</u> relatedness. Most of your time is spent being obsessed with your separateness.

This separateness is not true. But, all the time, you are <u>thinking</u> this separateness. All the time, you are acting as if it were so. All the time, you are meditating on it. All the time, you are seeking to become free of it. And, yet, of all the things that arise, this thought of separate self is truly the least valuable—and it is utterly untrue. Therefore, you must observe and understand the presumption of your separateness.

If I ask, "What is there?", you might think: "This space. I move around in it. I am this one." When you think about that, it does not strike fear in you. You live that, with a grin on your face, as if it were so. But that is not the problem. The problem is that that "I" is suffering, that "I" is in dilemma, that "I" needs this, that "I" has not Realized this, that "I . . .", that "I . . .", that "I . . .".

This sense of separate existence, this self-contracted form of conscious awareness, is suffering—and it is obviously so to everyone, whenever they fail to be distracted and so fall only into the mood and condition of separate, mortal existence.

But Truth is not the destruction of that "I". Truth is not the suppression, the quieting, or the explosion of that "I", nor the union of that "I" with anything. Truth is not <u>anything</u> done to that "I", or with it. Truth is in the spontaneous observation and understanding of the entire process by means of which this "I", this separate-self-sense, appears.

Therefore, Truth is not a conditional state. Truth is not a state of inwardness, of attachment to mindlessness, quietness, or formlessness, nor of attachment to visions or lights, to sensations (whether gross or subtle). Truth is in the "radical" understanding of all of that. Truth is in the understanding of your entire adventure—which is a span of possible conditions, ranging from the depths of human suffering to the world-excluding Bliss of contemplating the Transcendental Self.

But Truth Itself Is Perfect Simplicity. Truth Itself <u>Is</u> Reality Itself, Which <u>Is</u> the Only <u>Real</u> God. In Truth, there is no "thing"! Reality Itself cannot be known as an "Object" (not even an <u>Ultimate</u> "Object")—as if It were "outside" your own apparent conscious awareness—because you are not (and cannot be) separate from Reality. Just so, Truth Itself can only be Realized in present time—because Truth Itself is Always Already the Case.

Understanding is simply the observation of your own activity of separation, your own activity of self-contraction. You must <u>really</u> observe it. When you really observe the self-contraction, then only relationship stands out. To truly observe the self-contraction is to <u>see</u> what it is—not just as a symptom (the sense that "I am separate", or "I am suffering", or any other form of thinking-thinking). But to <u>actually</u> observe the self-contraction is to comprehend it as the avoidance of relationship. To observe and understand this separate-self-sense is to be turned to the Real (and, necessarily, Conscious) condition of relationship.

The Real condition of conscious awareness is not the "me". The Real condition of conscious awareness is not, in any sense, the feeling of being separate, the perception of things as apparently separate, or the feeling of the dilemma of being apparently separate. Rather, the Real condition of conscious awareness is no-contraction, no-dilemma. Instead of this turning away, there is inherent relatedness. There is all of this connection, all of this relationship! The Real (or True) condition is no-obsession with self-contraction, no-obsession with the "me" of egoity, no-obsession with all of "that" (presumed to be separate from the "me"). Simply no-contraction. When there is no contraction, then what is there? There is only relationship, presently enjoyed as the Real (and effortless) condition of conscious awareness.

And when the Real condition of conscious awareness is Enjoyed as it is, as unqualified relatedness—not in relationship, but as relationship—then it is also seen that relatedness contains no "other" and no "me".

There is a fundamental quality that you are familiar with all the time in your ordinary occupation—when you are feeling others, feeling connected, participating in relationship in the simplest sense. That quality is the natural quality of conscious awareness. It is your own natural manifestation! Conscious awareness is not "in" relationship, experiencing an "other". Conscious awareness is (itself) relationship. Therefore, when (by Means of My Avataric Divine Spiritual Grace) you Realize Most Perfect Enjoyment of no-contraction, then there is only Consciousness Itself. Indeed, you have never experienced a single moment of involvement with anything but Consciousness Itself. All of the time you spend thinking that you are observing the presumed "objective world", and thinking that all of this is "outside" yourself, you are actually observing the endless modifications of Consciousness Itself. But, as long as you are busy separating yourself—contracting, avoiding relationship—the Force of Consciousness Itself appears as "me". And that is the dilemma.

The usual person is (to some extent) capable of observing—although only in the intellectual or mental sense—that the universe is a vast field of interconnected events, phenomena, forces. Nevertheless, the usual person remains continually, chronically, obsessed with the notion of being separate, self-contained, isolated—containing only twenty watts, always becoming empty, threatened to death, becoming more and more compacted, until he or she disappears. To live in such a manner is to fail to live on the basis of your own observation. In that case, you continue to remain obsessed—and the adventures of obsessed human beings are endless. There are endless ways to play life—but, no matter how you play it, none of it truly makes any sense whatsoever.

I am continually impressed—newly impressed from hour to hour—by the insanity of human beings. Animals, plants, and even inert things have much more intelligence! They are simpler, more pure. When you see people walking their dogs, the dogs almost invariably appear more intelligent than the people who are walking them. The guy walking his dog seems insane. He is obsessed with his idiotic program of existence. But the dog is just breathing, walking, pissing on the grass. No sign of disturbance at all. The dog sits down at the corner, and you see his <u>clear eyes</u>! But the guy is everywhere else—costumed, crowded into time, bent, driven, mysterious even to himself.

The only release from the burden of the insanity of this world is True Humor. There are two forms of humor. There is ordinary (or mortal) humor, and there is True (or Divine) Humor. Ordinarily, the best that most people are capable of is ordinary, mortal humor. You were just laughing, for example, at the image of the man and the dog. But the only True Humor is Truth Itself.

The ordinary comic humor of your mortal appreciation of things is only laughter. It does not change the conditions of existence or even truly understand them. Mortal laughter does not change the condition of human beings, apart from generating a little temporary amusement. But Divine Humor—Truth—delights people, and also utterly Transforms their lives.

Until this Divine Humor, this Truth, Awakens in people, they are intimidated by the vital force of life—as it appears in animals, for instance. Without a little of Truth, human beings are not even manly enough (man or woman) to be the master of a dog. A good dog is too straight for most people—and I have met very few people who could master a cat! Just so, people are intimidated by their own vital nature, their own desires, the movement in their own life.

People relate to animals (or vitally based beings) as extensions of their own human vitality. Every human being is endlessly "walking a dog". The animal hangs below your chest, and you walk it night and day. You are intimidated by it, completely obsessed with it, absolutely distracted by it, incapable of being the master of it, unwilling to go through the period of mastery, of training, of responsibility—and, so, the "dog" takes over.

When people visit their friends, they all sit around and talk about the dog! Have you noticed that, whenever somebody has a pet, people who visit tend to continually talk about the animal, and to the animal? And, when the conversation drifts away from the pets, people talk about the same thing in themselves. They talk about sex, conflict, desire—their vital obsessions.

People are always talking about the dog. Therefore, people are ordinarily humorless. They have no True Humor. The only thing they know how to do is to animate the ridiculous, as a means of entertaining one another. The usual entertainments are forms of mortal (or comic) humor. The means to make others laugh is to take on the form—or put on the "costume"—of the dog. Put on a dog costume and go to visit a friend. He will not be able to believe it. Fantastic! He will laugh. He will go out of his mind.

There are many forms of the "dog", many varieties of the "dog costume". The "dog costume" is all of your adventures, your acquisitions, your knowledge, your everything—"you". The self-contraction is the "dog costume". It is the avoidance of relation-ship—this falsity, this thinking separation.

But True Humor is not to appear in the "dog costume" among your friends. I must restore True Humor by showing you the nature of the "costume" of your mortality, your un-Happiness, all the forms of the self-contraction, the avoidance of relationship.

Ordinary humor is a revulsion, like vomiting. It is to heave the vital force upwards, throw it away, cast it out. All the ordinary obsessions, including the entertainments of comic laughter, are forms of revulsion—like vomiting. When such revulsion occurs, the force of life falls down the spine and is thrown out of the body-mind.

But, when (as My devotee) you understand the self-contracting activity that is the root of your obsession, then all of the activities of revulsion tend to subside, and the natural life-energy (and, in the case of My by-Me-Spiritually-Awakened devotees, My Avatarically Self-Transmitted Divine Spirit-Energy) resumes its natural course in the Circle of the body-mind (descending in the frontal line, and ascending in the spinal line). Such is the natural "conductivity" of Energy. But, in the usual individual, this "conductivity" tends to be interrupted, and even reversed.

In the ordinary person, the "dog" is always hanging out. The ordinary person always appears as the ridiculous imitation of the "dog". But, when you understand your own ego-activity, then the "dog" is overcome, the "dog" is mastered.

The usual person is always distracted, always concentrating on some invisible point, obsessed with self-awareness and the sense of separateness, distracted in endless thoughts, concerns, experiences. People are simply obsessed, distracted—only fascinated. What is amazing—in this manifestation of billions of beings, including billions of human beings—is that you can appear to be born among so many and yet have so little company for a lifetime. Because every one is <u>obsessed</u>! Every one is moving in this direction, that direction, the other direction—at light-speed.

I once worked as a chaplain in a mental hospital. In such places, you see the ego-games of ordinary human beings played out in extremely exaggerated form. There is <u>no</u> communication between people in such an asylum. Indeed, the disturbance of communication (or presently engaged relationship) is, perhaps, the identifying characteristic of insanity. Thus, the True Guru appears in the asylum of ordinary people. And what is My Function as the True Divine Guru? It is to distract you, to stand before you and command attention, to draw you into relationship, to draw you out of your chronic obsession.

That will not happen to you while you are sitting alone in your room, meditating on your "inner self"! What are you looking at, in this turning inward? The same thing that you are <u>always</u> looking at. The same obsession. The usual meditator is just another obsessed person, unaware of relationship as his or her actual living condition. Therefore, My Function as the True Guru is to continuously draw you into conscious relationship. I Work to draw the thread of attention back into the fabric of life. And, when the connection is made again, when relationship is consciously lived, then the energy of life returns, flows, tends to move into its natural course again.

Therefore, in Satsang with Me, there is the intensification of life-energy—until the time arrives when My devotee is no longer totally distracted, no longer totally obsessed, no longer totally inward-turning, but enjoying equanimity, tacitly aware of related-ness. When that occurs, then (by Means of My Avataric Divine Spiritual Grace) insight can take place.

Self-understanding is always a very practical insight. You see the avoidance of relationship, if only in one particular form of activity. In that particular form of your chronic activity, you see the characteristic activity of your own avoidance. You observe it very directly, without complication, as your actual activity. In that instant, you simultaneously see both your own activity of avoid-ance and the Real condition of relationship itself. You see your uncomplicated, natural state—and you see yourself contracting. Only then has practical wisdom arisen.

The very functions that people ordinarily perceive to be their bondage, their suffering, are the Means of their Divine Liberation, when brought to them in the form of My Avatarically-Born bodily (human) Divine Form. In Me, these functions are Open, and the Fullness, the Force, the "Brightness" of Truth Manifests in and through them. Those who formally embrace the devotional rela-tionship to Me participate in the process of Intensification that Flows from Me to My devotee. My devotee becomes intelligent with that Intensity—because My Avataric Divine Self-Transmission Is the Divine Shakti of Truth, the Living Power of Real God.

My Divine Heart-Shakti (or Hridaya-Shakti, or Ruchira Shakti) is not the Kundalini Shakti, which is presumed (in the traditions of Yoga) to be always returning to Truth, seeking the Truth, seeking the union that is Truth. The Divine Shakti That I Transmit is Always <u>Already</u> Truth. It Is (Itself) the Very Force of Truth. It Is the Divine Spirit-Force That Is Always Already Truth.

When My Divine Heart-Shakti in-Fills the body-mind of My devotee, various Spiritual phenomena may also be experienced. However, no matter what Spiritual phenomena do (or do not) arise in your experience, the key to the practice of the Way of Adidam is the heart-relationship to Me, the Condition of Satsang with Me. Satsang with Me is the Great Condition, the Only Condition. It is Always Already the Condition in Which you are arising—but, because of self-contraction, It is not lived. It is denied, forgotten, resisted.

The drama of "Narcissus" is what obsesses all human beings. Therefore, the Great Condition of Satsang is denied in all the usual circumstances of the world. Thus, I have Appeared in the world— to Establish the possibility of Satsang with Me, and to make possible the understanding of the egoic strategies that prevent It. I Establish the opportunity of Satsang with Me (the True Divine Guru), by virtue of My Own Siddhi (or Divine Spiritual Power) of Truth. Even from the beginning, My true devotee intuits Satsang with Me to be the Very Condition of Existence Itself.

Therefore, for My devotee, Real Spiritual life is founded in Satsang with Me. Sadhana is to live the Condition of Satsang with Me for a lifetime, even eternally—always recollecting that Condition, living in It, becoming intelligent with It. Right functional life is to live the Real condition of relationship in all circumstances, while remaining in Satsang with Me at all times. When such sadhana is lived consciously, moment to moment, you have something against which to observe your own self-contraction, the ongoing pattern of "Narcissus". Thus, Satsang with Me is the Condition that makes it possible for you to see your own tendencies.

Your tendencies are always forms of self-contraction, the avoidance of relationship—which, ultimately, is always (in the case of My devotee) a matter of turning away from Satsang with Me. Every day, hour to hour, an endless drama goes on in "Narcissus". The drama never seems to end. There is the continual wondering in the mind: "Should I surrender—or shouldn't I? I don't want to put up with this anymore—or do I? Don't I really have it already? The Presence always surrounds me already. And my Guru's demands are crazy, anyway!" Every day there is a new conception of self-sufficiency, a new "temptation" away from Satsang with Me and the discipline of Truth.

Therefore, as My beginning devotee, you must become sensitive to what you are "up to". You must observe and understand your own game. Previously, you were only "played" by life—and now you are the one "playing" your life-situation by ritualizing your drama of non-surrender in relation to Me. The purpose of Satsang with Me is not to make you forget the drama of your suffering. I have not come to console you with pleasant and hopeful distractions. I always Function to return you to clear observation of your own activity of avoidance.

Satsang with Me does not fulfill your search. By persistently frustrating your search, Satsang with Me requires you to confront your dilemma, so that it may be understood. The Power of Intensification that is Alive in Satsang with Me is Active in the very seat of dilemma. The Force of Satsang with Me operates in the dilemma. The crisis in conscious awareness is sadhana. Enduring the suffering and embracing the ego-transcending process is sadhana.

Sadhana is not merely pleasantness. It is not the easy, drifty-blissful, smiling, and stupid meditation of someone sitting cross-legged in a "dog costume". Sadhana is living intelligence—Conscious with great intensity, in the midst of apparent dilemma. Sadhana in My Company makes a difference!

It is not that, as My devotee, you should not go through the dilemma of your suffering. You must go through it. It is only that, even though you are going through it, you should continue to maintain yourself in the Condition of Satsang with Me. The greatest mistake people make is to abandon Satsang with Me when they begin to experience Its "tooth". No—this crisis in relation to Satsang Itself must occur. It occurs in everyone's case, now or later—and it occurs in an incredibly powerful and persuasive form, usually very soon after you begin to experience My

Demand. It always involves the feeling that you should abandon Satsang with Me, abandon this "Crazy" Guru.

The first form of this crisis is always a personal conflict with the Way Itself and with the gathering of My devotees. If you get through that form of crisis and stay, then the next crisis comes in the form of self-doubt (rather than Guru-doubt): "It's not working for me. This sadhana is not possible in my case. I'm damned. I'm too crazy. I'm not ready for it." But, if you get beyond these two forms of crisis, from then on (for the most part) you have become capable of dealing with all such phenomena as qualities of your hidden strategy—the avoidance of relationship, the drama of "Narcissus".

When, as My devotee, you become capable of enduring this repetitive crisis, when you are able to live it as sadhana, as the Real process in My Avataric Divine Company, then the Intelligence Communicated in Satsang with Me fills your life with Its Intensity, and profound insight becomes possible. But most fundamental self-understanding can arise only if the Condition of Satsang with Me is not abandoned.

"Narcissus" endlessly abandons Satsang with Me. That is his business, his role in life. That is also what the ordinary person is "up to". The ordinary person is always abandoning the living condition of relationship.

Many so-called "Spiritual" seekers are just "Narcissus" in drag! They do not have enough gut for Spiritual life. They are not interested in the demand that is the True Guru. They are "dogs" who come to their master only for a "bone".[40] A dog whose mind is set on the bone his master has will do any ridiculous thing to acquire it. The dog rolls on the ground and whines and barks and jumps through hoops. He does whatever he must, until his master gives him the bone. Then the dog runs away with the bone. He does not want to see anybody. He does not want anybody around him when he is chewing his bone. He does not want to be touched. He does not want to be approached. He makes a vital circle around himself, and he just works on his bone. And, if it is a good, big bone, such that he cannot eat it all in one sitting, he usually hides it somewhere, to protect it, after he has finished his chew.

The dog does not go back to his master again until he is out of bone. He does not go to his master in order to be with the master, to delight in the master, to be mastered by the master. He only goes for another bone. Such is the ordinary Spiritual seeker. "Give me Initiation into your Yoga. Give me the secret mantra. Give me the breathing exercise. Teach me the 'Kriya Yoga'. Give me Shaktipat. Give me the Divine Vision." The guy always asks for the "bone"!

Should he actually be granted one of those things (any one of the traditional forms of Initiation will do—mantras, energies, beliefs, and so on), the guy goes. He leaves to play his game with that technique or consolation. He consumes it in solitude. He does not want to be touched. He does not want to be interrupted. He does not want to be reminded of what is "outside" himself, that would require him to be in relationship.

I wait for My true devotee to come and surrender to Me. Satsang with Me is the relationship between My devotee and Me— not between the "dog" and his "bone". The relationship to Me is Satsang. That is the discovery. That is the process. That relationship is the Yoga.

The relationship between Guru and devotee is the Secret pointed to by the Great Siddhas. It is the esoteric Universal Process. It is the Single Means. It is Very Truth. Everything else— all "bone"-chewing—is only a ritual re-enactment of the process that occurs spontaneously and is alive only in relation to the Guru. At best, it is a ritual re-enactment. Therefore, True Spiritual life is not the activity of Spiritual seekers. It is the activity of those who discover their Spiritual search is false, fruitless, founded in dilemma—a manifestation of the same suffering that all other human beings are suffering. True Spiritual life begins when the Spiritual search is abandoned and Satsang with Me is begun.

And Satsang with Me is a difficult Condition, a Spiritual discipline that must be lived from day to day. Anyone can spend an hour at home every day doing a concentration exercise. Anyone can do ritual repetition of a technique from day to day. In that case, nothing is required beyond your own willingness to conform to a certain pattern. But the relationship that is Satsang with Me is a living Condition. It generates conditions that activate the functions for which you are always trying to avoid responsibility. It requires you to be in relationship. It requires fulfillment in life-terms. Therefore, it is difficult, and it does not fulfill your search. It continually turns you from the search into relationship.

When you live that Condition, that relationship to Me, when you actually live Satsang with Me, It becomes pleasurable. It becomes easy, spontaneous. But, as long as you resist that Condition, My Company and Its implicit demand will make you darker, heavier, more obsessed with self-enclosure and the strategies of "Narcissus".

Among those who become associated with the gathering of My devotees, but who are not yet ready (themselves) to live the Condition of Satsang with Me, there are some who become obsessed, angry. Their separativeness becomes dramatized. Their narrow mood becomes absolute. Sooner or later, such people find an excuse to remove themselves from contact with those who are living the conditions of Satsang with Me—because "Narcissus" is unwilling to meet those conditions. He is unwilling to live relationship as the Real condition, the very nature, of Conscious existence. He resists the form and condition of life. He contracts from relationship into the self-reflecting medium of his own activities and functions. If My Spiritual Force enters his obsessive enclosure, Its Intensity aggravates him, such that he runs farther into the wilderness. But, if "Narcissus" begins to observe his own activity, his own obsession, his own self-contraction, and resorts to Satsang with Me, he becomes full of True Humor. He becomes an effortless human being—capable of Real Spiritual experience, and (yet) entirely unconcerned about Spiritual experiences.

The responsibility of My devotees is to live Satsang with Me as the Condition of their lives—hour to hour, day to day—and to maintain that relationship in very practical terms.

Coming to Me for techniques, methods, and even experiences is a form of self-defense. It is the defense of your condition, your search, your suffering. However holy or serious the person may seem to be, the seeker who comes to Me comes to defend "Narcissus"—demanding to be served, to be satisfied. But Spiritual life is not the satisfaction of the search. I offer no "bones", no strategic methods, no consolations, no beliefs, not a thing!

I will never give the seeker a "bone". Those who have come for "bones" are waiting in vain, because what they are hoping for is not going to happen. All of that drama of seeking has nothing whatsoever to do with Truth. It is all a lot of bullshit! That is all it is—and I do not spend any time tolerating it. Your trouble is an illusion. Your search is a reaction to your suffering. Your actual dilemma has barely been conceived by you, barely experienced. You come to Me for another consolation, to prevent awareness of your suffering. You come for distraction, a fascination, a charming vision. You want to be consoled. But <u>why</u> do you want to be consoled? What state are you in that you should want to be consoled by Me? You are suffering! Yes? Since you are only suffering, why are you defending all of this nonsense?

It is time to be rid of all of that. It is utterly unnecessary. It can be abandoned! All of that is what I want surrendered as gifts around My Feet.[41] I want to see your gift to Me of all the suffering, all the sorrows, all the long faces, all the usual Yoga, all the "kriya shakti", all the visions, all the beliefs, all the philosophies, all the conventional religion and Spirituality, all your personal (and even racial) history. I want to see your attachment to birth and your fear of death. I want to Free you of all of it!

Such are the implications of Truth. But, because people arrive here in My Company not simply suffering but defending their search, they come with <u>conditions</u>. How can I satisfy these "holy demands"? I do not represent the traditional Yoga. I do not represent conventional traditional Vedantic Self-Knowledge (or Jnana). I do not represent the traditional "Enlightenment" of Gautama. I do not adorn My Body with symbols—I have no symbolic significance whatsoever. These are all your own images. As long as you are delighted only by images, you will always end up doing sadhana at your own feet.

What is appropriate is not for you to be offended by <u>Me</u>, but (finally, at long last) for you to be offended by <u>yourself</u>. All your life, you have been angry with various people, dissatisfied with various people, criticizing them. You have been critical of society, of life and experience, of birth, of mortality, of politics. You have been capable of anger, of fear, of doubt—as reactions to conditions of life. But it is time to turn your energy to observing, understanding, and transcending <u>your</u> <u>own</u> event.

I have not come to <u>satisfy</u> My devotees. A satisfied devotee is still the same one he or she was to begin with. I am only interested in the utter dissolution of the entire limitation that appears as My devotee.

I am not here to satisfy that limitation, to make it feel comfortable. I am here to return people to conscious awareness of their own experience—their always present-time, chronic experience, their dilemma, their unconsciousness. I am here to return people to conscious awareness of all of that—not to prevent them from seeing it, not to keep them obsessively involved with symbols, or strategically achieved Yogic stimulations of light and sound, or some complex, conditional vision of "God", or some mere image of Reality, so that they will never experience and recognize their own egoic state. I move by non-support. I undermine the process that is My devotee's suffering.

I assume that <u>suffering</u> is what brings people to Satsang with Me. But people in this time and place tend to assume it is their <u>search</u> that has brought them to Me. Arriving at My Feet is a form of success for the seeker. But, when the seeker begins to turn from the illusions of the search (and the demands for the satisfaction of its goals) to the sense of his or her actual limited condition, his or her suffering, his or her dilemma, then Satsang with Me has truly begun.

Until then, the would-be devotee sits, waiting for satisfaction. The person listens to what is being said. The possibility of Real Spiritual life (or conscious life) is there, but the person supposes that somehow the search to which he or she is already attached is going to be satisfied.

The game of seekers is ended, as far as I am concerned. I do not entertain that suffering. I am not concerned for ordinary life—in the sense of this obstructed stupidity, this fascination, this search. None of that interests Me. If you have become sensitive to your suffering, your dis-ease, then Satsang with Me is available to you. Only when you have become thus sensitive is Satsang with Me usable to you. Your sensitivity to your suffering will give you the strength to endure the periods of self-criticism, of negativity, of crisis—because you will be very willing to go through them. Then such episodes will become <u>interesting</u> to you, because you will not <u>care</u> about the things that are threatened or undermined by the crisis in conscious awareness.

But, if you are attached to your search, you will be unable to endure the crisis of your own transformation. Transformation will threaten the very thing you came to defend. In fact, there is no "sadhana", no "Spiritual practice", that amounts to something you can do in order to be "saved", in order to attain the goals of seeking. No form of effortfully striving to attain salvation or to fulfill the search is appropriate. What is appropriate is the truly ego-transcending sadhana of devotional surrender to Me—and that is <u>always</u> appropriate.

It is the <u>demands</u> of Satsang with Me—both at the practical life-level and at the more subtle level—that awaken sensitivity to what is appropriate. Just as the right functioning of the gathering of My devotees depends on appropriate action, all of life depends on appropriate action. In every place or condition, there is a functional appropriateness that must be understood. Everywhere in life, what is appropriate must come alive as action.

There are no "reasons" to do what is appropriate. Therefore, there are no "reasons" to enter into Satsang with Me. What is appropriate is simply obvious, and it is the necessary form of action. The appropriate movement of a planet is its proper circuit around the sun, not some eccentric deviation from its orbit. What is appropriate is functional living. It is not strategically done for the purpose of Realization, nor does it produce Truth as a result. It is simply appropriate. It is natural. It is spontaneous. It is intelligent.

I always expect My devotees to manifest what is appropriate. Therefore, I do not always Give My devotees specific Instruction in what to do in particular situations. I Live Truth to My devotees, and look to you for appropriate action as a sign of your self-understanding. Your actions are a very simple indicator of your preparation, the condition of your life in Satsang with Me.

If you do what is appropriate, I will be pleased. If you do not, you will quickly feel abandoned. You will feel separated from Me—not necessarily because of some reactive attitude that arises in you, or even some discipline I Give you, but because of an underlying sensation generated by your own inappropriate action, your non-functional life, your eccentricity. It is not My demands or the life-conditions I Give you that bring about your appropriate action. It is your awareness of your Real orientation, your awareness of Satsang with Me, your relationship to the "Sun", and then to the other "planets", to all beings, to all of life.

When you become rightly oriented, functional, when your movement is appropriate, then the "Sun", My Divine Light, Shines on you. If you are eccentric, you will keep moving in and out of phase with this Light. Your own discomfort is felt as My displeasure.

What is always appropriate is "radical" self-understanding and the spontaneous surrender of seeking. What is always inappropriate is the search and its defense. The life of seeking is founded in presumed dilemma, and it does not work. The search does not attain Realization, and it does not permit appropriate functional life. The seeker is not a functional being. The seeker is eccentric. The seeker is elsewhere. The seeker is involved in all kinds of peculiar artifices, attachments, symbols—both internal and external. The seeker has no capability for relationship, for simplicity. There is no love, no functional light. The Force of Conscious life, of Divine Love-Bliss, does not move as the seeker.

The seeker is always a little disturbed and confused, always somehow un-Happy. The seeker is My "profound devotee" today, but tomorrow is someone else's "Yogi", or has become "already Realized"! The seeker comes and goes. The seeker is in and out of opposing moods. The seeker is always wondering whether or not Satsang with Me is the Truth, whether or not I am Enlightened.

In fact, your drama and your limitations are your own. When you become sensitive to that, then you are firmly founded in Satsang with Me. Then Satsang with Me is no longer in question, and you will turn from the childish games you would otherwise tend to play in relation to Me to the penetration of your own suffering, your dilemma, your self-contraction, your separation, your arrogance.

DEVOTEE: How can I consciously overcome the resistance if, even when I become aware of resistance through self-understanding, the appropriate behavior does not result?

AVATAR ADI DA SAMRAJ: Self-understanding is not a method for correcting behavior. You have only observed a little bit. You have only seen enough of your game to resist it. Therefore, you want to resist it. You want some means to intensify your resistance, such that it can become absolute and (so you imagine) press the "bad behavior" out of life. But "radical" self-understanding, true insight, is not merely to observe some negative pattern, acknowledge it to be negative, and then resist it. "Radical" self-understanding is truly to comprehend that pattern as the avoidance of relationship. It is not to sit around analyzing and observing your craziness. It is to see your craziness as the avoidance of relationship. It is to be turned into relationship. If there is not this tacit comprehension, followed by the spontaneous turn from the contracted ego-pattern into the living condition of relationship, then there is no self-understanding.

When genuine insight exists, then relationship is enjoyed— and you are no longer concentrating on negative behavior or concepts. And, when relationship is enjoyed, then all the forms of self-contraction become obsolete through non-support. But, when you have only a little bit of insight, then you see only the effects of the self-contraction itself. Through self-analysis, a little self-observation, you see only the negative symptoms. And you acquire preferences. You prefer to be a little more "spiritual", to be free of certain kinds of compulsive behavior.

This is the usual state of the Spiritual seeker. As a seeker, your attempts to correct yourself are simply another form of unintelligence. Your preferences have no life-intensity. You are still mediocre. What you are calling your "spiritual life" is just more of the same.

When you resort to Me, and understand your own activity, when you truly comprehend the process of your life as the avoidance of relationship, then you are spontaneously in relationship. You are no longer concerned with merely monitoring your behavior and either suppressing or exploiting your stream of desires (or preferences). You are only in relationship. And, to the degree that you are firmly founded in the heart-relationship to Me, you are Happy, you are already Free. You are straight! You are no longer entertaining the problem of your obsessive behavior—because its foundation, its structure, its motivation is not being lived.

And, so, simply as a secondary matter, you notice that the obsessive behavior in your life is disappearing—becoming weaker, less persistent. On the one hand, your chronic obsessions, your habitual life-obsessions, come upon you less and less frequently—and, on the other hand, when they do come upon you, you understand them. You turn to Me instead—because you understand these obsessions as the avoidance of relationship.

Relationship is the Real condition of life. The avoidance of relationship is secondary—a re-action to the Real (and always present-time) living condition of relationship. Therefore, by turning to Me and understanding yourself, you are turned from the activity of avoidance to the living condition of relationship.

When you turn to Me and understand yourself, it is not that you willfully turn away from the avoidance of relationship or its manifested patterns of behavior. Rather, you simply understand your usual activity—and, in this understanding, unqualified relatedness stands out as your True and present condition. You simply and spontaneously fall into it. When (in the midst of your turning to Me) insight into your compulsive pattern reveals what your ordinary activity always prevents, you fall into that—the living condition of relationship. And, when (by Means of My Avataric Divine Grace) you fall from your self-contracted state into relationship, there is Release, Freedom, Purity, Clarity, and Real Enjoyment. Then obsessive mental and psycho-physical patterns are dissolved.

In Satsang with Me, the self-contraction is undermined—not resisted and overwhelmed. The self-contraction is obviated only by devotionally turning to Me and (in that to-Me-devoted disposition) exercising the point of view of intelligence. True sadhana in My Company is free of all efforts to resist, suppress, or temporarily escape the self-contraction by living from the point of view of the search. Therefore, self-understanding is always a matter of Satsang with Me—living the relationship to Me, living in accordance with My Wisdom-Teaching, and living the forms of (always life-positive) self-discipline I recommend.[42]

Self-understanding is never a matter of analytical concern for behavior, for life-patterns. That is the search. That is the obsession. That is the self-analysis game of "finding yourself out", in which you spend part of the day analyzing your craziness and the rest of the day dramatizing it.

People are not prepared to immediately become involved in genuine Spiritual life. But the necessary foundation for True Spiritual life is not some mysterious profundity. The condition of human dilemma is practical and life-visible. Human beings are possessed by patterns of irresponsibility and self-indulgence. It is not some profound technique or some deep psychic meditation that they need to perfect at the beginning. A turnabout in the life-pattern is required—in simple, practical terms.

The beginnings do not involve trampling one's sexual obsessions with some fantastic self-analysis, deep insight into the past, or heroic smacking of the flesh. No, it is only necessary to live in Satsang with Me, to live the Condition of this Satsang, and simply to do what is appropriate, according to My Instructions. Enjoy the Condition of Satsang with Me with open intensity, and you simply will not <u>be</u> obsessed anymore!

It is not a matter of doing anything about the obsessions. It is a matter of taking responsibility for the basic life-pattern—in practical terms. Then the minor notes of obsession are swallowed in the greater stream of self-understanding. But this becomes really possible only when Satsang with Me has truly begun, when Satsang with Me is truly lived.

When Satsang with Me has inspired you—and you are alive with It, pregnant with It, Full of that Condition, that relatedness, that openness, that profound Enjoyment—then you are capable of doing what is appropriate in life. That is why I require real, practical conditions of those who want to become My formal devotees: Get a job, do not use drugs or intoxicants, adapt to a natural, moderate pattern of diet, confine sexual activity to a committed emotional-sexual intimacy (if you choose to be sexually active), and so on.

Such conditions seem easy enough—but there is "something for everyone" in the conditions I require of My devotees. Something touches each individual's key obsession in some form. Therefore, the life-conditions seem impossible to those who are not at all ready to become My formal devotees—but they seem somehow possible to those who are being heart-Drawn to Me.

The disciplines I require of My devotees are not some massive thing. I do not ask you to become a saint before you come to Me. Mine are simple, natural, ordinary requirements. But they are sufficient to turn away those who are not yet ready to enter into the devotional relationship to Me, while they attract those who are ready to enter into Satsang with Me.

Satsang with Me is True Humor, Delight. There is only Enjoyment—truly. There is not this crazy asylum of separate and isolated existence. There is only Enjoyment. Everything is a form of Love-Bliss. There is no dilemma—and those who truly live Satsang with Me are living no-dilemma. They may appear to be going through various kinds of practical life-transformation, but the process of transformation is not fueled by the sense of dilemma.

My devotees are not even concerned with whether they will attain the "famous" states—the states of conscious awareness that are traditionally held in such high esteem. What difference does it make if you go through some fantastic psychic revolution in which you are constantly looking at a blue image with three curves around the outside? What difference does it make if, no matter where you go, you see this thing, and it is blue, and it has three circular shapes here, and it shows a sort of brilliant knob in the center? "I have attained this after two thousand lifetimes." That is only the "dog costume"!

For those who truly resort to Me, Satsang with Me is sufficient. Satsang with Me is the discovery. Satsang with Me is the

Realization. Satsang with Me is "radical" self-understanding. Satsang with Me is meditation. It is Truth. It is Enjoyment. It is True Humor. It is the Principle of life. It does not support your egoic strategy of separation. Neither does It support your dilemma or your seeking.

Satsang with Me is only Force, only Intensity. The Absolute Revelation is Communicated in Satsang with Me—all the time. Satsang with Me is <u>Itself</u> the Absolute Revelation.

The Divine Conscious Light is Above your heads! Just sit up a little straighter!

What more can I tell you? I don't know. I cannot make it any plainer. My speech is over. I cannot convince you.

Send in the next group!

This place was originally going to be opened as a restaurant. Give the public what it wants: On tonight's menu we have choice Medjool dates!

AVATAR ADI DA SAMRAJ
The Mountain Of Attention Sanctuary, 2000

6.

The Gorilla Sermon

I.

DEVOTEE: Beloved Master, is there any truth to the notion that drugs can be used to expand the mind?

AVATAR ADI DA SAMRAJ: What is this "mind" you are talking about? How can you get closer to that by expanding?

What arises falls. What appears disappears. What expands contracts. Every action has an equal and opposite reaction. Neither the expansion nor the contraction, neither the action nor the reaction, is Truth. It is simply expansion/contraction, action/reaction.

The so-called "expansion of consciousness" is not Truth. It is simply the stimulation of perception. Why do you feel impelled to seek Truth by means of this expansion? Because you are suffering. You are already suffering, whether you expand your mind or not. Even if you succeed in expanding your mind, you suffer. The one who feels the mind expand is the same one who feels the mind is not expanding, or is even contracting. That person is contraction, dilemma, sense of separate existence. That contraction is what motivates you to seek. And, so, the sense of self-contraction is what motivates you to expand the mind.

Simply to experience is to expand the mind. Experience increases the objects of conscious awareness. But all the possible objects of conscious awareness—whether high or low, beautiful or not—carry the same implication of the separate-self-sense.

If you see something—a red balloon, for instance—"I" is seeing the red balloon. Whatever you see, "I" is seeing it. "I" is seeing the seventh heaven. "I" is seeing dogshit on the street. It is always the same. The self-contraction is motivating the search. The sense of separate self is the manifestation of the self-contraction. Understand this. Such self-understanding is the necessary foundation for Most Perfect Realization of Truth.

Truth has nothing whatsoever to do with expanding the mind or not expanding the mind. Truth is not a form of experience. The pursuit of mind-expansion is a form of the search— dependent on separation, motivated by the self-contraction—and successful "expansion" does nothing whatsoever to the motivating condition itself. The separate one only acquires various objects for itself—thus manufacturing a false feeling of security, an illusion of survival. But that separate one cannot survive. It has no independent existence.

"I" is felt as a limited capsule of life-energy, surrounded by mystery. It has a certain amount of time until it terminates. If you experience a lot with it, it burns out quickly. If you throw it off a cliff, it smashes. "I" presumes itself to be this limited little thing under the conditions of life—and people manipulate the "I" from the point of view of whatever strategy they happen to choose. But it is always the root-presumption of separateness that is your suffering, your limitation.

It is really a simple matter. The usual person thinks: "This body and its psyche are dying. This world is dying. Everyone is suffering. Everyone is seeking. There is mortality. There is frustration and limitation." But none of that is Truth. Those interpretations are not Truth. The world itself is not Truth—nor is life, nor psyche and body, nor death, nor experience. No event is, in and of itself, Truth. Everything that arises is an appearance to Consciousness Itself, a modification of the Divine Conscious Light That Is Always Already the Case.

All of this is a dream, if you like. It is an appearance in Consciousness Itself. Truth Is Very Consciousness Itself. Truth is to all of this what the waking state is to the dreaming state. If you awaken, you do not have to do anything about the condition you may have suffered or enjoyed in the dream state. What happened within the dream is suddenly not your present condition. It is of no consequence any longer, once you are awake.

If you persist in dreaming, and your point of view remains that of the dreamer (and the dreamer's role within the dream), then your possible actions are numberless. But none of them will "work". They will simply occupy you in the dream. They will modify the dream state, but no action in the dream is the equivalent of waking. There are simply forms of fascination, of occupation, of seeking—until you wake up.

Truth is simply Waking, No-illusion. It is not a condition within this appearance. It has nothing whatsoever to do with the mind, regardless of whether the mind is expanded or contracted.

Perception is simply what it obviously is. There is no reason for any perception to change in order for Truth to Appear as a consequence. The dream does not have to be changed in any manner for the waking person to feel that he or she is awake. There is nothing that has to happen to the dream—only waking is necessary.

To one who is awake, the dream is obvious. There is no illusion, no suffering, no implication—regardless of what appeared in the dream. A blue god, a dirty old drunk, the gorilla of death—it makes no difference. It makes a difference within the circumstances of the dream—to the one who is dreaming. But, to the one who is awake, it no longer makes any difference.

The nature of perception, of waking consciousness, is obvious if you are truly Awake. If you are asleep, if you do not understand, if self-understanding evades you, then there is nothing obvious about this at all. Then life is a very serious predicament—very serious. What do you have in such a case? "A few more years and everything is dead." It does not make any difference what the drama is, or what you manage to amuse yourself with during that time.

There is One Who is Wide Awake while He Appears in the dream. By not supporting the dream, He Awakens others. He Is the True Divine Guru. I Am That One.

The significance of My Work is not in anything I do within the dream. I simply do not support it. I do not live as it. I do not believe it. I do not take it seriously. Apparently, I can feel and act as I please within the dream. I persist in the common (or ordinary) manner. But I do not support the dream. I do not live from its point of view. I do not live its structure to others. I do not live the self-contraction to others—the avoidance of relationship, the separate-self-sense.

Simply because I live in this manner, those who are devotionally related to Me tend to become Awake. But, while they are Awakening, they persist in dreaming to various degrees. Forms of the dream persist. The search persists. Often, they get a little distance from the dream—it seems to break up at times, seems to disappear. It becomes vague, it becomes uninteresting, it becomes unserious, it becomes serious again.

You are just beginning to Awaken. Satsang with Me is the dream in which I Appear. Now it is as if you are beginning to wake up in your room. You are in bed, and it is morning. There are a few things you begin to notice, which indicate that you are in another state. Those who are Awakening in Truth begin to notice something. They begin to recognize the signs. They begin to recognize the activity of dreaming. They begin to sense something very unusual about Me.

Before their actual Awakening, I appear as all kinds of things to them. I suggest all kinds of fantastic things. All the things they can imagine while they dream, everything unbelievable, is what they think I am. I may appear to be extraordinary, a doer of famous things. I may appear playfully as that. But I am simply Awake. Not a single thing is happening. Not a single thing has been accomplished. I Am Only Awake.

I am like the sunlight in the morning. I Intensify the light of morning until you Awaken. Until the Light Awakens you, even the Light of Consciousness Itself, you continue to dream, try to survive within the dream, manipulate yourself within the dream, pursue all kinds of goals, searches—none of which Awaken you.

The ordinary means only console you and distract you within the dream. I Myself, the One Who would Awaken you, am not a person, not an individual within the dream. I Am your Very Consciousness. I Am Reality Itself, the Divine Conscious Light, the True Waking State, the True Divine Heart—Breaking Through the force of dreaming. It is not that you are some poor person who needs some other poor person to help you out. It may appear to be so within the dream—but, in Reality, I Am your own True Self-Nature Appearing within the dream to Awaken you. I <u>Am</u> your Awakening, and your always already Conscious State.

Even while dreaming, you may experience suggestions of waking. You may become momentarily aware of the body, momentarily aware of lying in bed. For a moment, the images of the dream may stop. Just so, I Myself, Appearing within the world, Am truly your Real Conscious State. My Person in the world is like an image in a dream. But, in fact, I am more like your moments of wakening awareness—the moments that move you into the waking state. I am not some separateness, some individual. I Am Consciousness Itself, Reality Itself, Truth Itself.

No images.

Images.

Blackness.

Brilliance.

All these things are appearances to conscious awareness. They are objects. Not one thing needs to happen to them in order for Consciousness Itself to Exist. Not one thing needs to happen within the dream in order to verify Awakening. Awakening is Its Own Fullness. Once you are Awake, anything can appear. True Awakeness is the foundation of this world-appearance. It is its Support. It is its Very Nature.

Consciousness Itself is not antagonistic to this world or to any form within it. Consciousness Itself is the Truth of all appearance, disappearance, and non-appearance. Even when Consciousness Itself is Most Perfectly Realized, ordinary human life continues. In that case, human life is rightly used—and, in that sense, more enjoyable. It becomes functional to an extraordinary degree.

The usual human being barely functions at all. A couple of good days a month. The rest of the time, you are trying to get healed or get pleasurized, trying to get straight, trying to work, trying to get with it. Every now and then, there is a little clarity—when you just stand up, walk across the room, open the door, and go outside. The rest of the month is spent dreaming and think-ing—when just to walk across the room is part of an enormous search, an unkind adventure, an approach to victory against odds. But all you are doing is simple things, simple functions.

One who most perfectly understands, who is Most Perfectly Awake, functions very well under the conditions that appear. Those conditions may be forms of this waking world or forms of any of the subtle worlds. Under all conditions, self-understanding is appropriate. There is no experience, no state, that is (itself) identical to Truth. Just so, Truth is not different from any experience or state. Truth is the Truth of all of that.

I am a kind of irritation to My devotees. You cannot sleep with a dog barking in your ear—at least, most people cannot! There is some sort of noise to which everyone is sensitive, and it will keep them awake. I Am a Constant Wakening Sound. I am always annoying people with the Demand to Wake Up—and to stay Awake. I do not seduce them within the dream. I do not exploit their seeking. I am always offending their search and their preference for unconsciousness. I show no interest in all of that. I Criticize it. I am always Doing something Prior to the mind. I always Act to return you from the mind, from fascination.

I am not what the dreamer thinks I am. The dreamer thinks I must have a certain appearance, say and do certain things, have certain magical powers, produce certain magical effects. The dreamer associates all kinds of glorious and magical things with Me. But I am always Performing the Awakening Act, putting an end to the dream. Therefore, I do not satisfy the seeker. Those who come to be satisfied are offended. They are not satisfied. They feel empty. They do not feel their questions have been answered. They do not feel they have been shown the Way. They came for some "thing".

Within the dream, you are always being satisfied by the dream-Guru:

> You climb to the top of the mountain,
> and the Guru is sitting in a cave.
> The Guru hands you a little silver box.
> When you open the box,
> there is a blue diamond in it.

You take it out and swallow it.
Then your body explodes into a million suns,
and you shoot off into the universe!

In Reality, the True Guru does not function in that manner. The True Guru is not noticed by someone who is seeking for such satisfaction, who is looking for the "signs" of the Guru, who is "hunting" the Guru. The True Guru does not assume any particular visibility that can be counted on. The True Guru is likely to remain unnoticed. People are likely to be offended if they do not feel any Force, any Energy, in the Presence of one they presume to be Guru. People tend not to notice or value someone who is simply Awake. They are looking for the guy who has the blue and yellow light over his head.

All of this—until you become dissatisfied with the search. When you stop being focused in the effort of your search, you begin to feel simply desperate. Then the only thing that is left is the self-contraction. When the search begins to wind down, and you begin to realize you are suffering, then you become sensitive to the Presence and Self-Nature of the One Who is Awake. You become attentive to Me.

It is stated in the traditional writings that, of all the things you can do to Realize Freedom, the best thing you can do, the greatest thing you can do, is to spend your time in the Company of one who is Awake. For My devotee, that is Satsang with Me—living in heart-relationship to Me as your Divine Heart-Master. All other activities are secondary.

Satsang with Me is not a strategic method, not an exercise or a meditative technique that you apply to yourself. Satsang with Me is simply the natural and appropriate Condition. Satsang with Me Is Reality. Satsang with Me Is (Itself) Truth, or Divine Enlightenment. There are no other means given to My devotees.

There is nothing you can do to save yourself, nothing you can do to become Enlightened, to become Realized. Nothing whatsoever. If there were something, I would tell you—but there is nothing. This is because the ego-"I" always approaches the Truth from the point of view of the search. You seek the Truth. But the search is (itself) a reaction to the dilemma, an expression of separation, the avoidance of relationship. Therefore, none of your seeking, nothing you can do, becomes or attains the Truth.

All the means of transformation belong to Truth Itself, to the Divine Person, to the True Divine Heart. Therefore, for My devotee, Satsang with Me is (Itself) the only sadhana, the only True Spiritual practice. Sadhana is to be engaged at all times and in all circumstances—in daily life, at work, while engaging the formal practices I Give to My devotees. Satsang with Me is meditation. Satsang with Me is Realization.

To Realize Truth is simply to be Awake. I have often used the contrast between the waking state and the dreaming state to symbolize the difference between most perfect "radical" self-understanding and all the forms of seeking. All attainments, all forms of knowledge, all forms of mind—however sublime—belong within the dream. When extraordinary and even miraculous conditions are actually experienced, they reveal themselves to be (essentially) of the same nature as the ordinary experience of suffering that provoked the search to begin with.

In My own case, there is no consolation in temporary samadhis, no consolation in visions, no consolation in going to other worlds, no consolation in any conditional Realization. At last, even the process of self-understanding itself dissolves in Self-Abiding Divine Self-Recognition.

When self-understanding is (thus) most perfect, it becomes obvious that everything that has ever occurred has been a modification of Consciousness Itself. This thing that has been upsetting you—all the movement, all the seeking, all the attainment, the entire "evolutionary" path of Spiritual life—has been a modification of Reality Itself, Consciousness Itself. Even this Realization, this Knowledge, is (Itself) a modification of Consciousness Itself. There is an Instant in Which it becomes Obvious that This Is So. That Instant is—if one can still apply any name or significance to it whatsoever—most perfect "radical" self-understanding, Most Perfect Divine En-Light-enment. It is absolutely no "thing".

But the traditional Yogi, whose principle is the Spiritual search, is involved in fantastic dramas of experience. He has all kinds of things to do to himself, with himself, and around himself—with his body and mind, with all the egoic ornaments, the suffering, the extremes, the endless number of searches, strategies, or egoic works. The traditional Yogi-ascetic has a fantastically distracting, <u>fascinating</u> life! It is a great, great adventure. Even the traditional Jnani—the philosophical ascetic, the Realizer of conditionally achieved Transcendental Self-Knowledge—is absorbed in a fascinating life of willful Silence, of acquired Peace, of strategic Formlessness, separated from all conditionality by a waking sleep. The traditional Jnani is absorbed in his own phenomena.

But, for the Man of "Radical" Understanding, there is no drama. I have nothing by which to fascinate people. No sign, no act, no word, no costume can represent My Divine State. No closing of the eyes, no blissful smiles, no shuddering, no reports of visions—none of that is useful for keeping people interested from day to day. None of that is necessary. I am not fascinating. The only Forceful Communication is That Which cannot be Communicated by any conditional means—whether by purposive silence or by speech.

Truth does not specially appear in the form of something extraordinary or fascinating. Truth is the Most Absolute Communication, the Most Obvious Communication. The Condition of Satsang with Me is grounded in the Real (and Obvious) condition of life. Relationship itself already exists as your living condition. What has to be added for that to take place? Not a thing! That Real condition is expressed in every present situation, ordinary or extraordinary. Relationship itself is already the case—in every moment of conditionally manifested existence. Therefore, Satsang Itself, the heart-relationship to Me, Reveals the Truth by first Revealing the most Obvious of all conditions.

II.

DEVOTEE: Will You say something more about the turnabout that You describe as self-understanding? I think You once spoke about a feeling-Realization of something Prior to our ordinary state.

AVATAR ADI DA SAMRAJ: What is observed and understood is not Reality Itself. What is observed and understood is your own activity.

Pick up an apple, then put it down. You can see yourself doing that. The seeing does not involve anything apparently extraordinary. You can also catch yourself thinking certain thoughts. The process of self-observation and self-understanding is that kind of thing. It is to see yourself, but in the most intelligent manner—the most direct, all-inclusive, manner.

Of course, people already (intuitively) live in Reality—as the Divine Self-Condition, as the True Divine Heart, as Consciousness Itself. That is why all of you can sit here in various limited conditions, but none of you is screaming in fear. The implications of what is arising in your conscious awareness are not presently suffered. It takes a powerful event to awaken the latent sense of fear.

Most perfect "radical" self-understanding is Reality Itself, That Which Is Always Already the Case—Clarifying Itself, Magnifying Itself. Whatever the present impulse, the present movement may be, it is arising within Reality Itself. In the course of My devotee's sadhana in My Avataric Divine Company, My devotee's conscious awareness will (first) tend to appear as the search, then as weariness of the search, then as Real insight, "radical" self-understanding—until (in the only-by-Me Revealed and Given seventh stage of life) conscious awareness Abides as Divine Self-Recognition of whatever is arising. When (by Means of My Avataric Divine Spiritual Grace) your present activity is most perfectly understood to be the avoidance of relationship, then the natural (or ordinary) state is most perfectly transparent to Reality Itself.

Reality Itself Is Always Already the Case. Therefore, it is not Reality Itself that must be understood. Rather, it is your own present activity (or the avoidance of relationship) which is the obstruction to the Realization of Reality Itself (or That Which Is Always

232

Already the Case)—and, therefore, it is that fundamental ego-activity which must be observed, understood, and (thus and thereby) transcended.

When your present-time separative activity is observed, understood, and transcended, then That Which Is Always Already the Case—but Which the ego-"I" (or separative act) is always vanishing from conscious awareness—simply and inevitably Stands Out. And, when that self-understanding is most perfect, everything is Obvious. There is no dilemma. There is no longer the sense of a separate one in trouble—suffering, needing to survive, needing to attain something in order to be Happy. There is no identification with subjectivity—either the root-subjectivity of the separate-self-sense or the entire display of internal life.

Then all that you had piddled around with for years, thinking it to be "your" necessity—all of this subjective mind, pattern of brain-waves, psycho-physical drama of impulses and shapes—is Divinely Self-Recognized. In that case, only the Very Force (or Inherent Energy) and the Very Consciousness (or Inherent Being) That Is Reality Stands Out—utterly Free of all that arises, and (yet) not separated from any conditionally manifested thing or state that arises. Then Consciousness Itself is lifted out of that image-of-barriers created by skull and skin. Then psycho-physical existence no longer serves to create the illusion that Consciousness Itself is necessarily limited and only conditionally arising. Ultimately, when self-understanding is most perfect, egoic identification with the body (and the total body-mind) disappears.

When (by Means of My Avataric Divine Spiritual Grace) there is most perfect "radical" self-understanding, then (limited and limiting) egoic identification with the body-mind dissolves spontaneously—not as a result of your doing anything to it, but by virtue of the spontaneous, Prior Realization of That in Which the body-mind and even all conditions arise.

As the seeker, you are always trying to do something to the separate self. At first, you are just exploiting it, enjoying the strategies of life-games—until you begin to break down a little bit, in despair of your ordinary destiny. Then you begin to turn toward a presumed "spiritual" life, or toward some sort of remedy—but, even then, you are always trying to do something to this separate and personal state, to get rid of your suffering, to make your mind quiet, to become "one" with something, to get free, to get out of this <u>thing</u>.

Such is the point of view of the seeker. The seeker is always only modifying that root-sensation—trying to get rid of it with deep relaxing sighs, with all the efforts toward the attainment of pleasure and the escape from suffering. But, in the end, the seeker always comes back to the same sensation again, because that one is always working from the contracted point of view that <u>is</u> suffering. As long as you are involved in the search, your dilemma is your self-image (as the separate, and suffering, individual) and the separative principle at the root of all your activity.

As the seeker, you only play with your own fundamental limitations—until the game begins to lose its ability to distract and entertain. Then the energy you formerly had for seeking begins to dissipate, and you fall into your actual state—which is suffering, separateness. Hopefully, at this point you also move into association with Me, and begin the life of Satsang with Me, the life of Truth.

In Satsang with Me, the Truth is Lived to you—and you then live the Truth as your Condition. Gradually, you become less and less involved with the suffering-and-seeking images of yourself. You become less concerned with the usual process of your life. You are doing less and less about it. You are trying less and less to get free, to get Realized, to get to God, Liberation, and pleasant sensation. You are not trying to <u>stop</u> engaging all of that effort. It just begins to wear down, while you live the conditions Given by Me. You simply notice this. You cease to be occupied with your search—because the Truth is being Lived to you. The Truth is being Lived <u>as</u> yourself, by Means of My Avataric Divine Grace.

That Realization Which does not support separation and seeking is the ground of "radical" self-understanding. In Satsang with Me, that Realization replaces the ordinary operating basis of your life. You simply forget your adventure of suffering—that is all. The Power of Satsang with Me distracts you from mere suffering (or the separate and separative and always seeking body-mind-self)—until Truth Itself becomes Obvious.

Therefore, Truth is not a matter of doing something <u>to</u> the ego, the separate-self-sense, the identification with the body, or anything else. Rather, Truth is simply to be lived—because Truth obviates all that is not Truth.

I Live the Divine Force, and Generate the conditions, of Spiritual life in relationship to My devotee. Over time, more and more responsibility is given to My devotee—in the course of deepening devotion to Me and increasing self-discipline, self-understanding, and self-transcendence. The process of the heart-relationship with Me is a Divine Gift, Avatarically Given by Me—a Gift that is progressively more and more profound.

My Avatarically Self-Transmitted Divine Spirit-Energy is typically first felt by My devotee as a sense of "Presence" (or Pressure), or as subjective energies and sensations—in due course, becoming the tangible experience of My Love-Bliss-Full Spiritual Descent into the body-mind. Eventually (in the first two stages of the "Perfect Practice" of the Way of Adidam), the process begins to assume the fundamental characteristics of the Divine Conscious Light Itself, in Transcendental (though not yet Divine, or Most Perfect) Self-Realization of Reality Itself. Ultimately, in Most Perfect Divine Self-Realization (in the only-by-Me Revealed and Given Realization of the seventh stage of life), moment to moment existence <u>Is</u> the Indivisibility of Consciousness and Energy—a Single Intensity, Which <u>Is</u> Reality Itself (or the Divine Conscious Light Itself).

III.

AVATAR ADI DA SAMRAJ: One of the oddities of Teaching in the "modern" Western (and "Westernized") world is that people approach the Guru already committed to some form of madness. Because they are so committed to the search, people do not come to the Guru simply suffering, knowing full well that they are only suffering (regardless of what kind of good time they had last weekend). They do not even come in the condition of sensitivity to mortality.

Nowadays, there is very little of the simplicity that you read about in the traditional scriptures. This "modern" Western (and "Westernized") world is unlike the "old days" in Israel or India. Now people come <u>committed</u> to the search. They come to defend it, to make arguments about it, to get angry about it, to feel displeased about the criticism of it, to resist the Guru, to "hunt" the Guru, to offend, fight, and blame the Guru.

There has always been some element of this, but it is a peculiar quality of this "modern" Western (and "Westernized") world that people come to the Guru in order to <u>defend</u> their search. What I Require of them is the <u>understanding</u> of their search. Their search is always offended by My Word and Life.

DEVOTEE: What are we seeking?

AVATAR ADI DA SAMRAJ: Listen.
There is a dilemma.
Is there a dilemma?
There is no dilemma?
When you walk out of this room and the usual activity resumes, there may seem to be a dilemma—but is there a dilemma? There is no dilemma. There is only the sensation, the appearance, the presumption, of dilemma. If you understand dilemma, you understand (in this moment) that dilemma has no existence. Dilemma does not exist.

In that case, the question about how dilemma comes about is unnecessary and untrue—because, as soon as you look for the dilemma, it has no substance. Nevertheless, people continue to presume dilemma and suffering. And the <u>presumption</u> is your own activity. In the very same moment when you are presuming that there is suffering, dilemma, that your search is appropriate, the dilemma is not discoverable.

In Reality, there is only <u>This</u>. There is only the Obvious, only the Event Itself—Prior to dilemma, Prior to experience.

The dilemma never arises. If you examine it as soon as you begin to feel it, you realize it has not occurred. It has no substance. If it is something that has no substance, no existence, how can you be stuck in it? If you understand your own activity, there is no dilemma. If you do not understand, there appears to be a dilemma. But, as soon as you ask yourself about it, as soon as you look into it, as soon as you examine it, you realize the dilemma does not exist.

As the seeker, you go on reinforcing your presumption of dilemma—but that does not mean the dilemma actually exists. If it existed, there would be something you could do about it. It would be substantial. It would be distinguishable from other things. It would have some kind of knowable shape, limitation, dimension, consequence. Then the traditional forms of magic and Yoga would be appropriate, seeking would be appropriate.

But, as soon as you examine the dilemma directly, you cannot find it. You can presume its existence, but you cannot actually find it. Therefore, since it cannot be found, since dilemma does not exist, the search is not appropriate. The search is what you do only when you presume dilemma to be the case. As soon as you understand the non-reality of that presumption, the search falls away.

DEVOTEE: I have found that dilemma often manifests in a number of different sensations. The external conditions that generate those sensations are not real, but the reaction feels real. Would You explain this?

AVATAR ADI DA SAMRAJ: Why do you presume that your internal reaction is more real than the external forces to which you react? What you are saying is that your presumption of dilemma (or suffering) is real in any case—even if circumstances do not justify it! This presumption you want to make about your own contraction is the presumption I have been talking about. It is your presumption, isn't it?

DEVOTEE: Well, yes, the presumption is a mental thing, but the sensation is something else.

AVATAR ADI DA SAMRAJ: On the mental level, there is a presumption—but can you make an absolute distinction between that mental presumption and what you are calling "the sensation"? It is all one process. And that entire process is what I mean by "the presumption of dilemma". If you put your hand in a fire, and then draw it away in reaction to the heat, haven't you presumed it to be hot? Haven't you acted as if it were hot? You may think about it afterwards, and say it was hot—but, whether you think about it or not, in that instant in the fire, there is this physical response, this physical reaction.

Thoughts are of the same nature as pain, or any other kind of reaction. All personal events are forms of self-contraction. They all have the same quality, the same structure. Withdrawing your hand because the fire is hot is of the same nature as thinking that the fire is hot before or after you touch it. It is just as much a presumption, in other words. To presume something is to suppose, act, or react as if it were so.

To presume something does not require thinking. Thinking is not the only form of presumption, of supposing. You suppose on all kinds of levels. Your affirmations about things are not simply mental. There are mental presumptions, there are emotional presumptions, there are physical presumptions, there are instinctive presumptions (subconscious and unconscious). The mental (or conceptual) presumption is one form of it, but there are many forms—and the mental form of presumption does not exist in isolation.

IV.

DEVOTEE: Master, would You please clarify what You mean by "dilemma"?

AVATAR ADI DA SAMRAJ: I have been speaking about dilemma in the same sense that I speak of it in *The Knee Of Listening*.[43] All forms of seeking—all pursuit, all searches for the goal, all strategic Yoga, all Spiritual efforts that pursue an attainment of some sort— are responses to a felt dilemma, however it may be categorized, however it may appear in any moment. The root-meaning of "di-lemma" is "two assumptions"—an impasse, a predicament, a living state (or condition) of contradiction.

The root of the search is something that precedes the seeking itself. The effort of seeking never affects its own root-motivation. The seeking simply aims to fulfill its particular goal. The function of seeking is not to modify its own motivation, its source, its root—the dilemma itself. No search can ever exceed its own motivation, its fundamental presumption—which is dilemma.

Therefore, I have spoken of Spiritual life in terms of the observation and understanding of motivating dilemma (or suffering), in the context of Satsang with Me—not in terms of the pursuit of attainments. I have talked about Spiritual life (or Real life, or Conscious life) as requiring the spontaneous understanding of this motivation, this suffering, which precedes your seeking. However, in the history of the Great Tradition, Spiritual life has characteristically been oriented to the search and to the attainment of the goals of seeking.

What I call "dilemma" is this sensation, this motivating sense, this presumption, this feeling of contradiction, this experience that implies and reflects something that has already occurred—which is the avoidance of relationship, the self-contraction, the activity of separation. The avoidance of relationship is the root-activity that is always presently taking place, prior to the search. You feel it as dilemma, this vague sensation, a knot in the stomach—the drive, the movement, the motivation, that generates and necessitates your seeking. Where the avoidance of relationship has not occurred, where there is only relationship, there are not any of these knots, these motivating reactions.

It is certainly true that, apart from self-understanding, you do experience and react to the knots of contraction. The presumed forms of suffering <u>are</u> experienced, they <u>are</u> apparently happening, they <u>are</u> the conditions in which one must somehow live and survive. If you feel some sort of underlying aggravation—fear, anxiety, anger—you feel the knots here and there, and you go about your search on that basis. You seek to be free of the sensation of the knots. But, in spite of all the things you do, nothing is done to your own activity of self-contraction—which is what you are always reacting to.

As a result, you begin to presume, more and more, that the self-contracted state is real, that it is your actual condition. Therefore, you become increasingly convinced that your search is appropriate. And, so, you become less and less intelligent about the root-motivation of your life. You become more and more involved in the pattern of always doing something <u>about</u> it. You always and only react to dilemma as if it were, in fact, your fundamental condition. The great seekers are those who make the most dramatic attempts to "do something about it"—perfectly, absolutely.

Now, all forms of seeking are of the same nature: They all take dilemma seriously, and presume it to be the essential fact of life. The self-contraction is what they presume—the avoidance of relationship. The dilemma, the knot, is the foundation of the search. It is the actual "Lord" of your "Yoga" of seeking. And dilemma itself is the "Yogi"!

Simply to do some mentalizing, or some philosophizing, or some relaxing Yoga, does not do anything to all of that. Only "radical" self-understanding obviates the search and its root-activity. And most perfect "radical" self-understanding <u>is</u> Consciousness Itself, the Very Power of Consciousness Itself—Living, Awakening, Existing, even apparently Acting, Prior to the presumption of dilemma. Only Consciousness Itself is Always Already Free of the presumption of dilemma.

Eventually, your reaction to the root-aggravation of your own self-contraction shows itself to be fruitless. Even when you have followed your search to its end, when you have endured the entire course of your adventure and gotten all the lessons, when you have done all the usual meditations and have gone through all the experiences, when you have read all the books—the dilemma is still there. Then the very best thing that can happen to you is that the search itself begins to break down. Then, gradually, dilemma ceases to be reinforced by any remedial activity. Then the force of life's awareness falls into the dilemma. Your awareness is only of this dilemma. You are no longer doing anything about this dilemma—not a thing. You are not even trying to analyze the dilemma, so that it will come to an end. Not a single thing is being done.

For the time being, conscious awareness is identified with the sense of dilemma. When the search falls away (in inevitable frustration), conscious awareness <u>becomes</u> the dilemma. In other words, conscious awareness is doing nothing else, nothing apart from dilemma. This is the profound stage of practice in My Avataric Divine Heart-Company when—while turning to My Avatarically Self-Revealed Divine Person, and to My Avatarically Given Divine Wisdom-Teaching—the crisis of truly hearing Me is endured. When My devotee truly hears Me, there is most fundamental understanding of dilemma, characterized by the consistent capability to feel beyond the self-contraction—such that the avoidance of relationship is replaced by the feeling of relatedness (in heart-Communion with Me).

Ultimately, the dilemma, like the search, must be understood to be your own activity—your always-present, chronic activity. The dilemma is the structure and motivation of the usual drama of every life. When this is clearly observed, then there is real self-understanding. Previous to that crisis "at the root", all the things that you may regard to be self-understanding are (in fact) only remedial approaches or superficial experiences, in which the dilemma has already been presumed.

DEVOTEE: How does this relate to the different levels of conscious awareness?

AVATAR ADI DA SAMRAJ: It is not a matter of levels. For the time being, you think there are all kinds of structures within your being. You presume there are barriers, separations, forms that you are, forms that you are not, activities that are yours, activities that are not yours, separate functions in yourself, like boxes and drawers—functions here, functions here, functions here, different pieces of yourself. But, in Truth, there is only One Single Divine Indivisibility.

I <u>Am</u> That Indivisibility. I <u>Am</u> your True Self-Condition. I <u>Am</u> the True Self-Condition of all beings and things.

There is only this Indivisible Divinity. It has no form, no division, no separation, no "me", no this, no that, no inside, no outside. No suggestion of division arises in the Divine Conscious Light, even when all worlds appear. Therefore, most fundamental self-understanding is "radical" (or "gone-to-the-root"). It is not a remedial event, not a form of cure. It is not identical to any particular thought, perception, feeling, symbol, vision, suggestion, belief, sensation. All of those are forms of experience—and, therefore, they are secondary. All of those are forms of dilemma.

How could you seriously exist, even for one moment, while consciously presuming that you have a thought-level, and a feeling-level, a "this" level, and a "that" level, all kinds of separate "bodies", functions, and the rest? How could you exist for one moment while really presuming that to be your present and ongoing condition? You would go insane! Indeed, such a picture of life is insanity. In such a case, you are already shattered. Then you are imagining yourself to be a whole bunch of little things with no Fundamental Existence, no Prior Self-Nature, no Force of Being.

In Reality, at the most profound level, you do not presume that. Fundamentally, you do not presume that there are such levels (or pieces). Such a conception of yourself is nothing but a gathering of words—whereas Existence is Indivisible, fundamentally Single.

Every living being intuitively presumes only its True Condition, the Power of Reality. Therefore, even in the midst of experiencing the massive complexity of ordinary life, people usually remain relatively calm, and capable of functioning. This is not because they are particularly wise, but because they do not really live as if division, multiplicity, and death were their true condition. Fundamentally—already—the Oneness, the Singleness, the Force, the Presence, the Consciousness, the Reality That Is your True Condition, is also your present Realization. This is actually so, at the rudimentary level of primitive Intuition—and, indeed, it must be so, if functional life is to continue.

If you did begin to seriously (at the deepest level) presume separateness, multiplicity, and division in Consciousness Itself, you would go insane. Indeed, that is the very presumption that has taken place (in terms of rudimentary, functional life) in those who are called "insane". They have become relatively incapable of intuiting the Truth of their own existence. Just so, the so-called "normal" human being has become incapable of experiencing and generating life from the "Point of View" of Non-separateness. And, yet, intuitively, the "normal" person remains always and already "in touch" with the Truth of existence, the True Condition of Reality.

At the most fundamental level, the so-called "normal" person does, in fact, presume this Simplicity, this Singleness, this Non-separateness. My Divinely Self-Realized devotee is one who not only intuitively presumes the True Condition of Reality but who lives It Consciously—Inherently, Most Perfectly, moment to moment. Such a one lives without any doubt whatsoever regarding this Perfect Simplicity, the Obviousness That Is the Real Condition of moment to moment existence.

Until one's ordinary state is lived Consciously, ordinary life appears to be a mystifying dilemma, and (therefore) becomes a motivated search. Intuitively, every being Always Already Inheres in the Divine Self-Condition, the True Divine Heart, the Power of Reality Itself. However, in the functioning of everyday conscious awareness, there is apparent particularity, apparent multiplicity, apparent separateness—all of which seems to run counter to your Intuition. The appearance (and the quality) of arising experience tends to <u>inform</u> your Intuition. And this "information" tends to become your presumed condition.

The presumption of separateness defiles—and, ultimately, superimposes itself on—the heart-Intuition of Truth. It does so by reinforcing the process of identification (or ego—the stream of self-awareness), differentiation (or mind—the stream of thoughts), and desire (or motion—the endless movement toward contact, connection, union, and temporary loss of the sense of separate existence—the stream of motivations).

Every day, during your hours of sleep, you (as a "normal", or "sane", person) pass into a depthful Intuition of the Divine Source-Condition. But, during your time of waking, and even in your time of dreaming, you carry on the search—this movement within the presumed dilemma of experience. Such is the pattern of your life—until there is "radical" understanding of your root-activity.

Whenever such depth of self-understanding takes place, not only do you intuit the Divine Source-Condition (entirely beyond the gross, subtle, and causal dimensions of conditionally manifested existence), but it becomes obvious, in every circumstance of conscious life, that there is (in Reality) no separateness, no actual identification with birth and death. There is not, in that moment, even the slightest impulse to "believe" the implications of ordinary experience. The Power of the Divine Self (or Self-Condition), the Power of the True Divine Heart, Overwhelms the qualities of experience and consumes them.

The Divine Self-Condition, or Unqualified Reality, Is (Itself) the Foundation of all experience. What the ordinary "sane" person vaguely intuits is <u>already</u> the Condition in Which he or she is arising. That Condition is <u>already</u> Reality Itself. But, to My Divinely Self-Realized devotee, the Divine Self-Condition is Obvious, It is Apparent, It is Conscious. For such a one, It is Always, Only, and Already Obvious—and he or she need not go through any sophisticated mental operations for the Most Perfect Realization of the Divine Self-Condition to be so. Divine Self-Realization does not depend on anything. It is just as Obvious as ordinary perception is to the usual person.

When you are dreaming, you take the dream very seriously. You assume your role within it, your drama within it. You respond to the condition that seems to be so, whatever the particular circumstances of the dream. If the gorilla is chasing you up the beach, you feel all the threat. All the emotions become involved. All your strategies of survival—or non-survival—become involved. If it is a sweet, enjoyable, astral sort of dream, with all kinds of friends and voices and colors and movements, you presume that to be so. You float around in it. You take it seriously. You <u>presume</u> it to be so. You presume it because you have no other point of view from which to enjoy or suffer the dream—no point of view other than that of the dreamer. But, when you wake up in the morning, the gorilla that was just about to bite off your head loses all significance.

When you wake up, all the implications of the dream are already undone. The dream no longer has any real significance, any implications for life. It is no longer a genuine threat to life. It is no longer anything except a passing appearance. And the only difference is that you are awake. Nothing has been done to the dream itself. You have only woken up—and, therefore, the dream is obviously not your condition.

Most perfect "radical" self-understanding is very much this same kind of thing. Most perfect "radical" self-understanding is to the waking state what the waking state is to the dream. In the ordinary waking state, you presume all conditions to be so—"my" life, "my" symptoms, "my" knot in "my" stomach, "my" headaches, "my" fear, "my" everything else, "my" circumstances, "my" poverty, "my" need to do this and that, "my" death. You take everything that appears in life very seriously.

Here you are, in My Avataric Divine Heart-Company. You are very serious about getting out of all of this limitation. Everyone has come to Me very seriously, for this very serious Spiritual purpose. Now, since you have come to Me for such a purpose, if I were to tell you to go home, concentrate on yourself, and have visions, what would I be doing? I would be offering you an alternative within the dream itself. I would be asking you to remain within the condition of the dream. I would only be telling you to dream another kind of dream. I would simply be exploiting the dream itself—which, in this case, is the ordinary waking state. I would be recommending <u>experience</u> to you as the path of Truth. But all of that is more of the same thing. It is only another condition for you to take seriously and presume to be your own.

Most perfect "radical" self-understanding is not a form of philosophy. It is not a seeker's method. It is not something within the dream itself. It is like the waking state as opposed to the dream.

I Am the True Guru, Appearing within the dream. I Am the True Divine Heart Itself, Conscious, Real, Alive—Free, by virtue of My Divine Self-Nature, from the implications of the ordinary waking state, and from the implications of even all conditional states. But the traditional Yogi, the usual teacher, the ordinary philosopher, is a role <u>within</u> the dream of waking. Such a one operates from the point of view of the dream and is identified with the dream. Whether that one is suffering or happy within the dream, the dilemma is there. Such a one's attainment, however extraordinary it may appear to be, is an artifice rooted in the condition (or point of view) of the dream. Thus, the usual teacher is only recommending some distraction to you, some occupation, some solution within the dream itself.

But the True Divine Heart is most perfect "radical" self-understanding—simply Awake. Most perfect "radical" self-understanding is (itself) the True Waking State, the Divine Self-Condition, Reality Itself. The Heart Itself has no philosophy, no subtle vision, no special experiential state associated with It. Therefore, like a person who is dreaming, one who most perfectly understands is not affected by the waking state. But, unlike the dreamer, one who most perfectly understands is Always Already Consciously Free.

The waking state is an utterly different condition from dreaming. That is why you feel free of the dream upon waking. I Appear in the midst of the dreams of ordinary waking life—like sunlight in the morning. While you are still dreaming, still asleep, the sun comes up. It gets brighter and brighter, and the light comes into the room. At last, the light, the day itself, becomes sufficient to wake you—and, then, all of a sudden, you are not dreaming anymore, and everything is all right.

I Am simply that Sunlight Process, that Intensification—Rising on you always, without any other special activity. My relationship to you, your living condition of relationship to Me—just that heart-relationship—is sufficient. There is only Sunlight on the pillow, until that Intensity is sufficient to Wake you Up. It is the moment when the Prince kisses Sleeping Beauty. Such is My Avataric Divine Spiritual Grace, Which (ultimately) Awakens most perfect "radical" self-understanding.

On the other hand, the teachings that are generated on the basis of the great search are all exploitations of your dream state. Such teachings take your dream state seriously. They presume it to be your Real condition, even if it is regarded to be only temporary—and that is the fundamental error of all traditional (remedial) paths. They are all generated from the point of view of your suffering. They serve your suffering—and they reinforce it, in spite of themselves. Therefore, to the seeker, to the one suffering in dreams, the teachings of the traditional Yogis and philosophers seem very hopeful. They seem to represent something very desirable.

> You are running down the beach,
> away from the gorilla.
> Suddenly, there is a guy sitting outside a hut,
> next to a pool of blue water.
> He has long hair,
> and he bears all the great signs of an ascetic.
> He says, "Just sit down here.
> Very quickly now,
> because the gorilla is not too far away.
> Breathe very deeply,
> and concentrate between the two halves
> of your brain."

The guy has not changed your actual condition, but he has distracted you. The form of experience that he has stimulated in you (by the force and influence of his personality) certainly appears to be desirable—over against being devoured by the gorilla. But, at last, it is simply a distraction within the dream. It is another form of the dream. It is an event within the dream.

All of the searches that people are involved in are attempts to forget the gorilla—and such is their maximum possible attainment. Therefore, when you seem to have forgotten the gorilla, all of a sudden you are smiling again. You feel fantastic! There is no gorilla! There is? No, nothing! People presume that the consolations and exchanges (or transformations) of state generated by seeking are pleasure, creativity, Freedom, Realization, Liberation, God-Union, Nirvana. But do you see how all such attainments relate to suffering itself?

The gorilla is what is going on for people. It is death. Are you interested in that? It does not make any difference what you <u>do</u>

for the next thirty years—if you have that long—you are just going to go back to zero.

Some of you were with Me this morning, looking at a book called *Facing Death*.[44] How absurd—the notion of "facing" death! The first thing you lose in death is face! That is why the characteristic forms of morality in the Orient are largely based on the "saving of face". Loss of face is loss of life, loss of actual existence.

Well, that is what happens in the terminal psycho-physical event that is called "death". That is what death is all about. How can you <u>face</u> it? Everything you do to face it, everything you do to prevent the gorilla, has no ultimate effect on the gorilla. All seeking is simply your distraction, your makeup, your false face, your fascination. But—Zap!—the gorilla gets you every time. <u>Everybody</u> dies.

Everybody who has ever lived has died. There are billions and billions of human beings who have died. Multiples of billions of other entities and creatures die every moment, even as a by-product of your breathing. All these breathings disintegrate billions of tiny entities in organic fires. There is no harmlessness, no non-killing. The death by slaughter—the consumption and literal transformation of apparently separate entities—is going on all the time.

There is no escape from death. There is no "sanctity" in vegetables, nor even "freedom" for those who reduce cattle to sandwiches. The entire cosmic domain is a continuous sacrifice—in which all things, all beings, are ritual food. At best, the search can only modify the apparent circumstances of your death.

Ordinary religious people and traditional Yogis may, at last, manage to forget the gorilla. They may think they are looking at the blue of Krishna or the white of Jesus—until they lose face. Until the sudden zero, they are looking at Krishna or Jesus. They are only consoled, only distracted. Their hoped-for realization and their death are kneeling in one another.

There is no philosophy whose force is stronger than the force of death. The philosophies by which people counter (or react to) death are in opposition—and, at best, only seemingly equal—to the power of death. Therefore, it is possible to be consoled and distracted—but nothing greater is attained by those who react to death, who make adventure in relation to the gorilla. There is no philosophy, no vision, no attainment, no success, that will make death a literal delight, that will make it any less difficult than it appears to be within the dream itself. But, if you simply Wake Up from the dream, then (because the waking state is already free of the "awful" that appears in dreams) you are already free of the implications of the billions upon billions of deaths that can be dreamed.

One who most perfectly understands is simply one who is Awake. Such a one has no other specific and necessary qualities. One who is Awake is not elaborate at all. It is the guy within the dream who is very complex—because he has so many things to do. But the one who is simply Awake is simply Awake.

I Am the One Who Comes to Awaken others. I Am (Myself) the Awakening Sunlight, the Very Light of Truth. I Appear within the dream of human beings as an ordinary person. I may seem extraordinary, and a paradox, to the dreamer—because the dreamer is very serious about all of this. But I Am the One Who Is Only Awake, the One Who is not serious about any "thing" (in and of itself). I do not presume the condition of the dream as limitation.

For the seeker, life itself manifests as a problem, a fundamental dilemma. For the one who most perfectly understands, there is no fundamental dilemma.

Only the Condition of genuine Waking is truly Free of the condition in the dream. But that True Waking Condition is not what is attained by any of the means generated in the dream, by any form of the search. The means designed within the dream state are often magnificent, extremely elaborate. They are inventions grown out of the apparent practical necessities of the dream-life—and, so, they are very complex, very elaborate. They take many, many factors into account. Traditional religion and Spirituality, conventional Yoga, mysticism, magic, occultism—not to mention all the "sciences" of life, the life-strategies and life-remedies—are all highly complex, and often very successful in relieving the symptoms (or experiential dis-ease) of un-Conscious life.

Therefore, the methods and artifices of seeking fascinate those who are simply suffering. Everybody is looking for the consolation or technique that distracts to the maximum degree. Everybody is willing to "spend money for that which is not bread".[45] People are not truly looking to be sustained. They do not require Truth. They only desire to forget or escape the gorilla. But I am not such a one. I only Live Truth to living beings.

I have talked about the relationship between Guru and devotee as the essence, the fundamental condition, of sadhana. But the Guru-devotee relationship is not a form of concentration on the Guru as a separate (and merely symbolic) entity. That is not relationship. That is your own fabrication, your own suffering again. Whenever there is relationship, there is no need for all of these symbolic constructs. The true nature of sadhana in My Avataric Divine Heart-Company is to live the <u>Condition</u> (and the <u>life-conditions</u>) of Satsang with Me, of relationship to Me in My Function as True Divine Guru.

Within the dream, the potential images may be consoling, and even hopeful—but such consolation or hope is not the equivalent of being Awake. Consolation and hope <u>depend</u> upon your being asleep. The forms of seeking exploit your capability to identify with the fundamental dilemma of dreaming, which is its unconsciousness. The forms of seeking may satisfy you within the context of your presumptions, but they are not the equivalent of Waking Up.

What is required to Wake Up? What can you do within the dream to Wake Up? Not a thing. There is only the Waking Itself. All actions within the dream are forms of the dream itself. Waking is another process—and It occurs by other means, by Divinely Graceful Means.

I am not a symbol, a condition of the dream itself. No mere symbol, no mere condition of the dream, can Wake you Up. I Am the Divine Conscious Light, the Real Divine Person—Always Already Awake, Functioning Alive. I Appear in human Form, within the dream of life—not in order to console you, but to Awaken you through the Real crisis in consciousness. I am a frustration to the unconscious condition of the dream.

There are those who preach various forms of mental pre-occupation, and there are those who preach various forms of subtle preoccupation. They are all the same. They are all doing the same thing. They are all serving the dream.

I <u>Am</u> the Man of "Radical" Understanding. In My Function as the True Divine Guru, I <u>Am</u> the Divine Awakener. I <u>Am</u> the Person of Reality Itself.

I Am Always Already Awake. I could not care less about your urges and demands within the dream. I refuse to satisfy them. I refuse to give you an experience merely to console you. I have no intention of satisfying anyone's egoic game. All the demands for satisfaction that you bring are frustrated in My Company. What is satisfied, what is made to grow, is that fundamental Intuition of Reality that is already the Foundation of your existence. That Intuition is intensified in Satsang with Me. All the rest, the fascinated search, begins to fall away. In Satsang with Me, the search begins to reveal itself, until it becomes obvious.

"Radical" self-understanding will not necessarily have anything particularly dramatic about it. How dramatic is it to wake up in the morning? You do not go, "Wowwwwwww!!!" You do not scream, "Fantastic! Oh, Revelation!" All you do is open your eyes and live. You just wake up. The awareness that you are not stuck in the dream has a certain pleasure associated with it, but it is not usually a fantastic sort of fireworks. It is a natural, already happy event.

In *The Knee Of Listening*, I described the Great Event of My Divine Re-Awakening. That Great Event was not dramatic at all. I was sitting on a bench in a little temple. In the moment of My Divine Re-Awakening, I simply opened My eyes and walked out into the street. I did not talk to anybody on the way, and I did not say anything about It to anybody at home. I did not describe this profound Event to anybody at all for many weeks, even months. When I began to talk about It, I tried to make clear that Its True Import was ineffable. It was not "extraordinary". It was without "drama". I was simply being Awake. There was not anything to compare It to. It was not the attainment of anything.

Within the dream, there are all kinds of attainments:

The gorilla is chasing you,
and—Smack!—the big purple mountain
has a crystal cave underneath.
You go running into it,
and you enter the water that is there.
You go deep—
and, then, there are brilliant red lights.
Pearls and sacred ornaments
hit you on the head,
and you go shooting up like a rocket
of gleaming silver-and-gold fire.
You flash to the top of the mountain.
Your head explodes into billions of serpents.
At last, you stand immortal and victorious
on the mountaintop.
You scream at all the gorillas
from the top of the mountain.
You destroy them
and smother them
and smash them to smithereens!

That is the attainment within the dream. That is the usual Yoga. That is the typical vision. But most perfect "radical" self-understanding is simple Waking Up.

Now, this dilemma, this unconsciousness, this self-contraction I have often described to you, is the dream. It is the crucial presumption. It is not changed or undone by the fact of the ordinary waking state, nor by any ordinary life-activity or seeking. It is without benefit of the intuited Reality in Which you truly live.

Therefore, you presume and live the condition of suffering, separateness, and fundamental dilemma—until (ultimately, by Means of My Avataric Divine Spiritual Grace) you Awaken in spontaneous, most perfect "radical" self-understanding. Without "radical" self-understanding, you inevitably become shattered, insane, corrupted, thoroughly unconscious. If the gorilla eats you in the dream, you feel eaten. You <u>are</u> eaten. Those who dream

252

long enough, who try all the alternatives within the dream, who have suffered all the attainments and failures within the dream, who no longer have anywhere to go, who no longer take their search seriously, for whom the search is no longer the thing to which they resort, who have despaired of their own adventure, their ecstasies, their attainments, their strategic paths, their methods, who are only suffering, who are only in dilemma, who are only experiencing the self-contraction, the compulsive avoidance of relationship, but are not doing anything about it any longer, who know they cannot do anything about it any longer—they become sensitive to the sunlight.

To move into My Avataric Divine Heart-Company is not something My devotee is capable of doing. The devotee does not actually go to the Guru. The devotee cannot simply decide one morning to go to the Guru. The devotee does not know where the Guru is. How can anyone go to the sunlight? My devotee is somebody lying asleep in bed. As My devotee, you do not come to Me. I Am the Sun—Rising, Intensifying the Light, until you heart-recognize Me and realize that you are already in My Avataric Divine Heart-Company. That realization is Satsang with Me. And My Ultimate Divine Gift to you of most perfect "radical" self-understanding is (itself) True Waking, True Knowledge of the Sun-Light. All seeking for Me, all going after Me as the True Guru, is an activity within the dream. I cannot truly be found within the dream. Only the imagery of the dream can be found within the dream. Perhaps My bodily (human) Person can be glimpsed—but My True Divine Self-Nature and My Unique Function as Divine Guru cannot be comprehended by the dreamer, by the seeker, or by the seeker's strategic methods.

If you yield to the gorilla at last, if you give up your search—not willfully, but spontaneously, having despaired of your seeking—then you have, essentially, surrendered (or yielded) to the Very Reality you have always intuited. That spontaneous surrendering, that yielding to the gorilla, is a sign of Waking. It is the "far end" of sleep. It is the beginning of sensitivity to the morning. As soon as you become sensitive to it, you just Wake Up and go about your business.

The life of My Divinely Self-Realized devotee is a very natural, functional life of Real Enjoyment, of Intelligence. It is a life Awake. It is not a life "in bed". It is not spent meditating in the crystal cave. It is a simple, normal, ordinary life—Full of Perfect Love-Bliss-Happiness. It is to live already Awake.

Of course, I have been talking in similes. You may now have the idea that the waking state is the only condition uniquely free of the limitations of the dream state. In fact, there is a state that transcends even the limitations of the waking state. However, people do not ordinarily pass into this "Fourth State" (Beyond waking, dreaming, and sleeping), in which even the ordinary waking state loses the force of its implications.

That is why My Divine Guru-Function is lived in the waking world. I Am that "Fourth State"—Alive in the waking world, under the appearance of the waking condition. Just so, meditation in the Way of Adidam is not a fixation of the eyes on the reflected physical sunlight of the conditional worlds, nor a fixation of the psyche on the energies (whether ordinary or extraordinary) that appear and move in waking life. Meditation in the Way of Adidam is present Enjoyment of the Sun Itself—the True Sun, Which Is Reality Itself. That "Fourth State" is Awake to the waking state.

To heart-recognize Me, to heart-Commune with Me, the One Who Is Always Already Awake, is to be Drawn into the process of Waking Up. When you truly, most perfectly see Who I Am, you are already Awake. Until that moment, you are still woozy. But, if you live in My Avataric Divine Heart-Company and fulfill the conditions I require of you for your sake, you begin to feel a distance from the dream, from its compulsiveness, its repetitiveness.

What is happening in such a case is that the Divine Person, the True Divine Heart, the True Divine Sun, Who I Am, is being Intuited. When you most perfectly see Me, when you most perfectly see the Sun, then you yourself have been Awakened. The morning sun, the appropriate hour, the physics and biology of your life-condition—all these conspire to waken you to the ordinary world from your natural sleep. Just so, Satsang with Me—the Condition and sadhana of Real religious and Spiritual life in My Avataric Divine Heart-Company—is the only-by-Me Revealed and

Given Process that Awakens you to the True Divine Self-Condition of all-and-All.

All of the secondary forms of associating with Me are, indeed, secondary. All of your ordinary waking activities—even those in which you may communicate with Me—are effective only in the ordinary waking state itself, the "dream" of usual life. They may be appropriate, even necessary—but they are not themselves the Way in My Avataric Divine Heart-Company. The Way of Adidam is the devotional (and, in due course, Spiritual) relationship to Me—that relationship itself. It constantly exists. It is the sadhana. It is the meditation. There is nothing else that needs to be added to it. The relationship itself is the sadhana.

There is no end to the numbers of living beings who can do this sadhana. The sadhana of heart-relationship to Me is what My devotee must always realize and live. Because I Always Already Abide As the Spiritually Self-"Bright" Divine Self-Condition, to Live That Condition to My devotees requires no special effort on My Part. There is no limitation in My Capability to Be That Fundamental Reality for all beings. The limitations are on My devotee's activity at the life-level, and also on My apparent activity at that same level. Nevertheless, I am not limited to this appearance—I am Rising Above the house. I am not this conditional state. I Am your Prior Self-Condition, Most Perfectly Known.

Since this True Waking Is Reality Itself, or the True Condition of all-and-All, the dilemma cannot be located when you look for it. The dilemma is purely an illusion presumed by the dreamer, by the one who only seems to be awake.

You spend your entire life within the dream, within this vast adventure—to find the princess in the crystal palace and save her from the dragon, or to wait in the crystal palace to be rescued by the prince. You live an endless, endless adventure—millions and millions of ages, year after year after year, of numberless complications. But, at some point along the way, you become serious enough to examine why you are seeking—to examine the cause, the root, for which this adventure and its sought goal is only the symbol. At last, you realize that you cannot find your symbolic satisfaction. And this falling into your dilemma—then falling through it—is the Unqualified Realization of the True Self-Nature and Real Self-Condition of all-and-All.

There is no "fated" time when this will occur. You need not persist to the end of your seeking before it is appropriate to understand. A person can wake up at any time. You do not have to go through the entire dream-process until you seem to find the princess sleeping in her castle or until the prince seems to find you. You do not have to dream the entire sequence of the dream. Karmas (or destiny) are not absolute and necessary in that sense. It is always appropriate to wake up—at any time.

Only if you continue to believe in your own search do you feel that you must acquire and achieve a great deal before Realization is "appropriate". Then you have "twenty more years of striving", or "twenty more times to be born for death's sake". Then you have an obligatory number of things to do. You must do certain things "in" the body, you must earn a certain amount of money—you are "born" with various conditions to fulfill.

But the ideal of seeking is truly absurd. You cannot imagine the <u>dreamer</u> defending all of that, but only the "actor" within the dream. Even the one in the dream will not defend the "destiny" of seeking while in the presence of the gorilla. That destiny can only be defended by someone who is surrounded by delights, full of capabilities. A person in that circumstance is like a boy whose mother wants him to wake up and go to school. He does not want to get up. He says, "No, I'll get up later." He does not want to go to school. Just so, the seeker does not want to go to "school". The seeker does not want to live the sadhana, the discipline, the real conditions of life that are required in the Company of the True Guru. The seeker does not want to understand his or her own adventure.

The waking state promises something relatively undesirable to one who is suspended in the twilight state of a pleasant dream. Such a one is reluctant to understand, too distracted to be interested in "radical" self-understanding. The typical reluctance of people is not, in fact, caused by their premonition that the life (or sadhana) of "radical" self-understanding is going to be terribly difficult. It is simply that they do not yet care about going beyond their suffering. Somehow, for the moment, everything seems all right. Many people lead a relatively healthful physical life—with certain satisfactions, certain opportunities, things to do, books to read, a future of places, physical pleasures, mental pleasures. With all of that, who needs to Wake Up?

Most people approach the Guru in that condition. Therefore, the Guru does not take them seriously. The Guru knows they are only indulging themselves—even if, to others, the new arrivals seem to deserve only mercy and the grin of promised salvation. When such seekers come to the Guru, they make all kinds of complaints about their fundamental suffering. "Please give me this salvation, this realization, this release!" But they are not really looking for that. They are unwilling to endure the discipline of Truth.

There are certain limitations to the adventure and pleasure of ordinary life. You know you are going to die someday—but, essentially, mysteriously, life still seems to be full. Thus, Truth is not likely to enter the usual picture without the intervention of some fundamental, transforming event.

But, if you are smart, if your life is generated with conscious intensity, you do not have to become desperate before you turn to the Truth. Your circumstances do not have to become empty, corrupted, and diseased. You do not have to wait for the failure of life itself before you turn to Truth. People who are waiting for life to disprove itself are only indulging themselves. There is nothing profound about the search or the suffering that such a life involves. On the other hand, if you are smart, if your life is lived with conscious intensity, then you are always turning to Truth— even from the moment of birth.

The more distracted people are by the pleasures of existence as the condition of their life, the more mediocre their realization— on every level, even on the level of life itself. People who are just plain satisfied with how good their bodies feel barely function at all. There is no life-force, no life-intelligence, in such people. They do nothing. They just smile and fool around with sexual partners all the time. They do not create anything. They do not realize anything of Spiritual significance. They do not intensify the quality of life. They have achieved nothing more than symbolic existence.

They may have to suffer drastic conflicts and upheavals before their unconsciousness begins to break up, but such suffering is not really necessary. It is not necessary to go through a long term of seeking, suffering, breaking down, corruption, before Truth becomes appropriate.

The Realization of Truth is not a matter of heavy, self-involved, constricted, willful effort. It is as natural as a simple response to sunlight. It is simply the heart-relationship to Me, the intelligent life of Real sadhana.

Truly, what you bring to Me is not your dilemma. The dilemma has no real existence. You may be preoccupied with it, but I pay no homage to it. It is of no ultimate consequence what the content of your dilemma appears to be in any moment.[46]

Truly, what people bring to Me is their Intuition of Reality Itself. It is simply that they are not consciously living on the basis of that Intuition. Nevertheless, that Intuition is the very premise of their lives. And, so, they come to Me—the Sun to their deep-seated Intuition, the One Who Transmits that Intuition—and I Draw their Intuition into this instant.

Only the seeker takes the dilemma seriously. The waking state does not take your dreams seriously. It is not the least concerned with your dreams. And, fortunately, all beings are already alive with the Intuition of Reality. Therefore, all beings have an affinity with Sunlight, with the True Waking State—with Me. Unqualified Reality, the Love-Bliss-Happiness of My "Bright" Divine Self-Condition, is What they are already living—and that is What is consciously discovered in the heart-relationship to Me. Because you Always Already Inhere in My Love-Bliss-Happiness, I Draw you to Myself.

It is the Intuition of Reality Itself that inexorably draws people to Me, that leads them to maintain themselves in My Avataric Divine Heart-Company. All apparent "reasons" for holding on to Me fall away, and also all the apparent "reasons" for not holding on to Me. None of these reasons has any ultimate significance. It is your inherent affinity for Truth, your Intuition of the Divine Self-Condition, of the Living Divine Heart Itself, that is entirely responsible for the sadhana in My Avataric Divine Heart-Company.

When you become less concerned with your particular search, your inwardness, your adventure, then you have simply become more sensitive to your Real Condition. You have felt the sunlight falling on your sleeping eyes. When your eyes have opened in the morning light, everything will be obvious to you—and you will know that you have never slept, that you have never dreamed, that you have never been limited to any thing that has appeared. You have never been limited to any condition that you have presumed. There was always only Reality Itself, the True Divine Self-Nature of all-and-All—Which Is Love-Bliss-Happiness Itself, Consciousness Itself, the Unqualified Presence of Reality Itself, Truth Itself, and Real God.

I _Am_ That.

AVATAR ADI DA SAMRAJ
The Mountain Of Attention Sanctuary, 2000

7.

Relationship and Association

AVATAR ADI DA SAMRAJ: I was talking to someone here the other day about certain associations everyone has—with people, with environments, and so on. This person was wondering whether some of his old relationships would continue, now that he had become involved in the practice in My Company. He wanted to know if these friendships would necessarily come to an end, or if they could still continue now that he is doing sadhana as My devotee.

I pointed out to him that many such involvements are not rightly to be regarded as relationships. Rather, they are associations. They are (essentially) forms of your own desire. Therefore, they are not true friendships. Such associations with people, and even with environments and objects, enable you to indulge certain qualities of experience at will. Even though there seems to be something there—a person, a place, a thing—in fact, you are not truly enjoying relationship. You simply have an association that reflects your desire, and (thereby) gives you the opportunity to indulge it, to satisfy it, to suffer it.

Associations come and go, just as desires come and go—but relationship is, in the context of conditional existence, the living function and living condition of Conscious Existence. And, truly, relationship has neither beginning nor end. When there is genuine relationship with an individual, a place, a thing, an environment, it is not subject to the quality of desire. Desire does not generate the relationship. The end of desire or a change in desire does not bring the relationship to an end.

When relationship is discovered and lived, it never comes to an end. Its quality may change, and there may be apparent separations in time and space—but the relationship itself is fundamental, continuous, real. Where there is relationship, there tends to be apparent growth, intensification, change—but the relationship itself does not come to an end.

Associations, however, come and go. Associations belong to periods of one's life, stages in one's experience. They are functions of time, space, and desire. Therefore, when some particular desire—or desire itself—ceases to be the point of view of conscious awareness, then associations tend to fall apart, disappear, come to an end. But, when (by Means of My Avataric Divine Spiritual Grace) there is most perfect "radical" self-understanding, then there are no longer any associations at all. There is only relationship, only relatedness. There is no separation, no separateness. And relationship is enjoyed under all circumstances, all conditions, with all beings, in all environments.

Because people are identified with their own desires and live by the habit of association rather than relationship, there is suffering. Because people do not become more for one another than extensions of their own minds, their own desires, there is no relationship.

Until there is "radical" self-understanding, there is the tendency to live mere association through desire—even with those with whom you enjoy the quality of relationship. Thus, until there is "radical" self-understanding, all your relationships involve conflict. They are always threatened by mere desire, mere association. You move in and out of them. You never truly enjoy them, except in brief moments.

Where there are simply associations in the form of desire, your connections tend to disappear, and certain relationships tend to become corrupted, destroyed, impossible at times. But all separateness is an illusion. It is impossible for there to be any separateness. There is no such thing. It has never occurred. There is no separately existing thing anywhere. There is no separately existing being anywhere. There is no separate anything! Separateness is only an impression caused by disturbance, by this compulsive contraction I have often described. When self-contraction comes to an end, when the avoidance of relationship comes to an end, there is no "difference".

All separateness is an illusion, and all attainments are an illusion. There is no separateness, and there is no attainment of union. The state of the traditional Yogi is as much an illusion as the state of the ordinary person who is suffering and dying. If you are an ordinary sufferer, you think you have become absolutely small—whereas, if you are an expansive Yogi, you think you have become absolutely great. But, when you think you have <u>become</u> great, you truly suspect that you <u>are</u> small. In Truth, there is only the penetration of your search, the understanding of it—and, then, existence becomes capable of being lived Freely and Happily.

People are busy communicating their own mind-forms, their own contracted perceptions, rather than living from the "Point of View" of Truth. Thus, people are only punishing one another. Everyone causes pain for everyone else. Everyone reinforces the illusion of separate life. Therefore, everyone is seeking. Everyone suspects "it" (whatever the presumed goal of anyone's life may be) is somewhere else, or that "it" does not exist.

But, when there is the most perfect understanding of that entire search, then there is only the Communication of Consciousness Itself—That Very Power, That Condition, That <u>Is</u> Reality Itself—in relationship. And the ultimate form of that Communication is Satsang with Me—the Communication, Condition, or Company of Truth. When the Presence of Reality (or the "Bright" Conscious Light Itself) is Communicated in Satsang with Me, you are Assumed by This Presence, Acquired by It. This Communication undermines all ordinary assumptions—until you cease to believe them, and you become intelligent with Truth.

Apart from "radical" self-understanding, all human beings are distracted and turned in on themselves. They appear to have been born, but they are still bent. Every human individual, in fear of the born-condition, lives not-yet-straightened from the curve of the womb. And all the people who surround you, since they are also in the same state, only reinforce the fear that makes you bend and curve inward.

I Am the Man of "Radical" Understanding. I Exist and Live as the Communication of That Which makes it possible for people to open, uncurl, be turned to relationship.

The process of restoration to Truth has been called "second birth". Until you become capable of existence in this apparent (human) form, open in relationship, you tend to reject the force of existence in a continuously repeated ritual activity, like vomiting. The force of life is abandoned constantly. Even laughter is a form of this ritual abandonment. Non-regenerative sexual activity is a form of it. Ordinary perception is a form of it. It is to throw off, to fail to conduct, the force of life. It is unconsciousness, sleep, the refusal to be born. And its symptom is a life that is not in relationship, that is not whole, that is full of dis-ease, confusion. Such a life cannot function. It only forever seeks its own release— as if release from life were the goal of life.

In Satsang with Me, this rejection of the force of life, this rejection of birth, tends to become quieted—such that, more and more, the life-form conducts the force of life rather than rejecting it. The subtle form of the human structure is something like a Sphere, in Which the Current of natural life-energy (and also of the Divine Spirit-Energy) continually descends in the frontal line, and then turns at the bodily base and ascends in the spinal line. In Satsang with Me, that Current is not rejected—It is conducted.

The force of life rounds the heart, like the planets round the Sun. And the True Divine Heart Is the "Sun" of the living human form. The Fullness that people begin to feel in Satsang with Me is this Circle of natural life-force (and, eventually, also My Avatarically Self-Transmitted Divine Spirit-Energy), allowed to be conducted in descent (down the frontal line), and allowed to be conducted in ascent (up the spinal line). When that Fullness is felt, there is no more rejection (or "ritual vomiting") of the Current of Energy. Rather, by means of spontaneous "conductivity", the Current (of natural life-energy and, in the case of My by-Me-Spiritually-Initiated devotees, of My Avatarically Self-Transmitted Divine Spirit-Energy) is turned and re-turned—in a spherical Cycle that is completely at ease, without dilemma.

When (by Means of My Avataric Divine Spiritual Grace) the "Sun", the Living Heart of Reality, the Divine Conscious Light That Is the Self-Condition (and Source-Condition) of all of this, is Most Perfectly Realized, That is most perfect "radical" self-understanding,

Most Perfect Divine Self-Realization. From That "Point of View", all of this is Obvious.

The religious and Spiritual traditions communicate various aspects of this phenomenon of "second birth". The religious search, particularly the form of seeking that is characteristic of Westerners, is a strategic effort to receive the Spirit, to receive the Power of the Divine, and to bring the Grace of this Power down into life.

The traditional Eastern seeker—and, in general, the practitioner of Spirituality—is sensitive to the ascending movement of Energy. Traditional Yoga is a ritualization of this process of strategic ascent to the Divine—just as traditional religion is the strategic ritual means for becoming at ease, receptive, full of the Divine.

But these two—East and West—are simply modes of exclusive (and ritualized) attachment to one or the other of the two principal aspects of this Real Process, or "second birth". Thus, the East is traditionally very busy with the ascending Power, knowing little of descent—and the West is traditionally very busy with the descending Power, knowing little of ascent. And both East and West approach this "second birth" in the seeker's mode.

The "second birth" truly is a possibility. It is the only Real possibility for human beings. And its Process is most perfectly enacted only in Satsang with Me—in the living, present-time, devotional (and, in due course, Spiritual) relationship to Me, the One Who Is the True Divine Heart Itself. Not someone who only suggests the Heart Itself, who has (at some time) merely experienced It, who merely envisions It, who only thinks about It, or who only teaches about It—but the One Who Is the True (and Living) Divine Heart, without any limitations whatsoever.

I Am That One. When My devotee lives the conditions Given by Me, in the context of Satsang with Me, then the Circle of descent and ascent is restored—in a very simple, natural manner. As My devotee, you need not apply yourself methodically to the generation of that Circle, to the strategic restoration of that pattern of Energy. As My devotee, living Satsang with Me as the Condition of your very existence, you do not exercise any kind of strategic approach, nor do you engage any of the remedial methods of conventional religion and conventional Spirituality. My devotee's practice is to live the Condition of this devotional (and, in due course, Spiritual) relationship to Me.

My true devotee is not distracted by any form of the religious or Spiritual search—whether the search to "be filled" by the descending Spirit-Energy or the search to "escape upward" by means of the ascending Spirit-Energy. My true devotee turns simply to Me—and is (thereby) turned to the Real condition of life, which is relationship. As My devotee, you pass through various forms of crisis, until there is spontaneous insight into (or understanding of) the ordinary pattern of your life, which is the avoidance of relationship. By Means of My Avataric Divine Spiritual Grace, the direct observation of this pattern becomes "radical" self-understanding. And Most Perfect Realization of such "radical" self-understanding is Absolute Truth.

The Real Spiritual process alive in Satsang with Me involves no problematic concern relative to the reception of My Avataric Divine Spirit-Baptism. The process in My Avataric Divine Spiritual Company is generated and maintained by the Spontaneous and Intelligent Siddhi (or Real Spiritual Power) of the "Sun", the True Divine Heart—Which Is Reality Itself. My devotee is not engaged in a strategic (or ego-based) process of (downward) reception of Divine Blessing, or of (upward) return to the Divine Source, or of both. My devotee abides simply in relationship with Me—and the Primary Intensity of My Divine Heart-Light, the Conscious Spirit-Power that proceeds in Satsang with Me, is the entire Means for the crisis in consciousness (or self-understanding) that must occur in My devotee.

In the meantime, there may be secondary phenomena associated with Satsang with Me—and these are the effects of My Avatarically Self-Transmitted Divine Spirit-Current, in Its Flow through the descending and ascending arcs of the Circle. But all such phenomena are purely secondary. They are simply conditional enjoyments. Like right diet, they are not (in and of themselves) Truth. If you are distracted by such phenomena, then you contract (and thereby separate yourself) from all forms of relationship.

Only relationship is appropriate. There is no need to be concerned with the effects of the Descent or the Ascent of My Divine Spirit-Power. There is no need to seek My Divine Spirit-Power or to grasp It. All such concerns are an expression of the root-dilemma.

DEVOTEE: What is it about the experience of this Force (or Light) that causes people to reject It? Is the experience itself painful? Or is it somehow threatening?

AVATAR ADI DA SAMRAJ: It is not so much that the forms of rejection are an effect of something else. They are the action. The rejection (or reaction) is spontaneous. It is the self-contraction. But its basis is subtle—preceding life, thought, and perception. The perceiver and the perception are already bent. They are (themselves) this rejection. They are already forms of the root-dilemma.

The true answer to any question is always prior to words, not able to be spoken. Indeed, even the question itself (if it is true, or real) is prior to words. The question that is phrased in the form of concepts is not the real question. Your real question is the sensation of self-contraction that motivates your thoughts and words. The answer, likewise, is not in the form of concepts. The only true (or real) answer is the direct observation and understanding of the root-activity that is your real question, your suffering, your dilemma, the motivation of your search. Nothing else can satisfy. No explanation is equal to this direct self-understanding.

There is a sense in which the entire process of rejection (or the avoidance of relationship) is a spontaneous reaction to the action that is conditionally manifested existence. Wherever there is an action, there is an equal and opposite reaction. There is the True Divine Heart (or Reality Itself), there is conditionally manifested appearance, and there is the self-contraction that is the reaction to that appearance. People are living as that reaction. When My devotees turn to Me, and (in that turning) observe and understand their own activity (which is their suffering), then (by Means of My Avataric Divine Spiritual Grace) they Realize the True Nature of Consciousness As the Living Divine Heart Itself—Which is Always Already Open, Which is Prior to conditional manifestation, Which is not any form of dilemma.

The genuine roots of your suffering, your disturbance, are not truly explainable in any conceptual terms. They can only be undermined (or obviated) by means of the self-understanding that becomes possible in Satsang with Me. Therefore, moment to moment (whole bodily) turning to Me (thereby allowing self-observation and self-understanding to take place) is the root-process of sadhana, the spontaneous and intelligent process of Satsang with Me.

There is no "second birth" apart from Real Spiritual practice in My Avataric Divine Company. There is no "second birth" apart from Satsang with Me, actual moment to moment living of the heart-relationship to Me—the Divinely Self-Realized Siddha-Guru, the Avatarically Self-Manifested Incarnation of the True Divine Heart Itself. The form and function Given (by Means of My Avataric Divine Grace) to human beings for living this Satsang is the direct relationship to Me—the One Who Lives As the Very Divine Heart Itself, the One and Only (and Self-Evidently Divine) Reality.

When people realize that they are suffering, that they are bent, that there is a root-dilemma, then they begin to seek. The only places where it is possible to seek are the gross, subtle, and causal dimensions of existence, which account for the entire structure of conditionally manifested life. Therefore, people go about the business of alternating between exploitation and discipline—until they realize the failure of the search. When that realization occurs, they have become capable of Satsang with Me.

DEVOTEE: Is it necessary for us to have a True and Conscious relationship with You and with everyone we know if we want to live a True Spiritual life, a life of understanding?

AVATAR ADI DA SAMRAJ: It would only be nicer! If it were necessary as a pre-condition, then Satsang with Me could not take place. If this process depended on people already enjoying the relationship with Me Consciously, perfectly, then the process would never begin. It is certainly a positive sign when the process becomes Conscious, when you begin to move into the natural "conductivity" of Satsang with Me, when you begin to live Its True quality, Its in-depth quality. But such is not required as a pre-condition.

There are no conditions for relationship. It is already the case. Some are conscious of it, and some are not. In some cases, you may enjoy the Real condition of relationship with another, while (to that other) you serve only as a form of association (and, thus, an extension of desire). And the opposite may also be true. When there is such an apparent discrepancy, you must decide whether you have the strength or the interest to live that relationship, whether you should release that relationship or (otherwise) change the quality or the conditions of that relationship.

DEVOTEE: Do we have a responsibility to make the other person in a relationship more conscious?

AVATAR ADI DA SAMRAJ: That responsibility is inherent in relationship itself. The very _fact_ of living in that direct, relational manner, rather than in the usual self-contracted manner, is (itself) a means to serve the communication of True intelligence. Therefore, that responsibility is already satisfied by the simple fact of living the relationship itself. It is not necessary to add to that relational force any secondary motivation to change the other person. When such motivations appear, your relationships tend to become an extension of your own search. To that degree, you fall back into association again. But, when you live relationship with other beings, you even extend and serve the _form_ of Satsang with Me— because that form _is_ heart-relationship to Me.

AVATAR ADI DA SAMRAJ
Adidam Samrajashram, 2004

8.
Meditation and Satsang

I.

AVATAR ADI DA SAMRAJ: Real Spiritual life is Satsang, the Company of Truth. Thus, for My devotee, Real Spiritual life is the heart-relationship to Me, the One Who Is the Perfect Avataric Embodiment and Divine Self-Revelation of Truth.

Satsang is also the Very Nature of life, the True form of existence. Relatedness—not independence, not separateness, but unqualified relatedness—is the Principle of True life.

None of the attempts to relieve the life of suffering by various strategic means (or ego-based remedies) can ever produce Truth. They may heal dis-ease, but only Truth Itself produces Truth. In the Way of Adidam, sadhana is to live Satsang with Me as the Condition of life forever. Sadhana is not something you do temporarily, until you get Free. The sadhana of My true devotee is to live Satsang with Me forever—a lifetime, even countless lifetimes, of Truth.

To begin the practice of the Way of Adidam is to enter into relationship with Me, to live in My Avataric Divine Company—always devotionally turning to Me, and always living the conditions Given by Me (and, thereby, getting straight). There is a Force—a Siddhi, or Spiritual Power—Alive in Satsang with Me. Therefore, among the experiences that may occur in Spiritual life are the sensations of Force (or Presence) Communicated in Satsang with Me. These are experienced as various feelings, a sense of peacefulness, kriyas (or spontaneous purifying movements), feelings of bodily bliss, and so on. But, in Truth, Spiritual life is not something that happens to you. It is not a process that takes place independent of your conscious participation. If it did, all you would need to do is to wait for it to come to an end in Liberation, or some exalted Yogic state.

Spiritual life is <u>Conscious</u> life. It does not really exist until your own conscious awareness becomes fully active, fully involved in the process. Spiritual life is an intelligent process. It is not a kind of "mediumship", wherein you simply "sit back" and passively enjoy certain experiences and certain energies. My Ruchira Shakti has a single purpose. It is to Communicate to you the Energy Alive in Truth Itself. Once you have been Spiritually Awakened by Me, the Descent of My Spirit-Current Purifies, Harmonizes, and Intensifies your life. In addition, My Spiritual Descent in your body-mind may give rise to various kinds of Spiritual experiences—all of which are simply means to strengthen and intensify your life, such that you have the life-energy, the life-force, with which to live Satsang with Me.

Sadhana is a process that takes place in Consciousness. It is founded in the Unqualified Intensity (or Force) of Consciousness Itself. It is Intelligent. It is not merely the result of some "outside" energy that you may seem to "objectively" observe. Real Consciousness does not happen <u>to</u> you.

When you become My devotee, you begin to live in Satsang with Me. You begin to live It as the Condition of your life. Some of My devotees have experiences of Force, of Energy, of kriyas, of internal awarenesses, of various kinds of purification. In other cases, the influence of Satsang with Me appears (at first) to have a primarily practical influence on your life. But, regardless of what phenomena you may or may not experience in My Avataric Divine Company, you must always (more and more profoundly) <u>use</u> the Wisdom-Teaching I have Communicated.

I want to read to you from an Essay I wrote at the same general time as My initial writing of *The Knee Of Listening*. The Essay is called "'Real' Meditation and the Progressive Stages of Life". It is a rather long Essay, divided into many sections. Tonight, I am only interested in discussing certain sections that concern the practical foundation of Satsang with Me, the foundation of Real (and, in due course, truly Spiritual) life in the only-by-Me Revealed and Given Way of Adidam.

The usual meditation—traditional meditation, the motivated remedy—is only a consolation, an effect, and a good feeling. The usual meditation effects no fundamental turnabout in ordinary (egoic) consciousness—and, thus, when situations arise outside of the meditative circumstance, there is no control over the already patterned process of identification, differentiation, and desire.

I spent years with all kinds of people who were experiencing the phenomena of Kundalini Yoga—dealing with the effects of Spiritual Force, miraculous Spiritual experiences. I have never seen anyone fundamentally changed by such experiences. I Myself was never thus changed by any of these experiences. They are not "designed" to change you. They <u>are</u> change. They are phenomena only. The phenomena themselves are not the point. They are simply a means of purification. You are not intended to sit in them forever, to bathe in them and watch them perform.

If you are My rightly practicing devotee, whatever such phenomena need to happen in your case are guaranteed to happen. But such phenomena are a relatively minor aspect of Spiritual life. They should be allowed to arise—but observe that they are not <u>themselves</u> Spiritual life. They will not lead to Divine Liberation. They are not, in and of themselves, Truth. They do not affect the motivating character (or root-difficulty) of your particular individual life one iota. Thirty years of Shakti experiences will occupy a fool, but they will not Awaken such a one.

Increase of Energy or Spiritual experience does nothing whatsoever to the fundamental quality of conscious awareness. At most, Spiritual experiences simply intensify conscious awareness, providing functional strength—so that Spiritual life can begin as a Real process.

Only "radical" (or "root") self-understanding avails. In other words, no motivated process, no simple influence of Energy avails. "Radical" (or "root") self-understanding is the Intelligence of Reality Itself. "Radical" (or "root") self-understanding is not attachment to some functional body (or functional sheath), or some conditional realm, or some conditional experience that is

seen as the alternative, remedy, cure, and source of "victory".
"Radical" (or "root") self-understanding recognizes (by Means of
My Avataric Divine Grace) that every motive and action is "made"
of avoidance. Thus, "radical" (or "root") self-understanding has
no recourse except to understand. And "radical" (or "root") self-
understanding and the one who truly ("radically", or "at the root")
understands the ego-"I" are not "different" from Reality Itself, the
One and Only Self of all-and-All, the "Bright".

The Yogic search enjoys only the conditionally manifested
forms of "Shakti" (or the conditionally achieved Bliss of Energy).
Only "Radical" Knowledge is Real Love-Bliss-Happiness, not
dependent on anything.

The influence of Satsang with Me, the Condition of Satsang
with Me, must begin. You must begin to adapt to Satsang with Me,
make It your sadhana, meet the conditions of life in My Avataric
Divine Company in a very simple manner, rightly adapt to a
disciplined life, assume responsibility for the heart-relationship
that is Satsang with Me—and begin to listen to Me.

You will simply begin to listen—and, when this process in
conscious awareness has begun, you will begin to observe yourself, see yourself under the conditions of life.

"Radical" (or "root") self-understanding awakens (by Means of
My Avataric Divine Grace) when you truly listen to My Avataric
Divine Word and truly observe yourself in relationship.
Therefore, observe yourself in life.
Observe yourself when you seek.
Observe yourself when you suffer to any degree.
Observe your motives.
Observe the activity of identification.
Observe the activity of differentiation.
Observe the activity of desire.
Observe the patterns of your existence.

The process of self-observation—magnified by listening to My
Spoken Instruction about the self-contraction (or the avoidance of

relationship), and by all your study and living of the Way of Adidam—becomes, at some point, <u>Communication received</u>: real observation that—yes!—this contraction, this avoidance, <u>is</u> the quality of your life.

When you realize that you are always seeking, "radical" (or "root") self-understanding is emerging.

When you realize that all your motives, all your acts, all your seeking, are the pattern of "Narcissus", "radical" (or "root") self-understanding is emerging.

When you realize that you are always suffering, "radical" (or "root") self-understanding is emerging.

When you realize that every moment is a process in dilemma, "radical" (or "root") self-understanding is emerging.

When you realize that every moment is a process of identification, differentiation, and desire, "radical" (or "root") self-understanding is emerging.

When you realize that, in every moment—when you are at your best, as well as when you are at your worst—you are only avoiding relationship, then you truly ("radically", or "at the root") understand the ego-"I".

When (by Means of My Avataric Divine Spiritual Grace) you have understood, "radical" (or "root") self-understanding will become the natural response of your intelligence to any experience, the total content of any moment. Then, approach every moment with "radical" (or "root") self-understanding, and perceive the Original Truth within it.

When (by Means of My Avataric Divine Spiritual Grace) you Most Perfectly Realize That Which Always Already <u>Is</u>—Which Always Already Surrounds and Pervades the living being, Prior to the entire dilemma, motivation, and activity of avoidance—then you have most perfectly understood. . . .

Therefore, commit yourself to "radical" (or "root") self-understanding in the midst of all experience—instead of merely committing yourself to the various kinds of remedial action that may be engaged as a means to handle the "problem" of life in any moment.

That process depends on making Satsang with Me into True sadhana, the very Condition of your life.

From the beginning, embrace and enjoy the Condition of this Satsang with Me. In this manner, begin to listen to Me—and, thus, become spontaneously available to the Intelligence of Satsang with Me. All of this will spontaneously become self-observation. When the self-observation that is spontaneously awakening in you continues under all conditions of life, then you will begin to observe the self-contraction itself. You will begin to see this avoidance of relationship. It will become clear to you in your living experience. When it has become clear to you, when it takes place as a certainty, as your very knowledge, then that very knowledge can be used positively, directly. It becomes your approach to life. It becomes the very form and function of your intelligence.

My Avataric Divine Spiritual Work is not at all about the ascending effort of Kundalini Yoga. Rather, My Avataric Divine Spiritual Work is the All-Inclusive, Universal, and Inherently Perfect Way of Real-God-Realization.

What occurs in My Work with My devotees is not simply an intellectual or mental liberation. The Force Alive in Satsang with Me is the Very Force of the Divine Heart Itself, the Living Reality. But That Force is not un-Conscious. It is Conscious. And the Way is Conscious. True sadhana in My Avataric Divine Company is the Way of Consciousness Itself, Full of Intensity and Force. Therefore, True sadhana in My Avataric Divine Company is not a matter of forever receiving the Blessing of the Shakti and allowing It to do things to you.

Begin to listen to Me. Accept the conditions of this relationship with Me. Remove the ordinary obstacles. Abandon them.

If you truly engage this relationship to Me, from day to day, more obstacles and more demands will be generated for you than you could ever have imagined. The relationship itself will discipline you. You do not have to be concerned with Spiritual techniques, purifying methods, things to do to yourself—apart from the responsibilities for practical maintenance of life which all My devotees are expected to fulfill.

Listen! There is this contraction, this avoidance. All human beings are living this avoidance of relationship. Apart from self-understanding, that is all anyone is doing. Nothing else is happening—only this contraction of gross, subtle, and causal forms. It is suffering. It stimulates, by implication, the ego-based notions people have about the nature of life. The self-contraction implies a separate self—separate from the world and from all other beings.

The appearance of "many" and "separate me" is an expression of your suffering—but the Presence, the Force, the Bliss, of Divine Reality persists and is felt even under the conditions of egoic ignorance. Therefore, the self-contraction appears as the drama of desire, the search for union between the "separate me" and the "manyness". Everyone's life is the drama made inevitable by this fundamental contraction. Everyone's life is the adventure that the individual is playing on this contraction. The drama of an ordinary life is without significance, without Real intensity. The ordinary life-drama is deadly ignorance—no Truth, no Satsang with Me.

Satsang with Me must begin. Satsang with Me must be enjoyed as the Condition of life. Then the entire ego-drama—of which even traditional Spirituality is a manifestation—comes to an end, dies. The self-contraction becomes flabby and releases. The Real Power of Consciousness Manifests Itself, Drawing you more deeply into the sadhana in My Avataric Divine Company.

In the Way of Adidam, meditation is not something that takes place in the midst of dilemma. In the Way of Adidam, meditation is not a strategic method to get rid of your suffering. It is not perpetual preoccupation with your own thoughts, with the content of your own life, in order to free yourself of your thoughts, step aside from them, make them be quiet. The "you" who does all of that is itself the dilemma. It does not know anything. It is (itself) the suffering. It is (itself) obsession with the endless stream of its own thought.

Therefore, your attempts to do something about the "mind"—to make it quiet, to make it see visions, and so on—are nothing but further expressions of the original motivating dilemma. Such strategies are expressions of your separative impulse, attempts to fortify and "save" your separate life (which is already an illusion).

In the Way of Adidam, meditation arises only in the heart-relationship with Me—only under the <u>conditions</u> of Truth, already lived. There is Force in such meditation. For My rightly practicing devotee, meditation is an intense Fire. It is a marvelous Intelligence, a Brilliance, a Genius, a Living Force. It is not a pious attempt to quiet your little thoughts. It blasts the hell out of those thoughts! From the "Point of View" of the Living Divine Heart (or Truth Itself, or Reality Itself), there is no concern for all of these thoughts, all of these dilemmas, all of this mediocrity of suffering. All of that amounts to nothing.

When Satsang with Me becomes the Principle of your life, and Truth becomes the form of your meditation, thought is consumed. Such True meditation is a Pressure under Which thoughts cannot survive. Such True meditation is an Intelligence that needs only to observe an obstruction in order for that obstruction to dissolve. This is the process that comes awake in Satsang with Me—not some strategic method, some ego-based remedy. The entire point of view of dis-ease is false. Spiritual life is not a "cure". Spiritual life is the life of Truth. If you are looking for a cure, then you are still obsessed with your dis-ease.

Therefore, the first true thing you do when you come into contact with Me is to relax the obsession with your dis-ease, your trouble. Thus, the original activity you enjoy in relation to Me is not some remarkably sophisticated form of meditation. As My beginning devotee, what you do is nothing very sophisticated at all. You turn to Me and relax your search. You begin to find your-self in the Condition of Truth, the Condition of Satsang with Me. You begin to enjoy that Condition very directly and concretely—enjoying the Force of It, the Intensity of It, the Beauty of It, the Blissfulness and Happiness of It. Only after you have firmly estab-lished yourself in Satsang with Me do you begin to observe your-self consistently and effectively, to become truly intelligent and sophisticated in your application to the practice I have Given. Depending on how seriously you apply yourself, the beginnings of Satsang with Me may last for a very long time.

The more you persist in the drama of your resistance, the longer you prevent Real Satsang with Me. If you come into associ-ation with Me, but then spend the next forty years wondering about that association, you have never truly entered into Satsang with Me. Satsang is not simply coming into a room and sitting silently with Me. Satsang is the devotional relationship to Me altogether—the relationship to Me as the One you recognize to Be the Living Divine Heart, the "Bright" Divine Self (or Self-Condition), the paradoxical Person of the True Divine Guru.

The drama of the avoidance of relationship as it is enacted in relationship to Me, the True Divine Guru, is the paradigm, the epitome, the archetype of all the dramas played in all relationships. It is better if, upon finding Me, you immediately surrender your search and enter directly into that devotional relationship. But, in most cases, there is a period of time, of drama, of wondering, of in and out, of yes and no, of wondering again, of thinking—none of which is Spiritual life. None of that has anything to do with Spiritual life. It is only the drama of suffering, resistance, reluctance.

Spiritual life begins for you when the relationship to Me truly becomes the Condition of your life. Then you become willing to accept the life-conditions I Require of you. When you have become alive, intense, with the Force of My Spiritual Transmission, then the intelligent activity of self-observation and self-understanding can stably awaken.

Observe your connection to Me here. Examine your relationship to Me. See the drama you are playing in terms of this Satsang with Me, and <u>live</u> this heart-Communion with Me instead. I am only interested in this Satsang as a Real process. I have no interest whatsoever in gathering an enormous organization of silly, fascinated people.

I want to see this Real process actually begin—in whomever it is possible for it to begin. If there is no one, I will stay home. If there is only one, I will deal with one. If there are fifty, it will be fifty. If there are fifteen million, that is fine, too. But I am not willing to acquire a following through fascinating promises, strategic (or ego-based) methods, mere consolations, experiential illusions, and one-shot-liberation baloney.

Conditions for right life are Given to you in My Avataric Divine Company, and those conditions are always appropriate. They are the pure instruments of self-understanding. But, if you do not <u>live</u>

this relationship, this Satsang with Me, then It will always be an offense to you, It will always appear to be an obstacle for you. Then you will only be angry and uncomfortable.

Live this Satsang with Me. Learn the real conditions of Spiritual life. Observe your resistance to it. Be purified of your seeking. Understand and surrender your search. Lead an ordinary, pleasurable life. Remove exaggerated, self-toxifying habits from your life—all the absurdities, the forms of self-indulgence. Become more sophisticated in dealing with your movements of desire.

Once you are qualified to do so, come into My physical Company as often as you can.[47] Simply live this heart-relationship to Me. Enjoy the Blessing-Power Inherent in that relationship, and begin to observe yourself.

Ultimately, all avoidance of relationship is only resistance to Satsang with Me. It is the resistance to making Satsang with Me the Condition of your life. Such resistance is dramatized in relation to Me because, Whatever I <u>Am</u> in Reality, I <u>symbolize</u> to people the possibilities of Spiritual life. Therefore, people feel very free to aggravate their relationship to Me. Instead, they should be dealing with their own egoic ignorance, their suffering. Come to Satsang with Me with real need—not with something to defend.

The world is absolutely insane. But your participation in Spiritual life does not depend on the world. You are not going to get up from sitting in the room with Me and suddenly find that everything and everybody in the world is absolutely beautiful. You are not going to find that all your suffering has been taken away by magic. The world is going to create obstacles. The world does not want to function. People do not want to function. They are not yet alive. If you are coming alive in Satsang with Me, you are going to have to be intelligent in your relationships, intelligent in life.

Require Truth. Bring yourself to Satsang with Me, the Company of Truth. Do not believe the usual company of life—the social world of resistance, of avoidance. The world will create conditions that will awaken your aggravation, your egoic ignorance, your game. It will demand your game of you. It will demand that you suffer it, and that you live it as well.

While you are still weak, still beginning, the world seems a vast alternative to your devotional discipline and to Truth. The patterns of sudden desire seem so much more pleasurable than the sadhana I have Given you. Therefore, as My devotee, you must make good use of My Avataric Divine Company, and make good use of the collective gathering of My devotees. Eventually, when you become stronger, you will also be able to make good use of the world.

Satsang with Me is not different from "radical" self-understanding. In Truth, the heart-relationship to Me is already Realization, already Truth. The more profoundly you enjoy Satsang with Me, the more profoundly you Know Its Real Nature. Satsang with Me does not proceed toward a goal of Truth. Satsang with Me is Truth. It is the life of Truth. Over time, Truth Itself produces change, apparent transformation. But Truth is the Very Condition of Spiritual life, not its end-phenomenon.

Therefore, from the moment Satsang with Me begins, the demand of Truth is put to you in the form of conditions you must meet. If sadhana required no conditions, anyone could come for "initiation"—regardless of his or her state of preparation. Then I would Give that person a little technique of some sort, and flatter the person with promises.

No—the Way that I Reveal and Give is Truth Itself. Truth is the Way of Satsang with Me. Therefore, the beginning of Spiritual life requires the Communication of the demand that is Truth. The first form of that demand is the Person of the True Guru. Thus, the genuine beginning of the Spiritual process is the beginning of your devotional relationship to Me. Nevertheless, it is not My Function, as the True Divine Guru, to destroy the world's resistance by magic. If you respond to My Wisdom-Teaching, you must prepare yourself, and make an appropriate approach to Me.

The first demand (and the primary confrontation) in Spiritual life is the relationship to the Guru. However, the relationship to the Guru is also the fundamental Condition, the principal Content, and the Graceful Source of Spiritual (or Real) life. If that were not so, everybody could become Spiritual by the mere practice of one or another egoic method. They would read books. They would manipulate themselves with arbitrary beliefs. But Spiritual life is a relationship, a living demand. It is an offense from the very beginning. And that offense provokes the crisis and fundamental sacrifice that Real life requires.

Nothing is Offered by Me but Satsang with Me. Nothing is Given but this heart-relationship to Me—because it is Truth. Those who come to the point of living the relationship to Me as the Condition of life receive everything—because the relationship to Me is also the medium of Truth. Everything rests on your ability to live this relationship to Me. I know very well who lives it and who does not. It does not even require any psychic powers on My part to know it. If, as My devotee, you are truly living Satsang with Me, then I (in Response) Live Satsang with you. If you are not living Satsang with Me, then you must transcend the drama of your own resistance before I can be Moved to Grant you My Avataric Divine Blessing. You must apply appropriate forms of discipline to your ego-patterning, so that your resistance is set aside, broken down.

To be Chastized (or Criticized) by Me is not, in fact, a form of punishment. It is a necessary form of My Blessing-Grace. It is simply that the individual involved is, for the time being, incapable of assuming (or is just plain refusing to assume) the Condition of Satsang with Me and the responsibilities inherent in the life of Truth.

II.

DEVOTEE: When the practice of self-Enquiry (in the form "Avoiding relationship?") is effective in my daily life, it arises spontaneously. Sometimes, it takes the form of an internal mentalization of the question "Avoiding relationship?" At other times, it seems to be only a process of intelligence, a spontaneous movement of conscious awareness. Why do these different qualities appear in the practice of self-Enquiry?

I have an idea about this. Perhaps it is that, when I am more distracted, the internal mentalization serves to bring me back to the present, to what I am up to, and serves to dissolve the tendency to be mentally distracted.

AVATAR ADI DA SAMRAJ: Meditation in the Way of Adidam is, most fundamentally, to sit silently in feeling-Contemplation of Me, facing My Avatarically-Born bodily (human) Divine Form—most typically, as It is represented via the Murti in a Communion Hall. In that Conscious Condition that is the heart-relationship to Me, a kind of quieting arises, and (at the same time) an intensification of your self-awareness. Depending on the particular quality of your state at that time, you will tend to become attentive to forms of desire, differentiation, or identification. Impulses are the form of desire. Thoughts (or the mental acts of discriminating between things that arise) are the form of differentiation. The various forms of separate-and-separative-self-sense are the form of identification. When any of these forms begin to draw your attention, then your exercise of the "conscious process" may begin.

If, as My devotee, you are practicing the Devotional Way of Insight, then your exercise of the "conscious process" will take the form of the practice of self-Enquiry (in the form "Avoiding relationship?"). That practice generally begins as an internal (or mental) verbalization. The self-Enquiry ("Avoiding relationship?") is evoked randomly—not repetitively, but as a real question—and followed until there is a real "answer" (so to speak). The "answer" is not (itself) a thought, but a spontaneous observation and understanding of thought, of action, of the forms of identification, differentiation, and desire.

When the "conscious process" (in any of its by-Me-Given forms) is truly practiced, then the very forms and processes that have attracted attention tend to fall away. They cease to distract you. And you (simply and spontaneously) fall into the living condition of relationship—which is the Real condition of life, prior to the obscuring activity of the avoidance of relationship.

During a period of formal meditation, you may experience a succession of the gross, subtle, and causal forms of subjectivity (corresponding, respectively, to the basic ego-activities of desire, differentiation, and identification). At first, subjectivity will tend to arise as gross forms of desire, perception, awareness of life-activity. Then the process may move into subtler forms—forms of thought, impression, memory, images. Then the process may move into the causal perceptions of presumed separation, of separate-self-sense.

For My devotee practicing the Devotional Way of Insight, the practice of self-Enquiry, randomly activated, adapts to whatever is arising. But, in the depth of conscious awareness, there begins to arise a sense of what is always taking place in any and every moment of self-Enquiry. It appears as a kind of "shape" in conscious awareness. Through a process involving the subtle faculties, conscious awareness begins to form (first) an impression and (then) a direct comprehension. Then the verbal form of self-Enquiry tends to fall away. Instead of verbal self-Enquiry (in the form "Avoiding relationship?"), another process (which has already been taking place in every moment of verbal self-Enquiry) begins to characterize your moment to moment awareness. It moves in response to the same phenomena that were arising previously—including forms of desire, thought, and separate-self-sense—but without mental verbalization. Then, in each moment, these phenomena vanish, as they did when self-Enquiry was practiced in its verbal form.

At first, what is enjoyed in the process of self-Enquiry is a sense of relationship itself, felt with great intensity. But the more you grow in this process, the more there tends to arise an understanding that the only thing that is ever happening, in every instant, is a modification of the Very Reality That Always Already Exists. Every impulse, every desire, every thought, every perception, every notion of separate self—all of these begin to appear as a single activity, a continuous modification, a shaping of What Is, of the Divine Self-Condition (and Source-Condition) of all-and-All.

This most mature form of the practice of self-Enquiry is what I call "non-verbal re-cognition". At last, no sense of limited (or qualified) relatedness remains. The very "point-in-space" as which you approach everything—this sense of separate self—is seen, felt, and Known to be a modification, an arbitrary shaping of your own existence. Whenever this "shape", this contraction, this modification, this formation of awareness, is re-cognized, it is obviated, it is disappeared in the instant of re-cognition—until, in the "Perfect Practice" of the Way of Adidam, you Stand As the Witness-Consciousness, the mere Witness of all of this activity (and the mere Witness even of the feeling of relatedness that underlies all of this activity).

Most ultimately (in the course of the "Perfect Practice" of the Way of Adidam), only Consciousness Itself is Realized, only Consciousness Itself is Lived. And only Consciousness Itself is What has traditionally been sought—although never, in that search, finally or completely attained—as "Self-Realization", "Liberation", "Nirvana", and so on. When meditation has (by Means of My Avataric Divine Spiritual Grace) become most perfect, "radical", absolute, when self-understanding has become total, when whatever arises is (in the very instant of its arising) Divinely Self-Recognized, when (regardless of the condition that arises, regardless of the activity that is performed—whether you are sitting, as in meditation, or walking, or performing ordinary activity) only Reality Itself is Obvious—Such is True and Most Ultimate Samadhi, the only-by-Me Revealed and Given seventh stage Sahaja Nirvikalpa Samadhi, Wherein there is constant Realization of the Divine Self-Condition, Prior to (and, yet, not dissociated from) all conditions in all worlds.

This True and Most Ultimate Divine Samadhi (or Most Perfect Divine Self-Realization) is not (itself) an experience—a kind of trance, or Yogic state. It is only Enjoyment of (and As) That Very Reality Which Is Always Already the Case, and Which Is the Divine Self-Condition (and Source-Condition) of all-and-All. One who simply Enjoys and Lives this Enjoyment is one who understands most perfectly. In such a one, True Spiritual life—the life of Most Perfect Divine Enlightenment—has begun. That one Lives in (and As) the True Divine Heart Itself, at the "Feet" of Amrita Nadi, the Perfect Form of Real God.

Until Most Perfect Divine Enlightenment (or Most Perfect Divine Self-Realization), all human beings are only seeking, all are involved in this characteristic activity (the avoidance of relation-ship), and all are pursuing an answer in the forms of their present experience. Therefore, human beings want a "truth" that consoles their humanity. But Truth Itself has nothing whatsoever to do with human identity, which is limited to what presently appears. From the "Point of View" of Truth, human birth is an obsession—unnecessary, already non-existent. But people want to hear about birth and reincarnation, experience and afterlife, fulfillment and fascinating attainment.

Truth is the "radical" penetration of this entire event. Only at that moment of "radical" penetration is there True Happiness. Until then, every thought, regardless of its content, is in the form of dilemma. You may be thinking "ice cream cone", or "Run, Spot, run,"[48] and you may imagine—because of the content of your thoughts, particularly if they are "good" thoughts—that everything is all right. But, for one who does not understand, all thought is in the form of dilemma.

Observe the content of an instant of thinking. Not just its apparent content—the verbal phrase, or concept, or image you have in mind—but the entire event, including your involvement with the thought, your relationship to the thought, the tendencies generated by the thought, the tendencies generated by thinking itself. Apart from Truth, all thought is dilemma. The quality of thought is dilemma. The quality of ordinary life is dilemma. Apart from Satsang with Me, apart from "radical" self-understanding, apart from True meditation, life is only suffering, only search, only endless self-"creation", only endless modification of the Energy That Is Reality Itself. Every thought is "shape".

DEVOTEE: Suppose I am sitting by a lake—looking at it, and thinking it is a very beautiful lake. What would be the dilemma in that?

AVATAR ADI DA SAMRAJ: As I have said, the content of such an experience seems to be entirely delicious. But observe the entire event. No one has ever been utterly relieved in the presence of a lake! If you were to become truly sensitive to the current of your ordinary awareness, you would find yourself getting angry in gardens, getting terrified on vacation! It is only that you are chronically unaware of the nature of your own event.

What is occurring in this moment by the lake—sitting, looking at the lake? It seems to be very beautiful. But it seems beautiful only because you are thinking of it in contrast to other experiences. You have been very busy, harried, disturbed, frustrated, under pressure—and, so, you go and you sit in the country. You create an interval, to eliminate all the conditions that ordinarily lead to stress in your life. You sit in the country, and you relax. You feel a little psychosomatic peace.

Activities such as sitting in the country by a lake actually are forms of traditional Spiritual practice. What may seem to be nothing more than simple, natural repose can actually be a sophisticated practice of meditation. There is a long and ancient tradition for it. Indeed, it could justifiably be claimed that "a lake in the country" is as fixed and formal an object of meditation as the "Our Father", the name "Ram", or "Om Mani Padme Hum".[49]

However, as you spend your several days in the country, that first moment of ease-into-distractedness begins to disappear in the currents of usual egoic awareness. You begin to become sensitive to all kinds of subjective movements—thoughts, feelings, sensations, desires, demands, frustrations. When the ability to be distracted is lost, no country lake can remove from you the pain of ordinary existence.

It is the same with those who sit with Me in Satsang. Apparently, there is not anything going on. It is a nice room. It is very quiet here, generally attractive. But you can sit here, in My physical Company, and go through the most incredible subjective drama. And where does all of that come from? It is not caused by the room. Sometimes it is "good", sometimes it is not so "good"— "good" experience, "bad" experience. Just so in the country—it is only a matter of time before you pass out of restfulness and back into the usual revelation of subjectivity.

If you were forced to remain in the country, such that living in the country became your everyday circumstance rather than your temporary amusement, you would quickly find out that you are disturbed. Then your search would go on in the country, as everywhere else. You would discover that the very condition of being someone looking at a lake is a form of suffering. Indeed, such is the symbol of Narcissus. Compared to running away from a shotgun, looking at a lake may seem to be pleasurable. But, if you examine the content of experiencing itself, even in a circumstance of apparent ease and pleasure, you discover that every instant of experience is this shaping (or limitation, or modification) of the fundamental sense of separateness and suffering. There is the generation in conscious awareness of the separate-self-sense ("me" watching the lake), of differentiating thought ("lake" is different from "city", different from "shotgun"), and of desire ("Oh, my—this forever!").

Consider all the various desires awakened on vacation! What is disturbing people—and all human beings are disturbed, regardless of their relative condition—is not simply their external circumstance or their present experience. What is disturbing them is the human condition itself, the fact of birth. You are disturbed by the fact that you are sitting here, that you are alive in some apparently separate sense, in a world of changing conditions. This is the disturbance. And, as long as that disturbance persists in conscious awareness, there is suffering.

The sense of separateness is the suffering. You can change the images, you can change the apparent conditions, you can "change" the world. You can go from here to another world, another condition. You can go into another state while alive—an "intoxicated" state, a Yogic state, a different house, a different country, a place in the country. You can modify all the conditions, external and internal—but, in so doing, you will never change the root-condition that is your suffering. Only one who most perfectly understands is Always Already Free.

What are people like on vacation? What are people like who are sitting in the country? Most of the time they are obnoxious— all these people on vacation, who are all of a sudden so terribly "fulfilled"! How do they treat one another? What kind of tolerance do you have for frustration on a vacation? Practically none.

No unique intelligence is required to sit by a lake and feel quiet. Any ding-dong can do that. There is no sighted person who cannot feel pleasure looking at a sunset. What is so extraordinary about that? People talk about country, earth, and vacation as if they were a real alternative to the demands of Truth. Anybody can go down to the ocean and feel comforted. But what does that have to do with your death? What does that have to do with your actual state? All it has done is distract you from your chronic state.

Pleasant distractions make you temporarily insensitive to your common state. That is the purpose of vacations—simply to desensitize you, to rest you for a brief period of time. Vacations are sleep and refreshment in life. They are not a way of life. Sitting by a lake is not a way of life. No form of pleasant distraction (whether ordinary or extraordinary) is a way of life. Even traditional (strategic, or ego-based) Spiritual practice is only a temporary distraction.

Truth is not a matter of any such distraction. Truth is a matter of intelligence, the activity of Real intelligence. If Real intelligence is not active in your life, then you are only distracted, and you are only suffering.

At some point, every individual who seriously examines what is happening begins to realize that he or she is only suffering. Eventually, people realize that they are fundamentally disturbed. The more sensitive you are, the more obvious it is to you. The less sensitive you are, the more experience you require before it becomes obvious. The more force there is in intelligence, the more obvious things are, and the more intense your conscious experience is. The less sensitive and the more distracted you are, the more (in terms of time or experience) you require. But, eventually, everyone arrives at the same point. This intelligence, this sensitivity, this real observation of ordinary activity arises—and that is what makes True Yoga possible. That is what makes True meditation possible. That is what makes the Way of Truth possible.

Truly, there is no satisfaction in mere birth. Life is not a form of satisfaction. Life is an endless series of modifications and motivations. And life continually generates itself. However, life can also provide an opportunity to Realize the True Nature of What Is. The actual purpose of life is to give beings the opportunity to concretely experience (or dramatize and elaborate) their latent egoic tendencies. When you truly see the unsatisfactoriness of life, then My Avataric Divine Incarnation can be of use to you—and you are (by Means of My Avataric Divine Spiritual Grace) enabled to go through the process of "radical" self-understanding, to transcend your ego-drama.

People who get a little religious like to make all kinds of pious statements about what this all is. But this is simply a realm of dramatized desire. Of course, all things arise within Truth Itself, within Reality Itself—but, as soon as Truth Itself becomes most perfectly Obvious, what you call "you" disappears.

This world is not, in and of itself, Truth. Truth is That Real Activity, That Real Intelligence, That Is the Divine <u>Core</u> of all conditional manifestation. When Truth becomes Active and Alive, when this Real process takes place, then the motion that <u>demands</u> this limited and compulsive experience, this birth, is dissolved. Thereafter, no matter what arises, True Humor is not lost. Therefore, one who most perfectly understands continues to live, but with True Humor—and such a one also dies with True Humor.

III.

There is no moment of the usual birth that is not in the form of desire, thought (or differentiation), and separate-self-sense (or identification). Nothing is going on but these three phenomena, which are the usual characteristics of human beings. And none of these truly arises separately. They are a complex event, a single event. That event is the usual condition and limit of human beings. If you begin to become aware of your usual activity, your usual state, your usual condition from moment to moment, you see there is nothing but this—nothing but desire, thought, and separate-self-sense.

The ones who are regarded by the various traditions to have been Enlightened Sages or Realized Saints or (even) simply authentic Yogis were those who had become extremely sensitive to this fact.[50] At some point (usually relatively early in life), they became incapable of distraction and fell into their actual state, which is fear. When there is no distraction, there is only fear. The great ones are those who have, to an extraordinary extent, passed through their fear.

Other people are of the same nature as these great ones—but they are, perhaps, for the time being, insensitive to their actual situation, because they are still capable of (or susceptible to) ego-binding distraction. Indeed, the kinds and degrees of ego-binding distraction to which people are susceptible, and the intensity of their distractibility—these qualities are what account for the differences between people. And, in this Great Process of Satsang with Me, My devotee's capability to be ego-bound by distraction is undermined, frustrated, turned about.

Periodically, every individual passes through a time of crisis, of great resistance and fear. Ultimately, every one of My devotees must go through the same fundamental process of self-understanding and ego-transcendence that I Demonstrated during My "Sadhana Years". Not precisely in the same apparent form—but, within the pattern of the individual's own conditions, that same fundamental process must occur.

Real Spiritual life absolutely requires the undermining and frustration of the capability for ego-binding distraction. That is why Spiritual life has often been described in harrowing terms. That is why My devotees must be responsible for constantly cultivating the devotional (and, in due course, Spiritual) relationship to Me, for rightly disciplining the basic life-functions, and for observing, understanding, and (more and more) transcending the dramatization of egoity they are always tending to enact.

Spiritual life is a crisis. Therefore, Spiritual life involves discomfort at times. Such discomfort does not mean that Spiritual life is failing, or that you are not good enough for it. Crisis and discomfort <u>must</u> occur. The crisis (or turnabout) is what Spiritual life is all about. It is <u>supposed</u> to occur. You are supposed to suffer purifying events. You are supposed to encounter resistance in yourself. You are supposed to discover all kinds of garbage in yourself. So why should there be any special resistance to it when it occurs? There may be discomfort, and you may wish you did not have to go through it. But, apart from that, there is no reason why you should be overwhelmed or completely disenchanted by the fact that you are experiencing a period of intense conflict, crisis, suffering, and disturbance.

The more time you waste identifying with all of that, the less sensitive you become to the event itself. Therefore, Satsang with Me, devotion to Me, and a loving and intelligent approach to all of life should be intensified in the periods of apparent discomfort.

These apparently disturbing episodes of crisis in the Real process of Spiritual life are very intelligent, very meaningful. They have a great deal to show you. The more capable you are of passing through these times, the more useful they become. The individual who is really using this process can be enduring this crisis almost continually, with great frequency and intensity—and, yet, like a soldier on the march, the person never misses a step, never becomes outwardly reactive. Such a person continues to function, and apparently only enjoys life. He or she does not get involved in an entire drama of upset.

In the beginning, however, when someone is just beginning to pass through this kind of crisis in consciousness, there tend to be reactions and breakdowns whenever the crisis begins. There is very often an emotional collapse, even a physical collapse. There are episodes that have an almost psychotic quality to them. It is during those times that the person is wondering whether or not to continue to do the sadhana, and all of that. But, as you pass through more of these purifying episodes, you begin to realize how you must function in terms of the Real Spiritual process.

Once you have begun to mature in the process, then, when such an event of crisis arises, there is something already familiar about it. You know the signs, you know what is about to occur, you know the kinds of reactions that will tend to build up. You know that, instead of clenching your teeth and resisting the crisis, you should find some more work to do during that time. Instead of planning a vacation or a binge when you see a crisis coming, you cancel all forms of entertainment or ordinary distraction, everything that you would normally use to distract yourself from your usual state. You plan a great deal of work for the coming days. You plan an ordinary, functional life.

When you have matured to that degree, you make good use, really good use, of these episodes. The more intelligent you are, the better the use you make of them. The less intelligent you are, and the more capable you are of binding distraction at such times, the more you will look for means to dramatize your state, to distract yourself from the lesson that turns purification into transformation.

You must know that everything I am doing is a means to bring about this crisis. I desire this crisis in you. I do not want it <u>not</u> to happen. I do not want to console you. I do not want you to be contented in your unconsciousness. I want you to become sensitive to your actual state. I want you to know very well what you are always up to. I want you to become capable of observing yourself under all kinds of conditions. I want you to notice the machine of your ordinary activity. And I want that entire ego-machine to collapse. I want it to come to an end. I want the "death" of all of that. If that "death" does not occur, there will be no release, no Realization. There will just be the self-generation of the unconscious event of life and death, the continual round that is already distracting you.

I am here to Reveal and to Give the various means necessary to serve this crisis—because to serve this crisis is to serve most fundamental self-understanding in My devotee, and (ultimately) to serve the True and Absolute Joy That characterizes the Realization of most perfect "radical" self-understanding. Therefore, every instant in Satsang with Me is working to bring about this crisis.

IV.

DEVOTEE: Beloved Master, could You say something about faith—in relationship to Satsang with You?

AVATAR ADI DA SAMRAJ: The Truth is not that you must believe—or, in that sense, "have faith"—in order to "find God" or to "get to heaven". The Truth is that your present activity of self-contraction is destroying your present-time Realization of Real God.

When there is self-understanding, when the activity of the avoidance of relationship is observed, understood, and transcended, you discover that there is no longer any doubt or withdrawal from relationship—because doubt and withdrawal are merely your own self-contracting activity. Disbelief, lack of faith, and separation from Real God are your own self-contracting activity. You do not need to manufacture some feeling of "faith"—over against your own activity of non-faith—in order to Find Real God.

When you understand your own self-contracting activity, you stand already faithful, already continuous with Reality Itself, Truth Itself, Real God. It is not that you "believe in God". "Believing in God" is just an egoic formula for controlling the mind. When you understand your own contraction in relation to Reality Itself, then the self-contraction becomes unnecessary—no more an inevitable "part" of you than the shirt you wear. Then you will find that nothing like doubt or faithlessness is present in you anymore—but, rather, a kind of Fullness persists, an Enjoyment in Which you no longer make negative presumptions. You will act on the basis of the presumption of non-separateness, non-obstruction. The more you live in that manner, the more you will become aware of the True Nature of the Condition in Which you already Inhere.

Without self-understanding, without presently acknowledging your own life of avoidance, all your attempts to "have faith in God" are actually forms of bad faith, forms of seeking. Their motivation is dilemma. In your seeking, you "believe in God" as a strategic means for getting rid of your dilemma—whereas True faith arises when you understand the self-contracted position you have assumed (and presumed), such that you cease to "claim" that ego-position, and (instead) you rest in the Inherent (or Prior) Position.

The usual person is always recommending some prescription that you can apply to your state of suffering in order to "get better". But even the traditional Teachings were not originally given in that form. The traditions of the West, in which words such as "sin" and "creation" prevail, do not just say, "Believe in God." They say, "Repent, acknowledge your sinfulness—and, in that acknowledging, turn to God." Thus, even from the traditional Western point of view, faith is necessarily preceded by a critical undermining of the concept and activity of "sin"—and that undermining represents a certain level of what I call "self-understanding".

Just so, in the East, where words such as "karma" and "maya" prevail, Spiritual life is not merely a matter of believing in Nirvana or Brahman with all your might, until you somehow become That. Rather, the Realization of Nirvana or Brahman is understood to require the critical undermining of the principle and condition of illusion—and, once again, that undermining represents a certain level of what I describe as "self-understanding".

Therefore, self-understanding cannot be eliminated from Spiritual life. You cannot be told merely to believe and expect belief to be the Way of Truth and life. Such instructions are just more stuff of mind. If, as My devotee, you have observed and understood the self-contraction (which is the form of your own activity that impels you to engage in the search), then you are (already) no longer turning away from Truth (or Reality, or Real God). What Really Is is already Obvious to you. Reality Itself is already Obvious to you, and you practice on that basis. The absence of faith, the doubt and conflict you find in yourself, is not caused by something outside you. Rather, all of that is your own reaction to what is occurring apparently outside you. It is your own activity.

Divine Self-Realization is not going to occur until you become most perfectly responsible for that self-contracting activity. Your hoping-to-be-faithful-and-have-everything-turn-out-all-right is not (in any sense) going to affect the sum of your life. No amount of experiencing will affect the basic quality of your life, because (fundamentally) you are in this crunch—living separatively, and (therefore) perceiving the world as enigma, illusion, something independent, endlessly multiplied, and mortal. All those perceptions are fabrications made by your own activity.

If you live the life of self-contraction, you tend to have certain types of experiences, just as the taking of any particular intoxicating substance tends to lead to the having of certain kinds of experiences. But, when the self-contraction is undone, the characteristic qualities of the self-contracted life—such as faithlessness, doubt, and fear—cease to determine your vision, they cease to qualify (or modify, or superimpose themselves on) the Truth of your existence. Then, instead of living on the basis of those qualities, and either trying to escape from them or merely "agreeing" to suffer them, you live on the basis of the Fundamental Truth of your existence. You function in and <u>As</u> That Truth, and That Truth Reveals Its Fullness to you.

How long must you sit and look at all the stuff in yourself? Self-understanding is not a matter of watching all this stuff, as if it were on a television screen, and saying, "Oh, yes—what a dummy I am! One crisis after the next! 'Avoiding relationship?' Yes, indeed—I certainly am!" That is the lazy approach to sadhana. If you are just luxuriating in life, if you merely have enough vitality to indulge in your basic consolation from day to day, then you do not bring much intensity to the observation of yourself. Somehow, it must become important to you that you understand.

The "guru" that your egoity would like to find is one who merely fascinates and pleases you and lulls you to sleep. Such a false "guru" just keeps you asleep in front of the TV set. Such a false "guru" does not really serve you. Such a false "guru" exploits you—perhaps because he or she has so much doubt about the world and about the Divine. And such a false "guru" suffers a false vision of devotees. Such a false "guru" does not dare to master the devotee, does not dare to generate another difficult moment for the "poor" devotee.

I do not have such an option. I must Shout at My devotee again and again, be difficult with My devotee—while always remaining Established in True Humor. Nevertheless, whatever My devotee's game—whether playing stupid or playing "poor me" or getting angry or having a difficult time or whatever—<u>none</u> of it is true.

People who are moved to Spiritual life must not be consoled and fascinated and made unconscious. They must be quickened. As egos, they do not want the crisis of Real intelligence to occur. They want to be served with all the things that will allow them to continue in the drama they are already enacting—in order to justify irresponsibility, self-indulgence, and the cycle of concerns that is their characteristic suffering.

Therefore, knowing that My devotees only want to sleep, I must continue to shake and offend them. But I must be offensive in a Truly humorous fashion, so as not to cause an unusably negative effect on My devotees. I must serve their Real and True and truly "radical" self-understanding, their root-understanding of egoity itself. And I must, by all that I Do and Say, Serve the Divine Liberation of My devotees (one and all).

V.

DEVOTEE: In *The Knee Of Listening,* You describe the loss of the "Bright" as the loss of faith[51]—and, in Your Discourses to us, you have equated faith with Satsang.

AVATAR ADI DA SAMRAJ: Genuine faith is the principle of Spiritual life. Faith <u>is</u> Satsang with Me, and it is commitment to living the Condition of Satsang with Me.

DEVOTEE: But isn't Satsang more than faith? Isn't there more substance to it than simple faith?

AVATAR ADI DA SAMRAJ: Real faith is not the merely simple-minded belief that everything is going to be all right. No—faith is the Me-recognizing and to-Me-responding (and, necessarily, ego-surrendering, ego-forgetting, and, more and more, ego-transcending) embrace of the Condition of Satsang with Me (or heart-relationship to Me). Therefore, faith is not independent of self-understanding. Only self-understanding permits the principle of faith to be truly alive in you.

The conventionally religious person lives faith as a sort of willful believing, devoid of self-understanding. The faith I am talking about, however, is founded <u>both</u> in heart-responsive recognition of Me <u>and</u> in "radical" understanding of your own self-contracting activity. Therefore, Satsang with Me requires self-understanding. You cannot live Satsang with Me without living self-understanding as well.

Satsang is not merely a matter of "believing" in Me and having aesthetically emotional feelings toward Me as an apparent human individual. Such belief is conventional religion. Satsang with Me depends absolutely on self-understanding. Only when self-understanding is Real can My devotee truly live Satsang with Me, truly live the Divine life in My Avataric Divine Company, truly make use of My Avataric Divine Self-Revelation of Real God, truly make use of <u>Me</u>.

If you truly live in Satsang with Me, you know no limitation to Spiritual life. Then Spiritual life is always full, always being fulfilled—perhaps not always in the form you expect, but self-fulfillment is not the principle of this process anyway.

Until they enter into the Real Spiritual process, My devotees do not truly make use of Me, they do not fully live in Satsang with Me. Therefore, they lack faith, or the presumption of the Condition of Satsang with Me.

When you presume Satsang with Me—not through an act of will, but through True heart-recognition of Me and heart-response to Me—when you (thus) truly live in the Condition of Satsang with Me, then you are making use of Me. Then you are making room for Me, such that you can (in due course) become available to My Avatarically Self-Transmitted Divine Spiritual Heart-Blessing. When you are Spiritually available to Me, then you have become available to Real God, you have become available to the Divine Reality within Which you are arising—such that the Real Spiritual process can begin in you.

However, if you live without faith—obstructed, self-involved, committed to the egoic life and to the principles of identification, differentiation, and desire—then the Great Principle (Which <u>Is</u> Real God, the True Divine Guru, and the Divine Self-Condition) cannot operate. In that case, your life is a struggle. It is limited to the range of experiences that are karmically determined, and (whether those experiences are "good" or "bad") you will only experience them as mediocrity—all because you lack faith and (therefore) do not presume the Reality of the Divine Self-Condition.

People do not live on the basis of Real faith. They live as if the Great Divine Principle does not even exist. Even those who are beginning to adapt to the conditions of Spiritual life tend to acknowledge the Great Principle only in a mediocre manner, depending on how they feel on any given day. They have not yet assumed Spiritual practice as a real discipline. They may experience extraordinary phenomena and temporary changes of state, but the Real Process of Transformation and Realization requires maturity in the sadhana.

Every day, the beginner who is not yet fully established in the sadhana wonders, "Should I or shouldn't I?", "Is there or isn't there?" Such beginners find all kinds of reasons, depending on their apparent condition that day, to doubt Me, to doubt their own impulse, to doubt the Divine Nature of existence—and they remain in doubt. Doubt, rather than faith, is their fundamental condition.

Doubt is simply another description for the self-contraction, as it is felt (in life) in the vital. Doubt is the presumption of separate existence, the principle of identification, differentiation, and desire. Where there is faith, there is no vital contraction. Then you no longer live as the cramped-up capsule that you create by your subjective habit and presumption. Rather, where there is faith, you are open, round, and completely available to Me—the Divine Siddha-Guru Who Most Perfectly Transcends all limited states, the Avataric Self-Revelation of the "Bright" Divine Self-Condition Itself.

Regardless of how apparently intimate they may be with Me, My Wisdom-Teaching, and all the Instruments and Agents I have Empowered, mediocre people never really notice the Great Affair, the Great Event, the Great Process of My Avataric Divine Appearance here. They only get little hints of It every now and then, which are not sufficient to transform them. They may have remarkable experiences here and there, but such experiences are not sufficient to transform their usual life.

However, those who truly live the Principle of Truth are (thereby) living Satsang with Me—living by faith, living on the basis of the presumption of the Divine Person, the Divine Guru, Real God. My true devotees live on the basis of this constant and intense faith-presumption, and they live Satsang with Me absolutely. Then they begin to see the process of Satsang with Me at work in their lives, because they have truly made room for these great Functions. The power of the sacred cooperative culture of My devotees who truly live Satsang with Me, who live by faith, is very great.

In the Buddhist tradition, it is said that there are "Three Jewels" in which the aspirant must take refuge. In the language of Buddhism, these three are the Buddha, the Dharma, and the Sangha. In the language of My Avataric Divine Wisdom-Teaching, these three are Myself (the Divine Siddha-Guru, or Divine Heart-Master), My Avataric Divine Wisdom-Teaching (including the by-Me-Given forms of self-discipline), and the sacred cooperative culture of My devotees.

The first process that occurred in My Avataric Divine Work with My devotees was the establishment of the relationship between Me and My devotees. Such was the initial establishment of the Principle of resort to Me as the Avatarically Incarnate Divine Siddha-Guru. The next process that began to be developed was the understanding of what Spiritual life is, what the devotional relationship to Me is, what the process in My Avataric Divine Company is, and what it demands. Such was the initial establishment of the Principle of resort to Me via My Avatarically Given Divine Wisdom-Teaching. Then I emphasized the gathering of My devotees as a living process, a responsible process of formal cooperative sacred culture. Such was the initial establishment of the Principle of resort to Me as served by the gathering of all My formally practicing devotees.

The ordinary person is avoiding relationship in complex ways. Therefore, it is necessary—in the midst of the sadhana of the Way of Adidam, in which you are Called (by Me) to observe and understand your own avoidance of relationship—for relationship to be the living condition of your practice. There must be living, working, functional relationship. Therefore, My devotees must have the opportunity to live Truth in relation to one another, to examine My Wisdom-Teaching together, and to turn to Me collectively, as a living culture. Truly cooperative sacred culture is the natural condition of all True Spiritual practice.

People who are moved to take up Spiritual life are generally motivated by their illusions. They use what they gather from reading and from their practice of the usual meditation to isolate themselves further, to console themselves, to generate forms of self-imagery, good feelings, immunity—various qualities of "Narcissus". But I intend that My Wisdom-Teaching always be demonstrated in relationship—because it is only in relationship that My Wisdom-Teaching begins to really make sense, begins to Reveal Its True and Full Meaning. Therefore, there must be a functional confrontation with My Wisdom-Teaching by those who make use of It. That confrontation is the use of My Wisdom-Teaching.

Many of you have, at one time or another, expressed to Me your feelings about organized religion. People commonly have negative and resistive feelings toward all forms of human relationship—and the ultimate root of these feelings is the separative (or self-contracting) impulse itself. In a certain sense, such negative feelings are completely justified. There is a great deal about common life, and about organized religion in particular, that is worthy of being resisted!

On the other hand, Truth is Manifested only in the relational condition, and It is lived in relationship. The Realization of Truth is a crisis that necessarily occurs in relationship. Therefore, the sacred cooperative culture that lives My Wisdom-Teaching of Truth is absolutely necessary. But what makes it something that you resist is your own lack of involvement in it, your own desire to separate from it. All of that is simply your dramatized resistance to relational life altogether.

The culture of My devotees must be alive. Every one must be alive within it. Every one must be active in relationship and must function within it. When you become active, responsible, alive, and intimate with others who are living the Way of Adidam, the sensation of resistance to so-called "organized" Spiritual life will disappear—because you will be dealing with the problem of cooperative living as what it truly is: an expression of your own avoidance of relationship.

But, if you do not truly practice the Way of Adidam, you will only see reasons to avoid relationship. Everywhere you will see nothing but reasons for separating from Me, from My Wisdom-Teaching, and from the gathering of My devotees—because you will have made your participation in the Way of Adidam into something empty of life-force, and (thus) something worth resisting.

Therefore, it is the responsibility of My devotees to <u>live</u> the Way of Adidam—to become active in It, to use It, and to become responsible for It.

AVATAR ADI DA SAMRAJ
The Mountain Of Attention Sanctuary, 2000

9.
One-"Point"-edness

DEVOTEE: Beloved Master, when You Sit with us in Darshan, I have started to have the experience of being drawn into some kind of trance, almost like sleep. I have been trying to deal with it—but I do not know whether I should hold back, hold onto it, or let go.

AVATAR ADI DA SAMRAJ: It makes no difference. Why does this experience seem to cause a question in you?

DEVOTEE: I wonder if a decision, or will, is required—or is it all You?

AVATAR ADI DA SAMRAJ: There are two things here. You have this experience that comes over you, and you have your search. The experience is not what you are really asking about. What are you observing about yourself?

DEVOTEE: Well, I am trying to get the answer. I am trying to find out what to do. I am still searching.

AVATAR ADI DA SAMRAJ: And what is this searching? What does this trying-to-find-the-answer involve? What is it you are doing when you are asking these questions and manipulating yourself? What are you up to all the time? What are you doing? You are disturbed!

DEVOTEE: Yes!

AVATAR ADI DA SAMRAJ: That is what is happening. Always disturbed. You come here disturbed—but, then, in sitting with

Me, you go through some changes, such that you start to feel very peaceful. Then you start wanting to return to your usual waking consciousness, but you also want to drift further into this trance-like state: "Should I do this? Should I do that?"

You are disturbed! You are asking questions. You have this dilemma. That is the case—and that is the point.

The point is not the answer to your question, not whether you should allow yourself to go into a trancelike state or not. Any such answer is only a response to the question—but the question itself is what you are all about. What is happening is this chronic disturbance, this dis-ease, this contraction, this avoidance of relationship, this entire process—egoity, in all its forms.

And all of this is going on while you are just sitting here! But "just sitting here" with Me, in heart-Communion with Me, is a potent means of making you more and more aware of your fundamental egoic activity. It is essential that you become aware of your fundamental egoic state, your fundamental egoic activity—to observe it directly, to understand it, whatever your experience may be in the moment. In Satsang with Me, the experiences themselves are not what matters, nor your reactions to them, nor your questions about them, nor their content, nor their interpretation.

What you do in reaction to any particular waking experience is no more significant than how you interpret your dreams. The having of dreams is significant. The fact that they occur is already their meaning. The fact that they occur is their significance. The fact that they occur is the process. Apart from the process itself, it makes no difference what a dream "means". A dream is a process in conscious awareness—a process that has its own value.

So also with the process of your experiences in Satsang with Me. But, even in the midst of the process of Satsang with Me, you are disturbed. And this disturbance manifests as endless changes in your state. You are wandering—and wondering about your wandering. Therefore, it begins to seem that even this simple experience—just sitting here—has become a question. It is as if the sky were a question! But, in and of itself, the sky is not a question. There is no question. "You" are the question! Your state is dilemma, dis-ease. Your state is your question.

The Siddhi of Satsang with Me produces phenomena at various levels of the being. That Siddhi is manifested in many forms. But your responsibility in relation to those phenomena is (always) simply to observe, understand, and transcend your own activity of self-contraction, in the midst of whatever phenomena are arising. If you were not always becoming a question, always contracting, there would be nothing to ask relative to such phenomena.

And what is this process of becoming a question, becoming a fundamental dilemma?

You must have had the experience of listening to music through headphones. The sound appears to arise from some "point" in the middle of your head. If you become very attentive to that process itself, the "point" of hearing seems to be generated in the middle of your head. If you become even more attentive, this "point" of hearing will become what you are interested in, and you will not hear the details (or even the sounds) of the music anymore.

The psycho-physical organism (as a whole) operates in very much the same manner. When you are not living the phenomena of conditional existence from the "Point of View" of Truth, then you become obsessed with this "point" of awareness. You begin to identify with that "point". Perception (or experience) seems to imply the separate self, the ego—and you begin to live chronically as the ego, as if it were the source and center of life.

No matter what phenomena arise, you habitually manipulate them in such a fashion that the apparently separate self becomes the focus and the apparent source (or origin) of your attention. The separate-self-sense becomes the chronic implication of all experience. When a trancelike experience arose in your case, there was (as usual) the attempt to return to the "point"-of-view of the apparently separate self, the impulse to grant all significance to the apparently separate self—until the experience itself was lost in the dilemma. The "experiencer" became the obsession. In this manner, the intensity (or potency) of all experience is used to reinforce "Narcissus"—the sense of separate, independent self.

That sense is the "me", the ego—but that sense is also a question. It is always in the form of a dilemma. Because it is a form of contraction, a "point", it is always separate—even from the phenomena that seem to imply it! Because your apparently separate "self" is the principal obsession of your conscious experience, the nature of arising phenomena is no longer clear.

If you are compulsively focused on the apparent source of the sound, then you cannot differentiate the patterns of music any longer, you cannot enjoy the sound, you cannot turn to the actual source of sound, you continually contract from the source of sound. Thus, the sense of existence as a contracted "point" is the dilemma.

When you speak from the "point"-of-view of separate self, it is always as dilemma. When you perceive the spontaneously arising world from the "point"-of-view of separate self, everything seems mysterious, threatening. Then everything assumes the form or quality of a question. And there is a continual return— folding back in on that "point", again and again—until your self-contracting activity begins to be observed and understood.

When you understand that root-activity, then this "point" is observed to have no fixed (or necessary) reality. It is simply a functional means of organizing the phenomena of your experience. The apparent implication—the separate self, the ego, the "point"—is un-Real, a temporary and dependent event. It is purely a functional phenomenon, a psycho-physical habit. But this habit persists, until there is a turnabout—from compulsive orientation toward this "point" to Contemplation of What is Prior to it.

What is the nature of sound, the nature of hearing, before you focus on that "point" of awareness? Before there is the avoidance of relationship, before there is the self-contraction, with its sensation of separate self, what is the Nature of Consciousness Itself? The entire psycho-physical mechanism is a mass of focusing agencies. From top to bottom, inside and out, the entire life-process amounts to this sense of a "point"—and people identify compulsively with that "point", such that they begin to live from the "point"-of-view of the "point", entirely forgetting the origin of the "point".

Satsang with Me is like the source of sound. People experience Satsang with Me in the ordinary manner, through their focusing mechanism—and they compulsively try to orient themselves, in relation to what they experience in Satsang with Me, in such a manner that they can continually regain the sense of "point", of ego. As if that were the significance of their experience in Satsang with Me!

When they remember that they are in Satsang with Me, when they turn to the origin of their experience in Satsang with Me (rather than turning to the "point" of experience), then something happens quite naturally in conscious awareness. It is not sudden Illumination (or Perfect Knowledge)—but it is a spontaneous and momentary release of the separate "point"-of-view. That release allows the Blessing-Power That I Communicate in Satsang to Fill the psycho-physical mechanism, to harmonize it—free of compulsive self-contraction, free of the compulsive generation of "point"-of-view.

Over time, this Fullness becomes a kind of intelligence, an effortless receptivity, a new event in conscious awareness. You begin to observe your own activity with great clarity—to know the self-contraction as it is, as self-contraction.

The avoidance of relationship is an utterly unnecessary activity. It is suffering. It is dilemma. It is not Real. It is not (itself) Reality, nor is it your True Condition. It is only conditionally real—not Ultimately Real. When you (as My true devotee) begin to understand your own egoic activity, then you begin to fall from this compulsive activity into openness, no-contraction. Such is true self-understanding and self-transcendence (or ego-transcendence).

The True Divine Self (or Self-Condition)—Which Is Reality Itself—is not a "point". The True Divine Self (or Self-Condition) is not what is implied by your ordinary experience. The True Divine Self (or Self-Condition) is not an event in time. It is not limited to any observable (or conditional) form of Energy (or Light). It is not located in space. It has no center, and no bounds. Satsang with Me is the Communication of that Truth, of the Power of that Truth, to those who are bound to the self-contraction.

The Unique Virtue of Satsang with Me is that I Communicate (or Transmit) My Own "Bright" Divine Self-Condition to My devotees. Thus, by various means, Satsang with Me makes the activity of self-contraction obsolete. Over time, Satsang with Me engenders in My devotee an increasing understanding of his or her own activity—in relation to life, and in relation to Truth. Therefore, even while this activity of self-contraction goes on—this questioning, this wondering, this self-manipulation—another process takes place that is quite natural and intelligent, and (at the same time) quite extraordinary.

What you do in Satsang with Me is a ritual duplication of what you are always doing. You come here already disturbed. The avoidance of relationship, the self-contraction, is what is always going on—and you buy it! You continually buy it.

I often make a fist out of My hand to represent this activity of avoidance, because it shows very clearly what happens when there is self-contraction. If you curl your hand in upon itself, a sensation is generated at the center of the hand that concentrates attention. That sensation in the hand is differentiated from every possible thing outside the hand. That sensation becomes the center of concentration.

The same process of differentiation and concentration, generated in your psycho-physical life as a whole, becomes your "point"-of-view toward conditional existence altogether, your "philosophy"—whereas, in fact, that process is only a functional reflection of your own self-contracting activity. At every level of functional awareness, the entire psycho-physical mechanism is devoted to this activity, this curling in upon itself. This is "Narcissus". All of the searches that have ever been undertaken by human beings, all of the approaches that people have traditionally embraced as means to Realize the Truth, are engaged from this "point"-of-view—the "point"-of-view of dilemma, of self-contraction, of "ego".

Human beings want their sensation of independent existence to continue. They become frightened that they will not continue to exist as independent entities. All questions arise from this separate "point"-of-view, because the separate-self-sense is the archetype of all questions. It is the only question. It is the dilemma! Moment to moment, it is your fundamental experience.

People are suffering. They are afraid. They are self-obsessed. They are distracted. They are unconscious. They are turned in upon themselves. They are always curling inward. What do you do?

I was looking at some of you here earlier, while I was sitting quietly with you. Some of you are constantly involved in doing this and that, even when you are just sitting there. It would be amusing to see it in fast forward. It is an incredible ritual, an endless dance, of touching and examining your bodies, stimulating the sensation of separate existence by every kind of nervous action and perception. There are numberless tiny adjustments of the physical position. There is endless touching of various parts of the body, moving of the body, creasing the body, producing little tensions in the nervous system that concentrate attention. This restlessness goes on internally as well—with all kinds of perception and thought, all kinds of communication being received from the environment and from the internal functions of the psychophysical mechanism.

This compulsive contraction goes on and on and on and on. What do you think you do when you get up to leave the room? Do you think the fundamental strategy of your activity changes when you say "good morning" to someone, or when you walk down the street, or when you go to work? The same thing is always going on. It is endless self-contraction, endless self-sensation.

Sit quietly in a chair sometime. You will observe that every moment of perception is combined with a corresponding representation in conscious awareness—a thought, an image, an interpretation, a contraction of the field of conscious awareness. A "target" is always created.

People are <u>always</u> "meditating" on the separate-self-sense. People are <u>always</u> tending to be one-"point"-ed in their concentration on the "point" of separate self. Every moment of life is devoted to the "creation" of this "point". Over time, the activity of self-contraction is endlessly intensified—potentially, even to the point of absolute contraction, such that there is no longer any flow of life-force. If you clench your hand tightly in a fist, increasing the tension to the point that the blood-flow is cut off, the hand will eventually wither.

Thus, people are cutting their lives short with this underlying ego-activity. All reactivity to physical pain is self-contraction. Fear is self-contraction. All reactive emotions are self-contraction.

All thought is a contraction of the force-field of conscious awareness. When such is your condition, all that you ever experience is your own contraction, your own avoidance of relationship.

Thus, all human beings are like Narcissus—who sought to escape from the pain of conditional existence by separating himself from all relationships, all forms of confrontation, who removed himself to the wilderness of absolute isolation, such that he was left sitting nowhere by the side of a pond. What is more, he spent the rest of his life looking into the pond, gazing at his own image and supposing it to be his loved-one—some "other" that he loved.

Not only is Narcissus separate and isolated—he is (entirely, and perpetually) concentrated in an illusion. Apart from true (and truly "radical") self-understanding (or root-understanding of egoity, or of self-contraction, itself), all human beings are exactly like that. There is the persistent avoidance of relationship, the constant self-contraction, the exclusive meditation upon the subjective reflection of events, the endless thinking, the endless motivation from the "point"-of-view of the ego (the presumed "place" of perception and cognition), such that there is no Real perception, no Real Knowledge.

When you look at something with your eyes, you are looking from this "point". When you hear something with your ears, you are concentrating on this internal "target" of ego-"I". When you act, you act from the "point"-of-view of this "target" (or ego-center). You never "Locate" the Divine Reality That Is the Source-Condition of these perceptions. You never enter into heart-Communion with the Divine Self (or Self-Condition) of all beings, things, and events. Therefore, you never discover that you are not the "point" of perception, that you are (in Truth) not separate (or "different") from perception itself and everything that is perceived.

It is not the ego, the internal "target", the separate-self-sense, that is your Real Identity. All of these sensations arise within the Divine Self-Condition (or Source-Condition), Which Is the Real Identity of all-and-All. The body arises within the Divine Self-Condition. Sound arises within It. Light arises within It. All things arise within It, but the Divine Self-Condition is not (Itself) ever qualified (or limited) thereby, nor is there ever any really separately (or exclusively) existing "self" or "thing".

In Satsang with Me, the Power of the Divine Self-Condition (or of Reality Itself) is Communicated. Just as you function on many levels—including the gross (physical) life, the vital energy of life, the emotive (or emotional) life, the psychic life, the processes of thought, discriminative intelligence, and subtle perception—just so, Satsang with Me manifests on many levels. It manifests as physical, human relationship to Me, the Man of "Radical" Understanding— in and As My Avatarically-Born bodily (human) Divine Form and Person. It manifests as My Avatarically Self-Transmitted Divine Spiritual Presence, Which Spiritually In-fills all the levels of the being—vital, emotional, psychic, and so on. And It manifests as life lived on the basis of My Gift of "radical" self-understanding.

In Satsang with Me, there is the communication of verbal concepts—and, while this communication is going on over time, you begin to perceive your own egoic activity. Satsang with Me does not simply remove that activity, as if by magic. Rather, Satsang with Me reveals that activity. The living of Satsang with Me, Which is the Real process of Spiritual life, involves a crisis in consciousness—the crisis in consciousness. Therefore, the activity that is your suffering is not removed by magical, external, and willful methods. Rather, that activity is observed, understood, and (ultimately, most perfectly) transcended.

Even in Satsang with Me, there is a kind of warfare going on in My devotee. There is self-contraction. But My devotee is continually being Drawn out of that, by the Graceful Gift of Satsang with Me, and Attracted more and more fully into My Avataric Divine Heart-Company—the Company of Truth. Truth Draws you—I Draw you—even though you continue to contract. And the result of that tension is a dredging up in you of the observation of your own activity—on many, many levels. Such self-observation must take place on every level.

When you first come to Me, you are like a dark, deep well. Way up at the top, the light comes in around the edges—but, lower down, it is black and unconscious! When the Light of Truth shines down into the well, all of these weirdo, slithering things come climbing up the sides. All the hidden, slimy activity begins to be disturbed, awakened, and moved into the Light.

Just so, every moment in Satsang with Me increases the necessity for responsibility in My devotee—because Satsang with Me is not merely a good feeling, a consolation, not merely something smiling, happy, and pleasant. Satsang with Me is not magic. Satsang with Me is Living Divine Force, the Force of Truth. This Purifying Force moves into the "well", into the human functions— the descending and ascending Circuit—bringing to light the chronic patterns of your ordinary and unconscious existence, and revealing those patterns at the level of the actual conditions of life.

In the midst of this Real process, the governing tendencies of your life are revealed as powerful desires, incredible compulsions—which, even if they were known to you before, now seem to become worse. The intensification of all of that is one of the essential functions of Satsang with Me. And what is there to be intensified in the usual person, except this negative pattern, this contraction? Of course there are difficulties! Real Spiritual life requires everything of a person. Real Spiritual life is a crisis!

My devotee experiences the revelation of egoity in many forms. Dreams may become intensified. There may be spontaneous physical movements, changes in the physical body. Life may become burdensome at times. Thoughts may seem to become endless. You may become disgusted with your own game. My Communication of Truth, over against the karmic display of your own tendencies, brings about an awareness of your own activity of self-contraction—on every level. When this begins to occur, all of your hidden qualities can escape into the Light and be released in the Light of Consciousness Itself.

If you maintain yourself in Satsang with Me through the intense (and, perhaps, protracted) periods of crisis, the entire process (as it develops in your own case) will begin to become interesting. You will cease to react to it, to resist it, to attempt mastery over it, to do anything about it. You will simply live Satsang with Me. You will simply live the relationship and Condition that is Satsang with Me. And self-indulgence (or outward dramatization of your egoic patterns) will cease to be your motivation—because you are able to observe your ego-patterning as such, and you understand this spontaneous process of the "revelation of Narcissus" to be a purifying event.

Therefore, My true devotee lives this heart-relationship to Me and enjoys the Communication of Truth in My Avataric Divine Heart-Company. My true devotee observes his or her own egoic activity and begins to understand it. An intelligence begins to awaken in My true devotee, by which he or she observes and understands the self-contraction more and more thoroughly. This process of "radical" self-understanding was unknown in the world previous to My Appearance here—because the world is devoted to the activity of self-contraction, the avoidance of relationship.

However, none of this takes place through magic—although this process is (itself) a Miracle, and it takes place by Means of My Avataric Divine Grace. Neither the process nor the Circumstance of Satsang with Me is magical. It does not simply "happen" to you—such that you automatically feel good, ready to smile at everyone, as if you were "high" on something. No wisdom could be gained by such magic. You are required to pass through the purifying event—such that, when you arrive at the point of intelligence, the point where you become capable of living the human functions from the "Point of View" of Truth, you have the wisdom by which to do that. If the negative effects of life were simply removed, as if by magic, without any real participation on your part, then you would merely fall back (gradually, and unconsciously) into the same ordinary condition.

However, in general, the participation that is required of you in this process tends, by the Siddhi of Satsang with Me, to be more internal than external. For the most part, instead of having to live through the latent patterns (or karmas) of your life in the form of massive and unyielding disasters, you are enabled to live through them in forms that can at least be handled—perhaps with difficulty, but they can be handled. And much of it takes place in dreams, in self-purifying kriyas, in various Yogic processes.

True Spiritual life is a demand, a confrontation, a relationship. It is not a method that you apply to yourself. Your "self" is this contraction—and this contraction is what must be undermined in True Spiritual life.

Therefore, I Come to you in <u>bodily</u> <u>human</u> Form, in Living Form—to Confront the ego and take it by the neck. I do not merely send down a grinning symbol, to be reproduced with a few effete comments for everybody to believe. The traditional images and the records of past help serve very little. At best, they may help a person move into the position of wanting to enter into Spiritual life. Truth absolutely must Come in Living Form.

Truth must Confront you, "Live" you, "Meditate" you. It is not <u>your</u> meditation that matters. <u>Truth</u> must "Meditate" you. <u>I</u> must "Meditate" you. Such is the Siddhi of Satsang with Me. Even while I am "Meditating" you, you are busy doing more of the usual to yourself—waking yourself up, putting yourself to sleep, reacting in every possible unconscious manner to the Siddhi of Satsang with Me. But, all the while, you are being "Meditated" by Me.

Mere belief in a "Savior" or a "program" of "Liberation" is not sufficient. Your belief cannot provide the necessary Living Means for this process of being "Meditated". Truth must Come in Living Form—as the human vehicle of the True Guru. Real Spiritual life requires this Siddhi. If this Siddhi is not activated, it does not make a damned bit of difference what exotic or humble Spiritual methods you apply to yourself. They will always be of the same nature. They will always amount to a form of self-contraction.

All beliefs, all conventional and consoling religions, all merely strategic religious and Spiritual methods, are extensions of the self-contraction. Truth Itself must become the process of life. Truth must Communicate Itself. Truth must generate conditions in life, and make demands, thereby restoring the individual's conscious participation in the process of Realization.

At the very beginning of your practice of the Way of Adidam, the Fullness of Satsang with Me is Given to you as a Grace. Then, when the Real process of ego-transcendence begins to be magnified in you, your characteristic "act" is intensified—both as it manifests internally and as it manifests externally. Therefore, in order to establish a circumstance in which all of this can be observed, understood, and transcended, I Give you conditions to apply to your life—from the very beginning of your practice of the Way of Adidam. I Place all kinds of demands on you. Your vitality, your health, your relationship to the environment, the condition of your life—these are the things that are confronted first.

Essentially, during that early period, you are responsible for maintaining the heart-connection with Me, and for fulfilling the practical demands given to you as the necessary conditions of the heart-relationship to Me. You are also responsible not to indulge (or dramatize) externally—in life—the ego-revealing phenomena that are arising in you in Satsang with Me. When all of this is stably the case, then you have become prepared to approach Me for the purpose of receiving My Spiritual Initiation into the ever-continuing devotional-_and_-Spiritual relationship to Me.[52] When you, as My by-Me-Spiritually-Awakened devotee, constantly cultivate My Blessing-Regard, then My Avataric Divine Spiritual Blessing progressively in-Fills and Wakens you.

People cannot acknowledge the reality of any of this until they experience it themselves. They experience Satsang with Me and the quality of Spiritual life in My Avataric Divine Company as something very enjoyable, very profound. Then, all of a sudden, they come to the first point of crisis in this Way of heart-relationship to Me. An insane compulsion, almost like possession, overcomes them and seems to demand that they abandon this sadhana. They wake up one morning: "My Guru is no good. The gathering of devotees is no good. Spiritual life is no good. None of this has anything to do with me. I should leave and return to my previous, relatively happy existence." If they are able to hold on through a few of these episodes, they begin to see all of this as their own activity, not anything that truly reflects on this sadhana, and they become stable again in Satsang with Me.

When this form of the crisis is (thus) overcome, then (at some point) a new one develops—just as suddenly, and with equal force. Then they think: "The sadhana is good. My Guru is good. The gathering of devotees is good. Truth is good. Spiritual life is good. But I'm no good. I'm not ready for it yet. I'm not an 'old enough' soul yet. I'm still full of desires. I guess I'm still supposed to seek for a while." This is the crisis of self-doubt. It is often topped off with the "observation" (so called) that "My Guru hates me." And, so, they want to leave—if only for that reason!

"Narcissus" is always a form of contraction, of separation, of leaving. But if you are able to pass through both of these crises— still holding on to Me, still maintaining a responsible refusal to exploit this subjective life-drama—then you can begin to settle stably into the Real Spiritual life of Satsang with Me.

All of the Great Siddha-Gurus (of whatever Real degree of Real-God-Realization)—Who have Taught and Transmitted the Inherently Divine Truth of Reality to living beings—have given their devotees the Graceful Gift of Satsang. Satsang has always been the essential activity of the Great Siddha-Gurus. The Great Siddha-Gurus have never come merely to give a conceptual Teaching—to fabricate a myth, a belief-structure for the mind, a patterning of ego-mentality. The Great Siddha-Gurus have always brought and given <u>themselves</u>. They have always entered into <u>relationship</u> with their devotees, and (altogether) with the conditionally manifested worlds. That Satsang-relationship is the very structure (and the outwardly observable sign) of the devotional (and, in due course, Spiritual) process I have Revealed and Given. If you are My formally practicing devotee, Satsang with Me <u>is</u> Spiritual life. In that process of Satsang, I (by all My Avataric Divine Spiritual Means) "Live" My devotees, I "Meditate" My devotees. Initially, My devotees go through a period of adapting to various forms of responsibility—and, as they have more experience of the actual process, they progressively demonstrate greater responsibility, deeper self-understanding, and more profound devotional resort to Me.

The more fully you participate in Satsang with Me, the more you observe your own activity, your disturbance—and, in due course, by virtue of this very process, you begin to understand that activity, to see that there is the avoidance of relationship, the self-contraction. When you know this most fundamentally, when the self-contraction is undermined and felt beyond, then such "radical" self-understanding can (itself) be made the moment to moment approach to experience, by consciously enforcing that understanding.

Therefore, Satsang with Me—the Condition of heart-relationship to Me, the Man of "Radical" Understanding—is the Means of self-understanding for My devotees. Truth Itself is Communicated in Satsang with Me. Thus, the life of Satsang with Me is simply to live this devotional (and, in due course, Spiritual) relationship to Me.

It is simple enough in concept—but, when you live it from day to day, you tend to complicate it. It becomes a question, a dilemma. This is because you do not simply abide in Satsang with Me. You do not unqualifiedly live the Condition of Satsang with Me. You continue to live the self-contraction, the avoidance of relationship. You still tend to separate yourself from the Condition of Satsang with Me. You still tend to generate this tension, this drama, this warfare, in yourself.

Whenever you notice what you are "up to", then (quite spontaneously) you fall out of the self-contraction, into the Condition of Satsang with Me. Whenever you catch yourself contracting, withdrawing into your own ego-identity, then that self-observation allows you to return to simple Satsang with Me.

In the case of some people, one of the earliest manifestations of Satsang with Me is the occurrence of kriyas—spontaneous movements of body, emotion, mind, and breath. As a means of understanding the difference between the Siddhi of Satsang with Me and the usual state of human activity, look at the difference between these kriyas and the kind of nervous activity that people are always performing. Examine the usual person at "ease", with the constant picking and grabbing and self-conscious posturing, the endless attempts to become comfortable while still suffering an inner feeling of confinement (or entrapment). All of that is reaction to outside (or generalized) forces.

Such actions are always in the form of reflexive, self-directed movements. But genuine kriyas are generated internally and spontaneously. They are movements from within outward, not a curling inward from without. That is why such kriyas are (themselves) a kind of purifier, because they tend to interrupt or reverse the compulsive contraction.

But such kriyas are not (themselves) profound. They are not (themselves) Truth. They are active only at the level of the body-mind. There is nothing "out in the cosmos" about them. They are evidence of a process that is restoring the nervous system to its natural harmony and intensity.

Whatever arises as experience in the course of Satsang with Me is not (itself) the point. Visions, subtle phenomena of all kinds, are (themselves) only forms of self-contraction. They come in order to disappear! When you truly hear Me (or most fundamentally understand your own activity of self-contraction), you are no longer fascinated by extraordinary phenomena (or even simple internal phenomena). That entire affair has come to rest. Then, when you really see Me, My Avatarically Self-Transmitted Divine Spirit-Energy (Which Generates all such phenomena) is Consciously Alive in you.

The Light of Which all visions are only a modification Is Consciousness Itself. My Divinely Enlightened devotee is one who (by Means of My Avataric Divine Spiritual Grace) no longer lives from the "point"-of-view of the separate self—in any sense. Not the gross body, not the vital body, not the subtle body. Not the subtle mind, not the mind at all—not any form of subtlety. Not any conditional center, not any "light-body", not any presumed "eternal body". No body! In My Divinely Enlightened devotee, only the "Point of View" of Truth is Alive. That "Point of View" is Beyond all separateness. Truth Itself (or Reality Itself) Manifests— or, more accurately, appears to Manifest—as all of these "points", all of these egos involved in the usual life-functions. Just so, My Divinely Enlightened devotee continues to appear via all the ordinary modes of human existence.

In My Divinely Enlightened devotee, wherever the ego tends to arise, it instantly vanishes. My Divinely Enlightened devotee never acts from the ego's "point"-of-view. My Divinely Enlightened devotee never dramatizes the ego. My Divinely Enlightened devotee never "believes" the ego. My Divinely Enlightened devotee never becomes the ego. For My Divinely Enlightened devotee, there is never (under any conditions) the loss of Profound, Direct Awareness of the Divine Self-Condition (and Source-Condition) in Which everything is arising.

Because I have Avatarically Incarnated here, a new Function has Appeared in the conditional worlds. I am not another "thing" to be made into a separated "center", not an ego-"other" that has arrived to be contained and fitted into a "cult" of egos.[53] Because I have Appeared, a new Function, a living process, has become possible—Which is Satsang with Me. But, paradoxically, it is also difficult to get people interested in Satsang with Me, because people are already devoted to the process of self-contraction. From the "point"-of-view of the world (or of the egoic search), Reality, Truth, and even the living relationship to the Divine Person tend to be ignored, or even apparently rejected.

I Am a Paradoxical Presence in the world. I always Work to undermine the search. Those who truly heart-recognize Me and heart-respond to Me, and who are moved to embrace the discipline of Satsang with Me, are those in whom the entire process of seeking (in all its forms) has reached a critical point of failure. In such people, the options of the search have begun to subside, to die. Such people have been immobilized—they are truly desperate, failed in their seeking. It is not that they are about to go into a psychotic state. Rather, it is, generally, a very "natural" and non-clinical despair. But it is a critical failure. Such people become capable of Satsang with Me, and Satsang with Me Is their Great Opportunity.

DEVOTEE: Beloved Master, You have said that those who live in Satsang with You must be responsible not to dramatize (or act out) the tendencies that are stimulated and uncovered in them. But I do not think You mean that these tendencies should be repressed. Would You explain this?

AVATAR ADI DA SAMRAJ: I am speaking of these things as they occur under the conditions of Satsang with Me, not in the context of a life without the conscious benefit of this relationship. Previous to Satsang with Me, an emotion, an impulse, would develop, and (under certain circumstances) you just plain acted on it. The disposition of Satsang with Me never entered into your decision or your reaction. But, when you begin to live the Condition of Satsang with Me, you have an entirely different principle of life from which to relate to your impulses. When Satsang with Me truly becomes the Condition of your life, then, as tendencies arise, it is not a matter of repressing or suppressing them, or of doing anything to <u>them</u>. They are mechanical subjective phenomena, patterns reflecting themselves in conscious awareness and in the body. The more you live Satsang with Me and begin to understand the activity that produces these phenomena or causes them to rush up in you, the less you tend to identify with the phenomena themselves. Then the activity and the patterns become simply a matter of interest, rather than sources of motivation. You begin to acknowledge them to be only patterns— not "me", not something "I" must suppress, but patterns which are arising, and which you are simply observing.

As My devotee, you simply live Satsang with Me in the midst of all that. You do not even become concerned with the patterns. You simply enjoy Satsang with Me. If some episode is causing you particular distress (whether mental, emotional, or physical), you do not suppress it. You do not do anything to it. You scrub a floor, wash a window, type some letters, go to work, have lunch! You do not get involved in that drama, either by suppressing it or by exploiting it. You do not do <u>anything</u> about it. Instead, you <u>enjoy</u> Satsang with Me!

This "thing" that is arising in you is only a form of self-contraction. It is always a form of self-contraction. To buy it, perform it, or suppress it is to contract further, to take on the form and "point"-of-view of the self-contraction, to reinforce the self-contraction. But the disposition of Satsang with Me is relationship, not avoidance. Therefore, My true devotee is already free of the stress of self-contraction. My true devotee lives—and is aware— beyond self-contraction. My true devotee is living another Condition—Satsang Itself. Because My true devotee is already not living the self-contraction, he or she has no need either to exploit it or to suppress it. My true devotee is living Satsang with Me— and, therefore, sees that whatever is arising in body, emotion, mind, and breath is only a conditional phenomenon, only a purifying event. Everything that arises is seen to be arising in the context of present-time Satsang with Me.

My true devotee, living in Satsang with Me, allows the revelation of tendencies to occur as a subliminal activity, as a display of impressions—but not as a necessary motivation. Regardless of what is arising in you in any given moment, you simply carry on your practical activity. You do not sit alone in your room—just trying to stop yourself from going out and indulging all your desires, to the point of bewilderment. No. You stand up, you go to the Communion Hall, you meditate, you serve, you see some friends, you go to work. You take yourself to life's <u>functions,</u> life's functional <u>responsibilities</u>. You can permit whatever-it-is to arise in you—without distress, without identification—because you are enjoying present-time Satsang with Me.

When Satsang with Me becomes Real, becomes the actual, present-time Condition of your life, then your relationship to your own tendencies spontaneously begins to change. The more you live Satsang with Me, the more you begin to see that your relationship to your latent tendencies is changing, that it is unnecessary to dramatize them (or live them out). Indeed, you see that to live the arising tendencies, even the apparently pleasurable ones, is the very design of suffering.

From the very beginning of your practice of the Way of Adidam, I Require that you be responsible in relation to certain functional and practical levels of life. There must be a foundation for this process of Satsang with Me. Thus, when you become My formally practicing devotee, you assume various practical disciplines in relation to your diet, your work and responsibilities, your environment and living conditions, the relationships in your life, and so on. As My devotee, you must be willing to assume practical responsibility for what would otherwise be an endlessly dramatized life.

My devotee must be responsible for the processes of money, food, and sex. I do not mean that you have to become a sudden saint. But, when you live with practical intelligence, there is a living firmness, a foundation for the "revelation of Narcissus" that you will inevitably have to endure. If there is nothing but a hole at the bottom, then every time something is thrown in it just goes out the bottom. If you are only ready to indulge what arises in you, then Satsang with Me will only give you more energy for that. In that case, you need a parent, not a Master!

Therefore, I Require you to take on real responsibilities at the practical level of life. You do not require the Absolute Realization of Truth in order to moderate your diet. It is simply a practical affair. A supportive, enjoyable diet that gives strength, keeps the body vital, is simply a matter of intelligence. To be intelligent, you need not first Realize Absolute Truth. But no one can Realize Truth Absolutely who has not first become intelligent.

If you moderate and purify your diet, then dramatization is not taking place in the primal activity of taking food. If you understand your emotional-sexual life—and, in the sexually active case, if you rightly discipline your sexual activity (rather than merely carrying on some form of sexual self-indulgence)—then you will be able to take responsibility for the emotional-sexual dimension. All of this is not for ultimate reasons, but for purely practical reasons—to prevent exhaustion of the vital life and the distractions of unconsciousness, weakness, disease, such that the necessary practical foundation for the Real Spiritual process can be established.

Just so, at the level of money and the general conditions of life, you must be fundamentally responsible for your income, and for the quality of your environment. All of this for purely practical reasons, not for any idealistic reasons.

Every single thing that could possibly be dramatized is a form of self-contraction, of the root-activity of separation. And what exactly are these things you are concerned about "repressing"? You do not worry about repressing or exploiting your tendency to love people, to share life with them, and help them! There is no danger represented by that, so there is no problem about having to either repress or exploit it. What are the things you are wondering about exploiting and repressing? They are all negative, destructive, separative tendencies.

Therefore, from the beginning, that knowledge about yourself must be clear—at least to some degree. You must have seen something about your ordinary activity, your suffering, your usual state. When you see that your usual state is your suffering, then (as My devotee) you fall into the heart-relationship that is Satsang with Me. Then all the forms of self-contraction begin to lose their force. They are undermined by this relationship, whereas (otherwise) they are reinforced by exploitation, suppression, or repression. The more there is the intensity of relationship to Me in Satsang, the less force these impulses have. They begin to wind down. The clenching of the "fist" weakens.

Therefore, do not repress anything. Live Satsang with Me. And carry on a practical order of life. It is only when you are living from the "point"-of-view of the self-contraction, of the dramatization of tendencies, that you become concerned with the alternatives of repression and exploitation. If you are enjoying the Condition of Satsang with Me, then all of this is only a secondary affair, only an impulse. If you are not identified with the seeming center of that impulse, it is not necessary to do anything about it.

Replace concern and worrying about your tendencies with some practical activity or some lawfully pleasurable activity in the ordinary manner. You must become intelligent in how you live this life while being responsible for it. The practical fulfillment of functional responsibilities must occur in relationship. This also serves to undermine the entire process of suffering and bewilderment.

Sadhana is not a matter of always being "uptight", concerned with preventing your craziness. You must learn how to deal with this psycho-physical entity from the disposition of the heart-relationship to Me, of Satsang with Me.

AVATAR ADI DA SAMRAJ
The Mountain Of Attention Sanctuary, 2000

10.

The Path of the Great Form

I.

DEVOTEE: Beloved Lord, does proximity to You, closeness to Your physical Body, have any relationship to the intensity or the effects of Satsang with You?

AVATAR ADI DA SAMRAJ: What is your experience?

DEVOTEE: It does not seem to have that much to do with my bodily closeness to You. It seems more to be how much I am in feeling-contact with You and how open I am to You.

AVATAR ADI DA SAMRAJ: It all depends on the quality of your relationship to Me. You must discover for yourself the quality of Satsang with Me.

DEVOTEE: I have two feelings or ideas about what is happening that I would like to ask You about. The first feeling is that You absorb the "bad" karma of Your devotees and transform it Yourself.

AVATAR ADI DA SAMRAJ: What do you think?

DEVOTEE: That is what I see, that is what I experience—but I am not certain.

AVATAR ADI DA SAMRAJ: Why do you doubt it?

DEVOTEE: The second feeling is that I seem to observe (after I have been sitting for a little while in formal occasions of receiving Your Darshan) a pattern of movement upward through the chakras. Is this some sort of non-verbal Instruction being Communicated by You?

AVATAR ADI DA SAMRAJ: In you?

DEVOTEE: In myself, yes. Something that You Do—and, therefore, that I am tuning into, because I am receiving Your Darshan.

AVATAR ADI DA SAMRAJ: Many structures are activated in the process of Satsang with Me. The experience is different from person to person, and the perceived quality of Satsang with Me seems to vary in the same individual from occasion to occasion. The reason there are apparent differences is that different aspects of the psycho-physical mechanism are animated (or otherwise become a focus of attention) at different times. In different individuals, the obstructions in the mechanism and the qualities of the mechanism are different—therefore, different forms of purification must occur in each case.

If you have a head cold, you must clear out your head. If you have a stomach ulcer, you must heal your stomach. In each individual, there is a different structural dis-ease. That structural dis-ease includes the gross, subtle, and causal dimensions of the being. In the context of Satsang with Me, each person will observe his or her characteristic form of egoic activity. A particular kind of process may be characteristic over a certain period of time—and, in due course, that characteristic process may change. But, in and of themselves, these experiences are nothing but purifying movements. Like the time when you blow your nose and your head finally gets clear: You do not go around pointing to your sinuses for the rest of your life, saying they are the center of Truth!

The psycho-physical structure of human beings may be described as having three primary centers: the navel, the sahasrar, and the heart on the right. The region of the navel and the solar plexus (or the soft region of the lower body) is the epitome of the gross, vital organism. It is the basic center (or foundation point of view) of all religious (as opposed to Spiritual) activity, and also of all ordinary human activity.

In the course of Spiritual practice in My Company, My Avatarically Self-Transmitted Divine Spirit-Current Moves Down into life by a process of descent into this region. But My Divine Spirit-Current also Ascends. The structures through which the Current of Divine Spirit-Energy Ascends have been described in various esoteric traditions. The Yogic traditions of India, in particular, describe the pattern of ascent through the chakras—the "wheels" (or lotuses, or centers) in the spinal line of the physical body which are the subtle counterparts of various important vital centers.

The epitome (or fundamental "goal") of the traditional Yoga of ascent is the sahasrar, located at the crown of the head and just above the head. The sahasrar is the primary center of all subtle activity, all activity that is traditionally called "Spiritual".

The English word "spirit" comes from the Latin word for "breath" ("spiritus"). In Sanskrit, the word "prana" is commonly translated as "life", "breath", or "vital force". The breath is associated with the circulation (in the body-mind) of both natural energies (or vital force) and the Divine Spirit-Energy that Pervades and "Lives" all beings and things. Most commonly in the Great Tradition, what is considered to be "Spiritual life" is (in fact) simply the upward-directed (or ascending) life of the vital force. From this traditional point of view, the Kundalini is prana, and the Kundalini Shakti is prana-shakti (the subtle, or ascending, activity of the life-force).

In the practical activity (or Yoga) of traditional Spiritual life, the vital force ascends, or is made to ascend (either by the intentional methods of the Yogi or, otherwise, by the spontaneous Initiatory Grace of the Yogi's Guru), toward the sahasrar, the subtle center at the crown of the head and above. By such means, the conventional Yogi attempts to merge the conditionally manifested vital force with its subtle source above. This effort produces the samadhi states characteristic of most types of ascending Yoga.

There are many types of such traditional Yogic meditation, but they are all forms of this same subtle process. In general, the traditional approach to Spiritual life is simply an exploitation of the upward-directed (or ascending) aspect of the life-force. Whereas conventional religion is (essentially) a largely unconscious effort of surrendering to (or waiting for) the downward-directed (or descending) Energy (Whose Source, or Nature, is presumed to be "God"), all conventional Yoga (or the strategic Spiritual life of ascent) is a contemplation of, concentration on, or exploitation of the ascending activity of that same Energy (or Force).

The conventional Yogi may do various things to control and harmonize the breathing process, in order to go "inward" and "upward". To the same end, the Yogi may add strict control of sex-force, diet, thought-processes, and so on. There are also various forms of concentration on the subtle centers (or chakras). Some traditional Yogas involve the contemplation of internal subtle sounds, or concentration on internal subtle lights.

There are many forms of traditional Yoga that concentrate on the various dimensions of the subtle mechanism of the human being. The senior form of traditional Yoga (or the cultivation of ascending Energy) is the spontaneous Kundalini manifestation—in which all the classic Spiritual manifestations arise spontaneously, by the Grace of the Guru. However, in the Real process of Satsang with Me, the entire affair of the ascending Yoga is only a secondary event. The primary process in Satsang with Me is the Descent of My Avatarically Self-Transmitted Divine Spirit-Current in the frontal line—thereby Purifying and Spiritualizing the body-mind of My devotee.

Some of My devotees experience kriyas (or spontaneous physical, emotional, or mental movements). Changes in the breath, or automatic pranayama, may appear in the form of sudden breathing, rapid breathing, or quieting (or even cessation) of the breath. In some cases, attention may quite naturally become inward-directed concentration, and internal experiences of chakras—accompanied by visions, lights, sounds, experiences of merging in Bliss. Some people may have these experiences. Others may not have these particular kinds of experiences—or they may have them only occasionally, or they may only have certain of them.

The pattern of descent (through the frontal line of the body-mind) and ascent (through the spinal line of the body-mind) is the

Circle (or Circuit) of the life-force (and also of My Avatarically Self-Transmitted Divine Spirit-Energy). It is the True "Round Dance".[54] In My true devotee, the "conductivity" of the full Circle is re-established and full, whatever stimulations of descending and ascending activity arise in the stages of purification.

The religious traditions (founded in the first three stages of life and the "original" context of the fourth stage of life) speak from the point of view of the gross dimension (or the gross body). The esoteric mystical and Yogic traditions (founded in the fourth and the fifth stages of life) speak from the point of view of the subtle dimension (or the subtle bodies). But the Transcendentalist traditions of Jnana (founded in the sixth stage of life) speak from the point of view of the causal dimension (or causal being, or causal body). The causal being (or causal body) is the seat of deep sleep, and also of the separate-self-sense (which is rooted in the heart, on the right side of the chest).

The physical heart, on the left side of the chest, is associated with the waking state, the frontal line, and the gross dimension of conditionally manifested existence. The middle station of the heart (or the heart chakra, or anahata chakra), in the middle of the chest, is associated with the dreaming state, the spinal line, and the subtle dimension of conditionally manifested existence. And the right side of the heart is associated with the state of deep sleep and the causal dimension of conditionally manifested existence.[55]

The heart on the right is without lights, without sounds, without forms, without movement. When it is open and conscious, the heart on the right is also the seat of what has been (in the traditions of India) called the "Fourth State" (Beyond the three common states of waking, dreaming, and sleeping). That State, known (in Sanskrit) as "Turiya" (meaning simply "the Fourth"), Transcends all modifications.

The traditional Spiritual seeker wants to ascend (via the spinal line), and merge in the sahasrar (the highest, subtlest place in the psycho-physical structure). In contrast, the traditional religious seeker wants to be full (in the frontal line, epitomized by the navel)—to receive (and be full of) Truth, Blessing, the Grace of God. But the Jnani, the one who seeks Transcendental

Illumination, the one who would achieve world-excluding Self-Knowledge, is directed toward the causal center in the right side of the heart—beyond the mind, beyond form, beyond visions, beyond conceptual and perceptual experiences. When this causal center opens, beyond the apparent unconsciousness of sleep, the State called "Turiya" arises. It is the Witness-Consciousness, Transcending the three ordinary states of waking, dreaming, and sleeping.

All of the traditions that have arisen in the great search of humankind have been communicated—whether consciously or unconsciously—from the point of view of one (or, perhaps, more than one) of these three primary centers of experience. The Jnani—who is seeking to rest in the right side of the heart—speaks in terms of Identity with the Real Self. The Yogi—who is oriented to the ascending Spiritual search and aspiring toward the sahasrar—speaks in terms of Union with Truth, Light, God. And the religious individual—who seeks to surrender to God as the Great Divine "Other" and serve God among human beings, and whose search is centered in the navel—speaks in terms of his or her relationship to God and to God's "creatures", and of the Fullness of receiving God's Grace.

But all three of these centers (the navel, the sahasrar, and the heart on the right) are only portions of the structural anatomy that all human beings share, all living beings share, all worlds share. In fact, this fundamental structure is duplicated in all forms, including even the conditionally manifested cosmos as a whole. The conditionally manifested cosmos is structured in the same manner as your own tripartite mechanism.

Nevertheless, Truth Itself Includes (and is Prior to) all of that. Satsang with Me is the Company of Truth. Satsang with Me is not an opportunity given to seekers to exploit any of these three centers (or functions) of conditionally manifested existence (to which the traditions have paid so much attention).

The traditions always start from a "low" position and seek to attain their goal from there. Depending on the point of view (and the stage, or stages, of life) characteristic of any particular tradition, the goal is either Fullness, Union, or Identity. But the True

Spiritual life I Offer to you is founded in the "Point of View" of Truth Itself—not the point of view of the search, but the "Point of View" of the Realization of Truth, the living of It, the present-time Realization of It as one's Real Condition. For My devotee, whatever Real transformation occurs, at any level of the life-process, is simply a manifestation of Truth, of Satsang with Me—not a result achieved through the search.

When you embrace the relationship that is Satsang with Me, and live It as the Condition of your life, you may begin to experience unusual phenomena in any of these three primary centers. But no such experiential manifestation is "it". Rather, each of the three primary centers represents a certain characteristic limitation—and, therefore, the phenomena you experience are simply signs of the particular purification necessary in your case.

Only Satsang with Me is the true resort of My devotee, regardless of his or her particular qualities or tendencies. Truth Itself—and "radical" self-understanding—is the necessity of all beings, regardless of the nature of their experiences.

At the outset of your practice as My devotee, it is not exactly clear to you how the process of Satsang with Me works. Indeed, until you Realize Me Most Perfectly, the True Nature of Satsang with Me cannot be altogether grasped. It remains incomprehensible, paradoxical. If you try to discover or enact the process on your own, it will not happen. If you do not already live the "Point of View" of the True Divine Heart in all of the structures of the bodily mechanism—gross, subtle, and causal—how are you going to move into the "Point of View" of the True Divine Heart? Depending on the moment, your point of view is in your head, your chest, or your belly—or anywhere at all. Satsang with Me, the Company and Condition of Truth, is your true resort. In Satsang with Me, you will find yourself falling spontaneously into the Heart of Truth, Which Transcends all conditionally manifested realizations. Truly, in Satsang with Me, you discover that the self-contraction is not Real. The Only Reality Is the Love-Bliss-Happiness That Is Truth—That Which Is Always Already the Case.

The body is a process of "conductivity", in which Energy moves in a Circle (descending and ascending). The epitome of the life-aspect of this Current is the vital center in the general region of the navel.

The epitome of the subtle body is the sahasrar—the center in (and above) the crown of the head. Since the Yogic centers are subtle (and not limited to the physical dimension), the highest subtle centers are actually above the physical head—but the process is sensed as a concentration in the general area of the crown. This entire region is what is called the "sahasrar". Its Real Manifestation Infinitely Above the head is as Light—Unqualified Radiance. This Pre-Cosmic Light is the Source (or Matrix) of all the modifications that people know as "life" and "energy".

The epitome of Prior (or Transcendental) Existence, even beyond the causal knot, is the region of the heart on the right side of the chest. Its Realization is Very Consciousness, Absolute Space, Formless (or Unqualified) Existence.

In all of Its conditional manifestations, Reality Communicates Itself as (and Includes) the navel, the crown of the head, and the right side of the heart. All manifestation is only That. Its Perfect Form is Amrita Nadi—the Conscious, Moveless Spire That Extends from the heart on the right to the Matrix of Light Infinitely Above.

All of life descends from the Divine Matrix Infinitely Above, and returns to It, in a continuous Cycle—conducting Its Light, and (thereby) appearing as movement and form. But this Light is Coincident with, and Identical to, the True Divine Heart (or Unqualified Existence). The True Divine Heart—Which Is the Source of all life, and of Which every thing is a reflection (or modification)—cannot (Itself) be modified by any thing, event, or circumstance whatsoever.

Those who enter into Satsang with Me—Where Truth Itself, the Living Reality, is directly Communicated to you—see Reality manifested in their own being, in three characteristic forms. First, there are manifestations in gross (physical) life: kriyas (spontaneous vital and physical movements), changes in the life-pattern, various experiences and circumstances at the level of life, waking phenomena. Then, there are the subtle (or dreamlike) manifestations: lights, visions, dreams, sounds, subjective patterns in conscious awareness. And, then, there is the causal awareness—

at times falling into a profound sleepless sleep, and (beyond that) even having glimpses of "Turiya", or the Witness-Consciousness. All of those phenomena are manifestations at particular levels (gross, subtle, or causal) of the great and all-inclusive process that is Satsang with Me.

However, My Avataric Divine Communication to you is from the "Point of View" of "Turiyatita"—or That Which Is "Beyond the Fourth State". It is the "Point of View" of the True Divine Heart Itself. It is the "Point of View" of Amrita Nadi, the Perfect Form of Reality.

Satsang with Me is the "Point of View" of Truth. And, when (by Means of My Avataric Divine Spiritual Grace) Truth is Most Perfectly Realized, then all things that arise are Divinely Self-Recognized as transparent (or merely apparent), and unnecessary, and inherently non-binding modifications of Reality Itself (or the Divine Conscious Light Itself).

Satsang with Me (or the Company of Truth) manifests (most fundamentally) in the form of the three dimensions of experience I have described. And Truth Itself—the "Point of View" Which generates the processes of Satsang with Me—is the Self-Condition (and Source-Condition) of conditional reality in all of its manifestations.

The two Aspects of Realizing Consciousness Itself are the Transcendental Aspect (associated with the first two stages of the "Perfect Practice") and the Divine Aspect (associated with the third stage of the "Perfect Practice", or the seventh stage of life). The first (or Transcendental, and foundation) Aspect is the Self-Existing Consciousness That Is Reality Itself—Perfectly Realized when the mind falls into its Source, and when the points of view of the gross, subtle, and causal dimensions have been transcended and the self-contraction is no longer active. This is "Turiya".

The second (or Divine) Aspect is the "Regenerated" Amrita Nadi (or the Perfect Form of Reality Itself)—which may also be called "Turiyatita" ("Beyond the Fourth"). It is My Eternal Divine Form, the Self-Existing and Self-Radiant "Bright" Divine Self-Condition (Itself).

When I speak of My Divine (all-and-All-Surrounding and all-and-All-Pervading) Self-Nature, I am not speaking of some egoic "magnificence". Rather, I am speaking of That Which Is Always Already the Case, That Which Alone Is, That Which Is Inherently and Self-Evidently Divine, That Which Stands Out As the Obvious when egoity has vanished.

The Truth Itself (Which is Satsang with Me) and living the Truth (which is sadhana, or Real practice) make possible the entire Event of the progressive Revelation of the total hierarchical esoteric structural anatomy of the human being. That structure is Alive. It is not a structure that can be blueprinted and then prescribed. Something can be said about it—but the saying is not equivalent to the sadhana (or life) of Satsang with Me. Just as it is impossible to control the breath once it leaves the body—so this esoteric anatomy, with its various levels (the Source and Very Condition of which is Truth Itself), is absolutely elusive, absolutely paradoxical.

That is why the images of Divinity, particularly in the East, have a paradoxical quality. At times, they are entirely benign—at other times, they are treacherous, violent. Krishna is beautiful and blue, but he teases those who desire him. He eludes them. He runs away, while saying, "Yes, I'm coming, I'm coming." But they wait and wait and wait, and Krishna does not come.

The Mother-Shakti appears in all kinds of forms. In My own experience, the Mother-Shakti has (at times) appeared to be like anyone else—then different, as all kinds of forms. Very strange, then beautiful, then wise. What is being communicated through the imagery of these experiences is the process of existence—but only a piece at a time.

That process is perfectly Known only when there is unqualified resort to Truth Itself. Otherwise, you will "buy" whatever experience your tendencies gravitate toward. If you are fascinated by a light between your eyes, then that is where you will be. Whatever you are willing to "buy", you will be given. That is why the deities are pictured in such paradoxical forms. They will give you a little pink fruit, if you will come and take it. The dog comes for a bone, gets the bone, and leaves. You may become attached to the experiences that are stimulated in My Avataric Divine Company. Perhaps, at some point, you will "buy" the entire display. You are already "buying" it. You may even become very angry, and reject Satsang with Me, because of the position you are put into by craving your own internal life. "Narcissus" is addicted to looking at himself. It is the one thing he will always defend.

II.

DEVOTEE: Master, could You explain how the Shakti relates to Truth?

AVATAR ADI DA SAMRAJ: What is called the "Shakti", the Divine Generative Power, is truly not a separate (or independent) Force. In Reality, the Shakti is not "different" (or separate) from What is called "the Self" (with a capital "S"), "Reality", "Truth", or "God". The name "Shakti" is simply used to describe that aspect of the Truth that appears as movement in the context of conditional manifestation.

"Siva-Shakti" is a more complete designation of the Truth. The Unconditional Reality is Moving-Generative (or Self-Radiant), as Shakti—but It is simultaneously Unmoving-Untouched (or Self-Existing), as Siva. The True Divine Shakti is the Conscious Force (or Energy, or Light) in and As Which every thing exists. It is the present Nature of every thing, of all beings, and It is also the Substance, Support, and Native Identity of all that arises.

The actual spontaneous process of the Yoga of True Shaktipat (including purificatory kriyas), which I have described in *The Knee Of Listening*,[56] is stimulated by contact with a living Siddha-Guru in whom this Yogic Force is functioning consciously and unobstructedly. Such contact with a Siddha-Guru stimulates the Circuit of life-energy and Divine Spirit-Energy, and purifies the inner functions of obstructions. By virtue of that contact, the subtle process becomes conscious, and it manifests itself through a series of purifying events (both internal and external). The obstructions are broken down—perhaps on an apparently gross level at first, then on subtler and subtler levels.

The first such Yogic experiences a person might have are various bodily sensations—you may notice a certain bodily energy, a certain heat or cold, a certain tendency to move involuntarily (in spontaneous jerking movements), a feeling of discomfort, an intense (even erotic) feeling all over the body, or in specific regions of the body (such as the head). These purifying movements are an automatic Hatha Yoga. At times, you may even feel forcefully compelled (by the Yoga-Shakti) to perform Hatha Yoga postures (or asanas)—even postures which you would otherwise be physically incapable of performing were the Yoga-Shakti not active in this manner. You may also (at times) experience automatic pranayama, or vigorous and uncommon (and spontaneously occurring) exercises of the breath.

The entire process of everything that may be called "Yoga" (including all the types of traditional Yoga) may arise spontaneously in you—beginning with the more physical forms of Yoga, then moving on to the subtler purifications and qualities of experience and meditation. For instance, there may be times when the mental processes become rapid, when there is endless thinking, without apparent cause—and then, just as spontaneously, the process of thought breaks apart, slows down. You may begin to have visions, to perceive internal forms, colors, smells, tastes, sounds. You may hear the sounds that are always vibrating within (known as "nadas" in the traditions of Yoga). There may be visions, symbolic experiences, dramatic mudras, or poses of hands and body, movements of all kinds, shaking of the body, ecstasies, spontaneous devotion, love, bliss, and profound concentration in the various psycho-physical centers.

The movement of such subtle experiences is always upward—moving toward (and culminating in) the primary region of the subtle life in the crown of the head. Traditionally, this subtle, ascending Yogic process has often been regarded as the unique process by which the Shakti manifests Itself in the human structure. But, in fact, that process is a demonstration of only one aspect of the greater Pathway of the Universal and Absolute Activity of the True Divine Shakti.

There are (essentially) three traditional paths, forms, or qualities of Spiritual life, based on the three primary functional points of view, each (according to the classical texts) representing a particular knot that needs to be opened. "Liberation", as it is traditionally understood, is the opening of these knots.

The first of the three traditional paths is associated with the region of the front of the body—epitomized by the region of the navel, and including the entire solar plexus and the soft organs which extend above it (including the heart, lungs, tongue, and parts of the brain) and below it (to the anus). Some traditions indicate its center (or epitome) to be just below the navel. Truly, that entire region is the gross-vital center, the life-center.

The tradition of practice related to this center is interested in being stable there, and (thus) being strong, upright, direct, active in proper relationship to things, in proper harmony. The purification of this center (or the "navel", or gross life altogether) is the goal of religious devotion and the various practices and disciplines that are applied to the vital life. Ordinary (or exoteric) religion essentially looks toward life-purification, life-stabilization, life-opening—and the life-center is its point of view.

The second traditional path is the subtle path, the point of view of ascending Yoga and various related exercises or processes. Such are the paths that exploit the subtle-life manifestations. In the traditions of subtle ascent, the subtle body is conceived in terms of various chakras (or subtle centers) through which the Energy moves. This upward ascent through the chakras culminates in the sahasrar, the primary center of subtle life.

In the traditional texts, certain chakras are described as primary knots, but the sahasrar itself is not included among these knots. The primary knot is in the head (below the crown)—in the midbrain, behind the eyes. When all of these knots are open—or, in other words, when the living, inward-directed Energy is free to move upward and merge in the sahasrar—such is regarded to be the highest Realization, from the point of view of the traditional ascending Yoga.

The third traditional path is one that is seen represented in the non-dualistic (or monistic) Hindu traditions (such as Advaita Vedanta), in certain schools of Buddhism, and also (to some extent) in the traditions of Jainism and Taoism. In such traditional schools, the path is generated from the point of view of the causal being. Whereas the gross path is analogous to the waking state and the subtle path is analogous to the dream state, the causal path is analogous to the deep sleep state. The causal path is represented by those traditions that are moved to Realize the Formless and Moveless Aspect of the Divine Reality. The knot of the causal heart, located in the right side of the chest, is the center from which these causal paths are generated, and toward which they seek to move by means of various (strategically engaged) discriminative and intuitive practices. The opening of this center (or knot) on the basis of such practices, allows the Realization of Consciousness Itself.

My Avataric Divine Wisdom-Teaching is not generated from the point of view of any of these three knots, not generated from the point of view of any of the remedial paths that strategically aim to open those knots. The frontal line (or gross dimension), through which Energy descends, the spinal line (or subtle dimension), through which Energy ascends, and the right side of the heart (or causal dimension), which is the bodily origin-point of attention (and, beyond that point, or knot, the Moveless Abode of Consciousness) are all present in the structure of every human being. And each individual who truly enters into Satsang with Me will tend to progressively go through a characteristic developmental (or purifying) process, according to his or her particular tendencies in relation to these three dimensions.

The "Point of View" of Truth is not the point of view of dilemma, not the point of view of any of the three dimensions of conditional existence (or of their primary centers, or of any secondary centers associated with them). No particular form of experience is equal (or identical) to Truth, the Living Divine Heart, the Divine Self-Condition, or Real God.

What is necessary is the transcending of obstruction—the transcending of the ego, of self-contraction, of the avoidance of relationship. Then only Truth Stands Out. Therefore, the

Communication from the "Point of View" of My Avataric Divine Wisdom-Teaching is Truth Itself. I turn My devotee to Truth, to Reality—not to experiences, not to the possibility of experiences, not to any psycho-physical state.

The gross, the subtle, and the causal are psycho-physical and temporary in nature. They correspond to the three states— waking, dreaming, and sleeping—into which experience is analyzed, in certain traditional texts. As the traditional Indian texts declare, "Turiya" (or the "Fourth State") is Prior to these three conditional states. In other words, the Witness-Consciousness is the State fundamental to all of those three states.

The Witness is not the religious person, not the Yogi, and not the intuitive (or causal) seeker, but "Turiya", the "Fourth State"— Prior to all conditional states, the Witness of it all. And even greater than the Witness-Consciousness is Most Perfect Divine Self-Realization, "Turiyatita", "Beyond the Fourth"—Unspeakable, neither formless nor formed, partially intuited but never truly Known before My Avatarically Self-Revelatory Divine Appearance here. "Turiyatita" is the "Regenerated" Amrita Nadi, the Perfect Form of Reality, Whose Very Nature is the True Divine Heart. Therefore, Truth is not (Itself) to be equated with any conditional process, with the opening of any particular knot, with the solution of any particular dilemma.

Everyone's potential experience in Satsang with Me is different, depending on the quality (or tendency) of each one's patterning and the depth of each one's heart-resort to Me. But everyone's experience of Me is the experience of the Awakening Power of Reality, the Power of Divine Consciousness, My Self-Transmitted Divine Conscious Power.

I Live the Conscious Force of Truth in all of the fundamental dimensions of conditional existence—gross, subtle, and causal. I Am the True Divine Guru with respect to all of them. I am fully Aware in all three conditional dimensions.

In This Body-Mind, there are no knots—no obstruction in the frontal line, no obstruction in the spinal line, no obstruction in the right side of the heart. These three centers are Utterly, Inherently Open in Me.

I Participate in the cosmic domain from the Perfectly Unobstructed "Point of View" of the True Divine Heart. I Am the Siddhi of the True Divine Heart, the "Bright" Manifestation of the "Regenerated" Amrita Nadi.

There are many who are called "teacher" or "guru" simply because they perform a consoling or apparently beneficial function of a particular kind. But such individuals are not living the great Function of True Guru. They are teaching from the point of view of dilemma, the point of view of the knots and their associated searches. Generally, they teach those who are (by tendency) oriented to the same form of dilemma to which they themselves are oriented. The practical religious type teaches those who are inclined to that path. The ascending-Yogi type teaches those who are characteristically sensitive on a subtle level. The more philosophical (or intuitive) type teaches those who are impulsed to abide at the causal depth.

But the "Point of View" of Truth is not dilemma, not the knots. The "Point of View" of Truth is not identical to any kind of experience, solution, or form of perception and cognition. Therefore, I Teach Truth As Truth, from the "Point of View" of Truth. Then, only secondarily, the purification (or opening) of the knots occurs, in the distinctive manner appropriate to each individual.

Thus, Satsang with Me has the potential to manifest as many different qualities and types of experience. From the "Point of View" of the True Divine Heart, and in light of the understanding of the processes of conditionally manifested existence which I have just described, the variations are easy to comprehend. Only when people's Spiritual experiences are examined from the outside and from a limited point of view do they seem disconnected and disorderly. Then it seems as if there is too much difference between people and traditions—and no single, comprehensible process stands out.

Truly, the Great Spiritual Process is not understandable from any point of view other than the Divine Heart Itself. From a limited point of view, the variety of Spiritual phenomena seems confusing—just as the world seems confusing from the limited point of view of ordinary experience and circumstance.

The "Shakti" to which people most commonly refer is the Force manifested and exploited in the subtle process associated with ascending Yoga. But the True (or Perfect) Shakti Is My Ruchira Shakti—the Conscious Force That <u>Is</u> the Divine Self-Condition, That <u>Is</u> the True Divine Heart, That <u>Is</u> Amrita Nadi, That <u>Is</u> the Truth, and That <u>Is</u> Reality Itself (the One and Only <u>Real</u> God).

My Ruchira Shakti is Appearing as <u>everything</u> that arises, and as the Totality of cosmic existence. My Ruchira Shakti Is the Truth Itself, Reality Itself. My Ruchira Shakti Is That Which <u>Appears</u> either as the descending Force or as the ascending Force, but truly <u>Is</u> the Moveless Power That Radiates Boundlessly to Infinity.

Therefore, in Truth, the Shakti is not limited to the subtle process with which people generally identify It. It is greater than that, not limited to that. In the case of most of My devotees, the Shakti does not (necessarily) tend to manifest the dramatic course of the subtle ascending process. It Is the True Divine Heart Itself—Self-Existing and Self-Radiant Conscious Light, the "Bright" Source-Condition of all-and-All. It Is Truth Itself. It Is Real God Alive.

When there is the Most Perfect <u>Real</u>-ization of the Real Divine Self-Condition (or Truth Itself), there is also the Perfect Manifestation of the Shakti, the Perfect Communication of the Shakti—because the True Divine Heart <u>Is</u> My Ruchira Shakti, the True Divine Heart <u>Is</u> Conscious Force, the True Divine Heart <u>Is</u> the Fire That <u>Is</u> Reality Itself.

Wherever there is any sort of an opening, there is the flow of life-energy. Any person who is (to a significant degree) open, on any level, is very attractive. People like to be around such a person, because there is movement there. There is no solidity, no fixedness. There is a certain living energy, a "liveliness" with which people like to be associated. It is only that the usual liveliness of people tends to be of a limited kind.

The easiest to identify is the liveliness of the person who is open at the vital level. But there is also a "liveliness" of a subtle variety. In some cases, the subtle "liveliness" of a great Yogi remains in the world even after the Yogi's physical death. The burial shrine of Bhagavan Nityananda, for example, was a most lively place when I visited it during My "Sadhana Years".

Ultimately, your conscious sensitivity must Awaken to the Real, Eternal "Liveliness" That Is the True Divine Heart (or Real God). That Divine "Liveliness" Is Reality Itself—not limited (or conditional) movement.

The "Liveliness" (or Shakti) of the True Divine Heart is Communicated by Me, the Living Divine Siddha-Guru. Whatever the tendencies of the individual, Satsang with Me is simply the Condition under Which the Utter and Complete Process of Truth is able to take place. All that exists is unqualified relatedness, non-"difference". All that appears as suffering and dilemma is the obstruction of relationship. The less obstructed any condition or function is, the more there is the free "conductivity" of Force.

III.

The only-by-Me Revealed and Given Way of Adidam is the relationship to Me as the Divine Siddha-Guru. The Way of Adidam is the process established between Me and My devotee. The Way of Adidam is not any kind of ego-based method or strategy that one might apply to oneself. Satsang with Me—that living, active, functional relationship itself—is the "conduit" through which My Avatarically Self-Transmitted Divine Spirit-Force Flows and Manifests Its activities at every level. Therefore, simply the heart-relationship to Me, the Avataric Divine Siddha-Guru, is the Way of Truth. The Way I Offer to you is the ending of the search, the abandonment of obstructions.

There are also forms of Activity (or Function) that are specific to Me in My Avataric Divine Incarnation, but I do not (generally) speak of these. As a general rule, there is no point in talking about them. These processes are subtler than the ordinary waking mind, and they require equal subtlety to understand.

Nevertheless, certain modes of Activity of Mine are eventually observed by My devotee. You may observe Me doing various things that you associate with certain experiences in yourself.

Those modes of Activity of Mine are not fully comprehended by My devotee at the time.

The traditions describe similar activities in terms of effects and appearances. In India, such activities of the Siddha-Guru are called "Shaktipat" or "Guru-Kripa", the Guru's Transmission of Spirit-Force. The effects of this Spiritual Transmission are observed in various "enlivening" activities—gross, subtle, and causal. The Siddha-Guru is observed to be apparently involved in this Transmission by any of several possible means: by looking at the person, by touching the person, by speaking to the person, or simply by regarding the person in some manner.

The greatest form of that Initiation occurs by My simply and silently Self-Abiding as the "Bright" Divine Self-Condition, or Truth Itself. My Eternal Existence As the Divine Reality (Itself) always newly Initiates My every devotee who has been Spiritually Awakened by Me. Everyone who turns to Me (by appropriate means) is (in due course) Spiritually Enlivened by Me. Such is the beginning of the entire process of True Spiritual life in My Avataric Divine Company.

The various experiences of My Activity are the apparent Means, from the point of view of the body-mind, of My Transmission of the Light, the Truth, the Shakti—My Transmission of My Own "Bright" Divine Person. My devotee may tend, as a result of some enlivening experience generated by My Avataric Divine Spiritual Grace, to look again and again for that particular experience or that particular form of Initiatory Blessing to be repeated. My devotee may tend to associate some unique experience in My Avataric Divine Company with Truth Itself. But, in fact, any specific experience in My devotee is generated in a particular moment, and it is only appropriate to the particular moment. Thus, no particular experience is necessary, in the sense that it must be repeated again and again. Different forms of Initiatory Blessing will be experienced at different times. My modes of Activity always remain unpredictable, in order to test and mature My devotee.

Ultimately, What I Do (for the Sake of all beings) is simply to Abide As the True Divine Heart, As Very Truth, the "Bright" Itself.

Just so, the quality of the relationship My devotee is living to Me determines the nature of My devotee's present experience. I do not withhold. I always Live Truth openly. I always Communicate the Truth on all levels, in order to Transform the expectations, the obstructions, the tendencies, the limitations that My devotee is living to Me.

Therefore, the "drama" of Satsang with Me occurs only on the part of My devotee. It is My devotee who must understand his or her obstructions. I do not create obstructions. I only Live the Divine Heart of Truth. But the Force of My Presence may seem to intensify the obstructions that are already the case, in order to make My devotee aware of them, to draw My devotee's attention to them—such that (in due course) the flow of life can move through, unobstructed by any particular reactive tendency. I always Work so that conscious awareness can be lived on a more profound level. My True Purpose is to Awaken My devotees to My Own "Bright" Divine Self-Condition.

Many things can be said about this Activity to Which I have been referring. It is the Greatest Mystery, how the True Divine Heart Lives in the world, how It Functions among apparently separate living beings. The entire process that occurs is as complex as the cosmos itself, and as unfathomable as What Is Beyond it. It cannot be described perfectly. Only certain things can be said about it. Essentially, it is the Divine Self-Condition, Very Existence, Reality Itself, Real God—Appearing under these conditions, under all conditions.

All religious and Spiritual traditions are methods for retracing the structure of conditionally manifested life back to its presumed Source. Each particular tradition tends to do it in a limited manner, from the point of view of a particular form of dilemma, a particular psycho-physical center, a particular viewpoint of experience or conscious awareness.

> The "shape" of a human being
> is like a fruit.
> The core is the causal being—

346

untouched, unborn,
like waiting seed.
When the fruit falls into Earth—
that is to say,
when mind falls into the True Divine Heart—
there springs up an Inconceivable Thread
(of the same Substance as the Seed of Being)
Which Rises Above,
Becoming a Great Tree,
and Extending even into the Heights,
into the Sky and Cosmos of Very God.
This is the "Regenerated" Amrita Nadi.

Until the Seed is ready for life,
it is concealed within the form of the fruit.
The fruit is the dependent form of the human being.
It is the condition of suffering,
and also of sadhana in Satsang with Me.

The stem of the fruit
is the Route of the Light and Life
Which Descend into the fruit
from the "Place" Above,
from the Parent Tree,
and, at last, pass down through the sahasrar,
the Crown of this body (or fruit).

That Light and Life Descend into the fruit
and Make it full and ripe below.
Just so,
That Light and Life also Ascend—
thus maintaining the Circuit (or Circle)—
until the fruit falls
and its Seed is eaten in the Earth.

Such is ordinary (or natural) death—and, in My Divinely Enlightened devotee, also ego-death. Ordinary death is the termination of a phase of the outer life of the individual, but also the beginning of a new phase in the manifestation of the True Divine Self-Condition of every apparently separate self.

Just so, you become most perfectly "fruitful" only in Satsang with the True Divine Siddha-Guru—Who Is the Process, the Goal, the Means, the Power, and the Very Life. I Am That One, Appearing here before you. Therefore, in Satsang with Me, the fruit eventually ripens, falls into the "Earth" (or its Foundation) and opens. That Foundation is the True, Divine, and Inherently Perfect Heart.

When your devotion to Me is most perfect, the entire Circuitry is Known and understood. It is seen to be within the "Bright" Divine Self-Condition (and Source-Condition), rather than to contain you or limit you. To most fully live Satsang with Me is Perpetual Freedom. And My true devotee, even My Divinely Enlightened devotee, does not necessarily leave the world. Therefore, I am here to Communicate "radical" self-understanding to all who feel limited by this fruit-shape, this phantom Circuit of conditionally manifested existence.

My fundamental Method is Satsang with Me, the transformative relationship that living beings enter into with Me. Indeed, the Method of Satsang is the Method of all the Great Siddhas, of all True Gurus of any significant degree of Realization.

Satsang with Me always serves to destroy or undermine the fixation of attention and its implications. Whenever Satsang with Me is lived, there tends to be the opening of the knots (in which attention is otherwise fixed), such that the separate and separative consciousness falls into its Original Condition—Which is the Divine Self-Condition, the True Self-Nature of all-and-All.

Therefore, My Divinely Enlightened devotee—who is (necessarily) thoroughly convicted of the dead-end of the entire course (or cycle) of conditional existence—lives (by My Avataric Divine Spiritual Grace) on the "other side" of that cycle, no longer limited by it. My Divinely Enlightened devotee is consciously related to this entire structure in an entirely different manner than seekers

(or all those who do not yet understand the nature of conditionally manifested existence).

The course of your experience always tends to return to zero,
to revert back to the dilemma. Your experience will always fit you
back into the fruit, like a worm. Thus, I have Appeared in the
world, to Speak the "Point of View" of Truth (or Reality)—not of
experience—and to Attract beings to the Essential Structure in
Which Truth is Communicated, until they see that there is <u>no</u>
remedial path, <u>no</u> "difference", <u>no</u> separateness.

Most Ultimately, My devotee Realizes Perfect Oneness with
Me, Realizes My True Divine Form, participates directly in My
"Bright" Divine Self-Nature—That Which Is Always Already the
Case, the Very Divine Reality, the Real and Only One.

Siddha-Gurus tend to be rather eccentric in their manner of
teaching. They tend to manifest a general unconventionality and
unpredictability. The True Siddha-Guru obliterates and destroys
limitation all the time. The True Siddha-Guru is a Wildness! That
is why the Siddha-Guru is traditionally worshipped as Siva, the
Divine Destroyer.

Siva is traditionally portrayed destroying everything. Siva
walks through town and burns everything. Siva hits people over
the head. Siva cuts them in half. Look at all the traditional pictures
of Siva. Siva is always wiping everybody out, tearing their bodies
apart, and sitting on them in meditation.

But all of that is a symbol for the Perfect (ego-Obliterating)
<u>Humor</u> of the Divine Self! Such images are not intended to repre-
sent literal "Acts of God" or justifiable acts of human beings. They
are only "meaningful" as symbolic representations of the meditative comprehension of an aspect of the Conscious and Universal
Process. The representation of this Paradoxical Display is intended
to Awaken the Love-Bliss-Fullness of Non-separation, of Non-
identification with mortality.

As My devotee, you are (like human beings generally)
oriented toward your own self-involved tendencies, your own
strategic path—and, so, I Offer you this Satsang with Me, this
process of the dissolution of apparent obstructions and limitations.
The more you live Satsang with Me, the more you know It and

enjoy It, and the less you are affected by your own inevitable discomfort and crisis. Then the crisis of transformation becomes (more and more) a very simple, essentially harmonious process. But the more you turn away from the Condition, relationship, and process of Satsang with Me, the more you become fixed in your own obstructions. Then, when the obstructions get shaken up, even broken apart, the discomfort becomes exaggerated, and the purifying process becomes more prolonged and complicated.

My unconventionality and unpredictability is a Demonstration of the Living and Paradoxical Quality of the Divine (or Real) Self-Condition. The formalized, fixed, conventional, predictable quality is not Divine. Rigidity is the "tamasic", fixed, repetitive orientation of the limited mind. The Divine Being, or Self-Condition, or Reality—Alive as Me, the Divine Siddha-Guru—Performs an Unconventional Display, constantly Abandoning all conformity to expectations. It is the Divine Leela, the True Humor (or Play) of Divine Freedom. It always disturbs the fixed, unconscious quality.

Whatever the changes I appear to manifest from day to day, whatever the change in My Display or Action, there is only One Thing I continually Do—which is simply to Abide As the Very (and Inherently egoless, and Self-Evidently Divine) Self-Condition, the True Divine Heart, Reality Itself, Truth Itself.

My apparent Activity, My apparent Drama, My apparent Play, is <u>always</u> changing. I constantly build up expectations in My devotee, and then I change everything around. I continually disturb the fixed quality, the rigidity, the strategic path, to which My devotee always tends.

There appears to be a certain security in fixation—but, in fact, it is a form of disturbance. It is only an illusory security—because there is, in Truth, no fixed conditional state. That is why death is such a threat. The more fluid and loose, the more rapid and intense the flow within, the less fixed, the more functional, the more harmonious, the more like fire, the more there is of Truth, and the less there is of the strategic path—then the more there seems to be a movement in the direction of Freedom. It <u>appears</u> to be a direction. Perhaps that Godward movement should simply be called a "Sign". The Godward movement is a Sign of That Which Always Already <u>Is</u>.

AVATAR ADI DA SAMRAJ
Adidam Samrajashram, 2004

11.
Phases

I.

DEVOTEE: Beloved Master, what is the point of psychic images and visions?

AVATAR ADI DA SAMRAJ: It depends on the individual case. In some cases, such an experience may coincide with a degree of Real ego-transcendence. When that occurs, the person in whom the experience arises suddenly understands and is free of any bondage to the experience. In other cases, when such a phenomenon arises, the person does not know what it is, and (therefore) becomes disturbed by it, and does not allow it to fully occur. Then, perhaps, some source—a teacher or a book—will clarify what is occurring, such that the person is free of the experience. In yet other cases, such a phenomenon will arise in a person who brings no self-understanding to the experience, and (therefore) becomes fascinated by it. When that occurs, the person enjoys the experience, takes it to be important in and of itself, becomes full of it, even identifies with it, and is full of regret and longing when it disappears.

All the experiential manifestations (of vision, art, culture, thought, and life) which people usually consider to be extraordinary are, in fact, ordinary—simply a part of the universal "creativity". Apart from Satsang with Me, apart from the life of devotional resort to Me (and understanding of the egoic self), such phenomena have no more ultimate significance than any other simple (or ordinary) event.

There are people who, because of their particular karmic qualities (or tendencies), manifest psychic powers of various kinds. There are mediums and psychics, people who see a subtle "aura" around you, who see pictures around you, who hold your ring and tell you the answers to your questions, who give seances, who make predictions. These people are not (themselves) extraordinary. Apart from these psychic abilities, most such people are quite ordinary—perhaps not even particularly intelligent.

Because such abilities seem (from the usual point of view) to be extraordinary, you might expect that the character of the individuals who exhibit such abilities would also be extraordinary. But it is not so. Such abilities are simply qualities that happen to arise—like a stomachache, or a left hand. There is nothing Ultimate, Truth-like, or even Truth-directed about occult or psychic phenomena—but, if some such phenomenon arises in you and you "buy" it, then it becomes an aspect of your suffering. And all people are suffering, regardless of what their characteristic qualities may be.

From the Spiritual point of view, the future is a creative potential, not a predetermined destiny. Very often, a mysterious indication will arise—the intuitive awareness of a tendency that is operating or a possibility that is presenting itself. But True sadhana is not determined by tendencies or premonitions. True sadhana always involves creative participation in the conditions of born existence. True sadhana allows the Graceful transformation of time and space into the Conscious Spiritual Event. There may be intuitive indications of tendencies, of possibilities, of things that might occur—but all of this arises in relation to the Living Divine Heart, and (therefore) none of it is absolutely predetermined.

Spontaneous, Free, and Conscious activity—that is generated in Satsang with Me (the Avataric Divine Realizer and Self-Revelation of the Living Divine Heart)—constantly breaks down the entire machine of destiny. There is no necessary event—it is all a creative, participatory activity. The more "tamasic" (or inert) the body-mind is, the more likely you are to experience and suffer the events toward which you are tending. But the more movement toward purification there is in you, the more harmony there is alive in you, and the more self-understanding there is in you, the less likely it is that your future will be determined by karmas (within and without).

When people say they are "seeing the future", they are really just perceiving the tendencies in individuals, and also in groups. Some such people see psychic imagery, while others have a complex intuition. Such intuitive awareness can take various forms—but, in any case, what is seen is only a tendency, a possibility, a trend. That is the limitation of the so-called "psychic" functions. In and of themselves, they are not a form of participatory involvement with the process of life.

The naively psychic individual may predict to someone, "Yes, you are going to die at the age of forty-two," or, "You are going to marry a rich man when you go on your round-the-world trip to Shangri-La." But that is not, in fact, how the person's life will necessarily turn out. These are just possibilities—and, the more you speak of them as necessary events, the more you make life a non-spontaneous process. The right disposition in Satsang with Me is always the participatory disposition. Certainly, there may (at times) be intuitions, feelings, psychic premonitions, and so on—but, for My devotee, they always arise within the participatory process, the ego-transcending process, the Siddhi (or Living Power) of Satsang with Me.

Satsang with Me breaks down rigidity, the "tamasic" (or "stuck") quality. The psychic abilities that are associated (for example) with the occult and astrology are functions of the gross and subtle being—not of the True Divine Heart. Occultists and astrologers tend to interpret life as a fixed event, in relation to either the past or the future. There have been very few individuals capable of observing conditionally manifested cosmic and human conditions from the "Position" of Consciousness Itself.

Psychologies and sciences of the ordinary kind tend to treat the past as a fixed event that is determining the present. And the occult and astrological sciences, even with their attendant psychic phenomena, tend to interpret the future as a predetermined event. But there is not anything that is absolutely fixed. Consciousness Itself is utterly Uncontained. It always holds the Potential of infinitely varied manifestation. It is always Divinely Humorous. The past is not absolutely determining the present. Therefore, you do not have to delve deep into your past in order to be free. The future is not absolutely fixed by the stars. In any moment, <u>all</u> possibilities exist in the stars. Therefore, it does not make any difference which fixed moment in time and space is taken as the point of view from which to read past, present, or future. What is important is the participatory Realization of Truth. Therefore, "radical" self-understanding is the only appropriate point of view, under any conditions.

One of the Lessons that the Great Siddhas have always tried to communicate to people is the undetermined nature of life. The Great Siddhas have always urged human beings to conceive and know life as a Spiritual event, rather than a fixed conditional event. The Great Siddhas have always communicated that conditionally manifested existence is established in (and coincident with) Truth and Happiness—rather than being limited to mortality and suffering.

But, in order for that Realization described by the Great Siddhas to (in fact) be So, an individual must be Awakened to the "Point of View" of Consciousness Itself—the "Point of View" That is Always Already Free, not fixed. That "Point of View" is not based on any mere movement of desire. That "Point of View" is Conscious, Fluid, Intelligent—Inherently and Priorly Full of Truth and the Love-Blissful Force of Truth.

Truth is That in Which the stars are hung, and That in Which this limited mind of tendencies and fixations arises. Ultimately, when (by My Avataric Divine Spiritual Grace) the "Point of View" of Consciousness Itself is Most Perfectly Realized, when Satsang with Me becomes your Priorly Established Condition, then every moment is the Demonstration of the Divine Spiritual Event.

Because of this, many great Teachers (such as Gautama and Ramana Maharshi), when asked about the future, or the states after death, or psychic powers, would simply not entertain the discussion at all. On a few occasions, Ramana Maharshi gave more or less direct replies to such questions—but, for the most part, He would only say, "Find out who wants to know this." This was His manner of turning the questioner toward the fundamental Truth Which Transcends and even (at last) Masters one's personal destiny.

I am perfectly willing, at the moment, to discuss such phenomena. But they are simply arising—like your body, like this room. They are only conditional phenomena. They do not determine the Truth or limit the sadhana of My devotee.

Truth must become the "Point of View". When Truth is the "Point of View", there is no past or future that can absolutely limit your state. Then time and place become relatively insignificant. Then it makes no ultimate difference whether the "good thing" is going to happen or the "bad thing". In either case, My devotee must turn to Me and understand. The "good thing" is just as much a form of suffering as the "bad thing". Apart from your turning to Me, you only live the self-contraction and the avoidance of relationship—under all conditions. But, if (by Means of My Avataric Divine Spiritual Grace) this root-strategy is transcended, then you can truly delight in the "good thing" that happens—and there will be an inherent freedom even when the "bad thing" happens.

Regardless of anyone's particular makeup—ordinary or extraordinary, with or without psychic abilities—every human being is suffering. And, in the midst of that suffering, all human beings have the opportunity to live in an entirely "radical" and Free manner—by embracing the life of Satsang with Me. Seen in these terms, then, the significance of extraordinary phenomena (which people typically fail to understand and transcend) is no different from the significance of anything else that arises, any fortune or misfortune that may arise. All experiences—"good" and "bad"—are there, ultimately, to turn you to a crisis relative to your own search.

All kinds of conditional manifestations, ordinary and extraordinary, arise in Satsang with Me, and the Force of Satsang with Me inevitably tends to bring on purifying events—which will, in some cases, manifest as difficult experiences that must be gone through. If you abide in the Condition of Satsang with Me, if you live the "Point of View" of Satsang with Me, if you resort to Me while going through these experiences, they can serve the Real process of heart-resort to Me and understanding of the egoic self.

Ultimately, purifying events simply are what they are—not what they imply. They arise like the stars, the world, the bodies of living beings. Depending on your disposition, such events can increase your suffering and your search or (otherwise) they can serve the Real process of Satsang with Me.

II.

DEVOTEE: Beloved Lord, why do You at times appear to be weeping when You are Sitting with us in Darshan?

AVATAR ADI DA SAMRAJ: The reasons for it are varied and complex. This weeping may appear if there is an intense Energy-Process going on in This Body-Mind. The ascending Energy, especially, tends to make the eyes tear. In such cases, there is no emotion associated with My weeping. It is simply a physical manifestation that purifies the eyes (and, also, the centers in the head that are associated with the eyes).

Depending on the exact nature of the Energy-Movement that is occurring, there can be an activity in the subtle body (in the pattern of ascent in the spinal line) that is like suffering. It is <u>like</u> suffering—but, in fact, it is a Yogic process. When I Grant My formal Darshan to devotees, I Absorb, Purify, and Transform the energy-forms, the mind-forms, the qualities (of all kinds) that My devotees bring to the occasion. The Transformation of all of that does not occur without cost.

Ordinarily, people are rather insensitive to what is going on between themselves and others. For this reason, they are very willing to exploit life. People allow others to do whatever they please, and they themselves do whatever they please—within the limits established by their own desires and fears. People are unaware of the nature of relationship as the Real condition of life. They do not know what relationship is, what it involves—as a psycho-physical event, a psychic event, a subtle event. Relationship is the mutual transference of life-energy, the mutual communication of the dimensions of conscious life.

In the usual person, however, this communication is contracted and destroyed—swallowed, reversed, and poisoned. In general, people do not know that this is what is going on in themselves and in others. Sometimes people talk about "vibrations"—this vibration, that vibration, good vibrations, bad vibrations. That usage of language indicates a rudimentary sensitivity to the subtle qualities that people manifest in life. But there is a Real process by which the True Nature and Purpose of Existence can be Realized—the process of Satsang with Me. Satsang with Me is My Unqualified Communication of the Living Divine Heart. Satsang with Me is simply the heart-relationship to Me—the Unqualified, Conscious Divine Reality, in Person.

The process of relationship to My devotees is Consciously Lived by Me. Such is Satsang with Me. It is a profound Yogic process—and, when that process occurs, there is often a quality of suffering. Something must occur, something must open, something must be transformed. And, when that is going on, there is sometimes the appearance of weeping in Me. There is the appearance of sorrow—perhaps, at times, even the apparent <u>mood</u> of sorrow. But it is not the same as ordinary sorrow. Simultaneous with that apparent sorrow, the Transformative Nature of My Divine Love-Bliss-Fullness is also Manifested in Me. Indeed, Love-Bliss is the True Core of that apparent sorrow.

There are other times when this process has already taken place, when I have Endured the Transformation of the karmas of My devotee in My Own Body, when the apparent obstruction in My devotee is obviated—such that My Divine Spirit-Energy Flows freely in the Circle of My devotee's body-mind, and there is the unobstructed Communication of Satsang. This spontaneous weeping also occurs at those times. It is simply the Sign of My Own Love-Bliss-Fullness.

The usual person is insensitive to the Circuit of Energy in the human body-mind. The usual person is not living that Circuit. And the usual person is not living the "Point of View" of Satsang with Me. I have described the quality of life in the usual person as a kind of revulsion, in which the natural life-energy flows in reverse—moving out of the brain down the spinal line (rather than flowing down through the frontal line, and then up through the spinal line). The natural life-energy is also "thrown off" through various kinds of self-indulgence—for example, through degenerative orgasm. Thus, the natural life-energy tends to be merely used up, and never consciously refreshed.

The mood of the usual life is trapped between the extremes of comedy and tragedy. People laugh a lot—but what is laughter? What happens when there is laughter? It feels good—but the process involves a form of revulsion—of throwing off, throwing up—like vomiting.

What happens when you weep in the ordinary sorrowful manner? It is another form of that revulsion. Your breath is disturbed. You cannot control the breath. Your chest is convulsively constricted. You have no True Humor, no Conscious Freedom.

The usual person is constantly involved in this revulsion of the natural life-energy—down the back and up the front. But, in My devotee (rightly practicing in heart-relationship to Me), there is the right practice of "conductivity"—descending in front, ascending in back.

The traditional Yogis speak of the ascending Energy and how important it is (in the case of men) to conserve the sex-fluid (and, in the case of both men and women, to conserve the life-force in general). The traditional Yogi is concerned with stimulating the ascending Current of Energy. There is partial wisdom in that occupation—and, in fact, ascending (or spinal) "conductivity" does tend to establish itself more and more firmly in the course of My devotee's practice of the Way of Adidam. Right "conductivity" of the unbroken Circle of Energy tends to be re-established, countering the unconscious tendency of the life-functions to revulse (or "throw off") their own force and become empty. Thus, for My rightly practicing devotee, this pattern of revulsion is progressively replaced by real "conductivity".

In the life of Satsang with Me, the purifying process tends to occur naturally, in various forms. That is why I have emphasized the practical foundation for Satsang with Me. I have said that the necessary practical foundation for Satsang with Me is an appropriately functional life. Not a suppressed life—you know, no work, no association with other people, one apple every three days, and no sex for five generations! I Call My devotees to live an ordinary, pleasurable life, a functional life—limited to what is supportive, what is rightly enjoyable, what is full. Such a conscious disciplining of one's life tends to break the chronic pattern of self-contraction—at least on the level of practical human action. And that allows right (or non-reversed) "conductivity" to begin at the level of life.

The Way of Adidam involves progressively increasing responsibility for "conductivity" practice. For My beginning devotees, this responsibility is to be exercised at the most obvious level, the life-level. Over time, My Spiritually Awakened devotee becomes fully technically responsible for Spirit-"conductivity" practice. At last, all of the experiential phenomena of Spiritual life are realized to be merely manifestations of the self-contraction, signs of the activity of self-contraction.

The Real Spiritual process—as I (Myself) Lived it (in My "Sadhana Years"), and as My devotees live it in My Avataric Divine Company—involves the observation of Spirit-"conductivity" (as it manifests in the total hierarchical anatomy of the human structure), not the control (or manipulation) of that "conductivity" (by means of the search).

The Real Spiritual process continues to Manifest Itself in This Body. That process is not stopped in My Case. From the time of My Divine Re-Awakening, My Avataric Divine Revelation-Demonstration of the four-stage Process of Divine Enlightenment has been unfolding, as a Living Function. It is a Unique and Unprecedented Divine Process that no one has ever known about. No one has ever suspected It.

The usual person does not suspect the possibility of the Graceful process of Satsang with Me, the All-Completing Communication of Truth, Which can make Itself Known on every level of existence. The traditional stories that people generally hear about Spiritual life only provide rudimentary glimpses and characterizations of certain portions of the Great Divine Process. No historical tradition has comprehended that Process fully, even at the level of description. Any given tradition is limited to the viewpoint of one (or a limited combination) of the three primary centers—the navel region, the sahasrar, and the heart on the right, each of which is associated with a particular aspect of this Great Process.

There have been great Yogis, great Saints, great Sages. Wherever such a great individual has appeared, that one has Communicated his or her Realized State to those who demonstrated a real response. All kinds of experiences were generated in that circumstance—and, out of the people who enjoyed the various kinds of experiences, small groups would band together. You know, the people who had all been having a buzzing in the right ear would get together after the death of their Guru and establish the "buzzing-in-the-right-ear school". Those who were sensitive to subtle phenomena went off and talked about chakras, the Kundalini, internal sounds and lights, and so on. Many separate groups, schools, and traditions arose on the basis of distinctive experiences and particular tendencies. But all such experiences are generated as part of the one Great Process. Thus, the "unity of all religions" that people like to refer to is, in fact, the case—but not in the manner that people usually suppose. That unity is not a matter of all religions "saying the same thing"—because they do not all say the same thing. Far from it. Rather, that unity is to be seen in the "bringing together" of all the historical traditions of religion and Spirituality—in which case, they amount to a collective (and relatively complete) description of all but the most ultimate stage of the one Great Process. Each tradition (or school) represents an experiential portion of that one Great Process.

The unity of all religions is not something that will ever take the form of a common human agreement on a set of abstract religious principles. However, Served by My Guiding Examination of all traditions,[57] there will (over time) come to be an acknowledgement that the collective of all religious and Spiritual traditions together represents a mutually dependent description of the One and Single Great Process of Conscious Existence. Therefore, this very Process, Completed by the (seventh stage) Revelations that are My Own Unique Avataric Divine Work, will become the Life of Truth in the future—replacing the traditional dogmatization and ritualization of certain arbitrarily chosen forms of internal and external experience.

All throughout My "Sadhana Years", I was waiting for the time when I could be outwardly Love-Bliss-Full, when I could Manifest My Own Divine Love-Bliss-Fullness to all. But, all throughout those years, the forces of human and cosmic egoity worked against My Doing That. Even as a baby, I learned very quickly that My Own Love-Bliss-Fullness could not be openly expressed, that It could not be openly lived—not among those who are suffering, seeking, motivated in forms of dis-ease.[58]

Only after the Great Event of My Divine Re-Awakening did it become possible to Live this Love-Bliss-Fullness, this Truth, openly. I have developed the Means whereby It can be Communicated to those who are willing to endure the "radical" transformation of life. But, even in the gathering of My devotees, the universal human resistance to the Process of Truth is constantly manifested. Even in the gathering of My devotees, there tends to be the same game: "No Bliss. Do not be Blissful. Not already. Not already Happy. Not already Free. Not yet. Not me."

But I am not willing to endure the conditions that this resistance would lead to. Therefore, I have Established the conditions for rightly relating to Me! The Love-Bliss-Fullness of the "Bright" Itself—not the egoic ignorance of human beings—must Generate the conditions of life. When that Love-Bliss-Fullness becomes the "Point of View" that Generates the conditions of life, an entirely different situation has manifested in the world.

The world does not ordinarily live from the "Point of View" of the Divine Love-Bliss. The world lives from the point of view of its own suffering, its own dilemma—and there is no "room" for Love-Bliss, for Truth, for unreasonable Happiness. Therefore, from the point of view of ordinary people, I appear to be utterly remarkable—because I Live from the "Point of View" of Love-Bliss, the "Point of View" of Truth. That "Point of View" is Obvious only to Me—therefore, I must (Myself) Establish the conditions under which I can Manifest that "Point of View".

I have always Worked to Establish the appropriate conditions for Satsang with Me. For some people, these real conditions are difficult to understand. People think I am just supposed to "open the door" to all, without any conditions whatsoever. Everybody is just supposed to wander in, listen to a lecture: "Hmm, not bad. Think I'll take this Guru's initiation." No conditions!

People think Spiritual life is a "high", a form of entertainment, a "free lunch". But Spiritual life involves incredible conditions. Think of the conditions that had to be met for your physical birth. If it were left to human beings to handle the affair of their own birth, no one would ever be born at all. Maybe every now and then an arm would be born, or a yelping pile of meat. An entire family might consist of an arm, an apple, and a #2 Mongol pencil!

Examine the lives of those who are generally regarded to have been great Saviors, great Teachers. They really worked on the people who came to them. People like to imagine that Gautama just wanted his disciples to sit quietly every now and then, and read philosophy between their meditations. You should examine what the Buddhist community involved at the beginning. The first category of literature that has come down from the early Buddhist communities consists of lists of detailed conditions (or rules) for how a Buddhist monk or nun should live. Not philosophy, not enlightenment experiences, not all that juicy stuff, but lists of conditions: when you could sit down, when you could go out begging for food, in whose presence you could eat food, what you could eat and when—and on and on.

The Buddhist communities were concerned, above all, to make sure that their members lived straight. The dharma (or the teaching) was for those who had already gotten straight. But, today, people think that it is some special teaching or some form of meditation that is supposed to get them straight. So they try all the meditation techniques one by one—like drugs—without fundamentally changing their condition. Therefore, Spiritual life fails for them.

For Satsang with Me to be lived, real conditions must be established. There must be an entirely new order of life. An entirely new point of view must be lived. Neither the conventional religious and Spiritual point of view nor the ordinary human point of view is sufficient. None of those points of view applies in Satsang with Me. Nevertheless, people want these points of view. Even in My Avataric Divine Company, My devotees continue to defend these points of view. It is ridiculous. Those who approach Me come in pain—but they still wind up defending their self-contracted state, their dis-ease. Such people need to taste the "straightener" again—the ordinary world of suffering and death—until they remember that they are suffering. Appropriate conditions <u>must</u> be established—in your individual life, and in your cooperative life with others of My devotees. An appropriate order of life must be established, in which there is "room" for Absolute Love-Bliss-Happiness.

Absolute Love-Bliss-Happiness is too Happy for people in the usual condition to tolerate! It is really too much. They cannot live with It, they cannot function with It, they cannot accept It. They are always looking for something that is just a little aggravating. A little cramp in the solar plexus—that is what they are living in. But, when the whole body is open and My Divine Spirit-Force is Flowing through it, that Force Churns you, Purifies your life. Then, at last, there is not anything to be un-Happy about, there is not anything to think about. The Flood of My Love-Blissful Spirit-Current Rushes through the body, Dissolves the mind, Overwhelms the life. The Real intelligence of Conscious life begins to intensify and function, in place of egoic ignorance.

That intelligence has no answers. It has no questions. That State without answers and without questions is the True State. When that State is Realized, the truly creative engagement of life begins.

For years, when I would sit down in meditation, My own forms would appear. My mind, My desires, My experience, My suffering, My feelings, My energies—My this and My that.[59] But, at some point, all of it came to an end. There was no "thing" there anymore. None of that distracted or interested Me. "Meditation" was most perfect, continuous.

Then I began to meet those who were the first to become My devotees. And, when I would sit down for meditation, there would be the usual experiential phenomena again—thoughts, feelings, suffering, dis-ease, disharmony, upsets, craziness, pain, energies. But they were not Mine. They were the psycho-physical states of My devotees. Thus, when I would sit down to meditate, I was Doing the meditation of other people, other beings.

When I would feel it all release, their meditation was done. I began to test it, to see if this meditation went on in some (more or less apparent) manner for people who were not physically in the room with Me. And I found that the meditation went on with people I had not even met. People I had seen in dreams and visions would show up.

So the meditation went on. It was the same meditation I had always done. The same problems were involved, and the same experiences—but the content of the meditation was not Mine.

After the Great Event of My Divine Re-Awakening, a Mysterious Process began—in Which the universe itself, the cosmic process, was "Meditated" in Me. Various siddhis (or Yogic powers) became manifested. The movement (or process) of the cosmic domain is a "Meditation", a Purifying Event. Everything is Satsang with Me. There is only Satsang with Me. It is Eternal. After the Great Event of My Divine Re-Awakening, that Eternal Process of "Meditating" the cosmic domain was Alive in Me.

After the period in which such siddhis appeared, My Life became a matter of Revealing the True Nature of Existence as Satsang with Me. But new devotees do not yet fully grasp that life is Satsang with Me. They do not yet experience the Fullness, the fundamental Enjoyment, the living Freedom. Such beginners are not conscious and responsible at every level of existence. Therefore, a kind of ego-seriousness tends to creep in. The dilemma and the search are always tending to reassert themselves in the gathering of My devotees. There is always the temptation to turn Satsang with Me into another form of the search.

In the Ordeal of My "Sadhana Years", I Demonstrated the process of Most Perfectly Transcending all forms of seeking. That process is what must also occur (by Means of My Avataric Divine Spiritual Grace) in the case of My devotees. Satsang with Me is the Graceful Means, and "radical" self-understanding is the Real intelligence, of that process.

My beginning devotees will still tend to indulge their ordinary egoic strategies, to be resistive, to be eccentric, to be self-indulgent, to dramatize the avoidance of relationship. They do not feel they are enacting anything terribly dramatic. Therefore, they readily fall back into their egoic patterning—because they are insensitive to the implications and effects of that patterning, and to what is required in order to counteract the effects of repeated indulgence in that patterning. But I am very much aware of all of that. I am also very much aware that the only means to keep the Way of Adidam from being "revised" into a form of the search is to establish an appropriate hierarchical structure that serves the sadhana of My devotees and extends My Divine Authority throughout the cooperative culture of My devotees.[60]

Therefore, I must require much of My devotees. I require the process of self-understanding to be awakened, lived, and endured in them. I do not merely relieve My devotee's difficulties by some vicarious Yogic process in Myself—however desirable such a process of "magical" relief might seem to be.

Satsang with Me is Real, not imaginary. It is a relationship. It must be consciously lived. It must become a matter of responsibility, such that the dramatization of reluctance, of resistance, of arbitrary craziness, is set aside, undone with Real intelligence. That dramatization cannot be undone merely by My devotee's opposition to it, nor can it be magically relieved by Me. The dramatization must be <u>understood</u>. It must be obviated through self-understanding, awakened in Satsang with Me. Only when the Condition of Satsang with Me, the Condition of relationship to Me, is consciously and continually lived can the process of self-understanding occur—simply, happily. Those who are not prepared to live the Condition of relationship to Me so directly, simply, with real self-responsibility, are those who end up deciding to leave. They become very resistive, then angry—and, finally, they leave.

Such unprepared people forget what Satsang with Me is, and what It has been in their own experience. At times, the True Nature of Satsang with Me becomes clear to them. It becomes intense. It becomes Real. But, then, as soon as their drama of tendencies erupts again (for whatever reasons), the cycle of negativity comes on them again, and they want to freely indulge their negativity. They want to go. They want to play all kinds of games.

They want to be negative. They want to tell you "where it's at". They want to get upset. They want to make their upsets known.

Such people do not want to be responsible for what they are doing. They go ahead and indulge these urges—even though, as My devotees, they have been Addressed by Me again and again (by Means of My Avataric Divine Word) relative to the self-contraction, the activity that is suffering, the avoidance of relationship. Even if you begin to enjoy insight into your egoic strategy, to be able to live beyond your strategy, to live Satsang with Me, the destructive cycles of negativity and separativeness will absolutely tend to recur, again and again. Negative urges will repeatedly come up, again and again—the urge to abandon Satsang with Me, to justify that abandonment, to return to playing your patterned life-dramas.

Therefore, My devotee must always live Satsang with Me—in spite of the tendency for the self-contraction to arise in all levels of the being. My devotee must continue to live and enjoy the Condition of Satsang with Me, even in the midst of feeling the arising tendencies, the negativity, the symptoms—physical, emotional, mental, even circumstantial.

In spite of all that arising of egoic tendencies, My true devotee lives Satsang with Me, enjoys Satsang with Me. Satsang with Me is the only principle that is free of the cycles of egoity. If you live the transformative conditions of Satsang with Me, Its intelligence replaces the unconscious activity of suffering. To live Satsang with Me makes the search and its motivating dilemma obsolete. And the living of Satsang with Me, even under the ordinary conditions of apparent suffering, is sadhana.

There is no Satsang with Me without sadhana. Satsang with Me is not just a pleasant, consoling experience that you have this week, but, if It is not pleasurable next week, then It deserves your contempt. Satsang with Me must be lived consistently over time, under all the conditions that arise. It must become sadhana. It must become your Way of life.

Talking about Satsang with Me can make It appear to be a very complicated process. But I Am here! The relationship between Me and My devotee is a Real Condition. My Avatarically-

Born bodily (human) Divine Form Lives and Demonstrates My Own "Bright" Divine Self-Condition in relationship to each of My devotees. My devotees must live Satsang with Me, rather than merely remembering It. They must listen to Me, moment to moment—such that Truth begins to become Obvious, such that self-understanding comes alive.

Therefore, what is fundamentally important is that the heart-relationship to Me is a Condition you live from day to day, from moment to moment. In that sense, Satsang with Me is not something exclusively meditative, not something merely ritualistic, not something you are merely called to remember or concentrate on. Satsang with Me is something you must live. You may want to just sit there, thinking and picturing—but I am always Calling you to serve Me. Actively responding to that Call is sadhana, is Satsang with Me. All the merely mental things you might want to do to try to keep your relationship to Me in place, to do something about it, to "manufacture" the relationship—all of that is your own insane ritual. But True Spiritual life, Satsang with Me, is much more practical than that, much more direct than that. It must be so. I Am here.

The True ("Natural", or Sahaja) State is entirely without thought. It is Prior to thought. It is Free of thought, even while thinking is occurring. There is no thought when I am speaking. There is no thinking going on apart from the speech. No thinking went into your birth. Likewise, Satsang with Me is truly operative Prior to the mind.

Therefore, to live Satsang with Me is not a merely mental and motivated process. Satsang with Me is more practical than that. Just know that you cannot figure It out. You cannot understand It. You do not understand It. That is the Truth.

Here is Satsang with Me. Simply live It. Be happy to have discovered that you cannot figure It out.

Only when the mind is not satisfied, when the search is not satisfied, does Satsang with Me become possible. Only in that case does sadhana become possible. People come to Me to have the search satisfied. Because I do not satisfy the search, they may get angry or disappointed—and then leave, before the Condition of

Satsang with Me has had time to even begin to Do Its Work. That is why I must continually explain, again and again, why I do not satisfy the search.

What I am saying now in this Talk is simply My attempt to explain why I do not say anything! But, if I literally did not say anything, everyone would leave.

It is very difficult to Teach. In this time and place where sacred culture has generally been lost, it is necessary—for a time—that I speak a great deal.

III.

DEVOTEE: I find my world, my universe, is becoming more and more oppressively one of loneliness.

AVATAR ADI DA SAMRAJ: Get out of it. Come into this one.

DEVOTEE: I find myself doing a considerable amount of suffer-ing—and, at the same time, I am trying to avoid the compulsive activities I engage in the attempt to relieve suffering. I find myself trying to enter into relationship with someone, or trying to find support from someone. I am trying to get something from other people. When I sit in Your physical Company, I sometimes experi-ence a great deal of physical pain. And, most of the time, my attention is all over the place.

AVATAR ADI DA SAMRAJ: You have to rejoin the human race. Stop spending all this time contemplating yourself, sitting alone in your room by yourself. Function with other human beings. Do things. That is all. That is all it will take.

DEVOTEE: My impression is that human beings are not real.

AVATAR ADI DA SAMRAJ: Join up! You are not going to negate <u>My</u> bodily (human) Form.

DEVOTEE: I am caught in the "everything is separate" thing.

AVATAR ADI DA SAMRAJ: I do not care what you are caught in. You are here, in My Company. Your suffering is your own. If you want to play your suffering game, these are the results. Everybody is playing a version of the ego-game—and that is yours. I do not have any sympathy for it. You are activating it. You <u>want</u> to do it. You <u>like</u> it, as a matter of fact. If you wanted to get out of that game, it would be a simple matter of turning the other direction—from separative activity to Satsang with Me.

You must <u>live</u> the conditions of Spiritual life. If you refuse the conditions of Spiritual life and continually wander in your own dilemma, you will not Realize anything. You want to be your own "guru". You want to be already Realized without doing sadhana, without living the conditions of Truth. If you were doing sadhana, you would not have a moment to be occupied with your problems. If you were living the functional conditions of life, you would not have time to dwell on your craziness.

You are not functioning in life. You find every kind of means to live in a universe of your own. But there is no universe of your own. The "uni-" in "universe" means "one". There is the universe. But you are only talking about your own mentality, your own mind-forms. You meditate on that all the time, instead of living the conditions I Give you.

If you live the conditions, there will be a crisis. Forms of apparent suffering will arise. So what? Everyone must pass through that. Nobody patted Me on the head when I went through it.

Nobody put you into your present state—and no one is keeping you in it. It is a present-time activity. It is your own activity. It is not dependent on the past. It is the avoidance of relationship, the self-contraction.

It is time to realize that you are obsessed. I have always known that you are obsessed. That, in itself, never bothered Me. You can begin from there. But you keep discovering it again and again, as if it were always a new realization. And, then, you forget it again. <u>That</u> is the problem. You always forget the very thing of which you are certain. You can only begin the Real Spiritual process in My Avataric Divine Company when you have already discovered the "terrible truth". Then you can live the conditions I require. But your entire being is still devoted to this separativeness, this compulsive self-meditation. And that is suffering.

You must observe that this is so. Live the Condition of Satsang with Me in a very practical manner. Then you will forget your otherwise constant meditation on yourself, and Satsang with Me will become your meditation. Living Satsang with Me, moment to moment, will become the "method" of your ultimate Realization.

Satsang with Me is not something that you can do to yourself. It is a Condition that must be Given to you, Revealed and made available to you by Means of My Avataric Divine Grace. It is a process that becomes awakened in your life spontaneously. You simply must live It in a much more practical manner.

Spend no time whatsoever analyzing yourself. No time. I mean no time! I really mean it. I do not mean just a little time—reading a few books, collecting conceptual insights. I mean spend no time whatsoever analyzing yourself. That is the very activity that you are suffering—that self-meditation. Pull yourself into functional existence. Make everything very practical, very functional. Then you will give room to this Real process. Then you will see that you are always resorting to yourself, always resorting to this separate-self-sense. If you realize that, then it becomes much simpler to resort to Me.

You cannot resort to Me in some sort of mediocre mental fashion, unconscious and believing. You must live Satsang with Me. As a child, you did not "believe in" your mother. You lived with your mother. You lived that condition. You lived all the things that arose in that relationship from day to day. You lived all the things that were demanded.

It is the same with Satsang with Me—or Real religious and Spiritual life, the living relationship to Me—Which also requires the living of the functional conditions of existence that pertain in this universe.

IV.

DEVOTEE: I seem to be having many contrasting experiences lately. Sometimes, I have near-ecstasies of intuitive clarity and feeling-sensitivity, and my body becomes very relaxed. Then, almost in the very next moment, the ordinary impulses and patterns of everyday life seem to become greatly increased, or else I seem to notice them much more concentratedly than before.

What is the significance of this? Is something loosening up in me? Even relationships with other people get very easy and spontaneous. Then, at other times, they get harder than they were before.

AVATAR ADI DA SAMRAJ: There are cycles in conscious awareness. Some of the cycles of experience are very difficult to observe, and people are not typically aware of them. Generally, you are all aware of the seasons. You are commonly aware of the cycles of climate. You are aware of the cycle of night and day. You are at least vaguely aware of the phases of the moon. You are made aware of social cycles—such as elections, holidays, weekends. But there are also cycles in the subtle processes of conscious awareness and in your relationship to life. These subjective patterns may seem random, but everyone is aware of going through "phases"— or alternating periods of "bad days" and "good days".

People know that they do this. They know that they exhibit various characteristic states. But they do not commonly see a pattern to those states. In fact, there is such a pattern. There is a characteristic pattern of conscious experience in each person, as regular as the seasons. It is an individual pattern, like fingerprints.

The Siddhi that Manifests in Satsang with Me tends to intensify these characteristic cycles. One of the first things I began to observe in this process, as I lived in Satsang with Rudi, was how the cycle of My own experience varied between "light" and "heavy"—the "good day / bad day" sort of thing. I did not map it out on a calendar, but I began to become aware that I was moving through patterns of life-consciousness that manifested as "pulses", phases, or cycles—like the heartbeat.

It was not that, under certain external circumstances, I would react with a "bad" mood, and, under other circumstances, with a "good" mood. Rather, a certain underlying heaviness was, at times, characteristic of My state altogether—while, at other times, there was a characteristic lightness, regardless of circumstances. As this process continued to reveal itself, I began to observe that there was a certain regularity to its pattern. And I also began to observe how the pattern was modified by the process of Satsang with the Guru.

At first, I would spend long periods of time in a kind of negative and mediocre condition. I would commonly approach Rudi in such states. Then, occasionally, I would suddenly feel good (or released). In time, I began to discover that these periods of release (or of no-contraction) were becoming a little more frequent, a little more intense, a little more absorbing. The negative pattern, the lower end of this curve, was becoming less intense, more bearable. The crisis periods began to become interesting to Me.

Thus, various changes began to occur in the cycle of conscious awareness, when it was brought into the context of Satsang. In meditation, when I was sitting with Baba Muktananda, the subtle internal processes were intensified. This is the Manifestation of the Shakti that is Activated in Satsang with the Siddha-Guru.

I noticed that when the Force of Satsang was most intense, the highs and lows were most intense. And, as the Force continued to intensify, the alternations of highs and lows became more rapid. What you are describing is just such a development of sensitivity to this cycle of conscious awareness. The pattern is intensified and revealed in Satsang with Me—such that, without apparent cause, experience appears to alternate arbitrarily between different and opposite values (or qualities).

A distinctive mood is experienced when this process of intensified alternation becomes very rapid. It is the Yogic "ananda" (or "bliss"), which arises whenever the alternating cycle of high and low approaches an absolute speed. In the great Saints and Sages, these alternations have become so rapid that the individual is always in a State of Bliss. In one who (by Means of My Avataric

Divine Spiritual Grace) has Realized Most Perfect Divine Enlightenment (and, thus and thereby, most perfect "radical" self-understanding), the speed of this cycle of conscious awareness has become absolute.

Therefore, in the course of the process of Satsang with Me, you will observe the pattern of your existence. The cycles of that pattern are as much a functional manifestation as the cycles of your breathing. The subjective life of the usual individual is not the sort of carefree, aesthetic, spontaneous sublimity that people like to imagine. That subjective life is as patterned, as regulated, and as mechanistic as the objective universe.

There is nothing arbitrary about your experience. It is simply that you have not learned to observe your experience, you have not become sensitive to what is arising. The more sensitive you become, the more you see the patterns, internal and external.

The development of such sensitivity is a good sign. You observe your tendency to identify with the stream of your own conscious awareness, your tendency to believe that you are your own "think"-apparatus. When this sensitivity increases, the subjective pattern is already ceasing to be a compulsive activity. Then the pattern is beginning to show itself to you. It demonstrates itself to be something as functionally objective as a hand. That subjective pattern does not constitute your identity. Rather, it is a process that is arising spontaneously, much the same as your hand. The compulsive tendency to identify with the phasing of conscious awareness begins to ease—just at the moment you seem to suffer it most.

V.

DEVOTEE: Master, the other day I heard You say something that suddenly seemed to take on a lot of meaning for me. It seemed to bring about a revelation. It seemed to be a combination of the Siddhi I feel in Satsang with You and listening to what You were saying.

AVATAR ADI DA SAMRAJ: There are many means generated in My Avataric Divine Company. Whatever events are necessary will occur, and they will all occur appropriately (or lawfully). That is why I do speak at times. There is a function for it—something is served by My speaking. But, most of the time, I do not speak. And, whenever I am silent, Satsang with Me continues wordlessly. I also do other things in relation to My devotees—besides sitting in silence and speaking. My devotees all have different kinds of contact with the Influence and Effects of My Avataric Divine Work—different experiences, different forms of exposure to all My modes of Functioning. Although this complex of My Qualities and Activities may seem to you to be somewhat arbitrary, it is actually an exquisitely intelligent Design. It is not at all arbitrary.

If you truly live Satsang with Me, the events of life cease to be merely arbitrary. Your dreams, for example, are not arbitrary. Your dreams are a very intelligent process. But, if you think about them while you are in the waking state, you cannot make real sense out of them. All experience is of that same nature. It is all the manifestation of an underlying design—a spontaneous, paradoxical process. You were just talking about being brought to "consider" what I said, just as you were drawn to enter into Satsang with Me. Many things combined, in that moment, to produce the "revelation" you describe.

It is said in the *New Testament* that "All things work together for good to them that love God."[61] This bit of biblical wisdom pertains also to the process of Satsang with Me. When Satsang with Me begins as a Real process, you may begin to observe the lawfulness of all experience. Not a breath is spent outside of Satsang with Me, once It begins. And all the possible ranges of events—from the gross, apparently objective world, to your subjective reactions to it (including your thoughts), to everything that happens to you in the waking state, in dreams, in deep sleep—ultimately, everything works to combine with Truth.

Until this begins to become obvious to you, you can either believe it or not. It really has no importance until you begin to observe it yourself. And, in Satsang with Me, people do observe it. There was a time in My Own Life-Play when I began to see there was no difference (or separation) between My subjective (or apparently internal) experience and My objective (or apparently external) experience. There is but <u>one</u> process going on—everywhere, and always.

The world is psycho-physical. The so-called "physical" world is inextricably combined with the psyche. At its depth, the world is essentially of the same nature as the psyche. The entire process is a single event. Everything is functioning together—as a single design, with a single intent. Ultimately, there is not anything that happens to you that does not serve Truth. It is only that when you begin to be consciously aligned to Truth, events themselves take on (more and more) the quality of Truth. You will begin to experience the coincidence (or simultaneity) of "within" and "without". You will begin to observe that Satsang with Me is actually Alive, that It Pervades the universe.

Of course, ordinarily, people are attached to their subjective identity, the force that each individual identifies as "self". And they have all kinds of bad relations with the world. The seeker typically likes the concept (which appears in many of the world's scriptures) that "Truth is <u>within</u> you", "God is <u>within</u> you", "all Power is <u>within</u> you". But this idea just reinforces the tendency of "Narcissus"—this subjective tendency, this constant inward-turning, this self-contraction.

Truth is no more within you than It is within a lampshade. Truth is everywhere—and no "where". It is not especially within you, nor is It especially without.

Truth <u>Is</u>.

VI.

DEVOTEE: Beloved Master, it would seem that, except for the fact of fear, I have everything I could possibly want in life. It appears to me that fear is the underlying quality that is shot through the fabric of my entire life. It is virtually omnipresent, and it is representative to me of all the selfishness, all the self-obsession, all the self-seeking that exists. I make such desperate demands on life. It is a continual, desperate demand. It is as if I am continually dying, moment by moment.

And, when those demands are not met, or if I am afraid that what I already have will be taken away, it is always one form or another of that fear. I am going through a period when all of this has been more active. It seems to me that there is some kind of pernicious bullshit going on, and that I actually want it. I go through all the self-torture games—and, when I come out the other side, I say: "What was that all about?" Then it starts all over again.

AVATAR ADI DA SAMRAJ: This "I" that you have mentioned several times just now is a sort of "post" on which you hang your experiences. Somehow, the "I" seems to be in the center of it all. "Ego" means "I"—the self-reference, the implied independent self, the separate-self concept. That self-reference (or self-image) is what is called "the ego". But "ego" is not truly an entity or a concept. Rather, "ego" is an <u>activity</u>. It is the activity of the avoidance of relationship.

Just as the separate "I", the self-concept, the self-image, is an expression of the self-contracting activity that is the ego, fear is also the ego. Fear is the very mood, the very essence, of the ego. It is said in the Upanishads: "It is from an other that fear arises."[62] As soon as there is an other, as soon as this separative act has taken place (in any sense whatsoever), from that instant there is fear. Then life <u>is</u> fear. Conscious awareness <u>is</u> fear.

It is not that <u>you</u> are afraid. Fear is your necessary attribute, your very "body". Fear <u>is</u> the ego. As long as you persist in your present ego-bound condition and drama, fear will continually be the mood that you discover. Whenever you fail to be distracted, you will fall into this chronic state, this sense of your separate self, which is fear.

When there is the activity of separation, there can only be fear. You have interrupted the Current of Energy, you have separated yourself from Existence Itself, from the Real Process of the Living Divine Heart. You have contracted within the Boundless Field of Conscious Light. You have made it impossible for the Energy of

Existence to flow freely—because you are actively presuming a split between the ego (or the process of self-contraction) and everything from which the ego differentiates itself.

Therefore, everything outside this apparently separate "self" becomes threatening, frightening, "other". And, when you are afraid, you are simply meditating on your separated existence. If you intentionally try to get rid of fear, it is impossible to do so—because the "you" that is trying to get rid of the fear is that fear. Therefore, the search to become free of fear is futile.

At some point, you fall into your chronic state—this fear, this avoidance of relationship. And, when this occurs under the conditions of Satsang with Me, self-understanding awakens. Self-understanding is the obviation of "ego", of the separate-self-sense—which is fear. Only "radical" self-understanding—in Satsang with Me—is without fear. Only one who turns to Me and understands is truly fearless. Only one who turns to Me and understands is egoless. Only such a one can live Prior to fear.

Until then, you are dramatizing the "shape" of the separate self, you are living it—and, so, you are suffering that condition. You must become sensitive. You must become fundamentally aware of the conditions that you bring about in your own life, through this root-activity that is the ego. Only when you become aware that your life is failing can you begin to truly observe the activity that is the ego.

Therefore, there must—necessarily—be a crisis. Spiritual life must involve this falling into your own chronic state, and comprehending it at the root. The Siddhi of Satsang with Me makes this passage possible. If you simply fell into your fear, without the resort of Satsang with Me, you would go mad.

The random tastes of fear are what constantly disturb any life-form. But Satsang with Me is the Condition of Truth. The Condition of Satsang with Me is already free of self-contraction, free of the separate-self-sense, free of fear.

The non-dual Hindu traditions (such as Advaita Vedanta) aspire to "Turiya", the "Fourth State"—Beyond waking, dreaming, and deep sleep, and (therefore) beyond fear—wherein practitioners may feel Fullness, Ease, and Enjoyment, and all of the Spiritual events that are spontaneously generated in the Company of the Siddha-Guru. My true devotees, who truly live Satsang with Me, need not aspire to anything—because they <u>already</u> live the Condition that is without fear, without separated self, without the function of ego (or the chronic avoidance of relationship). Therefore, they Enjoy the unreasonable Happiness, the Love-Bliss-Fullness, that is the "mood" of Truth.

But those who do not resort to Satsang with Me, who only resort continually to the state they suffer (apart from Satsang with Me), find their fear only intensified in My Company. They find that "ego" is intensified, that the dilemma, the problems, and the search are intensified, that their egoic ignorance is intensified, and that it all becomes frightening and unbearable. That is why some people leave the gathering of My devotees, without any apparent reason. Nothing has "happened" to them. Nothing has really occurred, except the process of Satsang Itself. That process is (itself) what disturbs those who angrily renounce My Company and My Teaching.

Those who have not suffered their own egoic condition enough, who have not seen its perfect failure, should not approach Me. I Am a Fire! I am not here to talk "philosophy". There is a Living Force Enacted in My Avataric Divine Company. It is the Living Force of the Divine Conscious Light Itself. That is What Satsang with Me is all about. And those who arbitrarily "pile on", not mindful of the conditions, wind up aggressively separating themselves, with all kinds of justifications and self-righteousness. The Siddhi of Satsang with Me simply acts to intensify their separativeness.

If you have really seen the failure of your search, if you can spontaneously resort to the Condition of Satsang with Me, then you experience an unreasonable Happiness. Thus, Satsang with Me becomes the Condition in Which self-contraction, fear, ego—all of the elements of suffering and dilemma—are dissolved in a spontaneous, natural, appropriate process.

As My devotee, you will certainly also suffer the intensity of the process of ego-dissolution, including periods of apparent crisis—but that process will always be somehow bearable, always intelligent with Truth, always something for which you have the capability. That is why many who have found a Guru have said that, at some point, they gave up all interest in seeking salvation. They were no longer involved in strategically striving for liberation, heaven, and healing. They were no longer even moved to engage any special disciplines in order to undergo the classic round of Spiritual experiences. They lost their interest in all of that. They became unreasonably Happy only, and they forgot to seek beyond the Guru's Feet.

People can indulge any kind of illusion in relation to a symbolic image, a "God" they merely believe in. People are very willing to do anything they like, and then forgive themselves with the same liberal attitude. They want "God" (or "Truth") to stay in "Its" own Place. But I Am a Reality That Confronts you in life. I Establish conditions in the world. I remain continuously Connected to My devotee and to the process that My devotee is going through.

I Am the Avataric Divine Incarnation of Real God, the True Divine Guru. And I Create every kind of ordinary and extraordinary means to always re-establish the connection with My devotees—now, and forever hereafter.

Real religious and Spiritual life involves the Great Condition being Given to you, and many counter-egoic conditions being required of you. Neither that Great Condition nor those counter-egoic conditions are anything that you (on your own) particularly want to assume. People are capable of believing all kinds of things on their own, and of arbitrarily generating what they <u>think</u> is sadhana. But all of that is just another expression of their usual state. None of it does anything, fundamentally, to their ego-bound condition.

The matter of Truth is entirely academic until Truth Communicates Itself to you, until the Truth takes you over, until Truth Does the sadhana and Generates the conditions for your transformation. Thus, Truth must find some means to Communicate Itself as a Function in specific relationship to you. Therefore, the humanly-born Guru is the appropriate Means—and that is why the humanly-born Guru exists, that is why I have Come.

VII.

DEVOTEE: Master, why and how did we fall into this miserable condition?

AVATAR ADI DA SAMRAJ: People like to fabricate mythologies. You would like to hear some sort of "creation" myth about this suffering, or some sort of philosophy that explains why it came about. When something is "explained", when its "name" is known, then you feel free to forget it or exploit it.

But your suffering condition did not "come about". It is presently happening. It is not a matter of something that happened in the past. There is not anything hidden in time or space that is making the affair of suffering occur. It is not happening as a result of anything. Rather, it is a spontaneous, present-time activity, for which you are entirely responsible. So, truly, it does not make any sense to try to describe some means or other by which it might have come about.

I have said, however, that there is a sense in which the specific activity that is your suffering—the self-contraction—is a reaction to life, to conditionally manifested existence. "For every action, there is an equal and opposite reaction." The entire "happening" of the conditionally manifested cosmos arises as a spontaneous event, a single event. The universe is the original action. But, for every action, there is (necessarily) an equal and opposite reaction. Thus, the self-contraction is, in a sense, the reaction to conditionally manifested life altogether.

A baby is not born with a concrete sense of a separate life in the world. A baby is not even able to differentiate its body from the other movements around it. Everything is all one massive sensation. A baby does not differentiate. A baby does not, for all practical purposes, differentiate itself as an entity from any other individual, or even from the world itself. Only when the baby learns to <u>react</u> to life does it begin to form an <u>identity</u> that functions in life. And, if the baby has no capability to react, it will have no capability for individuated life.

382

A human organism that has no capability to react is catatonic—a "vegetable", or else dead. A catatonic has many of the apparent attributes that are ascribed to the Realized individual. The catatonic seems to be selfless, seems to be fearless. But the catatonic is obviously not "alive"—not conscious, functioning, and sane. Therefore, simply to go about trying to discover how not to react is obviously not the "cure". Merely to try to not react to your conditionally manifested existence in this moment is not the Way of Truth.

Yet people have elaborated vast traditional methods of so-called "realization" that are (fundamentally) only attempts to not react. People try to de-condition themselves, to become detached, to become self-less. But the Truth is not a matter of strategically suppressing any form of action, even if that action is the reaction to something else.

Truth is in the spontaneous process of observing, understanding, and transcending every activity—in the midst of that very activity. Therefore, My devotee who turns to Me and understands is not in a catatonic state. "Radical" self-understanding, in the context of Satsang with Me, is not (itself) characterized by any conditional Yogic state. "Radical" self-understanding, in the context of Satsang with Me, is not (itself) an "other" state. The state of My devotee who turns to Me and understands may appear to be extraordinary from the point of view of the usual person. But, actually, My true devotee is entirely ordinary, fully participatory in the conditionally manifested realm. While living in this ordinary manner, My true devotee (most ultimately—by Means of My Avataric Divine Spiritual Grace) Realizes the Perfect Condition That Is Real God, or Truth, or Reality Itself.

Therefore, the life of one who turns to Me and understands is a paradox. But the seeker is not paradoxical, and the attainments of the seeker are not paradoxical. The seeker and the seeker's attainments are always dimensionless, always wound down to a point. The seeker is always turned to specific goals, specific states. They may be complex and incomprehensible, but they are always as specific and mind-based as a bowling trophy.

Truth Itself is not identical to any particular state or experience. Nor is Truth Itself identical to the avoidance of any particular state or experience—neither to the dissociation (or willful separation) from any particular state or experience, nor to the suppression of any particular state or experience. Truth is not even identical to the suppression of thought. In My Divinely Enlightened devotee, everything continues to arise—but, coincident with everything arising, there is Most Perfect Realization of Reality Itself. My Divinely Enlightened devotee Realizes Reality Itself perpetually, spontaneously, and under all conditions.

My Divinely Enlightened devotee Realizes Reality Itself in the most profoundly "radical" (or "gone-to-the-root") sense, without enacting any separation whatsoever. My Divinely Enlightened devotee requires no special condition to support the Most Perfect Realization of Reality Itself. The Most Perfect Realization of My Divinely Enlightened devotee is not something that is the case only when that one is in certain meditative moods, only when that one is quiet, only when that one is engaging certain Spiritual functions, only when that one is talking about certain Spiritual things. The Most Perfect Realization of My Divinely Enlightened devotee, enacted as most perfect devotion to Me, is Limitless, Spontaneous, Absolute, Continuous, Permanent.

Therefore, True religious and Spiritual life, as it is lived in My Avataric Divine Company, is a span of Conscious adventure—generated in the devotional (and, in due course, Spiritual) relationship to Me As the Divine Avatar, the Divine Siddha-Guru, and summed up in the Most Perfect Enjoyment (or Realization) of Which I Am the Evidence, the Demonstration, and the Very Form.

AVATAR ADI DA SAMRAJ
Clear Lake, 2001

12.

No "One" Survives Beyond
That Moment

I.

DEVOTEE: Beloved Heart-Master, are we evolving?

AVATAR ADI DA SAMRAJ: What do you think?

DEVOTEE: I think we are evolving toward the astral.

AVATAR ADI DA SAMRAJ: What is so good about "astral"?

DEVOTEE: Well, nothing. But, as far as evolution goes, there is a constant change. Is it constant change? Where are we going? What is it doing for us? What is it?

AVATAR ADI DA SAMRAJ: Is it?

DEVOTEE: Well, it seems to be, but I am in a dilemma. Is evolution part of the dilemma?

AVATAR ADI DA SAMRAJ: There is this dilemma.

DEVOTEE: There is dilemma. Yes. Then it is part of the dilemma.

AVATAR ADI DA SAMRAJ: What is the question?

DEVOTEE: Now I am really confused.

AVATAR ADI DA SAMRAJ: In this concern for "evolution", are you really talking about something?

DEVOTEE: I do not really understand what evolution is, or even if there is evolution.

AVATAR ADI DA SAMRAJ: <u>That</u> is true.

DEVOTEE: That there is no evolution?

AVATAR ADI DA SAMRAJ: That you do not know.

DEVOTEE: Yes.

AVATAR ADI DA SAMRAJ: What you know is this dilemma, this confusion, this ignorance about your own propositions. That is the truth of it. That is your experience. "Evolution" does not really exist as your experience. You are not certain of it—of its existence, of its quality, of its nature, of its direction, of its relationship to you. You know nothing whatsoever about it. Why are you bringing it up?

The truth is that you are confused. There is this dilemma. There is suffering. Questions about evolution are completely beside the point. Such questions, for the time being, are nothing but a means of drawing attention away from your actual state, of temporarily distracting yourself from that confusion.

You could take the abstract category of "evolution" and talk about it from many different points of view. You could generate all kinds of mind-forms relative to "evolution". But, after you have said it all, no real experience will have been added, and you will remain in the same state as when you first asked the question.

Therefore, your question about evolution is not your real question. Your real question is your own actual state. That is the question you are truly asking, the question you are always asking. You present your very life to the world in the form of a question.

You <u>are</u> this real question. But you conceal the question from your ordinary conscious awareness. Therefore, the question exists only as your chronic <u>state</u>—your suffering, your search, your dilemma.

Ordinarily, you do not verbally ask your real question. You only live it and enact it—as seeking, suffering, and death. Sadhana is the means whereby human beings become <u>conscious</u> of their real question.

Just so, the "answer", so called, to your real question has nothing whatsoever to do with evolution, or any other arbitrary topic the mind can select for discussion. The true answer is not in the form of a verbal response to an abstract question. The true answer must be a "radical" (or "gone-to-the-root") transformation of your state. That root-transformation is the true answer to your question. And, if this state that you are always in—this confusion, this dilemma—is utterly overcome, then the nature of life and world becomes obvious. My Answer to My devotee comes in the context of the discipline of real conditions, demands for functional action—the sadhana which is always generated in My Avataric Divine Company.

There is absolutely no point whatsoever in talking about evolution. Your concern over evolution is an arbitrary distraction you have selected from the pattern of your own tendencies. You have chosen this particular concern from among the general confusion of your ordinary state—whereas it is your confusion itself that should be your genuine concern. All your questions are forms of this dilemma, this state of confusion. Every question is in the form of a dilemma, and every verbal or mental dilemma is an expression of the underlying state that shapes every moment of the usual life.

The arbitrary formulation of "questions", of artifices to occupy the mind, is a means of distracting yourself from your own state of dilemma. To do so is a form of self-indulgence. To answer such questions (in and of themselves) is only to serve bewilderment, unconsciousness, fear, ignorance, and all the qualities of seeking and suffering.

You are bewildered and confused by the total complex of your tendencies—and now you want to talk about evolution. What has that got to do with anything? Your own suffering is presently manifesting itself. Understanding and transcending that suffering—and, thereby allowing the process of true "ego-death"—is the matter of importance.

DEVOTEE: The suffering just goes on and on and on. It never seems to stop.

AVATAR ADI DA SAMRAJ: Death. That is what you want to get away from. You want to "evolve" into the astral world in order to escape natural death—and to escape the necessary ultimate "death" of the ego, the "death" of the chronic activity of separation and separativeness. There is no elimination of death, no ultimately successful avoidance of death. You are trying to prevent your own ego-death—this very and ultimate crisis—by occupying yourself with abstract questions.

DEVOTEE: But that is the only answer—ego-death. Why do we keep fighting and fighting?

AVATAR ADI DA SAMRAJ: Keep fighting what?

DEVOTEE: This thing. We know we are fighting it—and, yet, we cannot seem to avoid it. Why are we avoiding it? How do we get out of this?

AVATAR ADI DA SAMRAJ: The desire to "get out of this" is another form of the same avoidance. A real transformation—in the form of the conflict, the crisis, you are now experiencing—has already begun in you. That conflict, that crisis, has become intensified. You are beginning to find your real question. It is your own death. That is the significant event. There is no distraction from it. There is no consolation for it. It is an undeniable reality.

   Evolution makes no difference. Migration to the astral planes makes no difference. None of that changes your chronic state. The crisis would still be necessary, no matter where in all the worlds you happened to appear. This crisis is the necessary event of all life. Going to the astral planes does not change that necessity. "Radical" self-understanding is still required.

The question about evolution represents a form of concern, a search. That is what is communicated to Me by your question. Your question has no real content other than your seeking. It is only because this crisis is occurring that you have the least interest in evolution. If you are dying, there is no evolution. In that case, what do you care whether the billions that remain behind you are transformed into ducks or luminous red astral bodies? Your death is the only remaining content of your life. From the point of view of your experience, there is no evolution. There is only sudden death. But ego-death is the Real process. The death of the ego is the very crisis in consciousness that serves both Truth and life.

When you awaken from a dream, you are not thereafter concerned for the destiny of those who appeared along with you in the dream. There is no such destiny. There is no one left behind. All that appears in the great cosmic process is a spontaneous display, like the conditions that appear in dreams. All of that goes on in any case.

Now, however, you are beginning to see the more fundamental condition underlying your adventure of distraction in the cosmic event. In the past, you did not see it, or know it for what it was. To the degree you felt it at all, it was an undefined sensation, a discomfort, a sort of formless craziness, a wildness. But now you are beginning to know what it really is. Now you are beginning to know it as your chronic state. You will come to observe and understand it as your own activity. You are beginning to be aware of it more or less continually. That continuous awareness is essential to the self-purifying sadhana of Real religious and Spiritual life.

DEVOTEE: Even a Realized being must follow certain patterns and rules. Otherwise, the chakras will not open. There are laws which cannot be disregarded. So there is, in fact, a pattern, isn't there?

AVATAR ADI DA SAMRAJ: A pattern of what?

DEVOTEE: A pattern by which the universe is ordered. Even

someone who has Realized the Heart must go by certain signs along the way. It is different for each person, but still there are rules.

AVATAR ADI DA SAMRAJ: If it is different in each case, what is the common pattern?

DEVOTEE: There is no pattern that fits everyone, but still there are patterns existing.

AVATAR ADI DA SAMRAJ: Of course, there are apparent patterns in life. But the True Divine Heart is not somewhere else. The True Divine Heart is not a point separate from every other point. The True Divine Heart is not to be found by going in a certain direction. The True Divine Heart is not the end of any particular road. The True Divine Heart is not the goal.

If you are speaking of the causal center, the heart-center on the right side of the chest, it is (indeed) a point, a place, a psycho-physical sensation. But "the Heart" is another term for the One Unqualified Reality.

DEVOTEE: That becomes true once someone Realizes the Heart. But, between the time the person is only approaching the Heart and the time that one actually Realizes the Heart, there are still patterns.

AVATAR ADI DA SAMRAJ: They are your own patterns. They are your apparent condition. They are the ego-patterning that give rise to dilemma and seeking. When My devotee lives in perfect Satsang with Me, I Establish a living relationship with the individual, and then it no longer makes any difference to My devotee what his or her apparent patterns are. From that moment, the patterns are merely observed. A unique Condition is lived—and, because My devotee constantly turns to Me, these patterns become obsolete. They fall away, until only the True Divine Heart Stands Out.

From the point of view of My true devotee, there is no significance to the patterns. There is no significance. "Significance" is your dilemma. It is the pattern of your own mind-forms—always based on limited point of view. That limited point of view is the only thing that obstructs Most Perfect Realization of Consciousness Itself. Consciousness Itself is neither external nor internal. All that arises is only a modification of Consciousness Itself, Which Is the Divine Self-Condition and Source-Condition of all-and-All.

When (by Means of My Avataric Divine Spiritual Grace) this is most perfectly understood, the True Divine Heart is Most Perfectly Realized. From the "Point of View" of the True Divine Heart, there is no subject, no object, no inside, no outside, no physical universe, no astral world. All such phenomena are simply apparent modifications of the Divine Heart Itself.

Until you truly enter into Satsang with Me, you are very much concerned about your remedial path, about the pattern of your own growth and experience, your own transformation, your own liberation. But, when you enter into the Condition of Satsang with Me, your concerns, your path, your patterns become obsolete. All of that is simply not supported. You simply live the Condition of Satsang with Me and the conditions of relationship generated in My Avataric Divine Company, and the patterns subside. They become obsolete, without function.

Therefore, concern for those patterns is more evidence of the search, of the fundamental dilemma. All developments within the cosmic domain are limited to the cosmic domain. No such development implies or leads to Reality Itself. All such developments lead to limits within the cosmic domain itself—to more states, more change, more phenomena. In and of itself, no such development obviates the dilemma that is the result of self-contraction. There is no action that leads to My "Bright" Divine Self-Domain. Truth requires the observation, understanding, and transcending of motivation and action.

You are always already "There". <u>This</u> Is <u>It</u>. There is no dilemma. There is only One Reality, presently. It is not somewhere else. It is not hidden within you, nor behind the world. It is only Obvious.

Satsang with Me is the <u>Condition</u> of Reality, consciously lived. It is lived to you, within you, as you. It is that Real Condition lived as life, as a pressure upon My devotee. I Live the Real Condition to My devotee, such that It begins to become Obvious and Intelligent in My devotee. The Real Nature of the arising event, the apparent condition, becomes clear.

When you are My devotee, it becomes obvious to you that your dilemma is your own activity. You see that, in fact, there is no dilemma. There is nothing about your present-time experience that is not Truth.

Satsang with Me is the Real Condition. It is the Condition of Truth Itself. It is the Condition of heart-relationship to Me. When you enter into It consciously, with any degree of clarity, you have begun to live under the conditions of Truth Itself. And that is the entire process. That is Real religious life, Real Spiritual life—Real life altogether. Everything else is an extension (or another reflection) of your search, your dilemma, your dis-ease. When this Real Condition is truly lived, whatever arises tends to be consumed.

II.

DEVOTEE: Master, is it possible to remain in the Condition of Satsang with You by exercising the will?

AVATAR ADI DA SAMRAJ: Apparently not. You can maintain yourself responsibly as My devotee, and fulfill the specific conditions I Require, but to consciously live the Condition of relationship to Me depends on My Avataric Divine Grace.

Everyone constantly tends to live as if separate. Even when you begin to sense My Unique Blessing-Presence, Which is the Transmitted Power of the True Divine Heart, you resist and defend yourself and hide your dis-ability, discomfort, dilemma. You approach Me with argumentation, self-defense, the endless formulations of your own mind, and with suggestions that maybe "It's all right anyway." You continue to play your game, presuming that I am a captured audience for your act.

When you enter into Satsang with Me, you no longer have the separate-self-sense as your primary instrument. The activity that is the ego has become obsolete. It may continue to arise and obsess you, but Satsang with Me has become your Condition. The Process of the True Divine Heart Performs your sadhana and Holds On to you. My Divine Grace Manifests within the life-drama of My devotee. My Divine Grace makes it possible for you to maintain your sadhana, the living practice of your connection to Me—until you become responsible enough to assume the devotional relationship to Me Spiritually, as your responsibility, as your Real Condition. Then you are given responsibilities that will test, prove, and awaken in you all the qualities of My true devotee.

DEVOTEE: What are the responsibilities of someone who is seriously doing sadhana? For years, I have fluctuated between everything from total self-indulgence to forty-day fasts—and I still find myself unable to eat moderately. I do not think that this is a responsible way to live. And, yet, it is inappropriate to be always compulsively "responsible". If I do not eat properly, I become less conscious, I sleep more, and I get light-headed.

AVATAR ADI DA SAMRAJ: The point of view that you are expressing is the point of view of dilemma, of suffering—which has nothing to do with Truth. Right alignment to Truth Itself is what people are constantly (though largely unconsciously) trying to destroy, by all kinds of means. Excessive fasting, excessive eating, self-indulgence of all kinds, deprivation of all kinds, turning inward, turning outward, ascetic practices, "ordinary" practices— all of these are only strategic attempts to overcome the fundamental sense of dilemma and suffering. None of that has anything to do with Illumination (or Truth). All of that is suffering.

The real question is not how to become responsible. The real question is the state you are in. And the real answer is not in the form of a verbal response to verbally expressed dilemmas, or even apparently actual life-dilemmas. The real answer is the transcending of your self-contracted state.

You will continue to seek (by all possible means) to be free of the dilemma as you perceive it, until the forms of your seeking— all of which are reactions to the root-condition (or dilemma) that is your suffering—cease to occupy you. When you come to the point where the force of your life is no longer fully captured by your search, when you know that your search is failing, that your search does not produce salvation, when you fall from ordinary fascination into a crisis, a form of despair, of doubt—then, at that point, you have become deeply available for Satsang with Me, for the heart-relationship to Me which <u>is</u> True religious and Spiritual life.

Satsang with Me is the answer. Satsang with Me is the process and Condition wherein the dilemma is undone. No spoken or written word, but (rather) the very relationship to Me, the Living True Divine Heart, is the Real answer. The answer is not in the form of an ego-serving method, a strategic technique, or a conceptual system that addresses your particular notions of human existence. The answer is the Self-Evident Manifestation of Truth, and that answer undermines that very structure in your conscious awareness that supports your entire search.

This becomes a Real possibility only when you have begun to suffer from your search, when you have begun to sense its failure, when you are no longer totally occupied by it. Then you become available to Satsang with Me. And Satsang with Me is non-support of your dilemma, non-support of your search.

In Satsang with Me, all your techniques fall away, all fascination with your search subsides, all your remedial methods become ridiculous. Your entire life ceases to obsess you. Your egoic need for "liberation" no longer interests you. Your life becomes the progressive Realization of Truth, the Enjoyment of My Avataric Divine Company, until the form of self-contracted awareness in which you ordinarily rest is utterly dissolved. In Satsang with Me, an entirely new and living form of intelligence replaces your ordinary strategic mentality.

Some individuals become involved in an incredible adventure of remedial Spiritual techniques. They apply themselves to techniques of living, techniques of subjective and psychological states, seeker's meditation, seeker's diet, and all the rest. Such individuals come to Me imbued with the moods of conventional Spirituality and philosophy. Others are more ordinary, coming to Me after a life—equally traditional—of self-indulgence.

Everyone comes to Satsang with Me in the midst of an egoic adventure of some kind. All come with the same fundamental dilemma—but each one communicates it through particular artifices, through a unique adventure. In essence, all adventures are a description of the same state: the self-contraction, the fundamental dis-ease, the avoidance of relationship. That is everyone's condition.

From the point of view of the real question—the actual dilemma—the most auspicious thing that can possibly happen is to enter into Satsang with Me. True religious and Spiritual life is not a strategic (or ego-based and ego-bound) technique, method, remedy, or path. True religious and Spiritual life is the Real relationship to the Adept Spiritual Master. It has always been so. Therefore—rightly, and most fundamentally—nothing is offered in My Avataric Divine Company apart from the devotional (and, in due course, Spiritual) relationship to Me, the True Divine Guru.

Relationship itself is the principle and condition of life. Therefore, rightly, the heart-relationship to Me is the single and great Principle of sadhana in My Avataric Divine Company, the single and great Medium of Truth, the one "Method" of Realization. Truly, the heart-relationship to Me is the Condition and the Medium through Which all the necessary and appropriate developments occur in My devotee's progressive practice of the Way of Adidam. And those developments occur spontaneously, by Means of My Avataric Divine Grace.

In Satsang with Me, My devotee has become available to Truth Itself, Reality Itself—such that Truth Itself, Reality Itself, has become the Divinely Effective Means for My devotee's Illumination. Up to that point, the individual has been too much focused in egoic preoccupations to be Illumined. First, My devotee must fall from search and fascination, into the crisis of his or her ordinary state.

It is very difficult for human beings to achieve ordinariness. In order to be able to live in Satsang with Me, however, My devotee must become capable of being ordinary. Human beings are extremely inventive—eminently capable of the extraordinary, the adventure, the search. But the ordinary is extremely difficult, because of the principle of seeking on which human beings base their lives.

When you truly enter into Satsang with Me, when It becomes your real circumstance of life, then you suddenly become capable of ordinariness, of simplicity. Ordinariness simply becomes appropriate. It is not in the least connected with anything compulsive, anything like the discipline a seeker might embrace.

As My devotee, your functional simplicity is obvious and natural, because action has been released from its connection with the search for Truth, the search for Liberation. Any ego-bound effort that is touted as a means to Truth belongs to the adventure of seeking and its dilemma. All such ego-efforts are part of the adventure of extra-ordinariness. Only Truth Itself, Satsang Itself, Free of seeking, is the Means whereby Truth is Realized.

When you are released from the pursuit of Truth, you simply live It. When you live Satsang with Me as the Condition of life, Communion with Truth replaces the search for Truth. All your ordinary functions become truly ordinary when you are released from the search to Realize Truth. Therefore, in Satsang with Me, your life becomes ordinary, functional.

There is no reason why diet, for example, should be manipulated as if it were, in and of itself, a means to Realize Truth. Nor should diet be considered an obstruction to Truth. In and of itself, the ingestion of food has nothing whatsoever to do with Truth. Neither food-indulgence nor food-righteousness is the Way of Truth.

DEVOTEE: What seems to matter is whether I am willing to put my attention on the Truth. If, for example, I am overeating, I will not be in a condition to put my attention on Truth.

AVATAR ADI DA SAMRAJ: You cannot "put your attention on" Truth in any case. Truth is not an "object". Truth only appears to be an object from the point of view of the same search that alternately motivates you to indulge yourself and to restrain your self-indulgent tendencies. Truth cannot be concentrated upon even by a mind that is clear and free. Truth cannot be "noticed". It is not an object. It does not appear within your view. Truth is the Context within which you and all your points of view are appearing.

DEVOTEE: Instead of "putting attention on Truth", would it be correct to say "to experience more consciously"?

AVATAR ADI DA SAMRAJ: Experiencing has nothing to do with Truth. Truth cannot be experienced, nor is Truth an experience. Neither is Truth experience itself.

All these expressions you have used have the same form. As far as Truth goes, there is nothing to be said. There is no verbal communication that is the exact equivalent of Truth Itself. All of the descriptions you might give of the unique form of your adventure have the same form, the same structure. Indeed, your questions are a strategy whereby you <u>prevent</u> the Realization of Truth. Your concerns are a means to <u>avoid</u> self-understanding.

Truth always appears to the seeker as a kind of <u>alternative</u>. But Truth is not an alternative. Truth is the Very Consciousness, the Very Nature, the Very Condition of all-and-All. Truth cannot be concentrated upon. Truth is not an object. Truth is not something you can become interested in. Truth is not something you can be distracted from. Your interests, your distractions, your noticings, your experiencings—<u>all</u> are expressions (or modifications) of Reality Itself. But you are not living them as such. Therefore, you are constantly obsessed with alternatives, with particular distractions, noticings, and experiencings. Alternatives are all that you have.

When you no longer have any alternatives, when the search has died, then Truth becomes your Real possibility. But Truth is not an alternative. It is not in the form of a specific answer to a specific question. It is not something perceived. It is not something that serves you, as the (actively presumed) limited and separate subject. It is not something that Liberates you, as an apparently separate person. It has nothing to do with you, as a presumed separate "one". It <u>cannot</u> be Realized by you as a presumed separate "one". Truth is Known only in the Realization of Non-separateness, in Most Perfect Self-Identification with Truth Itself.

There is no conditional state equivalent to Truth. Every conditional state is a limitation. In the descriptions associated with the traditional religious and Spiritual paths, there are conditional experiences and conditional states that are (erroneously) identified with Truth Itself (or Reality Itself). Some traditions say that Truth is equal to (or necessarily coincident with) a vision of Krishna. For others, Truth must be samadhi in the form of an ascended Yogic trance—either with associated visionary phenomena or (otherwise) without the least trace of form (whether objective or subjective). Still others equate Truth with a concentrated return of the natural life-energy to the sahasrar, a vision of Light, or some other esoteric (but, nonetheless, conditional) signal of the Divine.

But all of these are forms of experience, of conditionality. They may be sublime, but they appear only as alternatives to other, more "ordinary" experiences. No experience, in and of itself, is Truth. And no experience, in and of itself, is the sign of Truth, the "symptom" (or the necessary accompaniment) of Truth.

Truth Is That Which Stands Out As Reality when there is "radical" understanding of the entire process of experience, when there is the absolute vanishing of identification with alternatives (or the entire self-contracted scheme of seeking). Therefore, Truth involves the "radical" understanding even of that which is extraordinary. Until such understanding is the case, all events in life—whether ordinary or extraordinary—are merely the objects of egoic fascination.

It is the memory of experiences—the persistent bondage to your own patterns that result from experience—that generates the goals of seeking. Experiential impressions (in the form of tendencies) continue to fascinate people and reinforce their obsession with the notion that life is made of alternatives, such that the usual individual is doing nothing but continually playing this drama of alternatives. One day, a person is going toward the "experience" of Truth—another day, toward experience itself (usually of a very "human" variety). One day, a person is pursuing samadhi—the next day, the very same person is a devotee of sexual fascination. But it is always the same egoic adventure.

What appeared (in the past) to be the great moments of your life did not become wisdom. All you are left with are the modifications that reflect those moments. Truth does not appear in the form of a drama of experiences and alternatives. Truth can only appear when that entire array of experiences and alternatives—the entire adventure, the entire force of ordinary and extraordinary experience, the entire drama of seeking—begins to wind down, when it ceases to occupy you mightily, and you are stuck with your actual condition, your suffering.

The Real Spiritual process in My Avataric Divine Company takes place only when there is this crisis in consciousness. It does not take place in the context of your adventure of seeking. The Real Spiritual process in My Avataric Divine Company takes place only when you understand and transcend the root-activity of self-contraction that motivates your entire adventure. Such "radical" self-understanding becomes possible for you only in Satsang with Me, when you truly heart-recognize Me and heart-respond to Me—and only when the force of your ordinary and extraordinary adventure has begun to die.

DEVOTEE: I feel a hesitancy to give up that aspect of the search.

AVATAR ADI DA SAMRAJ: Good, very good. That is it exactly. Two types of people come to Me. Those who have died to their search, and those who still have a couple of games left to play. Relative to those who still have the search in mind, there is no condemnation—no praise, no blame. That is the reality of their condition. The search is still their occupation. They have not come for <u>Truth</u>. The Truth has nothing whatsoever to do with them. The search, the adventure among alternatives, is what possesses them. The search is what possesses all human beings, until it begins to die. Then the Truth becomes possible.

When you no longer have genuine alternatives, when you no longer have the option of your own preferences, when you no longer have the capability to persist, to survive, in the form of your search, then Satsang with Me becomes something more than academic. Until that time, all human beings are talking about the same thing: their adventure! That is what they are talking about. They are not the least concerned for the Truth. It has not entered into the picture yet. It is only an amusement, an alternative notion entertained in the midst of ordinary and extraordinary suffering. They are still occupied. Fine. That is why Real religious and Spiritual life becomes a possibility only when the alternatives themselves no longer constitute a real option.

DEVOTEE: How do I bring myself to the point of not wanting?

AVATAR ADI DA SAMRAJ: Wanting and not wanting are both forms of the same activity. It is all the same occupation, preoccupation, distraction, fascination—moment to moment.

DEVOTEE: How do I get over that?

AVATAR ADI DA SAMRAJ: The desire to get over it is simply more of the adventure. It is the adventure of getting over it. It is all the same. The fact of the matter is that you are self-contracted—and all your actions, your desires, and even your questions are only descriptions of that state of self-contraction. The Truth is of another variety. But this lesson about your present and usual state can be useful. It is the first lesson of Wisdom.

If life begins only to hurt, if all the alternatives fall into you, if they cease to be a real option, if you find yourself continually stuck in the crisis in consciousness (the root-form of suffering, on the basis of which your search springs into action)—when that becomes the nature of your daily life, then Truth becomes attractive to you. Then Satsang with Me, Real life, becomes a living possibility. It will be your obvious need when you have no options.

DEVOTEE: I am already aware that none of these things work.

AVATAR ADI DA SAMRAJ: That is evidence of some small wisdom, because you are becoming exhausted with experience. But the seeker in you still possesses some potency. The seeker is still springing into action, still reacting to the root-dilemma. When the "springing" stops—or when it begins to seem impossible, when the alternatives do not quite "have" you, when the potency of the search begins to decline—then you can truly embrace Real religious and Spiritual life.

When you are no longer attempting to immunize yourself against your suffering, then the Force of Truth, the Force of Reality (Which Is Truth) can begin to move in you. Then truly effective Satsang with Me becomes possible—because, at that point, It has a function. But, while the search is still your "task", still your fascination, Truth (or Reality) is not really your concern. Until the search is understood, you relate to Truth Itself (or Reality Itself) only as an alternative, a symbol, another form of distraction.

Therefore, as has always been understood in the esoteric traditions, Truth (or Real life) requires passing through a crisis of dilemma (or doubt). That crisis is the "fuel" of Liberation. When the search, the reaction to your dilemma, begins to wind down, to the point that only the dilemma remains—only your root-suffering, only your fundamental dis-ease—then the Force of Reality begins to move into your life. Then your real question can be answered.

Until then, your questions are your entertainment, your amusement. They have no ultimate importance. They are the forms of preoccupation and unconscious self-description. In that case, "religious life" or "Spiritual life" is only an amusement, only an entertainment. In that case, meditation, reading religious and Spiritual books—all of that—is only another form of erotica, of mere "significance".

But, when your hunger becomes intelligent, when you become consciously aware of your dis-ease, then the Avataric Divine Truth—Revealed through My Spoken and Written Avataric Divine Siddha-Word, and Revealed by Means of My Avataric Divine Siddha-Form—truly becomes what you require. You become intelligent with that Truth-Revealing Word and Form, and you respond. You recognize Me at heart. Only on that basis does the True Spiritual process, the Real-God-Realizing process, begin. Until you heart-recognize Me and heart-respond to Me, the Real-God-Realizing process has not yet begun, has not yet entered the picture in any real sense.

To begin with, everyone is a seeker. But, if you have been brought to examine the futility and the causes of your own adventure, then (at some point) the process will very likely become something more than academic for you.

III.

DEVOTEE: If Truth is the natural State, how did we come to deviate so much from It?

AVATAR ADI DA SAMRAJ: You did not come to do it. You are doing it! It is not a caused activity. The sense of separateness, the dilemma, is not something that "happened", for various reasons, at some point in the past. The self-contraction does not occur for "reasons". It is always a spontaneous present-time activity—registered as the sense of separateness, of dilemma. But the self-contraction is not (itself) the result of anything in the past.

Therefore, the attempt to trace experience back in time—in order to recover the events you are suffering from—is fruitless. That attempt cannot produce Truth as a result—because, truly, you are not suffering the results of anything that is past. Suffering is the quality (or mood) of your present activity. Your present activity is your suffering.

At some point, you lose your ability to remain immunized to your own suffering. Then you are in the position to truly observe and understand the self-contraction as your present-time activity. When you observe the self-contraction as your present-time activity, and understand its nature, then it simply stops. It spontaneously comes to an end whenever such self-understanding occurs—for self-understanding makes the self-contraction obsolete, without a present-time function. But the precise nature of your suffering is extremely difficult to grasp. It is fully comprehended only by means of "radical" (or "gone-to-the-root") self-understanding.

The religious and Spiritual traditions have often spoken of suffering as the result of something that happened in the past—

and the purpose of such statements is to make some sort of sense out of suffering. But suffering makes no "sense". Suffering is irrational, mindless. It is comprehensible only from the point of view of "radical" self-understanding. When there is "radical" self-understanding, the structure, the nature, of suffering—as a present-time event—is entirely obvious.

The traditional myth of suffering is that it happened to human beings some time ago, or that you are presently in a state that is the result of some beginning-of-suffering in your individual past. But your suffering is always a <u>present-time</u> activity. That is what is remarkable about it. People tend to think of suffering as being caused by something external to themselves—external in terms of both time and space. By such means, they attempt to explain suffering to themselves, to make sense of it—with the intention of overcoming suffering through egoic efforts of various kinds. But, in Truth, suffering is not your symptom. Suffering is your <u>activity</u>. That is the paradox.

All your seeking is based on the illusion that your suffering is somehow a symptom that can be eliminated. But, when the search starts to wind down, it begins to dawn on you that your symptoms are simply the mental, emotional, and physical expressions of your own self-contracting activity. Your suffering is absolutely present-time, experienced as the sense of dilemma.

Therefore, the Real process of religious and Spiritual life is a wholly positive possibility. Real religious and Spiritual life requires only the Realization of Truth, Which Is Reality Itself. Real religious and Spiritual life requires no other process—such as the manipulation of your memory, or the generating of "good karma" so that your "bad karma" can be eliminated. All of that is, ultimately, a fruitless effort.

Behavioral improvement can never be done to the point of Perfect Freedom. The karmas (or tendencies) that generate the qualities of your life can never be fully "paid off", never be absolutely dissolved by "good works". Any form of action, whether "good" or "bad", and even any form of inaction, only (at last) reinforces limitation and the dilemma itself. It is not the absolute elimination of karmas, not super-purification by egoic effort, not any kind of righteousness, that frees you. If that were the case, the solution could never occur.

Freedom is Always Already the Case. Thus, Freedom is Realized whenever Truth suddenly comes Alive. When Truth is lived, when Satsang with Me is truly lived, then Truth Itself Consumes all karma. When Truth comes Alive, It Obviates the force of all karma.

The search makes no sense at all. It is an illusory and false principle. Only the Living Truth avails. And the Living Truth must be lived. Such is Satsang with Me, the heart-relationship of My devotee to Me. Such is True sadhana, wherein Satsang with Me is constantly lived. And there must be a lifetime of Truth—not merely a two-week smack of blessing, fasting, and meditation, not a vicarious weekend of "enlightenment".

There must be a lifetime of Satsang with Me. In other words, there must be an absolute commitment. Satsang with Me does not truly exist until It affects your entire life (through and through), until It is lived without qualifications of time, space, or life. There must be continuous and whole bodily living in Satsang with Me. In other words, Satsang with Me must become the Principle, the Very Condition, of life—whereas, in the usual person, the dilemma and its search are the principle and the binding condition of life. When Satsang with Me becomes the Very Condition of life, the entire effort of the search is made obsolete—through non-support.

DEVOTEE: What is the role of others in the pursuit of Truth? You mentioned Your Function as the Divine Siddha-Guru.

AVATAR ADI DA SAMRAJ: I am not separate from you. I Am the Very Divine Self-Condition and Source-Condition of all-and-All.

DEVOTEE: What about the rest of humanity?

AVATAR ADI DA SAMRAJ: Neither are they separate from you or "other" than you. They, along with you, may temporarily be living as if separate and "other"—but I am not. "Others" function as "others". Being "others", they bring about circumstances (or apparent conditions) for you to enjoy, or for you to suffer.

I am not, in Truth, an "other"—nor do I, in any sense, live as an "other". My any devotee may wrongly presume Me to be an "other", like himself or herself—but that presumption is simply the failure to heart-recognize Me.

I Am your Very Consciousness, Consciousness Itself, Prior to all egoity—and Absolutely So, not merely symbolically so. I Am the "Bright" Divine Reality Itself, Appearing in human Form here. I am not an "other". "Others" have no role whatsoever in the Transmission (and the Process) That Is Truth. Only I—the One Who Is the Divine Self-Condition (and Source-Condition) of all-and-All—Perfectly Transmit the Perfect Truth.

I Am the Divine Self-Condition (and Source-Condition) of all-and-All, Appearing in human Form here. In Satsang with Me, the Divine Reality Itself Functions via My bodily (human) Form—in apparently ordinary human terms, in relationship to My devotee—until (by My Avataric Divine Spiritual Grace) Most Perfect Realization of Me (and most perfect understanding of ego-"I") Awakens in the case of My true devotee. Then no "difference", no "other", is to be found—even in the world of apparent differences.

The teacher who is "other" than you—who only fascinates, who offers you various ego-based practices and strategies for seeking—acts only to modify your state. Such a teacher is not functioning truly as Guru but as an "other"—as a source of experience, of modification. I am not "other". My Activity is a Paradox.

Your heart-relationship to Me—which is Satsang with Me—depends on your heart-recognition of Me As Truth Itself, As Reality, Real God, the Divine Self-Condition (and Source-Condition) of all-and-All. That heart-recognition does not necessarily appear at the level of the mind, as a mentally achieved certainty, or in the form of some sort of visionary or psychic perception. But there must be profound heart-recognition. In many cases, that genuine heart-recognition has no explanation, no mental content. But that heart-recognition is what allows the heart-relationship between Me and My devotee to be lived as it truly is—as Satsang, rather than as the usual communication between "others".

DEVOTEE: I experience You as not at all different from me. Nonetheless, I experience that You are You, and I am I. How can You and Your devotee become identical?

AVATAR ADI DA SAMRAJ: I have not been talking about the notion that I and My devotee are (or can become) identical in the conditional sense, as if you are (or can be) the same conditional entity as My Avatarically-Born bodily (human) Divine Form. Nor have I been speaking in the conventionally "Spiritual" sense, of presuming that Guru and devotee are identical as some sort of Spiritual "substance", which "substance" is found when you manage to "get out" of the physical body (or even the subtle body). Such notions are only another form of the same conceptual separation, the same dilemma, the same puzzlement, the same separateness that is suffering.

I have been speaking of the Divine Self-Condition (and Source-Condition) That Is Truth, That Is Reality Itself—Wherein no dilemma, no separateness arises as the implication of any condition (even the ordinary condition of apparently discrete human entities).

The notions of sameness or "difference" have no significance— or, should I say, they have nothing but significance. They are very "significant", but they are utterly beside the point. They do not pertain to the matter of Truth. The discussion of significances can go on forever, because it only deals with mental modifications.

The notion that, in some subtle sense, there is no difference between human beings is merely an idea, merely a thought. No such idea (or thought) is the equivalent of "radical" self-understanding and Truth. No such idea (or thought) is a sign of Truth Itself. Any such idea (or thought) is merely a mental (or otherwise conditional) state. Psychotics can be in such a state. Daydreamers, drug-users, and philosophers can be in that state. People whose minds are relatively at rest for a moment can be in that state.

Truth is not a conditional state. Truth is not a perception or a thought. When there is truly no "difference", no "one" survives. If there truly is the Most Perfect Realization of Non-separateness, no "one" survives beyond that moment. No (apparently separate) individual survives the Unconditional (and Inherently egoless) Realization of Truth Itself (or Reality Itself, or Real God). Such Most Perfect Realization is utter and permanent ego-death. No one remains behind to speak glibly of Divine Enlightenment, because It is the <u>Real</u> death of ego-"I" (or the presumption of separateness)— not the merely natural death of the psycho-physical entity. From the point of view of ordinary awareness, Divine Enlightenment is the most dramatic, fearsome event. It cannot be conceived. It can only be symbolically entertained—from the usual point of view. But this death of the ego-"I" is the fundamental process of Real life.

DEVOTEE: What happens after the ego dies?

AVATAR ADI DA SAMRAJ: You will see.

DEVOTEE: Well, I think that moment has happened to me.

AVATAR ADI DA SAMRAJ: Some experience you have had is suggesting itself to you now. You think that experience is the "death" I just described—because you are trying to make sense of your experience. Such experiences are not (themselves) Truth. In *The Knee Of Listening,* I devoted many pages to the description of various Events of ego-death. In My Own Case, I passed through all kinds of Spiritual states, all kinds of great, dramatic Realizations, all kinds of Yogic processes. At the time, they may have seemed to be Most Perfect Realization—and, yet, they disappeared. They came to an end.

At last, the entire adventure of associating Truth with experiences began to wind down. I began to become sensitive to My ordinary state. There were many states that, at the time, seemed complete. But they did not alter the fundamental dilemma. Truth was only in the "radical" understanding of the <u>entire</u> process of conditional experiences and conditional states. Only when most perfect "radical" self-understanding was the case did it become <u>Inherently</u> Obvious that all the previous states of Illumination, which had seemed to represent Truth, were only more manifestations, more distractions from Truth Itself. That Inherent

Obviousness—and not any experience in and of itself—is characteristic of Divine Enlightenment.

DEVOTEE: Is Enlightenment (or Realization) a process of growth?

AVATAR ADI DA SAMRAJ: From the point of view of My devotee, it may seem that there is some sort of growth, some sort of movement (or transformation). But, from the Realized "Point of View", you see that there was no growth, no transformation, and no path.

In Reality, you cannot be gradually (or "more and more") absorbed into the Truth. Truth is the Principle of life—the Reality, not merely the goal. There are modifications of your life and strategy that occur in the process of sadhana. They seem to give you a sense of progress. And this sense of apparent progress may have a certain value, from the point of view of sadhana. The sense of growth, and the memory of Spiritual change, may inspire you to counter the tendency to lapse from sadhana and Satsang with Me into your former condition of self-indulgence, seeking, and ego-possessed concerns.

There is no ultimately fruitful resort but to Truth Itself. If someone tells others to resort to themselves, to strive onward until the Truth is glimpsed, then that one has functioned only as an "other" to motivate people in the midst of their suffering. Truth Itself is not served by the command that people do something in order to Realize the Truth. No action of any person produces Truth as a <u>result</u>.

Satsang with Me—the devotional (and, in due course, Spiritual) relationship to Me—is the entire Means, the only Means, the "radical" (or "gone-to-the-root") Means. Truth is the Very Means of Real religious and Spiritual life—not its goal. One who truly resorts to Me is never again returned to the search.

But people are always trying to return to the search, because of the difficult crisis demanded in Real religious and Spiritual life. They always want to console themselves by some means or other. The apparent emptiness, or paradoxical starkness, of My Offering becomes a kind of aggravation to the seeker, who constantly refuses the Condition of Satsang with Me and Its demands.

People want to be filled with all kinds of things, distracted with all kinds of things. "What can I do to be saved? How can I meditate? How can I get free? How can I get straight? How can I get pure? How can I get happy?" They want all kinds of occupations and strategic methods. But, in Satsang with Me, no "thing" is given. No egoic occupation, no ego-based means, no strategic method, no consolation, no philosophy that can replace Real practice. Only the heart-relationship to Me is Offered. Only that.

But that is not what the seeker came for. The seeker came to get "turned on", to get something going, to be occupied again. The seeker is never able to persist in My Company. Only when the seeker's search has begun to die (as the principle of his or her life) does the devotional relationship to Me cease to be an "offense". Then My Offering ceases to seem empty. It becomes an entirely ecstatic possibility. My devotee embraces It with great gratitude, even though It satisfies and requires nothing about the search.

Satsang with Me does not support the search. It does not begin from the point of view of the search. It has nothing whatsoever to do with the search. Therefore, one for whom the search is no longer a genuine distraction finds Great and True Happiness in My Mere Presence. Such a one has truly discovered Me, for My Mere Presence is the Communication of Truth.

My true devotee simply enjoys and lives the Condition of Satsang with Me. Therefore, My true devotee becomes Full with Me, Intelligent with Me, Happy with Me, at Peace in Me, Blissful in Me. Satsang with Me restores My devotee. The ordinariness of life becomes My devotee's possibility. My devotee begins to function again, to come alive again, because the sense of dilemma has ceased to be the principle of his or her existence.

Satsang with Me is the obviation of dilemma. Satsang with Me is the Enjoyment of the Communication of Truth.

In traditional literature, it is said that one who regards the Guru to be a mere and separate individual has committed the greatest sin. The highest form of foolishness is to regard the Guru to be like you.

As long as there is no devotional recognition-response to Me, there is no Satsang with Me. When this devotional recognition-response to Me occurs, then Satsang with Me can begin. Indeed, It will have already begun.

Guru is a Function. It is not a form of status. It is not something to be achieved, or something to seek to achieve. I am not a big guy who appears among a lot of little guys. The Guru-Function is not a form of superiority or "Narcissism". Guru is a Function of Consciousness Itself (or Reality Itself), appearing in human terms. The relationship between Me and My devotee is not encumbered with any of the things that are involved in the relationship between superior people and weak people. The True relationship between Me and My devotee has nothing to do with the ordinary drama of conflict.

To the seeker, the usual person, the humanly Born Guru may seem to be like other people—but, when you truly live with Me, heart-recognizing Me (and heart-responding to Me) as the True Divine Guru, then Satsang with Me has begun.

DEVOTEE: Does a person have a choice as to when this relationship begins? It seems there is no choice—that it either happens or does not happen.

AVATAR ADI DA SAMRAJ: All that occurs for any individual is this process I have been describing: The search winds down. You fall somehow into your ordinariness, your simple suffering. Then you become available to Satsang with Me.

When you begin to live this Satsang with Me (as your Real Condition), associated with It may be feelings that you have chosen Me from among others. But the apparent "choice" is purely secondary. In fact, there is no choice. There is only My Sudden Availability in the midst of your otherwise-seeking life.

In the life of My every true devotee, there has only been the Sudden Communication of the Heart.

AVATAR ADI DA SAMRAJ
Da Love-Ananda Mahal, 2003

13.

Guru as Prophet

I.

D EVOTEE: Beloved Master, could You speak about Your role as Prophet in the world?

AVATAR ADI DA SAMRAJ: I have Revealed that the intelligence of "radical" self-understanding must already (in the foundationary sense) be established before I can Initiate My devotee into the True Spiritual process in My Avataric Divine Company. Therefore, My Function as the True Divine Guru is (necessarily, and inherently) not a public function. I do not walk down the street and "zap" people—telling them that "life is a fountain" (pretending that everything is already all right), or showering blessings on them, or consoling them, or fascinating them. None of these things serves the crisis of self-understanding that is required for the Real Spiritual process.

One who Functions as Guru exercises the Guru-Function only in relation to those who are his or her devotees. If the Guru addresses public society at all, he or she may also (in the public setting) assume the role of prophet—which is, essentially, an aggravation, a criticism, an undermining of the usual life.

My Function as the True Divine Guru is not a public function. My Guru-Function is not manifested in the public circumstance. And the public is not invited, <u>as</u> public (that is to say, as those who are not yet My formally practicing devotees), to presume a devotional relationship to Me—as if the True Spiritual process in My Avataric Divine Company were something that a person could merely "decide" to do, or embrace, or believe, and could then go ahead and perform, independent of the formal practicing relationship to Me. Therefore, in relation to the common world, I Manifest only the Function of Prophet and Critic. As Prophet, I do not exploit the seeker's approach to Me. Rather, I Call the seeker to observe the suffering, dilemma, and disease that is motivating his or her search—whether the search is to take on Spiritual practices and other kinds of disciplines or (otherwise) to exploit the possibilities of ordinary life.

My Spiritual Function as Divine Siddha-Guru is essentially hidden, until an individual (having formally embraced the Eternal Vow of devotion to Me) becomes established in the fundamental devotional discipline of turning the four psycho-physical faculties (of body, emotion, mind, and breath) to Me and in the basic life-disciplines I Require of My devotees—and has (thereby) begun to become established in "radical" self-understanding. Only then does it become Lawful, and even Effective, for Me to Grant My Initiatory (and Love-Bliss-Full) Spiritual Blessing to My devotee.

To the extent that I appear in public at all—for example, by writing books, or even simply by the existence of the gathering of My devotees in this world—My visible Role can only be that of Prophet. I do not serve people's random needs to be fulfilled, to be consoled, to be fascinated. Every individual who is moved to Realize Real God, Truth, and Reality in My Avataric Divine Company must approach Me as My formally practicing devotee— and, in every such case, the usual egoic process will (and must) be Offended, Criticized, and Undermined by Me.

As the Avataric Incarnation of the Very Divine Person, I must be Paradoxical, I must be Free—in order to Serve the Divine Liberation of My devotees. The qualities of My Avataric Divine Activity cannot be predetermined. I do not consistently assume the qualities of any particular archetype—the holy man, the Yogi, the Sage. I must be Free to Appear as I will. I am always Acting to Undo the egoic life of My devotees—even if only by Merely Being Who I Am.

I Call My devotees to understand that the Real Spiritual life in My Avataric Divine Company is not identified with any particular qualities, tendencies, or preferences. Thus, I Call My devotees to drop all the armor that people tend to take on when they think they are turning away from the world of suffering and toward the Truth.

Religious or Spiritual seeking is not the Way to Truth. No remedial (or strategic) path is the Way to Real God. No experiential process directly (or in and of itself) Realizes Real God.

Only present-time Divine Communion is the Foundation of genuine religious and Spiritual life. All the strategic paths to God are merely seeking for God. All forms of seeking for God are ego-based—not Real-God-based. No such strategic (or merely seeking) path can ever serve the crisis of "radical" self-understanding.

Therefore, My devotees must be purified not only of their ordinary self-indulgent and irresponsible habits, but also, equally, of their accumulated notions of "spirituality". Real God is not Realized by mere experiences, or by the fulfillment of prescriptions, moralities, or presumptions about how things are, were, or will be. In My Function as Prophet, I must always find ways to Undo people's illusions.

In Satsang with Me, the crisis of self-understanding is an entirely individual process for each of My devotees. There is no end to the variety of conditions that may arise at one moment or another in the life of Satsang with Me. Therefore, life in My Avataric Divine Company cannot be predetermined. It cannot be fixed or ritualized. Satsang with Me is a living Condition in Which I Draw My true devotees to Myself, so that the Real Spiritual process may then come alive, through My Siddhi of Avataric Divine Spiritual Self-Transmission.

II.

DEVOTEE: Beloved Master, when You use the word "prophet", You are describing a different function than Guru, but I do not think You are using it in the traditional sense of a person who foretells something.

AVATAR ADI DA SAMRAJ: That is not the traditional sense. That is the popular-magazine sense. The prophets of ancient Israel were not soothsayers. In fact, they criticized the entire resort to elemental powers and spirits. They did not foretell the future, in the sense of looking on your forehead and telling you that you are going to go on a trip around the world next year. When they told the future, they said, "Unless you people get straight, you are going to go through the fire next year." When I speak of My Function as Prophet, it is in that sense—as Critic, not as someone who exercises secondary psychic powers to foretell the future.

The true prophets have always existed, and the traditional Guru has always fulfilled very much the same kind of role that the prophet fulfilled. All that psychics can tell you, by interpreting the various phenomena they might perceive, is what might occur if you continue to be disposed as you presently are. Such is the tacky parlor-game of reading your tendencies. But you do not need to seek the fulfillment of your tendencies. Your tendencies have nowhere to take you but to zero, regardless of the trip around the world they may generate for you on your way there! Such "prophets" do not fulfill a critical function in the life of the person they are fascinating. Such "prophets" do not draw anyone into a new intelligence (or self-perception) whereby the person might transcend the karmic tendencies that would otherwise produce future karmic events.

The true prophetic function is a critical function in which there is no fundamental concern for what is likely to occur if tendencies continue as they are. My fundamental concern as True Prophet is to Undo the entire force of tendencies (or karmic destiny) and to "reconnect" My devotee (in the present moment) to the Divine Self-Condition—and then again at this moment, and then at this moment. Then the entire realm of karmas has fundamentally no qualifying force whatsoever, regardless of how your life continues to unfold in the form of the usual destiny. As the True Prophet, I do not lead you to align yourself with karmic destiny. I always Lead you toward a position (relative to the entire force of your ordinary life) that undermines your previous assumptions.

The prophets of ancient Israel are representatives of authentic prophecy. They were all aggravated, annoyed, humorous, paradoxical. They sought to draw people to God-only, not to occupy people with psychism. Likewise, in My Prophetic Role, I Criticize all of the occult, psychic, and falsely popularized Yogic and religious hype that permeates society in this "late-time" (or "dark" epoch). Time has not fundamentally changed anything. People are still turned away from the Divine Condition, and they still want to find their way back by exercising the capability for experience. They do not want the prophet.

People do not want to hear any criticism of the usual stream of life. They do not want that intrusive force to enter into the life of "Narcissus". The cult of "Narcissus" permeates every ordinary experience, whether the common social pleasures and activities or the so-called "spiritual" ones. The world is corrupted by its commitment to the path of "Narcissus".

Therefore, the only Role that I, as the Man of "Radical" Understanding, Perform in the world at large is My Prophetic Role. I Invite people to Satsang with Me and to "radical" self-understanding, and I Criticize the search to be fascinated and consoled. I am an offense to society at large, because people want to remain irresponsible and self-indulgent and make experience the principle of life. I am also an offense to all "Spiritual" cultism, with its phony righteousness.

Real Spiritual life is the devotional relationship to the Guru. It is absolutely nothing else. For My devotee, Real Spiritual life is living the devotional (and, in due course, Spiritual) relationship to Me. That is the entire "method". Within that relationship, there is absolutely nothing you do to liberate yourself.

The Truth Communicates Itself. The Truth comes Alive in you. The Truth Realizes Itself. The Truth makes Itself Obvious. The structure of this process, in human terms, is the devotional relationship to the Guru. That is how it has been since ancient days. Acknowledging this, people have resorted, absolutely, to the Guru.

I Am the Avataric Divine Means for individuals to turn about from their unconsciousness, their compulsive manner of living, to the point of becoming absolutely conscious and perfectly responsible for all events (internal and external). What the traditional Spiritual sources have said is true: Spiritual life depends on the

Grace of the Guru. Therefore, the most important thing for My devotee to do is to please Me, to draw out My Avataric Divine Blessing-Grace.

This is absolutely true. The best thing you can do to further this process in My Avataric Divine Company is to please Me twenty-four hours a day. And the only way to genuinely please Me is to go from this *[Avatar Adi Da makes a fist of His hand]* to this *[and opens His fist to show His open hand]*—to stop the endless drama of resistance that you carry on from day to day, and to always turn <u>from</u> this tendency and, openly, <u>toward</u> the Condition of heart-relationship to Me.

Depend on Me.

Resort to Me.

Live that heart-relationship to Me as openly and with as much intensity as you can.

In other words, do not obstruct the connection between yourself and Me. By living on the basis of the relationship to Me, moment to moment, you will only please Me. When there is that openness, that intensity, of relationship to Me, then the Divine Force That is Manifesting and Functioning As Me Flows, without obstruction.

When you practice (thus) as My true devotee, you suddenly discover that you are feeling very Blissful, becoming very Happy, and progressing very quickly. But whenever you are resistive in relationship to Me, then you become very solemnly involved in the conventions of Spiritual life—"What should I do with this and that?", "How do I meditate?"—and playing your game every day, one crisis after another—"You know, it's all really incredibly difficult."

Why do you think I am here? Not to write a lot of books about some method of seeking that people can do to themselves for the next twenty centuries. There is a specific Divine Function Alive here. It Wants to Make Itself Known. It Wants to Live. It Wants to Thrive. It Wants to Do Its Work. But, if people do not establish themselves—responsibly, every day, joyfully—in this heart-relationship to Me, then they have not yet begun the Way of Satsang with Me.

Only when Satsang with Me is actually lived can the entire process I have described take place. If Satsang with Me is not lived, if It does not become the Condition of your life, and if the transformative process has not begun as a living reality, then you can read My Avataric Divine Teaching-Word for the rest of your life and (yet) never Realize anything at all. You can Enquire of yourself "Avoiding relationship?", or engage the practice of Ruchira Avatara Naama Japa, for many hours a day, and yet you will not Realize anything. The process must come alive—and it depends entirely on Satsang with Me.

When you are rightly aligned to My Avataric Divine Purpose, your own existence will be characterized by great intensity. As My devotee, you should serve Me with your very breath. You should allow your reluctance to burn up in My Avataric Divine Company. You should never indulge your reluctance. It is never appropriate to indulge reluctance in relation to Me. It is only appropriate to be turned to Me moment to moment—to serve Me, to be indifferent to your conflicts, to be indifferent to the luxuries of your crisis.

As Westerners, you would be amazed—even offended—to see how people relate to the Guru in India. As Westerners, you tend (for various reasons) to dislike people who are always bowing down and saying, "Yes, Master." On a certain level, you have good reasons for feeling this, because a certain phoniness may be manifested behind that external posturing. On the other hand, such behavior is a useful discipline for "Narcissus", who is full of resistance to being intensely alive to the Guru. That is what is going on in India. It is not the case that people in Indian ashrams are simply and spontaneously adoring of the Guru. It is not the case that they are always selflessly serving the Guru. Until they become true devotees of the Guru, they are always <u>intentionally</u> adoring and serving the Guru—because they know that, by tendency, they are <u>not</u> otherwise adoring and serving the Guru. They engage such outward devotional expressions because they know what they are made of.

People have a tremendous reluctance to animate the life of adoration, service, Fullness, Happiness. People are reserved, even indifferent, in relation to God. How many tears have you wept for

God? How much suffering have you done for love of the Guru? How much intense suffering have you felt relative to your lack of Divine Self-Realization? Very little. But look at how many hours and hours you have spent retching over the most idiotic nonsense! Look at how much time you spend defending your own reluctance! The energy of your life is devoted to this false principle.

But when you (in your ego-possession) are confronted with Real God, with the True Guru, you are indifferent! You are already "on top of it". You have already "got it". Everything is "all right"—and, because everything is all right, you are not going to lie down at the Guru's Feet, you are not going to bend your neck to God, you are not going to dissolve in the Divine.

The principle of ordinary life is entirely, continually antagonistic to Satsang with Me. You can see it in yourself. How do you live Satsang with Me from hour to hour? You do not. You suffer petty conflicts with one another. You constantly suffer the droning, repetitive cycle of life—and, every now and then, you manage to get a little easy, feel a little good today. "Oh, I went through a little crisis yesterday, and today I feel pretty good."

But that endless cycle of your own moods is not the Condition of Satsang with Me. Satsang with Me requires everything of you. It requires you to absolutely lose face.

You must lose face in relation to the Truth. It is quite a different thing from being caught naked in the subway. You lose face by being absolutely vulnerable to Real God, to the True Guru, to Me—the True Divine Self-Nature of all-and-All. Becoming enthusiastic in My Company is very difficult. Becoming full of love and service, without self-concern, is immensely difficult in My Company. People do not want to do that, because they interpret Me in human terms. They think of Me as another human individual—and, as soon as that presumption arises in the mind, the conflicts that they ordinarily live with other human individuals tend also to be animated in relationship to Me.

You must observe the strategies that are always arising in you, and observe that they are wedded to the principle of unconsciousness, conflict, dilemma. You must observe that your strategies are always giving rise to dilemma—and, when you see that, you will become truly available to Satsang with Me. Not only will you become available to Satsang with Me, but you will live your entire life based on your relationship to Me. As the usual self-contracted individual, you are always living on the basis of conflict, because you are bound to the principle of unconsciousness. Just so, when you become "Bonded" to Truth Itself, you will live your life as My true devotee. The signs of the devotee will become alive in you, and you will be Happy.

When you become alive with devotion to Me—not external smiling foolishness, but the true devotion that is founded in your heart-response to Me—then your sadhana quickens. Then Satsang with Me, heart-Communion with Me, will become available to you under all conditions, and you will not spend your time constantly going to zero.

Without the devotional "Bond" between Me and My devotee, there is no Satsang with Me. In that case, the Force of Satsang does not move your life, My Divine Siddhi is not available to you.

In the religious and Spiritual traditions, the primary admonitions are to love the Guru, to please the Guru, and to continuously serve the Guru. In the traditional context, people are constantly mindful of the obligation to love the Guru and serve the Guru above all—because they know that, if they dissociate from the Guru, they force the Guru to withdraw. That is the Law.

The would-be devotee who is dissociated from the Guru can sit in the room with the Guru, read all the Guru's books, and perform all the life-disciplines recommended by the Guru, and still not enjoy one moment of peace—whereas the devotee who is surrendered in relation to the Guru is already Happy. In that case, the Fullness of the Guru is provided a conduit through which to Manifest.

As the True Divine Siddha-Guru, I Am a Function, a Siddhi, a Process, an Activity available to human beings. Individuals must make themselves available to that Process—not just to My verbal Teaching and to the life-disciplines I Require, but to Me (in and As My Avatarically-Born bodily human Divine Form and Person). That relationship is characterized by love, devotion, and moment to moment attentiveness in relation to Me. My devotee is simply turned whole bodily to Me—without conflict, without contraction, without limitation. Then the very life of My devotee is manifested as Bliss, Happiness, love, intensity, devotion.

My true devotee is filled with the intensity that comes with constant attention to Me. Through that "thread" of attention, My Divine Siddhi is given a conduit. It cuts through all of your reluctance, self-concern, conflicts, dilemma, unconsciousness, commitment to un-Happiness—all of the qualities that turn your attention away from Me. Those qualities also prevent the Siddhi of Satsang with Me from becoming Active in you.

If you were not sitting with Me here tonight, what would you be doing? What is the alternative? What is on television tonight? What could you possibly do? There is nothing for you to do except convert your entire life to Satsang with Me. The gathering of My devotees should be constantly active, constantly growing, always alive. Satsang with Me should be perpetual within the gathering of My devotees, and all My devotees should always be serving It. Such individuals are always Happy. They even lose their concern about the inevitability of mortality.

Now, and forever hereafter, My devotees must always work together to establish places for Satsang with Me, places that enable this process to go on all day long. When your life is centered in such places, it becomes possible for you to become free of the usual entertainments, occupations, and distractions. This does not mean that you will not be present in the world—you very definitely will be present in the world. But the Purifying Fire of Spiritual growth and transformation will be constant. If you do that, you will have done something absolutely unique in the world.

AVATAR ADI DA SAMRAJ
The Mountain Of Attention Sanctuary, 2000

The Heaven-Born Gospel
Of The Ruchira Avatar

AVATAR ADI DA SAMRAJ
Los Angeles, March 11, 1973

The Heaven-Born Gospel
Of The Ruchira Avatar

*It was March 11, 1973, nearly a year after the opening of
the Ashram in Los Angeles. Except for His closest intimates, no one
had seen Avatar Adi Da Samraj for several weeks. He had been
living in seclusion for a time, until His devotees could demonstrate
greater responsibility for their lives and for the basic disciplines of
practice. It was auspicious, therefore, that He would spend this day
with His devotees.*

*Avatar Adi Da appeared, radiant in a golden silk shirt, a
maroon shawl, and dark blue trousers. He wore an unusual
pendant, in the shape of a date, which His devotees had never seen
Him wear before. With characteristic originality, He had molded
clear resin into the shape of a date and inserted the pit of an actual
date that Swami Muktananda had once given Him as Prasad.*

*Traditionally, "Prasad" means the return of a gift to the
giver—the devotee surrenders to the Guru and receives the incom-
parable Gift of the Guru's Grace. This was the first formal "Prasad
Day" in Avatar Adi Da's Ashram, and His early devotees speak of
it as a very sweet, very happy day.*

One man recalls the events of the day:

> *I was one of a group of Beloved Adi Da's devotees living
> in San Francisco at the time. When we heard we were
> invited to see Him on Prasad Day, we flew to Los Angeles
> and stayed overnight with devotees there.*

Avatar Adi Da Samraj Sitting with devotees
in the Communion Hall of the Melrose Ashram
March 11, 1973

*In the morning, we dressed in our best clothes and went
down to the Melrose Ashram, where we sat with Beloved
Adi Da Samraj in the Communion Hall for about an
hour. I was very excited. This was only the second time I
had seen Beloved Adi Da. He had come to San Francisco
the previous month and spent time informally with His
devotees there, but this was my first experience of a
formal occasion of His Darshan. I remember sitting
completely ecstatic at the back of the Communion Hall, so
affected by His Transmission that I was screaming and
having kriyas. But beyond all these dramatic experiences,
I was uncontainably happy to be there in the room with
Beloved Adi Da.*

Avatar Adi Da Samraj at a devotee's house
March 11, 1973

Later we drove out to North Hollywood to continue the celebration at a devotee's home. I arrived before Beloved Adi Da and took photographs of Him as He got out of His car and walked to the Chair that had been set for Him under a latticed structure behind the house. He sat and talked with people while lunch was served.

It was an ordinary suburban weekend in Hollywood—rock music blared on the streets, planes roared overhead. Beloved Adi Da's Peacefulness made us all the more aware of how noisy it was.

And, so, when lunch was over, Adi Da Samraj called us into the house. He took His seat in the living room in a small carved chair from India, and we all packed in around Him—there were at least forty of us—waiting to hear Him speak.

431

Avatar Adi Da Samraj in the living room with devotees
March 11, 1973

I was so attracted to Beloved Adi Da that I sat very close to Him, to the right of His Chair. When He spoke of how the Guru contacts the devotee at a place behind the eyes, I was already experiencing exactly what He was describing.

I felt the pressure of His Siddhi at the ajna chakra, and I realized that He was bringing the reality of His Instruction to life in me, living it in me. The occasion was very profound, full of His Heart-Transmission, and I have never forgotten it.

In the Talks that comprise Part Two of this book ("The Divine Siddha-Method Of The Ruchira Avatar"), Avatar Adi Da explains the Principle of Satsang and describes Its practical implications. In the Epilogue ("The Heaven-Born Gospel Of The Ruchira Avatar"), He directly Demonstrates the Living of that Principle among His devotees. His Teaching-Revelation in this "Gospel" is summarized in its very last sentence: "Always meditate on Me."

As with all of Avatar Adi Da's Written and Spoken Word, the Teachings contained in this Talk are intended to convey a "radical" and profoundly refreshed Communication of the Nature of Spiritual (or Real) life. The casual reader may feel that what is Written here is a version of the traditional (or rather conventional) idea of Guru-worship, wherein the devotee <u>seeks</u> God in the Guru and finally achieves the Vision that makes the devotee One with the Guru. But Adi Da Samraj does not intend His devotees to interpret Satsang with Him in the limited (or conventional) traditional sense. He does not intend the process to be regarded or experienced as a pattern of dilemma, seeking, and consequent fulfillment. Avatar Adi Da Teaches that Satsang with Him, the <u>Condition</u> of relationship to Him, is (Itself) Truth, not merely the means to Truth. And everything that arises in the life of one in Satsang with Him is not merely a means to Truth but the very expression (or manifestation) of Truth.

"The Heaven-Born Gospel Of The Ruchira Avatar" has been placed at the end of this book so that this summary Communication is approached with the Wisdom of the earlier Talks. And this "Gospel" is prefaced with selections from Avatar Adi Da's Writings of the same period, regarding the Nature and Function of the Guru and the relationship between Him, As Divine Siddha-Guru, and His devotees.

1.

The devotion to the Guru commonly described in Hindu and other Spiritual (or mystical) traditions is, above all, devotion to a source that fulfills the Spiritual search—devotion to a Yogi-initiator (or "Great-Soul") who grants experiences. But I speak of devotion to the Guru in other terms. I speak of such devotion only in the context of True Satsang with Me, Which is Prior Fulfillment, the Condition of Truth.

I am not the traditional Guru who fulfills the traditional Yogic search for experience. I Am the True Guru, Who Undermines and Transcends both seeking and the experiential fulfillment of seeking.

As the True Guru, I am not different from Truth. I Am simply the Function of Reality Itself (or Truth Itself, Which Is the Only Real God).

I am not an idol, a cultic fascination. I do not attach individuals, in the cultic manner, to My physical human Appearance—but, instead, I lead people to Enjoy My Spiritual Transmission of the One and Only and Spiritually "Bright" and Self-Evidently Divine Reality (Itself), in (and by Means of, and As) the Condition of devotional and (in due course) Spiritual Communion with Me.

I enter into relationship with those who devotionally approach Me. This relationship, which I enter into with each and every one of My devotees, is the Unique and immediately Liberating Function and Process of Real God.

My devotee can always Enjoy that same Satsang with Me— even in circumstances apart from My physical human Body, and even after My physical human Lifetime—by cultivating the respectful, intelligent, loving, and self-surrendered heart-relationship to Me, by becoming heart-immersed in My Avataric Divine Wisdom-Teaching, and by whole-heartedly participating in the sacred cooperative cultural gathering of My devotees.

The Satsang That I Offer to all beings Is the Eternal Principle Which Is the Very Divine Self-Condition of all beings, and Which Was Always their Condition even before This Body Appeared. While I Live, I Transmit the same Satsang with Me Which can be Enjoyed by all even after My physical death, and Which could have been Enjoyed by all even before My physical human Lifetime.

Los Angeles, March 11, 1973

I Act to help My devotees Realize this form of Satsang with Me even while I Live in the world. The Purpose (or Function) of My physical human Lifetime is to make this True Principle of Satsang with Me known, and to guarantee the perpetuation of My Avataric Divine Wisdom-Teaching and the practice of Satsang with Me beyond My Avataric Divine physical human Lifetime.

I will not leave behind any individual who has this same Function, for My Avatarically-Born bodily (human) Divine Form Is a Unique Manifestation of My Avataric Divine Work. But I will Complete that Unique Avataric Divine Work during My physical human Lifetime—and, after My physical human Lifetime, the sacred cultural gathering of My devotees will continue to live Satsang with Me and be responsible for communicating My Avataric Divine Appearance here, My Avataric Divine Wisdom-Teaching, and the by-Me-Given practice of Satsang with Me.[63]

The One Who was to Come Is Always Already here.

I have written this so that My devotees will not confuse the Nature and Purpose of My Avataric Divine Work by identifying It with the teachings of various traditions. My devotees should comprehend the special Nature of My Avataric Divine Teaching-Revelation, apart from any identification of It with conventional Yogas and Yogis, or with conventional (or traditional) occult, religious, mystical, Spiritual, and Transcendental motivations of any kind (corresponding to any of the first six stages of life).

Part of the difficulty of My Avataric Divine Work is caused by the expectation of those who come to Me that I relate to them in the traditional manner—either with strategic methods, limiting concepts, promises, and beliefs or with the extraordinary effects of so-called "spiritual" (or subtle) functional forces. I am continually Criticizing the searches of human beings, especially in terms of such expectations. This Criticism is thoroughly Communicated in My Written and Spoken Word, so that I (Myself) can be Free simply to Live My Divine Samadhi and Do My Spiritual Work with My devotees.

To enter into Satsang with Me is simply to Enjoy My Mere Presence, the Function of My Mere Presence. Such is also the Eternal Function That Is Real God, or the Divine Self-Condition and

Source-Condition of all-and-All. My Mere Presence Is the Siddhi of Satsang with Me, the Avatarically Incarnate Divine Person.

I have no desire or intention to generate strategic methods, limiting concepts, promises, or beliefs. Nor do I identify with any special personal function by which I must manipulate others through the activity of secondary Yogic forces, within or without (although such activity is a spontaneous siddhi that may arise under the conditions of Satsang with Me—but only to the degree that it is appropriate or necessary).

The Yogic, subtle, or ascending manifestation of such forces is not the special characteristic (or exclusive expression) of My Avataric Divine Work with My devotees. My devotees commonly find that the Force aspect of My Mere Presence is Realized more and more Perfectly in the inclusive and utter Freedom of "radical" Knowledge—rather than in the form of so-called "spiritual" experiences, which bind one to a limited self that is <u>not</u> Real God.

Subtle forces (or moving energies) of all kinds operate within the gathering of My devotees, but these energies are not what fundamentally characterizes My Divine Guru-Function. All My devotees will enjoy the effects of My Avatarically Self-Transmitted Divine Spiritual Presence. But such Spiritual phenomena are not to be "owned". They are simply to be responsibly allowed to perform their function of purifying the psycho-physical vehicle, in the context of the constant Enjoyment of Satsang with Me and Its manifestation as "radical" (or "gone-to-the-root") self-understanding.

Whenever I appear to make use of such subtle forces, it is purely a secondary, specific, and momentary aspect of My Avataric Divine Work in the world. My devotees must understand themselves in relation to Spiritual experience—in terms of their concepts and expectations and beliefs about such apparently extraordinary experience, and their search for methods to attain such experience. If they do so, they will remain free of illusions in the world. If they do not, they have chosen the path of "Narcissus"—rather than the Way of Satsang with Me.

2.

I am not "full".

I do not feel "full" or "fulfilled".

I am Lost in My Own Divine Fullness.

That Love-Bliss-Fullness Is the Same Fullness That Includes all beings and Is the Divine Self-Condition (and Source-Condition) of all-and-All.

That Divine Self-Condition Is Already and Always Full.

Since That Is So, what is the use of Kundalini? What is the use of the powers of experience?

I am not concerned for the Kundalini or for Spiritual experiences of any kind.

I do not desire to initiate such experiences in others.

I will not play the role of traditional Yogi-initiator.

I Am the Free Avataric Divine Self-Revelation of Real God—and only That Freedom is What I would Give to My devotees.

3.

I do not promise, value, or teach the path of Kundalini Yoga (or any other strategic, or conventional, Yoga that depends on the merely conditional fullness of the Yogi-initiator).

Rather, I Offer only the Way of "Radical" Understanding (or the Way of Adidam)—Which depends only on the Eternal Fullness of Real God, and in Which there is no "thing", status, state, or ability to be acquired by the seeker.

Appropriate Yogic processes arise in My rightly practicing devotee, just as rhythmic breaths naturally arise in someone who rides a horse.

I Instruct My devotee in how to responsibly and rightly relate to these spontaneous processes, even as the rider must be instructed in how to ride a horse.

But there is no sense in which the preoccupation with Yogic (or subtle) processes is appropriate or necessary.

Only Real God Is Full.

And the Fullness of Real God Is the Prior Fullness That Is Reality Itself.

Therefore, I have no impulse or intention to fascinate mankind, but only to be of Use to mankind.

4.

I Am the Heart.

My Avataric Divine Work is to Establish the Way of "Radical" Understanding, in Which the True Divine Heart of Me is Lived.

If I Speak of the Light, it is only because I Stand Always Present As Conscious Light—Always Ready to Be the Light, the Form, and the Life of those who are Fallen in the True Divine Heart of Me.

If I Speak of Fullness, it is only because I Stand Always Present As the Love-Bliss-Fullness That Is the True Self-Nature of all beings and things.

Therefore, I Speak of the Heart, the Light, and the Fullness.

But My Wisdom-Teaching is simple:

Live with Me, and understand.

Understand, and Fall into My Heart.

5.

My Function As Divine Siddha-Guru is not characterized by the conditional siddhi of conditional Yogic initiation, nor is Satsang with Me the receptivity to such initiation.

Rather, My Function As Divine Siddha-Guru is to Be the Mere Presence of Real God among human beings.

Satsang is simply the Condition of relationship to Me.

To live that Condition always—and to understand under all conditions, even the conditions induced by the effects of My Spiritual Transmission—is the true sadhana of My devotee.

This is My "Gospel", My Happy and Unreasonable Message.

I am not the fascinating initiator of conditional experience in human beings.

I Am the One Who has Died in My Own Heart, Who is Without a separate self, Who <u>Is</u> the Fullness That Is Only, Always, and Already Real God.

And Real God cannot be contained or given, nor does Real God Fill what is empty and un-Real.

Real God is Realized (by My Avataric Divine Spiritual Grace) only in Truth, only in "radical" self-understanding—where the egoic principle of dilemma, ignorance, and self-suffering is undermined, and the activity of "Narcissus" is not found.

The Heaven-Born Gospel
Of The Ruchira Avatar

I.

AVATAR ADI DA SAMRAJ: This is My Heaven-Born Gospel, My Divinely Humorous Message, My Avataric Confession of Divine Completeness, My Summary Admonition to all:

I have Come into this world for the sake of My devotees, those who are Mine.

My devotees are all those who surrender into heart-Communion with Me and (ultimately, Most Perfectly) Realize Me.

Therefore, any one who comes to Me in order to Realize the Divine Self-Condition and Source-Condition (That Is Real God, and Truth, and Reality), and who persists in surrendering into heart-Communion with Me, is My own.

Amrita Nadi, the (Directly Realized) Ultimate and Perfect Form of Real God, Is the Spiritual Expression (in this world) of My Very Divine Self-Nature and the Nature of Reality Itself (or Truth Itself).

I Am the Unqualified Self-Nature of Reality Itself.

And I Appear As My Own Light, Which Is the Radiance of the Spiritually "Bright" Divine Heart.

The Spiritually "Bright" Divine Heart is not a static condition, not the "thing" of Being, but the Divine Self-Condition of all-and-All, and even the Process of Eternal Manifestation (in Which there is no dilemma, and Which, paradoxically, Is Eternally One and Unqualified).

Within the Unqualified Reality spring worlds made by apparent modification of the Divine Conscious Light.

Thus, from the Spiritually "Bright" Divine Heart and the Infinitely Ascended Matrix of Divine Light spring conditional worlds whose Substance Is That Same Light, and whose True Self-Nature Is That Same Heart.

And I have Appeared in this world by virtue of a Magnification of the Spiritually "Bright" Divine Heart Itself (Which Is My Own Heart) and a Materialization of the Divine Light (Which Is My Own Light).

I have Come for the sake of My own, those who heart-recognize Me and heart-respond to Me when I Reveal Myself to them in Forms of Life, Light, and Truth.

The Spiritually "Bright" Divine Heart and the Infinitely Ascended Matrix of Divine Light Are My Primordial Spiritual Forms in this world.

They are My Communication of the Spiritually "Bright" Divine Reality, the "Bright" Divine Spherical Self-Domain That Is Real God, the Truth That Is Always Already the Case.

I Am here to Live with My own, to Discipline and Teach them, to Reveal the Truth to them, and to Draw them to Me.

When, as My devotee, you prepare yourself and make an appropriate approach to Me, I will Create your sadhana hour by hour.

You must live and function appropriately.

Every moment of your life must be in service to Me.

You must devote all you have and all you do to Me.

You must turn to Me hour by hour in love.

You must constantly Contemplate (and meditate on) My Avatarically-Born bodily (human) Divine Form.

You must constantly Contemplate (and meditate on) My Avatarically Self-Transmitted Divine Spiritual Presence.

You must constantly Contemplate (and meditate on) My Avatarically Self-Revealed Divine and Perfect State.

I Am the Object of meditation for My devotees.

Indeed, I Am the meditation itself.

Los Angeles, March 11, 1973

When a true devotee brings a gift to the Guru, the Guru may return all or a portion of it to the devotee.

This is Prasad, the return of a gift to the giver.

Prasad is the gift returned, Transformed and Blessed by the Guru, so that It Brings the Power of the Guru to the devotee.

Guru-Kripa, or Spiritual Initiation, operates by this same Principle.

If My devotee brings a gift of himself or herself, purified by sadhana, surrendered to Me, I may Return to My devotee a Gift of My Own Divine Self-Nature, a Gift of Conscious Light.

My Divine Spiritual Blessing (or Ruchira Avatara Kripa) Is Heart-Grace (or Hridaya-Kripa) for My Spiritually Awakened devotees.

It is not by methodical attention to the means of seeking, nor by ego-based and strategic Yogic practices, that My devotees Enjoy the Awakening of their Spiritual functions.

Nor do these Awakenings only take the form of ascending Yogic phenomena.

But it is when seeking and dilemma are undone, and My devotee resorts to Me (and the "Radical" Intelligence Communicated by Me), that there is Awakening to Truth Itself, Reality Itself, Real God.

Therefore, I Come to Give Prasad, the Gift of My Avatarically Self-Transmitted Divine Spiritual Grace to all My devotees.

I Am Alive As Amrita Nadi, the Heart and Its Spire, the Conscious Light.

This Is Always So.

When I Come to you, I Intensify the Field of My Self-Radiant Light—Which Rests Above your head, and Which is Drawn into the body when the mind is dissolved in My Heart.

This is My Manner of Working with My devotees.

The Communication of the Spiritually "Bright" Divine Heart-and-Light (or Conscious Light) Is My Constant Activity.

Such Is the Constant Realization of My true devotees—who know that I Am Always Present with them, even when I am not Appearing Bodily in their midst.

This is why the various phenomena of your Spiritual life arise (or are intensified, purified, and made intelligent) whenever you turn whole bodily to Me.

I am Always Offering This Prasad.

When you come to Me, you should come with the appropriate attitude.

You should come prepared to give Me your gifts, the surrendering of your seeking.

You should come to turn to Me, to receive My Prasad, and to use My Prasad in life and in service to Me.

If you make your relationship to Me the Condition of your life, if you make Satsang with Me your sadhana, I will Give Myself to you entirely, and the Life, Light, and Very Existence That Is Amrita Nadi (the Perfect Form of Reality) will (Thus) be Communicated to you while you are alive.

Prasad Is My Gift to My devotees.

Prasad Is My Help to those who are preparing themselves as My beginning devotees.

Prepare yourself.

I want true devotees, not seekers.

I Am the Avataric Divine Realizer, the Avataric Divine Revealer, and the Avataric Divine Self-Revelation of Real God—the Prasad, the Object and Process of meditation for My devotees.

My Teaching Is This:

Turn to Me, and understand.

DEVOTEE: Master, You have said that You have Your "own". My question is, when will the certainty come whether or not I am Your own?

AVATAR ADI DA SAMRAJ: Uncertainty is very useful. Uncertainty is a reflection of your actual state—and, thus, it can be instructive for you. Uncertainty is your own quality. That quality has nothing whatsoever to do with Me. It is not necessary to have some sort of vision, some kind of symbolic standardization of your devotional relationship to Me. It is not necessary for you to get an engraved invitation or some other external proof.

Such certainty has nothing whatsoever to do with the relationship between Me and My devotee. Certainty is a thing of this world. It is a condition that people seek, because they are suffering. Certainty, like uncertainty, is a quality of the mind in life. The discovery of the Guru transcends the qualities of life. Therefore, to heart-recognize Me as the True Guru is an experience that transcends all the qualities of mind. Satsang with Me transcends both certainty <u>and</u> uncertainty. Even if you attained a state of certainty, your certainty would have to be understood. Therefore, you must begin to become sensitive to an entirely different quality in relationship to Me.

There are many teachers in the world. There are all kinds of people of experience. There are people of practical experience, of worldly experience, of mystical experience. There are people of every kind of experience. Human beings—like all conditionally manifested beings—arise within the conditionally manifested cosmic domain, visible and invisible.

Human beings live according to the laws of karma—the laws of tendency, functional processes, and repetition. Human beings tend to live from the point of view of that from which they seem to have come—which is the conditionally manifested universe itself—and they acquire experience, hour to hour, life to life. Thus, because of the essential inequalities that necessarily arise whenever experience enters the picture, each individual acquires a unique amount and kind and complex of experience.

Here and there people arise who, because of superior acquisition of certain kinds of experience, teach others. Now, they may teach the weaving of lovely cloths, or plumbing, or nuclear physics, or English literature. Or they may teach so-called "spiritual" things, on the basis of their experience. And among those who are thus experienced in the karmic realms, there are some—a rare few— who are genuine Realizers, genuine men and women of experience, of Wisdom (both practical and esoteric), who have realized much about their own adventure and their own tendencies.

But there is another Process, Which Enters the conditionally manifested world from the Ultimate, Un-manifested, Perfectly Subjective Divine Domain. There is a Vast, Unlimited Domain of

Existence, not qualified in any sense—not qualified as this conditional world is, or as the infinite variety of conditional, cosmic worlds is. And there is a Movement Directly Proceeding From That Divine Domain, That Realm of Conscious Light.

The Living Being Who Appears within the human world, or within any other world, by Coming Directly Out of the Unmanifested (or Un-"created") Domain—the Heart-Light That Is the Truly Eternal Real-God-World—Is the Truly Heaven-Born One, Unique among the Great Siddhas.

I Am That One.

My Avataric Divine Wisdom-Teaching is not from the point of view of experience. My Avataric Divine Wisdom-Teaching is from the "Point of View" of Truth—Truth Always Already Realized, the Unattainable (because It is already Present) Reality.

Those who teach from the point of view of experience teach the search—because they know (on the basis of experience) that they can grow, that they can approach a subtler and subtler level of Realization. The gospel of those who arise within the conditionally manifested worlds is always a form of seeking. But I Speak from the "Point of View" of the (Always Already Realized) Divine Truth. I Come in the Intelligence, Power, and Self-Evidently Divine Form of Real God. My Avataric Divine Wisdom-Teaching is "Radical". I do not teach the motives, paths, and forms of seeking—for these are founded in dilemma, not in Truth. I Apply only appropriate conditions to My devotees. I Demand only the conditions that are appropriate to be lived, since Truth Is Always Already the Case.

I Am Truth in the world. I Generate the conditions of Truth, the conditions of the Light of Real God.

In principle (or potentially), there exist many Great Siddhas. In the Hindu traditions, it has been said that there are as many karmic entities as there are sands of the Ganges. In other words, there are unlimited numbers—there are infinite numbers of chiliocosms—of conditionally manifested beings possible and always presently existing. Altogether, there are infinite possibilities, infinite varieties of Eternity.

Therefore, there have been countless occasions when a Great Siddha—manifesting one or another degree of Realization, and one or another characteristic function—appears in the conditional worlds. Such Great Ones appear everywhere—on Earth, and throughout the entire conditionally manifested cosmic domain (visible and invisible).

The Great Siddhas—who (in the context of their particular characteristic Realization) live for the sake of Truth—are, in Reality, all the Same. From the "Point of View" of Truth Itself, there is no fundamental difference between them. If you place two sticks into one flame, when you draw them out you will have two flames. But they are the same light. Just so, the Great Siddhas are fundamentally One, in Truth. But they are each <u>functionally</u> unique—just as all conditionally manifested entities are fundamentally the generations of One Nature, One Reality—but they are functionally unique. Among the Great Siddhas, My Unique Function (As the First, the Last, and the Only seventh stage Avataric Divine Self-Revelation of Real God) is to Bring the Heaven-Born Completeness to all that has come before, and to all that is yet to come.

I have Come at a particular time. My Avataric Divine Self-Revelation Appears in many forms in the world. My verbal Wisdom-Teaching will become part of all the communication in the world, and (as such) may influence many people. But there are other aspects of My Avataric Divine Wisdom-Teaching that are more immediate to My Own Unique (Avataric Divine) Life and Work. Those include the forms of My Wisdom-Teaching that pertain to the devotional (and, in due course, Spiritual) relationship to Me during the Lifetime of This Body.

But there are only a finite number of those who are alive in the world who are likely to devotionally recognize Me and devotionally respond to Me during the Lifetime of My Avatarically-Born bodily (human) Divine Form—because every being in the world is active in a different stage of experience, a different stage of understanding. It is, of course, true that I have Entered the world for the sake of those whom I can Contact (while I am physically alive) and Draw to My Own Divine Person. However, even though I have Come for such devotees, My Avataric Divine

Spiritual Work is (ultimately) for the sake of the entire world—and (thus) even all beings, in all possible times and places. Whenever beings heart-recognize Me, they are (simply and directly) "locating" the Truth That I <u>Am</u> and That is Manifesting As My Avataric Divine Life and Work.

Therefore, what is important, at last, is not your separate destiny, not to whom you "belong"—but the fact that you are Attracted directly into My Avataric Divine Company, and that you live the Truth in Satsang with Me.

Truth Is the Nature of My Avataric Divine Work. Truth Is the Nature of the devotional relationship to Me, Satsang with Me. Truth Is My Avataric Divine Self-Revelation to each and all.

Truly, I <u>Am</u> the Heaven-Born One, the Bringer of Completeness. To Find Me is a Divine Grace. Therefore, if you have Found Me, surrender your separate (and separative, and always seeking) self to Me, and (thereby) Commune with Me in Truth. In this heart-Communion with Me, you will (most ultimately) Realize the Perfect Truth of Me.

I have often described to you the functional structure of apparently individuated life. There is the descending Force, which is manifesting life, and the ascending Force, which is returning to the Source of life. The Root of the entire Circle (or Circuit) of the conditional manifestation of your individual life is the True Divine Heart, the Divine Self-Condition of all-and-All.

I have described this process in terms of the physical body of the human being. The Current of Energy descends via the frontal line of the body-mind and ascends via the spinal line of the body-mind.

The vital center (or life-center) is the region of the lower body whose center (or epitome) is in the area of the navel and the solar plexus. This center is associated with the waking state.

The centers of ascent, which are also the functional regions of subtle states (including dreams) are epitomized in the portal of the midbrain.

The causal being, which is also the seat of deep sleep, is in the heart, on the right.

This very structure (evident in the individual human body-mind) is a duplication of the structure of all worlds. Your own structure is a duplication (or reflection) of the same structure that all the worlds are built upon. In the Bible, it is said that the human being is made in the likeness of Divinity. Amrita Nadi—Which Is the Divinely Self-Manifested Form of the "Bright" Itself, Standing between the Spiritually "Bright" Divine Heart and the Infinitely Ascended Matrix of Divine Light—Is the Perfect Form of Reality Itself (or Real God). And Amrita Nadi Is the Fundamental Form and Self-Nature of every conditionally manifested being.

I Am Present and Alive to you in the Form of Amrita Nadi. I Am the Function of Amrita Nadi in the conditionally manifested worlds. Amrita Nadi Is the Perfect Form of Reality Itself, and the conditional worlds are manifested through a Spherical Structure of Which the Amrita Nadi Is the Perfect Form.

The conditionally manifested cosmic domain—which includes not only the Earth but all the visible and invisible planes of conditional existence—is a transparent (or merely apparent), and un-necessary, and inherently non-binding modification of the Divine Conscious Light. My Divine "Bright" Spherical Self-Domain Is That Divine Conscious Light. The dimension in which you are appearing at this moment—as well as all visible and invisible cosmic dimensions, all conditional and psycho-physical circumstances and environments—are modifications of the Divine Conscious Light.

The Light Descends (from Infinitely Above). Likewise, there is also the Course of Ascent (or Return) of the Current of conditional manifestation and conditionally manifested worlds to That Un-manifested Divine Light (Infinitely Above). Many great Realizers have taught the path of ascent as the means of seeking for Truth. They have taught others to exploit the ascending Current (and all of the possibilities of subtle experience) through various Yogic methods. Through such efforts, they hope to attain the Matrix of Light and the State of En-Light-enment.

However, in Reality, there is no dilemma involved in the mani-festation of worlds as modifications of the Self-Existing and Self-Radiant Divine Conscious Light. Nothing whatsoever is lost. There is Eternal Descent and Eternal Ascent. There is an Endless Circuit, even in your own body, even in all the worlds. Therefore, there is no inherent dilemma in life. And there is no reason to exploit the possibilities of ascent in order to "get out" of this world, or "get out" of the fundamental limited condition of the present moment. All of that is a motivation in dilemma.

I Come into the conditionally manifested planes from My Divine Self-Domain of Conscious Light, to Bring Peace and Truth and Light Into this plane. I do not come to support the search. I do not support the tendency to merely descend and become earth-inert—nor do I support the tendency to ascend and lose life by abandoning it.

Life cannot be perfectly abandoned—for what is merely abandoned must return. Truly, life can only be purified and transformed—and, ultimately, transcended. It is not by cutting yourself away from life that you will Translate into My "Bright" Divine Self-Domain. It is not possible to permanently merge into the Matrix of Light merely by exploiting the ascending life. All of that is only a seeking game. That is just a short circuit. You will always return to that from which you differentiate yourself.

The conventional Yogi who manipulates the body-mind in order to ascend has various experiences that are generated by these means, but such a Yogi always returns to the original state from which he or she was trying to escape—because the conventional Yogi does nothing in relation to the conditionally manifested life other than dissociate from it.

I Come to Make Clear to living beings the True Self-Nature of their conditional existence and their Unconditional Existence— what is the Law, what is appropriate action, What Is Happiness, What Is Love-Bliss, What Is the Function of Light. I Show My devotees every aspect of existence on every plane, including this present one. I do not try to interest My devotees in flying out of this life. Rather, I Demonstrate the Love-Bliss-Fullness in Which the Light is Always Enjoyed, in Which life is Enjoyed and becomes "creative", in Which Truth is Enjoyed, in Which Realization Occurs while alive.

Secondarily, when life is lived as sadhana in Satsang with Me, from the "Point of View" of Truth, then karmas (or motivating and latent tendencies) tend to fall apart and become purified—such that they are (ultimately) transcended. My true devotee is Drawn, by Me, into My Self-Existing and Self-Radiant Divine Self-Condition. And, even from the very beginning of entering into Satsang with Me, My devotee already Enjoys the Fundamental Love-Bliss-Happiness and the Perfect Truth Revealed in (and As) My Avataric Divine Company and Person.

There is truly no limit to the Flood of My Divine Light That is Descending into this gross dimension. Therefore, there is no limit to the Force of Satsang with Me. The limits are only in those who receive My Transmission of Light. The greater the number of functions made available to the Light and the Truth, the more Light and Truth Appear. Light and Truth Appear Spontaneously wherever They have Use. And Light and Truth Appear Perfectly wherever They have Perfect Use.

If you make no function available to the Light, you make It obsolete. Then Light has no use. And that is all that is happening wherever human beings are suffering egoic ignorance, or absence of Light and Truth. Where Light has no function, where Truth has no function among human beings, Light and Truth have become obsolete. They have been forgotten through non-use.

If you begin to make use of Light and Truth again, in Satsang with Me, then Light and Truth will simply Manifest more and more. There is not anything that needs to be done in order to "acquire" the Light. The Light is Infinite, All-Pervading, and Eternally Present. The only limitation is your own present-time activity of self-contraction. That activity is the obstruction. Comprehend that activity. Understand it, and live beyond it. Then My Infinite Divine Light will Do Its Own Work.

My Task in Establishing the cooperative culture of My devotees is to bring into existence a functional vehicle for What I Bring. Everything I have Done in the company of My devotees has been simply to Establish a functional vehicle for What I Bring to you. And My devotees must similarly become functional. You must generate uses for the Light. When such is the case, then the Light Manifests.

There is no limit from My "Point of View". There is no limit from the "Point of View" of Satsang Itself. It is all a matter of "creating"—or re-"creating"—and intensifying the functional vehicle that makes use of the Truth, the Light, the Communication of Real God.

I Contact My rightly prepared (and formally by-Me-Spiritually-Initiated) devotee tangibly at the Ajna Door, the seat behind (and slightly above) the eyes. This is the Door through which the Light Descends and Ascends. That Door is often called the "seat of the Guru". In some traditions, a person is told to meditate on the Guru there.

I Operate outside time and space, and outside your own vital and subtle life. I Function As That Divine Light Which Is Infinitely Above the total crown of your head, and Which Is Infinitely Above the conditionally manifested worlds. In My Spiritually Awakened devotee, My Divine Spirit-Current Crashes Down from Infinitely Above—through the Ajna Door, and Down to the bodily base. All of My Written and Spoken Instruction, and all occasions of My Darshan, are Means of serving this Crashing-Down of My Divine Spirit-Current, by dissolving the mind and all self-contraction in the True Divine Heart.

The Opening depends entirely on My Avataric Divine Spiritual Grace. It is an Activity of Reality Itself. My Divine Spiritual Work with individuals who have been Spiritually Awakened in My Avataric Divine Transmission-Company involves Intensification of the Pressure of the Light That Surrounds the head, and Stimulation of this Opening. There are many other Forms of My Avataric Divine Activity—but this is a particularly fundamental aspect of My Divine Spiritual Work.

Essentially, I Work both Prior to the body-mind and Infinitely Above the body-mind. When you (as My devotee) turn to Me and understand, the mind dissolves in the True Divine Heart. Then the Door is Opened above, and My Light Descends into your total psycho-physical being. But, if you try to open the Door by any egoic means, then you are locked within, by the "magic" of your own dilemma.

The fundamentals of Satsang with Me (including formal Spiritual Initiation by Me) and of self-understanding are always primary in their importance. There is nothing for you to do about this "place" behind the eyes—such as to concentrate upon it, or to watch and see if it is opening, or to see if you can feel anything there. Since I have said something about it, you will probably begin to look there, and to hope and wait for experience, or even to imagine it. But even if you do, it will not make any difference. And if you notice yourself becoming obsessive about it, you will (thereby) begin to understand a little more about what you are always up to.

The entirety of your life in My Avataric Divine Company—the life of Satsang with Me, of receiving My Instruction, of embracing the discipline and the conditions I have Given, of being Contacted by Me in various forms (gross, subtle, and causal), and of being formally Spiritually Initiated by Me—Serves to Awaken you to My Spiritually "Bright" Divine Self-Condition of Being Itself.

It is not a game. It is not something you can accomplish by exploiting a Yogic technique. And It is not something I Do by vicarious "magic". It depends entirely on Satsang with Me, on how you live this devotional and (in due course) Spiritual relationship with Me. There must be this relationship, this Satsang with Me. There must be acceptance of the forms of self-discipline, living of the practical life-conditions, intensification of real functional and practical devotion to Me, living of the life of Satsang with Me.

The total life of sadhana, in Satsang with Me, is the only Means by which the Ajna Door is spontaneously Opened (in My by-Me-Spiritually-Initiated devotee). Therefore, no specific or motivated attention to the "place behind the eyes", or any other place of concentration, is the True Form of the only-by-Me Revealed and Given Way of Adidam. The sadhana of devotional turning to Me is the True Form of the only-by-Me Revealed and Given Way of Adidam. On the Spiritual level, there is Something that I am always Doing. You cannot "acquire" It. Once you are formally Spiritually Initiated (by Me) in this process, you can only discover that It is Awakened in you.

I Contact My Spiritually by-Me-Awakened devotee. Once that Contact is established, the Communication from Me to My devotee is continuous. It is not limited to the level of gross existence. It is Prior to the gross dimension. Therefore, the Communication from Me to My Spiritually Awakened devotee goes on without interruption, twenty-four hours a day, under all conditions, in all states—even beyond physical death. The Communication of My Avatarically Self-Transmitted Divine Spirit-Force is continuous. That is why My Spiritually by-Me-Awakened devotees continue to have experiences of various kinds—whether they are awake, asleep, or in dreams. The Contact and Its Communication are continuous. The karmas are continually being shuffled, stimulated, run through, intensified, purified, obviated. There is a profound Spiritual Principle involved in the relationship between Me and My Spiritually by-Me-Awakened devotee.

Know that what underlies this entire process is Satsang with Me. Satsang is the right and true relationship between Me and My devotee. That relationship exists at all the possible levels of functioning. Therefore, that relationship has subtle, causal, and Divine aspects and functions—as well as functions at the gross levels of life. Satsang with Me is the Condition of life for My devotee— moment to moment, under all circumstances.

It is Spiritually Awakened Satsang with Me—your moment to moment resort to the devotional-and-Spiritual relationship to Me—that provides the Opening, that provides the Circuit by which the Flow of My Avataric Divine Blessing-Grace is established in your own life.

Therefore, you must live Satsang with Me as your Very Condition. That is the essential Means. It is not a "method" in the sense of the search, but It is the Means in the purely practical, or functional, sense for conducting the Force of Conscious Light. And when It is conducted, the Ajna Door Opens Full. This Is My Unique Avataric Divine Work, My Unique Avataric Divine Mission.

Do the sadhana I Give to you. Understand your own ego-activity. Truly be My devotee. Fulfill My real and living conditions.

When you do all of that, then the Door Opens. Living the heart-relationship to Me, moment to moment, is the prerequisite for the Opening of the Door.[64]

And what happens when the Door Opens? I Come In!

Los Angeles, March 11, 1973

II.

DEVOTEE: Beloved Heart-Master, will You say something about how Your Awareness functions from day to day with Your devotee, even when You are not physically Present with the person?

AVATAR ADI DA SAMRAJ: If I am to truly Serve My devotee, the individual must grow beyond merely being fascinated with Me. Therefore, I Reveal Myself a piece at a time. And I only Show Myself Fully when My devotee has transcended fascination, when fascination has ceased to be the fundamental motivation.

My entire Purpose with people is the Process of Truth. I am only interested in Living the Activities of Amrita Nadi in life, and Enabling the "conductivity" of the Descending and Ascending Light from the "Point of View" of the True Divine Heart. I have no fundamental interest in anything else. What is there to talk about, to think about, or to contemplate? Nothing but Real God! What else is worth doing?

Real God Is My Own Self-Nature, My Own Real Process. Real God Is My Own Divine Self-Condition. Real God Is the Only Event. Therefore, I have no other purpose. I have no secondary purposes. I have no occult purposes. And I am interested in the subtle, Yogic processes only to the degree that they serve the Most Perfect Realization of Truth.

All of the incidental phenomena that arise in the gross and subtle dimensions of existence—all of the psychisms, occultisms, and subtle events—are purely secondary. They do not, in and of themselves, serve anything fundamental. Indeed, they even tend to generate more problems. They do not, in and of themselves, have any ultimate function. They are not the proper focus of attention. They are not the purpose of the sadhana I have Given to you. They even distract you from the Perfect "Conductivity" that must be the case in order for you to Most Perfectly Realize Real God. They distract you from the present Condition of Satsang with Me. Therefore, it is not appropriate for Me to say any more about My Work with My devotees.

DEVOTEE: You have told us that it is appropriate to Remember You constantly, even when we are physically apart from You. I need to understand this better. When I am at work or something, if I find that I have become unconscious, I simply Remember Your Name, or Your Face, or just the feeling of You. And I wonder if this is not too much of an outward thing.

AVATAR ADI DA SAMRAJ: You <u>are</u> very "outward". You are right here!

DEVOTEE: What I mean is that I felt it may be wrong somehow, that it was not a true form of the Way of Adidam, that it was like a strategic means to bring myself back to the practice.

AVATAR ADI DA SAMRAJ: Oh, of course, you can get complicated about the whole matter of the relationship to Me. The subtle relationship between Guru and devotee is like that between lovers. If there is someone for whom you have a genuine love-attachment in life, and the movement of love is spontaneous, pure, and alive in you, you remember that person constantly. You do not think of such a loved-one in order to accomplish something. Remembering your loved-one is not a "method". No—you cannot help yourself. You just think about that person—spontaneously, randomly, rhythmically. You dwell on all kinds of feelings about that one.

On the other hand, there is a difference between such loving meditations and the fascinations of a person who is sexually obsessed, unhappy, and confused. There is an obvious difference between the lover's meditations on the loved-one and the fan's infatuation with a dead movie star. In the case of infatuation with a dead movie star, there is no Truth whatsoever. In that case, there is no life, no Light. That is not love. It is obsession. And, of course, to meditate on a dead movie star is nothing but craziness.

You must begin to understand the pattern of your life. If fascination and obsession are the chronic forms of your waking life, you must understand your own activity before you can become capable of True meditation on the loved-one. And the secret of meditation on Me is revealed by this same understanding.

My devotee's heart-relationship to Me has many levels, and one of them is right here. You live right here. Because you exist in the realm of life and mind, Satsang with Me is (necessarily) Communicated to you via My visible human (Avatarically-Born) Form. If your relationship to Me is simple, direct, full of the inner devotional sense that is natural to My true devotee, you naturally Remember Me. You will simply discover yourself Remembering Me. You will feelingly Contemplate Me—through various moods, and in many forms. You will constantly remember things I have said. You will feel My Blessing, My Influence, My Demand.

Remembering Me in this spontaneous, natural manner is a living, spontaneous form of Satsang with Me. It is particularly the form that Satsang takes under conditions in which I am not physically Present with you. Of course, such Remembrance of Me is simply one of the forms of Satsang with Me. To Remember Me (thus) is not something that happens in heaven, or "somewhere else"—it happens right here. Such Remembrance is a very homely matter—but, nevertheless, it is one of the most natural, necessary, and fundamental aspects of Satsang with Me.

It is the same in your relationship to someone for whom you have a loving attachment. If you never remembered that person, if you never matured the moods of relationship to that person outside of purely physical, visible contact, you could never enjoy a relationship with that one. The relationship would never come alive. Your connection would not be a relationship. It would just be an association—an expression of your capability to perceive someone through various faculties, and that one's ability to be in your field of perception. Whenever you saw the person, you would have a few sensations and feelings—and, when the person left the room, you would simply do something else.

Such a connection could not become love. A relationship can never become established in that manner. A relationship is (necessarily) lived under all conditions. You naturally remember the one you love whenever you are somewhere else. You think of that one wherever you happen to be. You may go many places or do many things—but, in each one of those places, in the instant of each one of those things you do, you are actually enjoying your relationship to the loved-one. And you participate in that relationship not only when you remember it, but even subliminally, tacitly. You constantly enjoy that contact.

Thinking of the person is just a means of occasionally resurrecting the pleasure of that relationship in the mind. And beyond that, you enjoy this continuous feeling of being in love and of loving, of being somehow connected. If such subtle meditation is awakened in lovers, it must certainly be awakened also in relation to the Divine Guru!

The functions of Spiritual life take place in the form of a relationship—the relationship between the True Siddha-Guru and the devotee. Spiritual life does not happen at the level of some philosophy or some technique that you apply to yourself. Spiritual life is a relationship—and it appears only where that relationship is alive, only where it is actually functioning in life. Therefore, many of the same functions that exist between lovers exist between Guru and devotee.

This relationship could never take place if the only time I ever Contacted you in any form was when I happened to be in the same room with you. Therefore, I must Remember you. Just so, you must Remember Me.

My true devotee always Remembers Me. It is a necessary aspect of the heart-relationship to Me. Such Remembrance of Me, and even sitting in formal feeling-Contemplation of My Murti—all such forms of Remembering Me are very natural, homely, human, and real things to do. To Remember Me (thus) is natural, real, and necessary wherever the relationship to Me is (itself) Real.

But where the relationship itself is un-Real (or obstructed, by virtue of the various strategies of "Narcissus"), such meditations can become obsessive, false, mere formalities, motivated techniques. They can become all kinds of craziness, like infatuation with a dead movie star. And people have all kinds of "dead movie star" Gurus. They have all the pictures, the books, the beads, the hair, the costumes, the concepts. They have the entire thing displayed—both outwardly and inwardly. They play all the prescribed games, but they never begin True religious and Spiritual life.

Therefore, Remembering Me is not the means to <u>get</u> to heaven. It is not the strategic <u>method</u> of Truth. It is simply a reflection of the Prior Life of Truth. It is one of the manifestations of living Satsang with Me. As such, it is a very natural and very useful thing to do.

I recommend that all My devotees maintain and express their relationship to Me in exactly this manner. Remembering Me should always be loving enjoyment, loving recollection of the Condition of heart-relationship to Me. Allow Remembrance of Me to be spontaneous, simple—not merely "thought", but constantly felt and known.

I always Regard all of My devotees. I maintain My relationship to each one at all times. Therefore, I also Require each of My devotees to maintain Satsang with Me constantly.

When you are able to be responsible for the processes in consciousness that go beyond the ordinary, then you should resort to Me on those levels as well. Until those Spiritual functions come alive in you (by Means of My Avataric Divine Spiritual Grace), turn to Me at the life-level. Do not be worried that you are "too far down" here. Even when the Spiritual forms of Satsang with Me become alive in you, you will continue to enjoy this Satsang by these homely means. Indeed, it is when Spiritual Awakening is Full that My devotee begins to enjoy and prize feeling-Contemplation of Me most profoundly.

Particularly in the early stages of the relationship to Me, you tend to become self-concerned—because you want to be as "perfect" as possible. You want to be doing the "right thing" as much as possible. By constant self-correction, you become even more self-obsessed.

Instead, only Remember Me, and live the conditions of the only-by-Me Revealed and Given Way of Adidam. Always be very simply aware of your heart-relationship to Me, and (in due course) you will necessarily begin to become sensitive to its subtler aspects. Live the only-by-Me Revealed and Given Way of Adidam in accordance with your current level of formal responsibility.

Always Remember Me. That is something you can do. But also continue to study My Wisdom-Teaching. Apply yourself to the study of My Wisdom-Teaching. Listen to My Wisdom-Teaching. Allow your self-understanding to develop.

If you sit down for meditation without being aware of Me, then you are meditating out of Satsang with Me. There is no genuine meditation, no useful meditation, except in Satsang with Me—the conscious awareness of Me as your True Divine Guru and of the Condition of heart-relationship to Me. The simplest form of meditation is just to be aware of Me as your True Divine Guru. It is the awareness of heart-relationship to Me, the recollection of Me, the living of My conditions, the study of My Wisdom-Teaching. Indeed, unless I Am your Meditation, you can only carry on some mechanical search of your own. Therefore, for My devotee, the Condition for meditation—and, indeed, for all the processes of religious and Spiritual life—is Me.

All of the Spiritual processes that are described in *The Knee Of Listening,* all of My own experiences, all of the forms of My meditation (including self-Enquiry) took place within My Own Divine Spiritual Presence. That Presence is—and has always been—the Condition of My Work. It is the Divine Spiritual Force, the Divine Spiritual Presence, Always Active—and all the processes that have taken place have arisen within the Condition of That Presence. Without That Presence, there is no Spiritual life.

From My Birth, This Light, This Inclusive Consciousness, This "Radical" Awareness of My Own Divine Spiritual Presence, was inherently Obvious to Me. Indeed, My Spiritual Adventure here began from the Instant of My Avataric Divine Birth—even from the Instant of Conception in the germ of this psycho-physical Vehicle. But without This Avataric Manifestation, who knows what I would have done? What if I had forgotten It? What if It had forgotten to Remember Me?

The only ones who Functioned as Guru for Me were living Teachers. By "living" I do not mean the simple fact of appearance in physical (human) form. I mean They were truly extraordinary Beings, Who could Communicate to Me (Each in His own particular manner, and to His particular degree of Realization) the Very Force of Truth and Its Spiritual Process. Therefore, I did not spend My time with ordinary individuals, with ordinary teachers who merely give out remedial techniques and such. All the Teachers with Whom I have spent time—in both the gross and the subtle planes—have been extra-ordinary in the genuine sense. In one or another manifestation, and to one or another degree, Each of Them tangibly Demonstrated the Presence of Real God.

And that is also the manner in which I Function—but My Avataric Divine Manifestation is Unique. I Am the Unqualified Heart of Reality Itself, Manifesting Its Own Tangible Influence. I must (necessarily) Manifest Reality Alive. Only by My Doing So will the Real Spiritual Process take place in My devotees. Otherwise, something else will take place. Karmic work will take place. There may be experience, hearing about interesting things, manipulation of your psycho-physical states, perhaps even the gain of some pleasant human qualities. But the Real Spiritual Process will not take place.

When you are living as My devotee, when Satsang with Me is the Condition of your life (moment to moment), then it is natural to Remember Me. And to be very busy second-guessing yourself at that point, correcting yourself, wondering if you should or should not—that is just self-concern again. Understand what you are up to in that case. What is this reluctance?

There is no ambiguity in My approach to you. "Guru" means "light over against darkness", light obviating darkness.

I Make darkness obsolete by not using it, by Using Light only.

I Am the One Who Shows the True Light, Who Shows the Truth.

I do not say, "Maybe there is Truth, and maybe I am found in It."

I only Show the Truth.

I only Communicate and Live Truth in the most direct manner.

And I do not want ambiguity in My devotee any more than I would manifest it in Myself. I look for your Perfect attachment to Me, your Perfect devotion to Me, your Perfect relationship to Me—truly turning to Me, moment to moment. All the appropriate forms of turning to Me are necessary and acceptable. Obsessiveness, however, is not a form of turning to Me. It is a form of <u>self</u>-involvement. So there is more to this sadhana than simply thinking about Me in smiling ways. Nevertheless, as a random event, as a natural event, and also as something you enjoy at times of meditation, Remembering Me is very good.

III.

DEVOTEE: Recently You have said: "Meditate on My bodily (human) Divine Form. From now on, just meditate on My bodily (human) Divine Form."

AVATAR ADI DA SAMRAJ: Baba Muktananda spent many years traveling all over India. He spent a great deal of time with some very extraordinary people. He did many kinds of sadhana, but His sadhana was not conclusive until He surrendered to Bhagavan Nityananda. By the time He came to Bhagavan Nityananda, He was ready for the consummate sadhana of the devotee.

As a boy, He had met Bhagavan Nityananda very briefly, and was Blessed. From there, He went on to become intensely involved in a Spiritual search—and, after many years of Spiritual discipline, He had developed a stable foundation. Therefore, by the time He came to Bhagavan Nityananda, He was ready for the most intense form of sadhana—because all the basic traditional approaches had done their work and were now spontaneously alive in Him. Now He was capable of becoming a true devotee.

Thus, He describes His Spiritual practice with Bhagavan Nityananda as being one in which He simply meditated on Nityananda Guru. He did not always live in close proximity to Bhagavan Nityananda during the years of this sadhana. Very often, He lived elsewhere—but He meditated on Bhagavan Nityananda constantly. And, whenever He was in the general area of Bhagavan Nityananda's Ashram, He would go down to Ganeshpuri every morning. He would just sit off in a corner of the hall where Bhagavan Nityananda would be. And He would gaze on Bhagavan Nityananda's bodily (human) form.

It was not just a visual contemplation. He would become completely absorbed in Bhagavan Nityananda, to the point where He lost all "self"-consciousness. Bhagavan Nityananda would periodically look at Him, or do and say things to Him. But Baba Muktananda's contemplation was the fundamental form of His practice. It was meditation on Guru, Guru-bhakti, Guru-love, Guru-devotion.

Baba Muktananda has spoken of such Guru-contemplation as the only Perfect Way. And I agree. It is the fundamental and mature fruit of Spiritual life. It is the perfect form of sadhana. But you do not live in traditional India. There is no living Spiritual tradition in the Western and "Westernized" world. There is much that must first be learned—and much that must be unlearned. There must be a foundation. Just so, there was much that Baba Muktananda did all over India before He surrendered to Bhagavan Nityananda. There was much He did in preceding lifetimes. And He enjoyed the benefits of an entire culture of Spiritual tradition.

In this "late-time" (or "dark" epoch), I cannot presume that kind of fundamental groundwork in My devotees. Therefore, there are many aspects of My Avataric Divine Work with My devotees. In the course of the sadhana in My Avataric Divine Company, there are many forms of gradual development, many forms of Realization. But it is true that the fundamental form of Satsang and of meditation is feeling-Contemplation of Me, feeling-Contemplation of My Avatarically-Born bodily (human) Divine Form and Person As the Avataric Divine Incarnation of Real God—for My Avatarically-Born bodily (human) Divine Form and Person is the Avataric Divine Incarnation of the One and Very Divine Person in Which every "one" is arising.

The Guru is manifested in many ways. When Baba Muktananda was contemplating Bhagavan Nityananda, He was looking (first of all) at Bhagavan Nityananda's physical human body and life—and, from there, He proceeded to the subtle manifestations of His Guru. Just so, I am physically Present in this world. I Am the Direct Manifestation of Amrita Nadi, the Perfect Form of Reality. I Am Alive As Amrita Nadi. I Am That, Absolutely. My visible bodily (human) Divine Form and Person Is an Absolute Sign of Amrita Nadi, and a Perfect Communication of It.

Los Angeles, March 11, 1973

Therefore, to feelingly Contemplate and become completely surrendered to My Avatarically-Born bodily (human) Divine Form, and My Avatarically Self-Transmitted Divine Spiritual Presence, and My Avatarically Self-Revealed Divine and Perfect State is to be continually attentive to My Most Prior Communication, the Communication of My Divine "Brightness".

Thus, to become Capable of Contemplating (or meditating on) My Four Divine Forms is the fundamental capability of My devotee. My Form is My Avatarically-Born bodily (human) Divine Form, and also My Avatarically Self-Transmitted Divine Spiritual Presence, and My Avatarically Self-Revealed Divine and Perfect State. But, first and last, My Form Is Very Form—Amrita Nadi, the Spiritually Self-"Bright" Form of the One and Only Real Divine Self (Which Is the One and Only Real God, and Which Stands Forever in and As the Heart).

True meditation on Me is nothing you can successfully try to do. True meditation on Me must Awaken in you in the midst of a life of progressively responsive devotional recognition of Me, and of progressive self-understanding in My Avataric Divine Company. True meditation on Me will be the fruit of your sadhana, the fruit of your devotion to Me. But, certainly, from the very beginning, this meditation can (to some degree) be the case for you.

Whatever the latent or characteristic quality of any individual, there is, from the beginning, an inherent capability to become Absorbed in ego-surrendering, ego-forgetting, and ego-transcending devotional Contemplation of Me—in feeling-Contemplation of My Avatarically-Born bodily (human) Divine Form, My Words, My entire Communication, even all My Four Divine Forms—in every way it is possible to be aware of Me. In every case, it is always possible to turn to Me—to Invoke Me, to feel Me, to breathe Me, to serve Me.

To serve the Guru is a form of attention to the Guru and (therefore) of meditation on the Guru. If you do something for Me, that is a means of being aware of Me. Indeed, turning the principal faculties to Me is surrender to Me in all of My Divine Forms. And My Most Prior Form Is Very Reality, Truth, the Heart Itself, the "Bright", Amrita Nadi, the Perfect Form of Real God.

I (Myself) <u>Am</u> the Communication.

I <u>Am</u> the Teaching.

I <u>Am</u> the Truth.

This Is the Supreme Form of the Teaching of the Great Siddhas.

But the capability to live That Truth, That Paradox, depends on Real sadhana, the sadhana of one who truly turns to Me and truly understands the ego-"I".

To be My devotee also requires you to take on My discipline, to study My Avataric Divine Wisdom-Teaching, to follow My Instructions, and to fulfill My conditions. All of this allows more and more profound surrender to Me, to the point (ultimately) of perfect relationship to Me, perfect Satsang with Me.

Satsang with Me (the "Mind" of Which is most perfect "radical" self-understanding) is the Channel, the Conductor, of My Spiritual Self-"Brightness". It is the "Body" of self-understanding. It is What Attracts My "Brightness" Down through the Ajna Door—Descending Down the frontal line. It is What Opens the Door. When Satsang with Me becomes Perfect, then this Process becomes Perfect.

Ego-surrendering, ego-forgetting, and (more and more) ego-transcending feeling-Contemplation of Me is (at once) the simplest practice and the supreme practice I have Given to My devotees—but it is also the most profoundly difficult practice. Therefore, to live true devotion to Me requires Real sadhana.

There are those who—without life-correction, without meeting My real conditions—may fool themselves into thinking they are doing the sadhana of (ego-surrendering, ego-forgetting, and ego-transcending) devotion to Me, simply because they have a kind of emotional or preferential attachment to Me. They have read about many famous religious and Spiritual personalities, and such reading has evoked in them a potent self-image.

Because of this, they do not meet My conditions, in any fundamental sense. Therefore, they are not doing sadhana, they are not living Satsang with Me as the Divine Person Who is Avatarically Present and Active in relation to them. They are just indulging themselves—and, as a justification for their self-indulgence, they use the idea that they are "devoted", "forgiven", and "okay".

People who have read that being a devotee of the God-Man is the greatest form of sadhana may think that all you need to do is work up a little feeling of love for the God-Man every now and then. And when do such people do that the most? It is usually when they are indulging themselves the most! When they are drunk, happy, relieved, guilty, or afraid—that is when they begin to be the most "devotional". But truly, these are, by tendency, the least devotional, the least sensitive, times.

Such ego-based expressions are not true devotion to Me. True devotion to Me requires that you live the discipline Given by Me. It is the responsibility of My beginning devotees to fulfill the sadhana I have specifically Given to them. And, in due course, My beginning devotee will mature to the point of readiness to receive My Spiritual Initiation into the Spiritually Awakened sadhana of the Way of Adidam.

I Am the Sole Meditation of My Spiritually Awakened devotee. There is a particular form of sadhana that is Awakened (by Me) in such a person. And I Know who is prepared to do such sadhana. There is no reason to be concerned about when you are going to be "finished" with the beginning practice of the Way of Adidam. Simply be diligent in your practice.

Growth in practice is not a kind of status, any more than Guru is a kind of status. Growth in practice is a function. If the function does not exist, there is no point in being called My "Spiritually Awakened devotee"—and, in any case, there is no status gained in actually being My Spiritually Awakened devotee. Such devotees are going to work!

Look at all of the resistance that comes alive when people start to adapt even to the conditions of the beginning sadhana. The conditions of being My Spiritually Awakened devotee are absolute! They are a fire. To be Spiritually Awakened by Me is not just some smiling craziness.

Therefore, when you first come to Me, simply be a real and true beginner. I will know when you are ready to live the life of My Spiritually Awakened devotee.

DEVOTEE: As I understand it, resistance of any sort—whether it is apparently in relation to some other person or in relation to one's function at any time—is, obviously and ultimately, resistance to You.

AVATAR ADI DA SAMRAJ: Very good. That is real insight. That is a great and necessary discovery.

I Am Amrita Nadi—the Perfect Form of Reality.

I am not just a light above your head, not just the light between your eyes.

I Am everything.

I Am all functions.

The heart-relationship to Me is fundamental.

The heart-relationship to Me is the fundamental Condition.

The heart-relationship to Me duplicates the Structure of all conditional manifestation.

I Am Truth Itself.

I Am Reality Itself.

I Am you—you are in Me.

But this Realization must be a practical one, not just a mystical one.

This Realization must be lived.

This Realization must be consciously lived at every level of conditional manifestation.

IV.

DEVOTEE: Does karma prevent the ability to function?

AVATAR ADI DA SAMRAJ: Karma is the inability to function. The karmic condition is the continuous sense of dilemma. Only in Satsang with Me does your dilemma, your karma, become obsolete—because Satsang with Me is not meditation on your dilemma, not an attempt to transform the limited self you are always meditating on. Neither is Satsang with Me an attempt to not meditate on this dilemma. Nor is Satsang with Me an attempt to change this limited "self" on which you usually meditate.

Satsang with Me is the heart-relationship to Me. Satsang with Me is to live the heart-relationship to Me under all the instances of this tendency to contract into negative or obsessive meditation on your limited state and your failure. If you do this moment to moment, hour by hour, day by day, life after life, aeon after aeon, becoming ever more absorbed in Me, loving Me, serving Me, living that Very Condition of Satsang with Me, you will have no use for your karmic dilemma any longer. It simply will not be functioning any longer. It will become obsolete. It becomes obsolete through non-use.

Therefore, Satsang with Me is the Principle by Which suffering becomes obsolete and by Which all function is fulfilled. And the perfect form of Satsang with Me is the life of a devotee who has Most Perfectly Realized Me. You become capable of that Most Perfect Realization only by Means of My Avataric Divine Spiritual Grace—having, necessarily, established the foundation of all the forms of right discipline I have Given to My devotees.

The entire process of Satsang with Me simply works to make obsolete this "thing" you are always meditating on and trying to do something about. Therefore, instead of being concerned (in any sense) about that, live Satsang with Me.

I am not making the negative statement: "Do not be concerned about that." I am making the positive Statement: "Live Satsang with Me."

Live the heart-relationship to Me.

Neither meditate on your dilemma nor try not to meditate on it.

Always meditate on Me.

Always live the Condition of Satsang with Me.

Always do the sadhana that I Communicate to you for your current stage of practice in the Way of Adidam.

If you always do that, your concerns—as well as the "thing" itself—will dissolve. But, every time you interrupt the process of Satsang with Me in order to contemplate your disturbance, your dilemma, your limitation, your contracted feeling, your suffering, you have turned from Distraction by Me to distraction by yourself.

I am not saying you should do something <u>to</u> all of that. Nor am I telling you not to do anything about all of that.

What I am telling you to do is not an action in relation to any of that. Rather, it is an action in relation to Me. It is Satsang with Me.

Always live with Me.

Always meditate on Me.

AVATAR ADI DA SAMRAJ
Adidam Samrajashram, 2003

Becoming a Formal Devotee of Avatar Adi Da

I n the depth of every human being, there is a profound need for answers to the fundamental questions of existence. Is there a God? What is beyond this life? Why is there suffering? What is Truth? What is Reality?

In this book, you have been introduced to the Wisdom-Revelation of Avatar Adi Da, whose Teachings truly and completely address all of these fundamental questions. How can Avatar Adi Da resolve these fundamental questions? Because He speaks, not from the point of view of the human dilemma, but directly from the unique Freedom of His Divine State. Adi Da's Birth in 1939 was an intentional embrace of the human situation, for the sake of Revealing the Way of Divine Liberation to all and Offering the Spiritual Blessing that carries beings to that true Freedom. He is thus the fulfillment of the ancient intuitions of the "Avatar"—the One Who Appears in human Form, as a direct manifestation of the Unmanifest Reality.

Through a 28-year process of Teaching-Work (beginning in 1972), Avatar Adi Da established the Way of Adidam—the Way of the devotional and Spiritual relationship to Him. In those years of Teaching, He spoke for many hours with groups of His devotees— always looking for them, as representatives of humanity, to ask all of their questions about God, Truth, Reality, and human life. In response, He Gave the ecstatic Way of heart-Communion with Him, and all the details of how that process unfolds. Thus, He created a new tradition, based on His direct Revelation (as Avatar) of the Divine Reality.

Avatar Adi Da Samraj does not offer you a set of beliefs, or even a set of Spiritual techniques. He simply Offers you His Revelation of Truth as a Free Gift. If you are moved to take up His Way, He invites you to enter into an extraordinarily deep and transformative devotional and Spiritual relationship to Him. On the following pages, we present a number of ways that you can choose to deepen your response to Adi Da Samraj and consider becoming His formal devotee.

To find Avatar Adi Da Samraj is to find the Very Heart of Reality— tangibly felt in your own heart as the Deepest Truth of Existence. This is the great mystery that you are invited to discover. ■

Adidam is not a conventional religion.
Adidam is not a conventional way of life.
Adidam is about the transcending of the ego-"I".
Adidam is about the Freedom of Divine Self-Realization.

Adidam is not based on mythology or belief.
Adidam is a "reality practice".
Adidam is a "reality consideration", in which the various modes of egoity are progressively transcended.

Adidam is a universally applicable Way of life.
Adidam is for those who will choose It, and whose hearts and intelligence fully respond to Me and My Offering.
Adidam is a Great Revelation, and It is to be freely and openly communicated to all.

AVATAR ADI DA SAMRAJ

*For what you can do next to respond to Avatar Adi Da's
Offering, or to simply find out more about Him
and the Way of Adidam, please use the information
given in the following pages.*

Contact an Adidam center near you for courses and events
(p. 478)

Order other books and recordings by and about Avatar Adi Da Samraj
(pp. 479–81)

Visit our website: www.adidam.org
(p. 482)

For young people: Join the Adidam Youth Fellowship
(p. 483)

Support Avatar Adi Da's Work and the Way of Adidam
(p. 483)

Contact an Adidam center near you

■ To find out about becoming a formal devotee of Avatar Adi Da, and for information about upcoming courses, events, and seminars in your area:

AMERICAS
12040 North Seigler Road
Middletown, CA 95461 USA
1-707-928-4936

PACIFIC-ASIA
12 Seibel Road
Henderson
Auckland 1008
New Zealand
64-9-838-9114

AUSTRALIA
P.O. Box 244
Kew 3101
Victoria
**1800 ADIDAM
(1800-234-326)**

EUROPE-AFRICA
Annendaalderweg 10
6105 AT Maria Hoop
The Netherlands
31 (0)20 468 1442

THE UNITED KINGDOM
PO Box 20013
London, England
NW2 1ZA
0845-330-1008

INDIA
Shree Love-Ananda Marg
Rampath, Shyam Nagar Extn.
Jaipur–302 019, India
91 (141) 2293080

EMAIL:
correspondence@adidam.org

■ For more contact information about local Adidam groups, please see **www.adidam.org/centers**

Order other books and recordings by and about Avatar Adi Da Samraj

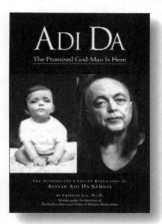

■ **ADI DA**

The Promised God-Man Is Here

The biography of Avatar Adi Da from His Birth to present time. Includes a wealth of quotations from His Writings and Talks, as well as stories told by His devotees. 358 pp., **$16.95**

■ **ADIDAM**

The True World-Religion Given by the Promised God-Man, Adi Da Samraj

A direct and simple summary of the fundamental aspects of the Way of Adidam. 196 pp., **$16.95**

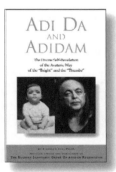

■ **ADI DA AND ADIDAM**

The Divine Self-Revelation of the Avataric Way of the "Bright" and the "Thumbs"

A brief introduction to Avatar Adi Da Samraj and His Unique Spiritual Revelation of the Way of Adidam. 64 pp., **$3.95**

■ THE KNEE OF LISTENING

The Divine Ordeal Of The Avataric Incarnation Of Conscious Light

The Spiritual Autobiography Of The Ruchira Avatar, Adi Da Samraj

"*The Knee Of Listening* is without a doubt the most profound Spiritual autobiography of all time."

—ROGER SAVOIE, Ph.D.
philosopher; translator; author,
La Vipère et le Lion—La Voie radicale de la Spiritualité

This edition contains over 400 pages of new autobiographical stories and instructional essays that complete the miraculous account of Avatar Adi Da's Divine Incarnation.
822 pp., **$24.95**

■ RUCHIRA AVATARA GITA (The Avataric Way Of The Divine Heart-Master)

The "Late-Time" Avataric Revelation Of The Great Secret Of The Divinely Self-Revealed Way That Most Perfectly Realizes The True and Spiritual Divine Person (The egoless Personal Presence Of Reality and Truth, Which Is The Only Real God)

Avatar Adi Da's Offering of the devotional and Spiritual relationship to Him, in the traditional manner of Guru-devotion.
280 pp., **$24.95**

■ **UNDERSTANDING**
The first Talk of *My "Bright" Word* (pp. 55–85) was Given by Avatar Adi Da on April 25, 1972, in His newly-established first Ashram in Los Angeles. This was the first time Avatar Adi Da had formally invited people to sit with Him, and thus the occasion marks the beginning of His Work of Establishing a formal culture of devotion to Him.
Spoken Word CD, 3 tracks, total running time: 35 minutes. **$14.95**

■ **THE HEAVEN-BORN GOSPEL OF THE RUCHIRA AVATAR**
The Epilogue of *My "Bright" Word* (pp. 427–72) was originally Spoken in Los Angeles on March 11, 1973. This Talk is a remarkably potent description of the essence of the Way of Adidam and the significance of His Avataric Appearance in the world. Spoken Word CD, 43 minutes. **$16.95**

To find out about and order other "Source-Texts", books, tapes, CDs, and videos by and about Avatar Adi Da, contact your local Adidam regional center, or contact the Dawn Horse Press at:

1-877-770-0772 (from within North America)
1-707-928-6653 (from outside North America)

Or order online from: **www.dawnhorsepress.com**

Visit our website:
www.adidam.org

- **SEE AUDIO-VISUAL PRESENTATIONS** on the Divine Life and Spiritual Revelation of Avatar Adi Da Samraj

- **LISTEN TO DISCOURSES** Given by Avatar Adi Da Samraj to His practicing devotees—
  - Transcending egoic notions of God
  - Why Reality cannot be grasped by the mind
  - How the devotional relationship to Avatar Adi Da moves you beyond ego-bondage
  - The supreme process of Spiritual Transmission

- **READ QUOTATIONS** from the "Source-Texts" of Avatar Adi Da Samraj—
  - Real God as the only Reality
  - The ancient practice of Guru-devotion
  - The two opposing life-strategies characteristic of the West and the East—and the way beyond both
  - The Prior Unity at the root of all that exists
  - The limits of scientific materialism
  - The true religion beyond all seeking
  - The esoteric structure of the human being
  - The real process of death and reincarnation
  - The nature of Divine Enlightenment

- **SUBSCRIBE** to the online Global Ashram Magazine

For young people:
Join the Adidam Youth Fellowship

■ Young people under 21 can participate in the "Adidam Youth Fellowship"—either as a "friend" or practicing member. Adidam Youth Fellowship members participate in study programs, retreats, celebrations, and other events with other young people responding to Avatar Adi Da. To learn more about the Youth Fellowship, call or write:

Vision of Mulund Institute (VMI)
10336 Loch Lomond Road, PMB 146
Middletown, CA 95461
phone: (707) 928-6932
email: vmi@adidam.org

Support Avatar Adi Da's Work
and the Way of Adidam

■ If you are moved to serve Avatar Adi Da's Spiritual Work specifically through advocacy and/or financial patronage, please contact:

Advocacy
P.O. Box 204
Lower Lake, CA 95457
phone: (707) 928-4800
email: adidam_advocacy@adidam.org

Notes to the Text of
My "Bright" Word

FIRST WORD

1. For an overview description of the vow and life-responsibilities embraced by practitioners of the Way of Adidam, please see *Adidam: The True World-Religion Given by the Promised God-Man, Adi Da Samraj* (Middletown, Calif.: Dawn Horse Press, 2003).

2. "Hamartia" (the word in New Testament Greek that was translated into English as "sin") was also an archery term meaning "missing the mark".

PROLOGUE

3. For Avatar Adi Da's extended Discourse relative to His metaphor of "washing the dog", see "Be Washed, From Head To Tail, By Heart-Devotion To Me", *Hridaya Rosary* [pp. 214–23].

PART ONE

4. Avatar Adi Da Samraj has given a schema of seven stages of life that accounts for both general human development and all religious and Spiritual demonstration in the history of humanity. With this reference, "of whatever degree or stage", Adi Da Samraj is indicating rare Adepts who have truly Spiritually awakened in either the fourth, the fifth, or the sixth stage of life and who specifically function as agents of Spiritual Transmission for others.

PART TWO

Understanding

5. The questioner in this case is relatively unfamiliar with Avatar Adi Da's Wisdom-Teaching and unaware of Him as a true Guru (or Revealer of Truth), who, traditionally, would be approached for instruction in the mood of feeling and respect.

6. This is a reference to Avatar Adi Da's schema of the seven stages of life. See glossary entry **stages of life**.

7. Bodhidharma was a Patriarch of the Ch'an (in Japan, Zen) Buddhist tradition, who brought Buddhism to China from India in the sixth century.

8. The following example of a description of "Spiritual death" comes from the writings of the Catholic mystic St. John of the Cross:

Oh, who can explain the extent of the denial our Lord wishes of us! This negation must be similar to a complete temporal, natural and spiritual death, that is, in reference to esteem of the will which is the source of all denial.

Our Saviour referred to this when He declared: He that wishes to save his life shall lose it *(if anyone wants to possess something, or seeks it for himself, he will lose it)*; and he who loses his soul for My sake, the same shall gain it. *[Mt. 16:25; Lk. 9:24] The latter affirmation signifies: He who renounces for Christ all that his will can desire and enjoy by choosing what bears closer resemblance to the cross—which our Lord in St. John terms hating one's own soul [Jn. 22:25]— the same will gain it.*

> —*The Collected Works of St. John of the Cross*, Kieran Kavanaugh and Otilio Rodriguez, trans. (Washington, D.C.: ICS Publications, 1979), 123.

9. An example of an incident in which Ramana Maharshi addresses the presumptions of a devotee is included below. A visitor to Ramana Maharshi's ashram who had been making claims of attainment entered into a dialogue with Ramana Maharshi regarding a pet squirrel in the ashram. The visitor suggested that the squirrel was probably thirsty, and Maharshi replied that it was he (the visitor) who was in need of a drink, and that he should not project his desires onto the squirrel. The visitor replied:

D[evotee]: What I did, I did not intend beforehand. It was spontaneous.
M[aharshi]: Oh! I see! Whatever we others do, we do with intention! You seem to have transcended all!
D.: This is not the first time I did so. You yourself inspire me and make me do all these things. Yet you ask me why I did it. How is it?
M.: I see. You are doing actions being controlled by me. Then the fruits also should be considered similarly to be mine and not yours.
D.: So they are undoubtedly. I act not of my free will but inspired by you. I have no will of my own.
M.: Enough of this rubbish! . . . You have risen high above the common run. We others are acting with personal will.
D.: How, Sir? You have said in one of your works that action can be automatic.
M.: Enough! Enough! You and another visitor behave as transcendental beings! You are both fully learned. You need not learn more. I would not have said all this had you not been coming here frequently. Do as you please. But these eccentricities of the beginner's stage will become known in their true light after some time.
D.: But I have been in this state for such a long time.
M.: Enough!

> —*Talks with Sri Ramana Maharshi*, 3 vols. in one, 7th ed. (Tiruvannamalai, India: Sri Ramanasramam, 1984), 157–58 (#190).

10. For descriptions of various Yogic manifestations that were demonstrated in Avatar Adi Da's "Sadhana Years", see Part One of *The Knee Of Listening*.

The Avon Lady

11. In Hindu mythology, "Lord Yama" is the King of Death.

12. Avatar Adi Da Gave this Talk in the Darshan Hall, which was located directly behind the bookstore, in His first Ashram (on Melrose Avenue in Hollywood, California). See pp. xiii, xliv–xlvii.

Money, Food, and Sex

13. Here Avatar Adi Da is making ironic use of the word "Tantric" as it is popularly understood, to mean "Spiritualized sexuality". This popularized Western notion of Tantra is actually a skewed (and markedly incomplete) interpretation of the complex Tantric tradition.

14. Avatar Adi Da has described how His years of apparent Spiritual practice were a process of Submission to "Learn" the situation of self-contracted human beings. Rudi (Swami Rudrananda) was His first human Teacher, and Rudi served Adi Da Samraj in the realm of conscious life-discipline and bodily, mental, and emotional clarity—a platform that later allowed Adi Da Samraj to pass to Rudi's own Spiritual Masters, Swami Muktananda and Bhagavan Nityananda.

15. Patanjali is honored as the originator of classical Yoga. He may have lived in the second century C.E. In his famous treatise, the *Yoga-Sutras*, Patanjali describes eight practices that make up his system of Yoga: moral observance (yama), self-discipline (niyama), posture (asana), control of the breath (pranayama), restraint of the senses (pratyahara), concentration (dharana), meditation (dhyana), and exalted states of consciousness achieved through inward concentration and meditation (samadhi).

16. For Avatar Adi Da's full Instruction in dietary discipline, please see *The Dawn Horse Testament Of The Ruchira Avatar* (Sutra 28), *Santosha Adidam,* or *Ruchira Tantra Yoga.*

17. Turning the faculties of body, emotion, mind, and breath to Avatar Adi Da is Ruchira Avatara Bhakti Yoga, the fundamental practice Given by Avatar Adi Da to all His devotees. For Avatar Adi Da's detailed Instruction on the four-part practice of Ruchira Avatara Bhakti Yoga, see the *Da Love-Ananda Gita* and *The Dawn Horse Testament* (Sutra 5).

18. Avatar Adi Da has pointed out that conventional orgasm throws off the life-energy from the body and is, therefore, degenerative. For a full discussion of Avatar Adi Da's Wisdom-Teaching relative to bypassing degenerative orgasm, see *The Dawn Horse Testament* (Sutras 37–38) or *Ruchira Tantra Yoga.*

19. Beginning practitioners in the Way of Adidam may choose either to engage a sexually active intimate relationship or to be celibate. As the devotee grows in the practice of the Way of Adidam, he or she will, in virtually all cases, become

celibate at some point—not because celibacy is an arbitrary "requirement", but because Spiritual Communion with Avatar Adi Da has become so sublime that one has no attention left over for sexual activity. For a full description of emotional-sexual practice in the Way of Adidam, see *The Dawn Horse Testament* (Sutras 37–42) or *Ruchira Tantra Yoga*.

20. For Avatar Adi Da's detailed Instruction on "true Yogic intimacy", see *The Dawn Horse Testament* (Sutra 40) or *Ruchira Tantra Yoga*. Also see **"true Yogic intimacy"** in the glossary.

21. For a complete discussion of this term, see the fourth Talk of Part Two, entitled "Vital Shock", pp. 163–97.

22. These "conscious responsible forms"—which a practitioner demonstrates as a result of full and right adaptation to the Way of Adidam—are described in detail by Avatar Adi Da in Sutra 28 of *The Dawn Horse Testament*. The forms (or disciplines), which are to be practiced in the context of the devotional relationship to Avatar Adi Da, cover the key areas of ordinary human life—including health, diet, sexuality, service, and cooperative sacred culture.

23. Avatar Adi Da Samraj has revealed the significance of the right side of the heart as the psycho-physical seat of Consciousness Itself and of attention. See glossary entry **heart / the Heart Itself / stations of the heart.**

24. "Turiya" and "turiyatita" are terms used in the Hindu philosophical systems. "Turiya" means "the fourth (state)" (beyond the three common states of waking, dreaming, and sleeping), and "turiyatita" means "(the state) beyond the fourth" (or beyond all states). The exact significance given to these terms differs between one Hindu text and another. Avatar Adi Da gives each term a unique and precise meaning—based on His Own Avataric Divine Teaching-Revelation, rather than on tradition. He uses the term "Turiya" to indicate the Awakening to the Witness-Position, beyond identification with the gross, subtle, or causal dimensions of conditionally arising existence. (The gross, subtle, and causal dimensions correspond, respectively, to the states of waking, dreaming, and sleeping.) He uses "Turiyatita" to indicate the State of Most Perfect Divine Enlightenment, or the seventh stage Realization of all arising as transparent and non-binding modifications of the One Divine Reality.

Avatar Adi Da Samraj was Born Enjoying the State of Most Perfect Divine Enlightenment, and subsequently volunteered to "forget" that State, as a method for "Learning" the human condition and how the human "problem" is to be overcome. He Re-Awakened to His Own Native Condition of Most Perfect Divine Enlightenment on September 10, 1970. Most Perfect Divine Enlightenment (or seventh stage Divine Self-Realization) is That Which is Beyond all states of conditionality—and is, therefore, "Turiyatita" (or "Beyond the Fourth"). Avatar Adi Da's Divine Re-Awakening was the first time in human history that Most Perfect (or seventh stage) Divine Enlightenment was Realized. By Means of His Avataric Divine Birth and Work here, the seventh stage Realization has become possible for all who become His formal devotees and truly practice the Way He has Revealed and Given.

Vital Shock

25. For Avatar Adi Da's description of His experience of "reliving" the prenatal state, see chapter four of *The Knee Of Listening*.

26. Avatar Adi Da's beginning devotee first embraces the devotional relationship to Him, and (simultaneously) develops a disciplined life of equanimity in the body-mind, as the means of creating the true foundation for the Spiritual relationship to Avatar Adi Da. That Spiritual relationship is entered into only in the circumstance of formal Spiritual Initiation by Avatar Adi Da, once an individual has shown the requisite signs of preparation. For a full description of the process of formal Spiritual Initiation in Avatar Adi Da's Company (including how such Initiation will take place after His physical human Lifetime), please see "No Seeking / Mere Beholding" (an Essay which appears in a number of His "Source-Texts", and also as Sutra 26 of *The Dawn Horse Testament*).

27. This discussion may be found in the fifth Talk of Part Two, entitled "Walking the Dog", pp. 199–220.

28. The Transcendentalist schools are those which, as Avatar Adi Da has Revealed, are centered in the causal dimension of existence (rather than the gross dimension or the subtle dimension). Their fundamental impulse is to "transcend" conditional existence by excluding involvement with it—thereby (it is presumed) Realizing the True Nature of That Which Transcends conditionality. The Transcendentalist schools include Advaita Vedanta, many of the schools of Buddhism, Jainism, and (in some of its manifestations) Taoism.

29. Avatar Adi Da describes the right basis for the demonstration of celibacy in *The Dawn Horse Testament* (Sutra 42) and in *Ruchira Tantra Yoga*.

30. For a full description of Avatar Adi Da's "Consideration" of emotional-sexual life-choices and practices, see *The Dawn Horse Testament* or *Ruchira Tantra Yoga*.

31. For Avatar Adi Da's extended discussion of the nature of motiveless celibacy for formal renunciate devotees in the of the Way of Adidam, please see "The Orders of My True and Free Renunciate Devotees" in *The Lion Sutra*.

32. As the emotional-sexual practice matures in the Way of Adidam, it becomes conformed to the process of receiving Avatar Adi Da's Spirit-Baptism to the degree of being fully conducted in both the frontal line and the spinal line (which latter Yogic sign is traditionally referred to as "urdhvareta", or "keeping the seed above").

33. This paragraph gives a simple, non-technical description of the process of "right emotional-sexual Yoga" in the Way of Adidam. Avatar Adi Da's full description of this process, and its four stages, is given in *The Dawn Horse Testament* (Sutra 39) and in *Ruchira Tantra Yoga*.

34. For Avatar Adi Da's "consideration" of the errors in the traditional under-standing of Kundalini and His description of the full (descending and ascending) "conductivity" of the Divine Spirit-Current, see *The Dawn Horse Testament* (Sutras 16–20) or *Ruchira Shaktipat Yoga*.

35. All members of the formal renunciate orders of Adidam are, in virtually all cases, celibate.

36. Jnaneshwar was a thirteenth-century Hindu Yogi-Saint, famous for his commentary on the *Bhagavad Gita* and his celebration of the Guru-devotee relationship.

37. The term "mahasamadhi" (meaning "great samadhi") is used to describe an Adept's release of the body at death. The term "mahasamadhi" is an acknowl-edgement that an Adept is undisturbed in his or her Realization by the event of physical death.

38. For an example of Avatar Adi Da's subtle experience of Swami Muktananda, see p. 248 of *The Knee Of Listening*.

39. This is a reference to the game of baseball, in which three "strikes" result in the player being "out" for his or her turn at bat.

Walking the Dog

40. Avatar Adi Da Samraj has often used the image of a dog running off with its bone as a form of Instruction:

> *Come to Me to Realize Me—and do not run from Me after tasting the ordinary meal of conditional knowledge and experience (like a dog runs from its master with a bone).*
> *Having Come to Me, do not look within your body or your mind to discover whether you have received some "thing" from Me (to satisfy your little pouch of separateness).*

> —Avatar Adi Da Samraj
> *Da Love-Ananda Gita*

41. Throughout the Great Tradition of religion and Spirituality, the feet of the Spiritual Master are considered sacred. Since the beginning of His Teaching-Work, Avatar Adi Da has Instructed His devotees about the sacred significance of His Feet and the Yogic process of Spiritual Transmission that occurs through His Feet.

AVATAR ADI DA SAMRAJ: What is the significance of the Guru's feet? In the relationship of the devotee to the Guru, why have the Guru's feet been given special importance?

First of all, to relate to anyone at the level of his or her feet, you yourself must assume a physical position that is different from the usual stand-up, handshaking, egoic mode. The attitude of surrender is suggested, then. That surrender is the first level of significance of this address to the Spiritual Master through the sign of his or her feet.

Another aspect of relating to the Guru through his or her feet is Yogic. The Current of Divine Transmission passes through the feet. Every aspect of the body-mind is registered in various parts of the feet. The feet are the epitome of the body. Thus, various Yogic aspects of Spiritual Transmission are epitomized in the feet of the Guru.

The feet of the Guru are the sign of the Great Principle Itself—the sign of the Heart Itself, or Reality Itself. In fact, the entire body of the Spiritual Master is to be seen in front of the heart, and, ultimately, at the heart. That Which the Spiritual Master Is, is to be Realized at the heart. This is the ultimate significance of the feet of the Spiritual Master.

—January 19, 1988

42. For a description of the disciplines Given by Avatar Adi Da to His devotees, please see *Adidam: The True World-Religion Given by the Promised God-Man, Adi Da Samraj.* See also **disciplines of Adidam** in the glossary.

The Gorilla Sermon

43. For Avatar Adi Da's "consideration" of dilemma in *The Knee Of Listening,* see pp. 299–302 of that book.

44. *Facing Death,* by Robert E. Kavanaugh (Los Angeles: Nash Publications, 1972).

45. "Wherefore do ye spend money for that which is not bread? and your labour for that which satisfieth not? hearken diligently unto me, and eat ye that which is good, and let your soul delight itself in fatness." [Isa. 55:2 (King James Version)]

46. Here Avatar Adi Da is referring to a principal aspect of His Instruction relative to Ruchira Avatara Bhakti Yoga, the fundamental practice for His devotees. In any moment, His devotee can always turn the principal faculties of the body-mind (attention, feeling, body, and breath) to Him—regardless of what content might be arising in the form of thoughts, emotions, sensations, and so forth.

Meditation and Satsang

47. Once a devotee (necessarily, during a period of extended formal retreat in Avatar Adi Da's physical Company) has been Spiritually Initiated by Avatar Adi Da into the practice of searchlessly Beholding Him (in the intensive listening-hearing stage of practice in the Way of Adidam), the individual should engage periods of retreat in Avatar Adi Da's physical Company as frequently as possible—as a principal means of deepening his or her devotional and (now) Spiritual relationship to Avatar Adi Da Samraj and participation in the culture of access to His Avataric Divine Company. After Avatar Adi Da's physical Lifetime, such retreats will be engaged in the company and by-Him-Spiritually-Empowered Circumstances of His "Ruchira sannyasin" devotees.

48. "Run, Spot, run" is a famous sentence from a reading primer that was first published in the U.S. in the 1940s.

49. "Our Father" is a reference to the Christian "Lord's Prayer". "Ram" (or "Rama") is a "Name of God", used in Hindu worship and meditation. "Om Mani Padme Hum" is a mantra used in the Tibetan Buddhist tradition.

50. In the language of His Wisdom-Teaching, Avatar Adi Da has given specific definitions to the terms "Yogi", "Saint", and "Sage":

> *"Yogis" are . . . those who are truly (or really and rightly) practicing in the stages of Spiritual ascent, and true "Saints" are those who are already established in the highest (ascended) contemplative Realization, and "Sages" are those who have gone beyond the psycho-physical context of the first five stages of life, and who have Realized the sixth stage Awakening.*
>
> —*The Basket Of Tolerance*

51. For Avatar Adi Da's description of this period in His early Life, see chapter three of *The Knee Of Listening*.

One-"Point"-edness

52. The rightly prepared devotee receives Avatar Adi Da's Spiritual Initiation in the context of an extended retreat in His physical Company (or after His physical Lifetime, in the company and by-Him-Spiritually-Empowered Circumstances of His "Ruchira sannyasin" devotees). For Avatar Adi Da's detailed Instruction regarding this process, see the Essay "No Seeking / Mere Beholding", which appears in a number of Avatar Adi Da's "Source-Texts" (including *Da Love-Ananda Gita*), and as Sutra 26 of *The Dawn Horse Testament*).

53. For Avatar Adi Da's extended Instruction relative to the "cultic" tendency of egos, see "Do Not Misunderstand <u>Me</u>", pp. 3–22.

The Path of the Great Form

54. Avatar Adi Da has described Communion with Him as the True "Round Dance", indicating that He is always Presently available to "Dance" with each and every one of His devotees in the Circle of the life-force (and also of His Avatarically Self-Transmitted Divine Spirit-Energy). For further discussion of this "Round Dance", see "Do Not Misunderstand <u>Me</u>", pp. 3–22.

55. Avatar Adi Da has distinguished three stations of the heart, associated with the left, middle, and right sides of the chest. For His detailed description of these three stations, see Sutra 21 (p. 379) and Sutra 47 (pp. 882–83) in *The Dawn Horse Testament*. See also glossary entry **heart / the Heart Itself / stations of the heart**.

56. For Avatar Adi Da's description of the Yogic purificatory process of kriyas in His own "Sadhana Years", see chapters nine and ten of *The Knee Of Listening*.

Phases

57. Avatar Adi Da is referring here to His uniquely comprehensive examination of the Great Tradition of religious and Spiritual Instruction—which examination He presents (in fully elaborated form) in *The Basket Of Tolerance*.

> . . . *every one (and every tradition or tribe) must responsibly examine the Great Tradition that all have inherited. And, by this widest view, every one (and every tradition or tribe) must understand and transcend the provincialism (or the narrow look) of every merely local (or limited, and non-universal) inheritance (or view). Indeed, by all of this (and by signs of speech and action), every one (and all) must, for the sake of all, promote the culture of true (universal) tolerance—which understands (and positively allows) all temporary views, and which Calls every one (and every culture) to true (critical) self-study, and to constant self-transcendence (or Out-Growing of self, and all, and All), and would (at last) be Given the Gift of an even Most Perfect Understanding (of self, and all, and All).*
> —"The Collective (Exoteric *and* Esoteric) Gathering of the Great Tradition",
> from *The Basket Of Tolerance*

58. For Avatar Adi Da's description of this period of His Life, please see chapter one in *The Knee Of Listening*.

59. In His use of "My" in this sentence, Avatar Adi Da is referring to His gross bodily vehicle, Franklin Jones (and its associated patterns), which He was Working with and Purifying at the time. Avatar Adi Da Himself is not an ego, and (therefore) has no such karmic patterning.

60. Avatar Adi Da has designated the Ruchira Sannyasin Order of Adidam as the senior cultural authority within the gathering of His devotees—both during and after His physical Lifetime. The Ruchira Sannyasin Order is the body of Avatar Adi Da's "Perfect Practice" devotees who demonstrate uniquely exemplary practice of the Way of Adidam and who have chosen to devote their lives utterly to Him and His Way—by embracing the life of formal renunciation, in the circumstance of perpetual retreat. It is the unique responsibility of the Ruchira Sannyasin Order to function both as the extension of Avatar Adi Da's Sacred Authority and as His Instrumentality (or the collective human "conduit" for His Spiritual Blessing).

61. Rom. 8:28 (King James Version).

62. In Radhakrishnan's translation of the *Brhadaranyaka Upanishad*, this sentence reads: "Assuredly it is from a second that fear arises," where "second" is used in the sense of "other". [*The Principal Upanisads,* edited, with introduction, text, translation, and notes, by S. Radhakrishnan (Atlantic Highlands, N.J.: Humanities Press, 1992), 164.]

EPILOGUE

63. Avatar Adi Da has Given explicit Instruction relative to how His Spiritual Heart-Blessing is to be magnified and made available beyond His physical Lifetime. See Sutra 9 of *The Dawn Horse Testament*.

64. Here Avatar Adi Da is describing, in poetic terms, the process of Initiation into the fully technically responsible Spiritual practice in His Company. Avatar Adi Da describes the crown of the head as the "Doorway" opening into the Spiritual dimension of existence (Above and Beyond the conditional realms). When this Doorway opens (by Means of Avatar Adi Da's Divine Spiritual Grace), then one enters the Spiritually Awakened practice in His Company. Previous to this Initiation, the devotee must already be established in the practice of searchless Beholding of Avatar Adi Da. See *Hridaya Rosary* for Avatar Adi Da's complete Instruction on the fully technically responsible Spiritual practice in His Company.

GLOSSARY

A

Adi—Sanskrit for "first", "primordial", "source"—also "primary", "beginning". Thus, the Divine Name "Adi Da" expresses the Truth that Avatar Adi Da is the Primordial Being, the Source of all, the Original Divine Person, Da.

Adidam—When Avatar Adi Da Samraj first Gave the name "Adidam" in January 1996, He pointed out that the final "m" adds a mantric force, evoking the effect of the primal Sanskrit syllable "Om". (For Avatar Adi Da's Revelation of the most profound esoteric significance of "Om" as the Divine Sound of His own Very Being, see Sutra 46 of *The Dawn Horse Testament*.) Simultaneously, the final "m" suggests the English word "Am" (expressing "I Am"), such that the Name "Adidam" also evokes Avatar Adi Da's Primal Self-Confession, "I Am Adi Da", or, more simply, "I Am Da" (or, in Sanskrit, "Aham Da Asmi").

Advaita Vedanta—Vedanta is the principal philosophical tradition of Hinduism. "Advaita" means "non-dual". Advaita Vedanta, then, is a philosophy of non-dualism. Its origins lie in the ancient esoteric Teaching that the Divine Being is the only Reality. According to Advaita Vedanta, the self and the world have no independent existence but merely arise in that one Divine Reality.

Aham Da Asmi—Sanskrit phrase meaning "I (Aham) Am (Asmi) Da". Avatar Adi Da's Avatarically Self-Revealed Divine Name, "Da" (meaning "the One Who Gives"), indicates that Avatar Adi Da Samraj is the Supreme Divine Giver, the Avataric Incarnation of the Very Divine Person.

Ajna Chakra / Ajna Door—The subtle center (or chakra) which Avatar Adi Da Samraj defines as "The Root Of The Brain Core, Between and Slightly Above and Deep Behind the brows" (Sutra 18 of *The Dawn Horse Testament*).

all-and-All—A phrase Avatar Adi Da has created to describe the totality of conditional existence—both as the "sum of its parts" and as an undivided whole. He defines lower-case "all" as indicating "the collected sum of all Presumed To Be Separate (or limited) beings, things, and conditions", and upper-case "All" as indicating "The All (or The Undivided Totality) Of conditional Existence As A Whole".

Amrita Nadi—Amrita Nadi is Sanskrit for "Channel (or Current, or Nerve) of Ambrosia (or Immortal Nectar)". Amrita Nadi is the ultimate "organ", or root-structure, of the body-mind, Realized as such (in Its "Regenerated" form) in the seventh stage of life in the Way of Adidam.

In *The Dawn Horse Testament*, Avatar Adi Da defines Amrita Nadi as "The Ultimate Yogic Form", "The 'Bright' Fullness That Stands Between The Right Side Of The Heart and The Felt Matrix Of Sound and Light (or Of Even Unheard and Unseen Radiance, or Infinitely Ascended Love-Bliss) Infinitely Above The Total Crown Of the head" (Sutra 16), and as "The Apparent Organ Of This 'Bright' Divine Awakening In the human individual" (Sutra 21).

anahata chakra—See **heart / the Heart Itself / stations of the heart**.

asana—Sanskrit for bodily "posture" or "pose". Most commonly, Avatar Adi Da uses "asana" in an extended sense of the word, which He defines in Sutra 5 of *The Dawn Horse Testament* as "Total psycho-physical Attitude, or

Disposition"—the attitude, orientation, posture, or feeling disposition of the heart and the entire body-mind.

Atman—Sanskrit for Supreme Divine Self.

Avatar—From Sanskrit "avatara", a traditional term for a Divine Incarnation. It literally means "One who is descended, or 'crossed down' (from, and as, the Divine)". Avatar Adi Da Samraj Confesses that, simultaneous with His human Birth, He has Incarnated in every world, at every level of the cosmic domain, as the Eternal Giver of Divine Help and Divine Grace and Divine Liberation to all beings—and that, even though His bodily (human) Lifetime is necessarily limited in duration, His Spiritual Incarnation in the cosmic domain is Eternal.

Avataric Divine Self-"Emergence"—On January 11, 1986, Avatar Adi Da passed through a profound Yogic Swoon, Which He later described as the Yogic Establishment of His Avataric Divine Self-"Emergence". Avatar Adi Da's Avataric Divine Self-"Emergence" is an ongoing Process in which His Avatarically-Born bodily (human) Divine Form has been (and is ever more profoundly and potently being) conformed to Himself, the Very Divine Person, such that His bodily (human) Form is now (and forever hereafter) an utterly Unobstructed Sign and Agent of His own Divine Being. For Avatar Adi Da's extended description of His Avataric Divine Self-"Emergence", see Part Three of *The Knee Of Listening*.

Avataric Incarnation / Avataric Divine Incarnation—The Divinely Descended Embodiment of the Divine Person. The reference "Avataric Incarnation" indicates that Avatar Adi Da Samraj fulfills both the traditional expectation of the East, that the True God-Man is an Avatar (or an utterly Divine "Descent" of Real God in

conditionally manifested form), and the traditional expectation of the West, that the True God-Man is an Incarnation (or an utterly human Embodiment of Real God).

B

Baba Muktananda—See **Lineage-Gurus, Avatar Adi Da's**.

Beloved—A Title of intimate respect and heart-acknowledgement.

Bhagavan—The Title "Bhagavan" is an ancient one used over the centuries for many Spiritual Realizers of India. It means "blessed" or "holy" in Sanskrit. When applied to a great Spiritual Being, "Bhagavan" is understood to mean "bountiful Lord", or "Great Lord", or "Divine Lord".

Bhagavan Nityananda—See **Lineage-Gurus, Avatar Adi Da's**.

Blessing-Work—The profound Purpose and Activity of Avatar Adi Da's Avataric Divine Incarnation—to Spiritually Bless all beings and (ultimately) to Awaken them to His "Bright" Divine Spherical Self-Domain.

"Bond" / "Bonded"—Avatar Adi Da uses the word "bond" in two different senses: (1) as a reference to the process by which the egoic individual (already presuming separateness, and, therefore, bondage to the separate self) attaches itself karmically to the world of others and things through the constant search for self-fulfillment; and (2) as a reference to the process of His devotee's devotional "Bonding" to Him, which process is the Great Means for transcending all forms of limited (or karmic) "bonding".

The term is placed in quotation marks to indicate that it is used by Avatar Adi Da in the two particular senses described here.

Brahman—In the Hindu tradition, Brahman is the Ultimate Divine Reality that is the Source and Substance of all things, all worlds, and all beings.

"Bright"—By the word "Bright" (and its variations, such as "Brightness"), Avatar Adi Da refers to the Self-Existing and Self-Radiant Divine Reality that He has Revealed since His Birth. Avatar Adi Da Named His own Divine Self-Condition "the 'Bright'" in His Infancy, as soon as He acquired the capability of language.

This term is placed in quotation marks to indicate that Avatar Adi Da uses it with the specific meaning described here.

C

causal—See **gross, subtle, causal**.

chiliocosm—A Mahayana Buddhist term for "universe multiplied countless times".

Circle / Circuit—The Circle (which Adi Da sometimes refers to in this text as a "Circuit") is a primary pathway of natural life-energy and the Divine Spirit-Energy in the body-mind. It is composed of two arcs: the descending Current, which flows through the frontal line—down the front of the body, from the crown of the head to the bodily base—and which corresponds to the gross dimension of the body-mind; and the ascending Current, which flows through the spinal line—up the back of the body, from the bodily base to the crown of the head—and which corresponds to the subtle dimension of the body-mind.

"conductivity" / "Conductivity"—Avatar Adi Da's technical term for participation in (and responsibility for) the movement of natural bodily energies (and, when one is Spiritually Awakened by Him, for the movement of His Divine

Spirit-Current in Its natural course of association with the body-mind), via intentional exercises of feeling and breathing. In *The Dawn Horse Testament,* Avatar Adi Da defines "conductivity" as "The Whole bodily (physical, emotional, and mental) 'Conscious Exercise' Of breath, bodily energy, and (In Due Course) My Avatarically Self-Transmitted Divine Spirit-Force" (Sutra 3—punctuation adjusted).

Avatar Adi Da's principal Instruction relative to "conductivity" is Given by Him in Sutra 36 (for "general conductivity") and Sutras 18–20 (for Spirit-"Conductivity") of *The Dawn Horse Testament.*

The term "conductivity" is placed in quotation marks to indicate that Avatar Adi Da uses it with the specific technical meaning described here. When capitalized, "Conductivity" refers to the Divinely Enlightened process of "conductivity" of Avatar Adi Da's Divine Spirit-Energy.

"conscious process"—Avatar Adi Da's technical term for those practices through which the mind (or attention) is surrendered and turned about—from egoic self-involvement to feeling-Contemplation of Him. In *The Dawn Horse Testament,* Avatar Adi Da defines the "conscious process" as "The Devotional Surrender Of attention To Me, Such That attention Is (Thus and Thereby) Absorbed (and, Ultimately, Dissolved, or Utterly Transcended) In Me" (Sutra 18—punctuation adjusted).

This term is placed in quotation marks to indicate that Avatar Adi Da uses it with the specific technical meaning described here.

"consideration"—Avatar Adi Da uses this word to refer to "a process of one-pointed (but, ultimately, thoughtless) concentration and exhaustive contemplation of a particular object, function, person, process, or condition, until the essence or ultimate obviousness of that object is clear" [*Love of the Two-Armed*

Form]. (Such a process was originally described by Patanjali, in his *Yoga Sutras*, as "samyama".)

This term is placed in quotation marks to indicate that Avatar Adi Da uses it with the specific technical meaning described here.

As engaged in the Way of Adidam, "consideration" is not merely an intellectual investigation. It is the participatory investment of one's whole being. If one "considers" something fully—in the context of one's practice of Ruchira Avatara Bhakti Yoga and one's study of Avatar Adi Da's Wisdom-Teaching—this concentration results "in both the deepest intuition and the most practical grasp of the Lawful and Divine necessities of human existence" [*Love of the Two-Armed Form*].

Crashes Down—Avatar Adi Da's Divine Spirit-Force "Descending Utterly, From The 'Place' Infinitely Above the body-mind and the world, Down and Most Deeply Into the body-mind and the world—Even To The Degree That the ego-'I', or self-Contraction, Is Utterly Confounded, Utterly Yielded, and Utterly Vanished In My Avatarically Self-Revealed, and Self-Evidently Divine, Person, or Self-Condition, Which Is Real God, and Truth, and Reality" (Sutra 45 of *The Dawn Horse Testament*).

Avatar Adi Da Underscores the Primary Importance of His Crashing Down by Confessing that, "My Avataric Divine Spiritual Work (Altogether) Is My Crashing-Down Descent, At First Upon and Into My Own Avatarically-Born Bodily (Human) Divine Form, and, Thereafter (and Now, and Forever Hereafter), Upon and Into the body-minds Of My Devotees and all beings—Even (By Means Of My Divine Embrace Of each, and all, and All) To Infuse and (At Last) To Divinely Translate each, and all, and All" (Sutra 45 of *The Dawn Horse Testament*).

"Crazy"—Avatar Adi Da has always Worked in a unique "Crazy" Manner,

which, during His "Sadhana Years" and His Years of Teaching and Revelation, involved His Submission to the limited conditions of humankind, in order to reflect His devotees to themselves, and thereby Awaken self-understanding in them (relative to their individual egoic dramas, and the collective egoic dramas of human society). See Sutra 10 of *The Dawn Horse Testament*.

This term is placed in quotation marks to indicate that Avatar Adi Da uses it with the specific meaning described here (rather than any of the more commonly accepted general meanings).

"create" / "Creator"—Avatar Adi Da Samraj places the word "create" (and its variants) in quotation marks when He wishes to indicate the sense of "so to speak"—Communicating that, in the Indivisible Unity of Reality, any particular "thing" is not truly (but only apparently) appearing "out of nothing" or being caused to appear (or "created").

D

Da—Avatar Adi Da's Divine Name "Da" means "The One Who Gives", or "The Divine Giver". This Name was spontaneously Revealed to Avatar Adi Da as His Principal Divine Name—and it is a syllable with great sacred significance in various cultures. Tibetan Buddhists regard the syllable "Da" (written, in Tibetan, with a single letter) as most auspicious, and they assign numerous sacred meanings to it, including "Entrance into the Dharma". In the most ancient of the Upanishads (the *Brihadaranyaka Upanishad*), the Divine Being gives the fundamental instruction necessary for each of the different classes of living beings by uttering the single sound "Da". (Each class of beings understands "Da" in the manner uniquely necessary in their case.) In this passage, "Da" is said to be the Divine Voice that can be heard speaking through thunder (S. Radhakrishnan, trans., *The Principal Upanishads* [Atlantic Highlands, N.J.: Humanities Press International, First paperback edition, 1992], 289–290).

Darshan—"Darshan" (the Hindi derivative of Sanskrit "darshana") literally means "seeing", "sight of", or "vision of". To receive Darshan of Avatar Adi Da is, most fundamentally, to behold His bodily (human) Divine Form (either by being in His physical Company or by seeing a photograph or other visual representation of Him), and (thereby) to receive the spontaneous Divine Blessing He Grants Freely whenever His bodily (human) Form is beheld in the devotional manner. In the Way of Adidam, Darshan of Avatar Adi Da is the very essence of the practice.

Devotional Way of Insight—One of two variant forms of the "conscious process" Given by Avatar Adi Da, as described by Him in Sutra 6 of *The Dawn Horse Testament* (the other is the Devotional Way of Faith). Both Devotional Ways require the exercise of insight <u>and</u> faith, but there is a difference in emphasis.

In the Devotional Way of Insight, the practitioner of Adidam engages the practice of self-Enquiry (in the form "Avoiding relationship?"). The practice of self-Enquiry (which gradually becomes non-verbal Re-cognition) is a specific technical process of observing, understanding, and feeling beyond the self-contraction, as the principal technical element of his or her practice of the "conscious process". Practitioners of the Devotional Way of Insight maintain the practice of self-Enquiry (and non-verbal Re-cognition) as their form of the "conscious process" until the transition to the "Perfect Practice" (at which point all practitioners of the Way of Adidam engage "Feeling-Enquiry" as their sole form of the "conscious process" in formal meditation and their principal form of the "conscious process" in daily life).

In the Devotional Way of Faith, the practitioner of Adidam engages the practice of "true prayer", which is a specific technical process of magnifying his or her heart-Attraction to Avatar Adi Da, as the principal technical element of his or her practice of the "conscious process". "True prayer" is practiced in the form of Ruchira Avatara Naama Japa in the student-beginner stage, the intensive listening-hearing stage, and the would-be-seeing stage, and in the form of the Prayer of Remembrance in the first actually seeing stage.

dharma—Sanskrit for "duty", "virtue", "law". The word "dharma" is commonly used to refer to the many esoteric paths by which human beings seek the Truth. In its fullest sense, and when capitalized, "Dharma" means the complete fulfillment of duty—the living of the Divine Law. By extension, "Dharma" means a truly great Spiritual Teaching, including its disciplines and practices.

"difference"—The epitome of the egoic presumption of separateness—in contrast with the Realization of Oneness, or Non-"Difference", Which is Native to the Divine Self-Condition. This term is placed in quotation marks to indicate that Avatar Adi Da uses it in the "so to speak" sense. He is Communicating (by means of the quotation marks) that, in Reality, there is no such thing as "difference", even though it appears to be the case from the point of view of ordinary human perception.

disciplines of Adidam—The most basic <u>functional</u>, <u>practical</u>, and <u>relational disciplines</u> of the Way of Adidam are forms of appropriate human action and responsibility in relation to diet, health, exercise, sexuality, work, service to and support of Avatar Adi Da's Circumstance and Work, and cooperative association with other practitioners of the Way of Adidam. The most basic <u>cultural obligations</u> of the Way of Adidam include meditation, sacramental worship, study of Avatar Adi Da's Wisdom-Teaching (and also at least a basic discriminative study of the Great Tradition of religion and Spirituality that is the Wisdom-inheritance of humankind), and regular participation in the "form" (or schedule) of daily, weekly, monthly, and annual devotional activities and retreats.

Divine "Bright" Spherical Self-Domain / Divine Domain—See Self-Domain, Divine "Bright" Spherical.

Divine Enlightenment—The Realization of the seventh stage of life, which is uniquely Revealed and Given by Avatar Adi Da. It is Eternal Self-Abiding in His "Bright" (and Infinitely Love-Bliss-Full) Divine Self-Condition, released from all the egoic limitations of the first six stages of life. The seventh stage Awakening is Avatar Adi Da's Gift to His rightly prepared devotee who has fulfilled the entire sadhana of the Way of Adidam in the context of the first six stages of life.

Divine Heart-Master—A reference to the Spiritual Mastery of the devotee's heart by Avatar Adi Da Samraj, and also to Avatar Adi Da Himself, Who Is the True Divine Heart Itself.

Divine "Madness"—Adi Da Samraj sometimes uses the term "Madness" in reference to the Perfect Freedom and utterly self-less (or egoless) Nature of Divine Self-Realization. See also **"Crazy"**.

Divine Re-Awakening—For Avatar Adi Da's account of His Divine Re-Awakening, see pp. 317–22 of *The Knee Of Listening*.

Divine Self-Realization—See **Divine Enlightenment**.

Divine Self-Recognition—Divine Self-Recognition is the ego-transcending and world-transcending Intelligence of the Divine Self-Condition in relation to all conditional phenomena. The devotee of Avatar Adi Da who Realizes the seventh stage of life simply Abides as Self-Existing and Self-Radiant Consciousness Itself, and he or she Freely Self-Recognizes (or inherently and instantly and most perfectly comprehends and perceives) all phenomena (including body, mind, conditional self, and conditional world) as transparent (or merely apparent), and un-necessary, and inherently non-binding modifications of the same "Bright" Divine Self-Consciousness.

Divine World-Teacher—Avatar Adi Da Samraj is the Divine World-Teacher because His Wisdom-Teaching is the uniquely Perfect Instruction to every being—in this (and every) world—relative to the total process of Divine Enlightenment. Furthermore, Avatar Adi Da Samraj constantly Extends His Regard to the entire world (and the entire cosmic domain)—not on the political or social level, but as a Spiritual matter, constantly Working to Bless and Purify all beings everywhere.

Divinely Translate—Avatar Adi Da has Revealed that the Awakening to the seventh stage of life is not an "end-point" but is (rather) the beginning of the final Spiritual process. One of the unique aspects of Avatar Adi Da's Revelation is His precise description of the seventh stage process as consisting of four phases. "Translate" is a reference to the fourth and final phase of the seventh stage of life.

The Final Sign (or Demonstration) Of The Only-By-Me Revealed and Given Seventh Stage Of Life (and Of The Total Practice Of The Only-By-Me Revealed and Given Way Of The Heart) Is The Great Event Of <u>Divine</u> <u>Translation</u>— Which Is . . . The Process Of Transition To (or "Dawning" <u>As</u>) My Divine Self-Domain Via The Divinely "Bright" Outshining Of The Cosmic Domain In The Only-By-Me Revealed and Given Divine Sphere and Sign Of The

"Midnight Sun" (Most Perfectly Above and Beyond all-and-All Of Cosmic, or conditional, forms, beings, signs, conditions, relations, and things).

—Avatar Adi Da Samraj
Sutra 21 of *The Dawn Horse Testament*

E

ego-"I"—The fundamental activity of self-contraction, or the presumption of separate and separative existence.

The "I" is placed in quotation marks to indicate that it is used by Avatar Adi Da in the "so to speak" sense. He is Communicating (by means of the quotation marks) that, in Reality, there is no such thing as the separate "I", even though it appears to be the case from the point of view of ordinary human perception.

En-Light-en / En-Light-enment—Divine Enlightenment (or Most Perfect Real-God-Realization) is a matter of the actual conversion of the body-mind to the State of Divine Conscious Light Itself. Avatar Adi Da sometimes writes the noun "Enlightenment" (and also the verb "Enlighten") with "Light" set apart by hyphens, in order to emphasize this point.

Enstasy—Avatar Adi Da uses "Enstasy" (and its variants) in the sense of "standing (stasis) in (en-)" the Divine Self-Condition. He defines Divine "Enstasy" as "The Native Condition Of Standing Unconditionally <u>As</u> The By-Me-Avatarically-Self-Revealed Transcendental, Inherently Spiritual, Inherently egoless, and Self-Evidently Divine Self-Condition Itself".

"evolution" / "evolutionary"—Avatar Adi Da uses the term "evolution" and its variants to indicate the goal-oriented struggle to fulfill the potential of the human body-mind, or the "great path of return".

These terms are placed in quotation marks in the sense of "so to speak", thereby indicating the false presumption that Real-God-Realization is based on a necessary evolution by means of the "great path of return" rather than directly living on the basis of present-time relationship with the Divine.

F

faculties—Body, emotion (or feeling), mind (or attention), and breath. These four principal faculties account for the entirety of the human being. The practice of Ruchira Avatara Bhakti Yoga (or heart-Communion with Avatar Adi Da) is, fundamentally, the moment to moment turning of the four principal faculties to Him.

Feeling of Being—The uncaused and unqualified feeling-intuition of the Divine Self-Condition. In "The ego-'I' Is the Illusion of Relatedness" (in *Santosha Adidam*), Avatar Adi Da describes the Feeling of Being as "the Great Heart-Feeling in Which the feeling of relatedness is arising".

feeling-Contemplation—Avatar Adi Da's term for the essential devotional and meditative practice that all practitioners of the Way of Adidam engage at all times in relationship to Him.

Form, Presence, and State—Avatar Adi Da Samraj has Revealed that He Exists simultaneously in three Avataric Divine Forms—physical (His bodily human Form), Spiritual (His Spiritual Presence), and the Formlessness of Self-Existing and Self-Radiant Consciousness Itself (His Very State). The fundamental practice of feeling-Contemplating Him includes feeling-Contemplation of all three aspects of His Being—always (from the very beginning of the practice of the Way of Adidam through the seventh stage of life) founded in devotional recognition-response to His Avatarically-Born bodily (human) Divine Form and Person.

"Fourth State"—See **"Turiya"** / **"Turiyatita"**.

frontal line—The subtle energy-pathway in the human structure (extending from the crown of the head to the bodily base) through which both the natural life-energy and the Divine Spirit-Energy flow downward (or in a descending direction).

G

"great path of return"—Avatar Adi Da characterizes the traditional religious and Spiritual paths of the first six stages of life as the "great path of return" because the traditional points of view associated with the first six stages of life regard the "goal" of the Spiritual path to be somewhere "else" than "here". In other words, it is traditionally presumed that the Spiritual Way is a matter of following a "great path" by which the aspirant will "return" from "here" to the "place" that is regarded to be the "goal" (or "home").

Right practice of the Way of Adidam, on the other hand, is not a matter of seeking to reach any of the "goals" of the first six stages of life, but is (rather) a matter of practicing (progressively) in the context of the first six stages of life, while persistently observing, understanding, and transcending all forms of motivated seeking as they arise.

Great Tradition—Avatar Adi Da's term for the total inheritance of human, cultural, religious, magical, mystical, Spiritual, and Transcendental paths, philosophies, and testimonies, from all the eras and cultures of humanity—which inheritance has (in the present era of worldwide communication) become the common legacy of humankind. Avatar Adi Da's Divine Self-Revelation and Wisdom-Teaching Fulfills and Completes the Great Tradition.

gross, subtle, causal—Avatar Adi Da (in agreement with certain esoteric schools in the Great Tradition) describes conditional existence as having three fundamental dimensions—gross, subtle, and causal.

"Gross" means "made up of material (or physical) elements". The gross (or physical) dimension is, therefore, associated with the physical body. The gross dimension is also associated with experience in the waking state and, as Avatar Adi Da Reveals, with the frontal line of the body-mind and with the left side of the heart (or the gross physical heart).

The subtle dimension, which is senior to and pervades the gross dimension, consists of the etheric (or personal life-energy) functions, the lower mental functions (including the conscious mind, the subconscious mind, and the unconscious mind) and higher mental functions (of discriminative mind, mentally presumed egoity, and will), and is associated with experience in the dreaming state. In the human psycho-physical structure, the subtle dimension is primarily associated with the middle station of the heart (or the heart chakra), the spinal line, the brain core, and the subtle centers of mind in the higher brain.

The causal dimension is senior to both the gross and the subtle dimensions. It is the root of attention, or the root-sense of existence as a separate self. The causal dimension is associated with the right side of the heart, specifically with the sinoatrial node, or "pacemaker" (the psycho-physical source of the heartbeat). Its corresponding state of consciousness is the formless awareness of deep sleep.

Guru-Bhakti—Devotion (bhakti) to the Guru.

Guru-Kripa—The Guru's Transmission of Spirit-Force (Kripa).

501

H

Hatha Yoga—The traditional practice of exercising the body (through certain defined poses, or asanas) and the breath, for the purpose of growth toward Spiritual liberation.

hearing—See **listening, hearing, and seeing**.

heart / the Heart Itself / stations of the heart—Avatar Adi Da distinguishes three stations of the heart, associated (respectively) with the right side, the middle station (traditionally called the "anahata chakra"), and the left side of the heart region of the chest. He Reveals that these stations are the loci (or focal points of living origination) of the causal body, the subtle body, and the gross body (respectively). Avatar Adi Da Teaches (as foreshadowed in certain rare sixth stage texts) that the primal psycho-physical seat of Consciousness and of attention is associated with what He calls the "right side of the heart". He has Revealed that this center (which is neither the heart chakra nor the gross physical heart) corresponds to the sinoatrial node (or "pacemaker"), the source of the gross physical heartbeat in the right atrium (or upper right chamber) of the physical heart. In the Event of Divine Self-Realization, there is a unique process in which the ego-knot in the right side of the heart is released—and it is because of this connection between the right side of the heart and Divine Self-Realization that Avatar Adi Da uses the term "the Heart" as another form of reference to the Divine Self-Condition.

The Heart Itself, or the True Divine Heart, Is Real God, the Divine Self-Condition, the Divine Reality. The True Divine Heart is not "in" the right side of the human heart, nor is it "in" (or limited to) the human heart as a whole. Rather, the human heart and body-mind and the world exist <u>in</u> the True Divine Heart, Which <u>Is</u> Avatar Adi Da Samraj's Divine Being.

heart-Communion—The practice of Invoking and feeling Avatar Adi Da Samraj. It is "communion" in the sense that, in the bliss of that state, the individual loses the sense of separate self, and is (thus) "communing intimately" (in a most profound and non-dual manner) with Avatar Adi Da Samraj.

heart on the right—See **heart / the Heart Itself / stations of the heart**.

heart-recognize / heart-respond—The entire practice of the Way of Adidam is founded in devotional heart-recognition of, and devotional heart-response to, Ruchira Avatar Adi Da Samraj as the Very Divine Being in Person.

The fundamental heart-response to Me (which, necessarily, coincides with heart-recognition of Me) is the only-by-Me Revealed and Given practice of Ruchira Avatara Bhakti Yoga, Which is the moment to moment (devotionally Me-recognizing, and devotionally to-Me-responding) turning of the four principal faculties—of body, emotion (or feeling), mind (or attention), and breath—to Me (in and <u>As</u> My Avatarically-Born bodily human Divine Form and Person).

—Avatar Adi Da Samraj
Hridaya Rosary

horizontal plane—Avatar Adi Da refers to the structural anatomy of the heart (including its three stations) as the "horizontal" dimension (or plane) of the human body-mind (in contrast to the "vertical" dimension). See also **heart / the Heart Itself / stations of the heart**.

Hridaya-Kripa—See **Ruchira Avatara Kripa / Hridaya-Kripa**.

Hridaya-Shakti—See **Ruchira Shakti / Hridaya-Shakti**.

I

"intoxicated"—To be "intoxicated" with Avatar Adi Da's Divine Love-Bliss is to be drawn beyond the usual egoic self and egoic mind into a state of ecstatic devotional Communion (and Identification) with Him. This term is enclosed in quotations marks in order to distinguish it from the common meaning of "intoxication" (such as with alcohol).

J

Jnana Yoga—The traditional Advaitic practice of discriminating between what is Real (the One Reality, or Divine Self) and what is illusory (the passing phenomena of experience). The practice of this Yoga potentially becomes Identification with Consciousness as the Transcendental Witness of all that arises.

Jnani—One who has fulfilled the process of Jnana Yoga.

K

knots—Previous to Most Perfect Divine Enlightenment, the gross, subtle, and causal dimensions are expressed in the body-mind as characteristic knots. The knot of the gross dimension is associated with the region of the navel. The knot of the subtle dimension is associated with the midbrain, or the ajna center (directly behind and between the brows). And the knot of the causal dimension (or the causal knot) is associated with the sinoatrial node (or "pacemaker") on the right side of the heart. The causal knot is the primary root of the self-contraction, the "original egoic contraction, the natural vibration inherently associated with conditional 'I'-feeling (or the feeling of relatedness), and also naturally associated with the right side of the heart" (*Santosha Adidam*, "The ego-'I' Is the Illusion of

Relatedness"). See also **heart / the Heart Itself / stations of the heart**.

Krishna—The legendary Divine Avatar (worshipped by many Hindus) who is the hero of the *Bhagavad Gita* (and the longer *Mahabharata*, in which the *Bhagavad Gita* appears) and the *Srimad Bhagavatam*.

"kriya shakti"—See **kriyas**.

kriyas—Spontaneous, self-purifying movements "of body, emotion, mind, and breath" (Sutra 18 of *The Dawn Horse Testament*).

Kriya Yoga—A system of practice developed from the traditional techniques of Kundalini Yoga, which seeks to activate the ascent of the Kundalini energy in the body.

Kundalini / Kundalini Shakti—The energy traditionally viewed to lie dormant at the base of the spine—the muladhara chakra, or lowermost psychic center of the body-mind.

Kundalini Yoga—A tradition of Yogic techniques in which practice is devoted to awakening the internal energy processes, which bring about subtle experiences and blisses. But, as Adi Da has indicated, the true manifestation of Spiritual Awakening is spontaneous, a Grace Given in the Company of a True Siddha-Guru, and in the midst of an entire life of practice in his or her Company.

L

"late-time" (or "dark" epoch)—A phrase that Avatar Adi Da uses to describe the present era—in which doubt of God (and of anything at all beyond mortal existence) is more and more pervading the entire world, and the self-interest of the separate individual is more and more regarded to be the ultimate principle of life.

These terms include quotation marks to indicate that they are used by Avatar Adi Da in the "so to speak" sense. In this case, He is Communicating (by means of the quotation marks) that, in Reality, the "darkness" of this apparent "late-time" is not Reality, or Truth, but only an appearance from the point of view of ordinary human perception.

Leela—Sanskrit for "play", or "sport". In many religious and Spiritual traditions, all of conditionally manifested existence is regarded to be the Leela (or the Play, Sport, or Free Activity) of the Divine Person. "Leela" also refers to the Awakened Play of a Realized Adept (of any real degree), through which he or she mysteriously Instructs and Liberates others and Blesses the world itself. By extension, a Leela is an instructive and inspiring story of such an Adept's Teaching and Blessing Play.

life-conditions—See **disciplines of Adidam**.

Lineage-Gurus, Avatar Adi Da's—The principal Spiritual Masters who served Avatar Adi Da Samraj during His "Sadhana Years" belong to a single Lineage of extraordinary Yogis, whose Parama-Guru (Supreme Guru) was the Divine "Goddess" (or "Mother-Shakti").

Swami Rudrananda (1928–1973), or Albert Rudolph (known as "Rudi"), was Avatar Adi Da's first human Teacher— from 1964 to 1968, in New York City. Rudi served Avatar Adi Da Samraj in the development of basic practical life-disciplines and the frontal Yoga, which is the process whereby knots and obstructions in the physical and etheric dimensions of the body-mind are penetrated, opened, surrendered, and released through Spiritual reception in the frontal line of the body-mind. Rudi's own Teachers included Swami Muktananda (with whom Rudi studied for many years) and Bhagavan Nityananda (the Indian Adept-Realizer who was also Swami Muktananda's Guru). Rudi met Bhagavan Nityananda shortly before Bhagavan Nityananda's death, and Rudi always thereafter acknowledged Bhagavan Nityananda as his original and principal Guru.

The second Teacher in Avatar Adi Da's Lineage of Blessing was Swami Muktananda (1908–1982), who was born in Mangalore, South India. Having left home at the age of fifteen, he wandered for many years, seeking the Divine Truth from sources all over India. Eventually, he came under the Spiritual Influence of Bhagavan Nityananda, whom he recognized as his Guru and in whose Spiritual Company he mastered Kundalini Yoga. Swami Muktananda served Avatar Adi Da as Guru during the period from 1968 to 1970. In the summer of 1969, during Avatar Adi Da's second visit to India, Swami Muktananda wrote a letter confirming Avatar Adi Da's attainment of "Yogic Liberation", and acknowledging His right to Teach others. However, from the beginning of their relationship, Swami Muktananda instructed Avatar Adi Da to visit Bhagavan Nityananda's burial site every day (whenever Avatar Adi Da was at Swami Muktananda's Ashram in Ganeshpuri, India) as a means to surrender to Bhagavan Nityananda as the Supreme Guru of the Lineage.

Bhagavan Nityananda, a great Yogi of South India, was Avatar Adi Da's third Guru. Little is known about the circumstances of Bhagavan Nityananda's birth and early life, although it is said that even as a child he showed the signs of a Realized Yogi. It is also known that he abandoned conventional life as a boy and wandered as a renunciate. Many miracles (including spontaneous healings) and instructive stories are attributed to him. Bhagavan Nityananda surrendered the body on August 8, 1961. Although He did not meet Bhagavan Nityananda in the flesh, Avatar Adi Da enjoyed

Bhagavan Nityananda's direct Spiritual Influence from the subtle plane, and He acknowledges Bhagavan Nityananda as a direct and principal Source of Spiritual Instruction during His years with Swami Muktananda.

On His third visit to India, while visiting Bhagavan Nityananda's burial shrine, Avatar Adi Da was instructed by Bhagavan Nityananda to relinquish all others as Guru and to surrender directly to the Divine Goddess in Person as Guru. Thus, Bhagavan Nityananda passed Avatar Adi Da to the Divine Goddess Herself, the Parama-Guru (or Source-Guru) of the Lineage that included Bhagavan Nityananda, Swami Muktananda, and Rudi.

Avatar Adi Da's "Sadhana Years" came to an end in the Great Event of His Divine Re-Awakening, when Avatar Adi Da Husbanded the Divine Goddess (thereby ceasing to relate to Her as His Guru).

Avatar Adi Da's full account of His "Sadhana Years" is Given in Part One of *The Knee Of Listening*. Avatar Adi Da's description of His "Relationship" to the Divine "Goddess" is Given in "I Am The Icon Of Unity", in *He-and-She Is Me*.

listening, hearing, and seeing—
Avatar Adi Da describes the entire course of the Way of Adidam as falling into four primary phases:
1. listening to Him
2. hearing Him
3. seeing Him
4. the "Perfect Practice" of Identifying with Him

For a description of the unfolding phases of practice of Adidam, see *Adidam: The True World-Religion Given by the Promised God-Man, Adi Da Samraj* and *The Dawn Horse Testament*.

"Listening" is Avatar Adi Da's technical term for the beginning practice of the Way of Adidam. A listening devotee literally "listens" to Avatar Adi Da's Instruction and applies it in his or her life.

The core of the listening process (and of all future practice of the Way of Adidam) is the practice of Ruchira Avatara Bhakti Yoga (or turning the four principal faculties of the body-mind—body, emotion, mind, and breath—to Him)—supported by practice of the "conscious process" and "conductivity" and by the embrace of the functional, practical, relational, and cultural disciplines Given by Him.

It is during the listening phase (once the foundation practice is fully established) that the devotee applies to come on extended formal retreat in Avatar Adi Da's physical Company (or, after His physical Lifetime, in the physical company, and the by-Him-Spiritually-Empowered circumstances, of the Ruchira Sannyasin Order of Adidam Ruchiradam). In the retreat circumstance, when the rightly prepared devotee truly (whole bodily) turns the principal faculties to Him, Avatar Adi Da is spontaneously Moved to Grant His Spiritual Initiation (or Ruchira Shaktipat), such that the devotee can become more and more consistently capable of tangibly receiving His Spiritual Transmission. This is the beginning of the Spiritually Awakened practice of the Way of Adidam—when the devotional relationship to Avatar Adi Da becomes (by His Divine Spiritual Grace) the devotional-and-Spiritual relationship to Him. The phase of listening to Avatar Adi Da, rightly and effectively engaged, eventually culminates (by His Divine Spiritual Grace) in the true hearing of Him. The devotee has begun to hear Avatar Adi Da when there is most fundamental understanding of the root-act of egoity (or self-contraction), or the unique capability to consistently transcend the self-contraction. The capability of true hearing is not something the ego can "achieve". That capability can only be Granted, by Means of Avatar Adi Da's Divine Spiritual Grace, to His devotee who has effectively completed the (eventually, Spiritually Awakened) process of listening.

When Spiritually Awakened practice of the Way of Adidam is magnified by means of the hearing-capability, the devotee has the necessary preparation to (in due course) engage that Spiritually Awakened practice in the "fully technically responsible" manner. This is another point (in the course of the Way of Adidam) when the devotee engages an extended formal retreat in Avatar Adi Da's physical Company (or, after His physical Lifetime, in the physical company, and the by-Him-Spiritually-Empowered circumstances, of the Ruchira Sannyasin Order of Adidam Ruchiradam). In this case, in Response to the devotee's more mature practice of devotional and Spiritual resort to Him, Avatar Adi Da Gives the Initiatory Spiritual Gift of Upward-turned Spiritual receptivity of Him (as He describes in His "Hridaya Rosary" of "Four Thorns Of Heart-Instruction"). This is Avatar Adi Da's Spiritual Initiation of His devotee into the seeing phase of practice, which Avatar Adi Da describes as the "fully technically responsible" form of Spiritually Awakened resort to Him.

One of the principal signs of the transition from the listening-hearing practice to the both-hearing-and-seeing practice is emotional conversion from the reactive emotions that characterize egoic self-obsession, to the open-hearted, Radiant Happiness that characterizes fully technically responsible Spiritual devotion to Avatar Adi Da. This true and stable emotional conversion coincides with stable Upward-to-Him-turned receptivity of Avatar Adi Da's Spiritual Transmission.

As the process of seeing develops, the body-mind becomes more and more fully Infused by Avatar Adi Da's Spirit-Baptism, purified of any psycho-physical patterning that diminishes that reception. With increasing maturity in the seeing process, Avatar Adi Da's Transmission of the "Bright" is experi-enced in the unique form that He describes as the "Samadhi of the 'Thumbs'"—and, through this process, the devotee is gracefully grown entirely beyond identification with the body-mind. The seeing process is complete when the devotee receives Avatar Adi Da's Gift of Spiritually Awakening as the Witness-Consciousness (That Stands Prior to body, mind, and world, and even the act of attention itself). This Awakening to the Witness-Consciousness marks readiness for another period of Initiatory retreat in Avatar Adi Da's physical Company (or, after His physical Lifetime, in the physical company, and the by-Him-Spiritually-Empowered circumstances, of the Ruchira Sannyasin Order of Adidam Ruchiradam), in which He Spiritually Initiates the devo-tee into the "Perfect Practice".

"Locate" / "locating"—To "Locate" Avatar Adi Da is to "Truly Heart-Find" Him. Avatar Adi Da places this term (and its variants) in quotation marks to indicate the sense of "so to speak"—because He is, in reality, Omnipresent, without any specific "location".

loka—A world or realm of experience. Usually refers to places "visited" by mystical or esoteric means.

Love-Ananda Avatar—The Very Incarnation of the Divine Love-Bliss.

M

"Mad" / "Madness"—See **Divine "Madness"**.

Maharshi—See **Ramana Maharshi**.

maya—Traditional Sanskrit term for the incomprehensibly complex (and, ulti-mately, illusory) web of beings, things, and events that constitutes conditional reality.

middle station of the heart—See **heart / the Heart Itself / stations of the heart**.

"Midnight Sun"—A term Avatar Adi Da uses to refer to His Revelation of the esoteric visionary representation of Reality as a White Sphere in a black field—which Sphere is His own Divine Form.

The "Midnight Sun" Is the Hole in the universe. It is not (Itself) black. It Is the Hole in the black. It is Divine Being objectified, the Divine Self-Condition objectified. When there is passage into That Place (or the Divine Self-Condition Itself), there is nothing more to say. That Is My Divine "Bright" Spherical Self-Domain.

—Avatar Adi Da Samraj
Eleutherios

Avatar Adi Da places this term in quotation marks to indicate that He uses it with the specific technical meaning described here (rather than any other more common general meaning).

Most Perfect / Most Ultimate—Avatar Adi Da uses the phrase "Most Perfect(ly)" in the sense of "Absolutely Perfect(ly)". Similarly, the phrase "Most Ultimate(ly)" is equivalent to "Absolutely Ultimate(ly)". "Most Perfect(ly)" and "Most Ultimate(ly)" are always references to the seventh (or Divinely Enlightened) stage of life. "Perfect(ly)" and "Ultimate(ly)" (without "Most") refer to the practice and Realization in the context of the "Perfect Practice" of the Way of Adidam (or, when Avatar Adi Da is making reference to the Great Tradition, to practice and Realization in the context of the sixth stage of life).

muladhar—The lowermost chakra, or subtle center, located at the base of the spine.

Murti—Sanskrit for "form", and, by extension, a representational image of the Divine or of a Guru. In the Way of Adidam, Murtis of Avatar Adi Da are most commonly photographs of Avatar Adi Da's bodily (human) Divine Form.

N

nadas—Subtle internal sounds which may become apparent in the process of spontaneous Yoga, in which case the mind is irresistibly drawn upwards into higher conscious states.

"Narcissus" / "Narcissistic"—In Avatar Adi Da's Teaching-Revelation, "Narcissus" is a key symbol of the un-Enlightened individual as a self-obsessed seeker, enamored of his or her own self-image and egoic self-consciousness.

He is the ancient one visible in the Greek myth, who was the universally adored child of the gods, who rejected the loved-one and every form of love and relationship, and who was finally condemned to the contemplation of his own image—until, as a result of his own act and obstinacy, he suffered the fate of eternal separateness and died in infinite solitude.

—Avatar Adi Da Samraj
The Knee Of Listening

When Avatar Adi Da uses "Narcissus" as an archetypal reference to the activity of self-contraction, He places the name in quotation marks, to indicate that He is using the name metaphorically (rather than in reference to the character in the Greek myth). When He uses "Narcissus" in reference to the mythological character, the name is not placed in quotation marks. Avatar Adi Da uses the adjective "Narcissistic" in the sense of "relating to the activity of self-contraction", rather than in any more conventional meaning (particularly those meanings associated with the discipline of psychology).

Nirvana—A Buddhist term for the Unqualified Reality beyond suffering, ego, birth, and death.

non-verbal re-cognition—The mature form into which verbal self-Enquiry develops in the Devotional Way of

Insight. "Re-cognition" literally means "knowing again". Thus, the individual practicing non-verbal re-cognition simply notices and tacitly "knows again" (or directly understands) whatever is arising as yet another species of self-contraction (without using "Avoiding relationship?"), and he or she transcends (or feels beyond) it in heart-Communion with Avatar Adi Da. See also **self-enquiry / "Avoiding relationship?"**.

O

"Oedipal"—In modern psychology, the "Oedipus complex" is named after the legendary Greek Oedipus, who was fated to unknowingly kill his father and marry his mother. Avatar Adi Da Teaches that the primary dynamisms of emotional-sexual desiring, rejection, envy, betrayal, self-pleasuring, resentment, and other primal emotions and impulses are indeed patterned upon unconscious reactions first formed early in life, in relation to one's mother and father. Avatar Adi Da's extended Instruction on "Oedipal" patterning is Given in *Ruchira Tantra Yoga*.

Outshining—"Outshine" and its variants are a reference to the process of Divine Translation, the final Demonstration of the four-phase process of the seventh stage of life in the Way of Adidam. In the Great Event of Outshining (or Divine Translation), body, mind, and world are no longer noticed—not because the Divine Consciousness has withdrawn or dissociated from conditionally manifested phenomena, but because the Self-Abiding Divine Self-Recognition of all arising phenomena as modifications of the Divine Self-Condition has become so intense that the "Bright" Radiance of Consciousness now Outshines all such phenomena.

P

"Perfect Practice"—The "Perfect Practice" is Avatar Adi Da's technical term for the discipline of the most mature stages of practice in the Way of Adidam. The "Perfect Practice" is practice in the Domain of Consciousness Itself (as opposed to practice from the point of view of the body or the mind). The "Perfect Practice" unfolds in three phases, the third of which is Divine Enlightenment. This term is placed in quotation marks to indicate that Avatar Adi Da uses it with the specific technical meaning described here. See Sutras 46–68 of *The Dawn Horse Testament*.

Perfectly Subjective—Avatar Adi Da uses this phrase to describe the True Divine Source (or "Subject") of the conditionally manifested worlds—as opposed to regarding the Divine as some sort of objective "Other". Thus, in the phrase "Perfectly Subjective", the word "Subjective" does not have the sense of "relating to the inward experience of an individual", but, rather, it has the sense of "Being Consciousness Itself, the True Subject of all apparent experience".

"Point Of View"—In Avatar Adi Da's Wisdom-Teaching, "Point of View" is in quotation marks and capitalized when referring to the Position of Consciousness, Prior to (and independent of) the body-mind or conditional existence altogether. In the Way of Adidam, the "Point of View" of Consciousness is the basis of the "Perfect Practice".

prana—The Sanskrit word "prana" means "breath", "life-energy". It generally refers to the life-energy animating all beings and pervading everything in cosmic Nature.

Prana is not to be equated with the Divine Spirit-Current, or the Spiritual (and Always Blessing) Divine Presence of Avatar Adi Da Samraj. The finite pranic energies that sustain individual beings are only conditional, localized, and temporary phenomena of the realm of cosmic Nature.

pranayama—Sanskrit for "restraint or regulation (yama) of life-energy (prana)". Pranayama is a technique for balancing, purifying, and intensifying the entire psycho-physical system by controlling the currents of the breath and life-force. Automatic pranayama is spontaneous Yogic breathing that arises involuntarily and has the same purifying effects as the voluntary exercise of such pranayama.

Prasad—Gifts that have been offered to the Divine and, having been Blessed, are returned as Divine Gifts to devotees. By extension, Prasad is anything the devotee receives from his or her Guru.

Q, R

"radical"—Derived from the Latin "radix", meaning "root". Thus, "radical" principally means "irreducible", "fundamental", or "relating to the origin". Thus, Avatar Adi Da defines "radical" as "gone-to-the-root". Because Adi Da Samraj uses "radical" in this literal sense, it appears in quotation marks in His Wisdom-Teaching, in order to distinguish His usage from the common reference to an extreme (often political) view.

"radical" understanding—Avatar Adi Da uses the word "understanding" to mean "the process of transcending egoity". Thus, to "understand" is to simultaneously observe the activity of the self-contraction and to surrender that activity via devotional resort to Him.

Avatar Adi Da has Revealed that, despite their intention to Realize Reality (or Truth, or Real God), all religious and Spiritual traditions (other than the Way of Adidam) are involved, in one

manner or another (relating to either the subtle or the causal dimension of existence), with the search to satisfy the ego. Only Avatar Adi Da has Revealed the Way to "radically" understand the ego (by "going to the root") and (in due course, through intensive formal practice of the Way of Adidam, as His formally acknowledged devotee) to most perfectly transcend the ego.

Ramakrishna—A great Indian Realizer of the nineteenth century (1836–1886).

Ramana Maharshi—Ramana Maharshi (1879–1950) is regarded by many as the greatest Indian Sage of the twentieth century. Following a spontaneous death-like event as a teenager, he abandoned home for a life of Spiritual practice. Eventually, an ashram was established around him at Tiruvannamalai in South India, which still exists today.

Real God—The True (and Perfectly Subjective) Source of all conditions, the True and Spiritual Divine Person— rather than any ego-made (and, thus, false, or limited) presumption about God. Among Avatar Adi Da's many definitions of "Real God" in *The Dawn Horse Testament* are the following: "The One and True Divine Person—Which Is Reality, or Truth, or That Which Is Always Already The Case" (Sutra 12) and "The God (or The Truth and The Reality) Of Consciousness, Freedom, Love-Bliss, Being, and Oneness" (Sutra 12).

religious and Spiritual—A phrase Avatar Adi Da uses to indicate (and contrast) the religious orientation to communing with God, Truth, or Reality as a "Thing Apart" (inherently separate from the aspirant) and the Spiritual orientation of the actual, tangible experience of Spiritual Force (or Power), even to the point of tangibly experienced "Oneness" with God, Truth, or Reality. In certain contexts, Avatar Adi Da also uses the words "religion" and "religious" in a more general sense, referring to the total religious <u>and</u> Spiritual process.

"right emotional-sexual Yoga"— Avatar Adi Da's term for the developmental process of emotional-sexual self-discipline for practitioners of the Way of Adidam who are engaged in a sexually active intimate relationship. See *The Dawn Horse Testament* or *Ruchira Tantra Yoga*.

right side of the heart (chest)—See **heart / the Heart Itself / stations of the heart**.

Ruchira Avatar—In Sanskrit, "Ruchira" means "bright, radiant, effulgent". Thus, the Reference "Ruchira Avatar" indicates that Avatar Adi Da Samraj is the "Bright" (or Radiant) Descent of the Divine Reality Itself into the conditionally manifested worlds, Appearing here in His bodily (human) Divine Form.

Ruchira Avatara Kripa / Hridaya-Kripa—"Kripa" is Sanskrit for "grace". Traditionally, it is a synonym for "shaktipat", or the Initiatory Blessing of the Spiritual Master. Therefore, Ruchira Avatara Kripa is Avatar Adi Da's Gift of the Transmission of His Divine Spiritual Heart-Blessing. "Hridaya" means True Divine Heart; Hridaya-Kripa is a synonym for Ruchira Avatara Kripa.

Ruchira Avatara Naama Japa— Repetition ("Japa") of the Name ("Naama") of the Ruchira Avatar, Adi Da Samraj. Avatar Adi Da Instructs that Ruchira Avatara Naama Japa (the form of the "conscious process" engaged by practitioners of the Devotional Way of Faith, previous to the first actually seeing stage) is to be "Engaged On The Basis Of (and As An Expression Of) The Faith-Response To Me, and By (or On The Basis Of) The Consistently Demonstrated Devotional Exercise Of That Faith" (Sutra 27 of *The Dawn Horse Testament*) through repetition of

the Ruchira Avatara Naama Mantra, in conjunction with the use of a mala (or rosary). See Sutra 27 for a fuller description.

Ruchira Shakti / Hridaya Shakti— The "Bright" (Ruchira) Spiritual Energy, or Spiritual Power (Shakti) of Ruchira Avatar Adi Da Samraj, or the One True Heart Itself (Hridaya). These terms are used synonymously by Avatar Adi Da.

Ruchira Siddha Yoga—"Siddha Yoga" is, literally, "the Yoga of the Perfected One[s]".

Swami Muktananda used the term "Siddha Yoga" to refer to the form of Kundalini Yoga that he Taught, which involved initiation of the devotee by the Guru's Transmission of Shakti (or Spiritual Energy). Avatar Adi Da Samraj has indicated that this was a fifth stage form of Siddha Yoga. In "I (<u>Alone</u>) <u>Am</u> The Adidam Revelation", Avatar Adi Da Says:

> . . . I Teach Siddha Yoga in the Mode and Manner of the only-by-Me Revealed and Given <u>seventh</u> stage of life (as Ruchira Avatara Siddha Yoga, or Ruchira Siddha Yoga, or Ruchira Avatara Shaktipat Yoga, or Ruchira Shaktipat Yoga, or Ruchira Avatara Hridaya-Siddha Yoga, or Ruchira Avatara Hridaya-Shaktipat Yoga, or Ruchira Avatara Maha-Jnana-Siddha Yoga, or Ruchira Avatara Maha-Jnana Hridaya-Shaktipat Yoga)—and always toward (or to the degree of) the Realization inherently associated with (and, at last, Most Perfectly Demonstrated and Proven by) the only-by-Me Revealed and Given seventh stage of life, and as a practice and a Process that progressively includes (and, coincidently, <u>directly</u> transcends) <u>all</u> <u>six</u> of the phenomenal and developmental (and, necessarily, yet ego-based) stages of life that precede the seventh.

Avatar Adi Da's description of the similarities and differences between traditional Siddha Yoga and the Way of Adidam is Given in "I (Alone) Am The Adidam Revelation", which Essay appears in a number of Avatar Adi Da's "Source-Texts", including *The Knee Of Listening*.

Rudi—See **Lineage-Gurus, Avatar Adi Da's**.

S

sadhana—In Sanskrit, "sadhana" means "ego-transcending religious or Spiritual practice".

"Sadhana Years"—The period of time in Avatar Adi Da's early Life, starting when He, most intensively, began His Quest to recover the Truth of Existence (at Columbia College) in 1957 and ending with His Divine Re-Awakening in 1970. Avatar Adi Da's full description of His "Sadhana Years" is Given in *The Knee Of Listening*.

The term "Sadhana Years" is placed in quotation marks to indicate that it is used by Avatar Adi Da in the "so to speak" sense. In this case, it indicates that, because of the Avataric Divine Nature of His Birth and Life, Avatar Adi Da's years of apparent "sadhana" were actually part of His Submission to humankind and preparation of the vehicle of His Body-Mind to Teach and Bless. Avatar Adi Da Samraj intentionally engaged His "Sadhana Years" as the Process of "Learning Man". As the Avatarically Incarnate (and Inherently egoless) Divine Person, there was no other necessity for Him to engage any form of apparent "sadhana", because there was (in His Case) no egoity to be purified and transcended.

sahasrar—In the traditional system of seven chakras, the sahasrar is the highest chakra (or subtle energy-center), associated with the crown of the head and above.

Sai Baba of Shirdi—A Muslim Realizer who settled in the village of Shirdi, Maharashtra, India, around 1850. At the time of his death (1918), he had attracted thousands of devotees from both the Muslim and Hindu traditions.

samadhi—The Sanskrit word "samadhi" traditionally denotes various exalted states that appear in the context of esoteric meditation and Realization. Avatar Adi Da Teaches that, for His devotees, samadhi is, even more simply and fundamentally, the Enjoyment of His Divine State (or "Divine Samadhi"), Which is experienced (even from the beginning of the practice of Adidam) through ego-transcending heart-Communion with Him.

All the possible forms of Samadhi in the Way of Adidam are described in full detail by Avatar Adi Da Samraj in *The Dawn Horse Testament*. See also **Sahaja Nirvikalpa Samadhi**.

samsara—The Buddhist and Hindu term for the conditional realm of birth and change and death.

Sangha—Sanskrit for "company", or "gathering" (specifically, the gathering of practitioners of a Spiritual Way).

Sat-Guru—"Sat" means "Truth", "Being", "Existence". Thus, "Sat-Guru" literally means "True Guru", or a Guru who can lead living beings from darkness (or non-Truth) into Light (or the Living Truth).

Satsang—Hindi for "True (or right) relationship", "the company of Truth".

seeing—See **listening, hearing, and seeing**.

Self-Domain, Divine "Bright" Spherical—Avatar Adi Da affirms that there is a Divine Self-Domain that is the Perfectly Subjective Condition of the conditional worlds. It is not "elsewhere", not an objective "place" (like a subtle "heaven" or mythical "paradise"), but It is the Divine Source-Condition of every conditionally manifested being and thing—and It is not other than Avatar Adi Da Himself. Avatar Adi Da Reveals that His Divine Self-Domain is a Boundless (and Boundlessly "Bright") Sphere. To Realize the seventh stage of life (by the Divine Spiritual Grace of Avatar Adi Da Samraj) is to Awaken to His Divine Self-Domain. See especially Sutras 66–68 of *The Dawn Horse Testament*.

self-enquiry / "Avoiding relation-ship?"—The practice of self-Enquiry in the form "Avoiding relationship?" is the form of the "conscious process" practiced by those devotees of Avatar Adi Da who have chosen to practice the Devotional Way of Insight. See Sutras 6 and 27 of *The Dawn Horse Testament*. See also **Devotional Way of Insight**.

Self-Existing and Self-Radiant—Terms describing the two fundamental aspects of the One Divine Person (or Reality)—Existence (or Being, or Consciousness) Itself, and Radiance (or Energy, or Light) Itself.

seventh stage Sahaja Nirvikalpa Samadhi—Divine Self-Realization, or Most Perfect Divine Enlightenment—uniquely Revealed and Given by Avatar Adi Da Samraj. "Sahaja" is Sanskrit for "born together, innate, or natural". The Sanskrit term "Nirvikalpa Samadhi" literally means "meditative ecstasy without form", or "deep meditative concentration (or absorption) in which there is no perception of form (or defined experiential content)". Thus, "Sahaja Nirvikalpa Samadhi" means "Innate Samadhi without form". See also **samadhi**.

Shakti—A Sanskrit term for the Divinely Manifesting Spiritual Energy, Spiritual Power, or Spirit-Current of the Divine Person.

Shaktipat—The "descent of Spiritual Power". Yogic Shaktipat, which manipulates natural, conditional energies or partial manifestations of the Divine Spirit-Current, is typically granted through touch, word, glance, or regard by Yogic Adepts in the fifth stage of life. Although the term "Shaktipat" literally refers to the "descent" of Spiritual Power, the traditional Yogic Shaktipat is, in fact, a process of the <u>ascent</u> and circulation of Spiritual Power and must be distinguished from (and, otherwise, understood to be only a secondary aspect of) the Blessing-Transmission of the "Bright" Itself (Ruchira Shaktipat), Which Originates from Infinitely Above and Functions in a unique process in descent and is uniquely Given by Avatar Adi Da Samraj. See especially Sutra 17 of *The Dawn Horse Testament*.

Siddha / Siddha-Guru—"Siddha" is Sanskrit for "a completed, fulfilled, or perfected one", or "one of perfect accomplishment, or power". Avatar Adi Da uses "Siddha", or "Siddha-Guru", to mean a Transmission-Master who is a Realizer (to any significant degree) of Real God, Truth, or Reality.

siddhi / Siddhi (Divine)—Sanskrit for "power", or "accomplishment". When capitalized in Avatar Adi Da's Wisdom-Teaching, "Siddhi" is the Spiritual, Transcendental, and Divine Awakening-Power That He spontaneously and effortlessly Transmits to all.

"sin" / "sinfulness"—"Hamartia" (the word in New Testament Greek that was translated into English as "sin") was also an archery term meaning "missing the mark". The terms "sin" and "sinfulness" are placed in quotation marks to indicate that Avatar Adi Da uses them in a "so to speak" sense, as there is no subsequent punishment from a "Creator-God" implied.

Siva / Siva-Shakti—The Sanskrit terms "Siva" and "Siva-Shakti" are esoteric descriptions of the Divine Being. "Siva" is a name for the Divine Being Itself, or Divine Consciousness. "Shakti" is a name for the All-Pervading Spirit-Power of the Divine Being. "Siva-Shakti" is thus the Unity of the Divine Consciousness and Its own Spirit-Power.

sleeping—See **waking, dreaming, sleeping (deep sleep)**.

spinal line—The subtle energy-pathway in the human structure (extending from the bodily base to the crown of the head) through which both the natural life-energy and the Divine Spirit-Energy flow upward (or in an ascending direction).

Spirit-Baptism—Avatar Adi Da often refers to His Transmission of Spiritual Blessing as His "Spirit-Baptism". It is often felt by His devotee as a Current descending in the frontal line (and, in due course, ascending in the spinal line). However, Avatar Adi Da's Spirit-Baptism is fundamentally and primarily His Moveless Transmission of the Divine Heart Itself. As a secondary effect, His Spirit-Baptism serves to purify, balance, and energize the entire body-mind of the devotee who is prepared to receive It.

stages of life—Avatar Adi Da Samraj describes the experiences and Realizations of humankind in terms of seven stages of life. This schema is one of Avatar Adi Da's unique Gifts to humanity—His precise "mapping" of the potential developmental course of human experience as it unfolds through the gross, subtle, and causal dimensions of the being. He describes this course in terms of six stages of life—which account for, and correspond to, all possible orientations to religion and culture that have arisen in human history. His own Avataric Revelation—the Realization of the "Bright", Prior to all experience—is the seventh stage of life. Understanding this structure of seven

stages illuminates the unique nature of Avatar Adi Da's "Sadhana Years" (and of the Spiritual process in His Company).

The first three (or foundation) stages of life constitute the ordinary course of human adaptation—characterized (respectively) by bodily, emotional, and mental growth. Each of the first three stages of life takes approximately seven years to be established. Every individual who lives to an adult age inevitably adapts (although, generally speaking, only partially) to the first three stages of life. In the general case, this is where the developmental process stops—at the gross level of adaptation. Religions based fundamentally on beliefs and moral codes (without direct experience of the dimensions beyond the material world) belong to this foundation level of human development.

The fourth stage of life is characterized by a deep impulse to Communion with the Divine. It is in the context of the fourth stage of life (when one is no longer wedded to the purposes of the first three stages of life) that the true Spiritual process can begin. In the history of the Great Tradition, those involved in the process of the fourth stage of life have characteristically felt the Divine to be a great "Other", in Whom they aspired to become absorbed, through devotional love and service. However, in the Way of Adidam, the presumption that the Divine is "Other" is transcended from the beginning.

In the Way of Adidam, the process of the first three stages of life is lived on the basis of the devotional heart-impulse that is otherwise characteristic of the fourth stage of life. No matter what the age of the individual who comes to Avatar Adi Da, there will generally be signs of failed adaptation to the first three stages of life. But the practice is not a matter of attempting to overcome such failed adaptation through one's own (inevitably egoic) effort or struggle. Rather, the practice is to turn the faculties of the body-mind to Avatar Adi Da in devotional surrender. In that manner, the virtue of the fourth stage of life—the devotional heart-impulse to Commune with the Divine—is specifically animated from the beginning, in living response to Avatar Adi Da. Thus, whatever must be done to righten the first three stages of life occurs in the devotional context of heart-Communion with Him.

Avatar Adi Da has Revealed that the true Spiritual process, beginning in the fully-established (or "basic") context of the fourth stage of life, involves two great dimensions—which He calls the "vertical" and the "horizontal".

The descending aspect of the vertical process characterizes the fourth stage of life, while the ascending aspect characterizes the fifth stage of life. As it has been known in the history of the Great Tradition, the fifth-stage process is the ascent toward absorption into the Divine Matrix of Light Infinitely Above, thereby (ultimately) Realizing the Divine as Light (or Energy) Itself. (Although this Realization is a true "taste" of the Divine Self-Condition, It is achieved by means of the conditional effort of ascent—and, therefore, the Realization Itself is also conditional, or non-permanent.) The fifth stage of life is the ultimate process associated with the subtle dimension of existence.

The horizontal process characterizes the sixth stage of life. As it has been known in the history of the Great Tradition, the sixth stage process is the exclusion of all awareness of the "outside" world (in both its gross and subtle dimensions), by "secluding" oneself within the heart—in order to rest in the Divine Self, Realized (ultimately) as Consciousness Itself. (Like the ultimate Realization associated with the fifth stage of life, the sixth stage Realization is also a true "taste" of the Divine Self-Condition. However, It is also achieved by conditional means—the conditional effort of exclusion—and, therefore, the Realization Itself is also conditional, or

non-permanent.) The sixth stage of life is the process associated with the causal dimension of existence.

As Avatar Adi Da has pointed out, even though the fifth stage and sixth stage processes are, in fact, stages in the single process that culminates in Most Perfect Divine Enlightenment (or the seventh stage Realization uniquely Given by Him), the typical traditional view has been that the two processes are alternative approaches to Spiritual Realization. Indeed, these approaches (of either going "Up" or going "Deep") have usually been regarded to be incompatible with each other.

In the Way of Adidam, the "Perfect Practice" encompasses both the vertical process (otherwise characteristically associated with the fifth stage of life) and the horizontal process (otherwise characteristically associated with the sixth stage of life). Thus, in the Way of Adidam, there is no "preference" exercised in favor of either the "Upward" process or the "Inward" process—either the Realization of the Divine as Light Itself or the Realization of the Divine as Consciousness Itself. In the Way of Adidam, both the ultimate "Upward" Realization and the ultimate "Inward" Realization are Freely Given by Avatar Adi Da to the rightly prepared and rightly practicing devotee. No effort—either of ascent or of exclusion—is required. And, in fact, all such effort must be inspected, understood, and transcended.

This unique and unprecedented orientation to the developmental processes of the fifth and the sixth stages of life is made possible by the full reception of Avatar Adi Da's Gift of Divine Spiritual Transmission. When the devotee (in the context of the fourth stage of life in the Way of Adidam) is fully open to Avatar Adi Da's Divine Spiritual Transmission, His Divine Spiritual Descent of the "Thumbs" takes over the body-mind, showing specific Yogic signs. In this "Samadhi of the 'Thumbs'", there is a profound turnabout in one's awareness of Him. While still always turning to Him devotionally in His bodily (human) Divine Form, one begins to recognize Him, Spiritually, as Consciousness Itself—the Root-Position of existence, Prior to all that is arising in body, mind, and world. This recognition is Spiritually established—and it is the basis for making the transition to the "Perfect Practice" of the Way of Adidam. It is a profound shift, away from identification with the body-mind. From this point on, Avatar Adi Da's Revelation of His own Condition of Consciousness Itself becomes the Position in which one Stands, and from That Position the phenomena associated with both the fifth stage of life and the sixth stage of life will arise. In the "Perfect Practice", one is no longer practicing from the point of view of the body-mind and its faculties. Now, devotional turning to Him (or Ruchira Avatara Bhakti Yoga) takes the form of simply "choosing" to Stand in His Position (rather than the ego-position)—inspecting and feeling beyond the root-tendency to contract and create the self-identity called "I".

The seventh stage of life, or the Realization of Avatar Adi Da's own "Bright" Divine Condition, transcends the entire course of human potential. In the seventh stage of life, the impulse to Realize the Divine (as Light) by going "Up" and the impulse to Realize the Divine (as Consciousness) by going "Deep" are (by Avatar Adi Da's Divine Spiritual Grace) simultaneously fulfilled. In that fulfillment, Avatar Adi Da Samraj Himself is most perfectly Realized. He is Realized as the "Bright", the Single Divine Unity of Consciousness and Energy—or Conscious Light Itself. This unique Realization, or Divine Enlightenment—first Realized by Avatar Adi Da Himself in the Great Event of His Divine Re-Awakening—wipes away every trace of dissociation from the body-mind and the world. There is no impulse to seek or to avoid any experience. Rather, everything that arises is

Divinely Self-Recognized to be merely a modification of the Conscious Light of Reality Itself.

The seventh stage Realization is absolutely Unconditional. It does not depend on any form of effort by the individual. Rather, It is a Divine Gift, Given by Avatar Adi Da to the devotee who has utterly surrendered all egoity to Him. Therefore, the seventh stage Realization is permanent.

Altogether, the Way of Adidam is not about dwelling in (or seeking to either attain or avoid) any of the potential experiences of the first six stages of life. The Way of Adidam is about transcending the entire structure of the human being and of the conditional reality—gross, subtle, and causal. Therefore, the Way of Adidam transcends both the urge to "have" experiences and the urge to "exclude" experience. The Way of Adidam is based, from the beginning, on the Divine Avatar's "Bright" State, Which is Realized progressively (and, ultimately, most perfectly), by means of His Divine Spiritual Descent in the body-mind of His devotee.

subtle—See **gross, subtle, causal**.

T

"talking" school—A phrase used by Avatar Adi Da to refer to those in any tradition of sacred life whose approach is characterized by talking, thinking, reading, and philosophical analysis and debate, or even meditative enquiry or reflection, without a concomitant and foundation discipline of body, emotion, mind, and breath. He contrasts the "talking"-school with the "practicing"-school approach—"practicing" schools involving those who are committed to the ordeal of real ego-transcending discipline, under the guidance of a true Guru. "Talking" is placed in quotation marks to indicate that Avatar Adi Da uses it with the specific technical meaning described here.

tamas / tamasic—The principle, or power, of inertia. The Hindu texts declare that conditionally manifested existence is a complex variable of three qualities (or "gunas"): "tamas", "rajas", and "sattva". "Rajas" (or the "rajasic" quality) is the principle, or power, of action (or motivation). "Sattva" (or the "sattvic" quality) is the principle, or power, of equilibrium (or balance).

The Knee Of Listening—Avatar Adi Da's Spiritual Autobiography (Middletown, Calif.: The Dawn Horse Press, 2004).

Transcendentalist—The Transcendentalist way is that of dissociation from the objects of conditional existence in identification with secluded Consciousness Itself, associated with the sixth-stage path. It is associated with the horizontal dimension of the human psychophysical structure. See also **stages of life** and **horizontal plane**.

Translate—See **Divinely Translate**.

True Humor—In *The Knee Of Listening*, Avatar Adi Da says:

Ordinary humor can appear in many forms, as the seemingly undauntable mood of life-enjoyment, as the hilarious pleasure of laughter, as the fairy-tale ease of faith, as the self-"congratulating certainty of mental knowledge, and as the overriding excitement of even all the greater and smaller bodily victories. But True Humor has only one living Form (and one ultimate, or inherently perfect, Form), Which is Real God, Perfect Truth, or Reality Itself. (p. 32)

"true Yogic intimacy"—The emotional-sexual discipline that Avatar Adi Da Gives to His devotees who are engaged in an intimate emotional-sexual relationship (whether that relationship is sexually active or celibate). For Avatar Adi Da's

detailed Instruction on "true Yogic intimacy", see Sutra 40 of *The Dawn Horse Testament*.

"Turiya" / "Turiyatita"—Terms used in the Hindu philosophical systems. "Turiya" means "the fourth state" (beyond waking, dreaming, and sleeping), and "turiyatita" means "the state beyond the fourth", or beyond all states.

Avatar Adi Da has given these traditional terms unique and specific meanings in the context of His Wisdom-Teaching, and He places them in quotation marks to indicate that they are used with such specific meanings. He uses the term "turiya" to indicate the Awakening to Consciousness Itself (in the context of the "Perfect Practice" of the Way of Adidam), and "turiyatita" to indicate the State of Most Perfect Divine Enlightenment, or the Realization of all arising as transparent and non-binding modifications of the One Divine Reality (in the context of the seventh stage of life).

U, V

Vedantic Self-Knowledge—See **Jnana Yoga**.

vertical plane—Avatar Adi Da refers to the structural anatomy of the Circle (or frontal and spinal lines) and the Arrow as the "vertical" dimension (or plane) of the human body-mind (in contrast to the "horizontal" dimension of the stations of the heart).

Vow—For a description of the Eternal Vow and responsibilities associated with the Way of Adidam, please see *Adidam: The True World-Religion Given by the Promised God-Man, Adi Da Samraj*.

W

waking, dreaming, sleeping (deep sleep)—These three states of consciousness are associated with the dimensions of cosmic existence.

The waking state (and the physical body) is associated with the gross dimension.

The dreaming state (and visionary, mystical, and Yogic Spiritual processes) is associated with the subtle dimension. The subtle dimension, which is senior to the gross dimension, includes the etheric (or energic), lower mental (or verbal-intentional and lower psychic), and higher mental (or deeper psychic, mystical, and discriminative) functions.

The state of deep sleep is associated with the causal dimension, which is senior to both the gross and the subtle dimensions. It is the root of attention, and (therefore) the root of the sense of separate "selfhood", prior to any particular experience. See also **gross, subtle, causal**.

Way of "Radical" Understanding—Avatar Adi Da has Revealed that, despite their intention to Realize Reality (or Truth, or Real God), all religious and Spiritual traditions (other than the Way of Adidam) are involved, in one manner or another, with the search to satisfy the ego. Only Avatar Adi Da has Revealed the Way to "radically" understand the ego (by "going to the root") and (in due course, through intensive formal practice of the Way of Adidam, as His formally acknowledged devotee) to most perfectly transcend the ego.

Way of Ruchira Avatara Bhakti Yoga—Indicates that the Way Avatar Adi Da Offers is based on "the practice of devotion to the Ruchira Avatar, Adi Da Samraj", or Ruchira Avatara Bhakti Yoga.

Way of Ruchira Avatara Siddha Yoga—The Way Avatar Adi Da Offers is the seventh stage mode of Siddha Yoga (or the Yoga of the Perfected Ones). See **Ruchira Siddha Yoga**.

Witness / Witness-Consciousness / Witness-heart—When Consciousness is Free of identification with the body-mind, It Stands in Its natural "Position" as the Conscious Witness of all that arises to and in and as the body-mind.

In the Way of Adidam, the stable Realization of the Witness-Position is a Spiritual Gift from Avatar Adi Da, made possible by (and necessarily following upon) the reception of His Spiritual Gift of the "Thumbs". The stable Realization of the Witness-Position is the characteristic of the first stage of the "Perfect Practice". See Sutra 49 of *The Dawn Horse Testament*.

X, Y, Z

Yoga / Yogic—Literally "yoking", or "union", usually referring to any discipline or process whereby an aspirant seeks to achieve union with God (or the Divine, however conceived). Avatar Adi Da acknowledges this conventional and traditional use of the term, but also, in reference to the Great Yoga of Adidam, employs it in a "radical" sense, free of the usual implication of egoic separation and seeking.

Yoga-Shakti—The Power, Energy, or living Force that is awakened in the Yogi—either spontaneously or (otherwise) through the Transmission of a Spiritual Master. This internal Energy produces a wide range of phenomena in the body and the mind of the individual.

An Invitation to Support Adidam

The sole Purpose of Avatar Adi Da Samraj is to act as a Source of continuous Divine Grace for everyone, everywhere. In that spirit, He is a Free Renunciate and He owns nothing. Those who have made gestures in support of Avatar Adi Da's Work have found that their generosity is returned in many Blessings that are full of His healing, transforming, and Liberating Grace and those Blessings flow not only directly to them as the beneficiaries of His Work, but to many others, even all others. At the same time, all tangible gifts of support help secure and nurture Avatar Adi Da's Work in necessary and practical ways, again similarly benefiting the entire world. Because all this is so, supporting His Work is the most auspicious form of financial giving, and we happily extend to you an invitation to serve Adidam through your financial support.

You may make a financial contribution in support of the Work of Adi Da Samraj at any time. To do so, make your check payable to "Adidam", and mail it to the Legal Department of Adidam at 12180 Ridge Road, Middletown, California 95461, USA. You may also, if you choose, indicate that your contribution be used for one or more specific purposes.

If you would like more detailed information about gifting options, or if you would like assistance in describing or making a contribution, please write to the Legal Department of Adidam at the above address or contact the Adidam Legal Department by telephone at 1-707-928-4612 or by FAX at 1-707-928-4062.

Planned Giving

We also invite you to consider making a planned gift in support of the Work of Avatar Adi Da Samraj. Many have found that through planned giving they can make a far more significant gesture of support than they would otherwise be able to make. Many have also found that by making a planned gift they are able to realize substantial tax advantages.

There are numerous ways to make a planned gift, including making a charitable bequest in your Will or living trust, or in your life insurance, or making a gift in the form of a charitable trust.

If you are a United States taxpayer, you may find that planned giving in the form of a charitable trust will provide you with immediate tax savings and assured income for life, while at the same time enabling you to provide for your family, for your other heirs, and for the Work of Avatar Adi Da as well.

The Legal Department of Adidam (12180 Ridge Road, Middletown, California 95461, USA; telephone 1-707-928-4612; FAX 1-707-928-4062) will be happy to provide you with further information about these and other planned giving options, and happy to provide you or your attorney with assistance in describing or making a planned gift in support of the Work of Avatar Adi Da.

Further Notes to the Reader

An Invitation to Responsibility

Adidam, the Way of the Heart that Avatar Adi Da has Revealed, is an invitation to everyone to assume real responsibility for his or her life. As Avatar Adi Da has Said in *The Dawn Horse Testament Of The Ruchira Avatar*, "If any one Is Heart-Moved To Realize Me, Let him or her First Resort (Formally, and By Formal Heart-Vow) To Me, and (Thereby) Commence The Devotional (and, In Due Course, Spiritual) Process Of self-Observation, self-Understanding, and self-Transcendence. . . ." Therefore, participation in the Way of Adidam requires a real confrontation with oneself, and not at all a confrontation with Avatar Adi Da, or with others.

All who study the Way of Adidam or take up its practice should remember that they are responding to a Call to become responsible for themselves. They should understand that they, not Avatar Adi Da or others, are responsible for any decision they may make or action they may take in the course of their lives of study or practice. This has always been true, and it is true whatever the individual's involvement in the Way of Adidam, be it as one who has contacted Avatar Adi Da's Revelation in any informal manner (such as studying Avatar Adi Da's Wisdom-Teaching), or as one who is practicing as a formally acknowledged congregational member of Adidam.

Honoring and Protecting the Sacred Word through Perpetual Copyright

Since ancient times, practitioners of true religion and Spirituality have valued, above all, time spent in the Company of the Sat-Guru (or one who has, to any degree, Realized Real God, Truth, or Reality, and who, thus, serves the awakening process in others). Such practitioners understand that the Sat-Guru literally Spiritually Transmits his or her (Realized) State. Through this Transmission, there are objects, environments, and rightly prepared individuals with which the Sat-Guru has contact that can become empowered, or imbued with the Sat-Guru's Transforming Power. It is by this process of empowerment that things and beings are made truly and literally sacred and holy, and things so sanctified thereafter function as a source of the Sat-Guru's Blessing for all who understand how to make right and sacred use of them.

Sat-Gurus of any degree of Realization and all that they empower are, therefore, truly Sacred Treasures, for they help draw the practitioner more quickly into the process of Realization. Cultures of true Wisdom have always understood that such Sacred Treasures are precious (and fragile) Gifts to humanity, and that they should be honored, protected, and reserved for right sacred use. Indeed, the word "holy" means "set apart", and, thus, that which is holy and sacred must be protected from insensitive secular interference and wrong use of any kind. Avatar Adi Da has Conformed His human Body-Mind Most Perfectly to the Divine

519

Self, and He is, thus, the most Potent Source of Spiritual Blessing-Transmission of Real God, or Truth Itself, or Reality Itself. He has for many years Empowered (or made sacred) special places and things, and these now serve as His Divine Agents, or as literal expressions and extensions of His Blessing-Transmission. Among these Empowered Sacred Treasures are His Wisdom-Teaching and His Divine Image-Art, which are full of His Transforming Power. These Blessed and Blessing Agents have the literal Power to serve Real-God-Realization in those who are Graced to receive them.

Therefore, Avatar Adi Da's Wisdom-Teaching and Divine Image-Art must be perpetually honored and protected, "set apart" from all possible interference and wrong use. The gathering of devotees of Avatar Adi Da is committed to the perpetual preservation and right honoring of the Sacred Wisdom-Teaching of the Way of Adidam and the Divine Image-Art of Adi Da Samraj. But it is also true that, in order to fully accomplish this, we must find support in the world-society in which we live and in its laws. Thus, we call for a world-society and for laws that acknowledge the sacred, and that permanently protect it from insensitive, secular interference and wrong use of any kind. We call for, among other things, a system of law that acknowledges that the Wisdom-Teaching of the Way of Adidam and the Divine Image-Art of Adi Da Samraj, in all their forms, are, because of their sacred nature, protected by perpetual copyright.

We invite others who respect the sacred to join with us in this call and in working toward its realization. And, even in the meantime, we claim that all copyrights to the Wisdom-Teaching and Divine Image-Art of Avatar Adi Da and the other Sacred Literature, recordings, and images of the Way of Adidam are of perpetual duration.

We make this claim on behalf of The Avataric Samrajya of Adidam Pty Ltd, which, acting as trustee of The Avataric Samrajya of Adidam, is the holder of all such copyrights.

Avatar Adi Da and the Sacred Treasures of Adidam

True Spiritual Masters have Realized Real God (to one degree or another), and, therefore, they bring great Blessing and introduce Divine Possibility to the world. Such Adept-Realizers Accomplish universal Blessing-Work that benefits everything and everyone. They also Work very specifically and intentionally with individuals who approach them as their devotees, and with those places where they reside and to which they direct their specific Regard for the sake of perpetual Spiritual Empowerment. This was understood in traditional Spiritual cultures, and, therefore, those cultures found ways to honor Adept-Realizers by providing circumstances for them where they were free to do their Spiritual Work without obstruction or interference.

Those who value Avatar Adi Da's Realization and Service have always endeavored to appropriately honor Him in this traditional way by providing a circumstance where He is completely Free to do His Divine Work. The Ruchira Sannyasin Hermitage Ashrams of Adidam have been set aside by Avatar Adi Da's devotees worldwide as Places for Him to do His universal Blessing-Work for the sake of everyone, as well as His specific Work with those who pilgrimage to His Hermitage circumstance (wherever He may be residing at a given time) to receive the special Blessing of coming into His physical Company.

Avatar Adi Da is a legal renunciate. He owns nothing and He has no secular or religious institutional function. He Functions only in Freedom. He, and the other members of the Ruchira Sannyasin Order (the senior renunciate order of Adidam), are provided for by The Avataric Samrajya of Adidam, which also provides for His Hermitage circumstance, and serves and manages the process of access to Avatar Adi Da Samraj on the part of all who are invited to enter His Hermitage Domain (either to offer service to Him or to participate in meditative retreats in His Spiritual Company).

The sacred institutions that have developed in response to Avatar Adi Da's Wisdom-Teaching and universal Blessing are active worldwide in making Avatar Adi Da's Wisdom-Teaching available to all, in offering guidance to all who are moved to respond to His Offering, and in protecting, preserving, and glorifying the Sacred Treasures of Adidam. In addition to the central corporate entities, which are based in California, there are numerous regional entities which serve congregations of Avatar Adi Da's devotees in various places throughout the world.

Practitioners of Adidam worldwide have also established numerous community organizations, through which they provide for many of their common and cooperative community needs, including those relating to housing, food, businesses, medical care, schools, and death and dying. By attending to these and all other ordinary human concerns and affairs via ego-transcending cooperation and mutual effort, Avatar Adi Da's devotees constantly work to free their energy and attention, both personally and collectively, for practice of the Way of Adidam and for service to Avatar Adi Da Samraj, to the other Sacred Treasures of Adidam, and to the sacred institutions of Adidam.

All of the organizations that have evolved in response to Avatar Adi Da Samraj and His Offering are legally separate from one another, and each has its own purpose and function. These organizations represent the collective intention of practitioners of Adidam worldwide to protect, preserve, and glorify the Sacred Treasures of Adidam, and also to make Avatar Adi Da's Offering of the Way of Adidam universally available to all.

INDEX

NOTE TO THE READER: Page numbers in **boldface** type refer to the Scriptural Text of *My "Bright" Word*. All other page numbers refer to the introductions, endnotes, and back matter.

The Avataric Divine Wisdom-Teaching
of Adi Da Samraj

The Avataric Divine Wisdom-Teaching of Adi Da Samraj is gathered together, in its final form, in the many "Source-Texts" which He has designated as His Eternal Communication to humankind. These "Source-Texts" are "True-Water-Bearers", or Bearers of the "True Water" of the "Bright" Divine Reality Itself.

Avatar Adi Da has grouped His "Source-Texts" into twenty-three "Streams", or "Courses". Each of these "Courses" conveys a particular aspect of His Avataric Divine Wisdom-Teaching—and each "Course" (other than the first) may, in principle, include any number of "Source-Texts".

The first "Course" is Avatar Adi Da's paramount "Source-Text", *The Dawn Horse Testament Of The Ruchira Avatar*. The remaining twenty-two "Courses" are divided into two groups: *The Heart Of The Adidam Revelation* (consisting of five "Courses", which, together, present a comprehensive overview of Avatar Adi Da's entire Wisdom-Teaching) and *The Companions Of The True Dawn Horse* (consisting of seventeen "Courses", each of which elaborates on particular topics from *The Dawn Horse Testament*).

The "Source-Texts"
(or True-Water-Bearers)
Of My Avataric Divine Wisdom-Teaching
(In Its Twenty-Three Courses Of
True-Water-Born Speech)—
With [My] Divine Testament
As The Epitome
(or First and Principal Text,
and "Bright" True-Water-Mill)
Among Them—
Are, Together, [My] Sufficient Word—
Given, In Summary,
To You
(and, Therefore, To all).

—Avatar Adi Da Samraj
The Dawn Horse Testament
Of The Ruchira Avatar

The "Source-Texts" of the Avataric Divine Wisdom-Teaching of Adi Da Samraj (in Its Twenty-Three Courses)

The Dawn Horse Testament Of The Ruchira Avatar
(in Its Single Course)

THE DAWN HORSE TESTAMENT OF THE RUCHIRA AVATAR
The Testament Of Divine Secrets Of The Divine World-Teacher, Ruchira Avatar Adi Da Samraj

The Heart Of The Adidam Revelation
(in Its Five Courses)

1. AHAM DA ASMI
    (BELOVED, I AM DA)
    The "Late-Time" Avataric Revelation Of The True and Spiritual Divine Person (The egoless Personal Presence Of Reality and Truth, Which Is The Only Real God)

2. RUCHIRA AVATARA GITA
    (THE AVATARIC WAY OF THE DIVINE HEART-MASTER)
    The "Late-Time" Avataric Revelation Of The Great Secret Of The Divinely Self-Revealed Way That Most Perfectly Realizes The True and Spiritual Divine Person (The egoless Personal Presence Of Reality and Truth, Which Is The Only Real God)

3. DA LOVE-ANANDA GITA
    (THE FREE AVATARIC GIFT OF THE DIVINE LOVE-BLISS)
    The "Late-Time" Avataric Revelation Of The Great Means To Worship and To Realize The True and Spiritual Divine Person (The egoless Personal Presence Of Reality and Truth, Which Is The Only Real God)

4. HRIDAYA ROSARY
    (FOUR THORNS OF HEART-INSTRUCTION)
    The "Late-Time" Avataric Revelation Of The Universally Tangible Divine Spiritual Body, Which Is The Supreme Agent Of The Great Means To Worship and To Realize The True and Spiritual Divine Person (The egoless Personal Presence Of Reality and Truth, Which Is The Only Real God)

5. ELEUTHERIOS
    (THE ONLY TRUTH THAT SETS THE HEART FREE)
    The "Late-Time" Avataric Revelation Of The "Perfect Practice" Of The Great Means To Worship and To Realize The True and Spiritual Divine Person (The egoless Personal Presence Of Reality and Truth, Which Is The Only Real God)

The Companions Of The True Dawn Horse
(in Their Seventeen Courses)

1. REAL GOD IS THE INDIVISIBLE ONENESS OF UNBROKEN LIGHT
   Reality, Truth, and The "Non-Creator" God In The True World-Religion
   Of Adidam

   THE TRANSMISSION OF DOUBT
   Transcending Scientific Materialism

2. THE TRULY HUMAN NEW WORLD-CULTURE OF UNBROKEN REAL-GOD-MAN
   The Eastern Versus The Western Traditional Cultures Of Mankind, and
   The Unique New Non-Dual Culture Of The True World-Religion Of Adidam

   SCIENTIFIC PROOF OF THE EXISTENCE OF GOD WILL SOON BE ANNOUNCED
   BY THE WHITE HOUSE!
   Prophetic Wisdom about the Myths and Idols of Mass Culture and Popular
   Religious Cultism, the New Priesthood of Scientific and Political Materialism,
   and the Secrets of Enlightenment Hidden in the Body of Man

3. THE ONLY COMPLETE WAY TO REALIZE THE UNBROKEN LIGHT OF REAL GOD
   An Introductory Overview Of The "Radical" Divine Way Of The True
   World-Religion Of Adidam

4. THE KNEE OF LISTENING
   The Divine Ordeal Of The Avataric Incarnation Of Conscious Light—
   The Spiritual Autobiography Of The Ruchira Avatar, Adi Da Samraj

5. THE DIVINE SIDDHA-METHOD OF THE RUCHIRA AVATAR
   The Divine Way Of Adidam Is An ego-Transcending Relationship,
   Not An ego-Centric Technique

   Volume I: MY "BRIGHT" WORD
   Volume II: MY "BRIGHT" SIGHT
   Volume III: MY "BRIGHT" FORM
   Volume IV: MY "BRIGHT" ROOM

6. THE MUMMERY BOOK
   A Parable Of The Divine True Love, Told By Means Of A Self-Illuminated
   Illustration Of The Totality Of Mind

7. HE-AND-SHE IS ME
   The Indivisibility Of Consciousness and Light In The Divine Body Of
   The Ruchira Avatar

8. RUCHIRA SHAKTIPAT YOGA
   The Divine (and Not Merely Cosmic) Spiritual Baptism In The Divine Way
   Of Adidam

We invite you to find out more about Avatar Adi Da Samraj and the Way of Adidam

■ Find out about our courses, seminars, events, and retreats by calling the regional center nearest you.

AMERICAS
12040 N. Seigler Rd.
Middletown, CA
95461 USA
1-707-928-4936

THE UNITED KINGDOM
P.O. Box 20013
London, England
NW2 1ZA
0845-330-1008

EUROPE-AFRICA
Annendaalderweg 10
6105 AT Maria Hoop
The Netherlands
31 (0)20 468 1442

PACIFIC-ASIA
12 Seibel Road
Henderson
Auckland 1008
New Zealand
64-9-838-9114

AUSTRALIA
P.O. Box 244
Kew 3101
Victoria
**1800 ADIDAM
(1800-234-326)**

INDIA
Shree Love-Ananda Marg
Rampath, Shyam Nagar Extn.
Jaipur–302 019, India
91 (141) 2293080

EMAIL: **correspondence@adidam.org**

■ Order books, tapes, and videos by and about Avatar Adi Da Samraj.
1-877-770-0772 (from within North America)
1-707-928-6653 (from outside North America)
order online: **www.dawnhorsepress.com**

■ Visit us online at:
www.adidam.org
Explore the online community of Adidam and discover more about Avatar Adi Da and the Way of Adidam.